# WELCOME

## to

## *Rapidex*®

## *Computer Course*

We welcome you as
another intelligent entrant for
joining the fast-growing family of
over 3 million 'Rapidex' readers.

More than one million copies in print,
benefitting over 3 million readers.

# Rapidex® Computer Course

## Windows 98/Me Edition

### Special Addendum on Windows XP

*Chief Editor*
**J.L. Neogy**
M.Tech.

*Editorial Panel*
**Dr. Ashok Gupta**
M.B.B.S.
**Amit Gupta**
B.E. (Electronics)
**Rohit Gupta**
B.E. (Electronics)

## PUSTAK MAHAL®

Delhi • Bangalore • Mumbai • Patna • Hyderabad

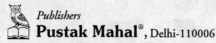

*Publishers*
**Pustak Mahal**®, Delhi-110006

J-3/16, Daryaganj, New Delhi-110002
☎ 23276539, 23272783, 23272784 • *Fax:* 011-23260518
*E-mail:* info@pustakmahal.com • *Website:* www.pustakmahal.com

*Branch Offices*
Bangalore: ☎ 22234025
*E-mail*: pmblr@sancharnet.in • pustak@sancharnet.in
Mumbai: ☎ 22010941
*E-mail*: rapidex@bom5.vsnl.net.in
Patna: ☎ 309419 • *Telefax:* 0612-2302719
*E-mail*: rapidexptn@rediffmail.com
Hyderabad: *Telefax:* 040-24737290
*E-mail*: pustakmahalhyd@yahoo.co.in

ISBN 81-223-0843-0

**Revised and Updated New Edition : July 2004**
**IIIrd Reprint Edition : July 2005**

---

*Printed at :* Unique Colour Carton, Mayapuri, Delhi-110064

# Preface

There are over a million copies of the *Rapidex Computer Course* in print. For computer users from the novice to those with mid-level skills, the existing book has provided comprehensive tutelage in computer basics and in popular software programmes such as the Microsoft Office suit. It has been well received and continues to sell very well. Why then have the publishers felt the need to bring out a new, completely revised and updated edition?

The answer lies in the rapid development in computer hardware and software. Instead of Microsoft Windows 95 and Microsoft Office 97 that were installed in most computers when the book was first published, today we hear of Windows 98 (or Windows Me) and the Microsoft Office 2000 software suit. Computers have become phenomenally powerful as well. Instead of 100 MHz Pentium Central Processing Units (CPUs), present-day computers have Pentium 4 CPUs running at 2 to 3 GHz.

The new millennium has seen changes that call for a complete overhaul of the contents of the book so that it remains in tune with the times. This edition, therefore, is based on Windows 98, Windows Me and also has a fully illustrated four colour chapter on Windows XP. Instead of FoxPro, information on anti-virus software has been included. To provide a richer, more interactive learning experience, the book comes with a CD-ROM that contains multimedia-learning courses that complement what you read in the book.

In the earlier edition, the mission of the book was to provide a step-by-step approach for self-learners and computer course instructors. Full of practical examples, the book stood out from a host of "teach yourself" books on the subject. This mission has not been lost sight of. While the contents have been thoroughly revised and updated, the style is the same friendly and familiar one that has endeared the earlier edition to thousands of readers in the past. If you liked the earlier book, you are going to love the present edition. Looking at the increasing awareness and advancement we have decided to include one complete chapter on Windows XP.

Revising and updating a book of this size is a major task, made more demanding by the need to meet and exceed the high standards of the earlier edition. The writer is indebted to the earlier and present editorial panel and to the publishers for their invaluable help in making this mission possible.

—**JL Neogy**

# Conventions and Contents

Conventions used in this book are aimed at improvements in readability and ease of identification of tips for better performance and of traps for the unwary. A tip is identified by a *Tip* symbol. In the same manner, pitfalls are identified by the *Trap* symbol. A paragraph of information deserving special attention is identified by the *Note* symbol. Read the information in a note for an in-depth understanding of what is being discussed. The CD-ROM supplied with the book aids your learning process by providing audio-visual explanations and lessons. The text is marked with the *CD-ROM* symbol and instructions are given there to tell you how to find what you need in the CD-ROM.

Examples below will clarify these aids to reading.

## Tips, Traps, Notes and the CD-ROM

**TIP**

The author has used his intimate knowledge of the Office Suit software and of his long experience as an EDP head to pick out tips, shortcuts and work-around. These will collectively aid in enhancing productivity, in resolving some knotty problem or showing the way to getting the job done in less time, with fewer commands. Look out for the wise owl who points the way. Read the tips carefully. Refer to them when a problem arises. Skim through a topic or a chapter to pick up tips about the topic. You will learn many useful tricks in a short time and with least effort.

**TRAP**

In a very large and complex software suit, it is natural that some situations will spell trouble. The author has drawn upon his own practical experience as well as the advice of computer gurus to post warning signs along the way so that you may benefit from the learning experience of others and thereby avoid making the same mistake! Look out for the familiar danger sign, skull and crossbones, to pick up pointers of what you must not do.

**NOTE** To help you pick up ideas of importance, and to provide you with a guide map of important points, a key paragraph will be identified by the Note symbol. Notes are additional important information or clarifications applicable to the matter being discussed. Read through the notes in this book for a clearer understanding of the subject.

**CD-ROM**

A special feature of this book is its accompanying CD-ROM, containing a set of interactive multimedia lessons covering most of the topics in the text. You can use the CD-ROM as a stand-alone computer-based learning tool. However, you can also add to what you learn from the text by jumping to the appropriate part in the CD-ROM. Thereby, you can see the same concepts explained to you with sound and animation. To help you find what you seek easily, directions are added to the text with the *CD-ROM* symbol.

# Instructions

This book contains several examples of step-by-step instructions, usually as numbered or bulleted text. For ease of comprehension, an action word such as *Click* or *Select* is followed by key words in bold script so that the instructions may be easily followed.

Here is an example:

To display the list of programmes installed in your computer, proceed as follows:

1. Click the **Start** button at the bottom left of your screen.
2. Click **Programmes**, the programmes menu is displayed.
3. Click the **Programme Name** that you want to launch.

Alternatively, a more compact form may be used from time to time, such as:

**Start → Programmes → Programme Name**

This shortcut procedure works with all versions of Windows from Windows 95 onwards.

Information to be entered is enclosed in angle brackets. Thus an instruction to enter your name will be written as <Your Name>. Enter your name *without* the angle brackets.

# What the Book Contains

This book is divided into seven sections for ease of identification of the topic that will interest a specific reader. Each section is self-contained and covers a particular topic. Each section is further subdivided into chapters.

Here is a brief layout of the arrangements of the sections:

Section 1 covers the basics. It includes chapters on computer hardware, the disk operating system (DOS) and the Windows operating system (Windows 98/Me/XP). Chapters 1, 2 and 3 form part of this section.

Section 2 covers communications using your computer. Here you will learn about the Internet, e-mail and Internet chat as well as Internet telephony and computer fax. Chapters 4, 5 and 6 form part of this section.

Section 3 introduces you to the powerful Microsoft Office 2000 software suit. You learn about common features of the applications that make up Office 2000. You also learn about Word 2000, the most popular word processing programme available to the personal computer user. You will find chapters 7 to 11 here.

In Section 4, you also learn about the calculating power of the spreadsheet programme, Excel 2000. Chapters 12, 13, 14 and 15 all deal with Excel.

In Section 5, you meet the database programme Access 2000. Chapters 16, 17 and 18 are all part of this section.

In Section 6, you are introduced to the premier presentation software, PowerPoint 2000 and you learn to manage your communications, appointments and schedules by using Outlook 2000. This section is spread over chapters 19 to 23.

Section 7 covers other software and accessories. Here you will learn about Windows accessories and anti-virus software. You will also be introduced to the CD-ROM-based interactive learning software that complements the written matter in this book and makes your learning process smooth, enjoyable and rapid. Chapters 24 and 25 and the Annexure are part of this section.

At the end of the book a special colour chapter on Windows XP has been added. This introduction chapter will help you learn about the differences between the earlier MS Operating Systems and Windows XP.

## In What Order Should You Read?

Each section is self-contained and you may start with any section. However, users new to the later Windows operating systems like Windows Me or Windows 2000 should read Chapter 1, *Introduction*, Chapter 2, *The Disk Operating System* and Chapter 3, *The Windows Operating System* in Section 1. Section 2 is primarily for those who are looking for mastery over communications. If you are new to the Internet, wish to use e-mail or communicate by using computer fax software, Section 2 is the place to start with.

Those who have not used Microsoft Office suits later than Office 95 will benefit particularly from Section 3. New users of Office 2000 will benefit particularly from Chapter 7, *Introducing Microsoft Office 2000* that deals with the common features of all the Office 2000 applications. If you need to master the word processor, start with Section 3. For spreadsheets, Section 4 is the place to start with.

For your convenience, the first chapter on any Office application summarises the basics. Thus, by reading Chapter 8, *Getting Started with Word 2000* in Section 3, you will get an overview of Microsoft Word 2000. You can then select the chapters that follow based on your specific needs. For other applications such as Excel, Access, PowerPoint and Outlook, you may start with sections 4, 5 or 6.

In Section 7 you are introduced to anti-virus software. You will learn to configure and use PC-cillin 2000 as described in this book and Norton Anti-virus as described in the CD-ROM. A very important feature of this book is the accompanying interactive package of on-screen learning supplied on the accompanying CD-ROM. Install this software in your machine for a learning guide that you can use at your convenience and at a speed that suits you. The lessons complement the written matter in this book. Taken together, you have in your hands the most effective computer course designed for the new millennium! We wish you luck and assure you satisfaction!

# Contents

# 1. Introduction

*In this chapter:*

☞ We look at a little bit of the history of personal computing.

☞ We explain how personal computers work.

☞ You are introduced to your computer's hardware.

☞ We work together to set up your personal computer.

☞ You learn how to start up and shut down your computer.

☞ We show you how to load software programmes in your computer.

☞ You learn how to add more hardware to your computer system.

# The Computer Gets Personal

## Overview

Look around you. Almost every thing you do today is influenced in some way by computers. Today computers do much more than simply compute. For example, supermarket scanners calculate our grocery bill while keeping store inventory; computerised telephone switching centres control millions of calls and keep lines of communication untangled while automatic teller machines (ATMs) let us conduct banking transactions from virtually anywhere in the world. Where did all this technology come from and where is it heading? To fully understand and appreciate the impact computers have on our lives and promises they hold for the future, it is important to understand their evolution.

## Early Computers

As early as 1000 BC, a device with a string of beads sliding on thin wires was the first calculating machine invented by man. Called the Abacus, it is still in use in some parts of the world such as China.

More sophisticated mechanical computers were invented between the 17th and the early 20th century. An Englishman, Charles Babbage (1791 to 1871) used steam power to run mechanical computers. However, commercial application of mechanical computers was the brainchild of Herman Hollerith (1860 to 1929), an American. *See Fig 01.01.*

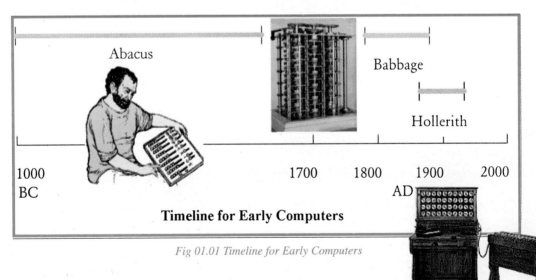

*Fig 01.01 Timeline for Early Computers*

## Modern Computers

Between 1945 and 1956, first-generation computers were built using vacuum tubes for calculations and magnetic tapes for memory. They were really huge in size and needed a team of specialised technical people to look after them. Each computer ran on its own unique programme, and was very unreliable and temperamental.

The second-generation computers (1956 to 1963) were of solid state design, and used transistors in place of vacuum tubes. They had all the components of a modern-day computer: printers, tape storage, disk storage, memory, operating systems, and stored programmes. The IBM 1401 was the most commonly used second-generation computer in business. By 1965, most large American businesses had moved financial accounting to second-generation computers.

Jack Kilby, an engineer with Texas Instruments, developed the integrated circuit (IC) in 1958, bringing the third generation (1964

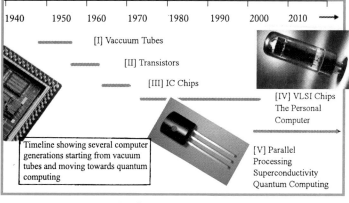

*Fig 01.02 Computer Generations*

to 1971) of computers into existence. The IC combined three electronic components onto a small silicon disc, which was made from quartz. Scientists later managed to fit even more components on a single chip, called a semiconductor. As a result, computers became even smaller as more components were squeezed onto the chip. Another third-generation development included the use of an operating system that allowed machines to run many different programmes at once with a central programme that monitored and coordinated the computer's memory.

*Jack Kilby*

After the integrated circuits, came large-scale integration (LSI) which could fit hundreds of components onto one chip. The fourth generation (1972 to present) of computers was born. By the 1980s, very large-scale integration (VLSI) squeezed hundreds of thousands of components onto a chip. Ultra-large-scale integration (ULSI) increased that number into the millions. The ability to fit so much onto a very small area helped diminish the size and price of computers. It also increased their power, efficiency

*Large-scale Integration (LSI)*

and reliability. The Intel 4004 chip, developed in 1971, took the integrated circuit one step further by locating all the components of a computer (central processing unit, memory, and input and output controls) on a minuscule chip. Whereas previously the integrated circuit had to be manufactured to fit a special purpose, now one microprocessor could be manufactured and then programmed to meet any number of demands. Soon everyday household items such as microwave ovens, television sets and automobiles with electronic fuel injection incorporated microprocessors.

*Fig 01.03 Early Computers*

In 1981, IBM introduced its personal computer (PC) for use in homes, offices and schools. The 1980s saw an expansion in computer use in all three arenas as clones of the IBM PC made the personal computer even more affordable. The number of personal computers in use more than doubled from 2 million in 1981 to 5.5 million in 1982. Ten years later, 65 million PCs were being used. Computers continued their trend toward a smaller size, working their way down from desktop to laptop computers (which could fit inside a briefcase) to palmtop (able to fit inside a breast pocket). In direct competition with IBM's PC was

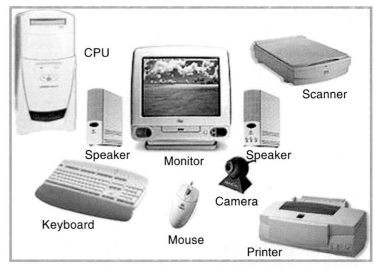

*Fig 01.04 Computer and its Components*

Apple's Macintosh line, introduced in 1984. Notable for its user-friendly design, the Macintosh offered an operating system that allowed users to move screen icons instead of typing instructions. Users controlled the screen cursor using a mouse, a device that mimicked the movement of one's hand on the computer screen.

*Laptop*

*Palmtop*

Many advances in the science of computer design and technology are coming together to enable the creation of fifth-generation computers. Two such engineering advances are parallel processing, which harnesses the power of many central processing units to work as one. Another advance is superconductor technology, which allows the flow of electricity with little or no resistance, greatly improving the speed of information flow. Computers today have some attributes of fifth-generation computers. For example, expert systems assist doctors in making diagnoses by applying the same problem-solving steps an experienced doctor might use in assessing a patient's needs. The future will see many wonders such as quantum computing.

While in the past computers were owned only by governments and very large corporations, the shrinking cost and size has brought computing power within the reach of individuals. From giant machines the computer has become personal in the form of a personal computer or PC.

## How Computers Work

### Computer Basics

We use the computer to carry out tasks. The tasks may be to calculate, to prepare a letter or a report, to find information on the Internet, to draw a picture, a chart or graph or simply to entertain us by playing music, playing a movie clip or by playing games with us.

In doing these tasks, the computer interacts with us. We tell the computer what to do by typing on the computer keyboard, or by pointing with the mouse. The computer responds by running an appropriate software programme and follows it up with messages or pictures on its monitor screen with or without sound from its speakers. Therefore, to accomplish a task using a computer, you need a combination of computer hardware, special programmes called software, and input from yourself.

*Fig 01.05 Input*

Hardware consists of devices, like the central processing unit (CPU), the monitor, keyboard, printer, mouse and speakers. Inside your computer there are more bits of hardware, including the motherboard, where you would find the main processing chips that make up the central processing unit (CPU). The hardware processes the commands it receives from the software, and performs tasks or calculations.

Software is the name given to the programmes that you install on the computer to perform certain types of activities. There is operating system software, such as the Apple Operating System for a Macintosh, or Windows 98 or Windows Me for a PC. There is also application software, like the games we play or the tools we use to compose letters or solve mathematical problems.

You provide the input. When you type a command or click on an icon, you are telling the computer what to do. That is called input.

## How They Work Together

In Fig 01.06, you can see a block diagram showing the relationship of the key components of a personal computer. Shown in the figure are:

1. The Monitor, through which the computer converses with you.
2. The Read Only Memory (ROM) chip that loads the boot-up programme when you start the computer.
3. The Hard Disk Drive (HDD) from which the computer loads the application programme or stored data.
4. The Central Processing Unit (CPU) which is the brain of your computer.
5. The Keyboard through which you talk to the computer.
6. The Mouse which is another device to send inputs to the CPU.

The arrows indicate the direction of signal flow.

First, you provide input when you turn on the computer. Then the system software tells the Central Processing Unit to start up certain programmes and to turn on some hardware devices so that they are ready for more input from you. This whole process is called booting up.

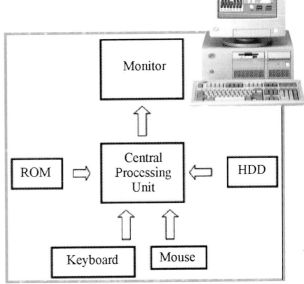
*Fig 01.06 How the Parts of a Computer Work*

The next step happens when you choose a programme you want to use. You click on the icon or enter a command to start the programme. Let us use the example of an Internet browser. Once the browser programme such as the Internet Explorer or Netscape Navigator has started, it is ready for your instructions. You either enter an address called a URL (Uniform Resource Locator), or click on an address you have saved already. In either case, the computer now knows what you want it to do. If you are already connected to the Internet, the browser software goes out to find that address, starting up other hardware devices, such as a modem, when it needs them. If you are not connected, a dialogue box opens on your monitor's screen asking you to provide more input (such as the telephone number of your Internet service provider) it needs to connect to the Internet. If the browser is able to find the correct address, it will then tell your computer to send the information from the web page over the phone wire or cable to your computer. Eventually, you see the web page you were looking for on your monitor's screen.

If you want to print the Web page you see, you can click on the printer icon. Again, you have provided input to tell the computer what to do. The browser software will check to see whether you have a printer attached to your computer, and whether it is turned on. It may remind you to turn on the printer, and then send the information about the web page from your computer over the cable to the printer, where it is printed.

In the next section, we will take a closer look at the different hardware components in a typical desktop personal computer and how the components are connected. After reading the next section the process of how the computer works will become clearer to you.

## The Hardware Parts

What we will describe here is a typical desktop personal computer complete with the ability to connect you to the Internet through your telephone line and play music and video for your entertainment. Virtually all personal computers (or PCs) available in the market will fall in this category, with some additions or omissions.

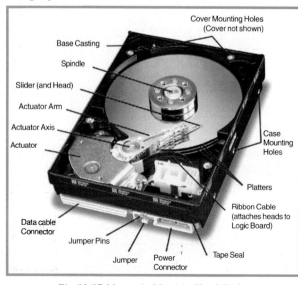

*Fig 01.07 Magnetic Memory Hard Disk*

Most PCs have a Central Processing Unit or CPU as their *brain*, a monitor as their output device and a keyboard plus a mouse as their input devices. In addition, the computer will have *permanent memory* known as Read Only Memory or ROM on fixed or hard disk drives and *temporary memory* as silicon chips called Random Access Memory or RAM. The permanent memory includes your computer's software programmes as well as data that you wish to retain for future use. The permanent memory is not lost when you switch off your computer. On the other hand, temporary memory is used by the computer's CPU while the computer is running. Everything in the computer's temporary memory is lost when you shut your computer down.

These hardware items form the bare essentials of the physical parts of a working PC. In your PC, there may be many additional hardware items called peripherals such as a CD-ROM drive or a printer. Let us now discuss the hardware items one by one.

*CD-ROM Drive*

The computer is box-shaped. It may be flat for use on the desktop, or a vertical tower for placing below the desk. It consists of:

1.  A Processor, such as Intel's Pentium or AMD's *Athlon*. These processors range from 100 MHz to the latest 2,200 MHz clock speeds. This is not the final speed, however. Processors continue to become faster relentlessly. According to Moor's law, the processor speed doubles every 18 months!

*InkJet Printer*

2.  A Motherboard, which functions as an organiser for the hardware parts that must work in unison with the processor. For example, the RAM, the ports for connecting the keyboard and the mouse, the video card that controls the monitor's display and many such components are mounted on or plugged into the motherboard. These components are electrically connected to each other through a *bus* or trunking of copper conductors etched on the motherboard. The processor speed is controlled by a quartz crystal *clock* that provides the pulses required to synchronise the working components.

*Motherboard*

3.  One or more Hard Disk(s) whose magnetic memory is used to save the data and programme files. Hard disks are fixed inside the computer cabinet and are not meant to be removed except for repair or replacement. Current hard disk drives may be anything from 40 to 120 Gigabytes in storage capacity.

4.  Memory chips of two kinds. The Read Only Memory or ROM chips contain permanently stored programme instructions that the computer reads as soon as it is switched on. The ROM programme, called the *bootstrap* programme, provides the start-up instructions. After the bootstrap programme is loaded, it instructs the computer to load the operating system such as Windows and many other programmes to make the computer ready to receive instructions from you. The Random Access Memory or RAM chips, on the other hand, assist the processor by loading bits of data and programmes for easy access. The data in the ROM is permanent. Unlike the data in the RAM, it is not lost when you switch off the computer.

5.  Some PCs have a Graphic Accelerator Card. This card is usually used for video games and for graphic rendering, which require a great deal of fast calculations to produce rapidly changing and complex pictures and graphics on the monitor's screen.

6.  To produce the stereophonic sound required for multimedia games and movies, the computer may have a separate sound card or, the sound capability may be built into the motherboard itself.

7. Components in the computer require power supply at different voltages. Power is supplied at the required voltage by a power supply unit installed inside the computer cabinet called a Switch Mode Power Supply or SMPS Unit.

For providing output to us, PCs have:

1. Monitors like small TV sets with a screen on which we can see the text or graphics that computers produce in response to the instructions we give.

2. Speakers to hear sounds and voices generated by the processor. This function can only be used if you have a Sound Card we have described earlier.

*Monitor*

3. Printers that provide us with printed data on paper, consisting of graphics or pictures in black and white or colour. Printers may range from lower quality dot-matrix printers to better quality ink-jet printers right up to the best quality laser printers.

4. Diskette Drives which can be categorised either as an Output device or an Input device. Diskette drives are magnetic storage devices where data or programme files can be stored. This data can be loaded into the computer or stored back on the disks after you have used the computer to create new data or modify existing data. Disk drives are of several types, starting with 1.44 MB capacity floppy disks to 100 or 250 MB Zip disks. There are also CD-ROM or DVD-ROM drives that handle much higher capacity disks. All these disks are removable and may be taken from one computer to another to provide an easy way for transferring data.

To instruct the computer or to input data into the computer, we use input devices such as a:

- Keyboard, which looks very much like the typewriter keyboard. We enter commands and data for the computer through the keyboard.

- Mouse, which is a small, hand-held device used to move the cursor around the screen. It can be used to execute programmes, or give instructions by clicking on specific *buttons* on the monitor's screen. The mouse is used extensively for graphics programmes such as Adobe Photoshop or AutoCAD. Video games require the use of a mouse, though you can use special *joystick* type games controllers as well.

If your computer has the necessary software and hardware installed, you can use the microphone to record dictation or enter voice commands. In Internet telephony, the microphone acts like the microphone of your telephone.

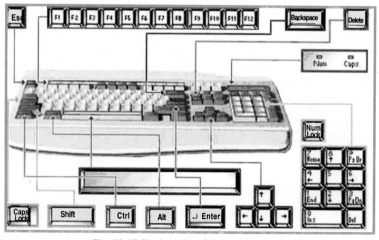

*Fig 01.08 Keyboard and its various keys*

A really important device for the Internet era is the modem. A modem is used to send and receive data from and to other computers around the globe through telephone lines or data cables. There are many types of modems such as internal and external modems, cable modems and so on. The speed of a modem can vary. Telephone modems are usually capable of transmitting data at the rate of 56 kilobytes per second (kbps). Cable modems are much faster.

In addition to the hardware we discussed here, there are many other peripheral devices that you can use to enhance the scope of what your computer can do.

# Setting Up Your System

## The Set-up

We will assume a configuration of hardware and software for this section. We have based it on the most common set-up found in homes today. If your own set-up is a little different, the difference will be small.

## Hardware

We will assume that your hardware is like this:

1. A vertical tower cabinet that houses:
   1.1. Central processing unit (CPU), possibly Pentium III or faster.
   1.2. Motherboard suitable for the CPU such as Intel 810E or 845.
   1.3. Memory chips, both RAM and ROM, the RAM being 128 MB or more.
   1.4. A Floppy Disk Drive (FDD).
   1.5. A 50x or so CD-ROM Drive.
   1.6. A 40 GB or so Hard Disk Drive (HDD).
   1.7. A 56 kbps internal or external modem.
   1.8. A sound card and a video card, either built-in or slotted in the motherboard.
   1.9. A power supply unit (SMPS).

2. A 14", 15" or 17" monitor that looks like a portable TV.
3. A pair of speakers.
4. A keyboard with 101 or more keys.
5. A pointing device called a mouse with two or three buttons.
6. A voltage stabiliser or an uninterrupted power supply unit (UPS).
7. A dot matrix or an ink-jet printer.
8. A set of power and data cables.

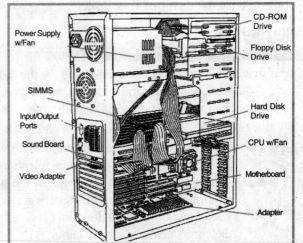

*Inside the Computer*

9. Wall sockets for connecting your voltage stabiliser or UPS.

10. A wall telephone jack for connecting the telephone line to your modem.

As we have already said, do not be too concerned if your own configuration is somewhat different. The set-up procedure we will discuss will still apply.

## Software

In addition to the hardware, we will assume that you have the following software either already installed on your machine, or you have the CD-ROMs and the instruction manuals for the software you intend to install. This will include:

1. The Windows Operating System (OS) such as Windows 98 or Windows Me.

2. The Microsoft Office Suit, perhaps MS Office 2000.

3. All *driver* software for the hardware items such as drivers for the CD-ROM drive, the Modem, the Printer etc.

4. Any additional antivirus or utility software such as Norton Antivirus and Norton Utilities.

**TIP**   If this is your first computer, it is advisable to have the dealer from whom you buy your machine to install the OS and the drivers for your hardware. This process is not ideal for beginners. You can also have all your software installed at your dealer's outlets. However, do make sure that you bring back all the CD-ROMs he has used. Many software programmes, such as MS Office, and even Windows have options not initially loaded in a typical installation. If you need them later, and do not have the CD-ROMs, you will be at the mercy of your dealer!

## Setting Up

Select a location away from an open window for your set-up. You will not want dust or sun to affect your machine. You will need a work table for the monitor, the keyboard and the mouse. If possible, have a sliding tray fitted to the table for the keyboard so that you can store it out of the way when not in use. You will need a special small table with shelves for your printer. The cabinet and the stabiliser or UPS can sit on the floor near the table.

**TRAP**   It is important to have 5 Ampere 3-pin wall sockets for power supply as well as a wall jack (RJ45 type) carrying your telephone line. Make sure that the 3-pin supply has a securely earthed third pin and that the neutral (usually black) line has zero voltage in relation to the third (earth, usually green) pin. It is important to ensure that the body of your computer cabinet does not become "live" and give you an electric shock, or damage the components inside the cabinet!

Remove all the components from their packing and set up as follows:

1. Put the tower cabinet and the stabiliser or UPS on the ground and connect the stabiliser/ UPS to the 5 Amp 3-pin wall plug. Make sure that the power supply switch on the wall is off.

2. Put the monitor, mouse and keyboard on the table. If you have a sliding tray for the keyboard, use it.

3. Put the printer on its table or stand. If you are using a dot-matrix printer with continuous stationery (that comes in continuous, accordion folded sheets perforated at the edges), you will need two additional shelves on the printer stand, one for the paper feed and the other for collecting the printed paper.

4. Locate the two speakers on either side of the monitor.

5. If you have an external modem, you may wish to place it on top of the tower itself.

Make sure that all items are securely placed and are not likely to be knocked over accidentally.

Now install the data cables. Data cables carry data from one item to the other. Most of them will be connected to the back of your computer's tower.

- Connect the jack from the speakers to the tower.
- Connect the flat printer cable to the 25-pin socket, the tower at one end and the printer at the other end.
- If you have an external modem, connect the modem cable to the tower at one end and to the modem at the other. The modem end will usually have 25 pins while you may choose a 9-pin or 25-pin socket for connection to your computer – depending on your machine's configuration, your dealer will tell you which to use.

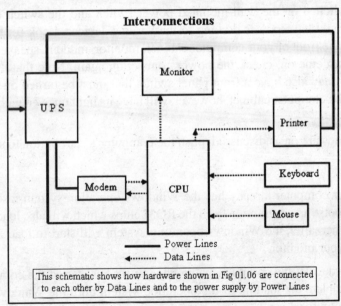

*Fig 01.09 Connection Diagram*

- Connect the telephone cable (with RJ45 jacks) to the modem (at the socket marked "line") at one end and to the telephone wall socket at the other end.
- If you have a telephone, use the second similar cable to connect the modem to the phone. The modem will have two sockets at its back, marked "line" and "phone" respectively. If everything is correct, you should be able to hear a dial tone when you pick up the handset of your telephone.

- Plug in the keyboard and the mouse data cables. Ask your dealer beforehand whether he is supplying you with serial or PS2 devices and have him point out the correct sockets to use.

- Now install the power cables. You will need to connect the computer, the monitor, the printer and, perhaps, the modem (if external) and the speakers to their own power supply sockets. Make sure that your stabiliser or UPS has sufficient sockets at its back. Usually, only three are provided.

- If you have a UPS and do not wish to lose data, connect the computer, the monitor and the modem to the three available sockets. You can afford to lose power to the printer and speakers in case of a power failure.

You are now ready to switch on power. To do so, you will use the wall-mounted power switch. A light in front of your stabiliser or UPS will come on to confirm that power supply is on. The stabiliser or UPS will have another switch (on the front panel or at the back) which you will then turn on to supply power to your computer system.

# Starting Up and Shutting Down

## Power On

Once you have switched on the wall-mounted power switch and the switch of your stabiliser or UPS is on, you should have power flowing to the various devices. Look for the indicating lamps (usually green) on the front of your computer cabinet, monitor, modem, speakers and printer. If any of the lights do not come on, check the power connection again. Note that the monitor, modem, speakers or printer may also have a front panel switch that must be turned on or pushed in for the light to come on. The computer cabinet, however, will have its light on even without your pushing its start button.

If all indicating lamps are on as discussed, push the computer's start button to start up your system.

## Log On

Assuming that your computer already has the Windows operation system installed, the computer will first load the bootstrap programme from the ROM chips which will also load the basic operating system or BIOS. Thereafter, the Windows operating system will start to load and you will see the Log-on screen on your monitor.

Enter your password to let the computer know which user has started the computer and Windows will proceed to complete the loading of the operation system until the Windows opening screen is displayed on your monitor.

We will discuss the Windows operating system in Chapter 3, *The Windows Operating System*.

## Log Off

After you have finished with whatever assignment you have begun on your computer, you may wish to shut your machine down. In order to make sure that the work you are doing has been saved on your hard disk and to avoid damaging your software programmes or your operating system, you should proceed in the following sequence.

1.  Shut down all programmes (except Windows) that may be running on your computer. We will learn about shutdown procedures in more detail later in this book.

2.  Close all open data files.

3.  Now click on the **Start** button at the bottom left of your Windows screen and select the **Shut down** option. Click **OK**. *See Fig 01.10.*

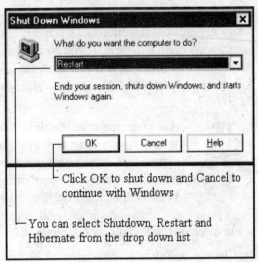

A message on the screen will inform you when shut down is complete. If you have an ATX machine, capable of being shut down by the Windows software, you have to do nothing except wait for the monitor's screen to go blank. If a manual shut down is required, you will see a message on your screen saying that it is now safe to shut down Windows.

*Fig 01.10 Windows Shut Down Screen*

## Power Off

Once log off is complete, you may shut your system down by simply switching off the power supply to the stabiliser. If you have a UPS and you wish to keep the mains supply on for battery charging, then switch off (or push off) the output switch on your UPS. It is generally unnecessary to switch each individual component of your computer off each time.

# Installing Software

If your computer has been pre-loaded with all the software you need by your dealer, then you may skip this section. As we have mentioned before, most of the modern software are fairly large and have a number of optional components that may not be installed automatically. Therefore, as you keep using the software, you may feel the need to add or remove certain software components. If so, it is useful to know the general procedure.

We will presume that the Windows operating system has already been loaded on your machine. Loading Windows and installing all the software drivers for your hardware requires some expertise. You will, of course, be able to do so after you have read through this book!

For this discussion, we will assume that you have a hard disk of 20 to 40 GB (Gigabyte)

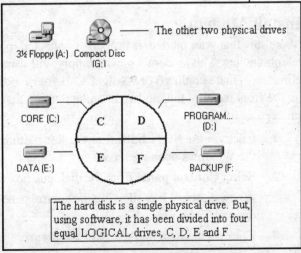

*Fig 01.11 Logical Partitions*

capacity. You should ask your dealer or computer supplier to format your hard disk and divide it into 4 logical partitions, labelled C, D, E and F. If you have a CD-ROM drive, it will be identified as G and your floppy drive will be A. If you do so, although you will still have only one hard disk, each logical partition will behave as if it is a separate disk. In other words, your computer will appear to have four hard disks, marked C:, D:, E: and F: each with 1/4th capacity of your physical disk. *See Fig 01.11.*

**TIP** Ask your dealer to install Windows on the root drive or drive C. You should install all your software programmes on drive D and save all your data files on drive E. Reserve drive F for saving back-up copies of your very valuable data. This arrangement will minimise the risk of corrupting your data or your software programmes as you use your computer. By backing up your most valuable data on drive F, you may really save the situation some day if your normal data drive (E) is corrupted by a virus attack or some mechanical damage to your hard disk.

In Chapter 7, *Introducing Microsoft Office 2000*, we will study the procedure of installing the Office 2000 suit of programmes in more detail.

# Installing and Adding Hardware

It is best to ask your dealer to install the software drivers of the hardware that is already installed inside the computer's cabinet. For example, he can install Windows and then install the drivers for the CD-ROM drive and the internal modem if you have one. If you have an external modem, you may wish to install its software driver after you have set up the computer in your home. The same goes for your printer and other peripherals you may have such as a Zip drive or a scanner.

In this discussion, we will study the installation of an external modem and a printer to illustrate the process. You can use the same basic steps for any other hardware peripherals that you may wish to add to your system.

We will assume that your computer has been powered up, you have logged on to Windows and the Windows opening screen is displayed on your monitor's screen.

## Install Modem

Make sure that your modem is properly connected to your computer, to the power supply and to the telephone line. The modem's power supply will usually be through a transformer/rectifier (battery eliminator) that supplies 6 or 9 volts DC to your modem. Make sure that the power indicating lamp on the front panel of the modem is on, indicating that power is being received by the modem. Now proceed as follows:

1. Click on the **Start button** at the left bottom corner of the Windows opening screen.
2. Select **Control panel** from the dialogue box that opens.
3. A new dialogue box showing the control panel will now open.
4. Click on the icon marked **Add hardware**.

*Modem*

See Fig 01.13 later in this section for a view of the *Add new hardware* icon.

Follow the instructions on the monitor's screen, inserting the CD-ROM containing the driver software for your modem when the computer asks you to do so.

After the installation is complete, you can test that the computer is able to communicate with your modem as follows:

1. Follow the instructions given earlier to open the control panel.

2. In the control panel dialogue box, click on the **Modem icon**.

3. In the dialogue box that opens, select **Modem properties**.

4. This opens a new dialogue box in which select **Query modem**.

5. A final dialogue box will appear after a few seconds showing the results of the modem test. None of the results should read *Failed. See Fig 01.12*

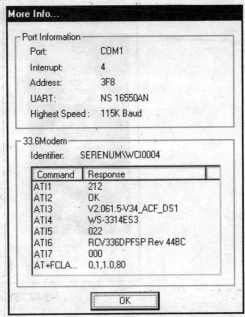

*Fig 01.12 Querying Modem*

Close all the dialogue boxes by clicking on the Close button ⊠ at the top right hand corner of the dialogue box. You can also click on the **OK** button at the bottom of the dialogue box.

If your modem is a current model and recognised by Windows, it is what is called a plug-and-play model. Installation is simpler then. For details, see the procedure for printer installation in the following section.

## Install Printer

Make sure that the printer is connected properly to its power supply and the data cable (a flat ribbon with 25-pin plug at one end and socket at the other) is connected to the computer at one end and to the printer at the other.

1. Switch on the printer and make sure that paper has been inserted properly.

2. Leave the printer on, but restart the computer as follows:

   • Click the **Start** button at the bottom left of the Windows opening screen.

   • Select **Shut down**.

   • In the dialogue box that appears, click **Restart** and then click **OK**.

*Laser Printer*

The computer will shut down and restart on its own. The computer will open the Add Hardware Wizard if it detects the new hardware you have added. If your computer is of the plug-and-play variety, Windows will detect the printer and either install the printer's driver from Windows' own collection of printer software drivers, or ask you to insert the CD-ROM supplied along with the printer.

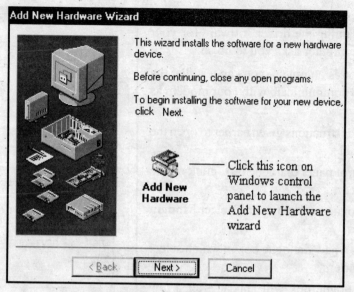

Fig 01.13 Add New Hardware Wizard

If the printer is an old (called *Legacy*) model, Windows may not be able to recognise it. If so, follow the steps described earlier in installing your modem for installing the legacy printer.

**CD-ROM**  To learn more about how personal computers work in a multimedia environment, insert the accompanying CD-ROM in your computer, select the **Interactive** mode in the opening screen. The main menu will appear. To go the section on Computer Fundamentals, click **Computer Fundamentals ➔ ABC of Computers**. You will see a sub-menu containing the following topics:

- How Computers Work
- Essential Components of Computers
- Optional Components of Computers
- Inside the Computer
- Functions of Computer Components

Click on the topic you want to view and follow instructions that will appear on your screen.

# 2. The Disk Operating System

# Who Needs DOS?

The answer to this question is "It depends!" The reason is that DOS or the disk operating system is at the core of all Windows Operating Systems (OS) right up to and including Windows 98 and Windows Me. It means that when you enter a command into your computer through the keyboard or your mouse, Windows transfers the command to the layer that lies below the DOS layer. You can picture a four-layer cake with you as the user at the top, followed by Windows, then DOS and finally, the central processing unit (CPU) of your machine.

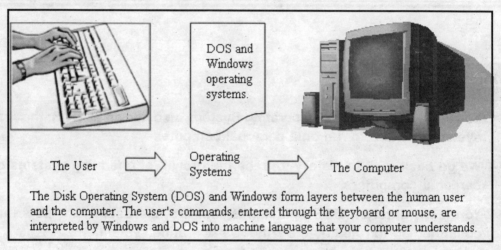

The Disk Operating System (DOS) and Windows form layers between the human user and the computer. The user's commands, entered through the keyboard or mouse, are interpreted by Windows and DOS into machine language that your computer understands.

*Fig 02.01 User/WINDOWS/DOS/CPU Layers*

We assume that you use Windows 98 or Windows Me like a majority of computer users in India. Therefore, you are using an operating system that is really running on a DOS kernel. For better control and in special circumstances, you have to go back to DOS. For example, assume that you have bought a new hard disk, or you had to completely destroy all files on your hard disk to get rid of a virus. In such cases, you have to format your hard disk using DOS. Even if your Windows operating system is working well, you may go down to the depth of DOS for faster, better response from your computer. In this section, we will explore DOS.

You will probably see a DOS icon on your desktop. If the icon is missing, do the following:

1. Double click the **My Computer** icon on your desktop to open its dialogue box.

2. In this, click on **C:** (for Windows 98 or Local Disk C: for Windows Me), opening the contents of the C: or the root drive where DOS and your Windows operating system files are located.

3. Locate the **Windows sub-folder** and click on this to display the sub-folder's contents.

4. Scroll down the list of contents (use the down arrow key on your keyboard to move the highlight down the list) till you highlight the **MS-DOS icon**.

5. Now position the mouse arrow on the **icon**, click the left button of your mouse and drag the **icon** down on your desktop.

6. When you release the left mouse button, a dialogue box will open asking you if you wish to create a shortcut of the icon on your desktop.

**MS-DOS
Prompt**

7. Click the **Yes** button of the dialogue box and a desktop icon for starting MS-DOS will be created on your desktop like the one shown in the previous page.

**TIP**

Now, anytime you wish to open a DOS window even if Windows is running, just click on the icon.

If you do not wish to create an icon on your desktop, you can also start DOS by clicking:

**Start → Programmes → MS DOS** from the Windows opening screen.

# A Bit of History

One of the first operating systems for personal computers was Disk Operating System or DOS. This operating system was originally designed by Tim Patterson for Seattle Computer Products. It was eventually licensed to Microsoft, who sold it to IBM in the early 1980s.

DOS 1.0 was first released in 1981 for the IBM-PC. DOS was upgraded and rewritten in many versions thereafter, passing through versions 2, 3, 4, 5 and 6. DOS 6.x was capable of supporting Microsoft Windows. In Windows Me, DOS 7.0 was introduced. Thereafter, Windows NT 5.0, Windows 2000 and Windows XP were all rewritten using a new core or kernel named New Technology or NT and DOS was no longer used to support these versions of Windows. *See Fig 02.02.*

DOS was really designed for running one programme at a time. However, as the user's need became greater, the PC was required to run more than one process at the same time.

For example, with later versions of Windows such as Windows 98 or Windows Me, you can edit one document while the computer drives your printer to print out another document in the background. However, such demanding performance was not very easy with DOS, which made errors and *crashed* from time to time. To solve this problem, and also to provide support for many advanced hardware and software technologies that were emerging, Microsoft rewrote its Windows

| DOS Version | FEATURES |
|---|---|
| Dos 1.0 | Released in 1981 for the IBM-PC. Supported 16K of RAM and single sided 5.25" 160K floppy disks. |
| DOS 2.0 | Released to support IBM's XT in 1983, with more than twice the commands of version 1.x. Also supported small hard disks of around 5 MB. |
| DOS 2.1 | Released to support IBM's PCjr with some minor improvements added. |
| DOS 3.0 | Released to support IBM-AT, with a few LAN features added. |
| DOS 3.1 | More LAN features and support added. |
| DOS 3.2 | Support for 3.5" floppy drives added. |
| DOS 3.3 | Released to support IBM's PS/2 and new 3.5", 1.44 MB floppy drives. New international character sets for 17 countries were added. |
| DOS 4.0 | A DOS shell was added and some minor changes and bug fixes were made. |
| DOS 5.0 | Released in 1991 with superior memory management, macro support and DOS shell enhancements. |
| DOS 6.x | Released to support Microsoft Windows, disk defrag, file compression, anti-virus etc. |
| DOS 7.0 | The last version of DOS supporting Windows 95, 98 and ME. |

*Fig 02.02 DOS Family Tree*

operating system using a new core or kernel named NT or New Technology. NT uses a different filing system from DOS, called New Technology Filing System or NTFS. NTFS and NT together perform a great deal faster and more reliably than DOS did.

With DOS, you could not point at small pictures on your screen (called icons) and click with your mouse to get the computer to do what you wanted. The Apple Macintosh range of computers had acquired this capability and Microsoft followed suit by introducing Windows. DOS remained below the Windows layer, hidden from the user. In Chapter 3, *The Windows Operating System,* we will look at Windows in more detail.

Initially, Microsoft launched Windows NT 4.0 in parallel with Windows 98, intending that home users would continue to use Windows 95 or 98 while the more reliable and robust NT technology would be used for business applications. This parallel situation continued till Windows Me was launched for home use while business was urged to buy Windows 2000, which had an NT kernel.

Recently, Microsoft merged these two separate styles of operating systems by launching Windows XP (for Experience!) which comes in two flavours, Home and Professional. Both varieties run on an NT kernel and DOS has been finally banished from the computer, although you can open a command window in XP that looks a great deal like the old DOS window and accepts many DOS commands.

As we have already discussed, if you use Windows 98, Windows Me or any earlier version of Windows, there is DOS under the hood of your machine and it will pay to become familiar with it.

# DOS Commands

## The DOS Prompt

After you launch DOS either by clicking on the MS-DOS icon on your desktop or by clicking on **Start ➔ Programmes ➔ MS-DOS**, a DOS window will open on your screen, which is a bit drab and severe looking. You will see a DOS prompt that looks like C:\>. This is the command line and to make DOS do what you want, you have to type the appropriate DOS command immediately after the C:\>.

The first character, a C in this case, tells you which drive is active. If your command is meant for another drive, it will be necessary to first change the drive to your target drive. For example, if you wish to change to your floppy drive which may have a floppy disk with files you wish to examine, type CD\A: and then press the Enter key on your keyboard. The DOS prompt will change to A:\>.

The next character, : (colon) indicates that C or A is a drive name. The next character, a backslash \, indicates the path within the drive

*Fig 02.03 DOS Window*

about which we will discuss shortly. The final greater than > sign is really the actual prompt. The cursor will appear immediately to the right of the prompt. It indicates exactly where you must begin typing your commands.

## The Command Language

The command language used by DOS is a little unfriendly and not easy to remember. That is one reason why operating systems added a Graphical User Interface (GUI) on DOS to make it easier for the user to give commands to his or her computer. DOS can only handle 8 characters as a command or the name of a file. That is one reason why both commands and filenames in DOS are cryptic and difficult to remember. For example you will come across commands such as ATTRIB, CHKDSK (also called SCANDISK in later DOS versions), MD etc or file names such as JAN02SLS. If you are curious, ATTRIB sets the attributes (such as hidden, read-only etc.) of a file. The JAN02SLS stands for Sales Report for January 2002!

One good thing is that DOS does not differentiate between a command like COPY, Copy or copy. That is, DOS commands are not sensitive to upper case or lower case letters in the command.

### *Examples*

To check that your hard disk (say the C: drive) is free from errors, while in the C: drive, you can enter a command at the C:\> prompt such as SCANDISK C:. This will cause the ScanDisk utility within DOS to run. A dialogue box will open displaying the progress of the checking process and, after a few minutes, you will receive a report of the status of the disk on your monitor's screen.

After you execute a number of DOS commands, the screen may accumulate a lot of text.

To clear the screen, at the DOS prompt C:\>, type CLS. The screen will clear immediately.

We will examine more DOS commands in the following section.

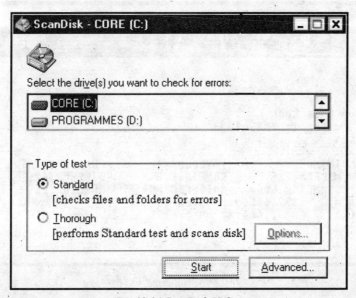

*Fig 02.04 ScanDisk Utility*

# DOS Commands

DOS is installed in a sub-directory on your root directory, usually on the C: drive. To execute any DOS command, you must either be operating from the C: drive, or you will have to set a "path" from your active directory to the directory that has the DOS sub-directory. You do so by executing the PATH command. For example, if you wish to run the CHKDSK utility on your floppy drive, which is usually the A: drive, while the A: drive is active, type the following (excluding the angle brackets):

    &lt;A:\&gt; Path=C\DOS&gt;        To bring CHKDSK on drive C on path

    &lt;A:\&gt; CHKDSK&gt;          To start the utility, hitting **Enter** ↵ each time.

The prompt you will see while in the A: drive is of course A:\>. At this prompt, type &lt;PATH = C:\DOS&gt;. By doing so, you establish a pathway from the A drive to C:\DOS, which is the sub-directory on your root C: drive in which the CHKDSK utility resides. Now you can ask DOS to check the floppy disk in your A: drive simply by typing &lt;CHKDSK A:&gt; at the A:\> prompt.

Let us look at a few more common DOS commands in this section.

## *The DIR Command*

To display all the files in your current drive (say C:), type &lt;DIR&gt; at the C:\> prompt and press **Enter** ↵. You will get a screen full of files and directories displayed. Files will carry an extension consisting of three letters indicating the type of the file. For example, all programme files carry an extension .exe. Similarly, all text files will have an extension of .txt and so on. Your drive may contain complete directories as well. Directories are collection of files. Directories are enclosed within square brackets like [WINDOWS] as you can see in Fig 02.05. On the other hand, files will appear without surrounding brackets such as MSCDEX.EXE.

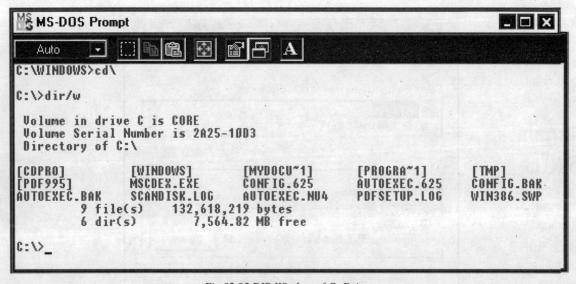

*Fig 02.05 DIR Window of C: Drive*

Additional information includes the drive name and its serial number. For instance, in Fig 02.05 you will see the following information:

*Volume in drive C is CORE*, which is the volume name and *Volume Serial Number is 2A25-10D3*, which is the serial number allotted automatically when the drive is first formatted.

### *The MD Command*

To organise files on your hard disk, you may create separate directories for each topic and store files related to that topic within that directory. For example, on your C: drive, you can create a directory marked Expenses, another marked Correspondence and so on. Then, all files related to expenses will go in the Expenses directory while all correspondence files will be saved in the Correspondence directory and so on. To create a directory named Expenses in the C: drive, proceed as follows:

1.  Make sure that you are at the root of the C: drive. This is done by typing <C:\> at the C:\> prompt. If you are in any directory in the C: drive other than the root, you will be taken to the root directory.

2.  Now type <MD Expenses> at the C:\> prompt and press **Enter** ⏎. The Directory named Expenses will be created.

### *The CD Command*

Having created a directory such as Expenses, you can easily navigate down to Expenses from the root directory by typing CD Expenses at the C:\> prompt and pressing **Enter** ⏎. The prompt will now change to C:\Expenses\> showing that now you are in the Expenses directory on your C: drive. If you now type the command <DIR> at the C:\Expenses\> prompt, only the contents of the Expenses directory will appear on the screen.

To move up back to the root directory, type <CD\ at the C:\Expenses\> prompt. Note how the prompt changes back to C:\>. Now if you were to type the <DIR> command, you will see Expenses with the extension <DIR> but the individual files within Expenses will not be displayed.

It is important to understand how directories and files are organised under DOS. In Windows too, the organisation is very similar. However, the commands are given differently. In the next section, we look at how DOS organises files and directories.

# Organising Directories and Files

## Directories and Files

On a personal computer, every programme and all data are saved on your hard disk as files. In DOS, files may have a name containing a maximum of 8 characters. In addition, file names have a three-character extension which identifies the type of the file.

Thus WINWORD.EXE is the programme file called WinWord (Word for Windows) and the extension .EXE indicates that it is a programme file. If you create a sales report for the month of January using WORD called SLRPTJAN, it will be saved on your hard disk as a file called SLRPTJAN.DOC where the extension .DOC is automatically added by Microsoft Word to identify the file as a formatted text document created by using Word.

In turn, files are collected together under a directory so that all files related to a subject, topic or project are kept together for convenience of location afterwards. Thus you may create a directory named Expenses and then sub-directories under Expenses titled Personal and Business respectively. Then you could group all your data files for personal expenses under C:\Expenses\Personal and all your business expense files under C:\Expenses\Business. You can navigate up and down from the root to the directory and the sub-directories using the CD command.

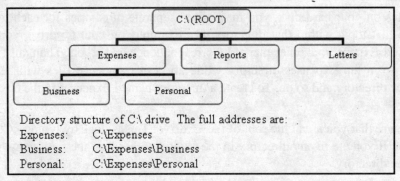

*Fig 02.06 DOS File Structure*

After you have used the DOS directory and file structures for a little while, you will begin to appreciate the convenience of being able to expand and contract the view of the files at will by using the CD and DIR commands so that you can either view a complete list of all files within a directory or just the list of directories in a drive.

## Partitions

Till just a couple of years ago, a typical PC would have a single hard disk of some 10 GigaBytes (GB) capacity. The entire hard disk would be used as a single drive, designated by the drive letter C:. The operating system files of Windows and DOS as well as all programmes and data files would be installed on drive C: under different directories. Since then, hard disks have really grown in size. At the time of writing this book, hard disks of 40 GB capacity are considered minimum requirement for a home computer and giant disks with 120 GB capacity are not unknown. With so much capacity available, it is possible to organise programmes and data even better.

**TIP**

Our advice to you is that you should ask your dealer to partition your 40 GB hard disk into 4 equal parts using the DOS FDISK programme. These 4 parts, though located on a single physical disk, will be recognised by your computer as 4 logical disks, exactly as if they were four separate physical disks of 10 GB each.

If you have a floppy drive and a CD-ROM drive, you will end up with the following set up:

A:  Floppy Drive
C:  Root drive on your hard disk. Windows and DOS will be installed here
D:  The next partition on your hard disk. Install all your programme files here
E:  The third partition (logical drive) where you can store all your data files
F:  The fourth partition (logical drive) for backing up your most valuable data
G:  A second physical drive which is your CD-ROM drive.

**NOTE** Note that you have only three physical drives, the floppy drive (A:), the hard disk (C:) and the CD-ROM drive (G:). However, by partitioning C: into 4 parts, you have created three additional logical or virtual drives labelled D:, E: and F:.

If you follow this suggestion you will find that your data will become logically arranged and well organised. A major benefit is that by separating the Windows system files (on drive C:) from the programme files (on drive D:) and the data files (on drive E:), you will minimise the risk of corrupting your Windows system files during hard disk read or write operations.

There are added advantages. For example, if you defragment your C: drive from time to time to improve your computer's performance, the defragmentation process will be limited to 10 GB instead of the entire 40 GB on the physical drive C:, saving you time. The backed up critical data files on F: can become invaluable if due to any reason some important original data file on E: gets corrupted and its data is lost.

While we have discussed partitions here, it is strongly recommended that you have your dealer do the partitioning before Windows, other programmes and data files are installed. This is a job for a professional software engineer!

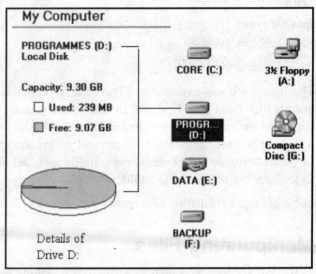

*Fig 02.07 Drives on Your Computer*

## Recommended Structure

In the earlier section we have discussed the procedure for creating sub-directories and the procedure for navigating from one drive to another and also down from root directories and sub-directories and up again. Let us look at a computer's filing organisation assuming that it has a single 40 GB hard disk with 4 partitions.

### C: Drive
\ (Root)
Sub Directory [Windows]
Sub Directory [DOS]
Sub Directory [Programme Files]

### D: Drive
\ (Root)
Sub Directory [MS Office]
Sub Directory [Norton Utilities]

*E: Drive*

\ (Root)

Sub Directory [Expenses]

Sub Directory [Correspondence]

Sub Directory [Reports]

*F: Drive*

\ (Root) .

Sub Directory [Backup]

Sub Directory [Win98]

Sub Directory [Off2000]

The names are self-explanatory. The F: drive contains a sub-directory called Backup for storing critical files from your E: drive. In addition, the entire contents of the Windows 98 CD-ROM are copied in the sub-directory called Win98. Similarly, the entire contents of your Office 2000 CD-ROM can be stored in the third sub-directory. This arrangement will allow you to easily add Windows or Office software components (not initially installed in a typical installation) without your having to look for the required CD-ROM.

For a graphic explanation of a multi-level directory structure, see Fig 02.06 earlier in this chapter.

# Manipulating Files

In the last section, we saw how virtually everything is stored in your computer as files. Each file has a name consisting of a maximum of 8 alpha-numeric characters, called a file name, followed by three more characters called extension. Since all your programmes and data are stored as files, you can easily see that to be good at computer operation, you must have a good idea of how to manipulate files. In this section, we will learn some basic file manipulation skills.

## Creating Files

You can create files in the DOS window by typing the command <Copy con filename.Extension>. The filename may be up to 8 alpha-numeric characters while the three character extension identifies the type of the file such as ".bat" for a batch file, or ".txt" for a text file and so on. The full name for "Copy con" is "copy to console", which tells the computer to display what you type on your computer's console or monitor. We will study this method of file creation in the next section on Start-up files.

However, most of the files you will come across are data files created by the software programme you use for a specific purpose. Thus, Microsoft Word will produce data files with the extension ".doc" while Microsoft Excel will create data files (spreadsheets in this case) with the extension ".xls" and so on. Graphic programmes such as Microsoft Paint will produce a bitmapped image file with the extension ".bmp" and so on. When you use a programme such as Word or Excel, for saving your file, it is only necessary to type in the filename. The programme will attach the appropriate extension automatically. Thus, if you save January 2002 sales data in an Excel spreadsheet, you have only to enter, say "JanSls02" and the programme will automatically add the extension ".xls" to the filename. Some typical filename extensions are shown in Fig 02.08.

| Extension | Sample | Generating Programme |
|---|---|---|
| *.txt | MyNotes.txt | Notepad |
| *.doc | ComputerBook.doc | MS Word |
| *.xls | MyCalculations.xls | MS Excel |
| *.ppt | MYCharts. | MS PowerPoint |
| *.mdb | MyDatabase. | MS Access |
| *.html | MSNHome.html | HTML Editor |
| *.bmp | MyLogo.bmp | MS Paint |
| *.exe | WinWord.exe | MS Word |

*Fig 02.08 Filenames and Extensions*

## Naming Rules

In addition to the restriction of a maximum 8 alpha-numeric characters for the filename and 3 for the extension, here are some additional basic rules you must follow while naming files:

- The filename may contain any alphabet from A to Z either upper case (capitals), lower case or a mixture of the two. Thus, JANSLS02, jansls02 or JanSls02 are all valid and all mean the same thing to the computer.
- You can also use any numeric character from 0 to 9, or a combination of alpha and numeric characters. Thus you can have a filename such as 981245 or JanSales or JanSls02.
- You can use any other special character on your keyboard except the following: ? / \ < > ; | or "".
- You cannot use any name reserved by a DOS command such as DIR, CD, MD etc unless you combine the command name with other letters or numeric. Thus you cannot name a file DIR.txt, but you can use FileDIR.txt.
- The dot or period (.) can be used only once in the filename. Thus you cannot name a file "JanSls.02.xls". Instead you can use the underscore "_" to separate parts of a filename for clarity. Thus you can use JanSl_02.xls as a valid filename.

## Copying Files

It is often necessary to copy files from one location to another. For example, you may create a data file containing a memo or letter using Microsoft Word that you wish to share with others. A simple way of doing so is to copy the file from your hard disk to a removable floppy disk and then send the floppy disk to the person with whom you may wish to share the memo or letter.

For copying files in DOS, you have to use the COPY command in DOS. Since this command is available in your DOS directory, usually located on your C:\> drive, you must either issue the command from the C:\> drive or set a path from the active drive to the C:\> drive. Let us take an example. Let us assume that you have saved your letter on E:\> drive, which is your data drive, with the filename MyLet.txt. You intend to copy this letter to your floppy drive which is normally A:\> drive and DOS resides in the DOS folder on your root directory, normally the C:\> drive; in a directory named DOS. You are on your E:\> drive when you begin issuing DOS commands. That is, you see the prompt E:\> in your DOS window. You will issue the following DOS commands for file copying:

    <PATH ₸ C:\DOS>      This sets the path from your active (E:\>) drive to the directory containing DOS.

    <COPY MyLet.txt A:>    COPY is followed by the filename (MyLet.txt) followed by the target drive, in this case, A:\>.

## Deleting Files

You can delete a file by the DEL (Delete) command. The procedure for specifying the path to the drive and directory containing DOS should be kept in mind. However, once you have specified the path, you need not do so in the same DOS session. Thus, if after copying the file MyLet.txt to the floppy disk on A:\> drive you wish to delete the copy of MyLet.txt on your hard disk drive, type:

    <DEL MyLet.txt>

Note that you are still in your E:\> drive after the file copying exercise and the path from E:\> to the DOS directory has already been specified. Therefore, you need not do so again.

## Wildcards in Filenames

In the example above, we have worked with just one file, copying it and then deleting it. If you need to copy or delete a number of files and they have similarity in name or in filename extension, then you can apply your DOS command to the entire batch of files at one time, saving you both time and typing effort.

Let us assume that you have ten memos on your E:\> drive titled MyLet01.txt, MyLet02.txt and so on up to MyLet10.txt and you wish to copy them all onto a floppy disk on your floppy drive A:\>. You can then get the copying done by a single command like this:<COPY MyLet??.txt A:\>

Here, the two question marks (?) are called wildcard characters since they can stand for any two permissible alpha-numeric characters. In this case, they stand for numbers from 0 to 9. The idea of a wildcard is borrowed from certain card games where a special card like the joker may stand for any card in the pack.

If your letters MyLet01.txt to MyLet10.txt were the only text files (with the extension .txt) on your E:\> drive, you could then use another wildcard character, the asterisk (*) to represent all the filenames with the .txt extension. Your command may then be:

    <COPY *.txt A:\>

Here the asterisk stands for all the filenames ranging from MyFile01 to MyFile10 since they all have the same extension, ".txt".

You must have noticed that the question mark (?) wildcard represents any single alpha-numeric character, whereas the asterisk (*) stands for any number of alpha-numeric characters, limited, of course to 8 in the filename and 3 in the extension. Therefore, if you wish to address all the files on a drive, you can issue a DOS command followed by a full wildcard such as either *.* or ????????.???. It will be obvious to you that it is more convenient to use the asterisk in such situations rather than the clumsier question mark.

**TRAP**

Since wildcards will address many files at one time, be very careful while using them, especially while deleting files. You can easily imagine the havoc you will cause if you issue a command such as C:\> DEL *.*.

This command will effectively destroy the operating system and all other files on the root directory of your computer and make the computer unusable!

## Navigation

Navigating up and down the drives and directories may appear confusing. However, if you remember the basic structure of your hard disk, you will be able to do so easily. Let us take an example to illustrate:

Assume that on your C:\> drive, you have the following directories and sub-directories:

- First the root directory designated as C:\.
- Under the root directory, you have two sub-directories named Letters and Bills.
- Under Letters you have two sub-sub-directories named Personal and Business.

See Fig 2.06 earlier in this chapter for a view of multi-level directories and files.

Now assume that you are in the root directory, that is, in C:\. To travel down to the first level of sub-directory (either Letter or Bills) you will type the DOS command <CD\Letters> to go to Letters.

To go down one more level to the sub-sub-directories (either Personal or Business) you have to type the DOS command <CD\Personal> to go to Personal.

Alternatively, from the root directory C:\> you can go down two levels to the sub-sub-directory by typing the DOS command <CD\Letters\Personal> to go directly to the sub-sub-directory Personal.

While moving up from the sub-sub level you can reverse the process. To go up one level, issue the DOS command <CD\Letters>.

**NOTE**

To jump up directly from the sub-sub level to the root level, issue the command <CD\>. You will then bypass the sub-directory level Personal and go right up to the root directory level, which is C:\.

It is really simpler to use the Windows interface called the Windows Explorer to navigate drives and directories. We will learn how to use the Windows Explorer in Chapter 3, *The Windows Operating System*, later in this book.

**CD-ROM**

To learn more about how personal computers work in a multimedia environment, insert the accompanying CD-ROM in your computer, select the **Interactive** mode in the opening screen. The main menu will appear. To go to the section on DOS, click **DOS** ➔ **Need of DOS and DOS Commands**. You will see a sub-menu containing the following topics:

- Use of DOS
- Accessing DOS
- Copying and deleting Files
- Displaying Files
- Creating Directory
- Using Check Disk Utility

Click on the topic you want to view and follow instructions on your screen.

# 3. The Windows Operating System

# A Typical Computer Set-up

What you see of the computer before you and can reach out and touch is its hardware. Your computer will usually include:

- The computer itself, housed in a flat rectangular box on your desk, or placed vertically, looking like a small tower, below the tabletop.
- The monitor, placed on the table, like a small TV.
- A keyboard, somewhat like a typewriter but provided with many more keys.
- A mouse with two or three buttons, usually sitting on a flat mouse pad.
- A printer.
- A modem used to connect your computer to the telephone line and on to the Internet.

In addition, you may have other hardware devices such as floppy drives installed in your computer, a separate zip-drive for storing data, an uninterrupted power supply unit or UPS etc.

A typical desktop set-up consisting of a computer on the left, complete with monitor and keyboard. For a more detailed view of individual components of your computer, see Fig 01.06 earlier in this book. Fig 01.09 that follows explains how the components are connected together.

We will presume that you already have some knowledge about your hardware, or can get some help and expertise about how to operate them.

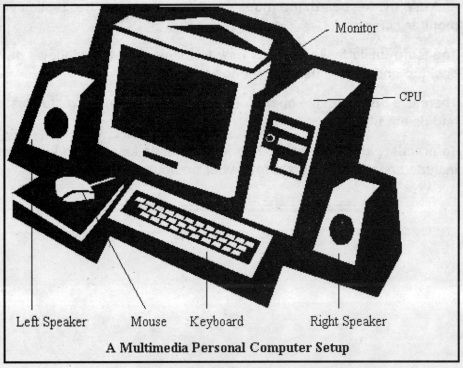

**A Multimedia Personal Computer Setup**

*Fig 03.01 A Typical Desktop Computer*

Essential skills that you need include how to:

- Switch the power to the computer, monitor, modem etc on and off.
- Type your commands on the keyboard.
- Move the mouse cursor (or pointer) and click your mouse buttons to send instructions to the computer.
- Operate the printer.

# Loading Instructions

For a computer, the instructions are written in a language that the computer can understand. A set of instructions put together is a programme. Windows 98 is one such programme. Microsoft Word, Microsoft Excel etc are other programmes that you may use on your computer. A programme enables the computer to carry out your commands. You send commands to the computer either by typing them on the keyboard or by clicking the buttons on your mouse. In turn, the computer responds by displaying its reply on the monitor screen, or by printing out its reply on the printer.

## Operating Systems

The starting programme (or set of instructions) that you load in your computer is the Operating System. When you switch on the computer, this programme will load automatically. The operating system that we are studying here is the Windows 98 operating system. However, the contents of this chapter apply equally to all Microsoft Windows systems such as Windows 95, Me, Windows 2000, Windows XP and so on. The operating system is the fundamental programme that controls your computer. All other programmes such as the Microsoft WORD word-processing programme act on your computer through the operating system. The word processor will not work unless Windows 98 or some other operating system has already been loaded.

# A Little Bit of History

## Unfriendly DOS

When first introduced, personal computers used a rather unfriendly operating system called Disk Operating System or DOS for short. The user had to type commands at what was called the DOS Prompt (usually C >). The commands were cryptic and difficult to remember.

## A Window Opens

Things became easier with the introduction of the Windows interface. Unlike DOS, Windows is pictorial or graphic in nature. Instead of having to type confusing commands, the user could now point with the mouse pointer and click with the mouse button on little pictures (called icons) on the monitor screen, to make the computer do things. The monitor screen, full of little icons, is called the Graphical User Interface or GUI for short. Apple Computers were the first to introduce GUI. With Windows, Microsoft introduced its own GUI.

# The Current Avatar

Since then, Windows has progressed through Windows 1, 2 and 3.x, 95, 98 and Me. For office use, where many computers are connected in a network, Windows 2000 is popular. The latest entrant is Windows XP, the Home edition as upgrade to Windows Me and the Office edition as an upgrade to Windows 2000. However, the overwhelming majority of Personal Computer users today have Windows 98 or Windows Me installed on their machines. Therefore, our focus will be on these two operating systems.

# Starting and Shutting Down Windows

## Starting Windows

You may wish to get some hands-on practise with starting and shutting down Windows. Follow the examples below:

Switch on your computer. In a short while, you should see the opening screen. Your screen may look different because you may have another version of Windows. In addition, the icons you see on your machine will depend on the software you have loaded.

If a Welcome to Windows 98 screen appears first, point at the Close button on this screen with your mouse pointer and click to close this screen.

A typical opening screen is shown here with a few short-cut icons on the left of the screen. The Task bar is seen along the bottom of the opening screen.

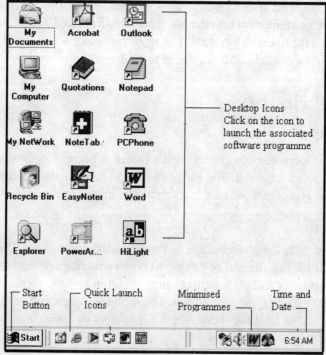

*Fig 03.02 Opening Screen*

At the bottom left hand corner of the opening screen is the Start button and the task bar icons. The Start button is on the extreme left. In addition, there are a number of programme icons on the task bar, also called quick launch icons.

On the desktop, you can see a set of short-cut icons for launching programmes directly from the opening screen. On the right bottom corner you can see some programmes already launched and running in the minimised state. At the extreme right is the time and date indication. Bring your mouse pointer over the time and the date will appear as a tool tip.

## Opening the Start Menu

Point and click on the Start button near the bottom right hand corner. A pop-up menu called the Start menu will appear. Using the Up and Down arrow keys of your keyboard, move the highlight on the Start menu up or down. Observe the sub-menus that appear. If you point and click on the Programmes option of the Start menu, a sub-menu listing all the programmes loaded in your computer will appear. *See Fig 03.03.*

The pop-up menu on the right appears when the Start button is clicked. In this example, the highlight has been moved to Programmes and the item has been clicked to display the Programme sub-menu on the right. You can now highlight a programme and click to launch it.

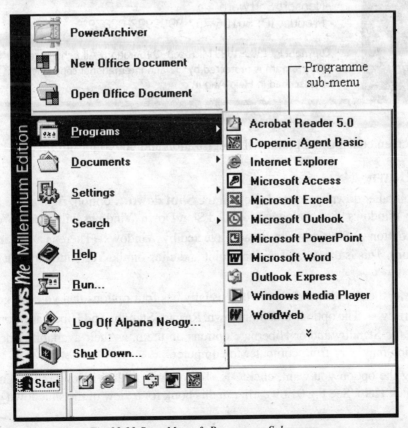

*Fig 03.03 Start Menu & Programme Sub-menu*

## Splash Screen

By pointing and clicking on any of the programme names (such as Microsoft Word) you can launch the programme you have selected.

Immediately, the opening screen will be replaced by what is called the Splash Screen of the programme you have selected. In Fig 03.04 you can see Microsoft's Word 2000 Splash Screen.

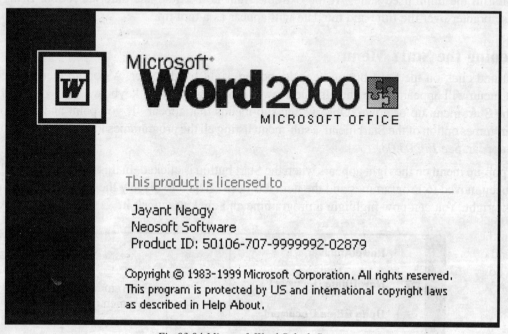

*Fig 03.04 Microsoft Word Splash Screen*

The Splash Screen contains the product ID, registration and copyright information.

## Shutting Down

To shut the computer down, point and click on the **Shut down...** option, right at the bottom of the Start menu. In Windows 98, a dialogue box titled Shut Down Windows will appear. You will notice that the radio button ⊙ Shut down is already selected by Windows. (There is a dot at the centre of the radio button). This is the default option. Point and click on the **Yes** button to shut the computer down.

In Windows Me, the shut down dialogue box usually has four options that you can get by clicking on the down arrow ▼. The options are: Shut down, Restart, Standby and Hibernate. Some computers may not have the Standby and/or Hibernate options on them, as their availability depends on the hardware, which may vary from computer to computer.

After selecting the option you want, click **OK**. To continue with Windows, click **Cancel** instead. To get help, click **Help**. See Fig 01.09 earlier in this book for a view of the shut down dialogue box.

# Conversing with Your Computer

## The Keyboard

The most common keyboard has 101 keys. In addition to all the letters of the alphabet and the numbers from 0 to 9, your keyboard will also include a set of Function keys marked F1 to F12, a set of navigation keys for moving the cursor, a keypad for entering numbers and keys to aid typing such as Insert, Delete etc.

The keyboard is your primary means of communicating with the computer. Therefore, spend as much time as you can to familiarise yourself with the layout of the keys. You will understand their operations with some practise. The time you spend now will pay rich dividends whenever you use your computer in the future!

## The Hot Keys

Since Windows 98 or Windows Me has a graphic or pictorial interface, the commands to Windows are usually given by pointing and clicking with the mouse as explained in the next section. However, much of the same results can also be obtained by using what is called the Hot Keys. If you look closely at the Start menu, you will notice that one letter of each option, often the first letter is underlined. If the Start menu is open, you will notice that the letter "u" is underlined in the Shut down option (Sh<u>u</u>t down). The letter "u" in this case is the hot key. You use the hot key by pressing down the Alt key, followed by the hot key you wish to use while the Alt key is still held down. Instead of pointing at the Shut down option with the mouse and clicking, you need only press and hold down the Alt key and press the "u" on the keyboard to start the process and call up the Shut Down Windows dialogue box. With a little bit of practice, you can actually work faster using hot keys than switching back and forth between keyboard and mouse.

## The Mouse

You may have either a two-button or a three-button mouse. The instructions that follow apply to both. In the three-button mouse, the middle button has special uses that we will disregard at present. Therefore, you need to concentrate on the left and the right mouse buttons only.

**Left Button Click:** With the mouse pointer on a command button such as the Start button (that we saw on the opening screen), a click on the left mouse button will activate the command. Click on the Start button using your left mouse button and the start menu will be displayed.

**Left Button Drag:** If the pointer is on an object that can be moved, such as any open window on your desktop, by pressing and holding down the left mouse button, the

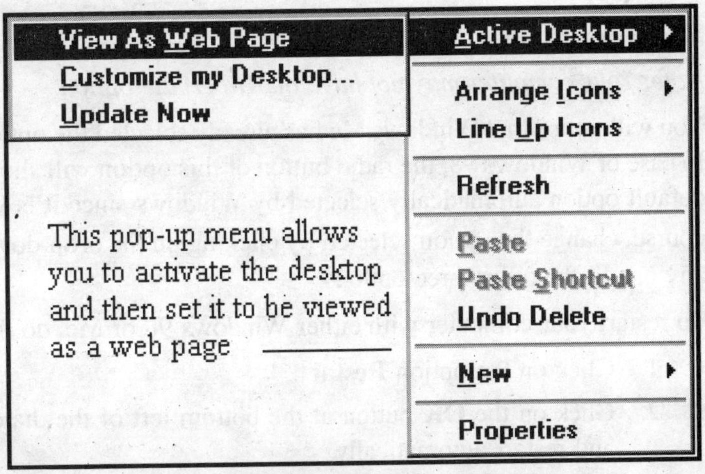

| View As <u>W</u>eb Page | <u>A</u>ctive Desktop ▶ |
| Customize my Desktop... | Arrange <u>I</u>cons ▶ |
| <u>U</u>pdate Now | Line <u>U</u>p Icons |
| | <u>R</u>efresh |
| This pop-up menu allows | <u>P</u>aste |
| you to activate the desktop | Paste <u>S</u>hortcut |
| and then set it to be viewed | <u>U</u>ndo Delete |
| as a web page | <u>N</u>ew ▶ |
| | P<u>r</u>operties |

*Fig 03.05 Pop-up Menu for Desktop*

window may be dragged across the screen. Release the left mouse button and the window being dragged is released as well. It will remain anchored in its new position.

**Right Button Click:** Clicking the right mouse button causes a context sensitive menu to pop up. By "context sensitive" we mean that the pop-up menu depends on the context. In other words, the menu depends on what programme is running. Thus, right clicking on any empty part of the desktop will bring out a pop-up menu that will allow you to arrange the desktop icons and change the desktop properties.

Right clicking anywhere on the desktop will cause the pop-up menu shown on the left to appear. Additional options of View as Web Page (the topmost pop-up menu item) are shown open in a second pop-up sub-menu on the right. *See Fig 03.05.*

## Navigation Tools

### *Dialogue Boxes*

Dialogue boxes will permit you to hold a dialogue, as it were, with Windows. The computer asks a question, such as, Shut down Windows? and gives you one or more choices such as Standby, Shutdown, Restart etc. After you have selected one of the choices, you may then tell the computer to go ahead and execute your selected choice by pointing to the OK button with your mouse pointer and clicking on the left button of your mouse.

### *Shut Down Options*

If you are using Windows Me, the shut down dialogue box will contain different options that you can display by clicking on the down arrow ▼ instead of radio buttons ⊙ as in the case of Windows 98. We look at the options for Windows Me now. Switch on your computer and wait for the Start screen to appear. Move the mouse pointer to the Start button at the bottom left hand corner of your screen. Click the left button on your mouse and the Start pop-up menu will appear. Now move the mouse pointer to the lowest option on this menu, which is Shut Down. Click on this option and the Shut Down Windows Dialogue Box will appear. You will notice the following choices listed serially in the drop-down list:

Shut down, Restart, Standby, Hibernate.

*Note: Your computer may not have the Hibernate option.*

You will notice that Windows Me has already selected the option Shut down shown in the text box. In case of Windows 98, the radio button of this option will show a dot inside the button. This is the default option automatically selected by Windows since it is your most likely choice. You can, of course, change the option selected by clicking on the drop-down arrow ▼ or the radio button ⊙ of any one of the other three options.

To restart your computer with either Windows 98 or Me, do the following:

1. Click on the option **Restart**.
2. Click on the **OK** button at the bottom left of the dialogue box. Windows will shut down and restart automatically.

Certain changes that you may make will only take effect after you stop and restart Windows so that the changed commands are loaded in your computer. The Restart command is useful in such situations. For example, restarting is usually necessary every time you install new software in your computer.

# Tabbed Dialogue Boxes

Tabbed dialogue boxes are a convenient way of displaying a number of options in a compact manner. A good cxample is the Windows Help Dialogue Box that appears if you choose the Help option from the Start menu.

## Open the Help Dialogue Box

Switch on your computer and wait for the opening screen to appear. Move the mouse pointer to the Start button at the bottom left hand corner of your screen. Click with the left mouse button of your mouse and the Start pop-up menu will appear. Now move the mouse pointer to the option marked Help and click. The tabbed Dialogue Box for Windows help will appear. *See Fig 03.06.* These commands may be shown in shorthand like this:

**Start ➔ Help**

The three tabs, Contents, Index and Search can be seen on the left of the Dialogue Box. The Contents tab is shown selected. This tab displays the contents of the help files grouped under major headings such as Exploring your Computer or Printing. You will notice three tabs marked Contents, Index and Search just below the title bar near the left hand top corner. Windows selects the Contents tab by default.

The top row contains navigation icons for the Help window. Just below, you can see the three tabs, Contents, Index and Search. The left pane shows a list of Help topics. The actual Help content is displayed on the right pane, which is shown only partially open in this picture.

*Fig 03.06 Tabbed Help Dialogue Box*

If Contents is selected, a list of Help topics will appear on the left hand pane of the Help Window. Click on a topic and sub-topics will be displayed in a tree structure in the right hand pane. Click on a sub-topic and the associated Help text will be displayed in the left hand pane.

If a topic in Search or a word in Index is selected, then clicking on the Display button will display the Help contents on the right hand pane of the Help screen. In all cases, to close the Help window, click on the top right hand corner button of the window that looks like this ⊠.

### Radio Buttons

Radio buttons are a convenient way for grouping a set of options that you can respond to in a Dialogue box. For instance, in *Shut Down Windows*, there are four options set up with their radio buttons. You can select only one of the options in a set of radio buttons. You will see a dot within the circle to the left of the selected option, like this ⊙.

### Command Buttons

In the Dialogue box, Shut Down Windows that you saw earlier, you would observe that below the array of the four radio buttons, there is a row of Command buttons. From left to right they read OK, Cancel and Help. Of these, the one on the left, OK is the default button. Clicking on this button or just pressing the <Enter> key will shut Windows down. The default button is the command button that is pre-selected by Windows. It will get activated when **Enter** ⏎ is pressed. Windows automatically assigns default status to the button you are most likely to use. Clicking on Cancel will remove the Shut Down Windows Dialogue box, an invaluable option if you want to change your mind about shutting down! Clicking on Help will pop-up the Windows Help system to give you more information of the options that you have.

## Scroll Bars

Scroll bars are devices located along the bottom and along the right vertical margins of certain types of windows.

Scroll bars help to display more written matter within a relatively small display window. By moving the scroll bars, the text in the window can be scrolled either horizontally or vertically as if the window is panning across the written text.

Scroll bars will appear automatically in windows that contain more text or graphic display matter than the window can show in full. Click on the scroll bar with the left mouse button. With the mouse button depressed, drag the scroll bar up, down or sideways to scroll the text inside the window.

Each scroll bar consists of two scroll buttons, one at each end of the scroll bar. In case of the vertical scroll bar, the buttons are at the top and at the bottom. In case of a horizontal scroll bar, the buttons are at the extreme left and right. In between the two scroll buttons is the square-shaped Scroll Box. *See Fig 03.07.*

The window may be made to scroll in three separate ways:

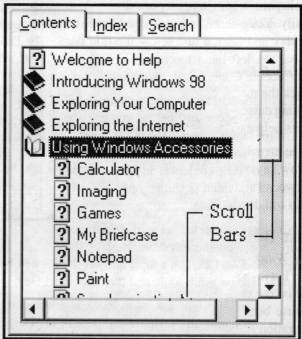

*Fig 03.07 Help Dialogue Box Scroll Bars*

- Click on any one of the **extreme scroll buttons** to make the window move in the direction of the arrow marked on the button.

- Drag the **scroll box** in the direction you want the window to move.

- Click **in between** the scroll box and one of the scroll buttons to make the window move in the direction of the arrow on the scroll button.

A click on the scroll button will move the display by one line while a click between the scroll box and the scroll button will move the display by one page. Clicking and dragging the scroll box will give you precise control of how much you want the window to move. See Fig 03.08 which shows a scroll box and a scroll button.

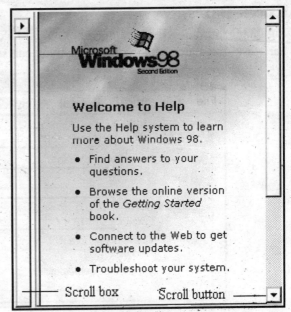

*Fig 03.08 Scroll Buttons and Scroll Box*

# Edit Boxes

The window inside a dialogue box in which you can insert a word or phrase is an Edit Box. When you search the help index, an edit box opens inside the dialogue box asking you to enter the word or phrase that you want Windows to search. What you type in the edit box can be edited by using the backspace or the insert key. If you do make a mistake in typing, you may correct your mistake easily. You can edit what you type inside the box, hence its name. See Fig 03.09 which has 3 edit boxes.

## *Using Edit Box*

Click the mouse button with the cursor anywhere inside the edit box. A vertical blinking typing or editing cursor will appear inside the edit box. You can now type the word you desire Windows to find in its help database.

Type <troublshooting>. As you can see, the letter "e" is missing between l and s. To correct, use the arrow keys to move the cursor back till it is between l and s (alternatively, you can point the cursor between l and s and click the left mouse button). Now type the letter e and press <Enter>. Windows help will display information on troubleshooting.

# List Boxes

The Windows help dialogue box in Fig 03.07 displays an index of help topics (under the Contents tab) as a list in the left pane. You can scroll up or down this list box, using the vertical scroll bar you will see on the right. Highlight the item in the list box by pointing to the item and clicking with the left mouse button. The item you clicked on will immediately appear in the edit box. Thereafter, the operation is the same as what you would do if you had typed the word in the edit box.

# Check Boxes

Fig 03.09 shows the Find dialogue box. This dialogue box is used to find files or folders on your hard disk that match certain criteria that you can select in the Find dialogue box.

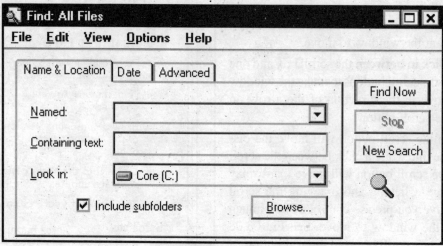

*Fig 03.09 Find Dialogue Box*

This dialogue box helps you locate files or folders on the hard disk(s) of your computer. In these days of huge hard disks running to 100 gigabytes or more, file location is indeed a difficult task!

Near the bottom left hand corner, there is a small white window with a check mark inside. The legend reads Include Subfolders. This window is the Check Box and the default condition is that Windows will look for the name of the file in folders as well as in subfolders. If you click on the window, the check mark will disappear. If you remove the check mark, Windows will search for the file or folder you have selected (by entering its name in the edit box) only in the main folders on your hard disk.

# Group Boxes

Open the Task bar properties from the opening screen of Windows 98 or Me as follows:

Click **Start → Settings → Task Bar and Start Menu**

The Task Bar properties dialogue box will appear. This dialogue box has two tabs, Task Bar Options and Start Menu Programmes in Windows 98. In Windows Me, the tabs are General and Advanced. Under the Task Bar Options tab, you will see four items, Always on Top, Auto hide, Show small icons in Start menu and Show clock. These four options together form

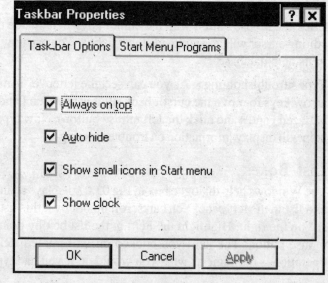

*Fig 03.10 Group Box in Task Bar Properties*

a Group Box. In case of Windows Me, the group box is under the General tab and contains 5 options.

You can select none, any or all the options by clicking on each option. When selected, a check mark will appear in the box to the right of the selected option. *See Fig 03.10.* Note that unlike a group of radio buttons, where you can select only one of the many options shown, in a Group Box you can select multiple options.

# Customising the Display

## Minimising, Maximising and Moving Windows

Display the Windows Help Dialogue Box as follows:

### Click **Start** ➔ **Help**

You will observe that the three small square command buttons are located along the top right hand corner. These are the Minimise, the Maximise and the Close command buttons at the top right hand corner of a window. [ _ ] [□] [⊠]. *See Fig 03.06.*

The Minimise command button shrinks the Help dialogue box window into an icon on the task bar. This is a convenient way of removing this window from the screen, exposing the window underneath, without shutting down the Help dialogue box window.

The Maximise command button expands the window to occupy the entire screen. This is useful when you wish to see more of the contents of the window at one time. The Close command button closes the window. In some windows, you may have

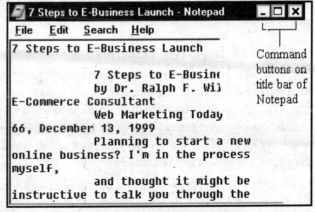

Fig 03.11 Title Bar and Command Buttons

a Restore instead of a Maximise command button. The Restore button will restore the window to its default size. Fig 03.11 shows Windows Notepad and its 3 command buttons.

To move a window, position the cursor anywhere along the title bar of the window, click the left mouse button and with the left mouse button held down, drag the window wherever you want on the screen. The dragged window will remain wherever you release the left mouse button.

## Resizing Windows

Apart from the three predetermined sizes that are controlled by the three command buttons as you saw in the previous section, windows can actually be adjusted to virtually any size within the boundaries of your monitor screen. Such fine-tuning of window sizes become necessary when you desire to have a number of windows open on the desktop at the same time and wish to adjust their sizes so that they fit in neatly on your monitor screen.

Open the Windows Help dialogue box by clicking **Start → Help**.

Observe that the window consists of two panes. When you select a topic from the narrow pane on the left (the list box or index window), the actual details of the topic will appear in the wider pane on the right (the contents box or data window). In Fig 03.12 only the right pane has been shown.

As you move the mouse cursor over the window, you will observe that the cursor changes to a double-headed arrow whenever it touches the edges of the window. The double-headed arrow will be horizontal when it touches a vertical edge of the window and vertical when it touches a horizontal edge.

Whenever the cursor changes to a double-headed arrow, clicking the left mouse button will allow you to drag the window edge in question up or down (in case the edge is horizontal) or, left or right (in case the edge is vertical). To anchor the window to its new size, release the left mouse button when you have reached the desired size. The right and the bottom edges of this window can be clicked by the mouse pointer and dragged to change the size of this window.

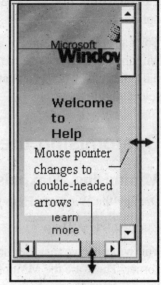

*Fig 03.12 Resizing the Help Window*

## Active and Inactive Windows

There are situations when you may want to have more than one window open on the desktop. If you wish to give commands to more than one window, you will have to address only one window at a time. To help you to know which window is ready to receive your command, Windows uses a convention of making one window Active at a time. Sometimes, we use the expression that a window has Got Focus. It means the same as that the window is Active. Similarly, a window is said to have Lost Focus when it becomes Inactive.

The title bar of the active window will darken as soon as it is selected. The title bars of all other windows will become light in colour. A glance at your desktop will tell you which window is active.

Once you have selected a window (its title bar is dark), you can give commands to that window as usual.

To understand these concepts, let us go through another practical exercise.

### Switching Between Windows

Switch on the computer (unless it is already on) and wait for the opening screen.

1. Click **Start → Find**. The Find dialogue box will appear. Drag the window to the right of the screen.

2. Now click **Start → Run** and the Run dialogue box will also appear on the screen. Drag the Run dialogue box below the Find dialogue box. Now your screen should look like Fig. 03.13.

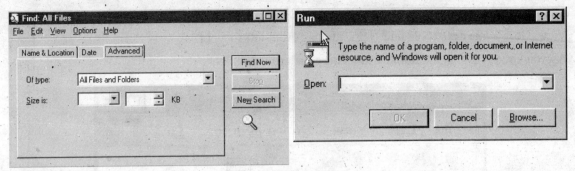

*Fig 03.13 Multiple Windows*

Giving focus to the window you select by just pointing at the title bar of the window and clicking the left mouse button. The selected window will become active and its title bar will become dark. At the same time, the title bars of all other windows open on the screen will lose focus and their title bars will become light in colour.

# The First Few Tasks

Having come this far, you are now ready to undertake a few simple tasks with Windows 98 and Me. We shall go over four common tasks that you will need to carry out regularly. They are:

- Using the Windows Explorer
- Finding Files
- File Operations
- Emptying the Recycle Bin

The exercises will help you sharpen the skills you have just learned, and make you comfortable with common Windows operations. Here we go!

## Using the Windows Explorer

Information (programmes or data) is organised in files in Windows 98. For convenience of finding and manipulating files, such as copying, moving and deleting files, similar files are grouped together under a folder or sub-directory.

Windows uses a special programme to view, sort, copy, move and delete files and folders. This is the Windows Explorer programme.

Launch the Windows Explorer programme as follows:

Click **Start** → **Programmes** → **Windows Explorer**

The Windows Explorer screen appears. The left window titled Folders shows folders and files organised in a hierarchical tree structure. The right window titled Name shows the names of files within a folder that you select in the left window. The Explorer Window Title bar shows the title, usually Exploring C: at the top left hand corner and the familiar three command buttons (Minimise, Restore and Maximise) at the top right hand corner.

Immediately below the Title bar is the Menu bar on which there are seven menu items, File, Edit, View, Go, Favourites, Tools and Help, running from left to right.

As you already know, the hot key letters are underlined.

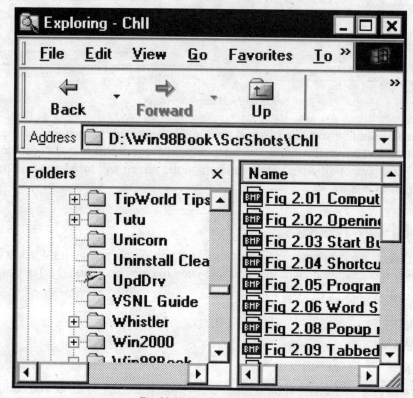

*Fig 03.14 Windows Explorer*

You can either point at the menu item and click or hold down the Alt key and strike the underlined letter to make the drop-down menu appear. Thus, to activate the file drop-down menu, you can either point and click on the file menu item or hold down the Alt key and type the letter f.

Below the Menu bar is the Icon bar containing icons for moving Back, Forward, Up (all navigating tools), Cut, Copy, Paste, Undo, Delete, Properties and Views.

The Windows Explorer is your main programme for working with files. Since all data in your computer is organised in the form of files, your skill in manipulating them will greatly influence your proficiency in working with Windows.

Small triangles ▼ called Drop-down arrows next to the Back and Forward arrows can be clicked on to show a list of past moves. However, past moves will only show after Explorer has been moved back and forward. On a fresh screen, these arrows will be greyed out to indicate that there is no history of past moves to display.

Clicking on Edit will cause a Drop-down Edit Menu to appear. This menu lists the different options with which files and folders can be manipulated. The options are Cut, Copy, Paste, Paste Shortcut,

Select All and Invert Selection. You would have observed the underlined letters and recognised them as hot keys. The Edit box titled Address is located in the area below the Icon bar. By default, the Edit box will show the C:\ drive. *See Fig 03.15.*

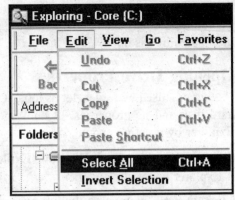

The drop-down arrow at the extreme right of the Edit box will display all the drives on your computer plus some icons such as Desktop, My Computer, Control Panel etc. The exact list will vary from computer to computer.

The area below the Address Edit box is divided into two panes. The narrower pane on the left shows the folders

*Fig 03.15 Windows Explorer Edit Menu*

and sub-folders on the C: drive in a tree structure. The wider pane on the right shows folders, sub-folders and files depending on what folder or sub-folder is selected in the left pane. Folders or sub-folders are selected in the left pane by pointing and clicking with the mouse, as usual.

To the right of the drive letter the folders are listed. A (+) plus sign to the left of the folder indicates that the folder contains sub-folders.

If you click on the (+) plus sign, the sub-folders or files within the selected folder will be displayed. The (+) plus sign will change to a (-) minus sign. You will need to open sub-folders and files if you are looking for a particular file. However, the window will get too crowded. So, to get only an overview, click on the (-) minus sign to get a summarised view of only the folders or directories.

The right pane can be configured to show folder and files as large or small icons and also as a detailed list containing information such as file size (for files only, not for folders), file or folder type, creation date etc.

The Windows Explorer will open with the highlight on the C drive on the left pane and the contents of the C drive, showing folders and files in the right pane in all computers, by default. The actual

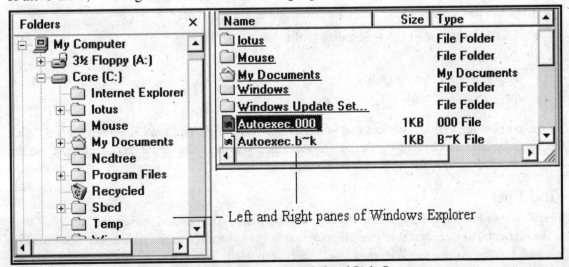

— Left and Right panes of Windows Explorer

*Fig 03.16 Windows Explorer Left and Right Panes*

list of folders and files will vary from computer to computer depending on the programmes loaded. Therefore, the lists and details you see on your computer screen will not tally with the contents of the figures in this book. *See Fig 03.16.*

## Opening Drive Properties

Having practised with files, let us look at your hard disk and its properties. Open Windows Explorer by pointing and clicking:

**Start → Programmes → Windows Explorer**, if Explorer is not already open.

Click on the C:> drive on the left pane. Now click on the Properties icon on the icon bar. The C: Drive Properties window will drop down. This window has two (or more) tabs. The default, General tab includes an Edit box for entering or changing the name you wish to give to your C drive.

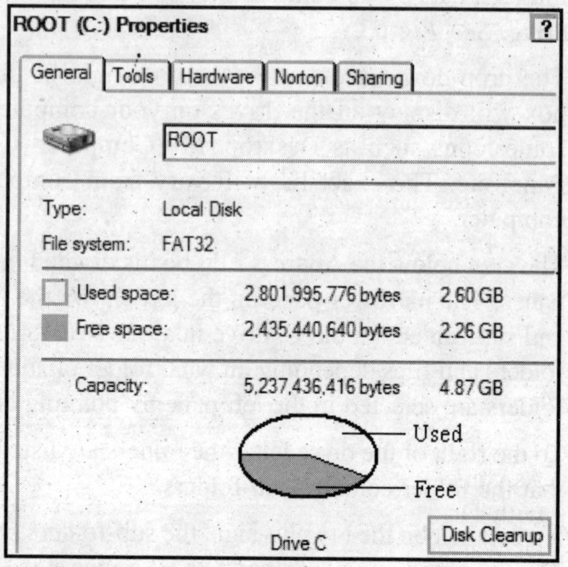

Fig 03.17 Drive Properties for Drive C

The Properties window for the drive will show the disk statistics. The statistics include:

- The Used Space
- The Free Space
- The Total Space on the Hard Disk

Figures are shown in Bytes and Gigabytes. *See Fig 03.17.*

The Command Button at the bottom right triggers a Disk Cleanup Utility that deletes unwanted files.

The Tools tab has a set of tools for Disk maintenance. They include:

- Check Drive for Errors – Scandisk Utility
- Back Up Drive
- Defragment – Defrag Utility
- Disk Cleanup Utility

To get to know the various services that you may access through Windows Explorer, you can click the Tools tab and experiment with each service. Once you have finished experimenting, close the Properties window to return to Windows Explorer.

## Find Files

The Windows Explorer is like a map of all your hard disks. All files and folders will be listed both in the hierarchical tree format in the left pane and in the list format in the right pane. Sometimes it is much quicker to use the Windows Find utility, especially if you know the file names you are looking for.

We are now ready for an actual file finding exercise, a task you may have to do quite often! Open the Find dialogue box as follows:

1.  Click **Start ➔ Find ➔ Files or Folders**.
2.  The Find dialogue box appears. In the Edit box, type the <name of the file> that you want to locate. *See Fig 03.09.*
3.  Let us assume that you want to locate the programme Dr Watson, which is a diagnostic programme shipped with Windows 98. Type <Drwatson> in the Edit Box titled Named. The default drive shown in the drop-down box marked Look in should read C drive by default. Do not change this.
4.  Now click on the Find Now command button. A List box opens below the Find dialogue box and after a brief moment, three items are listed in the List box:

    a.   Dr Watson            Folder            In C:\Windows Directory
    b.   Dr Watson.exe        Programme         In C:\Windows Directory
    c.   Dr Watson.vxd        System file       In C:\Windows\System sub-directory

As you can see, the result of the search is rather general. Folder, programme file and system file, all with Dr Watson in their names, have turned up. To limit the search only to the programme Dr Watson, we will use the Edit box titled Containing Text. Type <exe> in the Edit box Containing Text and click the Find Now command button once again. The List box will clear and this time, only the Dr Watson.exe programme file will remain in the List box. Success is achieved at last!

## File Operations

All information on your hard disk is arranged in files. In turn, files are grouped in folders (called sub-directories in the days of DOS). Thus, a programme may consist of several files that are collected together under a folder. Very large programmes may consist of several folders, each containing several files. In order to run any programme, a good working knowledge of files and folders will be of great help to you. The following sections will give you some practice in this basic but vital aspect of computer operations.

## Folder and File Operations

We shall go over some basic file operations in this section. You will:

*   Create a folder named TestFolder in the C drive, also called the Root drive.
*   Create a File named TestFile in the TestFolder in the C drive.
*   Erase the file TestFile.
*   Erase the Folder TestFolder.

**TIP**     It is much easier to do all these file operations in Windows itself by using the Windows Explorer, although it is possible to open a MS-DOS window on the Desktop and use DOS commands in Windows 98. In later versions of Windows such as Windows XP, opening a DOS window is not easy!

## Create Folder and File

Open the Windows Explorer unless it is already open, as follows:

1. Click **Start** ➜ **Programmes** ➜ **Windows Explorer**.

2. Click on the C drive letter to ensure that it has focus. The right hand pane will show the folders and files installed on drive C. Now click on the drop-down arrow next to the Views icon and select the option Details if this option is not already selected.

3. Click on the **C drive letter** in the left pane.

4. Click **File** ➜ **New** ➜ **New Folder**.

A folder icon with the name New Folder will appear at the very bottom of the list in the right pane.

1. Right click on the name **New Folder** and select **Rename** from the pop-up menu that appears. The name will change into an Edit box with a blinking cursor.

2. Type <TestFolder> and hit **Enter** ↵. The Folder name will change to TestFolder. Shrink Windows Explorer to an icon on the task bar by clicking on the **Minimise** command button at the top right of the Explorer window.

3. Launch the Windows accessory Notepad as follows:

4. Click **Start** ➜ **Programme** ➜ **Accessories** ➜ **Notepad**.

5. In the Notepad window that appears, type <This is a Test File>.

6. Now select **File** ➜ **Save As**. In the Save As dialogue box that appears, click on the drop-down arrow to the right of the Save in edit box that appears.

7. Select C ➜ **TestFolder**. Click on the Open command button at the bottom right and then type the name of the file <TestFile> in the File name edit box and click the **Save** command button.

8. Close Notepad.

Restore Windows Explorer by clicking on the Task bar icon for Windows Explorer. Now observe that the folder TestFolder appears both in the tree in the left pane and at the very bottom of the list of files and folders in the right pane. Click on the TestFolder name on the left pane. The right pane will clear and will now show the file TestFile that you have just created. By repeating the steps listed after opening Notepad, you can create several files under the same folder if required. Files may also be created by other software programmes such as Word or Excel.

## Copy Files or Folders

1. Open Windows Explorer.

2. If the file or folder you want to copy is not located in My Documents or its subfolders, use Search to find it. To open Search, click **Start**, and then click **Search**.

3. Click the **file or folder** you want to copy.

4. Under File and Folder Tasks, click **Copy this file** or **Copy this folder**.

5. In Copy Items, select the **drive or folder** you want to copy to, and then click **Copy**.

You can copy more than one file or folder at a time. To select consecutive files or folders, click the first item, press and hold down SHIFT, and then click the last item.

To select non-consecutive files or folders, press and hold down CTRL, and then click each item.

### *Erase Folder and File*

Since you do not actually need either the folder TestFolder or the file TestFile, delete them as follows:

1. Move to the right pane and right click on the file name **TestFile**.
2. In the pop-up menu that appears, click on **Delete**.
3. Confirm **Yes** in the Confirm file delete dialogue box that appears. The file is deleted and it disappears from the right pane.
4. Move to the left pane and right click on the folder name **TestFolder**.
5. Select **Delete** from the pop-up menu that appears.
6. Confirm the delete action by clicking on the **Yes** command button in the Confirm folder delete dialogue box that appears. The folder is deleted and it disappears from the left pane.

Congratulations! You have just successfully carried out a reasonably complex set of file operations in Windows Explorer!

Now that you have created and deleted a file and a folder, you will find that they are temporarily stored in a special space called the Recycle Bin. You can restore the contents back to your computer if you need them again. If not, you can permanently delete them, as we shall now see.

## Empty Recycle Bin

The files that you delete from time to time collect in a special folder on your hard disk called the Recycle Bin. If you want to recover a deleted file, you can open the Recycle Bin and retrieve the deleted file. If you are quite sure that you do not need the deleted files in your Recycle Bin, you can empty the bin.

To do so, proceed as follows:

1. Close the Windows Explorer and any other window that may be open on the Desktop.
2. On the desktop, locate the Recycle Bin icon and click on the **icon** to open the Recycle Bin.
3. The Recycle Bin dialogue box appears. You will see a list of files and folders on the right pane. Instead of a list, you may see icons or nothing if the bin is empty. *See Fig 03.18.*

*Fig 03.18 Recycle Bin Dialogue Box (Bin is Empty)*

4. Click on **Empty Recycle Bin** to permanently remove the deleted items from your hard disk and reclaim disk space.

5. You will have to click on the **Yes** command button in the Confirm File Delete dialogue box that will appear.

6. Click **File** then click **Close** on the drop-down menu.

Files or folders deleted by emptying the Recycle Bin cannot be recovered after you have closed the dialogue box. In case you wish to undo the action of emptying of the Recycle Bin, click on the Undo icon on the icon bar of the Recycle Bin window. However, the Undo action will only work so long as you have not yet closed the Recycle Bin window. Be careful, therefore, before you empty your Recycle Bin!

## Windows Accessories

Windows comes with a number of accessories or utility programmes. The most commonly used ones are:

• **Notepad**, a simple text editor.

• **Calculator**, which comes in two versions, standard and scientific.

• **Paint**, which is a simple painting and retouching programme.

• **WordPad**, which is a more sophisticated text editor.

You will learn about these accessories in Chapter 24, *Utilising Windows Accessories*, later in this book.

 **CD-ROM** To learn more about the Windows operating system in a multimedia environment, insert the accompanying CD-ROM in your computer, select the **Interactive** mode in the opening screen. The main menu will appear. To go to the section on Windows, click the button marked **Windows**. You will see a sub-menu containing the following topics:

• Windows Overview, which covers the basics of Windows 98.

• Getting Control over Windows, where you learn about Windows Help.

• Windows Utilities, where you learn how to set wallpaper and screensaver and other Windows environment variables.

• Power of Windows Unleashed, where you learn about programme shortcuts and the calculator.

Click on the sub-menu item you want. Another level of sub-sub-menus is displayed from which you can select the particular topic you want to see. Click on your selected topic and follow the instructions on your screen.

# 4. The Internet

*In this chapter:*

☞ You are introduced to different types of Internet connections.

☞ We look at your hardware and software needs.

☞ We go over the installation procedure of your modem in detail.

☞ We review the information you need from your ISP.

☞ You are given detailed guidelines for installing and configuring a dial-up connection on your computer.

☞ We give you tips on Web surfing.

☞ You learn about the Internet Explorer and effective ways of surfing the Internet.

# Introduction

The Internet requires no introduction. Increasingly, it is becoming the biggest source of information, entertainment, communication and even business. Communication in the form of e-mail has now become all pervasive. If you have access to cyber cafes, you will probably use e-mails and Internet chats as the preferred means to communicate with your business associates and friends.

It is almost unthinkable to do serious research without going on the Internet and though e-business (electronic business) over the Internet is still in its infancy in India, it is growing slowly but surely. In this chapter we look at the Internet basics. In the next two chapters, we will explore Internet surfing and communications in detail.

# Types of Connections

Just as computers and their operating systems have increased in numbers and variety, so have the different means now available to a subscriber to the Internet. In India, you are no longer confined to the familiar telephone line for your Internet connection. You have (especially if you live in a metro city) many options. Let us look at some of them.

## Dial-up Networking

We begin with the most familiar one, a connection to your Internet Service Provider (ISP) over your existing telephone line. You connect your computer to the Internet by opening an account with an ISP such as *Videsh Sanchar Nigam Ltd* (VSNL) or select from half-a-dozen service providers such as Mantra Online. You dial a special number using the dial-up network (DUN) software in your computer to connect to your ISP via a telephone modem. Your ISP then connects you to the Internet after you type in your username and password. Now you can launch your Web browser and your home page opens. From there, your odyssey begins. You are limited only by the time you have and the telephone bills that you can afford! Currently, DUN has a connection speed of around 40 kilobytes per second (Kbps).

However, before you can connect to the Internet, you will have to install your modulating-demodulating unit or modem and configure the communications software in your computer. We shall look at the mechanics of installing your modem and configuring your software for Internet connection later in this chapter.

## ISDN

The telephone line carries your conversation as an analogue message. The variations in air pressure created as you speak are converted into analogous changes in electrical current that flows along the telephone lines. These electrical signals can be distorted by magnetic fields such as the ones that surround power lines. Distortion degrades the quality of transmission and reduces transmission speed. One way to improve transmission quality is to replace the electrical analogue signals by digital ones. Digital signals do not pick up interference or deteriorate. Digital networks are called Integrated Services Digital Network (ISDN). Since the equipment cost of a digital system is very high, digitisation is progressing rather slowly in India. At present, this service is largely limited to

Both the telephone instrument and the ISDN modem are different from, and more expensive than, their dial-up counterparts.

If you can afford ISDN, you will not only get speeds of either 64 Kbps or 128 Kbps, but will also be able to transmit both voice and data on the same line at the same time. In other words, you can surf the Internet and receive a normal telephone call at the same time, on the same telephone line.

## DSL

Digital Subscriber Loop (DSL) sends high-speed digital signals over your existing telephone lines. ISDN is actually a special case of DSL. You can have a DSL setup where the upload speed, used for sending data to the Internet, is slower than the download speed. As most of us download data from the Internet much more frequently than uploading data, this setup (called an asynchronous setup) makes sense and costs less than having the same speed both ways. Like ISDN, you can simultaneously transmit analogue voice and digital data over the same line at the same time. This service too is expensive and meant for commercial users.

## Cable Modem

Also called Net over cable, this service is provided by your cable operator, who utilises the spare capacity (called bandwidth) in the co-axial cable over which you get movies, news and music on your cable TV. Like ISDN and DSL, Net over cable requires special cable modems as TV set-top boxes. Signals coming from your cable operator are split in two. The TV signals enter your TV set and the digital data signals go to your computer. These digital data signals allow you to surf the Internet while the TV signals let you watch your favourite programme at the same time!

High cost of set-top boxes and heavy investment by cable TV providers are the reasons for slow growth of this attractive alternative to dial-up networking. An additional problem with Net over cable is that data transfer really slows down if too many people (connected to the same provider) begin to surf the Internet at the same time.

## The Right Choice

So which one is the right choice for you? Actually, you may not have too many options at present. If you are a business concern, you will probably use ISDN or DSL, depending on what is available near you. If you are a private user, you will be using dial-up networking over your existing telephone line. Perhaps, as the subscriber base grows, you may switch to a cable modem in the near future. Since this book is written primarily for the home user, we will assume from here onwards that you have a dial-up connection. Let us now look at your hardware and software needs for connecting to the Internet.

# Hardware & Software Needs

We will assume that you have a computer and a telephone line. Your computer should have a Pentium II (or better) Central Processing Unit (CPU) with a clock speed of at least 100 MHz or faster. At least 32 MB of Random Access Memory (RAM) is recommended along with a hard disk drive with, say about 100 MB of free space to hold temporary Internet files. These figures are the bare minimum requirements. Better specifications will give you better performance. Chances are that if you have bought your machine in the last couple of years or so, it is much more powerful.

While more RAM and a faster CPU will speed up Internet surfing, the limit usually is the speed at which data can be transferred on telephone lines. Therefore, you will probably get connection speeds between 40 and 45 Kbps on a dial-up network, no matter how powerful your computer or modem is!

## Operating Systems

As your Operating System (OS), you should be using Windows 98 or a later version. If you are an individual home user, the chances are that you will not be using Linux or UNIX as your operating system. When we discuss specifics of configuration, we will cover the needs of all the popular Windows operating systems such as Windows 95, Windows 98 and Windows Me.

## Analogue Modems

The only additional piece of hardware you will need is a modem that acts as an interface between the telephone line that transmits only analogue signals (in a dial-up setup) and your computer that only understands digital data.

The conversion works both ways, from analogue to digital and vice versa, when you are downloading as well as when you are uploading data.

Modems may be internal, mounted inside your computer, or external, sitting separately on your computer or on your desk. Fig 04.01 shows an external modem.

Since computers are of many different makes and so are modems, a special piece of software code, called a software driver, has to be installed and configured just right so that your computer and your modem can exchange information in a way that both devices understand. Drivers are usually provided by the modem manufacturer. Many drivers are also available on the CD-ROM that contains your operating system.

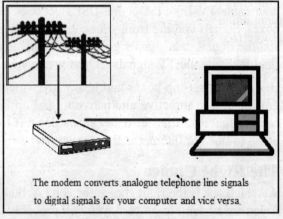

The modem converts analogue telephone line signals to digital signals for your computer and vice versa.

*Fig 04.01 External Modem*

### Selecting a Modem

As a home user, you will probably have a dial-up connection over your telephone line. To connect your computer to your telephone line, you will need an analogue modem. Currently, all modems sold are capable of 33.3 Kbps upload speed to the Internet and 56 Kbps download speed. In addition, many modems have voice and fax capabilities. You may decide to buy a modem with these additional features. A voice capable modem can be used for setting up a voice-mail system. Keep these tips in mind while selecting your modem:

- Select a modem that is Microsoft Windows compatible and designated for plug-and-play installation. If you are using Windows 2000 or Windows XP, make sure that the modem you buy is listed in the compatibility list of these operating systems. If in doubt, check the Website http://www.microsoft.com/hcl, where you can view the hardware compatibility lists.

- Choose a modem that is compatible with the fastest service protocol that is used by your ISP. For 56 Kbps modems, a V90 protocol compliance is desired.

**TRAP**

Do not buy a Win Modem. These types of modems do not have any on-board processing power. They depend on the computer's CPU to encode and decode the signals. Therefore, they slow down the performance of your computer.

### *Internal or External Modem?*

You will also have to decide between an internal and an external modem. Internal modems are faster and cheaper. However, external modems are more robust. In addition, external modems keep the relatively higher voltages of the telephone lines out of your computer.

If you have a DSL connection, it is very likely that your Internet service provider will supply you with a DSL modem and an Ethernet card or a USB (Universal Serial Bus) port connection, to connect the modem to your computer. Therefore, you will not have to choose anything!

If you have an ISDN connection, choose an internal ISDN modem. Internal modems are treated by your computer as a network adapter. As a result, the modem can be configured directly by the computer's hardware, and your Windows operating system will have more control over the functioning of your modem. ISDN modems will come with either U or S/T wiring interfaces. The U interface is recommended.

The importance of compatibility with your Windows operating system increases if you have a DSL or ISDN service. So make very sure that the equipment you get is compatible with your version of Windows.

## Installing and Configuring Your Modem

We shall assume that you have a dial-up connection, an external modem and your computer is running Windows 98. The same procedure will also apply to Windows 95 or Windows Me.

Make sure that you have the modem, the power cable with adapter, the data cable, the software driver for the modem (in a floppy disk or a CD-ROM), Windows CD-ROM and the telephone jack ready. Now follow the step-by-step instructions given below:

1. Switch off power to the computer.
2. Connect the data cable (either 9 pin or 25 pin) to your computer's COM port (usually COM1) at one end and to the back of the modem at the other end.
3. Connect the telephone line jack at the rear of the modem in the socket marked "Wall" or "Line". If you have a telephone, connect it to the socket marked "Phone".
4. Plug in the power adapter at the rear of the modem and connect the input of the adapter to 220-volt power supply. Turn on power to the modem.
5. Turn the computer on.

What happens next will depend on whether you have a plug-and-play modem and on the operating system loaded in your computer. In most cases, the modem will be detected automatically. With Windows Me, 2000 or XP, if you have selected a compatible modem, Windows will install the appropriate software drivers by asking you to insert the Windows CD-ROM in your CD-ROM drive. If Windows does not have appropriate driver software, you can install the one supplied by the manufacturer on the floppy disk or CD-ROM by the following procedure.

1. From the Start menu, select **Settings** ➔ **Control Panel**.
2. Double click the **modem icon** and select **Install New Modem**. *See Fig 04.02*.
3. Check **Don't detect my modem, I will select it from a list** then click **Next**.
4. Insert the modem manufacturer's floppy disk or CD-ROM in its drive and then click the **Have Disk** button. If no software is available, select the modem from the manufacturer's name in the left pane and then select the model from the right pane.

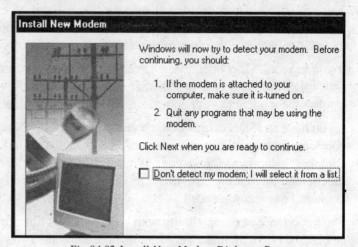

If you have Windows 98, once the modem software has been installed, you will need to select the communications or COM port to which the modem is connected. In the later versions such as XP, Me or 2000, Windows will automatically detect the COM port to which you have connected your modem.

To select the COM port, proceed as follows:

*Fig 04.02 Install New Modem Dialogue Box*

1. Select the port to use this modem by clicking on the **COM ports** listed and then click **Next**.
2. On the screen that appears, saying that the modem has been successfully installed, click **Finish** and then click **OK**.
3. Restart your computer for the changes to take effect.

Congratulations! Your modem is now ready for use. However, before you begin to surf the Internet, it is necessary to test your modem and configure your Windows software so that your computer can connect you to the Web via your ISP. We will tackle these steps next, one after the other.

## Testing Your Modem

You can test your modem even before you have configured your Internet connection. You do so by asking your Windows operating system to communicate with your modem and display the test result on your monitor's screen. By carrying out this test, you ensure that the modem, the COM port (through which your modem is connected to your computer) and the modem driver software are all working properly.

To test your modem, proceed as follows:

1. Make sure that the modem is powered on.
2. Click **Start** ➔ **Settings** ➔ **Control Panel** and in the control panel, right click the **modem icon**.

3. In the drop-down menu, click **Properties**.

4. Click on the **More Info** tab to run diagnostics. *See Fig 04.03.*

A report is displayed in a short while, indicating problems, if any.

## Information from Your ISP

We shall soon take up the job of configuring your computer for the Internet and set up your Internet connection so that you can start savouring the joys of the Internet! However, before we begin, you must get the following information from your ISP:

- Telephone numbers to dial-up your ISP, for example, 172226 for VSNL in New Delhi.

- The Domain Name Server (DNS) addresses of your ISP. Usually, there will be a primary and a secondary DNS address. These are generally in the form of digits such as "202.54.15.1" or "202.54.1.30". Some ISPs assign DNS addresses automatically when you connect to them. In that case, you will not need the DNS addresses in advance.

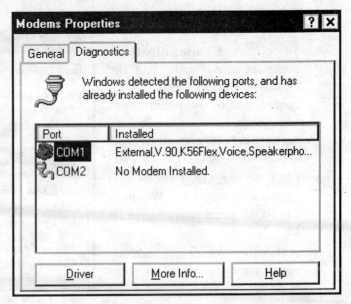

Fig 04.03 Modem Properties Dialogue Box

- The type of the post office server that your ISP has, such as a POP3 or IMAP server. These are the servers you will use for e-mail, Newsgroups etc. To subscribe to Newsgroups, you will also need the NNTP server address (such as, news.vsnl.net.in) of your ISP.

- Names (or addresses) of the SMTP mail server, the post office server and the news server. Names such as mail@vsnl.net.in or addresses may be like 202.54.15.1.

- You will also need your account name and your account password.

# Setting up Windows for the Internet

## Dial-up Networking

We will study the procedure applied to Windows 98 here. With Windows 98 onwards, things have become simpler so that some of the steps are done automatically. The simplified procedure applies to Windows Me as well. In general, if you know how to set up dial-up networking in Windows 98, you can easily handle the later version of Windows.

While setting up Windows, the Dial-up Networking component may or may not have been installed. You can verify its presence by double clicking the My Computer icon on your desktop. When the My Computer window has opened, look for the Dial-up Networking icon. If it is not there, proceed as follows:

Make sure that you have your Windows CD-ROM handy and follow these steps:

1. From the Start menu, select **Settings** ➔ **Control Panel**.

2. In the Control Panel window, click the **Add/Remove Programmes** icon to display its properties dialogue box.

3. Select the **Windows setup** tab. Components of Windows already installed on your computer will be displayed.

4. Select the **Communications** component and click on the **Details** button. The sub-components of Communications will appear. Click on the **Dial-up networking component** so that its check box is checked.

5. Click on the **OK** buttons that appear and insert the Windows CD-ROM when prompted to do so.

6. Follow the prompts on screen and restart the computer when asked to do so.

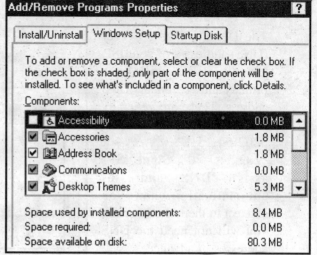

*Fig 04.04 Add/Remove Programme Properties*

## Configuring TCP/IP

As before, we will describe the procedure you have to follow if you have Windows 98 or Me installed. Matters get simpler if you have later versions such as Windows Me, where some of the tasks have been automated.

1. Select **Start** ➔ **Settings** ➔ **Control Panel** and click on the **network icon** to cause the network dialogue box to appear. *See Fig 04.05.*

2. Click the **Add** button and the Select Network Component Type dialogue box will appear.

3. Click the **Protocol** option and the Select Network Protocol dialogue box will appear. In the list of manufacturers in the left pane, select **Microsoft**. A list of network protocols will appear in the right pane of the window. Select **TCP/IP**. *See Fig 04.06.*

4. Click **OK** and insert your Windows CD-ROM in its drive if prompted. The Network dialogue box will reappear showing that TCP/IP has been selected as one of the network components.

5. Click the **OK** button.

The Network protocol has now been installed in your computer.

**TIP** In Fig 04.05, the Network dialogue box can be seen with the configuration tab open. The Client for Microsoft Networks component is shown selected in the pane captioned *The following network components are installed.* The default tab is Configuration. If this tab is not open, click on it to open the tab.

You select the Network protocol in the Select Network Protocol dialogue box, which is shown in Fig 04.06.

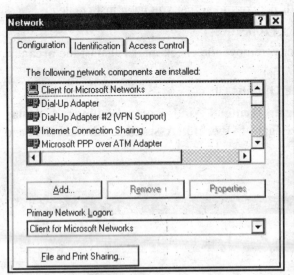

*Fig 04.05 Network Dialogue Box*

*Fig 04.06 Networking Protocol Tab*

## Creating an ISP Connection

You are now ready to create a connection to your Internet Service Provider or ISP.

After creating the connection, you will configure the properties of the connection so that you can be connected to the Internet.

All ISPs will have their own protocols and procedures. Many will provide you with software on a CD-ROM that you have to install on your computer. The software will automate the creation and configuration of your connection.

### Creating the Connection

1. Click **My Computer** and then click the **Dial-up Networking icon**.
2. In the Dial-up networking dialogue box that will open, click the **Make New Connection icon**.
3. The Make New Connection dialogue box appears. Type the name <VSNL> of your service provider. Do not press **Enter** ↵. Instead, in the Select the Modem pull down list below, select the **modem** that you have installed. Now click **Next**.
4. In the dialogue box that appears, enter VSNL's <access telephone number>. Enter your <area code> and your <country code> in their appropriate boxes.
5. Now click **Next** and then click **Finish**.

**NOTE** Most of us depend on VSNL for our Internet connection. Unfortunately, the user has to configure his computer with very limited help from VSNL. We have, therefore, described here the procedure for VSNL. If you subscribe to some other ISP, you will get a CD-ROM from them that will greatly simplify the process.

Follow these steps to configure the connection:

1. Click **My Computer** and then click the **Dial-up Networking icon**. The Dial-up Networking window appears showing the new VSNL network icon that you have just created.

2. Right click on the **VSNL icon** and select **Properties**.

3. If you are dialling VSNL in your own city, remove the check marks against the **area** and the **country code** check boxes.

4. Click the **Configure** button and then the **Options** tab.

5. Now check the check boxes against **Bring up Terminal Window after Dialling** and **Display Modem Status**. Uncheck the check box against **Operator Assisted** or **Manual Dial** and click **OK**.

### Configuring the Connection

6. Click on the **Server Type** tab and make sure that the selection under the title Type of Dial-up Server is **PPP Internet Windows NT Server Windows 98**. Under Advanced Options, uncheck **Log on to network** and **Require encrypted password**.

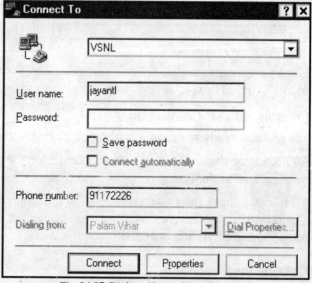

7. Under Allowed network protocols, uncheck all protocols except **TCP/IP**. *See Fig 04.07*.

8. Click **TCP/IP** Settings and in the dialogue box that appears, select the radio button marked **Server assigned IP address**. Now select the radio button marked **Specify name server addresses** and fill

*Fig 04.07 Dial-up Networking Connection*

in the <primary and secondary DNS addresses> of VSNL appropriate for your city. *See Fig 04.08.*

9. Click **OK** and as the previous dialogue box reappears, click **OK** again.

Congratulations! You have now done all that is necessary to set up your Internet connection. You can now move on to techniques for using the Internet, such as sending and receiving e-mails or surfing the World Wide Web!

**Test Your Connection**

To test your connection, follow these steps:

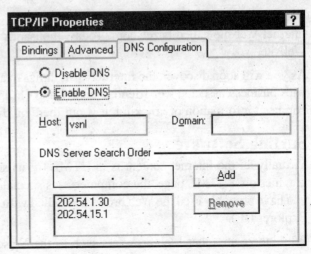

1. Click your **connection icon** (marked VSNL) and the connection dialogue box will appear. *See Fig 04.07.*

2. Enter your <username> and <password> and click **Dial**. The phone number will also appear if you are running Windows 2000 or XP.

3. After VSNL is contacted and a connection is established, the After Dial dialogue box will appear. Enter

*Fig 04.08 VSNL's DNS Addresses*

your <username> and <password>. VSNL will respond with a message such as *Switching to PPP....* followed by a row of characters. Click **Continue**.

4. A connection icon will appear on the task bar near the bottom right hand corner.

If you right click the connection icon, you will see two options:

- Disconnect – Hang up the connection.
- Status – View connection status (dialogue box).

Clicking on Disconnect will hang up your phone line. Clicking on Status will display information of your connection such as the connection speed, the elapsed time, and the bytes sent and received.

If all works well, you are ready to surf the Internet at last!

**TRAP** If you do run into a problem, first make sure that the instructions given here have been followed correctly. In particular, double-check all the entries you have made, such as the DNS server addresses etc. If the problem persists, uninstall the connection by right clicking on the **connection icon** (see step 4 above) and selecting **Delete**. Now, repeat the entire installation process once again.

# Web Surfing

## Why do we Surf?

Why is the Internet so addictive? To answer that question, we begin by looking at the main reasons for surfing the Internet. A moment's thought will convince us that our purpose is usually one of the following:

- To gather information
- To be entertained
- To do business on the Web (e-business)

The last item is recent, but its influence is growing. Until last year, few had heard of the Indian Internet Website called bazee.com. Today, thousands of surfers buy or sell products online at this Website.

As you will soon discover, the Internet is all things to all people. Whether you want to communicate with business associates or friends quickly and cheaply, or you are looking for entertainment, or you need information of any kind, it is out there on the Internet!

## Surfing Software

Virtually all the Internet content is in HTML (or its successor XML) format. To read the text and graphics on a HTML page, the computer uses specialised software called a Web browser. Most of you have probably used the Web browser bundled with your Windows operating system, the Internet Explorer (IE).

While there are other Web browsers such as the Netscape Navigator and the Opera, for Windows users the Internet Explorer is the de facto industry standard. Since it is bundled with your operating system, it is very well integrated with Windows. In fact, the code of the Internet Explorer is also used to run the Windows Explorer, the device you use to view the contents of your computer. The Netscape Navigator (NN) is also a popular Web browser. If you want to use it, you will have to install it separately.'Since the majority of Windows users will run IE on their machines, this chapter is based on the Internet Explorer. If you have Netscape Navigator, you will find that what we discuss here applies equally to NN as well, with only minor variations.

Just as you have Windows available in several flavours, IE too comes in several versions. If you have Windows 95 or 98 installed, you may have IE 4.x. With Windows 2000, you will get IE 5.0, with Windows Me, IE 5.5 and with Windows XP, IE 6.0.

Fortunately, IE can be downloaded (or obtained from CD-ROMs sold with computer magazines) free of cost. If you have IE 4.x, it is strongly recommended that you upgrade at least to IE 5.0. You will see great benefits in speed, find more features and experience greater stability and security.

## Components of Internet Explorer

### *Navigation Tools and Home Page*

While installing Windows, the software selects the Microsoft Network (MSN) home page as your default home page. Therefore, the chances are high that if you were to connect to the Internet and click on the Internet Explorer icon, you will be taken to the MSN home page. However, you can change the home page, say, to the VSNL home page as described later in this chapter. Note that home page designs keep changing and the current home page may look different from what you see in this book.

In Fig 04.09, starting from the top, below VSNL's name, you will notice the menu bar, the tool bar and then the address bar. The links bar is usually on the same line as the address bar and is not visible here. If you wish to add Websites that you visit frequently to the links bar (as icons), you may wish to drag the links bar lower so that it forms a full-length bar just below the address bar.

## Menu Bar

The menu bar contains the items File, Edit, View, Favourites, Tools and Help. The menu items are very similar to the ones that you will encounter throughout Windows programmes. Clicking on each item exposes its drop-down menu. Of special interest to Web-surfing is the Favourites menu item. *See Fig 04.10.*

Clicking on Favourites will open a drop-down menu. The first option in this menu will allow you to add frequently visited Websites to your list of favourites so that you can find them easily afterwards. The second option lets you sort and organise your list of favourites. In addition, the favourite Websites are displayed here.

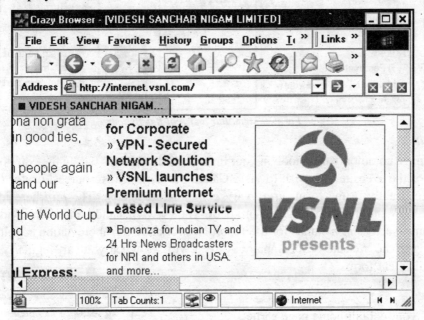

*Fig 04.09 VSNL Home Page*

## Tool Bar

The tool bar contains important buttons (or icons) for navigation. At the extreme left, you have two arrows that allow you to move back or forward amongst the Web pages that you have visited. Subsequent buttons allow you to:

- Stop a Web page or graphics download
- Refresh (or reload) the page you are viewing
- Go to your Home page
- Search the Web by launching the Search Assistant
- Display your list of Favourites
- Display the History of your Web surfing, going back to weeks or even months.

You may have several other buttons on the tool bar, depending on your version of IE and other Web surfing programmes installed. Many such programmes such as Copernic or Download Accelerator will install their own quick launch buttons on the Internet Explorer tool bar so that you can launch these programmes without leaving IE.

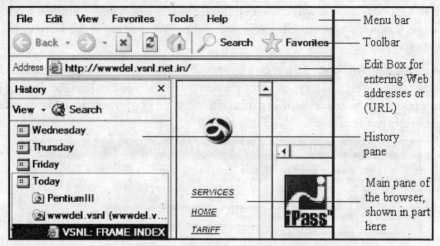

*Fig 4.10 Menu Bar and Tool Bar Buttons*

## Address Bar

Perhaps the most commonly used tool on your browser is the address bar. In the edit box, you enter the address of the Website you wish to visit. Called the Uniform Resource Locator (URL), Web addresses are usually in the form: *http://www.company-name.com.* The *http* here identifies the Website to follow the hypertext transfer protocol. The "www" stands for World Wide Web. The company-name, such as *msn* stands for Microsoft Network and the abbreviation *com* indicates that you are going to the Website of a company. As you will see when you surf regularly, URLs may have many different forms.

## Home Page

We spoke of your default home page earlier.

Most probably, this will be the Microsoft network home page, which gets set when you install the Windows operating system on your computer. However, you can easily change your home page as follows:

1. Go to the Website you wish to open automatically whenever you launch Internet Explorer by typing its URL in the address bar.

2. Click **View → Internet Options** in the menu bar of your browser, the Internet Properties dialogue box will appear.

3. Click the **General** tab and then click on the **Use Current** button.

Your selected Website will now become your home page.

*Fig 04.11 Address Bar for BBC, UK*

### *Using AutoComplete*

To speed up entering URLs, Internet Explorer has a built-in feature that reviews your browsing history and displays a number of possible matches based on URLs you have entered in the past. These options are displayed in a drop-down list that appears immediately below the address bar as soon as you begin to type a fresh URL. You will frequently spot the URL you want in this list before you have completed your typing. If so, you can select the wanted URL by clicking on it. If the options you see do not match what you want, simply keep typing the complete URL and then click the "Go" button.

### *History*

Browse through a list of Web pages you recently visited by clicking the "History" button on the tool bar. You can rearrange or search the History list to find the address of a site that you wish to visit again. See Fig. 04.10 earlier in this section for a view of the history pane.

## Surf Faster

We have already seen how to use the AutoComplete feature, or the history button to find Websites you have visited quickly. Here are a few more tips to speed up surfing and downloading.

### *Speed Up Downloads*

Unless you have a very fast Internet connection, it will take you a long time to load Web pages. It is not for nothing that many long-suffering Internet users have renamed WWW as the World Wide Wait!

Here are some tips to speed up downloading pages. No need to worry, the changes you make can be restored easily by clicking the Restore Defaults button!

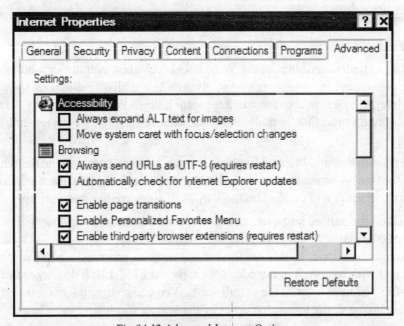

*Fig 04.12 Advanced Internet Options*

**Turn Off Unwanted Multimedia Options**

1. Open Internet Explorer and click on **Tools ➔ Options**.

2. In the Internet Properties dialogue box that appears, click on the **Advanced** tab. *See Fig 04.12.*

3. Scroll down to the Multimedia section. You will see several options for displaying sound, video, animation, pictures etc. Turn off all the options that you do not need by clearing their check boxes.

4. Click **OK**.

**NOTE**

Though you can considerably speed up page download by turning off pictures, in some Web pages you will find that the pictures themselves form links to more information. In such cases, you will require the pictures to navigate further, so you should not turn them off.

**Use Favourites or Bookmarks**

When you reach a Website that you want to visit repeatedly, you can add its URL to your list of favourites as follows:

1. With the Web page open, click on the **Favourites** button on the tool bar. A special window opens to the left of the main page.

2. Click the Add button near the header of the special window. The URL of the Web page you have opened is added to your list of favourites.

If you are using Netscape Navigator, URLs are bookmarked by a similar procedure so that you can find them easily in the future.

**Use the Find Feature**

Yes, you can find virtually anything on the Web. However, when you are in a hurry, you seem to find everything else except the one thing you really want! Actually, finding exactly what you need quickly on the Internet is a fine art. You can get useful help in Web searching by using the Search Assistant, a sub-programme that is built into your Internet Explorer (version 5.0 or later). *See Fig 04.13.*

After you have gone online and Internet Explorer is open, you can summon the Search Assistant by clicking on the tool bar. A separate search window opens to the left of the main window. What you see in your search window will depend on the way your software has been set up.

If you have installed specialised software such as Copernic, the search window will be formatted to show the Copernic search options. However, in its default setup, the search assistant will display MSN Web search as seen here. In this configuration, you can enter a description (called a search string) of what you wish to search in the edit box captioned *Find a Web page containing*. Click the Search button after you have entered the search string. You can change the default setup by clicking on the Customise button at the top right corner of the search window.

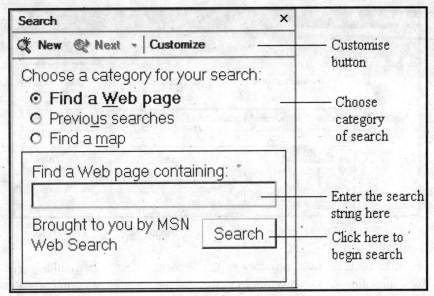

*Fig 04.13 IE Search Assistant*

## Browse Off-line

When you make a Web page available off-line, you can read its content without connecting to the Internet. You can quickly download all pages that appear interesting without having to take the time to read them through. Later, after going off-line, you can go through the pages and delete the ones you do not need. Apart from allowing you to study the downloaded pages at your convenience, this method minimises the time you have to stay online, reducing your telephone bills! You can specify how much content you want available, such as just a page or a page along with its entire links. You can also choose how you want to update the downloaded content on your computer.

If you just want to view a Web page off-line, and you do not need to update the content, you can save the page on your computer. You can save the Web page in several ways. For example, you can just save the text, or you can save all of the images and text exactly as it appears on the Web. If you have saved Web pages at work, you can read them at home by copying them on a floppy disk and carrying the disk home.

## Make Current Page Available Off-line

While browsing the Internet online, you may see a page that you wish to study in detail. In order to be able to browse the page off-line, at your convenience, you have to mark the page. Do the following, while still online:

1. On the Favourites menu, click **Add to Favourites**.

2. Select the **Make available off-line** check box.

3. Click **Customise** to specify a schedule for updating that page and to determine how much content to download.

4. Follow the instructions on your screen. *See Fig 04.14.*

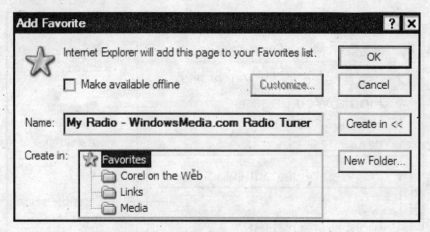

*Fig 04.14 Add Favourites Dialogue Box*

## Update a Favourite

A Web page is often updated by the owner of the Website. This is particularly true if you are browsing a stock quotation page, an online newspaper page or a page containing item lists with prices. If you have added such a Web page to your list of favourites, you may wish to update the page from time to time. You can do so while online, as follows:

1. On the Favourites menu, click **Organise Favourites**.
2. Click the **page** you want to make available off-line.
3. Select the **Make available off-line** check box.
4. Click **Customise** to specify a schedule for updating that page and to determine how much content to download.
5. Follow the instructions on your screen.

In Fig 04.15, you can see the Favourites Search dialogue box. The example shows the setup for browsing the Internet for Windows media files, that is, files containing music and video. The right pane contains the Web sources while the left pane has a list of featured stations for each Web source.

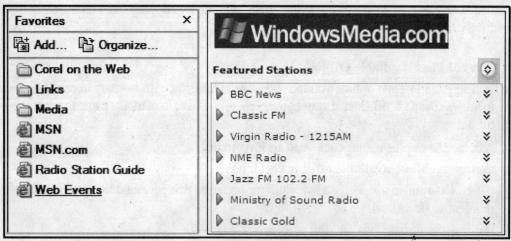

*Fig 04.15 Favourites Search Dialogue Box*

## Save a Web Page

Some Web pages, such as the text of a speech or a magazine article, do not change over time. Therefore, you need not update the page. You may save the page on your hard disk for future browsing without adding it to your list of favourites. To do so, proceed as follows:

1. On the File menu, click **Save As**.
2. Double click the **folder** in which you want to save the page.
3. In the File name box, type a **name** for the page.
4. In the Save as type box, select a **file type**.

The more details you save, the longer will the saving process take. Also, a page saved with pictures, style sheets etc will occupy more hard disk space. Select the option you need (graded from high to low) from the ones below to suit how much details you need and the time and hard disk space you can spare.

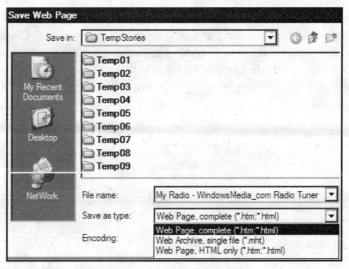

*Fig 04.16 Save Web Page Dialogue Box*

Here are some options for saving Web pages. *See Fig 04.16.*

- To save all the information needed to display this page in a single Multipurpose Internet Mail Extensions or MIME-encoded file, click **Web Archive**. This option saves a snapshot of the current Web page.

- To save all the files needed to display this page, including graphics, frames, and style sheets, click **Web Page, complete**. This option saves each file in its original format.

- To save just the current HTML page, click **Web Page, HTML only**. This option saves the information on the Web page, but it does not save the graphics, sounds, or other files.

- To save just the text from the current Web page, click **Text Only**. This option saves the information on the Web page in straight text format.

What we have discussed so far about the Web browser may appear, at first, to be a little confusing. However, as you continue to browse the World Wide Web, you will become quite familiar with these techniques. As you select the areas that interest you, you will build up your own list of favourites and will become familiar with the websites that hold the information you need. As your experience grows, Web surfing will become easier, more rewarding and a lot of fun!

**CD-ROM**  To learn more about the Internet and to observe Web surfing in a multimedia environment, insert the accompanying CD-ROM in your computer, select the **Interactive** mode in the opening screen. The main menu will appear. To go to the section on the Internet, click the button marked **Internet**. You will see a sub-menu containing the following topics:

- Power of Internet Unleashed
- Working with Outlook Express

Click on the first sub-menu item, *Power of Internet Unleashed*. Another level of sub-sub-menus is displayed from which you can select the particular topic you want to see. Click on your selected topic and follow the instructions on your screen. The second sub-menu shown above deals with material covered in Chapter 5, *E-Mails and Chat* that follows.

# 5. E-mails and Chat

☞ You are introduced to Outlook Express, the built-in e-mail software (client) that comes with your Windows operating system.

☞ You learn how to set up your e-mail account and select the default dial-up connection for your e-mail.

☞ You learn how to reply to an e-mail message, or compose new e-mail, then send e-mails to one person or an entire group.

☞ In the Address Book, you learn how to add, edit or delete entries. You also learn to set up and use distribution lists.

☞ You learn how to filter incoming messages, sorting them into folders and blocking unwanted messages.

☞ You learn how to get free e-mail accounts and how to access your e-mails while away from home.

☞ You are introduced to the finer points of netiquette, so that your e-mails are well behaved!

# Introduction

If you need any proof of the impact of the Internet on communications, you need to just think of e-mail. Post offices in cities today are desperately looking for additional services that they can offer to the public because the income from ordinary postal services has fallen rapidly. The cause is e-mail! There is no doubt that the effort required to buy postage, write letters and then post your composition is far greater than to use e-mail instead. Even without a computer of your own, you can use a cyber café.

E-mail began in the 1970s when engineer Ray Tomlinson developed a way for users of the *ARPAnet* (predecessor to the Internet) to leave messages for each other. E-mail is used today by individual users to send messages to others all over the world. Within an organisation, a Local Area Network (LAN) can be used for company-wide e-mail communications that are conveyed from the sender to the recipients almost instantaneously. Messages such as notices for meetings, minutes of meetings or company information can be broadcast to all employees in minutes. Both personal communication and the business world have been transformed by the power of e-mail.

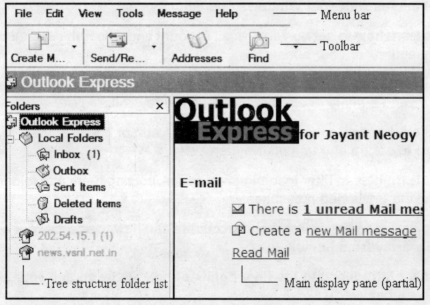

*Fig 05.01 Outlook Express Opening Page*

# Outlook Express

In order to send and receive e-mails, you need special software called an e-mail Client. While there are a number of such software, many free, that you can download from the Internet, it is difficult to match the performance of Outlook Express that comes bundled with your Windows operating system. Even if you still use Windows 95 or 98, you can easily upgrade your Internet Explorer by downloading IE 5.0 or later, free of cost. If you have done so, you will get Outlook Express 5 (OE 5) along with IE 5. OE 5 is powerful, has all the features you need, and it is free. If you use Netscape Navigator, your computer will then have Netscape Messenger, which has the same capabilities as Outlook Express. For the purposes of this book, we will assume that you are using OE 5 or OE 6.

# Launch Outlook Express

You launch Outlook Express by clicking on its icon on your desktop. If there is no icon on your desktop, you will find one in the quick launch tool bar next to the Start button at the bottom left of your desktop. You can also launch Outlook Express by choosing **Start → Programmes → Outlook Express**. *See Fig 05.01.*

The opening page of Outlook Express is not very useful. You can configure it to open directly in your inbox by checking the checkbox at the bottom of the opening page that carries the message When Outlook Express starts go directly to my inbox.

# The Inbox

On the opening page, click the Inbox icon in the left pane under Local Folders. When the Inbox opens, the right side of the window will show the headers (titles) of the e-mail you have received in the top half of the window while the bottom half, called the Preview Pane, will show part of the e-mail. Unopened e-mail headers will be displayed in bold script. If you prefer to see the entire message and not just a preview, double click its header in the top half of the window. Here you see only the default list of local folders. You can add your own folders to the list. *See Fig 05.02.*

You can remove the preview pane to create more space for the headers. To customise Outlook Express, try the following with Outlook Express open:

1. Choose **View → Layout**.
2. In the Window Layout Properties dialogue box that appears, select or deselect elements according to what you wish to display or hide.
3. Click **OK** when the window looks the way you want.

*Fig 05.02 Folder List of Outlook Express*

# Setting Up an E-mail Account

Before you can start sending or receiving e-mail, you have to set up your e-mail account. Make sure that you have the information from your Internet Service Provider (ISP) at hand. This includes the ISP's phone number you have to dial, their Internet Protocol (IP) address for both incoming mail (POP3) and outgoing mail (SMTP). In addition, you will need the username and password allotted to you by your ISP.

You can start setting up your e-mail account from within Outlook Express by following these steps:

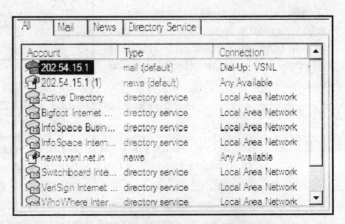

*Fig 05.03 Internet Accounts Dialogue Box*

1. Choose **Tools** ➔ **Account**.

2. The Internet Accounts dialogue box opens. *See Fig 05.03.* Click the **Mail** tab to open that page.

3. Click **Add** ➔ **Mail**.

4. The Internet Connection Wizard opens. The dialogue box asks for your Display name, the name that the recipients of your e-mail will see. Enter your <name> and click **Next**.

5. The next dialogue box asks you for your e-mail address (provided by your ISP). At this time, you can choose to sign up for a free Hotmail account if you so wish. Click **Next** after entering your <e-mail address>.

6. In the next dialogue box, you are asked to enter the names or IP addresses of your incoming mail (POP3, IMAP or HTTP) and your outgoing mail (SMTP) servers. This information would also have been supplied by your ISP. Click **Next** after entering the required information.

7. In the next dialogue box, enter your login name and your password (supplied, again, by your ISP). Do not select the option Remember Password if others use your computer and you do not want them to access your e-mail. Select the Secure Password Authentication option only if your ISP requires it. Enter the required information and then click **Next** and then click **Finish**.

**TIP**

If you choose to apply for a Hotmail account, you will get the opportunity to do so in step 5 described above. The procedure is extremely simple. All you have to do is furnish some personal details and follow the prompts on your screen. Being free, hotmail is a popular e-mail account that many opt for.

## *Selecting the Default Dial-up Connection*

The only other information required is the dial-up connection that Outlook Express must use to connect to the Internet. If you have already configured your dial-up connection, Outlook Express will automatically assign your default Internet connection to your mail account. If you have more than one Internet connection installed in your computer, you can select one as the default connection.

Choose the default connection for Outlook Express as follows:

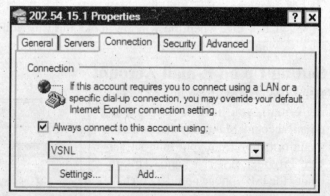

*Fig 05.04 Connection Tab on Properties Dialogue Box*

1. In the Internet Accounts, click the **Mail tab** to open the Mail page. Select the account that you want to change and click the **Properties** button to the right of the dialogue box.

2. In the Properties dialogue box that opens, click the **Connections** tab. Select the **connection** you want to use from the drop-down list. If you wish to use the selected connection exclusively for your e-mail account, then select the option **Always Connect to This Account Using**. *See Fig 05.04.*

3. Click **OK** and then click **Close** to exit all dialogue boxes.

## Incoming Messages

To download incoming e-mail messages, launch Outlook Express. If you are not already online, you will be prompted to activate the dial-up connection. As soon as you are connected, Outlook Express will automatically download your incoming e-mail messages and the headers will appear in the top half of the right window. You can expand any message by clicking twice on the header. If message download does not start automatically, click the Send/Receive button on the tool bar.

## Replies

You can conveniently reply to any message by first selecting it and then clicking on the Reply or the Reply All button. If the original message has been marked to others either in the address or in the CC column, the Reply All option will send your reply to all these addresses.

**NOTE** The default setup will display the original message in your reply window with an angle bracket (>) at the beginning of each line. Thereby, you can see the original message in the same window as you compose your reply. When you send your message, the original message and the reply are sent together to your recipient. This arrangement is very convenient in business situations where the recipient will have both documents together without having to go through his own correspondence. If you wish, you can delete the original by selecting all the text that begins with an angle bracket and then pressing Delete.

In the Reply window, type your own text and then click the Reply button. If you are online, the message will be sent immediately. However, it is more common to download all incoming mail and go off-line. Later, at your convenience, you can compose the replies to one or all the messages and then click the Reply button one at a time. Each time you do so, the reply is saved in the Outbox. They will be sent automatically and together, the next time you launch Outlook Express and go online.

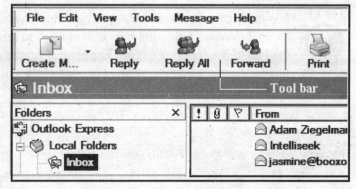

*Fig 05.05 Inbox and Tool Bar*

## Delete Messages

You can delete a downloaded message from your inbox by right clicking on the selected message and selecting Delete from the drop-down menu. Outlook Express removes the messages you delete from your Inbox folder and stores them in the Deleted Items folder. To remove these messages permanently, right click the Deleted Items folder icon and select Empty 'Deleted Items' folder in the pop-up menu that appears.

If you wish to automate the permanent deletion of unwanted messages, do the following:

1. Click **Tools** ➔ **Options**.

2. In the Options dialogue box that appears, click on the **Maintenance tab**.

3. On the Maintenance page that appears, under Cleaning Up messages, select the option **Empty Messages from the 'Deleted Items' folder on exit** by clicking on its checkbox.

**TRAP** Do note that when you delete items, they bypass the Recycle Bin. Therefore, once deleted, you will not be able to recover the messages. Move important messages to a separate local folder for safekeeping. You can create a new folder by right clicking Local folder, selecting New Folder from the drop-down menu and typing a name in the New Folder dialogue box, then clicking OK.

## New Mail

From the opening page of Outlook Express, you can launch a new e-mail composition window in several ways. For instance, you can:

1. Click on the **Create a New Mail Message icon** in the main right pane.

2. Click on the **Create Mail icon** on the Outlook Express tool bar.

3. Click on the **name of the person** you wish to send the message to. After names have been added to your Outlook Express address book, they will be listed in the bottom half of the left pane of your opening page.

4. After you have completed the message, click the Reply button. If you are online, but do not wish to send the message right away, click **File ➔ Send** later. The message will be stored in your Outbox folder, ready for despatch the next time you go online.

**TRAP** It is important to address the e-mail correctly. Even one wrong letter, a hyphen instead of an underscore or a missing period, is enough to send the e-mail to the wrong person, or cause it to bounce back to you. The general format of an e-mail address looks like this – mailto: account@domain name. For example, a valid e-mail address on a VSNL account is jlneogy@vsnl.com.

Note that it is not necessary to enter the "mailto:" since all modern e-mail software assumes it to be there in the address.

The reply window has spaces (fields) for the following:

- **To**: This may contain one or more addresses separated by semi-colons.
- **Cc**: May contain one or more addresses of those who will receive copies of the message.
- **Subject**:
- The text of the message, entered in the space provided below the tool bar.

Of the four fields, only the To field is required to be filled before you can send the e-mail. All the other fields, including the body of the message is optional! In other words, you can send a completely blank e-mail message to someone if you wish!

## Attachments

One of the most useful features of e-mails is that you can send entire files along with your e-mail message as attachments. The files may be Microsoft Word documents, Excel spreadsheets, pictures and graphics or even video clips! In short, almost anything that can be stored on your computer's hard disk can also be sent as an e-mail attachment.

## Sending Attachments

To send an attachment, carefully note the filename and the path to the file to be attached. For example, "C:\Reports\Jan2002.xls" is a Microsoft Excel file named Jan2002, available in the sub-directory "Reports" on the hard disk named "C".

To attach this file to your e-mail, do the following:

1. Open the message composition window and type your e-mail message as usual. Now click the **Attach** button on the tool bar. The Insert Attachment dialogue box opens. *See Fig 05.06.* Now locate the file you want to send as attachment.

*Fig 05.06 Insert Attachment Dialogue Box*

2. Click **Attach**. The file attachment will appear in a new header that will open just below the Subject header.

3. Click **Send**.

Since most of us have relatively slow dial-up connections and because many harmful viruses are often transmitted as attachments to e-mails, it may be a good idea to keep a few things in mind:

- Do not send an attachment larger than 2 MB especially if you or the recipient uses dial-up modems. The time required to upload or download will be too long.

- It is a good idea to compress the attachment using some file compression utility such as WinZip. It will minimise transport time. However, the recipient must also have a similar utility to expand the compressed attachment after it is received. A good solution may be to zip your file as a self-extracting .exe file. Such files will expand without the need for WinZip when your recipient clicks on the file.

- Check beforehand if the ISP at either end prohibits attachments. Due to the risk of virus masquerading as an attachment, some ISPs may block attachments. If so, your e-mail will not go through.

## Receiving Attachments

You will see the icon of a paper clip to the left of any e-mail message you receive if the message has an attachment. If you trust the sender, you can right click the icon and open the attachment, or select Save As, to save it on your hard disk.

**TRAP** Do not open an attachment from a source you do not trust for fear of a virus. E-mail viruses can be devastating. Try to save the attachment on a floppy disk and then scan the attachment for virus using good anti-virus software. If a virus warning is triggered, you can delete the file without risking contamination of your computer.

## The Address Book

The Address Book in Outlook Express stores e-mail addresses and other information for you. E-mail addresses such as *jlneogy@del01.vsnl.net.in* can be very tiring to type. They are difficult to remember and can be easily mistyped. Fortunately, the built-in Address Book makes your job much simpler by remembering and automatically inserting the selected e-mail addresses for you.

You can open the Address Book from Outlook Express at any time by clicking the Addresses icon on the tool bar. The Address Book opens with the list of addresses listed in your Main Identity list exposed in the right pane. Other addresses such as Shared Contacts can be accessed by clicking the appropriate folder in the left pane. *See Fig 05.07.*

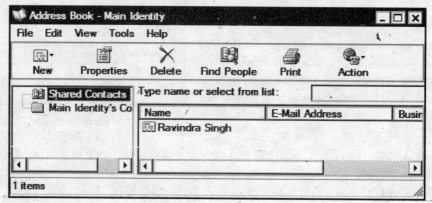

*Fig 05.07 Address Book*

### Adding or Deleting Entries

You can open the Address Book by choosing **Tools** ➔ **Address Book** in Outlook Express. The Address Book will open in its own window. Entries can be added to your Address Book in two ways:

1.  When you reply to an e-mail that you have received by clicking on the Reply button, the sender's name and address is automatically entered in your address book. Right click on the **sender's name or e-mail address** in the message header and choose **Add to Address Book**. The Properties dialogue box will open where you can enter additional particulars about the sender.

2.  You can click on **Contacts** in the bottom left pane of the opening page of Outlook Express and select **New Contact**. The Properties dialogue box opens where you can enter name, e-mail address and other particulars of the person you wish to add to your Address Book.

As items are added to your Address Book, they will appear as a list in the Contacts panel. Double click on any entry and an e-mail composition window opens with the address from the entry already filled in.

You can right click on any **unwanted entry** and select **Delete** to remove the entry from your Address Book.

### Distribution Lists

Suppose you are the secretary of a club. You may need to send the same e-mail announcement to several members. To do so, you can enter several addresses in the To and the Cc fields from your

Address Book. The addresses will have to be entered one by one and they will appear separated by semi-colons. However, a better way is to set up a distribution list.

You can set up a distribution list as follows:

1. Open the Address Book by clicking **Tools ➜ Address Book** while Outlook Express is open.

2. Click **New** and select **New Group** from the drop-down list.

3. In the Properties dialogue box that appears, select a name for the group such as <Photography Club>.

4. Click the **Select Members** button on the right of the Properties dialogue box.

5. The Select Group Members dialogue box appears. *See Fig 05.08.* In the left pane of this dialogue box, you will see a list of all the contact addresses that you have in your Address Book. Highlight the entry you wish to transfer to the group and click the **Select >>** button to transfer the contact to the right pane. Repeat the process until you have transferred all the names you wish to include in your group.

6. Click **OK**.

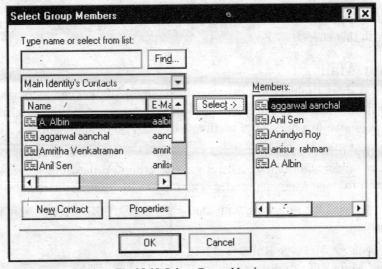

*Fig 05.08 Select Group Members*

A listing with the group name that you have selected will now appear in your contact list. The next time you wish to send an e-mail to all the members of the group, simply select the group name in your e-mail and Outlook Express will automatically send the message to all the members in the group.

## Organising Your Mail

If you receive a large number of e-mails regularly, you will find that your Inbox gets crowded very quickly. When you can no longer easily find the e-mail you want, it is time to organise your e-mail into folders much as you organise the files on your hard disk. To create folders and to store messages in folders, proceed as follows:

1. Right click the **Inbox folder icon** in the first page of Outlook Express and choose **New Folder** from the menu that appears.

2. The Create Folder dialogue box appears. *See Fig 05.09.*

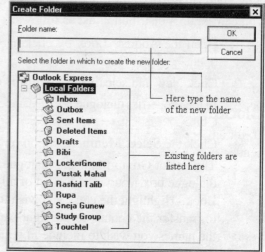

3. Type the <name of the new folder> in the edit box and click **OK**. The new folder will appear in the list of local folders displayed in the bottom half of the Create Folder dialogue box.

4. You can now drag and drop selected messages to the new folder. You can also right click on a **message header** and select **Move to Folder**.

5. In the Move dialogue box that appears, you can select the folder in which you would like to store the message.

*Fig 05.09 Create Folder Dialogue Box*

If an e-mail does not fit into the list of folders you have, you can always create a new folder as discussed earlier in this chapter.

## Filtering Your Mail

If you have created special folders to store your incoming mail, you can automate the process of distributing your incoming mail to separate folders. If you receive very large number of e-mails (for example, if you subscribe to a number of mailing lists), this bit of automation is a real time saver.

You can also use mail filters to delete mail that you do not wish to see at all. Mail can be filtered by content, subject or sender information. Therefore, by setting up the filter appropriately, you can make sure that mail from an annoying sender is automatically deleted.

To set up a filter, perform the following with Outlook Express open:

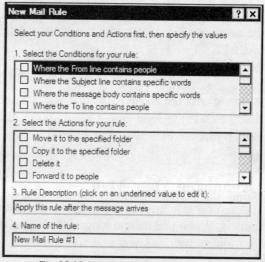

1. Choose **Tools ➔ Message Rules ➔ Mail**. The New Mail Rule dialogue box will open. *See Fig 05.10.* If you already have rules, the Message Rules dialogue box will open instead. Click **New** to open the New Mail Rule dialogue box.

2. Select one condition at a time from Box 1 of the New Message Rule dialogue box. Then, in Box 2 select the action you want Outlook Express to perform. In Box 3, click what you want to specify (such as names of people or words on the subject line) and then click the folder option to select the

*Fig 05.10 New Mail Rule Dialogue Box*

folder where you want Outlook Express to store the e-mail. In Box 4, enter the name of the Mail Rule you have just set up. Click **OK** when you have finished.

Repeat steps 1 and 2 for each mail rule that you want to set up. These rules will appear in the Message Rules dialogue box with a check mark against each the next time you click **Tools** ➔ **Message Rules** ➔ **Mail**. You can open this dialogue box at any time to edit or delete a message rule that you have set up.

## Blocking a Sender

If, for any reason, you wish to block mail being sent to you by a specific sender, you can block the sender as follows:

1. Click **Tools** ➔ **Message Rules** ➔ **Blocked Sender's List** in Outlook Express to open the Blocked Sender's List.

2. Click on the **Add** button on the right. The Add Sender dialogue box will ·open. *See Fig 05.11.*

3. Enter the <address of the sender> to be blocked in the edit box and then select whether you wish to block mail messages, news messages or both by clicking on the **appropriate radio button**.

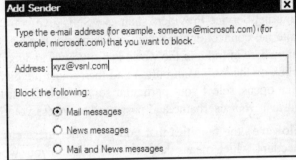

*Fig 05.11 Block Sender Dialogue Box*

4. Click **OK** twice to close the window.

You can open the Blocked Senders dialogue box at any time to edit or remove the sender's name you have blocked.

## Compacting and Backing Up Folders

Do you experiment with new software or upgrade your computer from time to time? If so, you will be no stranger to lost e-mails and e-mail addresses! The answer is to back up your important e-mails! Even if you leave the inner workings of your computer strictly alone, you may wish to conserve precious hard disk space by compacting your e-mail folders. Let us see how:

1. Select an **e-mail folder**.

2. On the File menu, point to **Folder**, and then click **Compact**.

3. To back up the folder, find the folder file, and then copy it to a backup folder, floppy disk, or network drive. Outlook Express e-mail folders have a .dbx extension (for example, *Sent Items.dbx*).

Some message files might be too large to back up onto a floppy disk. If so, you can use some commercially available file splitting software that will allow you to break up the file into smaller ones that may fit on several sequential floppy disks. Alternatively, you can use larger capacity back-up devices such as a Zip disk or a Jazz disk.

# Free E-mail Accounts

If you do not have a computer at home, you can still use e-mails by using the facilities of a cyber café and creating a free e-mail account for yourself. You will have to pay the cyber café's charges though! A very popular Website that offers you free e-mail is the Yahoo Website. You can also subscribe to *rediff.com* or *indiatimes.com* and to many other such e-mail agencies.

The main problem with such accounts is that you have to read and reply to your e-mails while online, which is expensive. To cut down online time, you can pre-compose your e-mail letters using a simple word processor such as Notepad. Save your e-mail on disk. When you are online, you can open the composing window of your e-mail client to cut and paste the text of your letter.

# Check E-mails Away from Home

Internet Service Providers such as VSNL give you the facility to log on to their Website from any Internet connection anywhere in the world. For VSNL, the Website for connecting to e-mail from anywhere in India or the world is http://www.del.vsnl.net.in. Once you have opened this Web page, click on the Web Mail button and then select the city where your account is registered. In the page that opens, select your particular server such as nda1 or bom2, as applicable. You will be asked to furnish your username and password to access your e-mails.

However, the facilities that you get under these circumstances are similar to the user of a Yahoo account, which means that you have to do all your work online. See the tip in the previous paragraph on how to cut down your online time.

# E-mail Etiquette

For both personal and business use, e-mail is rapidly becoming the preferred means of communication. It is cheaper and faster than a letter, less intrusive than a phone call and less trouble than sending a fax. Differences in location and time zone are no obstacle to e-mailed communication. Your correspondent will tell you that the e-mails they receive from you appear to be friendlier and less intimidating than formal letters.

Because of these advantages, the use of e-mail is growing exponentially. Chances are that you will be using e-mails as your only means of communication in the near future if you are not doing so already. As a result, the image you project about yourself to your friends, or of your company to your business associates, will depend increasingly on how effectively you can handle your e-mail correspondence.

Often, our difficulties about e-mail correspondence arise because we do not have a clear idea of how e-mails differ from other, more familiar means of communication. As a first step towards understanding the special nature of e-mails, we look at what sets e-mails apart from all the rest.

## E-mails are Different

E-mails are closer to telephone calls than to letters. This is because you will usually receive a reply overnight, much faster than what is possible through post, sometimes called snail-mail! Because of the long time that letters take, it is important that you say what you have to say clearly the very first time. It takes just too long for clarifying questions to be asked and answers to be received.

E-mails let you seek clarifications and get answers much faster and easier. Because your correspondent expects a swift response, and it is quick and easy to clarify matters if things are not clear the first time, it is customary to sacrifice a bit of accuracy to get a quick reply out as soon as possible. In other words, do not hold up your e-mailed reply while you track down the smallest detail that you want to include.

While e-mails are fast, like a conversation, remember that you cannot convey expressions and feelings like you can when talking face-to-face. Therefore, there is a greater risk in being misunderstood. People have used little icons called emoticons to add feelings. For example, you can convey happiness by typing symbols such as :-) or :). You can also convey sadness by typing :-( or :(.  In addition, many word processors will allow you to insert symbols such as ☺ or ☹. It will be obvious to you, however, that these additions are generally limited to personal e-mails.

Another difference between e-mail and other media is that what the sender sees when composing a message might not look like what the reader sees. When you speak, you will sound the same to yourself as to your listener.  The written letter will have the same formatting when you write and when your correspondent reads it. However, with e-mail, the software and hardware that you use for composing, sending, storing, downloading, and reading may be completely different from what your correspondent uses. Your message's visual qualities can therefore be quite different by the time it gets to someone else's computer screen. For example, if your recipient has a different word processor, the inserted symbols we saw in the earlier paragraph may not display at all on his computer.

# Internet Chat

## What is Chat?

E-mails allow you to be in touch with your friends and relatives. However, replies to your e-mails usually take some time, perhaps days. Newsgroups allow you to become a member of groups with interests similar to yours, but the interaction is not immediate. You post a query and wait for replies. There is no real time interaction. However, the Internet does provide you with a tool for instant communications, the "chat" facility. You have a conversation by typing in text on your keyboard and get an immediate reply! Since the conversation happens in real time, it is like chatting on the phone.

You can chat over the Internet using the "Chat Rooms" of online services such as Yahoo! MSN, CompuServe or AOL. You can also use specialised software such as Internet Relay Chat (IRC). In all cases, conversations are held in real time. Chat need not be restricted to just two persons; you can join a Chat Room and take part in a multi-party interaction. What is more, by using special icons included in chat programmes, you can convey a smile, a hug or sorrow along with the text you type. Chats can be fun. They are also very addictive!

While there are many ways of chatting, we will look at Yahoo! Chat as an example of an online service chat room and IRC as an example of specialised chat software. You can go to Yahoo's Website at http://www.yahoo.com and sign in to use its chat services. Similarly, you can download the IRC software from the Internet free of cost.

# The Yahoo! Chat

We will assume that you have not used Yahoo! Chat before and, therefore, do not have a Yahoo! Identification, called an ID, or password. Do the following to register:

1.  Open your Web browser, connect to the Internet and navigate to the Website http://www.yahoo.com.

2.  Click the **chat** option. Click **Sign me up!** Read and accept the service terms agreement that will appear.

3.  In the new window that opens, enter a <User ID> and a <Password> that you like. If the ID is already assigned to someone, you will be asked to enter a different one.

4.  After an ID and Password have been agreed upon, you will be asked to provide personal information including name, e-mail address, gender, profession, address etc.

Once all information has been supplied, Yahoo! will sign you in and welcome you as a member.

You are now ready to begin chatting. Proceed as follows:

1.  Click **Go to Yahoo! Chat**. The chat page opens.

2.  You can select between Java and HTML-based chat. If you select the HTML-based chat page, the page will load quickly but you will have to click the refresh button to see other's responses to your messages. Java-based chats load slower, but get automatically refreshed so that messages and replies are always updated. You can now choose your area of interest. Areas include sports, romance, science fiction, general etc.

3.  Click **Complete Room List**, to see a list of chat rooms available. Select the **room** you want to enter.

After you select a room, you will see a list of chatters on the right of your screen.

Here are some of the settings you can change in Yahoo! Chat:

*   You can change the display of text on your screen (such as font, colour, font size) by clicking **Preferences** and selecting what you want.

*   You can send a private message to another chatter by clicking **PM**. A new window opens in which you can type your private message.

*   To know more about another chatter, click **Profile**.

*   If you want to block messages from a chatter, click **Ignore**.

Chatting online is the best way to get familiar with all the options and commands available to you. So get chatting!

# Using IRC

Internet Relay Chat or IRC software can be downloaded free from a number of Websites. The IRC programme that you download is called the **Client** part of the programme. Several Internet Websites have **Server** chat software installed. When you connect to one of these servers, you can get access to many clients through the network of servers. IRC is so popular that there may be as many as 2,000 interconnected clients on the Web at one time! See Fig 5.12 for a view of the IRC.org website.

## Basic Operations

After installing and launching IRC, you will usually select a nickname for yourself, select a server, list the currently open channels on the server you have chosen and listen in to the conversation that is going on. The nicknames of the current participants as well as what they are saying will appear in your IRC screen as text. If you wish to contribute to the conversation, you can join in.

*Fig 05.12 Website of IRC.org*

## IRC Commands

All commands in an IRC chat session begin with forward slash like this "/". If you type anything without the forward slash, it is taken as text. If you have joined in, the text you type will appear as your message on the screens of all who are active in the chat room. Some of the important IRC commands are shown in the table below. Remember that all commands must begin with a "/" or forward slash.

| | |
|---|---|
| /server | Selects the server you want to use. |
| /list | Lists the current channels open on the server you have selected. The number of current users is also indicated. |
| /nick | To assume your nickname or to change your nickname. |
| /join | To join any of the channels on the network. |
| /whois | Shows information of a fellow chatter on your channel. |
| /msg | Allows you to send a private message to another chatter that others cannot see. |
| /invite | Invites another chatter to join you in another channel. |
| /notify | You will be informed when the person you specify joins your channel. |
| /help | Seek online help. |
| /quit | Ends your chat session, you can add a reason for leaving if you wish. |

## Some IRC Servers

After launching IRC, you will have to connect to one of the many IRC servers on the Internet. You can choose servers such as:

- Irc.portal.com
- Irc.voicenet.com
- Irc.colorado.com
- Chat.talkcity.com

**CD-ROM**  To learn more about different aspects of e-mails using Outlook Express in a multimedia environment, insert the accompanying CD-ROM in your computer; select the **Interactive** mode in the opening screen. The main menu will appear. To go to the section on e-mail, click **Internet**. You will see a sub-menu containing the following topics:

- Power of Internet Unleashed
- Working with Outlook Express

Click on the second sub-menu, *Working with Outlook Express*. The sub-sub-menu will be displayed showing you a list of topics including:

- Setting up an e-mail account.
- Checking and replying to e-mails.
- Attaching files.

Click on the radio button of the selected topic.

# 6. Internet Telephony and Computer Fax

*In this chapter:*

☞ We explain the new technology of Internet telephony.

☞ You learn about Voice over Internet Protocol used in Internet telephony.

☞ We explain the hardware and software you will need to call up your friends and relatives overseas using Internet telephony.

☞ You learn about using your computer as a fax machine for sending and receiving fax.

☞ We show you how to set up a well-known computer fax software to let you send faxes over the telephone line to other similarly equipped computers or to standard fax machines.

# Communication Techniques

We have already seen how communications can improve spectacularly by using the computer and a telephone line. Earlier in this book, we have discussed the Internet, e-mail and Internet Chat. In this chapter, we look at some more communication techniques that you can use with your computer. In addition to your computer, a modem, a phone line and an Internet connection, you will need some additional hardware and software. In this chapter, we look at Internet telephony and computer faxing.

# Internet Telephony

## Introduction

Because of the high tariff of international phone calls, users have long looked for cheaper alternatives to International Subscriber Dialling (ISD). With improvement in quality and speed of Internet connections, Internet telephony now provides this alternative.

We make everyday telephone calls on a dial-up connection using a standard analogue telephone line and a telephone instrument. Since standard analogue phone lines are available worldwide, we can call a friend or business contact overseas almost as easily as our next door neighbour. The networks we use are called PSTN (Public Switched Telephone Network) or POTS (Plain Old Telephone Service). Although easy, the cost of an overseas call is indeed very high.

If you have a computer with a modem and an Internet connection, a cheaper solution lies in installing Internet telephony in your computer. Through this system, we can call anyone connected to the PSTN system even if the recipient has only an ordinary analogue telephone. We have to register with a service provider for Voice over Internet Protocol or VoIP. The charges are considerably lower than the normal overseas telephone call charged by your telephone company.

## VoIP Architecture

The VoIP technology utilises the same TCP/IP protocol that you use for e-mails and to surf the Internet. However, before it could be widely used, VoIP technology had to improve the voice quality and integrate seamlessly with the existing PSTN network that interconnects the existing telephones all over the world. A schematic view of the VoIP architecture can be seen in Fig 06.01.

The VoIP gateway or voice switches allow computers to interface with the worldwide telephone network and also to regular telephones and fax machines. To do so, packets of information flow from the computers, through appropriate software on to the Internet and back to the PSTN telephone network.

In Fig 06.01, you can see two illustrations. In the left hand illustration you can see PCs with Fax or Voice software (1) accessing either phones or faxes (2) through a voice switch via the Internet.

Alternatively, the PCs at the top (1) can access fax machines or telephones after travelling via the Internet, through the voice switch, into a private voice network before connecting up to our everyday PSTN service (3).

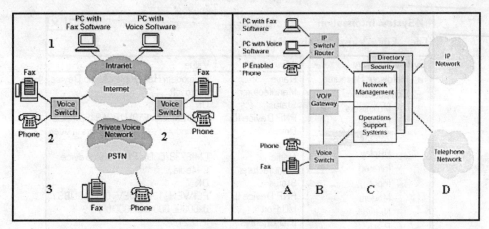

*Fig 06.01 VoIP Architecture*

On the right, you can switch PCs, enabled telephones and fax machines (A) connecting to the Internet Protocol (IP) or the telephone network (D) passing through layers of either IP Switches, VoIP Gateways or voice switches (B) and network management software (C).

There are now service providers in India with tie ups with international providers who will let you download free software from the Internet. You have to then buy a phone card, much like mobile phone cards that contain a code number that you must enter at their Website to get registered. Before you do so, however, you must have the required hardware installed in your computer. We look at the equipment you will need in the section below.

# Hardware

Most multimedia-enabled computers these days come equipped with sound capability. It may be built directly into your motherboard, or installed as a separate sound card. You have to determine whether the sound card or capability you already have will support full duplex operation. If your motherboard has sound capability, it is very likely to be only half duplex, that is to say that it will support only one-way communication. You can either speak, or listen, but not both. Half duplex capability is not really satisfactory for Internet telephony. You have to wait between speaking and hearing the reply. Therefore, you should get a separate sound card with full duplex rating.

### *Detecting Sound Card Capability*

You can display your audio devices by the following steps:

1. Click **Start** ➔ **Programmes** ➔ **Accessories** ➔ **System Information** to display the system information dialogue box.

2. Click the **+ sign** next to Components and then click **Sound Devices**. The sound devices installed in your system are displayed in the right pane of the dialogue box. *See Fig 06.02.* As you can see, the main sound device listed in this example is half duplex and will not be suitable for Internet telephony.

If this is true in your case, you will have to install a separate sound card such as *CREATIVE* or an equivalent make. Usually, you will buy a set comprising a sound card along with a good speech quality headphone/microphone set which are not only compatible with each other, but will also suit your Windows operating system.

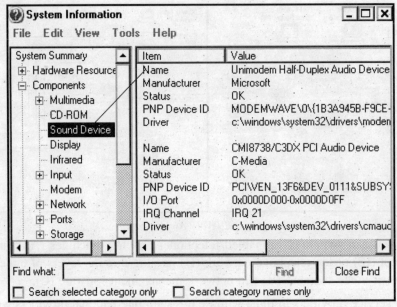

*Fig 06.02 Your Audio Devices*

## Headphone and Microphone Set

You will require appropriate headphone-microphone set, complete with jacks to connect the headphone and the microphone to your sound card at the rear of the computer. Select a good quality set with padding around the earphones so that you may be insulated from ambient sound. See Fig 06.03 for an illustration.

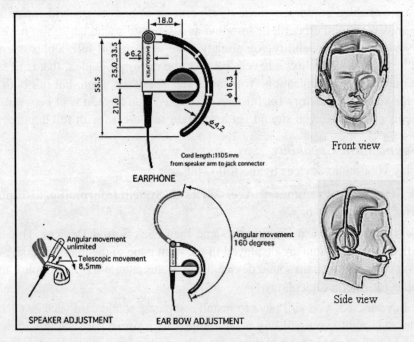

*Fig 06.03 Headphone and Microphone Set*

# Telephony Software

After you have made sure that you have the right hardware, you can download the software from a service provider such as *phonewala.com* and install the software. There are many other vendors. Choose one that has been in operation for some time and, hence, can be expected to remain in service. See Fig 06.05 later in this section showing one setup Wizard for Internet telephony. The setup wizards will vary according to the software you download.

During the installation process you will also set up the speaker/headphone and microphone volumes for clear conversation.

The *Phonewala* dialogue box and phoning options are shown in Fig 06.04. After you have purchased a telephone card of suitable value (ranging from Rs. 100 to Rs. 1000), you have to access their Website to download their dial-up programme. With the dial-up programme installed, connect to their service site and enter the pin code that is revealed when you scratch the card you bought.

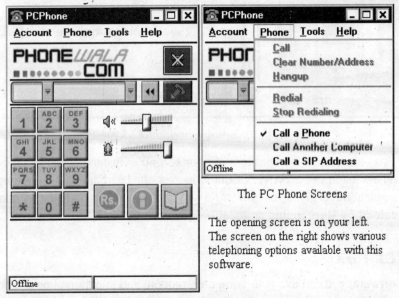

*Fig 06.04 PC Phone*

After entering personal details, you can begin the process of adjusting your sound levels and then you can dial the number you want by following the instructions on your screen.

After installing the software, you can set up your speaker/headphone and microphone using their Setup Wizard. See Fig 6.05 for a view of the Setup Wizard.

## *Calling*

The actual operation is simple. Follow these steps to connect to a remote party:

1. Connect your computer to the Internet through your modem as usual.
2. Click the **icon** of your Internet phone provider on your desktop. The programme's dialogue box opens. *See Fig 06.04.*
3. Enter the international code, the area code and the number to be dialled.

4. Click the **dialling icon** and wait for the connection to be made.

5. Speak and listen using the headphone and microphone set.

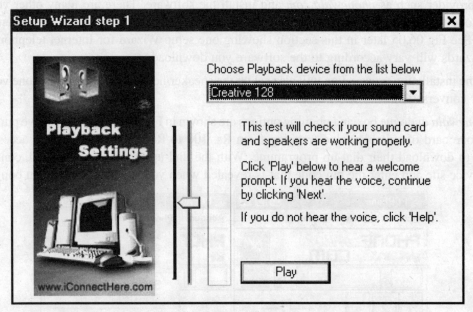

*Fig 06.05 Setup Wizard for Internet Telephone*

**TIP** You can activate the speakers of your computer instead of the headphone if you wish others listen to the conversation. However, the headphone must be unplugged first. A headphone set gives you greater privacy and permits you to listen without the distraction caused by surrounding ambient sound.

# Computer Fax

With proper software, you can use your computer, modem and telephone line as a fax machine that will send or receive faxes either from another computer with similar capabilities, or a regular fax machine. For fax operation, you do not require to connect to the Internet. However, if you send a fax to an overseas number, your telephone service must be enabled to make ISD calls.

**NOTE** Make sure that the internal or external modem installed with your computer has fax capabilities. Check the documentation of your modem. It should read something like "Voice, Fax Modem". You can look up your modem specification by following the same steps as you did earlier to check your sound card capability. This time, however, select Modem in the left pane instead of Sound devices. The modem specifications will appear on the right pane. See Fig 06.02 earlier in this chapter.

If you have the correct modem, you can use your computer as a fax machine by using appropriate software. In Windows 98, Windows 2000 or Windows XP, your Windows operating system will have a built-in fax service. It is not included in Windows Me. You have to ensure that this Windows component is installed on your computer. To confirm that fax service is installed, proceed as follows:

1.  Click **Start** ➔ **Control Panel** ➔ **Add or Remove Programmes**. The Add or Remove Programmes dialogue box is displayed.

2.  Click **Add or Remove Windows Components** and the Windows Components Wizard is displayed. *See Fig 06.06.*

3.  The Fax services component will be listed here. Make sure that there is a check mark in the check box next to this component. If not, check the **box** and click **Next**.

4.  Follow instructions on screen. You may be required to insert your Windows CD-ROM during the installation of the fax service.

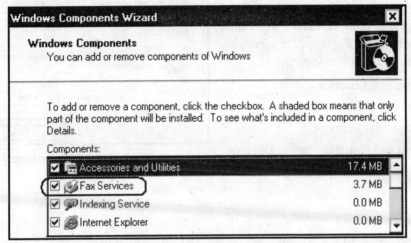

*Fig 06.06 Windows Components Wizard*

Windows Me does not include the Windows fax service. However, if you have Microsoft Office 2000 installed, then along with Outlook (a component of MS Office) Symantec's WinFax Starter Edition will be available. You can use this software instead of Windows fax service. You can read how to use WinFax Starter Edition in Chapter 22, *Communicating with Outlook* later in the book. If you use fax regularly for communication, you can install a more powerful version of Winfax, the Symantec WinFax PRO (the current version is 10), which we will discuss in the next section.

# WinFax PRO

WinFax turns your computer into a fax machine that sends and receives fax. Using WinFax, you can fax documents from your computer to any fax number in the world, anytime. In addition to being able to send and receive fax using your computer, WinFax also provides a wide variety of features for personalising and automating your faxes.

With Winfax PRO you can assemble your faxes just like you assemble traditional fax. You can preview and modify them while you are creating them. You can also check for new faxes in one place and conveniently access fax numbers directly from your WinFax phone-book or any other contact manager such as your address book in Outlook.

Winfax PRO lets you fax right from your computer to one or more people. Fax will transmit faster with improved fax compression software that is built into WinFax. As a fail-safe measure, WinFax detects and corrects conditions that could otherwise cause faxes to fail.

If you are sending faxes long distance within India, you can reduce telephone charges by scheduling WinFax to automatically dial the number and send the fax during off-peak hours. You have to only leave your computer on, but need not be present during the fax transmission.

### Configuring WinFax

Upon installation, the software opens a dialogue box that gives access to various parameters that you would like to set up for the programme to function correctly. Mainly, you are required to enter data in appropriate dialogue boxes that you can open from the WinFax PRO Programme Setup dialogue box. *See Fig 06.07.* In particular, you have to set up the following:

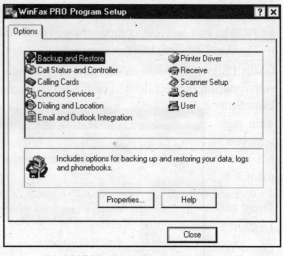

- Dialling and Location
- E-mail and Outlook Integration
- Message Management
- Modem and Communication Devices
- Receive
- Send
- User

*Fig 06.07 WinFax PRO Programme Setup*

The WinFax PRO programme setup Wizard is launched automatically as soon as you finish installing the software. You are required to follow the instructions on your monitor's screen, filling in personal information and details of phone and fax line numbers to complete the installation.

If your modem is installed, WinFax will carry out self-diagnostics and will display a report that the modem is suitable for fax transmission and fax receipt. If there is a problem with the modem, you will have to consult the documentation that came with your modem. See Fig 06.08 for the Modems and Communication Devices Properties dialogue box. You are required to merely select your modem by clicking on its name in the drop-down list.

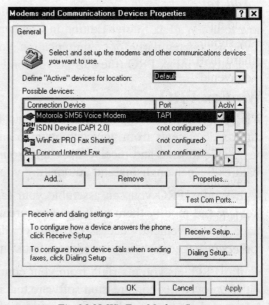

Once installation is complete, you can access the WinFax PRO Message Manager window shown in Fig 06.09. The Message Manager window is very similar to the Outlook Express window that we have already seen. You can organise your faxes here much like the e-mails in Outlook Express.

More details on using the Message Manager is given in the subsequent sections under Sending faxes, Receiving faxes etc.

*Fig 06.08 WinFax Modem Setup*

# Sending Faxes

WinFax is a versatile fax software that is not confined to sending faxes to other fax machines alone. You can also send a fax as an e-mail. We look at different sending procedures below.

### *Send and Forward Faxes by e-mail*

If your recipient does not have a fax machine, but does have an e-mail account, you can send him a fax using WinFax from your computer as an e-mail attachment. You can send or forward a fax in self-viewing format to any e-mail address. The recipient simply double clicks the attached file to launch the fax document in its own viewer. Your message arrives looking exactly the way you want it to, and your recipients do not need any special software or equipment.

### *Drag and Drop Documents for Instant Faxing*

Open Windows Explorer and select the document you want to fax. Then, simply drag the selected document to the WinFax Drag and Drop Depot desktop icon. The WinFax Send dialogue opens automatically, with your document all ready for faxing. You need only address your fax and click **Send.**

*Fig 06.09 WinFax Message Manager*

### *Add Your Signature*

Add a personal touch by signing outgoing faxes. You have to first import or capture your signature by signing on a sheet of paper and scanning it. You can then save the signature as an image on your hard disk. Thereafter, you can import the signature image at the bottom of your fax. To do so conveniently, you can use the handy new Signature button to add it to your outgoing faxes.

# Receiving Faxes

You can receive faxes manually or set up WinFax to intercept any call on the connected telephone line and attempt to download it automatically as a fax. The automatic reception works best if you have already been advised that a fax is on its way, or you have a dedicated telephone line connected to your computer's modem setup solely for receiving and sending faxes. We look at both the methods below.

### *Receiving a Fax Manually*

1. If you answer a fax call on a shared voice/fax line, do not hang up the handset right away.

2. Do either of the following:

2.1. **From Message Manager**: On the Receive menu, point to **Manual Receive Now** and click the **modem** you want to use.

2.2. **From the Controller**: Right click the **Controller icon** on the Windows task bar, point to **Manual Receive Now** and click the **modem** you want to use.

3. Do not hang up the handset. The Manual Receive dialogue appears.

4. Click **Yes**.

5. When you hear your modem pick up the line and the message *Answering...* appears on the Line Status dialogue, now hang up the handset. WinFax prepares your modem and begins receiving the fax.

If you have only one modem and one phone line connected to your computer, click the **Manual Receive Now** command. You do not have to select a modem.

### *Receiving a Fax Automatically*

Do either of the following:

- **From Message Manager**: On the Receive menu, point to **Automatic Receive** and click the **modem** you want to use.

- **From the Controller**: Right click the **Controller icon** on the Windows task bar, point to **Automatic Receive** and click the **modem** you want to use.

With automatic reception enabled, WinFax will receive incoming messages automatically as long as either Message Manager or the Controller is running. You can change the default automatic reception options (for example, the number of rings before WinFax answers and the time periods during which automatic reception is enabled) in the Receive Properties dialogue (start **Programme Setup**, double click **Receive**, and then click the **General** tab). If you have two phone lines and two modems connected to WinFax, you can set separate automatic reception options for each line.

## Using Outlook for Fax

If you have installed Symantec's Fax Starter Edition as part of Microsoft Office 2000 installation, you need not use WinFax PRO. Although limited in capability in comparison to the PRO version, you will find the starter edition adequate for almost all your personal or business fax needs. Furthermore, being part of the MS Office 2000 suit, the starter edition is very well integrated with Outlook. It can use the Address Book in Outlook and the Outlook Journal can be set up to automatically track all the Faxes you send and receive.

Read about Outlook and the incorporated fax service in Chapter 22, *Communicating with Outlook*. Read about faxing directly from Word 2000 in Chapter 11, *Using Word Efficiently*.

# 7. Introducing Microsoft Office 2000

☞ You are introduced to the Microsoft Office 2000 software suit.

☞ You learn about elements common to all Office applications. Mastery over these elements will help you use all the individual Office applications efficiently.

☞ We show you how to select and edit text.

☞ You learn how to handle objects such as graphics, moving and copying them as desired.

☞ You are introduced to the Office Assistant, how to use the assistant and how to turn it off.

☞ We show you how to get online help while using any one of the Office software applications.

☞ You are shown how to use the special features that make programmes accessible.

# Microsoft Office 2000

Until the arrival of Office XP, Microsoft's Office 2000 was the most powerful suit of business application software available to personal computer users. Although Office XP has a number of added features such as the Task pane and multiple cut and paste capability, Office 2000 has virtually all the software capabilities that a normal user is likely to need. In this part of the book, we explore the software suit that makes up Microsoft Office 2000. *See Fig 07.01.*

| Application Name | Also Called | Used for |
|---|---|---|
| Word | Word Processor | Document Writing |
| Excel | Spreadsheet | Calculations, graphs and charts |
| PowerPoint | Display Software | Slides, Charts, Graphs, handouts etc. |
| Outlook | PIM | Communication, information management |
| Access | Relational Database | Business applications using substantial data |

*Fig 07.01 Office Applications*

Office 2000 comes in five varieties. They include:

- Office 2000 Standard which includes Word 2000, Excel 2000, Outlook 2000 and PowerPoint 2000.

- Office 2000 Small Business which includes Word 2000, Excel 2000, Outlook 2000, Publisher 2000 and Small Business Tools.

- Office 2000 Professional which includes Word 2000, Excel 2000, Outlook 2000, PowerPoint 2000, Access 2000, Publisher 2000 and Small Business Tools.

- Office 2000 Premium which includes Word 2000, Excel 2000, Outlook 2000, PowerPoint 2000, Access 2000, Publisher 2000 and Small Business Tools, FrontPage 2000 and PhotoDraw 2000.

- Office 2000 Developer which includes everything in the premium edition as well as tools and documentation for building, managing and deploying software solutions (programmes) with Microsoft Office.

As you can see, the packages are designed to meet the needs of different users. Of course, they are priced differently too. Based on our experience of what the average user requires most, we have selected to cover Word 2000, Excel 2000, Outlook 2000, PowerPoint 2000 and Access 2000 in this book. As you know, Word is a word processor while Excel is a spreadsheet. With Outlook, you can communicate and organise your work while PowerPoint is ideal for presentation of your ideas to others. If you run a small business, the Access database programme will be very useful to you. You will get much more information on all these applications later in this book.

## Starting and Exiting

You can start and exit all applications in the Office suit in the same way. If you have installed and configured the Office shortcut bar, it is a convenient location to launch an Office application. If you have not installed the shortcut bar, you can launch an Office application as follows:

1. Click **Start** ➜ **Programmes** from the Windows opening screen.

2. In the menus that appear, select the application you want to launch.

Alternately, you can activate the Office shortcut bar by clicking **Start** ➜ **Programmes** ➜ **Microsoft Office Tools** ➜ **Microtct Office Shortcut Bar**. The shortcut bar is launched. You can now add the icons for the applications you wish to launch from this bar. You can also add additional programmes such as the Notepad or the Calculator (Windows Accessories) to the bar to create a convenient launching platform for programmes that you use most frequently. *See Fig 07.02.*

You can exit an application either from the drop-down menu by clicking on **File** ➜ **Exit**, or by clicking on the close button ☒ at the upper right corner of the application window. Make sure that you have saved the work file of the application before exiting the application.

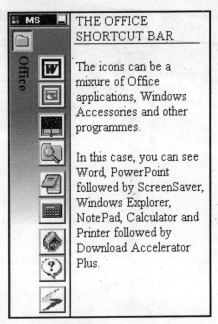

*Fig 07.02 MS Office Shortcut Bar*

# Common Office Elements

Office 2000 applications share many common elements between them. This feature is very convenient to you as a user since what you learn in Word will help you with similar features in Excel or Access.

## Screen Elements

In Fig 07.03, you can see a typical Word 2000 window. Many elements in this window are common to the other Office 2000 applications we will study in this book.

We take a look at each of these elements in the section below.

**Title Bar**: The title bar shows the application and the file that is currently open. For instance, Fig 07.03 shows a document titled *AccOff120701* opened in Word. If more that one file is open (Word opens each document in its own window), then the window with a dark border is the active window in which you can work.

**Control Icon**: Click this icon to control the open application. For instance, a drop-down menu appears after you click. It will let you restore, move, size, maximise, minimise or close the application.

**Menu Bar and Tool Bar**: These appear below the title bar. We discuss menus and tool bars in detail later in this chapter.

**Status Bar**: The status bar is located at the bottom of the application window. It displays information, warning messages and status. The information varies according to the software in use. For instance, with Word, you will see the line and column number of where the cursor is on an open document. In Excel, you will see whether the spreadsheet is in the ready or the edit mode. In PowerPoint, the slide number and in Access, the record number will be displayed and so on.

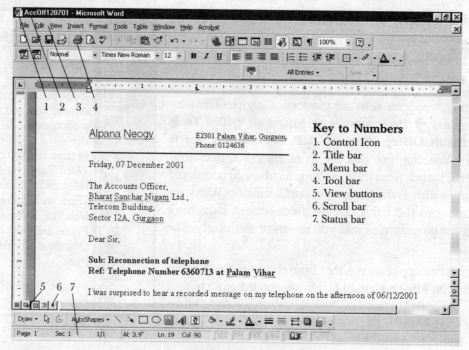

Fig 07.03 Typical Screen Elements

**Key to Numbers**
1. Control Icon
2. Title bar
3. Menu bar
4. Tool bar
5. View buttons
6. Scroll bar
7. Status bar

**Scroll Bars**: These appear at the bottom and right of a window if the contents are more than a full page.

**View Buttons**: They appear in some programmes such as Word and PowerPoint where the same document can be displayed in different views. For instance, in Word you can look at a document in Normal view which shows text only. You can also see the document in Page Layout view in which information on margins, headers, footers, page numbers etc are displayed.

See Fig 07.04 which shows the menu items and tool bar icons of a Word window.

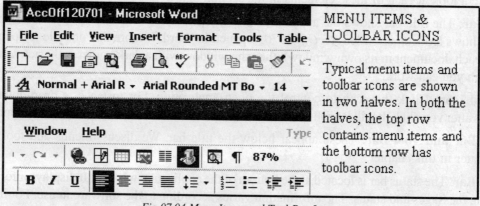

Fig 07.04 Menu Items and Tool Bar Icons

# Menus

There are many menu elements common to all the Office applications. For instance, except for Outlook, the first four menu items for the remaining four applications are File, Edit, View and Insert. Depending on the context, a Format menu item will appear. If the application opens more that one window (like Word) then there is a menu item called Window. For all the applications we are discussing, there is also a Tools and a Help menu item.

In addition, there are some specific menu items for particular applications. For instance, there is a Favourites menu item in Outlook and a Slide Show menu item in PowerPoint. See Fig 07.05 for examples of a number of application menu bars that have common menu items and icons.

We emphasise the menu structure of the applications because they are similar and therefore if you learn one, you are already familiar with most of the menu items of the other applications. We discuss the common menu items in detail below.

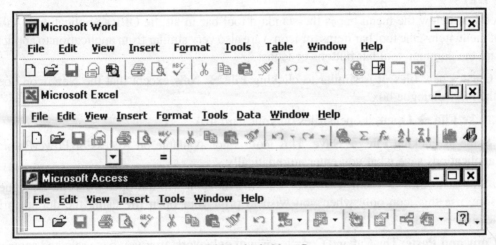

*Fig 07.05 Multiple Menu Bars*

**File menu**: Use commands in this menu to create and open files, to set printing parameters and print files and to exit the application.

**Edit menu**: You will observe that many edit functions are greyed out (unavailable) unless you have selected an object (like text) in the document to be edited. The Edit menu contains the Undo, Cut, Paste and Copy commands. In addition, you will see the Find and Replace commands in the Edit menu.

**View menu**: You will find commands for displaying tool bars, and changing between views where appropriate.

**Insert menu**: You can insert different objects using the Insert command depending on the application. Thus, you can insert clip art in Word, PowerPoint or Excel, a new record in Access or a new appointment in Outlook.

**Tools menu**: The Options menu item is applicable to all Office applications. In addition, the spelling checker is here for appropriate applications. To display the default options for any Office application, click **Tools ➔ Options**. You can also change options in the multi-tabbed dialogue box that opens.

**TRAP**  Be careful about changing default options. If you do, it is a good idea to note down the default settings so that you can reset the defaults if your changes do not work as expected.

**TIP**  You will note that all menu items on the menu bar have a single letter underlined. In any drop-down menu, you can either point at the menu item with your mouse pointer and click, or you can press the Alt key followed by the underlined letter for the same effect. Thus to open the Edit drop-down menu in any of the applications, you can either position your mouse pointer in Edit and click, or type **Alt + E** on your keyboard. In the drop-down menu, the items can be accessed by typing **Ctrl + the underlined letter**.

## Tool Bars

Located just below the menu bar is the standard tool bar in all the Office applications. As in the case of menu items, the tool bar items (or icons) are also very similar from application to application. Here are the common tool bar buttons or icons:

**New**: Creates new files. It is similar to clicking **File ➜ New** except that the New icon does not open the New dialogue box.

**Open**: Like **File ➜ Open**, it opens files on your hard disk.

**Save**: Same as clicking **File ➜ Save**. This icon is not available on Access or PowerPoint since these applications save what you enter automatically.

**Print**: Similar to **File ➜ Print**. However, clicking the icon will not open the Print dialogue box. Therefore, use this icon only when you wish to print your open file using the default printing parameters.

**Cut, Copy and Paste**: The Cut and Copy icons will only work after you have selected some object on the open file. The Paste icon will only work after you have previously cut or copied some item to the Windows clipboard. It is the same as clicking **Edit ➜ Cut**, **Edit ➜ Copy** or **Edit ➜ Paste**. You can also achieve the same result by typing **Ctrl + X**, **Ctrl + C** or **Ctrl + V** respectively.

**Undo**: The same as clicking **Edit ➜ Undo**, this command allows you to rollback your last action in many cases. You can also type **Ctrl + Z** for the same effect.

There are some special formatting icons or buttons that do not appear on Outlook, but appear on the remaining four applications. They are:

**Bold, Italic and Underline**: You can apply the relevant attribute to the selected text by clicking these buttons. You can also click **Format ➜ Font** and choose these attributes from the Font dialogue box.

**Align Left, Align Centre, Align Right and Justify**: You can click these buttons after selecting text to apply these formattings.

**Font and Font Size**: These are drop-down boxes rather than buttons. After selecting text, you can apply the desired font or font size by clicking on the option you want in the drop-down box.

# Selecting and Editing Text

As in the case of tool bars, menu items and screen elements, there is much in common in the ways you can select and edit text in any of the five applications we are discussing. We look at the most common actions you have to perform with any Office application.

## Insert Text

Position the cursor between the two characters where you wish to insert text. Click to anchor the cursor and then type the text you wish to insert. If the text is contained within a graphic object, you may have to click to select the graphic object first.

## Delete Text

To delete a single character, position the cursor next to the character. If your cursor is just before the character, press the delete key. If your cursor is just behind the character, press the Backspace ← key. The character will be deleted.

## Select Text

If you wish to work on a block of text (a word, a sentence or a whole paragraph) you must first select it. You can do one of two things:

- Drag the mouse cursor (left click, hold down button and move the mouse) over the text to select it.
- Position the cursor at the beginning of the text block, hold down the Shift key and use the arrow key to move the highlight till you reach the end of the text block.

In either case, after selecting the text block, you can easily delete your selection by pressing the Delete key. This is normally the easiest method of getting rid of large amounts of unwanted text.

**TIP**

To replace text, it is best to select the unwanted text as described above and just type the replacement text right over the old text. The new text will replace the old selected text. It is not necessary to delete the old text first.

## Copy and Move

The Windows clipboard is a temporary storage where you can store any object that you acquire by either copying or cutting the original. In case of copying, the original remains while in cutting, the original is removed. The clipboard is available with all the Office applications we are discussing. Start by first selecting the text you wish to cut or copy. Then move the insertion point where you wish the text to appear. Right click for the shortcut menu to appear and click **Paste.** There are other options:

- Choose **Cut, Copy** or **Paste** from the Edit menu of the application in use.
- Click the **Cut, Copy** or **Paste** buttons on the standard tool bar.
- Select the text and then right click the selection for the shortcut menu to appear. Click **Cut, Copy** or **Paste** from the shortcut menu. *See Fig 07.06.*
- Press **Ctrl + X** to cut, **Ctrl + C** to copy or **Ctrl + V** to insert using the keyboard.

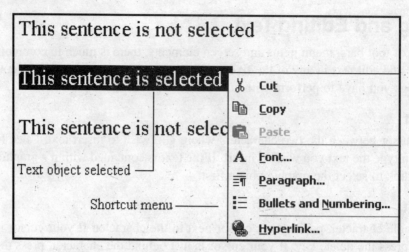

*Fig 07.06 View of Selected Text and Shortcut Menu*

# Selecting and Manipulating Objects

You will deal with a variety of graphic objects such as clip art, charts and pictures in a number of Office applications such as Word, Excel or PowerPoint. While creating drawing objects is quite complex and the moves depend on the software you use, the actions required to select and manipulate objects (delete, move, size, cut and paste) are quite similar across the Office applications that we are discussing. We look at these moves.

### Selecting and Deleting

Click on a graphic object and it is selected! Eight black (or white on a black background) squares (called handles) appear around the selected graphic object. See Fig 07.07 for a selected graphic object.

After selecting an object, you can delete it by pressing the Delete key. You can also right click on the object and display a shortcut menu that will allow you to Cut, Copy or Paste the object. You can click Edit to launch a drawing programme (such as Microsoft Paint) to alter the object. You can also format or resize the object as we see in the next section.

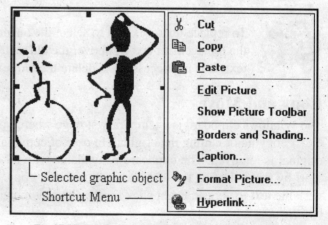

*Fig 07.07 Selected Graphic Object with Shortcut Menu*

### Moving and Sizing

After an object has been selected, 8 handles will appear around the object. If you move your mouse pointer on any of the handles, the pointer changes shape to a double-headed arrow. You can now drag the selected handle to change the size of the object.

To move an object, you may first have to format the object using the Format command in the shortcut menu that appears after you have right clicked a selected object. Click as follows:

**Format ➔ Layout ➔ Tight ➔ OK**. The solid black square handle will turn into small circles.

If you now move your mouse pointer inside the selected object, the pointer will turn into a four-headed arrow. Now you can drag the object to any other position on your document.

### Cutting and Pasting

The moves are the same as for text objects. You have to first select the object and then display the shortcut menu. If you click on Cut or Copy, the object is stored in the Windows clipboard. Move the cursor to the desired insertion point on the same or a different document, right click to display the shortcut menu and click on Paste to insert the object at its new location. *See Fig 07.08.*

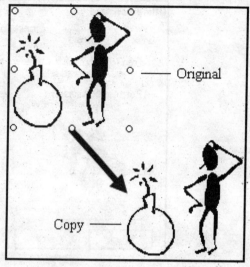

*Fig 07.08 Moving a Drawing Object*

# Getting Help

All Office applications have the same four basic Help systems. You can get help from the Office Assistant, the Help system, the "What's This?" feature and the Office on the Web. We look at each feature one by one.

## Office Assistant

The Office Assistant is an animated cartoon figure. The default one is called *Clippie*. It pops up to answer questions, offer tips and provide help with different features of an Office Application. The Office Assistant is a feature that is turned on by default. That is, in a fresh installation of Microsoft Office, the Office Assistant will be active. However, advanced users often turn the Office Assistant off. We explain how you can do so later in this section.

If it is turned on, the Office Assistant can give you six different kinds of help, tips and advice as explained below.

**Specific Help**: This is related to the task you are performing. For instance, in Word, the Assistant may recognise that you are writing a letter and offer to open a letter template for you.

**Productivity Tips**: You may see a yellow light bulb icon appear in the Office Assistant. If you click the Assistant, you will get a tip on a shortcut or a suggestion for using an application feature more effectively.

**Response to Request**: If you click on the Office Assistant window, a discussion bubble opens with some suggested help topics. An edit box also opens where you can type in a question. You can click on one of the topics or type your question. The question can be framed in normal English such as

"How do I create mailing labels?" The Office Assistant interprets the question by picking up key words such as "Mailing", "Labels", "Create" and provides you with a useful answer.

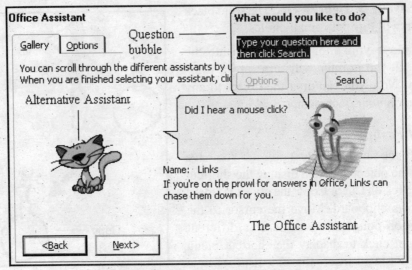

*Fig 07.09 Office Assistant with Bubble and Options*

**Warnings**: If you try to exit an application without saving your work file, the Assistant will pop open to ask you if you want to save your work first.

**Daily Tips**: The tip of the day appears when you first start an application. Click on the light bulb icon to see the tip.

**Newcomers**: When you enter an Office application for the first time, the assistant will ask if you want help with the application.

### Turning On or Off

In case the Office Assistant comes in the way, you can turn it off by Clicking **Help** ➔ **Hide the Office Assistant**. You can turn it on again by clicking **Help** ➔ **Show the Office Assistant** on the opening screen of any of the Office applications. When the Office Assistant icon appears, you can turn the help bubble on or off by clicking on the icon.

To change the Office Assistant icon to a different one, click the **icon** and choose **Options**. You will see two tabs. The Gallery tab will permit you to choose a different Office Assistant. If the one you choose is not already loaded, you may be prompted to insert the Office 2000 CD-ROM. Follow the instructions on the screen.

To reset the options of the Office Assistant, click on the **Options** tab and check or uncheck the options as you wish. Click **OK** to complete the exercise.

## The Help System

For a general description of the Help system, see Chapter 3, *The Windows Operating System* that describes the Windows Help system. The Office 2000 Help system is very similar. You have the same two-pane structure with the right pane providing the details while the left pane has three tabs.

The tabs are labelled Contents, Answer Wizard and Index. This arrangement too is the same as for Windows help. The PowerPoint help window is shown in Fig 07.10.

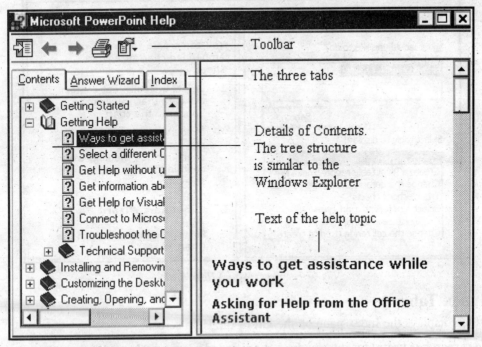

*Fig 07.10 Help Window in PowerPoint 2000*

## The Contents Tab

The Contents tab (first tab from the left) reveals the topics in the help files. You see the main headings displayed in a tree structure as you see folders and files in the Windows Explorer. The text is grouped under topics, each with a book icon and a heading. If you click on the plus sign (+) to the left of a book icon, sub-topics are displayed. The information documents are revealed when you click on any document icon that is revealed below a topic or sub-topic. In Fig 07.10, you will see a list of topics under the Contents tab.

If you do not have much information on a subject, the contents are the best place to begin your search. Browse through the topics and the sub-topics till you find the information you want.

## The Answer Wizard

The next tab displays the Answer Wizard. If you do not know the exact name of what you are looking for, you can use the Answer Wizard. Enter your question in the edit box captioned *What would you like to do* and click the **Search** button. You can type your question in simple English much as you would in the bubble of the Office Assistant as we saw earlier.

In the pane on the left, the Answer Wizard, all topics relevant to your question will be displayed. Scroll down the highlight amongst the topics to see a more detailed explanation on the right pane of the help window. *See Fig 07.11.*

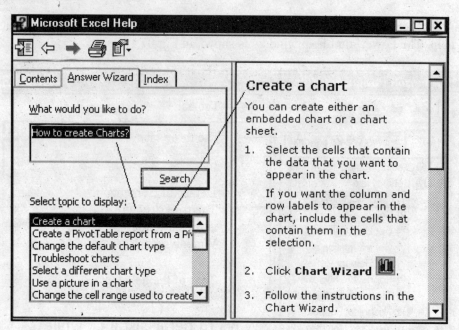

*Fig 07:11 Answer Wizard Help Window*

## The Index Tab

The last tab displays the Index pane on the left of the Help screen.

The Index search is useful for intermediate to advanced users who know the exact term to look for. Otherwise, use the Contents if you know what topic you wish to look up. If you are not sure of the exact term you want, frame a question in the Answer Wizard.

As you type the first few letters of the item of your interest in the box captioned *Type keywords*, the Help programme displays matching keywords in the list box captioned *Or choose keywords*.

If a matching topic is found by Help, it will be displayed in the list box captioned *Choose a topic (if found)*. Highlight the item or topic that is appropriate to your search. The details appear in the right pane of the Help window.

See Fig 07.12 for a view of the Help window with the Index tab selected.

## What's This?

To find out more about a button on a tool bar or options in a dialogue box that you have opened, you can use the What's This? feature. There are three ways to do so:

- In any Office application, click **Help ➔ What's This?** The mouse pointer changes to an arrow and a question mark. Click the item that interests you with this changed mouse pointer and a pop-up Help for that item will open. Press Esc to close the pop-up.

- In a dialogue box, first select the item of interest and then press **Shift + F1**. A pop-up Help appears (if available for that item). Press **Esc** to remove the pop-up.

- Many dialogue boxes have a "What's This?" button. Click on that to display the What's This? pointer. Then proceed as in the first option above.

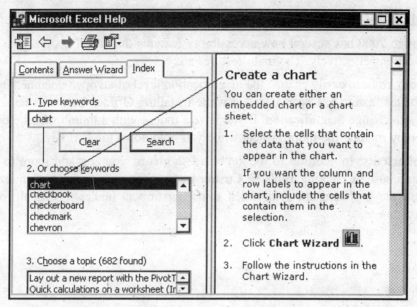

*Fig 07.12 Index Tab in the Help Window*

**TIP**

You can make the mouse pointer hover above a button to cause a Tool tip to appear, which explains the purpose and function of the button. For instance, if you hover the mouse pointer above the "*I*" button on a formatting tool bar, a tool tip appears that says *Italic* explaining that the button will format the selected text in italics. Where available, this is faster than What's This?

## Internet Help

If you click on the Help menu item on the standard tool bar of any application, the drop-down menu carries an option captioned *Office on the Web*. If you are unable to get the information you seek from the Help files and you are connected to the Internet, you can click on this option to connect to the Microsoft Office 2000 Website. Search features help you find more information from the Website on topics of your interest. *See Fig 07.13.*

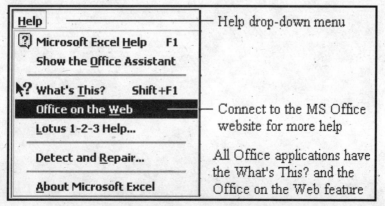

*Fig 07.13 Office on the Web Option*

# Accessibility Features

Microsoft Office 2000 has several new accessibility features that assist people with handicaps to use the applications effectively. The main features are:

**Magnification**: You can easily change the magnification level of an open document to improve its readability. If this feature has been installed while installing Office, there will be an icon on the menu tool bar to change magnification. If you have a mouse with a thumb wheel, you can change magnification by rotating the thumb wheel while you hold down the Ctrl key.

**Keyboard Shortcuts**: In addition to the keyboard shortcuts, you can add more to replicate the action of your mouse by clicking **Tools ➜ Customise** from the menu bar. This feature lets the user work with just the keyboard and is useful if some impairment makes it difficult for the user to operate with a mouse.

# 8. Getting Started with Word 2000

## In this chapter:

☞ We introduce you to the "flagship" of the Office 2000 suit of programmes, Microsoft Word 2000.

☞ We walk you through the basics of Word 2000, starting with a description of the opening window in Word.

☞ You create your very first document using Word 2000.

☞ We show you how to save your document and to print out your work.

☞ We move on to your next document, which may be another new document or opening of an existing document.

☞ You learn how to select text in a document, the first step before you can modify the text on your document.

☞ We show you how to insert and delete text.

☞ You learn how to move and copy text from one location to another or from one document to another.

☞ You learn to use the drag and drop method for manipulating text.

# Getting Started with Word 2000

Word is a powerful word processing software. You can use it to prepare simple notes or complex documents, reports and publications. Whether simple or complex, all documents begin in the Word window and use the large array of menu items and tools that you get with Word 2000. Therefore, we must begin by opening Word and becoming familiar with its rich collection of features.

## Starting Word

You can start Word in three ways. If you see a Word icon on the opening screen of your computer, then you can start Word by clicking on it. Word will open with a blank document. If you have the Office Shortcut bar installed on your computer, you can click on the Word icon on the shortcut bar instead to open Word with a blank document. If you have been using Word already, and have saved documents created with Word, you can navigate to the document you want to open using the Windows Explorer and click on the document file. Word will open with the document you have selected.

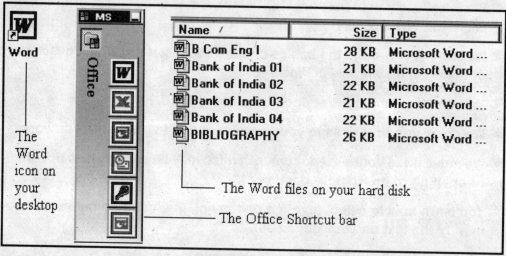

*Fig 08.01 Starting Word*

## The Word Window

Regardless of the way you start Word, the Word window will open either with a blank document, or with the document you have selected. In Chapter 7, *Introducing Microsoft Office 2000*, you have already become familiar with the common window elements of all Office 2000 applications. In addition, some elements of the Word window are special. They include:

**Ruler bar**: Located near the top of the screen, you can use this bar to set the document's margins, indents and tabs.

**Status bar**: Located at the bottom of your screen, this bar shows the page number, section number, current page and total pages in your document. There are status indicators to show if Word is in the overwrite mode or insert mode.

**View buttons**: Located at the bottom left corner of your screen, these buttons let you switch views of your document. You can cycle through Normal, Web Layout, Print Layout and Outline views of your document. We will discuss these terms in later chapters.

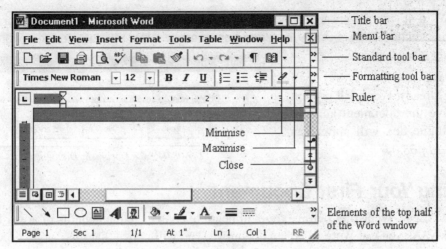

*Fig 08.02 Word Window Top Half*

See Fig 08.03 later in this section for a view of the bottom half of the Word window.

## Exiting Word

When you have finished working with a Word document, you can exit Word by clicking **File ➜ Exit** from the menu bar and the drop-down menu. If you have not already saved the document, Word will prompt you to do so. In the dialogue box that appears, click on Yes to save the document. The other options, No will not save the changes you have made while Cancel will allow you to continue to work with the document.

**TIP**

You can also close the Word window by clicking on the Close button at the top right of the Word window. *See Fig 08.02.*

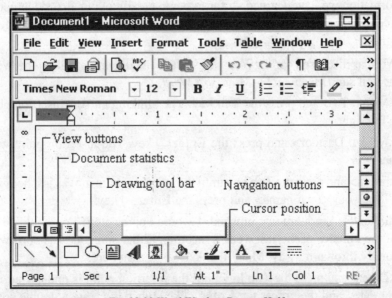

*Fig 08.03 Word Window Bottom Half*

To close Word, if your fingers are on the keyboard, use keystrokes to close Word. If your fingers are on the mouse button, then click on the Close button of the Word window. In other words, use the more handy means.

If you have not saved the open document already, Word will prompt you to save the document and the Save dialogue box will appear as shown in *Fig 08.04.*

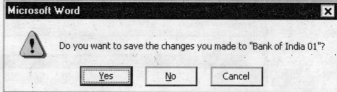

*Fig 08.04 Save Document Dialogue Box*

# Creating Your First Document

If you have used a typewriter before, you will begin to appreciate the benefits of a word processor very quickly. As you use Word to type a document, you will notice that there is no need to hit the carriage return. The sentences wrap around by themselves as the right margin of the page is reached. You will also like the ease with which you can correct a typing error. Simply hit the backspace key to erase the error and type the correction!

There are of course many more features that Word has that make document preparation so much easier. For instance, the Tab key will let you line up lines in your text one below the other with a precision difficult to achieve with the space bar alone. As you type and reach the end of the page, you can continue typing. Word will automatically insert a page break, creating a blank page for the document to continue.

As you read these chapters on Word, you will come across many other sophisticated tools that Word possesses for formatting, editing and preparing documents.

## Hands on Document Creation

We use the information we have learned so far to begin creating your first document. We work on a short memo requesting a copy of the minutes of last week's meeting. Proceed as follows to create your first document:

1.  Start Word as discussed earlier. You will see a blank document filling the Word screen. The title bar will say *Document1 – Microsoft Word*.

2.  Type <Memo To:> and press the **Tab key**. The blinking cursor (insertion point) will move 1/2" to the right.

3.  Type <Mr J P Dastoor> and press the **Enter** ⏎ key. The insertion point will move down one line.

4.  Type <From:> and press the **Tab key** until the insertion point moves just below the recipient's name. Type your <own name> and press the **Enter** ⏎ key.

5.  Type the text of the memo: <Jamshed, I would appreciate if you could send me an extra copy of the minutes of the last week's meeting. Either someone has borrowed it, or I have accidentally thrown it away. Many thanks!> as shown here.

6.  Type <Date:> and press the **Tab key** until the insertion point is under your name. Type the <current date> and then press the **Enter** ⏎ key twice to create a double space.

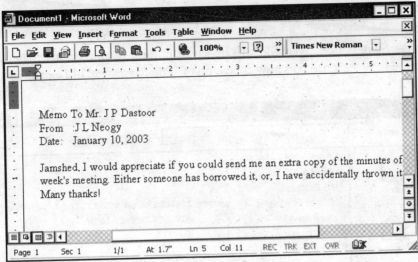

*Fig 08.05 Your First Document*

**TRAP**

Remember not to press the **Enter** ↵ key in between. The paragraph will stay "together" and it will be easier for you to format it later. You will notice how Word will wrap the sentences as the right margin is reached.

Congratulations! You have just created your first Word document.

# Saving and Printing Your Work

To preserve your document, it is necessary to save it. When you do so, the document is written as a file on your hard disk (or floppy disk, if you so desire). You can reopen the document at a later date by navigating to the document file in Windows Explorer and clicking on it.

If you want to physically send your document to someone else, you will have to print your document using your printer. In this section, we look at how you can save and print your document.

## Saving Your Document

When you open a new document in Word, it has the default name of *Document 1*. You have to assign a name to the document in order to save it. Word will automatically add a file name extension of *.doc* while saving the document.

As we have discussed, you can save your document on a fixed hard disk or on removable media such as a floppy disk, a Zip disk or on a back-up tape drive if you have one installed. If you are connected to a network, you can also save your document on the hard disk of the network server. This is useful if you are part of a team and other members need to access your documents.

For our first exercise in saving the memo you have created earlier, we will use the hard disk of your computer. Do the following:

1. Click **File** ➔ **Save** on the menu bar and the drop-down menu that appears. Alternatively, you can click on the **file icon** on the standard tool bar. Since this is the first time you are saving the file, the Save As dialogue box appears. *See Fig 08.06.*

2. In the File Name list box, type the name you wish to give to the memo, say <Memo Dastoor 001>.

3. Click the **Save** button. Your file will be saved in the My Documents folder and the new name you have assigned will now appear on the title bar instead of *Document 1 – Microsoft Word*.

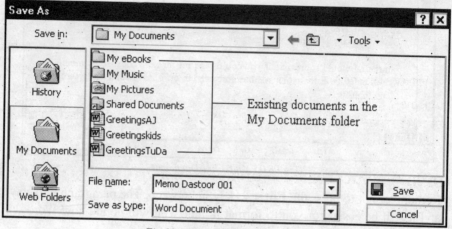

*Fig 08.06 Save As Dialogue Box*

**NOTE**

Depending on how your Office suit has been installed, the default folder in which files are saved will probably be the My Documents folder. If you edit your work, it is necessary to save your document again. Otherwise the changes you have made will be lost. When you save your document a second time, the Save As dialogue box does not appear if you click **File -> Save** or click on the **Save** icon.

# File Name Extensions

As we have seen, Word assigns a three-letter extension .*doc* to your document while saving it. The file name (*Memo Dastoor 001*) will be separated from the extension by a period (.). Though all Word documents carry this extension, you will normally not see it when you look at the file names using Windows Explorer. *See Fig 08.06.*

If the extensions are displayed, you may find them distracting. Hide them as follows:

1. Click **Start ➔ Settings ➔ Control panel**. The Control panel opens.

2. In the Control panel, click the **Folder Options icon**. The Folder Options dialogue box appears. *See Fig 08.07.*

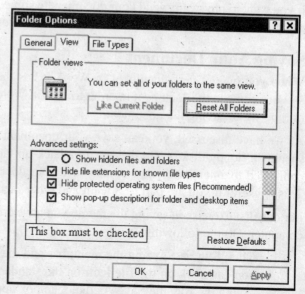

*Fig 08.07 Folder Options Dialogue Box*

3. Click the **View** tab and if the box for Hide file extensions for known file types is not checked, then click to **check** the box.

4. Click **Apply** followed by **OK**. Close all open windows and reopen the Windows Explorer. The extensions will be hidden now.

# Saving Different Versions

If you are sending a memo to a number of persons, you may wish to send a special copy to a particular recipient with a personal message. A simple way of achieving this is to first save the memo with its normal name containing the text as you want all but a particular recipient to see. Thereafter, reopen the memo and add your personal note. Then save the memo with a different name so that you have two versions, one for every one and the second for a particular recipient. This is how you save two versions of the same document:

1. Save the memo as described earlier with the name *Memo Dastoor 001*. The name on the title bar changes as described earlier.

2. Click **File** -> **Save As** from the menu bar and the drop-down menu. The Save As dialogue box appears. The original name, *Memo Dastoor 001* will appear highlighted in the File Name list box.

3. To change the file name to *Memo Dastoor 002*, click the **File name list box** to remove the highlight. Position the insertion point (blinking cursor) at the end of the file name (just after 001).

4. Press the backspace key to erase the "1" and type "2".

5. Click **Save** to save the second version of the file.

**TRAP** If you make any changes and click **Save** instead of **Save As**, the Save As dialogue box will not appear and the revised version will replace the original version. The original version will be lost. Hence, if you want to save multiple versions, save the current version, make the changes you want and then save the changed version by the Save As route.

# Printing Your Work

To send out what is called hard copies, you will have to print out your document on the printer attached to your computer. You may also use a networked printer if your computer is part of a network. Before you print your document, you will probably want to preview the document on your monitor's screen just as it will appear in print. We discuss previewing and printing in the following sections.

## Previewing

In the preview mode, you will get to see the document as it will appear in print. You can select a special view so that you can see several pages, reduced in size, at one time on the screen. This view is useful when you are looking through a large document to check for uniformity of the format and placement of the graphics and wish to quickly run through the pages. If you do notice an error, you can edit the document while still in the preview mode by clicking on the magnifier button.

In order to save on paper and printing ink, it is a good idea to preview your document before printing it. Here is how you can preview the memo you have just created. Refer to Fig 08.08 while going through the descriptions.

1. Make sure that the *Memo Dastoor 001* document is open in Word. Click **File ➜ Print Preview** on the menu or click on the Print Preview button on Word's standard tool bar. The preview window opens. *See Fig 08.08.*

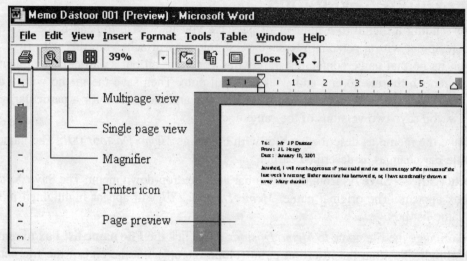

*Fig 08.08 Print Preview Window*

2. To view a magnified image, click on the **Magnifier button**. The mouse pointer will change to the icon of a magnifying glass with a plus sign (+) in the middle. Click anywhere in the document to enlarge it. You will now be able to read the text but the page will become too large to fit into your monitor's screen.

3. You can move around the page to see all of the text by using the scroll bars.

4. You will notice that the mouse pointer has now changed to a magnifying glass icon with a minus sign (–) in the middle. Therefore, if you click the document again, it will revert to its default full-page view. Click the magnifier button again and the pointer returns to its default shape.

5. Click the **Multiple pages button** and select the 2 x 2 page option from the drop-down menu. The preview will shrink to a small size. If your document had more pages, you would have seen four pages on your screen at a time.

6. Click the **One page button** to revert to the default single-page view.

7. When you have finished, click the **Close** button to close Print Preview and return to the document window.

**TIP**

If you are previewing your document in the one-page mode, you can use the next page and previous page buttons near the bottom of the vertical scroll bar (at the right hand border of the preview window) to page through your document.

## Printing Your Document

When you are satisfied that the document looks all right in the preview window, you are ready to print the document. Word can print the document in the background while you continue to do other work using Word.

To print your document, follow these steps:

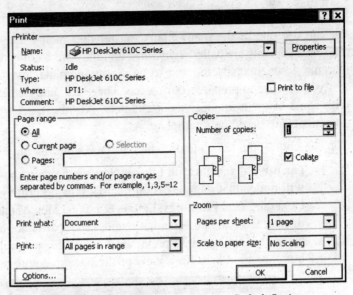

*Fig 08.09 Print Dialogue Box Showing Default Settings*

1. Make sure that the document you want to print is open in Word. From the file menu, click **File ➔ Print**. The Print dialogue box opens. *See Fig 08.09.*

2. To print using the default settings, simply click the **Print** button. Your document is printed out on the currently selected printer. Later with more experience, you will be able to change the default print settings. The options will allow you to select a different printer (under the caption Printer), select the page range (under the caption Page range), select the number of copies to be printed (under the caption Copies) as well as to select the document to print (under the caption Print What) and to determine the number of pages to be printed per sheet (under the caption Zoom).

## Closing Your Document

It is usually a good practice to close your open document when you have finished with it. However, it is possible to open multiple documents at the same time. If you need to jump from one document to another while working on a project, you can open additional documents while the earlier one is still open. Having a number of documents open at the same time will, however, use up a great deal of memory and slow down your computer.

To close your document, you can click on **File ➔ Close** from the menu bar or click on the document close button, located immediately below the window close button. If no changes have been made since the document was last saved, it will close immediately. If you have made changes but have not saved them, Word will ask you if you want to save the changes. Select **Yes** if you want to save the latest changes. Click **No** if you want to abandon the changes and revert to the earlier, saved version.

# Handling Documents

Having created, saved and printed our first memo, we are now ready to handle documents that are somewhat more complex. In this section, we will tackle the creation of new documents of different types and the opening of existing documents.

# Creating New Documents

We can use one of the many blank master documents that come with Word 2000. These blank master documents are called *Templates* and they are a collection of formatting information such as margins, fonts, line spacing and so on. Some templates may also contain *To:* and *From:* headings that you can use to prepare your memo. There are many other types of templates and we will deal with some of them in subsequent chapters. At this stage, we need only remember that all Word documents are based on a template.

You can choose the template on which to base your document by following these steps:

1.  Open Word and click on **File** ➜ **New** on the menu bar. The new dialogue box appears. You will notice that there are a number of tabs describing different types of templates such as General, Legal Pleadings, Letters & Faxes, Memos and so on. By clicking on a tab, you can display the templates available under that particular category. When you select a template by double clicking it, a preview (if available) will appear in the right pane of the dialogue box. See Fig 08.10 for a view of the New dialogue box.

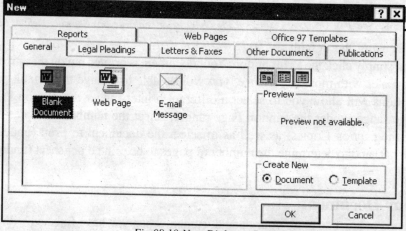

*Fig 08.10 New Dialogue Box*

2.  Click the **General** tab and then double click on the **Blank Document template**. A blank document opens with a default name such as Document 2. The document is blank with scroll bars on the side of the window.

3.  Type the text you want to enter just as you did for the memo you created earlier.

4.  Save and print your work as before and close your document.

**TIP**

To use the most commonly used blank document template for your new document, you can directly click **File** ➜ **New** from the menu bar to bypass the New dialogue box. If you do so, a blank document will open based on the default, Normal template.

# Opening an Existing Document

There are many reasons for you to open an existing document. If you are having correspondence with another party, you may wish to recall what you had written. You can create a follow-up letter quickly and efficiently by opening the last correspondence, modifying a few lines such as the date, the reminder number etc and have a brand new letter prepared in very little time which will already contain addresses, names and so on that you had written earlier.

To open the memo you have just created, proceed as follows:

1.  Open Word and either click **File ➜ Open** on the menu bar or click on the File open icon on the standard tool bar. The Open dialogue box appears. See Fig 08.11 for a view of the Open dialogue box.

2.  Since you have saved your memo in the default folder, its name will appear in the dialogue box.

3.  Double click the file *Memo Dastoor 001* and the memo will appear in the Word window.

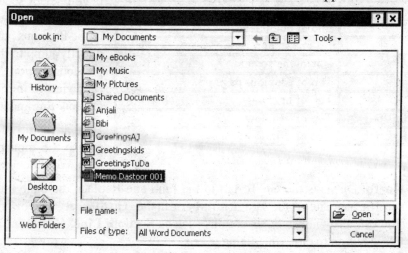

*Fig 08.11 Open Dialogue Box*

# Editing Your Document

As we have just discussed, you can harness the power of Word if you can edit an existing document to create new ones saving a great deal of time and effort in the process. To edit a document efficiently, you have to learn to do the following well:

*   Navigate to the correct place of your document.
*   Insert new text you need to modify the document.
*   Delete text that you no longer need.
*   Move or copy text to another place.

We will use the rest of this chapter to develop these four skills.

## Navigating in a Word Document

You can use the scroll bars and the mouse to navigate a Word document as you do in any Office 2000 application. The procedure is the same as in any Windows screen. For those of you who may have learned word processing with DOS-based applications such as the early versions of Word Star, Word also supports a complete range of keyboard shortcuts. These are listed in Fig 08.12.

| Keystroke | Result |
|---|---|
| Left Arrow | One character to the left |
| Right Arrow | One character to the right |
| Ctrl + Left Arrow | One word to the left |
| Ctrl + Right Arrow | One word to the right |
| Up Arrow | Up one line |
| Down Arrow | Down one line |
| Ctrl + Up Arrow | Up one paragraph |
| Ctrl + Down Arrow | Down one paragraph |
| Home | Beginning of line |
| End | End of line |
| Ctrl + Home | Beginning of document |
| Ctrl + End | End of document |
| PgUp | Up one screen |
| PgDn | Down one screen |
| Ctrl + PgUp | Top of previous page |
| Ctrl + PgDn | Top of next page |
| Ctrl + Alt + PgUp | Top of Window |
| Ctrl + Alt + PgDn | End of Window |

*Fig 08.12 Keyboard Navigation Shortcuts*

If you prefer a mouse, you can configure the Next and Previous buttons (at the bottom of the vertical scroll bars) to jump from page to page or section to section or comment to comment etc. You do so by clicking on the Select Browse Object button on the scroll bar and then selecting the object that you wish to jump from or to. Thus if you select section, at every click of the mouse on the Next or the Previous button, you will directly jump to the next or the previous section. See Fig 08.13 for a view of the Select Browse Objects Sub-menu.

Here are some additional ways to use the mouse to navigate your Word document:

**TIP**

**Go To**: Displays the Go To tab in the Find and Replace dialogue box. To go to a specific page, insert the **<page number>** in the "Go to what" list box and click **Next**. You can also choose other options such as **Section, Line, Comment** etc. Click the **Close** button to close the dialogue box.

**Find**: Displays the same dialogue box. Type the exact word or phrase you are seeking in the "Find what" text box and click on Find Next to go to the word or phrase you have selected.

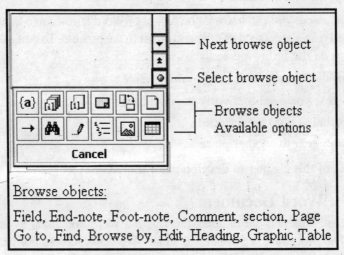

*Fig 08.13 Select Browse Object Sub-menu*

# Selecting Text

Before you can edit and format a letter, word, line or paragraph, you must select the text you want to work on. When you select text, it is highlighted on your screen. You can use either your mouse or keyboard to select text.

## Selecting Text with a Mouse

If the text you want is short enough so that all of it is visible at one time on your screen, then the simplest way to select text with your mouse is to click and drag. However, when working with large blocks of text, you may find that some portions of the text is off-screen and will require you to use the scroll bars to expose the hidden portions.

In this situation, you can use the click and shift click methods. We discuss both these methods now.

### *Click and Drag*

1. Click to the left of the first word or letter of your intended selection and keep the left mouse button pressed down.
2. With the mouse button held down, drag the mouse pointer over the text (from left to right) till all the intended text is highlighted.

You can also begin with the last word or letter. Click to the **right of the last point** and drag from **right to left**. To deselect the selected text, simply click the mouse **anywhere** else on your document.

To select by increments of letters or whole words, you have to set the appropriate options. To do so, click **Tools** ➔ **Options** in the menu bar of a Word window. In the Options dialogue box, click on the **Edit** tab and then do one of the following:

- Check the box "When selecting, automatically select entire word" to incrementally select whole words.
- Uncheck the same box to select letter by letter, incrementally.

You may have to experiment with both options to see what suits you.

### *Click and Shift Click*

If not all the text you want to select is visible at one time, do the following:

1. Click **on the left of the first letter or word** you wish to select.
2. Scroll down using the scroll bars until you see the end-point (letter or word) of the text you wish to select.
3. Press and hold down the Shift key on your keyboard.
4. Click at the **end-point** and the entire text you want will be selected and highlighted.

As in the case of click and drag, you can deselect or select backwards in the same way as for click and drag described above.

## Selection Shortcuts

Here are some additional text selection shortcuts you can use with the mouse:

- To select a single word, double click on the word.

- To select an entire line, click on the left margin next to the line.
- For a large block of text, you can click on the left margin next to the first line and drag the mouse cursor to the left margin next to the last line of text you wish to select.
- To select an entire paragraph, either double click on the left margin along the paragraph or triple click the text anywhere within the paragraph.
- To select the entire document, triple click on the left margin anywhere along the document.

There are a number of keyboard shortcuts for text selection as well:

If you are a touch typist and already have well-developed typing skills, you may wish to keep your fingers on the keyboard rather than alternate between the keyboard and the mouse. See Fig 08.14 for a list of keyboard shortcuts you can use to select text without having to use the mouse.

| Press this shortcut | To select |
| --- | --- |
| Shift + Left Arrow | One character to the left of the insertion point. Continue pressing the left arrow to select additional characters |
| Shift + Right Arrow | One character to the right of the insertion point. Continue pressing the right arrow to select additional characters |
| Shift + Ctrl + Left Arrow | To the beginning of the word to the left of the insertion point. Continue pressing left arrow key to select additional words |
| Shift + Ctrl + Right Arrow | To the beginning of the word to the right of the insertion point. Continue pressing right arrow key to select additional words |
| Shift + Up Arrow | From the insertion point to the same position in the previous line |
| Shift + Down Arrow | From the insertion point to the same position in the next line |
| Shift + Ctrl + Up Arrow | From the insertion point to the beginning of the current paragraph |
| Shift + Ctrl + Down Arrow | From the insertion point to the beginning of the next paragraph |
| Shift + Ctrl + Home | From the insertion point to the beginning of the document |
| Shift + Ctrl + End | From the insertion point to the end of the document |

*Fig 08.14 Keyboard Shortcuts for Text Selection*

## Inserting and Deleting Text

Having selected the text you want to work with, you can insert replacement text simply by typing over the highlighted text. The old text will be deleted and what you type will take its place. To delete the selected text, just press the Delete key on your keyboard.

However, it is not strictly necessary to select text before inserting new text or deleting old text. For instance, you can move the insertion point where you want new text to appear and simply type the additional text. As you type, the old text will be pushed either back to the right, or will be overtyped depending on the mode you have selected for Word.

**TIP** You can set the mode of Word by toggling between Insert and Overtype by pressing the Insert key on your keyboard. The mode indicator at the bottom of the Word window will indicate the current mode. In the insert mode, new text pushes back the old text to the right but does not delete it. This is useful if you wish to add just a letter, word or line to the existing text. In the Overtype mode, each new letter will replace one old letter. This is useful if you are replacing a letter, word or line.

Here are some more methods for inserting and deleting text:

- Press the **Delete** key to delete letters to the right and press the **Backspace** key to delete characters to the left of the insertion point. This is useful for deleting a letter or word or two.
- Press **Ctrl + Delete** or **Ctrl + Backspace** to delete the entire word instead of letters.

If you delete a letter or word by mistake, you can restore it by clicking the Undo button on the standard tool bar of Word. This only works if you have not typed anything else already before clicking on the **Undo** button.

# Editing Your Memo

We can now practise some of the things we have learned on the memo you have prepared, *Memo Dastoor 001*. Proceed as follows:

1. Open the memo if not already open. If you locate the memo in the My Documents folder and double click on the **filename**, Word will be automatically launched and the memo will appear in the Word window.

2. Double click on *Dastoor* to highlight the name. Now type <Barucha>. The name will change to *J P Barucha*.

3. Click just before the phrase *last week's*. Press **Ctrl + Delete** three times to delete these three words. Type a space and then type <March>.

4. Click before the word *Either*. Press and hold down the Shift key and click after *thrown it away*. The sentence is selected.

5. Press the **Delete** key and the selected sentence is deleted.

6. Click on **File ➜ Close** on the menu bar to close the file. Do not save the changes! The original file should remain intact on your hard disk.

# Moving and Copying Text

After selecting the text as we have discussed earlier, you can move or copy the text to another part of the same document or to another document. To do so, you have to temporarily store the text in what is called the Windows clipboard. Actually, you do not see the clipboard at all. When you select text and cut or copy it, a copy of the text is automatically stored in the clipboard until it is pasted elsewhere. All you need to remember is that whatever is in the clipboard will be lost when Word or Windows is shut down. Therefore, you must paste the cut or copied material before exiting Word or Windows.

You can use two different methods for moving or copying text. We look at them one by one.

## Cut and Paste

This is a two-step process. In the first step, you select the text and then cut or copy it to the clipboard. In the second step, you paste the text from the clipboard to the insertion point. The basic difference in copying and cutting is that in copying the original text remains unchanged in the original location. In cutting, however, the original text is removed. Cutting and pasting, therefore, are equivalent to moving the original text.

After selecting the text to be copied or moved you can do one of the following:

- Click your right mouse button on the **selection**. A shortcut menu appears. Click on **Cut** or **Copy**, as appropriate. Move the insertion point to the new location and click your right mouse button again. Now click on **Paste** to insert the text at the new location.

- Click on **Edit ➜ Copy** or **Cut** on the menu bar. Move the insertion point to the new location and click **Edit ➜ Paste** on the menu bar.

## Cut and Paste Exercise

We can practise the cut-and-paste method with the memo document you have already prepared. Proceed as follows:

1.  Open *Memo Dastoor 001,* if it is not already open.

2.  Select the text *Either someone has borrowed it* by clicking in the word *Either* and dragging to the word *it*. Do not include the period after the word *meeting* or the comma after *it*.

3.  Click the **right mouse button** to display the shortcut menu and click **Cut**. The selected text disappears and the comma appears just after the period following *meeting*.

4.  Click after the period following *meeting* but before the comma. The insertion point is now positioned here.

5.  Click the **right mouse button** to display the shortcut menu and click on **Paste**. The words *Either someone has borrowed it* appear in their new position.

6.  Repeat the process to move the words *I have accidentally thrown it away* to its new position where *Either someone has borrowed it* used to be. The two phrases are interchanged.

7.  Click the **Undo** button twice to undo the changes you have made.

## Drag and Drop

To drag and drop text to a new position, proceed as follows:

1.  Select the **text** you want to move. The text is highlighted.

2.  Position the mouse pointer anywhere within the **highlighted text**.

3.  Click and drag the **text** to its new location.

**NOTE**

This method is effective if you can see both the existing and final position of the text you want to move. If your mouse cursor strays outside the visible window, the window begins to scroll, usually too fast for you to control the movement and dropping the text accurately becomes very difficult. To move text outside the visible window, it is better to use the cut-and-paste method described earlier.

You may lose control of the mouse and accidentally drop the dragged text before you have reached its final location. If that happens, click the **Undo** button.

**CD-ROM**

To learn more about Microsoft Word 2000 in a multimedia environment, insert the accompanying CD-ROM in your computer, select the **Interactive** mode in the opening screen. The main menu will appear. To go to the section on Word, click the button marked **Word**. You will see a sub-menu containing the following topics:

*   Getting Started in Word
*   Getting Control over Word
*   Creating Professional Documents
*   Power of Word Unleashed

Click on the first sub-menu item, *Getting Started in Word*. Another level of sub-sub-menus is displayed from which you can select the particular topic you want to see. Click on your selected topic and follow the instructions on your screen.

# 9. Formatting and Managing Documents

## In this chapter:

☞ You learn how to format text in Word so that your document looks more attractive. You learn about the formatting tool bar, choosing fonts and changing text alignments.

☞ You learn about formatting with menus and dialogue boxes, which give you more control over formatting.

☞ You are introduced to paragraph formatting and to the techniques for changing the alignment of your text.

☞ You learn about borders and shadings and learn how to set tabs and indentations.

☞ You learn how to work with several documents at the same time. You open several documents, switch back and forth between them and display multiple documents on your monitor's screen at the same time.

☞ You are shown how to manage the environment of Word. You learn about using different views, zooming documents, displaying hidden formatting codes and how to split your document.

# Formatting Text

In Chapter 8, *Getting Started with Word 2000*, you have been introduced to Word basics, adequate for creating simple inter-office memos. However, Word is capable of much more. You can design your own letterhead, create newsletters, produce reports or even write books like the one you are reading just now by using the rich capacities of Word 2000. In this chapter, we will explore how you can format text and manage complex documents.

After you have written your document, you can improve its appearance in many ways. For instance, you can emphasise certain words, change line spacing, try a different text alignment or reset the margin and tab settings. You can select just the changes you need to make your document more attractive and your message more hard-hitting. You make all this happen by formatting text just the way you want. Formatting changes the appearance only, the words and sentences themselves remain unchanged.

**TIP**

The important thing to remember about formatting is that you must select the text first. If you do so, the formatting changes are easy to apply and will affect only the selected text, leaving the rest of the document unchanged.

## Using Tool Bars

The easiest way to format text is to use the Formatting tool bar buttons. Select the text and then click the appropriate formatting button and the work will be done. If you need complex formatting options, then it is better to use the menu bar items and their associated drop-down menus.

If you cannot see the formatting tool bar near the top of your Word window, do the following to make it visible:

1. Click on **View** on the menu bar and then click **Tool bars** on the drop-down menu. The tool bars sub-menu opens.

2. Click on **Formatting**. A check mark will appear to the left of the tool bar name. The formatting tool bar will now become visible. See Fig 09.01 for a view of the tool bar sub-menu.

## Emphasising Text

The three most common ways to emphasise a letter, a word, a sentence or an entire paragraph are to use boldface, italic or underlining. Here are some general guidelines:

- Use boldface to attract the reader's attention to a word, a phrase or a heading.

- Use italics in a paragraph to identify foreign words, names of books etc.

Underlining is a carry over from our handwriting and typewriting habits. It is still used to identify the subject

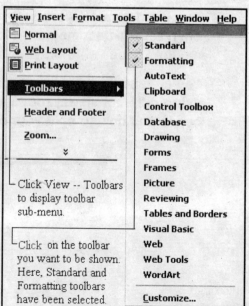

*Fig 09.01 Tool Bar Sub-menu*

and reference of a business letter. However, it is somewhat old-fashioned and should be generally avoided.

To apply these formats, proceed as follows:

1. Open the document in Word.
2. Select the **text** to be formatted.
3. Click the **B** (bold), <u>U</u> (underline) or *I* (italics) button to format the selected text.

## Choosing Fonts

The Windows 98 or Windows Me operating system installed on your computer has a very wide selection of typefaces or fonts. Each font comes in several sizes. Most of the fonts can be made bold, italicised or underlined. You can see, therefore, that you have a very wide selection of formats available that you can apply to anything ranging from just individual letters to the entire document!

While it is tempting to experiment with the rich assortment of fonts available to you, it is important to make sure that variety does not distract the reader from what you are trying to say in your document. Too many different fonts and too many sizes may become irritating to the reader.

**TIP** Graphic designers recommend that on a single page, do not use more than two different typefaces (or fonts) and not more than three different sizes of the same font. A good rule of thumb is to use a font such as Arial for headings and the more readable Times New Roman for the body of your document. You can use a large size for headings, a regular size (such as 11 point) for the body and a smaller size for footnotes in your document.

To change fonts, proceed as follows:

1. Select the **text** you want to format.
2. Click the **drop-down arrow** ▼ next to the font window in the formatting tool bar. A drop-down list of fonts available on your computer will appear. See Fig 09.02 for a view of the Fonts drop-down list.
3. Click on the **name of the font** you want. The selected text changes to the new font.

You will notice the TT abbreviation to the left of some of the font names. These are True Type fonts. These fonts will look the same whether you view the document on your screen or you print your document. It is safer to use True Type fonts whenever possible.

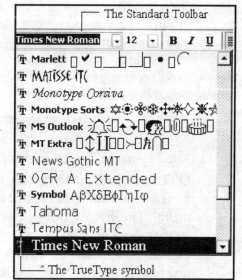

*Fig 09.02 Fonts Drop-down List*

## Changing Text Alignment

The text in your document will normally be aligned along its left margin while the right margin will appear ragged. However, there are situations where you may want to change the alignment of the entire document or that of a particular line. For instance, when you type the heading of a document, you may want it centred, not aligned with your left margin. Similarly, for some applications (such as the pages of this book), you may want both the left and the right margins to be straight and the spacing between words adjusted accordingly. This is called justified text.

Right alignment is not very common, but it is used sometimes for datelines, letterheads and in some specialised desktop publishing.

**TRAP** You cannot apply alignment to individual letters, words or sentences. The entire paragraph (to which the letter, word or sentence belongs) will be affected by any alignment change. Therefore, if you want a heading to have a different alignment than the following text, then you must press **Enter** ↵ after the heading to break it from the following text.

To apply alignment to selected text, proceed as follows:

1. Select the **text** you want to align.
2. Click the **Left**, **Right**, **Centre** or **Justify** button on the formatting tool bar. The alignment of the selected text will change to match your selection.

# Formatting with Menus and Dialogue Boxes

You can also use menus and dialogue boxes to do all your text formatting. Although not as simple and fast as the formatting tool bar buttons, menus and dialogue boxes give you more options and allow you to fine-tune your formatting tasks.

### The Font Dialogue Box

Instead of the font drop-down list, you can use the font dialogue box for more font formatting options. For instance, you can select a font, change its character spacing and add text effects. You can also change the font style, change its size, its colour or add effects such as a shadow, show the font in outline or in the embossed mode. All these options become available to you by opening the tabbed Font Dialogue box.

Follow these steps to open the Font Dialogue box:

1. Select the **text** you want to change.
2. Click on the **Format** menu item and then click on **Font** in the drop-down menu. The Font Dialogue box appears. *See Fig 09.03.*
3. Choose the **options** you want. You may have to click on the appropriate tab such as **Font**, **Character Spacing** or **Text Effects** to find the options you want. You can observe the effect you have selected in the preview pane.

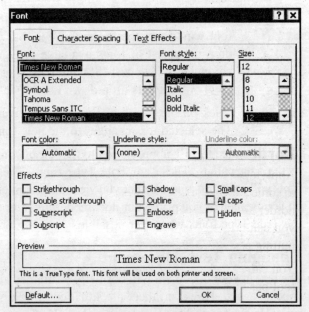

*Fig 09.03 Font Dialogue Box*

4. When satisfied with your selection, click **OK**. You will return to your document where you can observe the effect of the change.

## Paragraph Formatting

If you are writing a long document with many paragraphs, you should use the Paragraph dialogue box to specify the options you want to apply to each paragraph. For instance, you may want the first line of each paragraph to be indented. Or, you may want to use a non-standard line spacing (say 1.5 lines space between two lines) in each paragraph. You may also want to specify the exact distance between two paragraphs. All these, as well as margins, can be set by using the Paragraph dialogue box.

Here is how you can apply paragraph formatting:

Select the text you want to change.

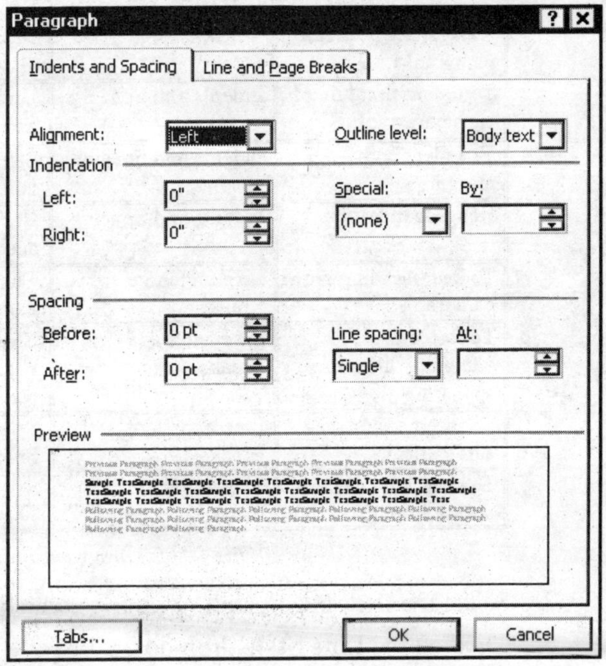

*Fig 09.04 Paragraph Dialogue Box*

1. Click **Format** on the menu bar and click on **Paragraph** in the drop-down menu. The Paragraph dialogue box will appear, open at the Indents and Spacing tab. *See Fig 09.04.*

2. Select the **Indents and Spacing** options you need.

3. Click on the **Line and Page Breaks** tab. The dialogue box opens at the selected tab.

4. Select the **Line and Page Break** options you need.

5. Click **OK** to close the dialogue box and return to your document.

To understand the options available on the Paragraph dialogue box, see Fig 09.05.

## Borders and Shading

Applying borders and shading to selected text is another attractive way to draw the reader's attention to some part of the text that you wish to highlight. For instance, you may wish to put a double-lined border around the name of the author on the first page of a report you have prepared. Alternatively, you can draw attention to some important information in a particular paragraph in your report by putting a border around it.

You can easily put borders or add shading by using the Tables and Borders tool bar. To make this tool bar visible, proceed as follows:

1. Right click on any **visible tool bar** and then select the **Tables and Borders** tool bar from the drop-down list. The Tables and Borders tool bar appears. *See Fig 09.06.*

| To do this | Use the Tab | And do this |
|---|---|---|
| To change line spacing | Indents and Spacing | Select appropriate spacing from the line spacing list box |
| To have 12 point blank space between paragraphs | Indents and Spacing | Either choose After and select 12 points or choose Before and After and select 6 points under Spacing |
| To indent first line of each paragraph | Indents and Spacing | Under Indentation, click Special → First Line and select $\frac{1}{2}$" in the By window |
| To indent both margins | Indents and Spacing | Select $\frac{1}{2}$" for both right and left under Indentation |
| Hanging indents | Indents and Spacing | Under Indentation, click Special → Hanging and select $\frac{1}{2}$" in the By window |
| To keep heading with paragraph | Line and Page Breaks | Click Keep with Next check box under Pagination |
| To stop one paragraph line appearing alone | Line and Page Breaks | Click Widow/Orphan control check box under Pagination |
| To insert page break automatically | Line and Page Breaks | Select heading and then click Page Break Before check box under Pagination |
| To keep long heading on one line | Line and Page Breaks | Select heading and then click Keep Line Together check box under Pagination |

*Fig 09.05 Paragraph Formatting Options*

2.  Select the **text**, **paragraph** or **page** to which you wish to apply border or shading.

3.  Click on the **Line Style** drop-down arrow ▼ and select the **line style**.

4.  Click on the **Line Weight** drop-down arrow ▼ and select the **line weight** you want.

5.  Click on the **Border Colour** drop-down arrow ▼ and select the **colour** of the border line from the colour palette that appears.

6.  Click on the **Border** drop-down arrow ▼. You will see a selection of available border styles. If you hold your mouse pointer above the icons, a tool tip will appear explaining the nature of the border. Select the **type of border** you want or select **No Border** to remove a border.

7.  Click the **Shading Colour** drop-down arrow ▼. The shading colour palette will appear. Select the **shading colour** you want from the palette.

*Fig 09.06 Tables and Borders Tool Bar*

In case you wish to access more options for borders and shading, instead of using the Tables and Borders tool bar, you may wish to use the Borders and Shading dialogue box. You can open this dialogue box as follows:

1. Select the **text** you wish to format.

2. Click on **Formats** on the menu bar and click **Borders and Shading** in the drop-down menu. The Borders and Shading dialogue box will open. *See Fig 09.07.*

3. Select the **Border** (for text or paragraphs), **Page Border** (for the entire page) or **Shading** tab (for fill colours and fill style) as appropriate.

4. In Borders (page or text), you can choose the **Setting**, the **style** and whether the changes should apply only to the selected text or the entire paragraph. In the Preview pane on the right, you can see a preview of your choice.

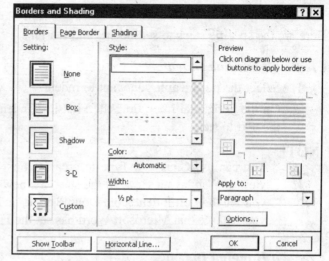

*Fig 09.07 Borders and Shading Dialogue Box*

5. In the Shading tab, you can choose a **fill colour** or a **pattern** for the selected text. If you select a pattern, you can also choose a colour for the pattern. Thus, if you choose Lt. Down Diagonal in style and Orange in Colour, the selected text will acquire a background of light orange diagonal lines.

## Setting Tabs and Indentations

Word comes ready with default tab and indent settings. Both are ½" or the metric equivalent and usually you will not need to change either. However, for special documents, you may want to set up your own tab and indent values. It is easiest to use the Ruler to set tabs and indents. The Ruler is the graduated bar near the top of the document window which also carries small icons and shading for the indents and margins.

If you do not see the ruler, click **Ruler** on the View menu.

You can set the following on the ruler by dragging the corresponding icon or shading with the mouse pointer:

- First Line Indent: Marker is a downward arrow near the left edge of the ruler.

- Hanging Indent: Marker is an upward arrow near the left edge of the ruler.

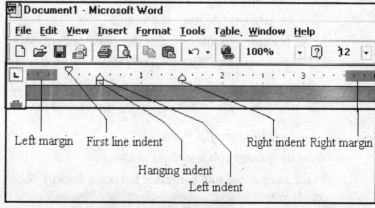

*Fig 09.08 Ruler with Indent and Margin Markers*

- Left Indent: Marker is a small square near the left edge of the ruler.
- Right Indent: Marker is an upward arrow near the right edge of the ruler.

In addition, the left margin is a shaded bar at the left of the ruler and the right margin is a similar bar at the right edge of the ruler. *See Fig 09.08.*

Here are the specific steps to set indents and margins.

### Create a First-line Indent

1. Select the **paragraph** you want to indent.
2. On the horizontal ruler, drag the First-line Indent marker to the position where you want the text to start.

**NOTE**

You can use Click and Type to create a First-line indent. First, switch to Print layout view or Web layout view. At the start of a new paragraph, move the I-beam pointer until you see the Left Indent icon. Double click, and then start typing your text. As you type, you will see that Microsoft Word has set the First-line indent where you double clicked.

### Create a Hanging Indent

1. Select the **paragraph** in which you want to create a hanging indent.
2. On the horizontal ruler, drag the Hanging indent marker to the position at which you want the indent to start.

### Create a Negative Indent

1. Select the **paragraph** you want to out-dent or extend into the left margin.
2. On the horizontal ruler, drag the Left Indent marker to the position where you want the paragraph to start.

To change the right indent for all lines of text in the selected paragraph or paragraphs, drag the Right Indent marker.

### Decrease the Left Indent of a Paragraph

1. Select the **paragraph** you want to change.
2. On the Formatting tool bar, click **Decrease Indent**. Word decreases the indent by one tab stop. If you want to change the position of the indent, you can first set a different tab stop.

To change the right indent of a paragraph, on the right side of the ruler, drag the Right indent marker to the position where you want the right indent to occur.

### Increase the Left Indent of a Paragraph

1. Select the **paragraph** you want to change.
2. On the Formatting tool bar, click **Increase Indent**. Word increases the indent by one tab stop. If you want to change the position of the indent, you can first set a different tab stop.

To change a paragraph's right indent, drag the Right Indent marker to the position where you want the right indent to occur.

### Set an Indent by Using the TAB Key

1. On the Tools menu, click **Options**, and then click the **Edit** tab.
2. Select the **Tabs and backspace set left indent** check box.
3. In the paragraph you want to change, do one of the following:
   3.1. To indent the first line of a paragraph, click **in front of the line**.
   3.2. To indent an entire paragraph, click **in front of any line but the first line**.
4. Press the **TAB** key.

To remove the indent, press **BACKSPACE** before moving the insertion point. You can also click **Undo** on the Edit menu.

## Greater Precision

You can set indents by dragging the indent markers. However, it is sometimes necessary to use greater precision. For setting first-line indent and hanging indent, we give below some more precise methods.

### First-line Indent

Select options on the Indents and Spacing tab (**Format ➜ Paragraph**). In the Special list under Indentation, click **First Line**, and then set the other options you want. For Help on an option, click the question mark and then click the option. A preview shows the results of your adjustments, so you can experiment before making your final decision.

### Hanging Indent

Select options in the Indents and Spacing tab (**Format ➜ Paragraph**). In the Special list under Indentation, select **Hanging.** In the By box, set the amount of space for the hanging indent. A preview shows the results of your adjustments, so that you can experiment before making your final decision.

See Fig 09.04 earlier in this section for a view of the indents and spacing options available on the Paragraph dialogue box.

# Working with Several Documents

There are occasions when it is convenient to have more that one document open in Word at the same time. For instance, you may want to prepare a new document by combining portions of text from two older documents. Alternatively, you may wish to write a reply to a letter while keeping the original letter open before you for reference.

In this section, we will look at Word's special capability of handling several documents at the same time.

## Opening Several Documents Simultaneously

By opening several documents at the same time but each in its own separate window, you can open, close, scroll, save and close each document independently. If you maximise one of the documents, its window fills your screen and the others are hidden behind it. You can switch between the documents or arrange the documents so that they are all visible in separate small windows.

It is very simple to open multiple documents. You have to just open a new document without closing the one that is already open. You can open as many documents as your computer system's memory will support.

**TIP** To open several documents at once, in the Open dialogue box, click the first document you wish to open. Then, hold down the Ctrl key and click on the additional documents one by one. If the documents you wish to open are in a continuous list, after clicking the first document, hold down the shift key and click on the last document you want to open.

## Switching Between Documents

When several documents are open in Word at the same time, you can see the names of the open documents by clicking on Windows on the menu bar. A drop-down menu appears listing the names of all the open documents. You can navigate from one document to another by clicking on the name of the document you wish to open. *See Fig 09.09.*

Instead of the Windows menu item, you can also use the task bar at the bottom of your screen. Each open document appears as a small icon on the task bar.

You can also switch from one document to another by clicking on the icon of the document you wish to open.

If you have several documents open at the same time and wish to close the document currently occupying the screen, click on the Document

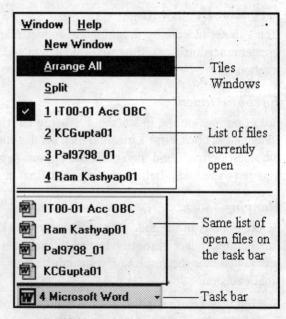

*Fig 09.09 Windows and Task Bar Open Files*

Close button on the right side of the menu bar. To close Word, close all documents and then click on the Application Close button.

## Displaying Multiple Documents Simultaneously

To display several documents at the same time, do the following:

1. Click **Windows** on the menu bar. The Windows drop-down menu appears.
2. Click on **Arrange All** on the drop-down menu. Windows arranges each open document in its own window arranged like tiles. You can see four individual windows in Fig 09.10.

You can resize, minimise, maximise or close individual windows as required.

# Managing Your Word Environment

As you can see, in this chapter we have progressed beyond the basics. However, you must customise Word to your exact needs before learning advanced uses. By customising, you will be able to use Word with greater ease, speed and comfort. In this section, we will concentrate on customising Word.

## Using Views

You can view the document you are working on in four different ways. Each way is called a view and you can call up the view you want by clicking on the appropriate View Button. The four View Buttons are located at the bottom left corner of your screen, left of the horizontal scroll bar. You can switch back and forth amongst the four views by clicking the View Buttons. The four views are:

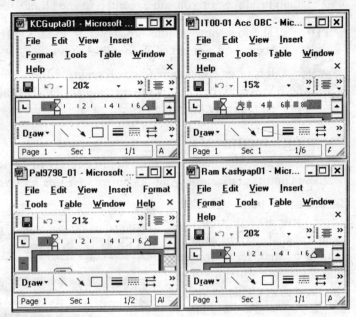

*Fig 09.10 Set of Tiled Word Documents*

- **Normal View**: This is the default view in which a document will open initially. In Normal View, material in the top and bottom margins, such as headers, footers, pagination and footnotes are not shown on the screen. Normal View gives you the largest viewing area for seeing the text of your document.

- **Web Layout View**: Shows you how your document will appear if it is published on the Internet. This view is also useful for reading documents on your monitor's screen. The font is larger and the text wraps at the margins.

- **Print Layout View**: Shows how your document will appear after it is printed. All printable text, including headers, footers, page numbers and footnotes are displayed. It is a good view for checking a document just before printing.

- **Outline View**: In Outline View, Microsoft Word simplifies the text formatting to help you focus on the structure of your document. Work

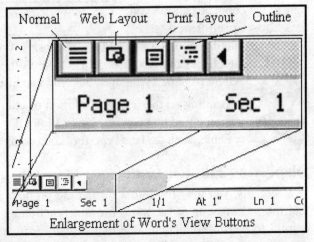

*Fig 09.11 Four View Buttons*

in outline view to look at the structure of a document and to move, copy, and reorganise text by dragging headings. In outline view, you can collapse a document to see only the main headings, or you can expand it to see all headings and even body text.

**TIP**

The four view buttons are shown in Fig 09.11. For ease of viewing, the buttons have been shown enlarged in the illustration.

It is often convenient to do all typing, editing and formatting work in the Print Layout View. Since the document appears at all times as it will print, you get what is colloquially known as *what you see is what you get.*

## Zooming Documents.

If you have a large document that does not fit entirely into one screen of your monitor, you can use the zoom command to shrink your document to a smaller size to fit into the screen.

On the other hand, to take a closer look at a section of a document that may have small fonts or a small icon, you can enlarge the view using the zoom command to get a better look at a selected part of the screen.

When enlarged, you can move the document up, down or sideways to display the portion that interests you. *See Fig 09.12.*

You use the Zoom box on the standard tool bar to change the displayed size of your document. The drop-down arrow ▾ on the right of the Zoom box allows you to choose predefined sizes

*Fig 09.12 Magnified Portion of a Document*

ranging from 10% to 500%. You can choose other percentages by typing the number directly in the Zoom box. There are other options such as Page width, Text width, Whole page or Two pages that you can also select.

**TRAP**

Depending on the screen resolution of your monitor and the font used in the document, you may find that certain sizes will not display properly. Unless the fonts used are fully scalable, such as TrueType fonts, zooming may distort what you see on the screen.

## Displaying Hidden Code

Occasionally, you may run into a formatting problem while preparing a document. You may find that the indentations or tab stops are not functioning as you expect. In this situation, it may be helpful to reveal the hidden code that actually formats your document. These codes may specify where spacing will appear between words, where a sentence will wrap to the next line and how margins or tabs are set.

To reveal hidden code, click on the Show/Hide [icon] button on the standard tool bar in Word. The button toggles. Therefore, clicking the button will reveal code if it is hidden or hide code if it is visible. *See Fig 09.13.*

**NOTE** The paragraph mark at the end of a paragraph on your document contains not just an instruction to wrap text, but all other formatting instructions for that paragraph. These instructions include spacing, margins, alignment and indentation. So, while codes are revealed, you can copy the paragraph by including the paragraph code in your selection, so that the copied text will also carry with it all formatting instructions. Alternatively, you can select the text without the end of paragraph code so that only unformatted text is transferred when you paste the paragraph.

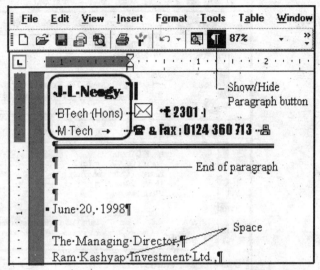

*Fig 09.13 Document with Code Displayed*

## Splitting Your Document

It is often useful to be able to see the top part of a long document while writing the middle or the end. This situation will arise when the document is too large to fit in one screen. You may want to see what has been written already at the beginning while writing the middle, to make sure of consistency. Word allows you to do this by splitting your document into two parts and displaying each part in its own window. You can scroll the text in each window independently. Thereby, one window can show you an already written part while the second window can let you write a latter part of the same document. You can even drag or drop text from one window to the other, thereby moving or copying text from one part of the document to another. This is how you can split your document:

1.  In Word, open the document you wish to split.

2.  Click **Windows** on the menu bar and click on **Split** in the drop-down menu. The Pointer changes to a double-headed arrow with a double horizontal line in the middle of your screen.

3.  You can move the pointer up or down until the split is positioned where you want. Then click the mouse button to anchor the split. Your document becomes visible in both the windows, each with its own vertical scroll bar.

You can now scroll the two copies of the document independently. After you have finished, you can remove the split by clicking **Window ➜ Remove Split**. You can also drag the split line to the bottom of your screen. See Fig 09.14 which shows a letter split into two independently scrollable windows.

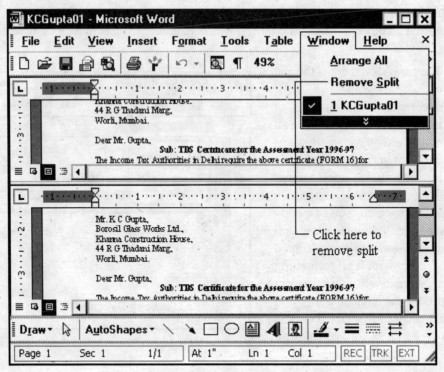

*Fig 09.14 Split Document*

## CD-ROM

To learn more about Microsoft Word 2000 in a multimedia environment, insert the accompanying CD-ROM in your computer, select the **Interactive** mode in the opening screen. The main menu will appear. To go to the section on Word, click the button marked **Word**. You will see a sub-menu containing the following topics:

- Getting Started in Word
- Getting Control over Word
- Creating Professional Documents
- Power of Word Unleashed

Click on the second sub-menu item, *Getting Control over Word*. Another level of sub-sub-menus is displayed from which you can select the particular topic you want to see. Click on your selected topic and follow the instructions on your screen.

# 10. Managing Long Documents

## In this chapter:

☞ You are introduced to long documents, covering a large number of pages such as research reports and books.

☞ You learn how to use outlines to organise your thoughts, so important for writing long documents.

☞ You learn how to format long documents, to use styles for uniform looks and to divide the document into sections.

☞ You learn how to include bulleted and numbered lists and to incorporate tables in your documents.

☞ You are introduced to the table of contents and indexes, important for books and reports that contain many chapters or sections.

☞ We discuss how to provide footnotes and endnotes to your documents.

☞ You learn about headers and footers that give a distinctive look to the documents you create.

# Managing Long Documents

Reports and other long documents require a distinctive, professional look. They are, therefore, planned and formatted quite differently from a short document such as a memo or a letter. You have to organise your thoughts and plan the different sections or chapters of your document so that they follow the topics logically. You have to ensure that separate chapters have their own distinctive formats and yet retain an overall uniformity of style. In fact, you have to combine several formatting features to produce an outstanding long document. You will find that the skills required to incorporate these features will take you to a higher level of proficiency in using Word. We examine some of the important features that you will learn in this chapter. They include:

- Organising Your Thoughts.
- Formatting Long Documents.
- Adding Special Features.

In this chapter, we will show you the best way to produce outstanding long documents easily and quickly. Although advanced in comparison to what we have discussed so far, what you will learn in this chapter is not difficult.

## Organising Your Thoughts

A simple document such as a memo or a letter will usually revolve around a central idea. It is generally not necessary to plan out your sequence of thoughts, it is usually only necessary to write the memo or letter so that your thought is conveyed effectively. In large documents such as a study report or a research paper, many trains of thought have to be organised in their proper sequence so that there is a proper introduction, development of your theme and a conclusion. Such documents require that you first organise your thoughts.

We are accustomed to jotting down our thoughts on paper, then arranging them in the correct sequence and finally fleshing out our thoughts to produce the final document. Word can help you to do the same, using outlining and introducing the concept of master and subdocuments. We will deal with these concepts in detail later in this chapter.

### *Formatting Your Long Document*

Long documents have special formatting needs. Firstly, we want the entire document to have a consistent look. We achieve this by using styles and templates consistently throughout the document. At the same time, we may want some formatting elements to change from one part of the document to another. We accomplish this by dividing our document into sections. For instance, we may select a header style (font and font size) that remains consistent throughout the document. At the same time, we can use different header text for each section of our document.

### *Adding Special Features*

Large documents such as reports usually require special inclusions such as a bulleted or numbered list or tables of data. *See Fig 10.01.* We learn how to include them. In an academic report, it is customary to provide footnotes and endnotes for annotation.

A good example of a long document is a book, like this one. The reader will need guidelines so that he may find what he seeks quickly and easily when reading something as voluminous as a book. To help the reader, we have to provide a table of contents and an alphabetical index. In this chapter, we learn how to do so.

This is an example of a bulleted list that you may include in your document:

> ➤ This is the first item
> ➤ This is the second item
> ➤ This is the third item
> ➤ This is the fourth item

You can have several levels in bulleted lists and you can choose several types of bullets.

If the list describes a sequence of instructions or events, you may prefer to use numbers instead of bullets.

Table of Contents

| | |
|---|---|
| Introduction | 1 |
| Chapter I | 4 |
| The Internet | 5 |
| Hardware Requirements | 15 |
| Chapter II | 16 |
| Choosing a Modem | 17 |
| Selecting an ISP | 25 |
| Connecting to the Net | 35 |

*Fig 10.01 Sample of Special Formatting*

## Seeing the Broad Picture

Large documents stretch across several hundred pages, several chapters and sections. It is often difficult to get a bird's-eye view of the main headings because details obstruct our view. We need to see the forest without being obstructed by the trees!

There are two effective techniques built into Word that help us see the broad picture without being overwhelmed by details. These techniques also allow us to concentrate on the details when we want. Thus, to prepare the broad outline of our document, we use the outline view or the master document. To actually write and then edit the text, however, we can switch to the full view or go down to each subdocument.

The two techniques we will learn to help organise our thoughts and yet not lose sight of the details are:

- Using Outline Views.
- Using Master and Subdocuments.

## The Outline View

As we have seen earlier in this chapter, for a long write-up or a research report we usually jot down our thoughts on paper. These thoughts are the outline from which we develop our document. Word helps us develop our outline electronically by introducing the Outline View.

When you display your document in the outline view, you have the option of collapsing your document so that only the headings show. The uncluttered view helps you focus on the big picture so that you can make sure that your thoughts are consistent. You can also expand the view to include all the text. To focus on just that section, you can expand the text under a particular heading.

### Outline a Document

See Fig 10.02 for a view of the Outline Tool bar.

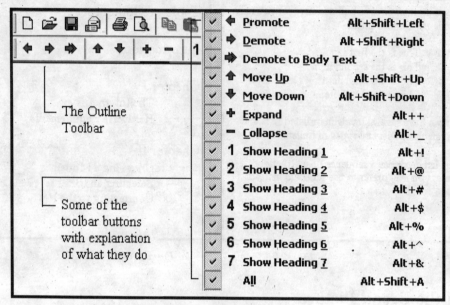

*Fig 10.02 Outline Tool Bar*

To prepare the outline of a document, proceed as follows:

1. In outline view, type headings for the document title and each subdocument. Make sure to press **Enter** ↵ after typing each heading. Word formats the headings with the built-in heading style Heading 1.

2. Assign a heading style to each heading (for example, use Heading 1 for the title and Heading 2 for each subdocument). To do this, drag the heading or outline symbol as follows:

   • To demote a heading to a lower level, drag the outline symbol to the right.

   • To promote a heading to a higher level, drag the outline symbol to the left.

**TIP** You can apply heading styles by using buttons on the Outlining tool bar or by using the Style box.

You can use outline levels instead of heading styles to set up the master document outline.

## Navigating in the Outline View

To use the Outline View, your text should be formatted with the built-in heading styles (Heading 1 through Heading 9) or outline levels (Level 1 through Level 9). In outline view, you can easily rearrange this text by dragging the outline symbols for the headings and body text to a new location or level. See Fig 10.03 for a document in Outline View.

- To move text to a different location, drag the outline symbols up or down. As you drag, Word displays a horizontal line. Release the mouse button when the line is where you want to move the text.

- To change a heading level, drag the outline symbols to the left or right. To promote a heading to a higher level, or to change body text to a heading, drag the outline symbol to the left.

- To demote a heading to a lower level, or to change a heading to body text, drag the outline symbol to the right. As you drag, Word displays a vertical line at each heading level. Release the mouse button to assign the text to the new level. Word applies the corresponding heading style to the heading, or applies the Normal style to the body text.

When you drag a heading's + symbol, the subheadings and body text under it also move or change levels. To move or change only the heading, first display any subordinate text that is collapsed under the heading. Then click the heading text to select just the heading paragraph. To move the heading, click Move Up ▲ or Move Down ▼ on the Outlining tool bar. To promote or demote the heading, click **Promote** ➜ or **Demote** ⬅.

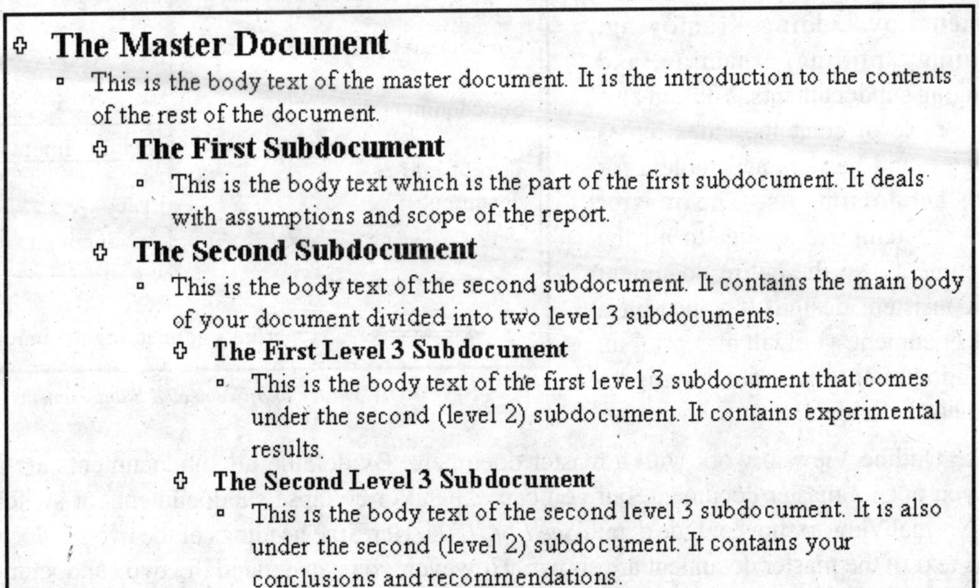

> ✪ **The Master Document**
> ▫ This is the body text of the master document. It is the introduction to the contents of the rest of the document.
> ✚ **The First Subdocument**
> ▫ This is the body text which is the part of the first subdocument. It deals with assumptions and scope of the report.
> ✚ **The Second Subdocument**
> ▫ This is the body text of the second subdocument. It contains the main body of your document divided into two level 3 subdocuments.
> ✚ **The First Level 3 Subdocument**
> ▫ This is the body text of the first level 3 subdocument that comes under the second (level 2) subdocument. It contains experimental results.
> ✚ **The Second Level 3 Subdocument**
> ▫ This is the body text of the second level 3 subdocument. It is also under the second (level 2) subdocument. It contains your conclusions and recommendations.

*Fig 10.03 A Document in Outline View*

# Master and Subdocuments

It is often convenient to break up a long document into a master and a number of subdocuments. We can then work with the subdocuments individually and after they are ready, combine all of them with the master.

This is very convenient when several members work on a project as a group. The master document lays out the overall structure including the formatting parameters. Thereby, each member can work separately with subdocuments without losing consistency of format or layout.

## A Master Document

A master document is a document that contains a set of related documents. Use a master document to organise and maintain a long document by dividing it into smaller, more manageable subdocuments. For example, use a master document to organise chapters of a book. In a workgroup, the book's master document can be stored on a network. The master is then broken up into individual subdocuments that can be worked on by all the members of the workgroup simultaneously.

## Creating a Master Document and Subdocuments

To create a master document, you start with an outline in Outline View (see the earlier section on Outline View) and then designate headings in the outline as subdocuments. When you save the master document, Word assigns names to each subdocument based on the text you use in the outline headings. You can also convert an existing document into a master document and then divide it into subdocuments, or you can add existing documents to a master document to make them subdocuments.

### Working with a Master Document

In a master document, you can quickly change the top level structure of the document by adding, removing, combining, splitting, renaming, and rearranging subdocuments. You can also create a table of contents, index, cross references, and headers and footers for all the subdocuments. The master document's template applies to all the subdocuments, so the entire document has a consistent design. If you print a master document, you will also print all the subdocuments without having to open them individually.

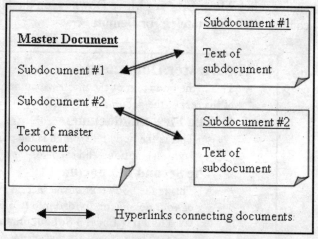

*Fig 10.04 Master and Connected Subdocuments*

You use Outline View to work with a master document. By default, all subdocuments are hidden when you open a master document, but you can expand or collapse subdocuments or switch in or out of Normal View to show or hide detail. *See Fig 10.04.* Here, the headings of the two subdocuments and the text of the master document are shown. However, you can expand the two subdocuments to see the full text of each.

### Working with Subdocuments

In a subdocument, you can work just as you would work in any other Word document. You can add, remove, and edit text and graphics; check spelling, print part of the document and so on.

To work with the contents of a subdocument, open it from the master document. When subdocuments are collapsed in the master document, each subdocument appears as a hyperlink. When you click the hyperlink, Word displays the subdocument in a separate document window. A hyperlink allows you to jump to the subdocument directly from the master document when you click on its associated hyperlink.

# Formatting a Master Document and Subdocuments

A major advantage of using master and subdocuments is that while you retain a consistent format across all the documents, you can vary some formatting aspects from one subdocument to the next. Thus, while the font and style of the header remain the same, you can vary the actual text of the header from one subdocument to the next. To get consistency in formatting, you use document templates as explained later in this chapter.

### Using Subdocument Sections to Vary Formatting

When you create or insert a subdocument in the master document, Word places it in a separate section by inserting section breaks before and after the subdocument. You can change the section formatting (such as page numbers, borders, headers, margins, or number of newspaper columns) for individual subdocuments, change the type of section breaks, and add section breaks. You can also change section formatting by opening individual subdocuments and then making the changes. For example, insert page numbers in a footer in the master document to number pages for the entire document, and then in each subdocument, create a header that contains the chapter title.

# Working with Subdocuments

Here are some of the skills you need to work with subdocuments within a master document. We study them one by one.

### Expand or Collapse Subdocuments

To expand or collapse a subdocument, do the following:

1. Display the master document in Outline View.
2. To expand subdocuments, click **Expand Subdocuments** on the Outlining tool bar.
3. To collapse subdocuments, click **Collapse Subdocuments** on the Outlining tool bar.

### Open a Subdocument From Within a Master Document

You can open a subdocument within its master document. To do so, proceed as follows:

1. Display the master document in Outline View.
2. If the subdocuments are collapsed, double click the **subdocument icon** of the subdocument you want to open. Click **Master Document View** on the Outlining tool bar if you cannot see the subdocument icon.
3. When you finish working on the subdocument, save it. To close the subdocument and return to the master document, click **Close** on the File menu.

### Rearrange Subdocuments within a Master Document

To change the order of the subdocuments within a master document, proceed as follows:

1. Display the master document in Outline View.
2. Expand the subdocuments.
3. To select the subdocument you want to move, click its **subdocument icon**. To select multiple adjacent subdocuments, click the **first icon**, and then hold down SHIFT as you click the **last icon** in the group.

4. Drag the subdocument icon to a new location.

You can also move text or graphics between subdocuments. First, expand the subdocuments and switch to Normal View, or Outline View, and then move the item as usual. See Fig 10.05 for example of moving objects between documents.

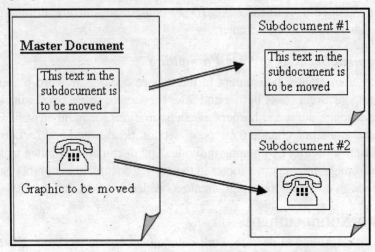

*Fig 10.05 Move Objects from One Subdocument to Another*

## Combine Subdocuments

You may wish to combine two or more subdocuments into a single one. For instance, you may have two colleagues write one subdocument each on different parts of the same topic, which will combine to form one chapter in your master document. To combine subdocuments, proceed as follows:

1. Display the master document in Outline View.
2. Expand the subdocuments.
3. Move the subdocuments you want to combine next to one another.
4. Select the first subdocument you want to combine by clicking its **subdocument icon**.
5. Hold down SHIFT as you click the **last icon** in the group of subdocuments that you want to combine.
6. On the Outlining tool bar, click **Merge Subdocument**.

**NOTE** When you save the master document, Word saves the combined subdocuments with the file name of the first subdocument.

When you combine subdocuments (for example, documents A, B, and C), the uncombined versions of the subdocument files (documents B and C) remain in their original location. If you do not need them, you can delete these subdocument files.

### Remove a Subdocument from a Master Document

While finalising your master document, you may decide to remove a subdocument. If so, proceed as follows:

1. Display the master document in Outline View.
2. Expand the subdocuments.
3. Click the **subdocument icon** for the subdocument you want to remove.
4. Press **Delete**.

When you remove a subdocument from a master document, the original subdocument file will remain in its original location.

If you want, you can delete this subdocument file if you do not need it separately any longer.

## Formatting Long Documents

Long documents are usually divided into sections or chapters. One of the special formatting needs of a long document is that while you want a uniform style for the entire document, you will need some differences from chapter to chapter or section to section. For example, you will probably want the same font and font size for headings and text in all the chapters. However, you will want to provide different chapter headings and a common book name heading.

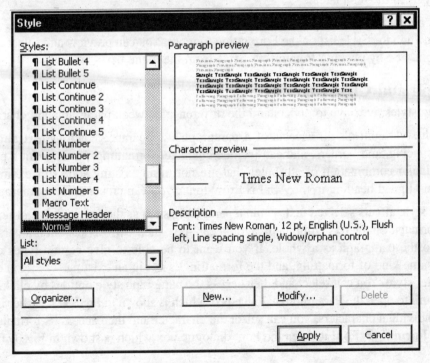

*Fig 10.06 Style Dialogue Box*

The Style dialogue box is seen in Fig 10.06. To understand details of formatting, you have to become familiar with the following topics:

- Using Styles
- Using Templates

- Dividing into Chapters or Sections
- Adding Headers and Footers

We discuss these formatting issues in this section.

## Using Styles

A style is a set of formatting characteristics that you can apply to text in your document to quickly change its appearance. When you apply a style, you apply a whole group of formats in one simple task. For example, you may want to format the title of a report to make it stand out. Instead of taking three separate steps to format your title as 16 pt, Arial, and centre-aligned, you can achieve the same result in one step by applying the Title style to your title.

When you start Microsoft Word, the new blank document that opens is based on the Normal template, and text that you type uses the Normal style. This means that when you start typing, Word uses the font, font size, line spacing, text alignment, and other formats currently defined for the Normal style. The Normal style is the base style for the Normal template, meaning that it is a building block for other styles in the template.

There are a number of other styles besides Normal available in the Normal template. A few basic ones are shown in the Style list on the Formatting tool bar. You can preview and select others in the Style dialogue box by clicking **Format** ➔ **Style** from the menu bar.

## Paragraph and Character Styles

Before using styles, we have to understand the difference between paragraph and character styles.

A paragraph style controls all aspects of a paragraph's appearance, such as text alignment, tab stops, line spacing, and borders, and can include character formatting. If you want a paragraph to have a particular combination of attributes that are not in an existing style (for example, a bold, italic, centre-aligned heading in the Arial Narrow font), you can create a new paragraph style.

A character style affects selected text within a paragraph, such as the font and size of text, and bold and italic formats. Characters within a paragraph can have their own style even if a paragraph style is applied to the paragraph as a whole. If you want to be able to give certain types of words or phrase the same kind of formatting, and the formatting is not in an existing style, you can create a new character style. You can select and then access the paragraph style options by clicking **Format** ➔ **Paragraph** to open the Paragraph dialogue box which is shown in Fig 09.04 earlier in this book. In case of individual characters, you can select the character and then access its formatting options by clicking **Format** ➔ **Font** to open the Font dialogue box which is shown in Fig 09.03 earlier in this book.

## Modify a Style

1. On the Format menu, click **Style**.
2. In the Styles box, select the style you want to modify, and then click **Modify**.
3. Click **Format**, and then click the **attribute**, such as Font or Numbering that you want to change.

4. Click **OK** after you have changed each attribute, and then repeat for any additional attributes you want to change. See Fig 10.06 for a view of the **Style** dialogue box, earlier in this chapter.

**NOTE** To use the modified style in new documents based on the same template, select the Add to template check box. Word adds the modified style to the template that is attached to the active document.

When you change a formatting element of the base style in a document, all styles that originate from the base style in that document will also reflect the change.

You can also have Word modify a style automatically, meaning that Word detects when you alter the formatting of text containing a style, and then automatically updates the style. When Word automatically updates the style, all text formatted with that style is updated to match the formatting of the text you have just changed.

## Redefine a Style

To change all the text formatted with a particular style, you can redefine the style. For example, if your main headings are 14 pt Arial, flush left, and bold, and you later decide you want your headings to be 16 pt, Arial Narrow, and centred, you do not have to reformat every main heading in your document. Instead, just change the properties of that style in the Style dialogue box. See Fig 10.06 earlier in this chapter.

## Delete a Style

To delete a style, do the following:

1. On the Format menu, click **Style**.
2. In the Styles box, click the **style you want to delete**, and then click **Delete**.

**NOTE** If you delete a paragraph style that you had created, Microsoft Word applies the Normal style to all paragraphs that were formatted with that style and removes the style definition from the template.

If you click Styles in use in the List box, you can delete some built-in styles from a particular document. However, you cannot delete the Normal style and built-in heading styles. Word applies the Normal style to all paragraphs formatted with the style you deleted but retains the built-in style definitions in the template. You can make the built-in style available again by clicking All Styles in the List box.

## Use the Style Gallery

You can use the Style Gallery to see how your entire document would look if you applied styles from a different template. If you want, you can then apply the styles directly from the Style Gallery.

To display the Style Gallery, click Theme on the Format menu and then click the Style Gallery button. *See Fig 10.07.* When you select a template in the Style Gallery dialogue box, a preview window shows how your document would look like. You can also view sample documents showing styles from the selected template, or see a list of the styles used in the template. View or apply the styles from another template by using the Style Gallery.

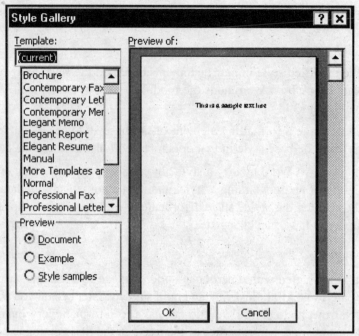

*Fig 10.07 Style Gallery Dialogue Box*

## Using Templates

To format long documents, in addition to styles, we need to understand the concept of templates. Every Microsoft Word document is based on a template. A template determines the basic structure for a document and contains document settings such as AutoText entries, fonts, key assignments, macros, menus, page layout, special formatting, and styles. The two basic types of templates are global templates and specific document templates. *See Fig 10.08.*

Global templates, including the Normal template, contain settings that are available to all documents. Document templates, such as the memo or fax templates in the New dialogue box, contain settings that are available only to documents based on that template. For example, if you create a memo using the memo template, the memo can use the settings from both the memo template as well as the settings in any global template. Word provides a variety of document templates, and you can create your own document templates. Fig 10.08 shows how a fax document can be constructed using a global template for general formatting and a fax template for special formatting.

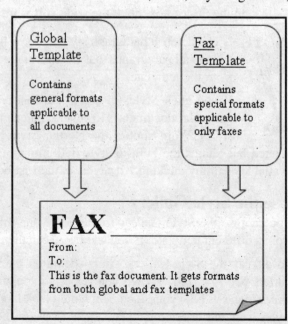

*Fig 10.08 Global and Specific Templates*

# Working with Global Templates

When you work on a document, you can typically use only the settings stored in the template attached to the document or in the Normal template. To use any such items that are stored in another template, you can load the other template as a global template. After you load a template, items stored in that template are available to any document during the remainder of the Word session.

The templates that you load are unloaded when you close Word. To load a template each time you start Word, copy the template to the Start up folder, whose location is specified on the File Locations tab. To display the File Locations tab, click Tools on the menu bar and then click Options. On the Options dialogue box, click on the File Locations tab. *See Fig 10.09.*

# Locating Templates

Templates you save in the Templates folder appear on the General tab. If you want to create custom tabs for your templates in the New dialogue box, create a new subfolder in the Templates folder and save your templates in that subfolder. The name you give that subfolder will appear on the new tab. When you are saving a template, Word switches to the User templates location, which by default is located in the Templates folder and its subfolders. If you save a template in a different location, the template will not appear in the New dialogue box.

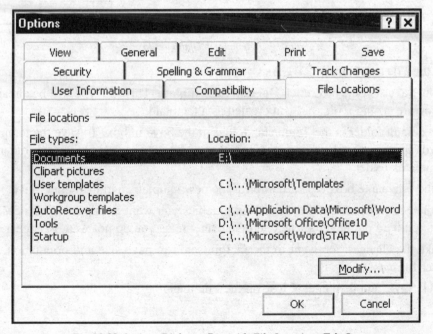

*Fig 10.09 Options Dialogue Box with File Locations Tab Open*

# Create a Document Template

In addition to the global templates such as the Normal template, you may wish to create a distinctive document template for use with your reports or stationery. Proceed as follows to create a document template:

1.  Do one of the following:

    *   To base a new template on an existing document, click **Open** on the File menu, and then open the document you want.

    *   To base a new template on an existing template, click **New** on the File menu. Click a **template** that is similar to the one you want to create, click **Template** under Create New, and then click **OK**. See Fig 10.10 for a view of the **Template** dialogue box.

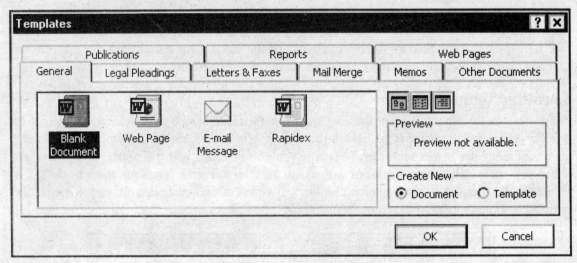

*Fig 10.10 Templates Dialogue Box*

2.  On the File menu, click **Save As**.

3.  In the Save As type box, click **Document Template**. This file type will be already selected if you are saving a file that you created as a template.

    The default folder is the Templates folder in the Save in box. To save the template so that it will appear on a tab other than General, switch to the corresponding subfolder within the Templates folder.

4.  In the File name box, type a **name** for the new template, and then click **Save**.

5.  In the new template, add the text and graphics you want to appear in all new documents that you base on the template, and delete any items you do not want to appear.

6.  Make the changes you want to the margin settings, page size and orientation, styles, and other formats.

7.  Click **Save**, and then click **Close** on the File menu.

## Sections

To separate the book into parts or chapters, you can use a section break. By using a section break, you can alter some of the formatting characteristics from chapter to chapter without losing overall uniformity of things such as fonts, margins, titles and so on, which remains the same throughout the book. For example, you may notice that while fonts, margins and heading styles are the same throughout the book you are reading, the header titles (chapter names) vary from chapter to chapter.

## *Section Breaks*

You can use sections to vary the layout of a document within a page or between pages. Just insert section breaks to divide the document into sections, and then format each section the way you want. For example, format a section as a single column for the introduction of a report, and then format the following section as two columns for the report's body text.

### *Types of Formats You Can Set For Sections*

You can change the following section formats: margins, paper size or orientation, paper source for a printer, page borders, vertical alignment, headers and footers, columns, page numbering, line numbering, and footnotes and endnotes.

Keep in mind that a section break controls the section formatting of the text that precedes it. For example, if you delete a section break, the preceding text becomes part of the following section and assumes its section formatting. Note that the last paragraph mark ¶ in the document controls the section formatting of the last section in the document; or of the entire document if it does not contain sections.

The three examples of section breaks are shown in Fig 10.11. Each of these three types of section breaks is described in detail in the following section.

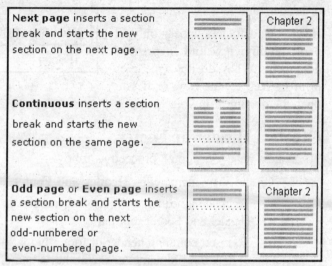

*Fig 10.11 Types of Section Breaks*

### *Types of Section Breaks*

The following examples show the types of section breaks you can insert. In each illustration, the double-dotted line represents a section break.

**Next page**: Inserts a section break and starts the new section on the next page.

**Continuous**: Inserts a section break and starts the new section on the same page.

**Odd page** or **Even page**: Inserts a section break and starts the new section on the next odd-numbered or even-numbered page.

# Headers and Footers

Headers and footers are typically used in documents you intend to print. You can create headers and footers that include text or graphics. For example, you can insert page numbers, the date, a company logo, the document's title or file name, or the author's name in the header or footer. In short, you can use any material that is usually printed at the top or bottom of each page in a document. A header is printed in the top margin and a footer is printed in the bottom margin.

You can use the same header and footer throughout a document or change the header and footer for part of the document. For example, use a unique header or footer on the first page, or leave the header or footer off the first page. You can also use different headers and footers on odd and even pages or for part of a document. See Fig 10.12 for samples of headers and footers.

Headers and footers appear only in print layout view and in printed documents. They do not appear or print in Web layout view or if you open the document in your browser.

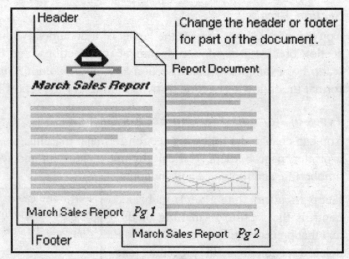

*Fig 10.12 Example of Header and Footer*

## Create a Header or Footer

To create a header or footer, proceed as follows:

1.  On the View menu, click **Header and Footer**.

    *   To create a header, enter text or graphics in the header area. Or click a **button** on the Header and Footer tool bar.

    *   To insert common header or footer items, such as running total page numbers (Page 1 of 10), the file name, or the author's name, click **Insert AutoText** and then click the **item you want**. *See Fig 10.13.*

    *   To create footer, click **Switch between Header and Footer** to move to the footer area. See Fig 10.13 for details of what you can insert and how.

2.  When you finish, click **Close**.

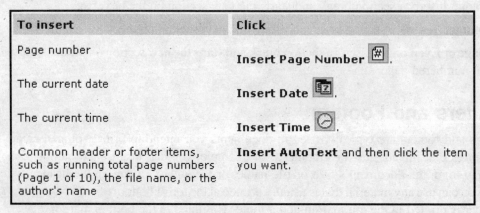

*Fig 10.13 Inserting Objects in Header or Footer*

**TIP**
The text or graphics you enter in a header or footer is automatically left aligned. You may want to centre the item instead or include multiple items (for example, a left-aligned date and a right-aligned page number). To centre an item, press TAB; to right align an item, press TAB twice.

## View, Edit, or Format a Header or Footer

To view a header or footer, switch to Print Layout View. To edit or format a header or footer, you need to display the header or footer you want. Do the following:

1.  On the View menu, click **Header and Footer**.
2.  Make your changes to the header or footer.

To move from header to footer, or to move to the header or footer you want, click the appropriate button on the Header and Footer tool bar.

**NOTE**
When you change a header or footer, Word automatically changes the same header or footer throughout the entire document. To change a header or footer for part of a document, divide the document into sections and break the connection between them.

In Print Layout View, you can quickly switch between the header or footer and the document text. Just double click the dimmed header or footer or the dimmed document text to jump to the header, footer or the text as required.

See Fig 10.14 for a view of a sample header. The bottom half contains a description of the three navigation buttons used to navigate headers and footers.

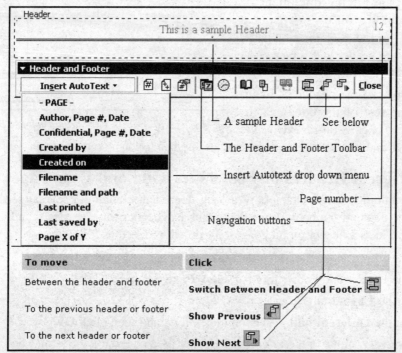

*Fig 10.14 Header and Footer Tool Bar*

## Create a Unique Header or Footer for the First Page

It is customary to have a different header or footer for the first page or the title page of your document. Sometimes, headers and footers are inserted from the second page onwards if the first page is a title page.

To create a unique header, proceed as follows:

1. If your document is divided into sections, click in a **section** or select **multiple sections** you want to change.

2. On the View menu, click **Header and Footer**.

3. On the Header and Footer tool bar, click **Page Setup**. See Fig 10.15 for a view of the Page Setup dialogue box.

4. Click the **Layout** tab.

5. Select the **Different first page** check box, and then click **OK**.

6. If necessary, move to the First Page Header area or First Page Footer area.

7. Create the header or footer for the first page of the document or section. If you do not want a header or footer on the first page, leave the header and footer areas blank.

8. To move to the header or footer for the rest of the document or section, click **Show Next** on the Header and Footer tool bar. Then create the header or footer you want.

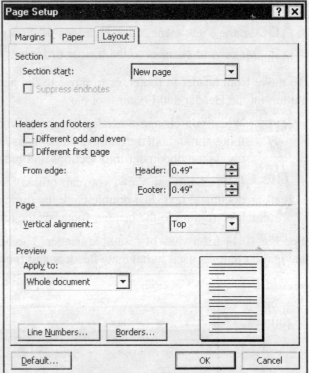

*Fig 10.15 Page Setup Dialogue Box*

## Create Different Headers or Footers for Odd and Even Pages

In a book containing several chapters or a long document containing several sections, you may wish to use the name of the book or the document as a header for even pages and the name of the chapter or section as a header on odd pages. To do so, proceed as follows:

1. On the View menu, click **Header and Footer**.

2. On the Header and Footer tool bar, click **Page Setup**.

3. Click the **Layout** tab.

4. Select the **Different odd and even** check box, and then click **OK**.

5. If necessary, move to the Even Page Header area or Even Page Footer box.

6. Create the header or footer for each even-numbered page.

7.  To move to the header or footer for each odd-numbered page, click **Show Next** on the Header and Footer tool bar. Then create the header or footer you want.

**NOTE**

Word inserts the odd and even headers or footers throughout the entire document; you cannot create odd and even headers or footers for part of the document. However, if you divide the document into sections and break the connection between them by inserting a page break, you can set different odd and even headers or footers for each section.

# Adding Special Features to Your Document

In the previous section, we have discussed special formatting needs of long documents such as a research report or a book. In addition to formats, such long documents also use special features as part of the document. Some of the inclusions such as lists or tables can be used in short documents as well. Some other features such as a table of contents, an alphabetical index or footnotes, however, are useful only in reports and books. We discuss these special features here so that you can include what you need in your Word document.

## The Lists

Lists are either numbered or bulleted. Numbers are used to indicate a sequence. For example, if you are describing steps to carry out a task, you will number your list of tasks. However, if you are listing a collection of statements in no particular order, you will probably bullet the items just to separate them.

### Add Bullets or Numbering

If you have typed a list of items in your document and wish to bullet or number them, proceed as follows:

1.  Select the items you want to add bullets or numbering to.
2.  On the Formatting tool bar, do one of the following:
    *   To add bullets, click **Bullets**.
    *   To add numbering, click **Numbering**.

**TIP**

To create a bulleted or numbered list automatically as you type, type 1 or * (asterisk), press **Spacebar** or **Tab**, and then type any text you want. When you press **Enter** ↵ to add the next list item, Word automatically inserts the next number or bullet. To finish the list, press **Enter** ↵ twice. You can also finish the list by pressing **Backspace** to delete the last bullet or number in the list.

### Convert Bullets to Numbers and Vice Versa

After bulleting or numbering your list, you may realise that what you have numbered should have actually been bulleted, or vice versa. If so, to change, proceed as follows:

1.  Select the items that have bullets or numbers you want to change.
2.  On the Formatting tool bar, click **Bullets or Numbering**.

### *Modify Bulleted List or Numbered List Formats*

Word will apply the last format that was used for bullets or numbers. However, you may want to change the format. For instance, you may want to use a, b, c instead of 1, 2, 3.

To make the changes you want, proceed as follows:

1. Select the paragraphs that have the bullet or number format you want to change.

2. On the Format menu, click **Bullets and Numbering**. The Bullets and Numbering dialogue box opens.

3. Click the **tab** for the type of list you want to modify. You can choose from Bulleted, Numbered or Outline Numbered formats.

4. Click the **list format** that matches your list's existing bullet or number format.

5. Click **Customise**. The Customise dialogue box appears, depending on the format you have selected. *See Fig 10.16.*

6. Select the formatting options you want.

7. Click **OK** to return to your main document.

Fig 10.16 shows the Customise dialogue box that will appear if you are customising a bulleted list. For a numbered list, a similar dialogue box containing the options available for numbers will appear instead.

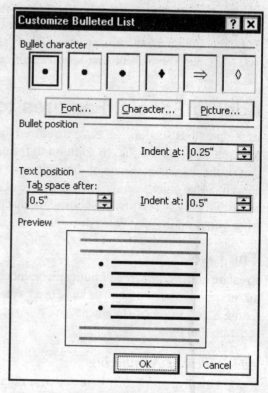

*Fig 10.16 Customise Dialogue Box*

# About Tables

While a bulleted or numbered list can display information in an organised manner, it is often necessary to use a table with several rows and columns to arrange a large amount of data. To do so, Word provides you with a structure called a Table.

A table is made up of rows and columns of cells that you can fill with text and graphics. Tables are often used to organise and present information, but they have a variety of other uses as well. You can use tables to align numbers in columns, and then sort and perform calculations on them. You can also use tables to create interesting page layouts and arrange text and graphics.

## Parts of a Table

Before we begin building tables, it is necessary to become familiar with the parts of a table. *See Fig 10.17.* The parts are described in detail in the following section.

The main parts are:

**Borders and gridlines**: By default, tables have a black ½-pt, single-line, solid-line border that will be printed. If you remove this border, you will still see the gridlines that form the cell boundaries. Gridlines are not printed.

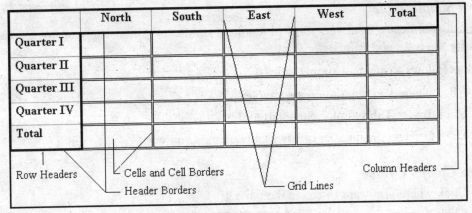

*Fig 10.17 Parts of a Table*

**End marks**: End-of-cell and end-of-row marks are non-printing characters that, like gridlines, appear only on the screen.

**Cell spacing and margins**: If you are using a table to arrange text and graphics, for example, on a Web page, you can add spacing between table cells. You can also add cell "padding" (spacing between the boundary of the cell and the text inside the cell) by changing the cell margin.

**Nested tables**: If you use a table to lay out a page, and you want to use another table to present information, you can insert a nested table, that is, a table within a table.

**Table move handle and resize handle**: Use the table move handle to move the table to another place on a page, and use the table resize handle to change the size of a table.

## Creating Tables

We will discuss creating a simple table and then a more complex table. We will also see how to navigate within a table and how to format a table in the following sections.

You can use the Table AutoFormat command to quickly give a table a polished look by using a variety of borders, fonts, and shading. *See Fig 10.18.*

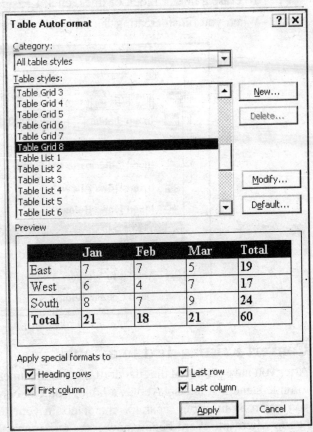

*Fig 10.18 Table AutoFormat Dialogue Box*

### Create a Simple Table

For most of your needs, however, you will require a simple table, consisting of rows, columns and headers for the rows and columns.

Proceed as follows to create a simple table:

1. Click where you want to create a table.
2. Click **Insert Table** on the Standard tool bar.
3. Drag to select the number of rows and columns you want.

### Create a Complex Table

1. Click where you want to create the table.
2. Click **View** on the menu bar and click **Tool bars** on the drop-down menu. Click the **Tables and Borders** item. The Tables and Borders tool bar appears. *See Fig 10.19.*
3. On the Tables and Borders tool bar, click **Draw Table**. The pointer changes to a pencil.
4. To define the outer table boundaries, draw a rectangle. Then draw the column and row lines inside the rectangle.
5. To erase a line or block of lines, click **Eraser**, and then drag over the line.
6. When you finish creating the table, click a **cell** and start typing or insert a graphic.

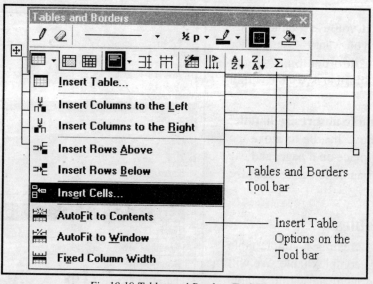

*Fig 10.19 Tables and Borders Tool Bar*

## Convert Existing Text to a Table

After you have produced the first draft of your document, you may find that some text will be easier to understand if it is displayed as a table. You can convert the existing text into a table. To do so, you begin by inserting separator characters in your text to indicate where a new column should begin. Microsoft Word begins new rows at paragraph marks. Choose paragraph marks as your separator character to convert your text into a table with one column.

After inserting separators, proceed as follows:

1. Select the text you want to convert.
2. On the Table menu, point to **Convert**, and then click **Text to Table**.
3. Under **Separate text at**, click the **option** for the separator character you want.
4. Select any other options you want.

## Move Around in a Table

You can use special keystrokes to move around in a table. *See Fig 10.20 for details.*

| Press | To |
|---|---|
| The TAB key anywhere in a table except at the end of the last row | Move to the next cell |
| The TAB key at the end of the last row | Add a new row at the bottom of the table |
| SHIFT+TAB | Move to the preceding cell |
| UP ARROW or DOWN ARROW | Move to the preceding or next row |
| ALT+HOME, or ALT+7 on the numeric keypad (NUM LOCK must be off) | Move to the first cell in the row |
| ALT+END, or ALT+1 on the numeric keypad (NUM LOCK must be off) | Move to the last cell in the row |
| ALT+PAGE UP, or ALT+9 on the numeric keypad (NUM LOCK must be off) | Move to the first cell in the column |
| ALT+PAGE DOWN, or ALT+3 on the numeric keypad (NUM LOCK must be off) | Move to the last cell in the column |
| ENTER | Start a new paragraph |
| ENTER at the beginning of the first cell | Add text before a table at the beginning of a document |

*Fig 10.20 Type and Move Around in a Table*

## Delete a Table or Delete Items from a Table

You can delete individual or multiple cells, rows, or columns, or you can delete an entire table. You can also clear the contents of cells without deleting the cells themselves.

To delete a table and its contents, proceed as follows:

1. Click the **Table**.
2. On the Table menu, point to **Delete**, and then click **Table**.

To delete cells, rows, or columns from a table, proceed as follows:

1. Select the **cells**, **rows**, or **columns** you want to delete.
2. On the Table menu, point to **Delete**, and then click **Columns**, **Rows**, or **Cells**.
3. If you are deleting cells, click the **option** you want.

To clear the contents of a table, proceed as follows:

1. Select the items you want to clear.
2. Press **Delete**.

## Modifying Tables

After you have set up a table and are entering data in it, it happens that you find that you need to resize the table or add more rows or columns. We discuss how you can change an existing table.

### Add Rows or Columns

1.  Select the same number of rows or columns as the number of rows or columns you want to insert.

2.  On the Tables and Borders tool bar, click the **drop-down arrow** ▼ next to Insert Table, and then click the **Insert command** you want.

**NOTE** You can also use the Draw Table tool to draw the row or column where you want.

To quickly add a row at the end of a table, click the **last cell** of the last row, and then press the **Tab** key.

To add a column to the right of the last column in a table, click **just outside the rightmost column**. On the Table menu, point to **Insert**, and then click **Columns** to the Right.

As you can see, there are many different ways to draw or modify a table. After a little practice, you will be able to decide which method suits you best.

## Resize a Table

To fit a table on a page containing text, it is sometimes necessary to resize the table. Follow these steps to resize a table:

1.  Rest the pointer on the table until the table resize handle appears on the lower right corner of the table.

2.  Rest the pointer on the table resize handle until a double-headed arrow ↔ appears.

3.  Drag the table boundary until the table is the size you want.

**TIP** If you are working on a Web page or in Web layout view, you can set the table to automatically resize to fit in a window when you change the window size. Click inside the table. On the shortcut menu that appears, point to AutoFit, and then click AutoFit to Window. The table will adjust itself to the window size.

## Merge Cells into One Cell

You can combine two or more cells in the same row or column into a single cell. For example, you can merge several cells horizontally to create a table heading that spans several columns. Do the following to merge cells:

1.  On the Tables and Borders tool bar, click **Eraser**.

2.  Drag the eraser over the cell dividers you want to remove.

**TIP** You can quickly merge multiple cells by selecting them and right clicking to display the shortcut menu. Click Merge Cells in the shortcut menu. The selected cells are merged together into a single cell. After merging cells, it is often necessary to change the heading direction from the normal horizontal to vertical. To do so, right click the merged cell again and the text direction dialogue box appears. Click the vertical text direction option to realign the heading vertically.

# Formatting Tables

To enhance the appearance of a table, you can format the table. You have already seen the use of the AutoFormat command earlier in this section. The AutoFormat command gives you a preset number of enhancements. The section below describes how you can format individual attributes of the table to suit your exact needs.

## Display or Hide Gridlines in a Table

In Word documents, all tables have a black ½-point, single-line, solid-line border by default. This border will get printed. Even if you remove this border, the gridlines remain until you deliberately hide them. To hide or show gridlines, do the following:

1.  On the menu bar, click **Table**. The drop-down menu appears.
2.  On the drop-down menu, click **Show Gridlines** or **Hide Gridlines**. This command toggles. That is, if gridlines are visible, the option will hide gridlines and vice versa.

## Positioning Table on a Page

Like many other drawing objects, you can move a table on your document's page for the best layout. To move a table, proceed as follows:

1.  Rest the pointer on the table until the table move handle appears on the upper-left corner of the table.
2.  Rest the pointer on the table move handle until a four-headed arrow ⟷ appears.
3.  Drag the table to its new location and release the mouse button to anchor the table.

## Footnotes and Endnotes

Typically, footnotes and endnotes are used in printed documents to explain, comment on, or provide references for text in a document. You can include both footnotes and endnotes in the same document. For example, you might use footnotes for detailed comments and endnotes for citation of sources. Footnotes appear at the end of each page in a document. Endnotes typically appear at the end of a document or at the end of each section or chapter.

A footnote or an endnote consists of two linked parts. They are the note reference mark and the corresponding note text. You can automatically number marks or create your own custom marks. When you add, delete, or move notes that are automatically numbered, Word renumbers the note reference marks and adjusts the numbers as needed.

## Insert a Footnote or an Endnote

To add a footnote or an endnote to your document, proceed as follows:

1.  In Print Layout View, click the **mouse button** where you want to insert the note reference mark.
2.  On the menu bar, click **Insert**. In the drop-down menu that appears, click **Footnote**. The Footnote and Endnote dialogue box appears.

3. In this dialogue box, select location of footnote or endnote, and the number format.

4. Click the **Options** button to display the Note Options dialogue box where you can select the start number (the default is 1) and whether the numbering will be continuous throughout the document or start afresh at each section. See Fig 10.21 for a view of the two dialogue boxes.

5. Click **OK** and then **OK** again. Word inserts the note number and places the insertion point next to the note number.

6. Type the note text.

7. Scroll to your place in the document and continue typing.

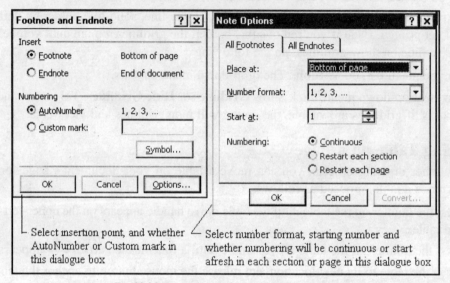

*Fig 10.21 Footnote and Endnote Dialogue Box*

**TIP** The default locations are footnotes at the end of each page and endnotes at the end of the document. You can change the placement of footnotes so that they appear directly below the text. Similarly, you can change the placement of endnotes so that they appear at the end of each section. However, you may wish to accept the default settings in most cases.

In Fig 10.22, you can see a typical example of a footnote at the bottom of the page.

## View Footnotes and Endnotes

In the document, rest the pointer on the note reference mark to view a footnote or an endnote.

The note text will appear above the mark in a Screen Tip. *See Fig 10.22.*

**NOTE** To scroll through all footnotes or endnotes in the note pane, switch to normal view, and click Footnotes on the View menu. If a message appears, click View footnote area or View endnote area, and then click OK. In the note pane, click All footnotes or All endnotes.

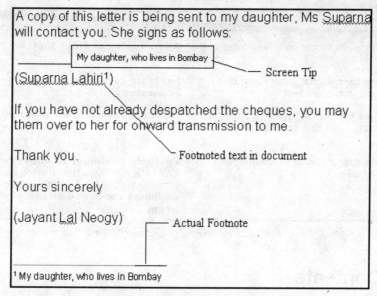

*Fig 10.22 Example of a Footnote*

## Delete a Footnote or an Endnote

When you want to delete a note, you have to delete with the note reference mark in the document window, not the text in the note pane. Proceed as follows:

1. In the document, select the note reference mark of the note you want to delete, and then press **Delete**.

2. If you delete an automatically numbered note reference mark, Word will renumber the notes in the new order.

## Footnote and Endnote Options

To display the note pane, switch to Normal View and click **Footnotes** on the View menu. If a message appears, click **View footnote area** or **View endnote area**, and then click **OK**. The options are listed in Fig 10.23.

# Table of Contents and Index

A large report or a book contains a great deal of information. The reader needs some means of navigation so that he or she can get to the information required easily and conveniently. There are two navigation aids that you can provide your readers, the table of contents and the index.

If the reader wishes to locate a topic, it is easier to find the topic by going through a table of contents. Tables of contents are arranged in the same sequence in which the topics are listed in the main document.

If, however, the reader is not sure of the topic, but wishes to find out more about a word or term used in the document, it is easier to use the index. Indexes are arranged alphabetically to help with the search.

| To | Click |
|---|---|
| Display all footnotes or all endnotes in the document | **All footnotes** or **All endnotes** |
| Change the line that separates notes from the document text | **Footnote separator** or **Endnote separator** |
| Create a line that separates document text from notes that continue onto the next page | **Footnote continuation separator** or **Endnote continuation separator** |
| Add a notice that notes continue to another page | **Footnote continuation notice** or **Endnote continuation notice**, and then type the text — for example, type **Endnotes continued on the next page**. |

*Fig 10.23 Footnote and Endnote Options*

# Table of Contents

We look first at the table of contents and learn how to create them.

### Use Built-in Heading Styles

By default, Word has 9 built-in heading styles, ranging from Heading 1 up to Heading 9. You can display the headings by clicking on the drop-down arrow ▼ next to the Style dialogue box on the standard tool bar of Word. If the Normal template has been altered, there may be other heading styles available as well. However, we will assume that you are using the default headings in this case. In Fig 10.24 you can see the Table of Contents dialogue box and the Table of Contents options available.

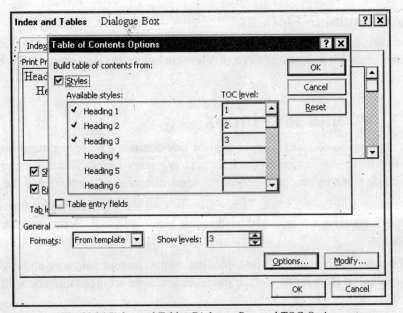

*Fig 10.24 Index and Tables Dialogue Box and TOC Options*

To use the built-in heading styles for your table of contents, proceed as follows:

1. In your document, apply built-in heading styles (Heading 1 through Heading 9) to the headings you want to include in your table of contents.

2. In your document, click where you want to insert the table of contents. The normal location is right at the beginning of your document.

3. On the Insert menu, click **Index and Tables**, and then click the **Table of Contents** tab.

4. Do one of the following:

   • To use one of the available designs, click a **design** in the Formats box.

   • To specify a custom table of contents layout, choose the options you want.

5. Select any other table of contents options you want.

6. Click **OK**. Word creates your table of contents and places it at the insertion point you had selected.

## *Use Outline-level Styles*

An easy way to create a table of contents is to use the built-in outline level. Outline level is a system of paragraph formatting that you can use to assign a hierarchical level (Level 1 through Level 9) to paragraphs in your document. For example, after you assign outline levels, you can work with the document in outline view or in the Document Map.

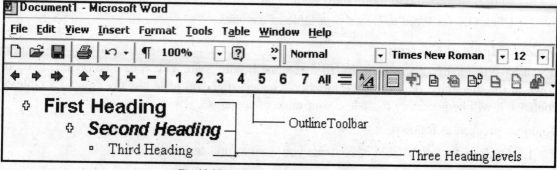

*Fig 10.25 Outlining Tool Bar Heading Levels*

In Fig 10.25, you can see the Outlining tool bar along with a document fragment showing three levels of headings.

To use the built-in outline level, do the following:

1. On the View menu, point to **Tool bars**, and click **Outlining**. *See Fig 10.25.*

2. Select the **first heading** that you want to appear in the table of contents.

3. On the Outlining tool bar, select the **outline level** that you want to associate with the selected paragraph.

4. Repeat steps 2 and 3 for each heading that you want to include in the table of contents.

5. Click where you want to insert the table of contents.

6. On the Insert menu, point to **Reference**, and click **Index and Tables**.

7. Click the **Table of Contents** tab.

8. To use one of the available designs, click a **design** in the Formats box.

9. Select any other table of contents options you want.

10. Click **OK**. Word builds your table of contents and inserts it where you chose the insertion point in your document.

### *Create a Custom Design*

You can customise your table of contents if you do not want to use the default styles we have discussed so far. To do so, proceed as follows:

1. On the Insert menu, click **Index and Tables**, and then click the **Table of Contents** tab. See Fig 10.24 earlier in this section.

2. In the Formats box, click **From Template** in the drop-down list, and then click **Modify**.

3. Under Styles, click the **style** you want to change, (say, TOC 1) and then click **Modify**. The Modify Styles dialogue box opens.

4. Make changes to font, formatting etc as required. If you wish to add the new style definition to your template, select the **Add to template** check box.

5. Click **OK** to return to the Style dialogue box.

6. Repeat steps 3 to 6 to modify any additional style such as TOC 2, TOC 3 etc.

7. Click **OK** for Word to create your table of contents.

### *Update a Table of Contents*

If you have to modify your document so that some headings are added, deleted or moved up or down in the hierarchy, or if the page numbers change after you have already created a table of contents, it will be necessary to update your table of contents.

To do so, proceed as follows:

1. Click to the left of table of contents you want to update.

2. Press **F9**. The table of contents is updated.

### *Delete a Table of Contents*

You can delete an unwanted table of contents as follows:

1. Click to the left of the table of contents you want to delete.

2. If you do not see a field code, press **Shift + F9**.

3. Select the field code, including the curly brackets { }, and press **Delete**. The table of contents is deleted.

# Index

To locate individual words or terms used in your document, the reader will probably find the index to be more useful than the table of contents, especially if the reader is not sure which topic to open to view the word or phrase.

To help such readers, you will want to provide an alphabetical index usually placed at the end of your document. We study indexes in this section.

An index lists the terms and topics discussed in a printed document, along with the pages they appear on. You can create an index entry:

- For an individual word, phrase, or symbol.
- For a topic that spans a range of pages.

A spanning topic may refer to another entry in the index. For example, you can have an entry called Transportation that says *Transportation. See Bicycles.*

If you create numerous index entries for a specific topic area, you might want to create multi-level index entries. For example, you can create the main index entry "Transportation", and then group the subentries *Bicycle* and *Automobile* under it.

## Creating Index Entries

To create an index, you must first mark the words or phrases that you wish to use as index entries in your document. To mark an entry, just select the text, assign it an index entry name, and then watch Word insert a special XE or Index Entry field such as {-XE-"Urgency"-} is an index entry for the word "Urgency".

You can manually mark each index entry, or you can automatically mark each occurrence of the index entry. To speed up indexing, you can also use a concordance file to automatically mark multiple index entries at the same time. We look at the task of marking index entries and then designing and building an index in the sections that follow.

## Mark Index Entries for Words or Phrases

The first step in index building is to mark the words or phrases that you want to appear in your document index. To mark, proceed as follows:

1. Do one of the following:
   - To use existing text as an index entry, select the **text**.
   - To enter your own text as an index entry, click where you want to insert the index entry.
2. Press **Alt + Shift + X**.
3. Do one of the following:
   - To create a main index entry, type or edit the **text** in the Main entry box.
   - To create a subentry, specify the main index entry, and then type the **subentry** in the Subentry box.
   - To include a third-level entry, type the **subentry text** followed by a **colon (:)** and the text of the third-level entry.
4. Do one of the following:
   - To mark the index entry, click **Mark**.
   - To mark all occurrences of this text in the document, click **Mark All**. You will only see this button if you have selected text before opening the dialogue box. The button will not be visible if you have typed your own text in the dialogue box.
   - To mark additional index entries, select the **text** or click immediately after it.

5. Mark Index Entry dialogue box, and then repeat steps 3 and 4.

**NOTE**

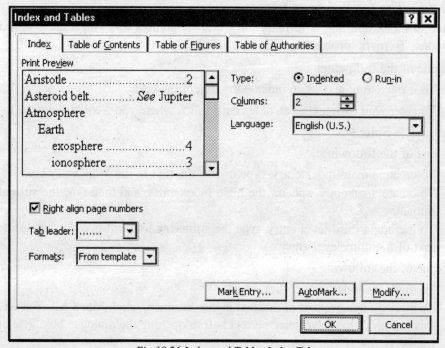

Mark All marks the first occurrence in each paragraph of text that exactly matches the uppercase and lowercase letters in the entry.

Word inserts each marked index entry as an XE (Index Entry) field in hidden text format. If you do not see the XE field, click the Show/Hide Icon on the Standard tool bar.

### Design and Build an Index

After all the desired index entries have been marked, you can proceed as follows to design and build an index:

1. Mark the **index entries** in your document.
2. Click where you want to **insert** the finished index.
3. On the Insert menu, click **Index and Tables**, and then click the **Index tab**. *See Fig 10.26.*
4. Do one of the following:
   - To use one of the available designs, click a **design** in the Formats box.
   - To design a custom index layout, choose the **options** you want.
5. Select any other index **options** that you want.
6. Click **OK** and Word inserts the index entry at the chosen point.

To make sure that the document is paginated correctly, you must hide field codes and hidden text. If the XE (Index Entry) fields are visible, click the Show/Hide icon on the Standard tool bar.

*Fig 10.26 Index and Tables Index Tab*

## *Edit, Format, or Delete Index Entries*

When you mark an index entry, Word inserts an XE (Index Entry) field. To change an index entry, you need to modify the text in the index entry field. Proceed as follows:

If you do not see the XE fields, click the **Show/Hide icon** ¶ on the Standard tool bar.

Do one of the following:·

- To edit or format an index entry, **change the text** inside the quotation marks.
- To delete an index entry, select the **entire index entry field**, including the brackets { }, and then press **Delete**.

### TRAP

Do not modify the index entries in the finished index; otherwise, the next time you rebuild the index, your changes will be lost.

# Create a Concordance File

A convenient way to mark the indexes in your document is to first create a separate Word document containing a two-column table. The table is filled with words or phrases that you wish to use as indexes in your main document. Then you use the new document called a Concordance File, to mark your main document automatically. Thereafter, the index for your main document is produced as usual. This is the recommended method for indexing any large document such as this book.

To create a concordance file, proceed as follows:

1. Click the **Insert Table icon** on the Standard tool bar. The table grid appears.
2. Drag to select two columns and click to create a two-column table.
3. In the first column, enter the **text** you want Microsoft Word to search for and mark as an index entry. Make sure to enter the text exactly as it appears in the document. Then press **TAB.**
4. In the second column, type the **index entry** for the text in the first column. Then press **TAB.** If you want to create a subentry, type the main entry followed by a colon (:) and the subentry.
5. Repeat steps 3 and 4 for each index reference and entry.
6. Save the concordance file.

To make sure Word marks all the text you want to index, list all forms of the text you want to search for. For example, type erupt, erupting, and eruption in three separate cells in the left column, and then type volcanoes in the matching cells in the right column.

### TIP

To speed up the creation of a concordance file, first open both the concordance file and the document you want to index. To see both documents at once, click Arrange All on the Window menu. Then copy text from the document you want to index into the first column of the concordance file.

In Fig 10.27 you can see a sample concordance file using the procedure outlined above.

After you have created the concordance file, proceed as follows to mark the entries:

1. Open the document you want to index.

2. On the Insert menu, point to **Reference**, click **Index and Tables**. The Index and tables dialogue box appears.

3. Click the **Index tab** and then click the **AutoMark button**. The Open index AutoMark File dialogue box appears.

4. In the File name box, enter the **name** of the concordance file you have created and saved.

5. Click **Open**. Word searches through the document for each exact occurrence of text in the first column of the concordance file, and then it uses the text in the second column as the index entry. Word marks only the first occurrence of an entry in each paragraph.

| Words in Text | Entry in Index |
|---|---|
| erupting | Volcanoes |
| eruption | |
| erupt | |
| cars | Automobiles |
| sedans | |
| hatchback | |
| motorcycles | Two Wheelers |
| scooters | |
| mopeds | |

**A Sample Concordance File**

*Fig 10.27 Sample Concordance File*

6. Click where you want to insert the finished index in your main document. The index is created and inserted.

**NOTE**

To make sure that the document is paginated correctly, you must first hide field codes and hidden text. If the XE (Index Entry) fields are visible, click **Show/Hide ¶** on the Standard tool bar. This icon toggles and will hide the field codes if they are displayed and vice versa.

## Formatting and Updating Indexes

The procedures are the same as what has been described earlier for table of contents. Use the Index tab in the Index and Tables dialogue box to change formats or modify indexes. See the procedures outlined under table of contents earlier in this section. Also see Fig 10.24 earlier in this chapter.

As in the case of table of contents, if the text in the document changes so that the page-wise location of indexed words is changed, you will need to update the index. To update the index, click to the left of the field and press F9.

**CD-ROM**

To learn more about Microsoft Word 2000 in a multimedia environment, insert the accompanying CD-ROM in your computer, select the **Interactive** mode in the opening screen. The main menu will appear. To go to the section on Word, click the button marked **Word**. You will see a sub-menu containing the following topics:

• Getting Started in Word
• Getting Control over Word
• Creating Professional Documents
• Power of Word Unleashed

Click on the third sub-menu item, *Creating Professional Documents*. Another level of sub-sub-menus is displayed from which you can select the particular topic you want to see. Click on your selected topic and follow the instructions on your screen.

# 11. Using Word Efficiently

*In this chapter:*

☞ You are introduced to various features of Word that make your word processing more efficient.

☞ You learn about formatting documents using AutoFormat and other automatic formatting techniques.

☞ We show you how to shrink documents to fit into a page while printing your document.

☞ You learn how to prepare automatic summaries of your long documents and how to troubleshoot problems while preparing automatic summaries.

☞ We show you how to use the AutoCorrect feature and how to automatically carry out spelling and grammar checks while typing, or after you have finished composing your document.

☞ You learn how to automate your correspondence, using templates and Wizards. You also learn about quick and efficient ways of drafting memos and faxes.

☞ You learn about mail merging, a technique that allows you to send out several copies of a form letter to a list of customers or clients and yet, personalise each letter.

# Increasing Efficiency

After learning the basics of Word, we have already moved on to more complex aspects of word processing in Chapter 10, *Managing Long Documents*, where we have learned about the special needs of long documents and about special inserts in Word such as lists and tables. We are now ready to improve our working efficiency with Word.

In this chapter, we learn how to use Word faster and more effectively. We work with long documents once in a while. But we write memos and letters almost daily. It is the short but oft-repeated tasks that take up most of our time. Therefore, to be able to use Word more efficiently, we need to learn how to do these daily tasks faster and more effectively, to use shortcuts and automation wherever possible. With this objective, we learn about:

- Automatically formatting documents
- Automatically summarising documents
- Automatically correcting spelling and grammar
- Automating your correspondence
- Mail merging techniques

As you can see, it is all about using your computer to create letters, memos and faxes more efficiently.

# Formatting Documents Automatically

### *How AutoFormat Works*

By using AutoFormat, you can quickly apply formatting such as headings, bulleted and numbered lists, borders, numbers, symbols, and fractions to your text. Microsoft Word can also:

- Automatically format Internet, network, and e-mail addresses as hyperlinks.
- Apply bold or italic character formatting to text surrounded by asterisks (*) or underscores (_).
- Replace two hyphens (--) with an em dash (—).

You can automatically format a document either as you type or after you have written it. Word analyses each paragraph to see how formatting has been used on an item in a document. For example, Word will determine if an item is a heading or an item in a numbered list. Word will then apply a style that is appropriate for that item.

# Two Ways to Use AutoFormat

Word offers two ways to automatically format a document. You can:

### *Format Text Automatically as You Type*

To format text as you type, set the formatting options beforehand as follows:

1. Click **Tools** on the menu bar and click **AutoCorrect** on the drop-down menu. The AutoCorrect dialogue box opens.

2. Click the **AutoFormat As You Type Tab**. A page containing several options will open. *See Fig 11.01.*

3. Click to select the formatting options that will apply to your document as you type.

4. Click **OK** to return to the document window.

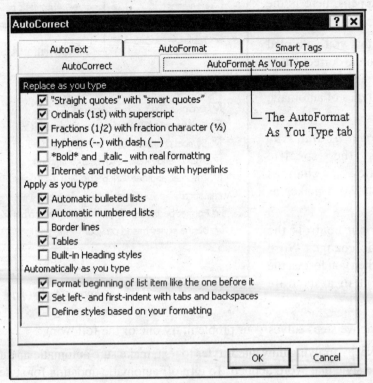

*Fig 11.01 AutoFormat Tab on AutoCorrect*

Word will now automatically format text as you type your document. For example, if you type a number followed by a period or hyphen, followed by a space or tab, followed by text, Word will make the text into a numbered list.

### *Format Documents Automatically After Writing*

If you prefer it, you can type your document without any special formatting. After typing is over, you can format the document as follows:

1. Click **Format** on the menu bar and then click **AutoFormat** on the drop-down menu. The AutoFormat dialogue box opens.

2. Click **Options** to open the AutoCorrect dialogue box with the AutoFormat tab open. *See Fig 11.02.*

3. Open the AutoCorrect dialogue box as shown earlier.

4. Select the appropriate options grouped under *Apply, Replace, Preserve* and *Always AutoFormat*.

5. Click **OK**. Word applies the selected formats to the document that is open.

## *Troubleshooting*

You can run into a problem while using AutoCorrect. You may find that automatic formatting does not turn off. If it happens, here is the remedy.

First, make sure that you've turned off the options on the correct tab in the AutoCorrect dialogue box. You can turn off two types of automatic formatting:

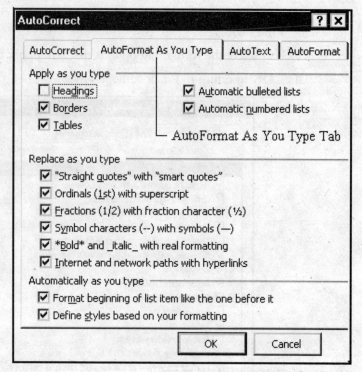

Fig 11.02 AutoFormat As You Type Tab

1. *AutoFormat as You Type* controls the specific automatic changes Microsoft Word makes as you type.

2. *AutoFormat* controls the automatic changes Word makes when you format the document in a separate pass.

If neither of the above steps solves your problem, try one of the following:

- If Word keeps applying unwanted styles to text, make sure automatic updating is not turned on for the style that Word applied. To turn off automatic updating for styles, click **Style** on the Format menu, select the **style** in the Styles box, and then click **Modify**. Clear the **Automatically update check box**.

- If Word continues to format text as headings even after you've cleared the Headings check box on the *AutoFormat As You Type* tab (Tools menu, AutoCorrect command), clear the **Define styles based on your formatting** check box under *Automatically as you type*.

- Make sure that the Bold and _italic_ with real formatting check box is selected on both the AutoFormat As You Type and the AutoFormat tabs.

# Shrink to Fit

You may find that one or two lines of your document spill over to an additional printed page. You will naturally like to reformat the document to avoid this spill over. Word has a Shrink to Fit feature to help you.

Try to reduce the amount of text that appears on the last page. If only a small amount of text appears on the last page of a short document, you may be able to reduce the number of pages by clicking Shrink to Fit in print preview. *See Fig 11.03.* This feature works best with documents that contain only a few pages, such as letters and memos. In order to shrink the document, Word decreases the font size of each font used in the document. You can undo a Shrink to Fit operation by clicking

Undo Shrink to Fit on the Edit menu. However, if you save the document and close it, there is no quick way to restore the original font size after that.

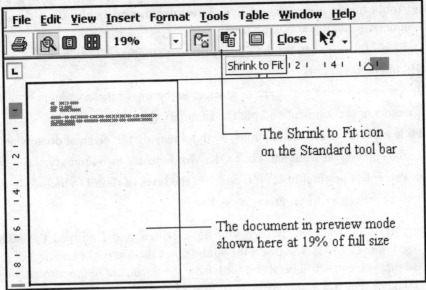

*Fig 11.03 Shrink to Fit Icon*

## Automatically Summarise a Document

There are many occasions when it becomes necessary to prepare a summary of your document. This is particularly so when your document is long and a summary (sometimes called an executive summary) is needed to brief, let us say, people attending your meeting.

Word provides you with a useful feature called AutoSummarise, which will automatically prepare a summary. This is how it works:

- AutoSummarise identifies the key points in a document for you.

- The key points are determined by analysing the document and assigning a score to each sentence. Sentences that contain words used frequently in the document are given a higher score. Word then lets you choose a percentage of the highest-scoring sentences to display in the summary.

- AutoSummarise works best on well-structured documents such as reports, articles, and scientific papers.

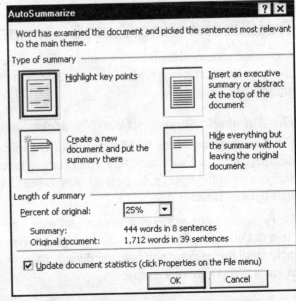

*Fig 11.04 AutoSummarise Dialogue Box*

## Create an Automatic Summary

To use AutoSummarise, do the following:

1.  Click **Tools** on the menu bar. Click **AutoSummarise** in the drop-down menu. The AutoSummarise dialogue box appears.

2.  You will see four choices for the display of your summary. They are:
    *   Highlight key points
    *   Insert an executive summary or abstract at the top of the document
    *   Create a new document and put the summary there
    *   Hide everything but the summary without leaving the original document

3.  Select the choice you want and click **OK**. Word creates the summary.

4.  In the Percent of original box, type or select the level of detail to include in the summary.

5.  To cancel a summary in progress, press **Esc**.

**TIP**

In the initial stages, before you have edited and finalised the summary, it is recommended that you insert the summary at the top (or beginning) of the document so that you can scroll back and forth from the document to the summary and make any changes that you want.

Once you have created the executive summary or abstract, it is a good idea to review the summary to make sure it covers your document's key points. If it does not, click Undo to delete the summary, and then repeat the previous procedure and choose a higher percentage of the original document.

You can also modify the summary yourself. Keep in mind that the summary text is a "rough draft" and you will probably have to fine-tune it.

# Troubleshooting AutoSummarise

Automatic summarising is not an exact science. After you have produced a summary automatically, you may find that it is not what you expected. We discuss some of the common problems you may run into and their solutions.

### The Automatic Summary Does Not Make Sense

The summary may need to be fine-tuned. Depending on the text you summarise, the automatic summary may include everything you need, or it may just serve as a starting point or rough draft that you need to improve. In general, AutoSummarise works best on documents that have a clear, well-defined structure.

Every line of text you summarise may end with a paragraph return. If you try to summarise a list or other document made up of one-line paragraphs (such as an e-mail message), the summary may not include all the relevant points in the document, or it may contain sentences that combine keywords in ways that do not make sense.

Check for extra paragraph marks. If the document contains extra paragraph marks, you may be able to improve the summary by removing them. You can use options in the AutoFormat dialogue box, or options in the Find and Replace dialogue box to remove unwanted paragraph marks and then run AutoSummarise again.

### *The Summary Text and the Highlighted Text Look the Same*

When you select Highlight key points in the AutoSummarise dialogue box, summary text is highlighted in yellow. If other text in your document is highlighted in yellow, that text may appear to be part of the summary.

Although you cannot change the colour used to highlight summary text, you can remove yellow highlighting from the original text in the document or use a different highlight colour to remove the confusion. Select the highlighted text, and click the **arrow** ▼ next to Highlight. Click **None** to remove highlighting, or click a colour other than yellow. *See Fig 11.05.*

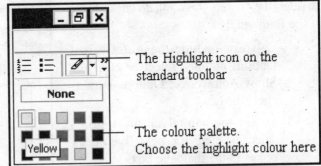

*Fig 11.05 Highlight Icon on Standard Tool Bar and Colour Palette*

# AutoCorrect and Spelling Check

One of the major drudgeries in life is to have to check for spelling and grammar errors in the document that you produce. A short memo or fax may require little time to edit and remove errors manually. However, if your document is several pages long, the editing may become tedious.

Apart from fatigue, the longer you have to check your document word by word, the greater is the chance that some error will slip through. Recognising this, Word has provided several powerful ways to electronically edit your document and minimise the risk of errors getting through.

A very handy feature for automatic correction of common spelling errors is to use Word's AutoCorrect feature. We discuss this feature and then look at other techniques for spelling and grammar check.

## Using AutoCorrect

We have just seen how you can configure Word so that the spelling and grammatical errors are displayed as you type. You have to correct the errors manually. However, Word has another feature that corrects errors automatically as you type. This is the AutoCorrect feature which will automatically detect and correct typos, misspelled words, grammatical errors, and incorrect capitalisation. For example, if you type "teh" plus a space, then AutoCorrect replaces what you have typed with "the". You can also use AutoCorrect to quickly insert text, graphics, or symbols. For example, type (c) to insert ©, or type ac to insert *Acme Corporation*.

## Setting AutoCorrect Options

Before you use AutoCorrect, you must make sure that the required correction options are turned on and the unnecessary options are turned off. Since AutoCorrect will automatically correct what you are typing without warning you, you must be certain that the appropriate options have been set to avoid unexpected results. Here is how you set the options:

Click Tools on the menu bar and click AutoCorrect Options on the drop-down menu. The AutoCorrect dialogue box opens showing the language in use (usually US English) to which AutoCorrect is currently set. *See Fig 11.06.*

To select the options you want, do one or more of the following:

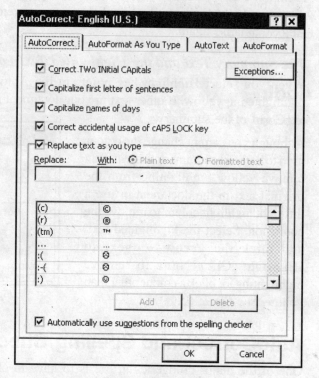

Fig 11.06 AutoCorrect Dialogue Box

- To show or hide the AutoCorrect Options buttons, select or clear the Show AutoCorrect Options buttons check box.

- To set the capitalisation options, select or clear the next five check boxes in the dialogue box.

- To turn on or off the AutoCorrect entries, select or clear the Replace text as you type check box.

- To turn on or off the spelling checker corrections, select the Replace text as you type check box, and then select or clear the Automatically use suggestions from the spelling checker check box.

**TIP**

If you are using the spelling checker corrections, make sure that you turn on automatic spell checking.

You can undo a correction or turn AutoCorrect options on or off by clicking an option on the AutoCorrect Options button. The button first appears as a small, blue box when you rest the mouse pointer near text that is automatically corrected, and it changes to a button icon when you point to it.

## Using AutoCorrect to Correct Errors as You Type

As we have just discussed in Chapter 10, *Managing Long Documents*, first set the AutoCorrect options you need. In particular, make sure that the following options are set the way you want them:

- **Capitalisation options**: For example, AutoCorrect can capitalise the first word in a sentence or the names of days of the week.

- **AutoCorrect entries**: AutoCorrect can use a list of built-in corrections, called AutoCorrect entries, to detect and correct typos, misspelled words, grammatical errors, and common symbols. You can easily add your own AutoCorrect entries or remove unwanted ones.

- **Spelling checker corrections**: For enhanced spelling correction, AutoCorrect can use corrections that are generated by the spelling checker's main dictionary (in addition to the built-in list of spelling corrections).

Once you have set the AutoCorrect options, type the text that you want to correct, followed by a space or other punctuation.

# Adding or Editing AutoCorrect Entries

AutoCorrect comes with a list of built-in entries that are used for correcting your typing. However, you may want to add to the AutoCorrect entries, or edit some of the existing ones. Word provides a quick way to add entries during a spelling check.

### *Add an AutoCorrect Entry*

To add to the built-in AutoCorrect entries, you may wish to first identify the common typing errors that you make. For instance, you may often type "teh" for "the". To catch your typos, do the following:

1. Open a document in Word which is typical of what you type regularly such as a memo, a fax or a monthly report. Locate your mouse pointer at the **beginning** of the text.

2. Click **Tools** on the menu bar and then click **Spelling and Grammar** on the drop-down menu.

3. When a word you often misspell or mistype is identified, right click on the **misspelled (red underlined) word**. A pop-up menu appears.

4. Click the **AutoCorrect** option. A sub-menu appears with the correct spelling.

5. Select the **correct spelling**. AutoCorrect adds the misspelling and the correct spelling to its built-in list.

The next time you type, AutoCorrect will correct the typo automatically. *See Fig 11.07.*

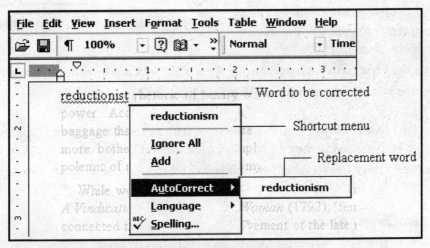

*Fig 11.07 Adding an Entry in AutoCorrect*

### Edit an AutoCorrect Entry

To edit an AutoCorrect entry, open the AutoCorrect dialogue box as explained earlier in this section. Now proceed as follows:

1. In the scrollable pane below the captions *Replace*: and *With*:, select the **item** you wish to modify. The item will appear in the edit box above this pane.
2. Type in the **change** in the *With:* part of the edit box.
3. Click the **Replace** button and then click **OK**.

See Fig 11.01 for a view of the AutoCorrect dialogue box that contains the edit box and scrolling pane described here.

You can also type new entries into AutoCorrect by typing the wrong spelling under *Replace* and the correct spelling under *With* to add a new entry.

### Preventing AutoCorrect from Making Specific Corrections

There are several conventions that AutoCorrect will follow in its default setting. For instance, it will capitalise the first letter of a word that follows a period (.). However, you may want AutoCorrect to make exceptions to suit your typing style. For example, you may want to prevent AutoCorrect from capitalising a word that you type after the abbreviation "info.".

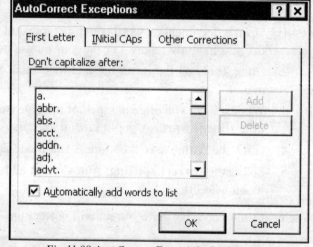

Fig 11.08 AutoCorrect Exceptions Dialogue Box

To change the default settings in AutoCorrect, follow these steps:

1. Open the AutoCorrect dialogue box as explained in the previous section.
2. Click the **Exceptions** button. The AutoCorrect Exceptions dialogue box opens. *See Fig 11.08.*
3. Select the **First Letter** tab to enter the word after which you do not want capitalisation.
4. Enter the word you want (such as "info.") in the edit box under the caption Don't capitalise after:.
5. Select the **INitial CAps** tab to enter the word with more than one initial capitals you do not want to be corrected in the edit box under the caption Don't correct:.
6. Select the **Other Corrections** tab to enter any other special words with a non-conventional spelling that you do not want automatically corrected.

### Delete an AutoCorrect Entry

For any reason, if you wish to remove any AutoCorrect entry, proceed as follows:

1. Open theAutoCorrect dialogue box as explained in the previous section.

2. In the scrollable list under the Replace box, click the **entry** you want to remove.

3. Click **Delete**.

# Spelling and Grammar Check

Microsoft Word provides several ways to check spelling and grammar. We look at the key points of some options in this section.

To correct spelling and grammatical errors without having to confirm each correction, you can use the AutoCorrect feature as we have just discussed in the previous section. For example, if you type "definitly" and then type a space or other punctuation, AutoCorrect replaces it with "definitely".

However, you may prefer to be shown the errors (usually by a wavy line below the misspelled word) rather than leave the correction in the hands of AutoCorrect. You may also wish to prepare the first draft of your document without interference from AutoCorrect and check and correct spellings only after your draft has been edited and refined.

You can still use Word's capability for automatic spelling and grammar check without auto-correction. We discuss these techniques in the following sections.

## *Automatically Check Spelling and Grammar as You Type*

Use automatic spelling and grammar checking to have Word check for these errors automatically and in the background. As you type, the spelling and grammar checkers check the text, and then mark possible errors with wavy underlines. To correct an error, right click on the underlined word. A shortcut menu is displayed. You can either select the suggested correct spelling, or, if it is a proper name, add it to the dictionary.

If you find the wavy underlines distracting, you can temporarily hide the underlines until you're ready to make corrections. To do so, proceed as follows:

1. Click **Tools** on the menu bar and then click **Options** on the drop-down menu. The Options dialogue box opens. *See Fig 11.09.*

2. Click the **Spelling and Grammar** tab of the dialogue box. The tab is revealed.

3. Under Spelling, make sure that the checkbox **Check spelling as you type** is selected. Similarly, under Grammar, make sure that **Check spelling as you type** is selected.

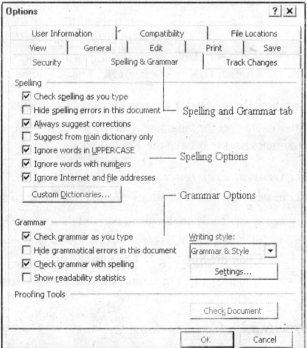

*Fig 11.09 Spelling and Grammar Tab*

4. Clear the checkboxes **Hide spelling errors in this document** under Spelling and **Hide grammatical errors in this document** under Grammar. Word will track the errors but will not display the wavy lines.

5. When you are ready to edit your document, you can follow steps 1 to 4 and check these two checkboxes to reveal the errors for your correction.

# Customising Spelling and Grammar Check

### *The Default Language*

Although Word comes with a set of default options set for spelling and grammar checking, you may want to reset some of the options. It is important to remember that the default language for Word (or any other application of the Office suit) is US English, different from UK English that we normally use in India. It is important that both the Windows and Office languages are set for UK English to avoid annoying corrections to the spellings, such as "customize" instead of the more familiar "customise".

Proceed as follows to set the language:

1. Click **Tools** on the menu bar and then click **Language** ➜ **Set Language** on the pop-up menu and sub-menu that appear. The Language dialogue box opens. *See Fig 11.10.*

2. In the scrollable pane, scroll down to select **English (UK)** and click **OK**. The language is selected.

*Fig 11.10 Language Dialogue Box*

## Set Spelling and Grammar Preferences

After having set the language, you can proceed with setting options that will make the spelling and grammar checker behave the way you want.

### *Set General Preferences*

Begin with the general settings. Do the following to set general preferences:

1. Click **Tools** on the menu bar and then click **Options** on the drop-down menu. The Options dialogue box appears.

2. Click the **Spelling & Grammar** tab.

3. Under Spelling or Grammar, select the options you want. See Fig 11.09 for a view of the Spelling and Grammar tab.

### *Specify a Preferred Spelling*

You may wish to specify a particular spelling for some technical words or proper names. To do so, you can add variations of the word's spelling to the exclude dictionary. Proceed as follows:

1. Click **File** ➔ **New** on the menu bar and the drop-down menu that appears. A blank document opens in the Word window.

2. Type the words you want to include in the exclude dictionary. Press **Enter** after each word.

3. On the File menu, click **Save As**.

4. Locate the folder to save the exclude dictionary in. The location varies depending on your version of Windows. It is usually:

   "C:\Windows_folder\Profiles\User_name\ApplicationData\Microsoft\Proof_folder" for Windows Millennium Edition (Me). The location must be the same as for the main dictionary.

5. In the Save As type box, click **Plain Text**.

6. In the Filename box, type a **name** for the exclude dictionary.

7. Click **Save**.

8. In the File Conversion dialogue box that appears, select the **options** you want, and then click **OK**.

9. On the File menu, click **Close**.

The exclude dictionary that you have just created will come into effect only after you shut down and restart Word. Check the location of the main dictionary beforehand to make sure that both dictionaries are in the same directory.

**NOTE** If you have Windows 98, then save in the "C:\Windows_folder\Application Data\Microsoft\Proof_folder". You can also save the exclude dictionary in the folder: "C:\Windows_folder\Profiles\User_name\ApplicationData\Microsoft\Proof_folder", all depending on where your main dictionary is located.

Make sure to give the exclude dictionary the same name as the main language dictionary it is associated with. However, the filename extension must be ".exc." For example, the English (United States) dictionary is called Mssp3en.lex, so name the associated exclude dictionary Mssp3en.exc.

## Skip Text During a Spelling and Grammar Check

If your document contains a quotation or a passage in another language, you may not want Word to check this text as you will get many unwanted error messages. Proceed as follows to exclude the other language text during spelling check:

1. Select the **text** that you do not want to check.

2. Click **Tools** on the menu bar and click **Language** ➔ **Set Language** on the drop-down menu and sub-menu. The Language dialogue box appears. See Fig 11.10 for a view of the Language Dialogue box.

3. Select the **Do not check spelling or grammar** check box.

4. Click **OK** to close the dialogue box and return to the document. The selected text will not be checked during the spelling and grammar check.

## *Select a Grammar and Writing Style*

Just as Word comes with a default language [English (US)], Word also comes ready with a default grammar and writing style. Some of the style options may not suit you. For instance, Word may keep underlining all sentences that you write in the passive voice. You can alter the style as follows:

1. Click **Tools** on the menu bar and then click **Options** on the drop-down menu. The Options dialogue box opens. Click the **Spelling and Grammar** tab. The tab opens. *See Fig 11.09.*

2. In the Writing Style box, select whether you want to check grammar and style, or grammar only.

3. Click the **Settings** button under the section captioned *Grammar*. The Grammar Settings dialogue box opens. *See Fig 11.11.*

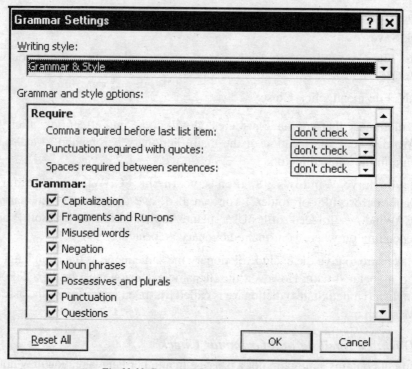

*Fig 11.11 Grammar Settings Dialogue Box*

4. In the Grammar Settings dialogue box, do one or both of the following:

   - Under **Require**, select the options you want for serial commas, punctuation within quotation marks, and number of spaces between sentences.

   - Under **Grammar and Style**, select or clear the check boxes next to the rules you want the grammar checker to check or ignore.

To restore the original rules of the selected grammar and writing style, click **Reset All.**

## *Turn On or Off Automatic Spelling and Grammar Checking*

Many users do not like to be distracted by Word's spelling or grammar checking that keeps underlining words or sentences by wavy underlines. Instead, they prefer to concentrate on the composition and run the spelling and grammar check only after the document has been drafted to their satisfaction. You may also prefer to shut the checking off and switch it on later. To turn checking on or off, do the following:

1. Click **Tools** on the menu bar and click **Options** on the drop-down menu. The Options dialogue box appears.

2. Click the **Spelling & Grammar** tab. The Spelling and Grammar tab opens. *See Fig 11.09.*

3. Do one or more of the following:
   - To turn on or off automatic spelling checking, select or clear the **Check spelling as you type** check box.
   - To turn on or off automatic grammar checking, select or clear the **Check grammar as you type** check box.

 **NOTE** When you turn on automatic spelling and grammar checking, Microsoft Word clears the **Hide spelling errors in this document** and **Hide grammatical errors in this document** check boxes. This enables the spelling and grammar checkers to mark possible errors with wavy underlines. If you find the wavy underlines distracting, you can **select** these check boxes to suppress the underlines.

## Look Up Words in the Thesaurus

To improve your writing, you may often look for words with similar meanings called synonyms. You may also want a word with the exactly opposite meaning to another word, called an antonym. Similar words help you to avoid using the same word again and again, whereas words with opposite meanings enrich the vocabulary you use. To look for synonyms and antonyms, you require a thesaurus. Word has a built-in thesaurus. To start it, proceed as follows:

1. Select or type a word in your open Word document for which you want to find a synonym, an antonym, or related words.

2. Click **Tools** on the menu bar and then click **Language →  Thesaurus** on the drop-down menu and sub-menu that appear. The Thesaurus dialogue box opens. The current language setting is shown on the dialogue boxes title bar.

3. The meaning of the selected word appears in the text box captioned *Meanings* and the synonyms appear in the right pane under the caption *Replace with Synonym.*

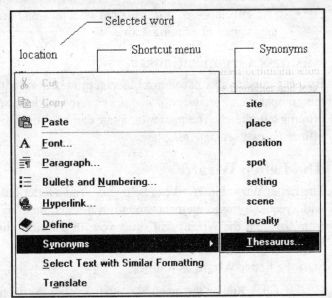

*Fig 11.12 Selecting Synonyms from Shortcut Menu*

4.  Select the synonym you want and click the **Replace** button. The original word is replaced by the synonym you have selected.

If you are mainly concerned with common synonyms for a word, you can find these by a quicker method, using the shortcut menu. To do so, proceed as follows:

1.  Right click the **word** for which you want a synonym. The shortcut menu appears. *See Fig 11.12.*
2.  Click on **Synonyms** on the shortcut menu, a pop-up menu appears with available synonyms.
3.  Click the **synonym** you want. The original word is replaced by the selected synonym.

## Automating Your Correspondence

In this chapter, we have begun by concentrating on efficiency and productivity. We now examine ways and means for extending these concepts to correspondence that you can handle using Word 2000. If you work in a business establishment, you will find that automating letters is the single biggest way to cut down time and raise efficiency. To automate letters, memos and faxes, you have to design a good system first. Here are some guidelines.

## Individuals and Home Offices

Use Word's letter Wizard or the three built-in templates to design your personal or home office letterhead. If you want to design your own letterhead, here are a few tips:

*   Use a simple and uncluttered design. Use the WordArt feature to design the company name or company logo.
*   For printing use a LaserJet printer. Inkjet, bubble jet and dot matrix printers will not give your letterhead the professional look it deserves.
*   Use envelopes with transparent windows and pre-printed return address. It will save you the trouble of printing addresses.

## Business Organisations

By using good quality paper on a LaserJet printer along with a specially designed letterhead template, the company can produce all business correspondence on plain paper and save the cost of pre-printing letterheads. The master template can be altered to incorporate addresses of head and branch offices on two separate templates.

## The Letter Wizard

The Letter Wizard in Word can help you write a letter quickly and easily. The Wizard provides you with frequently used elements found in a letter, such as salutations and closings. You can select from lists that the Wizard will show you. In addition, the Wizard helps you structure your letters based on built-in, popular letter styles.

Start the Letter Wizard as follows:

1.  Click **File** on the menu bar and then click **New** on the drop-down menu. The New dialogue box opens. See Fig 08.10 earlier in this book for a view of the New dialogue box.

2. Click the **Letters & Faxes** tab, and then double click the **Letter Wizard icon**. An outline letter and a small Letter Wizard dialogue box opens. *See Fig 11.13.*

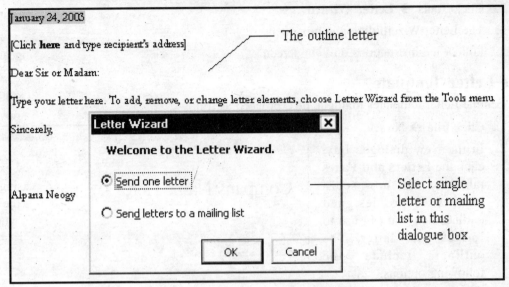

*Fig 11.13 Outline and Letter Wizard Dialogue Box*

3. Select if you want to send a single letter or send to a mailing list. Select the **single letter option** for this example and click **OK**. The first step of the Letter Wizard opens. *See Fig 11.14.* Follow the instructions in the Letter Wizard.

4. You will be taken through 4 steps to help you complete the letter. The steps are:

   - Selecting a letter format
   - Entering recipient information
   - Inserting other elements
   - Entering sender information

5. If you want to skip a step or go to a specific step, click the appropriate tab.

6. Click **Finish** after you have used the steps you want. The Letter Wizard will close leaving you with the outline of your letter in which, between "Dear Sir or Madam" and "Sincerely" you can type the body of your letter.

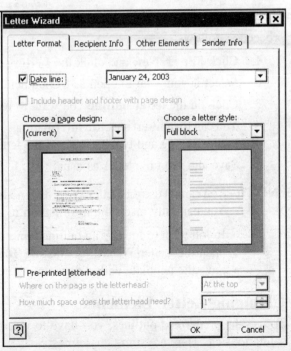

*Fig 11.14 Letter Wizard*

You can also modify or complete an existing letter. To do so, follow these steps:

1. Open the letter in Word.
2. Click **Tools** ➜ **Letter Wizard**.
3. The Letter Wizard dialogue box opens.
4. Follow the instructions on your screen.

## The Letter Template

To open the Letter templates dialogue box, proceed as follows:

1. Click **File** ➜ **New**.
2. In the New dialogue box, click the **Letters and Faxes** tab. You will now see a number of pre-designed outlines that you can use to format your letter. The outlines include the following options:

   - Contemporary letter. *See Fig 11.15.*
   - Elegant letter.
   - Professional letter.

Fig 11.15 Outline of Contemporary Letter

To use any one of these outlines, proceed as follows:

1. Click **File** ➜ **New** and click the **Letters and Faxes** tab.
2. Select if you want to open as a document or template.
3. Click on the **letter outline** you want to use.
4. You can then insert specific information such as name, address, return address etc as guided by the outline and type the text of the letter to complete it.
5. Save and print the letter as usual.

**NOTE** You cannot use the Letter Wizard to modify an outline that you have opened as a document. You can only insert the information requested and type the text.

If you wish to modify an outline template, open the outline as a template. Now you can open the Letter Wizard by clicking **Tools** ➜ **Letter Wizard** and modify the template. Save the template with a different name such as *My Contemporary Letter*.

## Changing Letter Elements

To use the predefined outlines, you have to insert or change several elements such as addresses, salutations etc. Here are some guidelines:

- To change elements such as the addressee or salutation in an individual letter, the simplest thing to do is to type the new element over the old one.

- To use some elements over and over in your letters, use the Letter Wizard which comes with many standard letter elements, such as the salutation or closing stored as AutoText entries. These can be quickly inserted or changed in your letter.

- As you modify a letter that you have created using the Letter Wizard, you can change names and text in standard letter elements by right clicking the element and then selecting a different entry from the list that appears.

- To add a new entry to the list, select the letter element in the document and type the text you want. Then, right click the letter element and click Create AutoText. To quickly see which letter elements you can change, display fields with a grey background.

## Office Assistant

If you start a new document with a salutation such as "Dear Sir," and the Office Assistant is turned on, it will appear and offer to help you with the letter. See Fig 07.09 and read about Office Assistant in Chapter 7, *Introduction to Microsoft Office*, earlier in this book. If you accept help by clicking on the option that reads **Get help with writing the letter**, the Office Assistant launches the Letter Wizard and guides you through the steps of the Letter Wizard. See Letter Wizard earlier in this section for more information.

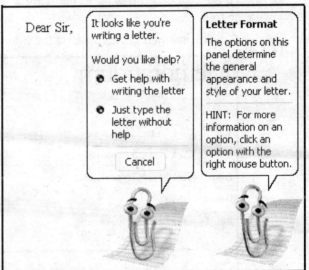

*Fig 11.16 Office Assistant*

## Create a Document Template

While the Letter Wizard is useful for drafting letters by individuals, for an organisation you may want to set up standard in-house templates that can be used by all personnel companywide.

A great deal of time can be saved and uniformity achieved by designing such standard document templates such as templates for reports, internal memos, faxes and standard letters to be used companywide. A Memo template is shown in Fig 11.17.

To prepare a document template, proceed as follows:

1. Do one of the following:
   - To base a new template on an existing document, click **File ➔ Open** in the menu bar, and then open the document you want.
   - To base a new template on an existing template, click **New** on the File menu. The **New** dialogue box opens. Click the Office 2000 Templates tab. You will see a number of built-in Word document templates. Select a template nearest to the one you want. You can

see how the template will look in the preview pane. Click Template under the caption *Create New:* and click **OK**.

2. On the File menu, click **Save As**.

3. In the Save As type box, click **Document** Template. This file type will already be selected if you are saving a file that you created as a template. The default folder is the Templates folder in the Save in box. If you want this newly created template to appear in some other subfolder rather than the General folder, switch to the corresponding subfolder within the Templates folder before saving.

4. In the File name box, type a **name** for the new template.

5. In the new template, add the text and graphics you want to appear in all new documents that you base on the template, and delete any items you do not want.

6. Make the changes you want to the margin settings, page size and orientation, styles, and other formats.

7. Click **Save** and then click **Close** on the File menu.

---

# Memorandum

**To:**      [Click **here** and type name]

**CC:**      [Click **here** and type name]

**From:**  [Click **here** and type name]

**Date:**   1/24/2003

**Re:**      [Click **here** and type subject]

---

**How to Use This Memo Template**
Select text you would like to replace, and type your memo. Use styles such as Heading 1-3 and Body Text in the Style control on the Formatting toolbar.

To delete the background elements—such as the circle, rectangles, or return address frames, click on the boundary border to highlight the "handles," and press Delete. To replace the picture in this template with a different one, first click on the picture. Then, on the Insert menu, point to Picture, and click From File. Locate the folder that contains the picture you want to insert, then double-click the picture.

To save changes to this template for future use, choose Save As from the File menu. In the Save As Type box, choose Document Template. Next time you want to use it, choose New from the File menu, and then double-click your template.

---

*Fig 11.17 Sample Memo Template*

## Addressing Correspondence

Entering names and addresses in letters can take a lot of time. In addition, there is always the chance that something is omitted or misspelled. Much of this exercise can be automated by configuring Word so that the Address Book, which is one of the built-in features of Office 2000, can be accessed from within Word.

Once you have done so, you will be able to import the recipient's names and addresses from the Address Book directly into your letters, envelopes and mailing labels.

To be able to open the Address Book easily while working with Word, you will need to insert a special button on the standard tool bar. Here is the procedure to add this button:

1. Right click any empty space on the Standard tool bar and click **Customise** on the shortcut menu that appears.

2. On the Customise dialogue box that appears, click on the **Commands** tab. *See Fig 11.18.*

3. Select **Insert** from the Categories list and then scroll through the Commands list till you find the Address Book item.

4. Drag the Address Book item from the Commands list to the Standard tool bar.

5. Click the **Close** button to close the Customise dialogue box and close your document.

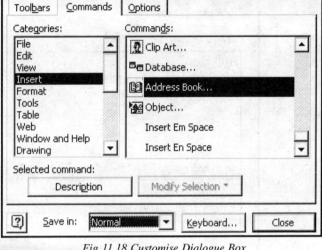

*Fig 11.18 Customise Dialogue Box*

6. If you are prompted to save the changes to the Normal template, say **Yes**.

The Insert Address tool bar button will now appear on your Standard tool bar. Now that you have created an Insert Address button, you can insert the recipient's names and addresses from a number of sources by using this button as we explain in the next section.

## Electronic Address Books

You can insert addresses from the following electronic address books: a Microsoft Outlook Address Book or Contact List, or the Personal Address Book.

To use the Insert Address button to insert an address onto an envelope or mailing labels, follow this procedure:

1. Click **Tools** on the menu bar and then click **Envelopes and Labels** in the drop-down menu. The Envelopes and Labels dialogue box appears. *See Fig 11.19.*

2. Click the **Envelopes or Labels** tab.

3. Click the **Insert Address** button. The Select Name dialogue box appears.

4. If you have more than one source (such as Outlook and Personal Address Book) then in the Show Names from the box, click the **address book** or **contact list** you want.

5. In the Type name or select from list box, enter a **name**. Or click **a name in the list** and click **OK**. The name and address is transferred to the Envelopes and Labels dialogue box.

**TIP** To quickly insert an address you have used recently, you can click the down arrow ▼ next to the Insert Address button. A drop-down list will display all the names you have in your Address Book. Click the name you want and it will be transferred to the Envelopes and Labels dialogue box.

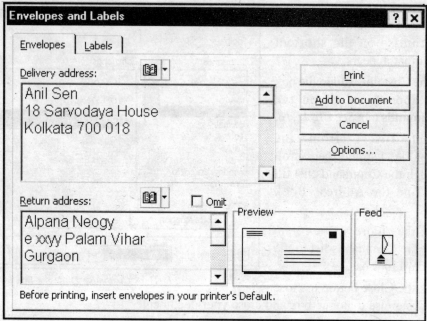

*Fig 11.19 Envelopes and Labels Dialogue Box*

## Printing Envelopes

To create and print a mailing envelope in Word, proceed as follows:

1. Click **Tools** on the menu bar and then click **Envelopes and Labels** on the drop-down menu. The Envelopes and Labels dialogue box appears. *See Fig 11.19.*

2. Click the **Envelopes** tab.

3. In the Delivery address box, do one of the following:

   • Enter or edit the **mailing address**.

   • Insert a mailing address from an electronic address book.

4. In the Return address box, you can accept the default return address or do one of the following:

   • Enter or edit the return address.

   • Insert a return address from an electronic address book.

   • Omit a return address by selecting the Omit check box.

5. To select an envelope size, the type of paper feed, and other options, click **Options**. The Envelope Options dialogue box appears. *See Fig 11.20.* Select options such as envelope size and the font to be used for the addresses.

6.  Click **OK** when done. You are returned to the Envelopes and Labels dialogue box.

7.  In the Envelopes and Labels dialogue box, do one of the following:

    *   To print the envelope now, insert an envelope in the printer as shown in the Feed box, and then click **Print**.

    *   To attach the envelope to the current document for later editing or printing, click **Add To Document**.

**NOTE**

If you wish to print immediately, you must make sure that your printer is turned on, connected to the computer and printing paper has been inserted. If you want to print later, add it to the document as described above. The envelope settings will be saved along with the letter or document.

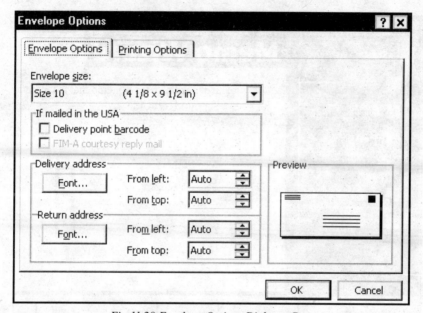

*Fig 11.20 Envelope Options Dialogue Box*

## Memos and Faxes

As we have seen in the case of letters, a quick and simple way to create memos and faxes in Word is to use Wizards. Not only will the Wizard help you put together a professional looking memo or fax, but you can also use the Insert Address button to insert names and addresses in memos and names and fax numbers in a fax.

The alternative to the use of the Wizard is to customise a template for your memo or fax. The advantage in customising a template is that you can incorporate your company's logo and create unique and distinctive templates. However, Word's templates are designed by professional graphic artists and it is not easy to produce attractive templates on your own. In addition, the Wizards are much easier to use. For individuals and small offices, therefore, the Wizard will be the preferred choice. We discuss the memo Wizard and the fax cover page Wizard in the following sections.

# The Memo Wizard

### *Create a Memo*

To create a memo automatically, you can use the Memo Wizard in Word. The very first time you use the Wizard, you will be asked to fill in some personal details. Word will remember the information so that you will not have to enter it again when you use the Memo Wizard in the future.

To start the Memo Wizard, follow these steps:

1. On the File menu, click **New**. The New dialogue box opens.
2. Click the **Memos** tab. You will see the Memo Wizard icon along with three icons for predefined memo templates.
3. Double click the **Memo Wizard icon**. The Memo Wizard appears. *See Fig 11.21.*

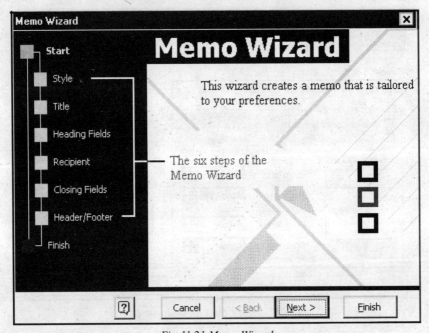

*Fig 11.21 Memo Wizard*

4. Follow the 6 steps of the Memo Wizard. The steps are briefly described below:
   - **Style:** Choose from Professional, Contemporary or Elegant.
   - **Title:** Accept the default or form your own title.
   - **Heading Fields:** Insert headings such as Date, From, Subject and Priority.
   - **Recipient:** Type the recipient's name and address. You can also insert this from your Address Book by clicking the Insert Address button.
   - **Closing Fields:** Insert Writer's initials, Typist's initials, Enclosures and Attachments.
   - **Header/Footer:** Insert header and footer information.

5. When you have completed the steps you need, click Finish. The Memo Wizard displays the outline document on your monitor's screen. *See Fig 11.22.*

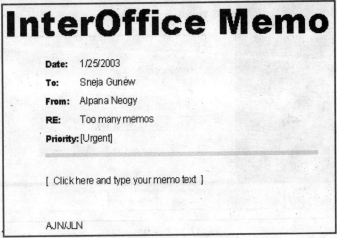

# InterOffice Memo

**Date:**  1/25/2003

**To:**  Sneja Gunew

**From:**  Alpana Neogy

**RE:**  Too many memos

**Priority:** [Urgent]

[ Click here and type your memo text ]

AJN/JLN

*Fig 11.22 Memo Wizard Output*

**NOTE**  You can skip any step you do not need by clicking on the next step's button on the Memo Wizard. To skip all click **Finish**.

You can use the Memo Wizard to send the memo by e-mail or fax. However, to do so, your computer must support these services and be configured to send items by e-mail or fax.

# Sending a Fax

We have already discussed sending faxes in Chapter 6, *Internet Telephony and Computer Fax*, on e-mails and faxes. However, you can send faxes directly from Word using your fax capable modem even if you do not have separate fax software such as WinFax Pro installed in your computer. Although not as versatile, powerful or reliable as WinFax, the Fax Wizard in Word can handle most of your routine faxes without having to launch special fax software.

## Using the Fax Wizard

To create and send a fax with the Fax Wizard, follow these steps:

1. On the File menu, click **New**. The New dialogue box opens.
2. Click the **Letters and Faxes** tab. You will see the fax icon amongst the set of icons.
3. Double click the **Fax Wizard icon**. The Fax Wizard appears. *See Fig 11.23.*
4. Follow the 5 steps shown in the Wizard. The steps are briefly summarised below:
   - **Document to fax:** Select the document, with or without a cover sheet. If the fax is very short, you may select just the cover sheet with a note and insert the text in the note.
   - **Fax software:** Select the fax software you want to use. Since you have Office 2000 installed, you may wish to use the Symantec Fax Starter Edition that comes with the Office 2000 suit.

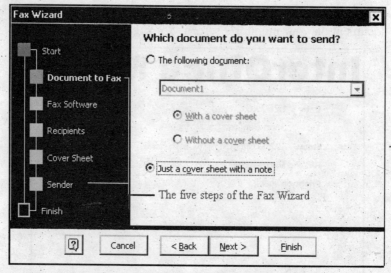

*Fig 11.23 Fax Wizard*

- **Recipients:** Select recipients and their fax numbers. You can use the Insert Address button for this step.

- **Cover sheet:** Select a cover sheet design. Choose from Professional, Contemporary and Elegant.

- **Sender:** Furnish sender's name and other details.

5. When you have completed the steps you need, click **Finish**. The Fax Wizard displays the outline fax on your monitor's screen. *See Fig 11.24.*

NEOSOFT SOFTWARE

Fax Wizard ☒
**Send Fax Now**

**FACSIMILE TRANSMITTAL SHEET**

| TO: | FROM: |
|---|---|
| Sneja Gunew | Alpana Neogy |

| FAX NUMBER: | DATE: |
|---|---|
| 01 234 5678 | January 25, 2003 |

| COMPANY: | TOTAL NO OF PAGES INCLUDING COVER: |
|---|---|
| [Click here and type company name] | [Click here and type number of pages] |

| PHONE NUMBER: | SENDER'S REFERENCE NUMBER: |
|---|---|
| [Click here and type phone number] | [Click here and type reference number] |

| RE: | YOUR REFERENCE NUMBER: |
|---|---|
| [Click here and type subject of fax] | [Click here and type reference number] |

☐ URGENT ☐ FOR REVIEW ☐ PLEASE COMMENT ☐ PLEASE REPLY ☐ PLEASE RECYCLE

NOTES/COMMENTS:
[Click here and type any comments]

*Fig 11.24 Fax Wizard Output*

6.  After you have inserted the text and made any other changes you want, click the **Send Fax Now** button to start fax transmission.

Your computer must be equipped to send faxes. The primary requirements are that:

-  You have fax capable modem.
-  You are connected to a telephone line with STD and ISD facilities if you want to send you faxes to other cities or abroad.
-  You must have appropriate fax software such as Microsoft Fax that comes with Windows 98, Symantec Fax (Starter Edition) that comes with Office 2000 or stand-alone fax software such as WinFax Pro. The software should be installed and configured.

# Mail Merge Techniques

We have discussed e-mails in Chapter 5, *E-mails and Chat*, earlier in this book and fax in Chapter 6, *Internet Telephony and Computer Fax*. Both provide you with means of fast and efficient communication. In both cases, however, the recipient must have the capability to receive e-mails or faxes. If not, you have to fall back on the mail. There are also some situations where you have to reach a large number of recipients through the mail. For example, if you manage a club or a business, you need to correspond with members or customers on a regular basis. While it is possible to create a standard circular and mail it to all concerned, it is more attractive if you could personalise the message so that each recipient feels that the mail is specially designed for him or her. The mail merge facility of Word allows you to do just that.

## Simple Mail Merge

A mail merge operation consists of three steps. These are:

-  Select an existing document or create a main document or a form letter that you want to send.
-  Create a new data source (a mailing list) or open an existing data source that contains the names and addresses of the recipients you wish to send the form letter to.
-  Merge the main document with the data source to create individual form letters, one for each of the recipients.

The data source provides the field names (such as names, addresses and so on) that are inserted in the merge fields positioned on the main document. During the mail merge, you will move back and forth between the data source and the main document to do this.

You can use mail merge to create the letter, mailing labels or mailing envelopes. The labels and envelopes pick up information from the data source.

To assist you in mail merge, Word has a built-in feature called a Mail Merge Helper. We take a look at the helper in the following section.

See Fig 11.25 for an explanation of Mail Merge fundamentals. Note how the main document has merge fields in which information from the data source is inserted to create the merged form letter and the mailing envelopes.

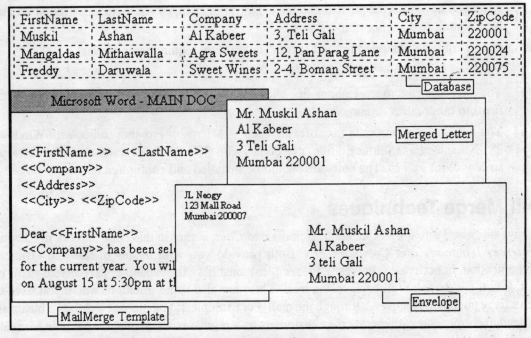

*Fig 11.25 Mail Merge Fundamentals*

# The Mail Merge Helper

To carry out the mail merge process as we have just discussed, you can use a feature in Word called the Mail Merge Helper. To open the helper, click **Tools** on the menu bar and click **Mail Merge** on the drop-down menu. We go through the steps for using the helper one by one.

## Step 1: Create a Form Letter

To open an existing main document (or form letter) or to create a new main document, proceed as follows:

1. Either open an existing letter or create a new letter to be used as a main document. This is the active document.

2. On the Tools menu, click **Mail Merge**. The Mail Merge Helper appears. *See Fig 11.26.*

3. Under Main document, click **Create**, and then click **Form Letters**.

4. Click **Active Window**. The active document becomes the main document.

In Fig 11.27, you can see a portion of a main document. In this view, the merge fields have not been shown. It is an invitation to the members of a study group to attend a talk.

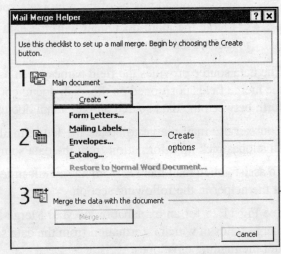

*Fig 11.26 Mail Merge Helper Dialogue Box*

| SPEAKER: | Mr. HARI DANG |
|---|---|
| TOPIC: | EDUCATION: TWENTY FIRST CENTURY |
| DATE: | SATURDAY, 14TH DECEMBER |
| VENUE: | JAIPUR ROOM, CHANCELLOR CLUB |
| PROGRAMME: | 6:00 PM- TEA;   6:30PM- TALK |
| SINGLE: | Rs. 30   COUPLE:  Rs. 50 |

*Fig 11.27 Main Document*

### Step 2: Open or Create Data Source

To open or create a new data source (mailing list) move to step 2 of the Mail Merge Helper. To create a new data source, proceed as follows:

1. In the Mail Merge Helper dialogue box, click on the down arrow ▾ next to Get Data and select Create Data source from the drop-down list. The Create Data Source dialogue box opens. *See Fig 11.28.*

2. Delete the fields from the right pane that you do not need by selecting the field and clicking on the **Remove Field Name button**. In this instance, to keep the example uncluttered, only the following field names have been retained:

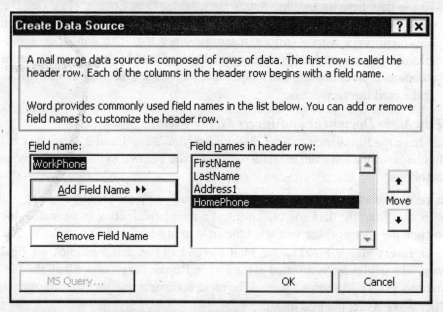

*Fig 11.28 Create Data Source Dialogue Box*

- FirstName
- LastName
- Address1
- HomePhone

Note that you can use a different set of field names to suit your own purpose.

To add field names, type the name in the text box captioned "Field name:" and click the Add Field Name ▸ button below it. *See Fig 11.28.*

3. Click **OK** to open a Word table containing the field names you have just selected. Insert data in the Data Source table as shown in Fig 11.29.

| FirstName | LastName | HouseNumber | HomePhone |
|-----------|----------|-------------|-----------|
| Anjali | Singh | C 1234 | 236 1234 |
| Goutam | Parasar | B 2345 | 236 2345 |
| Anand | Bindra | E 5432 | 236 5432 |
| Bipin | Behari | B 4567 | 236 4567 |

A Data Source Table is created in Word containing the same field names that appear in the main document or form letter. Mail merge will replace each field by picking up data from this table.

*Fig 11.29 Data Source Table*

**NOTE** To use data from an existing data source, under Data Source, click Get Data, and then click Open Data Source. As your data source, you can use either a Microsoft Word document, or a worksheet, database, or other list. The data source must have the information you need for your merge fields separated by some form of delimiter such as a comma or a semicolon. Click Open and then click Edit Main Document to start step 3 of the mail merge process.

### Step 3: Edit Main Document and Insert Merge Fields

You already have the form letter and the mailing list from steps 1 and 2. You must now tell Word where individual information from the data source is to be inserted in the main document. To do so, proceed as follows:

1. In the main document, insert **merge fields** where you want to merge names, addresses, and other data from the data source. To insert a merge field, click in the **main document** and position the cursor where you want the field to appear.
2. Click **Insert Merge Field** on the Mail Merge tool bar, and then click the **field name** you want. The field name is inserted at the cursor. Repeat the process till all the field names are inserted. Fig 11.30 shows a part of the main document and the Mail Merge tool bar.
3. Click **Save As** on the File menu.
4. Name the document, and then click **Save**.

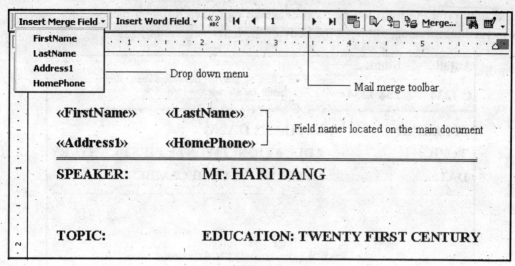

*Fig 11.30 Insert Merge Fields*

## Step 4: Merge the Data

You are now ready to actually merge the data using the Merge dialogue box. To do so, proceed as follows:

1. Click the **Tools icon** in the menu bar and then click **Mail merge** in the drop-down menu. The Merge dialogue box appears. *See Fig 11.31.*

2. To merge only part of the data, select **From:** and **To:** under the caption *Records to be merged*. To select all the records, select **All** instead.

3. Click **Merge** when done. You are returned to the Mail Merge Helper dialogue box.

4. In the Mail Merge Helper dialogue box, click **Merge** under Merge the data with the document.

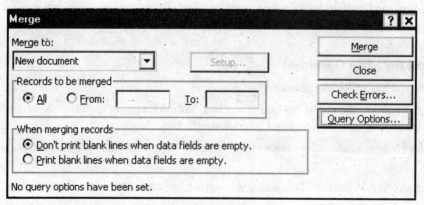

*Fig 11.31 Merge Dialogue Box*

Word creates the individual form letters, each with one set of data from the data source table. See Fig 11.32 showing a portion of a form letter with the merge fields inserted in place.

You can now print the form letters, each of which will have different names, addresses and any other merged information, although the body of the letter will be the same.

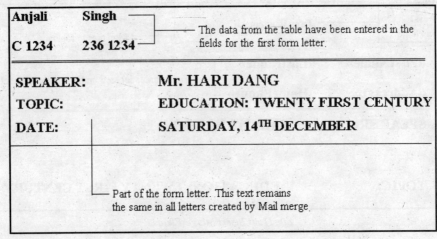

*Fig 11.32 Sample Form Letter*

# Other Mail Merge Tasks

We have just seen how the mail merge technique can create a set of form letters for a list of recipients. In similar ways, you can create and print a set of mailing labels or envelopes carrying the names and addresses from a mailing list.

The basic technique is the same: you combine a mailing list with the sub-programmes that prints mailing labels or prints envelopes. For instance, we list the main steps in creating a set of envelopes for the form letter (main document) and the mailing list (data source) we have already created.

## Create Envelopes

Creating mail merged envelopes is a three-step process, very similar to the process for creating the merged document. The steps are described below.

### Step 1: Select the Main Document

1. Open the main document in Word.
2. Click **Tools** on the menu bar and then click **Mail Merge** on the drop-down menu. The Mail Merge Helper opens. See Fig 11.26 earlier in this chapter.
3. In the Helper, under Main document, click **Create**, and then click **Envelopes** in the drop-down list.
4. Click **Active Window**. The active document becomes the main document.

### Step 2: Open the Data Source

1. In the Mail Merge Helper dialogue box, under Data Source, click **Get Data**, and then click **Open Data Source**.

2. Select the Word table you have already created and then click **Open**. See Fig 11.29, the Data Source table earlier in this chapter.

3. Click **Set Up Main Document**.

**Step 3: Select the Envelope Options and Insert Merge Fields**

1. On the Envelope Options tab, select the **envelope size** you want, and adjust the address format and position on the envelope.

2. On the Printing Options tab, make sure that the selected envelope feed options are appropriate for your printer, and then click **OK**.

3. In the Envelope Address dialogue box, insert merge fields where you want to merge delivery addresses from the data source. To insert a merge field, click **Insert Merge Field**, and then click the **field name** you want. *See Fig 11.33*.

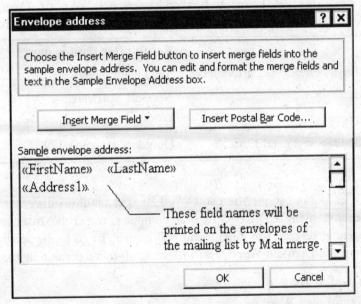

*Fig 11.33 Inserting Merge Fields*

4. Click **OK**.

5. In the Mail Merge Helper dialogue box, under Main document, click **Edit**, and then click the envelope main document. Verify the return address, or delete it if the envelopes have a pre-printed return address.

6. On the Tools menu, click **Mail Merge**.

7. Do one of the following:

   • To send the merged envelopes directly to a printer, click **Printer** in the Merge to box, and then click **Merge**.

   • To store the merged envelopes in a new document, so you can review, edit, and print them later, click **New document**.

## Tips on Inserting Merge Fields

Inserting merge fields in your mail document or in the envelope address box can create a few problems unless you take precautions. Here are some hints and tips to make the job smoother.

- Before you insert merge fields, make sure that you have already set up the main document and selected a data source.

- You must insert merge fields by clicking Insert Merge Field on the Mail Merge tool bar.

- You cannot type the merge field characters « » or insert them by using the Symbol command on the Insert menu.

- To emphasise merged information, you can format the merge fields. For example, you might want to make an address bold or use a different font for a product name.

- To display the merged data correctly, make sure to type spaces and punctuation between the merge fields, outside the merge field characters « ». To place a merge field on a new line, press **Enter** ↵. For example, you can insert the merge fields for an address as follows:

| Merge Fields | Result after data is merged |
|---|---|
| <<Title>> <<FirstName>> <<LastName>> | Mr. Jayant Neogy |
| <<Company>> | NeoSoft Software |
| <<Address1>> | E 9998 Palam Vihar |
| <<City>> <<State>> <<Postal Code>> | Gurgaon, Haryana 122017 |

**CD-ROM**

To learn more about Microsoft Word 2000 in a multimedia environment, insert the accompanying CD-ROM in your computer, select the **Interactive** mode in the opening screen. The main menu will appear. To go to the section on Word, click the button marked **Word**. You will see a sub-menu containing the following topics:

- Getting Started in Word
- Getting Control over Word
- Creating Professional Documents
- Power of Word Unleashed

Click on the third sub-menu item, *Power of Word Unleashed*. Another level of sub-sub-menus is displayed from which you can select the particular topic you want to see. Click on your selected topic and follow instructions on your screen.

# 12. Introducing Excel 2000

*In this chapter:*

☞ You are introduced to Office 2000's worksheet programme, Excel 2000. You learn about workbook and worksheet, the Excel window and modes of operation of Excel with keyboard and mouse.

☞ We show you how to open and navigate a worksheet using the mouse and keyboard and to save and close a worksheet when you are done.

☞ You get hands-on experience in creating a worksheet, to enter labels and data, formulas and functions.

☞ We show you how to edit a worksheet, to change cell content, to switch to the edit mode, to copy and move data, to select cells and to insert and delete.

☞ You learn how to format a worksheet, to format cells, cell contents, to change fonts and to format columns and rows.

☞ We show you how you can preview and print your worksheet.

# Getting to Know Excel

In this chapter we introduce you to the spreadsheet in the Office application suit, Microsoft Excel 2000. You will learn the basics and create a worksheet called Budget.

You can start Excel from the Microsoft Office Shortcut bar. See Fig 07.02 earlier in this book for a view of the shortcut bar. If the shortcut bar is not available, then start Excel by clicking **Start** ➔ **Programmes** ➔ **Microsoft Excel**. A blank spreadsheet appears on your screen.

## Workbook and Worksheet

In Microsoft Excel, a workbook is the file in which you work and store your data. Because each workbook can contain many sheets, you can organise various kinds of related information in a single file. Each workbook will contain one or more worksheets as well as charts and other Excel objects such as macros. See Fig 12.01 for a view of the main components of a worksheet.

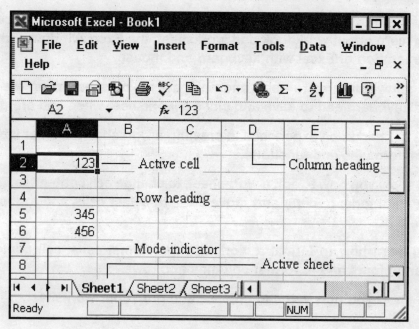

*Fig 12.01 Worksheet Components*

Use worksheets to list and analyse data. You can enter and edit data on several worksheets simultaneously and perform calculations based on data from multiple worksheets. When you create a chart, you can place the chart on the worksheet with its related data or on a separate chart sheet.

The names of the sheets appear on tabs at the bottom of the workbook window. To move from sheet to sheet, click the sheet tabs.

Each spreadsheet is a matrix of rows identified by numbers and columns, identified by letters. Each cell in a worksheet is defined by its address, its row and column. Thus, a cell may be addresses such as (3, B) indicating that it is at the junction of row 3 and column B.

# The Excel Window

To use a worksheet and to move around in it, it is necessary to become familiar with the Excel window. Here are the important elements in a spreadsheet window. See Fig 12.01 earlier in this section.

**Active Cell**: When you click on a cell, it is selected and becomes active. You have to select a cell before you can enter data in it or enter a formula in it. A dark frame called a cell selector appears around the active cell.

**Column and Row Headings**: Usually, the column headings are alphabetical such as A, B, C etc while the row headings are numerical such as 1, 2, 3 etc.

**Sheet Tab**: Although the default names for the sheet tabs are Sheet 1, Sheet 2 etc, you can change the names of the sheet tabs. Click on these tabs to move from one worksheet to the next.

**Tab Scroll Buttons**: These buttons appear as arrows. You can navigate by one sheet at a time or move to the first or the last sheet ⏮ ◀ ▶ ⏭.

**Formula Bar**: The Name list box appears to the left of the Formula bar. If the active cell has a name assigned, the name appears in the Name box. Otherwise, its cell address (row, column) appears here. The contents of the cell are shown on the right side. If the active cell contains a formula, it will be shown here. If the cell has a number, the raw (unformatted) number will appear in the formula bar.

## Modes of Operation

When you open a worksheet, it is in the Ready mode. That is, it is ready to accept data from you. As you begin to enter data, the worksheet changes to the Enter mode. It will go back to the Ready mode after you press the Enter ↵ key or an arrow key to complete the data entry. The spreadsheet will go to the Edit mode when you edit the contents of a cell. For all the menu commands to be available, you must be back in the ready mode. See Fig 12.01 where the worksheet is shown in the Edit mode.

# Navigating a Workbook

We have already seen how you can move from one worksheet to the next by clicking on its tab. To move within a worksheet, you may either use your mouse or the keyboard.

## Using the Mouse

Click on the cell you wish to move to. The cell becomes the active cell. If the cell you want is not visible on your screen, use the window scroll bars to move to the cell and then click to select it.

## Using the Keyboard

To move large distances in a very big worksheet, it is more convenient to use the Go To dialogue box. Display this dialogue box by pressing the **F5** function key on your keyboard. Enter the cell address you want to go to and click **OK**.

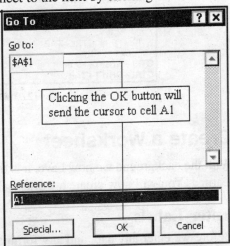

*Fig 12.02 Go To Dialogue Box*

Alternatively, you can use the keyboard shortcuts shown in Fig 12.03 later in this section to move around on your worksheet. The choice of whether to use the mouse or the keyboard for moving around in the worksheet is a personal one. If you are entering data and are familiar with keyboard shortcuts, you will find it convenient to keep your hands on the keyboard instead of alternating between keyboard and mouse. Read about the common features of all Office 2000 windows in Chapter 7, *Introducing Microsoft Office 2000*, earlier in the book.

## Exit Excel

After you have familiarised yourself with the elements of the Excel window, you may wish to exit Excel. You can click **File ➔ Exit** from the File menu item to exit Excel. If the workbook you are working with has not been saved, you will be prompted to do so. A dialogue box opens asking you if you wish to save the worksheet. Click on **Yes** to save and exit. If your work is not finished, click **No** to keep working.

| Press | To |
|---|---|
| Arrow keys | Move one cell up, down, left, or right |
| CTRL+arrow key | Move to the edge of the current data region |
| HOME | Move to the beginning of the row |
| CTRL+HOME | Move to the beginning of the worksheet |
| CTRL+END | Move to the last cell on the worksheet, which is the cell at the intersection of the rightmost used column and the bottom-most used row (in the lower-right corner), or the cell opposite the home cell, which is typically A1 |
| PAGE DOWN | Move down one screen |
| PAGE UP | Move up one screen |
| ALT+PAGE DOWN | Move one screen to the right |
| ALT+PAGE UP | Move one screen to the left |
| CTRL+PAGE DOWN | Move to the next sheet in the workbook |
| CTRL+PAGE UP | Move to the previous sheet in the workbook |
| CTRL+F6 or CTRL+TAB | Move to the next workbook or window |
| CTRL+SHIFT+F6 or CTRL+SHIFT+TAB | Move to the previous workbook or window |

*Fig 12.03 Keyboard Shortcuts for Navigation*

# Create a Worksheet

With the background we now have, it is time to create a simple worksheet to practise what we have learned. You will now create a worksheet for budgeting household expenses we will call *Budget*.

## Enter Labels

Before we enter any data and any formula for calculation, it is necessary to build the worksheet's structure, much as we would do with pencil and paper. We create the structure by entering labels which explain what the cells will contain. Follow these steps to enter the labels for the Budget worksheet:

1. Start Excel. You will see a blank worksheet.
2. Click cell **B1** and type <**January**>. Press tab and the cursor moves to cell C1.
3. Type <**February**> and press **tab** again to move to cell D1.
4. Type <**March**> and press tab to move to cell E1.
5. Type <**Average**>.
6. Click on cell **A2** and type <**Salary**> and press **Enter** ↵ to move to cell A3.
7. Type <**Rent**> and press **Enter** ↵ to move to cell A4.
8. Type <**Food**> and press **Enter** ↵ to move to cell A5.
9. Type <**Transportation**> and press **Enter** ↵ to move to cell A6.
10. Type <**Insurance**> and press **Enter** ↵ to move to cell A7.
11. Type <**Medical**> and press **Enter** ↵ to move to cell A8.
12. Type <**Total**> and press **Enter** ↵.

You have completed labelling your worksheet, which should look like the left side of Fig 12.04 shown earlier. If there are any differences, move to the cell which does not have the correct label and enter corrections.

You will note that the word *Transportation* runs into the next cell. We correct it by clicking on the top of column A, and moving the mouse pointer to the partition between columns A and B. The

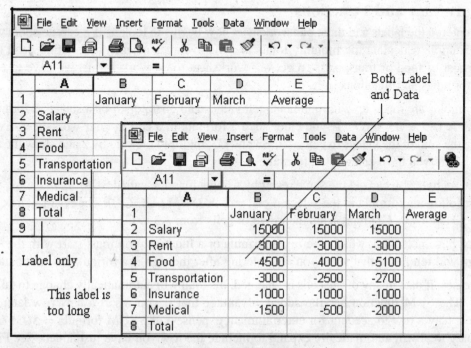

*Fig 12.04 Labels and Data*

pointer changes to a double-headed arrow ↔. We now drag the partition to the right till all of *Transportation* fits into the enlarged column. See the right hand worksheet in Fig 12.04.

## Enter Data

We will now enter some numeric data in the *Budget* worksheet we have created. We are already familiar with the Tab function which moves the cursor sideways and the **Enter** ⏎ key press that moves the cursor one line down. Using the skills we have learned while entering labels, enter the data you see in the right hand worksheet fragment in Fig 12.04.

At this stage, we will enter the raw data, not worrying about its format, which we will learn later. Remember to enter the (-) signs as shown. A formatted worksheet will look like Fig 12.05. As you can see, the width of column A has been adjusted to fit the word *Transportation*.

| | A | B | C | D | E |
|---|---|---|---|---|---|
| | | January | February | March | Average |
| 1 | | | | | |
| 2 | Salary | 15000.00 | 15000.00 | 15000.00 | 15000.00 |
| 3 | Rent | -3000.00 | -3000.00 | -3000.00 | -3000.00 |
| 4 | Food | -4500.00 | -4000.00 | -5100.00 | -4533.33 |
| 5 | Transportation | -3000.00 | -2500.00 | -2700.00 | -2733.33 |
| 6 | Insurance | -1000.00 | -1000.00 | -1000.00 | -1000.00 |
| 7 | Medical | -1500.00 | -500.00 | -2000.00 | -1333.33 |
| 8 | Total | 2000.00 | 4000.00 | 1200.00 | 2400.00 |

Column A has been broadened to fit "Transportation"

Numbers have been formatted to have two decimal places

*Fig 12.05 Formatted Worksheet*

## Use Formulas and Functions

Having entered the labels and data, our worksheet now begins to look as if it can do some work for us, for example, calculate the monthly totals and the averages of each accounting head (such as average cost of food or transport). To get our worksheet to do work for us, we have to enter the correct formulas and functions in it.

Excel formulas are made up with numbers, cell values and operators. For instance, a formula may read = 2 ✗ (A3 + B3 + C3). If you enter such a formula in a cell in your worksheet, Excel will calculate the sum of the values in cells A3, B3 and C3, multiply the sum by 2 and show the result in the cell where you have entered the formula.

As an alternative, you can get the same result by using a function called SUM. In that case, you will enter the following formula in the selected cell = 2 ✗ (SUM (A3...C3)). The result will be exactly the same. Here (A3...C3) represents the range of cells from A3 to C3.

You must have noted that while entering a formula or a function, you must start with the (=) sign. This sign will tell Excel that what you are entering after the sign is a formula and not data.

In both cases, if data in any of the cells is changed, the total will automatically change to take it into account. The SUM function has the added advantage that if you insert a new row later in your worksheet (say a row to account for entertainment expenses), the SUM formula = SUM (B3...B7) for January total will automatically expand to include the row you have just added. See Fig 12.06 illustrating the SUM function.

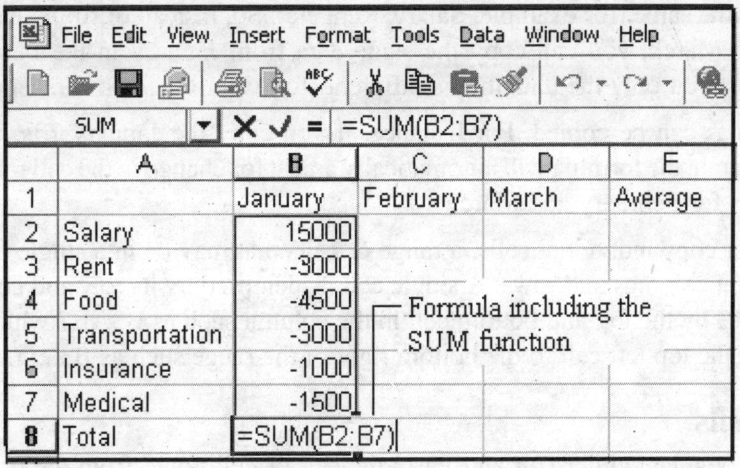

*Fig 12.06 SUM Function*

For calculating averages for the three months, you can use the AVERAGE function just as you used the SUM function earlier.

# Edit a Worksheet

As you keep using your worksheet, you will have to change many of its elements from time to time. For instance, you may wish to change some data or a formula. To do so, you must edit your worksheet. We look at how we can change cell contents and copy or move data.

## Change Cell Content

Before you can work with cell contents you have already entered, you must get to the Edit mode. You can do so in two ways:

- Select the cell you want to edit and either double click the **cell** or press the **F2** function key. The insertion point will appear in the selected cell.

- Select the **cell** and then click the **Formula bar** near the top left of your worksheet. The insertion point will appear in the Formula bar.

In both cases, you will go to the Edit mode as shown by the status indicator at the bottom left of your worksheet. While in the Edit mode, the right and left arrow keys will move the insertion point forwards or backwards within the cell entry instead of moving to the adjacent cells. Similarly, the Home and End keys will move you to the beginning and end of the cell entry.

You can insert characters in the cell entry just as you would in any other Office 2000 application and the backspace and delete keys work as usual. When you finish editing, go back to the ready mode by pressing the **Enter ↵** key. To abort any editing you have done, press the **Esc** key.

## Copy and Move Data

You may require to copy data from one part of the worksheet to another. You may also wish to move data to rearrange your worksheet. Here is an example of use for the Copy facility. Go back to the Budget worksheet. You will notice that the values in the columns marked January, February and

March are often the same (for example, Salary, Rent etc). So, instead of filling each cell separately in February and March, you can copy the same data from January in the February and March columns and then edit only the data that is different (for example, Food, Transportation etc).

Even the formulas can be copied. For instance, if you copy the January *Total* cell's formula in February and March, the formula will automatically adjust for change in the cell ranges and calculate the correct totals for February and March.

You can move or copy individual cells, a range of cells that may be in a single column or a range occupying several columns and rows. A single cell is identified by its row and column such as B3. A column of cells by the top and bottom cell in the column such as B3...B7 while a range of rows and columns by the top left cell to the bottom right of the range such as B3...D7.

## Selecting Cells

To move a cell, you can either Cut and Paste the cell or cell range from the origin cell(s) to the destination cell(s). Or you can Drag and Drop (when the pointer is an arrow) the cell or cell range. To copy a cell or range, use the Copy and Paste method. You can also use the Drag and Drop method (when the pointer is a + sign). In case of copying, you have a third method called AutoFill. In all cases, you begin by selecting the cell or cells you wish to copy or move.

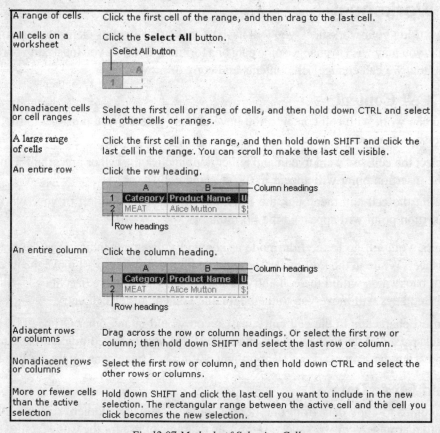

| A range of cells | Click the first cell of the range, and then drag to the last cell. |
| All cells on a worksheet | Click the **Select All** button. |
| Nonadiacent cells or cell ranges | Select the first cell or range of cells, and then hold down CTRL and select the other cells or ranges. |
| A large range of cells | Click the first cell in the range, and then hold down SHIFT and click the last cell in the range. You can scroll to make the last cell visible. |
| An entire row | Click the row heading. |
| An entire column | Click the column heading. |
| Adiacent rows or columns | Drag across the row or column headings. Or select the first row or column; then hold down SHIFT and select the last row or column. |
| Nonadiacent rows or columns | Select the first row or column, and then hold down CTRL and select the other rows or columns. |
| More or fewer cells than the active selection | Hold down SHIFT and click the last cell you want to include in the new selection. The rectangular range between the active cell and the cell you click becomes the new selection. |

*Fig 12.07 Methods of Selecting Cells*

You can select single cells, a range, or even cells in ranges that are not contiguous. Different methods are needed for these. In Fig 12.07, you can see a list of the common methods. While the list of options is quite long, the swiftness with which you can work in Excel depends on swift cell selection and navigation.

## Copy, Cut and Paste

Apart from the procedure for selecting cells (instead of text or graphics) the rest of the procedure for cutting, copying and pasting of cells and cell ranges is the same for such operations in any Office 2000 application.

## Drag and Drop

Dragging and dropping is somewhat different in Excel than for the other Office applications. After selecting a cell, position the mouse pointer on the border of the selected cell. The shape of the pointer changes from a cross to an arrow.

To move the selection, click the border and move the selection to its new destination. To copy the selection, press and hold down the Ctrl key while dragging the selection.

## Use AutoFill

The AutoFill feature will allow you to fill cells quickly and efficiently. Here are some examples.

### Copy Data within a Row or Column

1. Select the **cells** that contain the data you want to copy.
2. Drag the fill handle across the cells you want to fill and then release the mouse button. The existing values or formulas in the cells you fill are replaced, and formatting is copied.

### Fill in a Series of Numbers, or Dates

1. Select the **first cell in the range** you want to fill, and then enter the starting value for the series.
2. To increment the series by a specified amount, **select the next cell in the range** and enter the next item in the series. The difference between the two starting items determines the amount by which the series is incremented.
3. Select the **cell or cells** that contain the starting values.
4. Drag the **fill handle** over the range you want to fill.
5. To fill in increasing order, drag down or to the right. To fill in decreasing order, drag up or to the left.

### Insert and Delete

Occasionally, you may require inserting or deleting an entire row or column in your worksheet. To do so, proceed as follows:

1. Select the **entire row** by clicking on the row number or the entire column by clicking on the **column letter**. The entire row or column is highlighted.
2. Right click on the **selection**. A shortcut menu appears.

3. Choose **Insert** or **Delete** as needed. The inserted row will appear above the selected row and the inserted column will appear to the left of the selected column.

You can also select the row or column and right click to display the shortcut menu shown in Fig 12.08. You can then click the **Insert** or **Delete** menu items in the shortcut menu.

# Formatting a Worksheet

So far, we have been entering data in the Budget worksheet in its raw form, that is, without formatting. We know, however, that numerical data have comma separators and show decimals. In the same way, labels can also be enhanced to improve the looks of your worksheet. Column widths can be adjusted to fit labels and we can enhance labels by changing fonts, using bold or italics in the lettering as well as a host of other features.

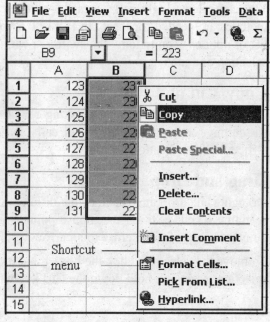

*Fig 12.08 Shortcut Menu for Insertion or Deletion*

We need formatting to enhance and to draw attention, to make important information stand out. We learn the basics of formatting cells, rows and columns in this section.

## Format Cells

The format of a cell determines how the data will appear in the cell although Excel may store the data as you have entered it. For instance, you may enter 1.2345 in cell A1. If you format A1 to show only two decimal figures, then A1 will show 1.23 though Excel will store the number as 1.2345. You can format empty cells also before you have entered any data.

## Format Numbers

Formatting decides decimal places, how negative numbers will be shown and if currency or percentage symbols will be displayed. Dates are also considered as numbers by Excel.

To format numbers, proceed as follows:

1. Select the **cell** or **cell range** to be formatted and click on **Format** on the menu bar. Then click **Cells** in the drop-down menu. The Format cells dialogue box appears. *See Fig 12.09.*

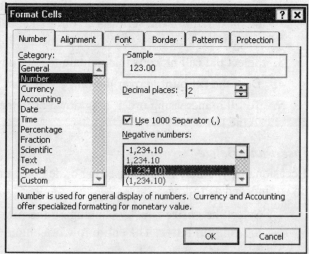

*Fig 12.09 Format Cells Dialogue Box*

2. Click the **Numbers** tab if required.

3. Scroll down the list box under the caption *Category* and select **Number**. The options available are displayed.

4. Select options such as number of decimals, whether to use commas as separators and style for negative numbers. A sample will appear in the pane captioned *Sample*.

5. Click **OK** and formatting is applied to the selected cells.

## Set Alignment

You can set alignment for the contents of the selected cells by clicking on the Right, Centre, Left or Justify buttons on Excel's standard tool bar. For more complex alignments, you require the Format Cells dialogue box we saw in Fig 12.09.

To set alignment, follow these steps:

1. Repeat step 1 of the previous section to open the Format Cells dialogue box.

2. Click the **Alignment** tab to display the alignment options. *See Fig 12.10.*

3. Select the alignment options you want and click **OK**.

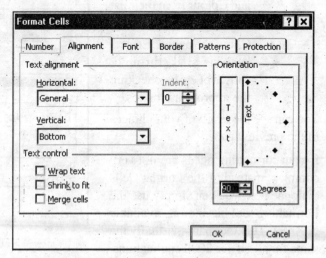

*Fig 12.10 Format Cells Alignment Tab*

In the Alignment tab, you have the following options:

* **Horizontal**: Decides side-to-side alignment.

* **Vertical**: Required if cells are more than one row in height. It decides whether the data will be closer to the top edge, the bottom edge or in the middle.

* **Wrap Text**: Useful for wrapping text to break it up in several lines rather than spread out.

* **Shrink to Fit**: Smaller fonts are used to fit the text in the space available.

* **Merge Cells**: Combines cells to allow long labels such as titles to fit in an expanded cell.

* **Orientation**: You can angle the headings of a worksheet to fit more headings in a limited space. You can even make the headings vertical by setting the degrees to 90.

## Format Fonts

Fonts in Excel can be formatted for font, font style and size just as in Word 2000. If you are producing a book or report that contains both Word documents and Excel worksheets, you can co-ordinate the fonts in both to maintain uniformity in your work.

To format fonts, proceed as follows:

1. Display the Format Cells dialogue box as before, after selecting the cell or cell range.
2. Click the **Font tab** to display the font options. *See Fig 12.11.*
3. Select the options you need and click **OK**. You can choose from:

   - Pick from the list boxes to choose Font, Font Style and Size.
   - Similarly, pick Underline and Colour from their list boxes.
   - Choose Special Effects such as strikethrough, subscript etc by checking the appropriate boxes.

You can see the result of your choices in the preview pane.

If your formatting needs are not very complex, instead of the Format Cells dialogue box, you can simply use the Formatting tool bar buttons available in Excel. This tool bar is virtually the same for all Office 2000 applications.

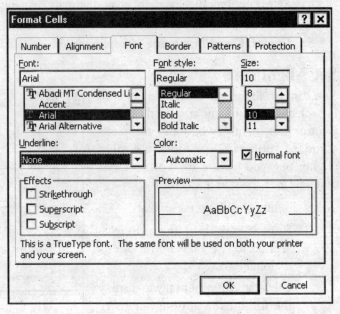

*Fig 12.11 Format Cells Font Options*

## Create Borders

You can set borders around selected cells to make important data stand out. For instance, you may wish to put a box around the final results of your worksheet calculations.

To create borders around selected cell or cells, proceed as follows:

1. Display the Format cells dialogue box as before after selecting cell or cells to be formatted.
2. Click the **Border tab** to display the border options. *See Fig 12.12.*
3. Select the options you need and click **OK**. You can choose from:

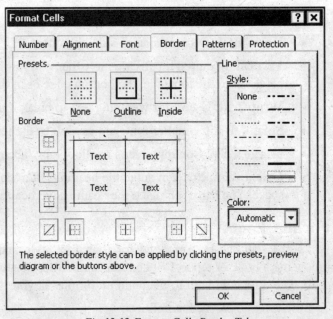

*Fig 12.12 Format Cells Border Tab*

- Border type under the caption *Presets*.
- Border alignment under the caption *Border*.
- The style and the colour under the caption *Line*.

As we have seen in the case of formatting, you can use the Borders button on the formatting tool bar of Excel for simple borders around cells.

## Use Patterns

In addition to or instead of borders, you can emphasise cells also by filling them with a selected colour or a pattern.

To set cell colours and patterns, proceed as follows:

1. Select the cell or cells and display the Format cells dialogue box as before.
2. Click the **Patterns tab** to display the Cell colour and shading options. *See Fig 12.13*.
3. Select the colours and/or the patterns and click **OK**.
   - Choose colour under the caption *Colour*.
   - Choose Patterns and its colour from the list box that appears after you press the drop-down arrow ▼ next to the *Patterns* caption.

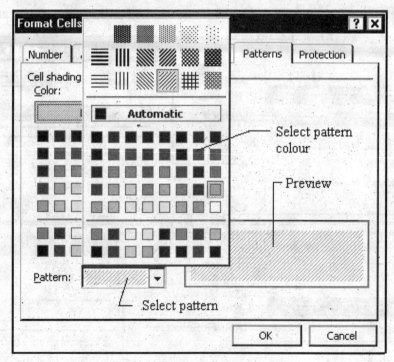

*Fig 12.13 Format Cells Patterns Tab*

## Format Columns and Rows

To complete our session on the formatting of the worksheet, we have to become familiar with the procedure for adjusting column widths and row heights to accommodate labels or data that do not fit into the default-sized columns and rows. We have already had occasion to adjust the column width to accommodate the label "Transportation" in the Budgets worksheet we have prepared at the start of this chapter. We complete the formatting exercise here.

## Row Width and Column Height

Change the width of a column as follows:

1. Move mouse pointer in the column heading (A, B, C etc) to the border of the column you wish to widen. The pointer changes to a two-headed arrow ↔.

2. Drag the pointer to widen or narrow the column. A yellow label is displayed showing the width of the column in cm (or inches) and pixels as you move the pointer.

Use the same procedure to make rows taller or shorter, positioning the mouse pointer on the row number area, at the border of the row that you wish to alter.

**TIP** Alternately, you can click on Format on the menu bar and select **Column ➜ Width** or **Row ➜ Height** to accomplish the same thing. In both cases, a dialogue box opens where you can enter the desired height or width. *See Fig 12.14*. It is a composite picture in which the top half deals with row height and the bottom half shows the procedure for changing the column width.

In both cases, enter the desired height or width in the text box of the dialogue box and click **OK**.

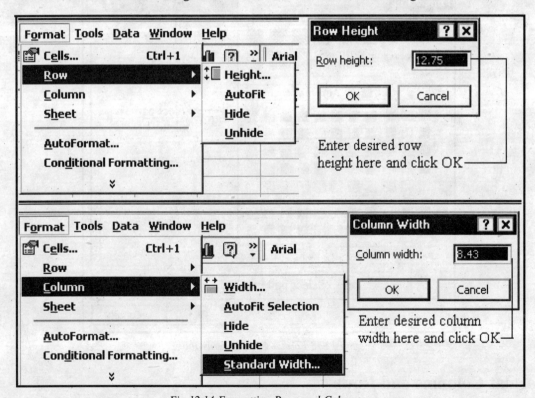

*Fig 12.14 Formatting Rows and Columns*

# Use AutoFit

The AutoFit feature takes the guesswork out of adjusting rows or columns to the data already entered into a worksheet. Do the following to AutoFit columns:

1. Move mouse pointer in the column heading (A, B, C etc) to the border of the column you wish to widen. The pointer changes to a two-headed arrow ↔.

2. Double click with the mouse and the column width adjusts to the widest data entered in that column.

**TIP**

Since rows size themselves automatically to fit in the data as you enter it, you will need to use AutoFit on rows only rarely. If you do want to, the procedure is just the same.

To AutoFit all rows and columns in a worksheet at once, first select the entire worksheet by clicking on the Select All button at the junction of column header A and row 1. Then repeat the AutoFit procedure for rows or columns as described above.

# Hide Rows and Columns

There are situations where you may not wish to display certain data. For instance, you may have a worksheet that shows discounts to certain dealers, information that you do not want to share with others. In such cases, you can hide the row or column containing the sensitive information.

To hide and display (unhide) a column, proceed as follows:

- Right click the **heading of the column** you want to hide and choose **Hide** from the shortcut menu.

- To display the hidden column, right click the **heading of a neighbouring column** and click **Unhide** in the shortcut menu. See Fig 12.14 earlier in this section in which the Hide and Unhide options are shown.

# Use AutoFormat

If you do not want to apply each format feature one by one, you can tackle the entire worksheet in one go by using Excel's AutoFormat feature.

To format your worksheet automatically, proceed as follows:

1. Select the **range of cells** you wish to format.

2. Click **Format** ➔ **AutoFormat** from the menu bar. The AutoFormat dialogue box is displayed. *See Fig 12.15.*

3. Select the options for formatting that you wish to apply and click **OK**.

Even if you use AutoFormat to provide you with a basic style, you can individually alter any of the worksheet's parameters afterwards to suit your needs. AutoFormat can, therefore, provide you with a good starting point for worksheet formatting.

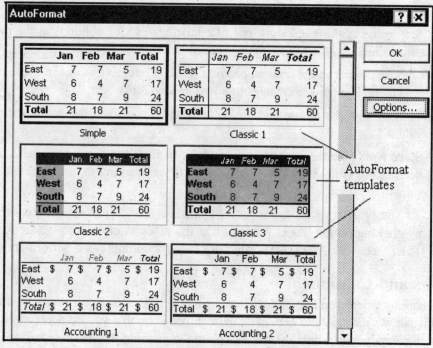

*Fig 12.15 AutoFormat Dialogue Box*

## Conditional Formatting

This is a powerful feature of Excel that allows you to highlight changes in data in your worksheet. For instance, if you are looking at a range of loan amounts, you may set up a worksheet where the monthly repayment amount is calculated for different loan amounts. You can conditionally format the repayment amount cell data to turn red if it exceeds say, Rs. 5,000.00. That way, you can easily change loan amounts and interest rates and stop as soon as your limit of repayment is reached.

To conditionally format a cell or a range of cells, proceed as follows:

1.  Select the **cell** or **the range** you wish to format.

2.  Click **Format ➜ Conditional Formatting** from the menu bar. The Conditional Formatting dialogue box appears. *See Fig 12.16.*

    The dialogue box has three conditions specified:

    *   Cell value between        Rs. 4,000 and 5,000
    *   Cell value equal to          Rs. 4,900
    *   Cell value less than         Rs. 2,000

    You can make up many other combinations, choosing the cell value or the formula, selecting operators such as greater than (>) or less than (<) and the upper and lower limits of value.

3.  After selecting the format conditions, click the **Format button** to display the Format Cells dialogue box that we have seen in Fig 12.09 earlier.

4.  Select the cell format you want, such as the colour of the data and click **OK**. See the earlier sections in this chapter for more information on cell formatting.

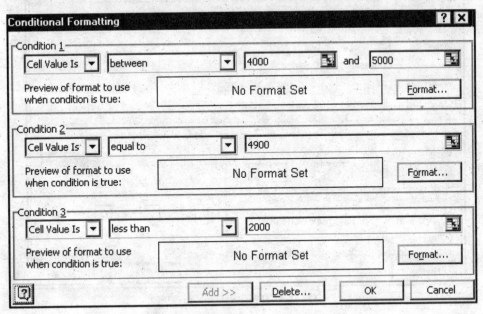

*Fig 12.16 Conditional Formatting Dialogue Box*

# Printing a Worksheet

Printing a worksheet is similar to printing documents created by other Office applications. We discuss some of the special features of printing Excel worksheets here.

## Printing

You can print an entire worksheet or print only selected portions of the worksheet.

To do so, proceed as follows:

1.  If only a part of the worksheet is to be printed, select the **print area** in the usual way of selecting cells or cell ranges that we have discussed earlier in this chapter.

2.  In the menu bar, click **File ➜ Print**. The Print dialogue box appears. *See Fig 12.17.*

3.  In this dialogue box choose from:
    - **Printer**: If you have more than one printer installed on your computer or network, select the one to be used.
    - **Print Range**: Specify all pages or particular pages.
    - **Print What**: Here decide if the entire workbook, the active worksheets or only the active sheets are to be printed.
    - **Number of Copies**: Choose from 1 to multiple copies.

4.  Click **OK** to commence printing.

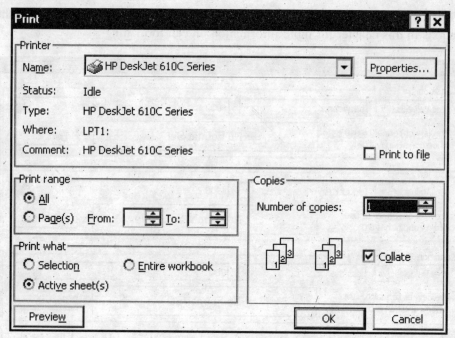

*Fig 12.17 Print Dialogue Box*

## Define Print Options

It is sometimes necessary to modify the default print options to improve the looks of your worksheet. One common problem most of us face is that, unlike Word documents, worksheets tend to be wider than their height. As a result, you can better utilise your printing paper if you turn the printing around and print in the landscape mode rather than the default portrait mode.

There may be other changes you want for the printed document. To view and modify these options, you have to open the Page Setup dialogue box. Proceed as follows:

1. Click **File ➜ Page Setup** in the menu bar. The Page setup dialogue box opens. *See Fig 12.18.*

2. Click the **Page tab** if required.

3. Choose from the following options:
   - **Orientation**. Portrait or Landscape
   - **Scaling**. To a percentage of full size or to fit a page of specified height and width
   - **Paper size**. From a drop-down list
   - **Print quality**. From a drop-down list
   - **First page number**. From a drop-down list

4. Click the **Margins** tab to display the Margins dialogue box. Here you can select the different margins and also the centring of the page. *See Fig 12.19.*

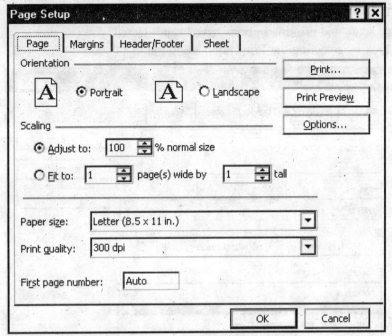

*Fig 12.18 Page Setup Dialogue Box*

5. Click the **Header/Footer button** to open the Header/Footer dialogue box. *See Fig 12.20.* Here enter Headers and Footers that you may wish to include on each page of your printed worksheets.

6. Click the **Sheet tab** for the Sheet dialogue box. Here you can select column and row titles that you want repeated in each worksheet. You can also select if the gridlines and the row and column headings should be printed.

7. After selecting all the options you want, click the **preview button** for a display of the worksheet as it will look after printing. We discuss previewing in more detail below.

8. If all seems in order, click **OK**.

You will be returned to the main Page Setup dialogue box, Fig 12.18. From here, you can start printing the worksheet as usual.

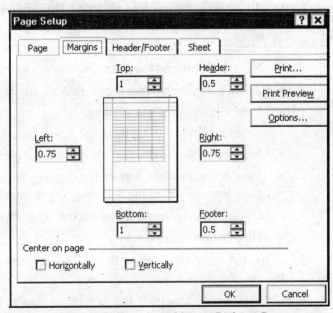

*Fig 12.19 Page Setup Margins Dialogue Box*

# Preview Printout

After all the page setup and printing options have been selected, you can preview how the printed worksheet will look by selecting the Print Preview option.

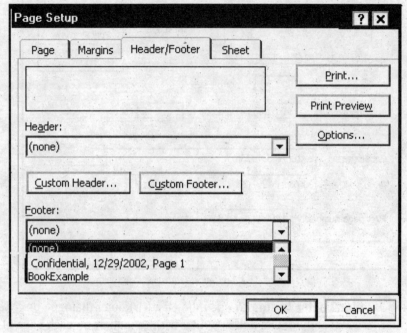

*Fig 12.20 Header Footer Dialogue Box*

Proceed as follows:

1. On the menu bar click **File ➔ Print Preview**. The Print Preview appears on the screen with a number of option buttons along the top of the page. *See Fig 12.21.*

2. The options include:
   - Next and Previous buttons to navigate a multi-page preview.
   - Zoom button to enlarge the worksheet image.
   - Print button to initiate printing.
   - Setup button to call up the Page Setup dialogue box.
   - Margins button to display margins on the preview screen.
   - Page Break Preview button that displays page break layout and allows you to modify page breaks by clicking and dragging them with your mouse. *See Fig 12.22.*
   - Close button to return to the normal worksheet window.
   - Help button to display help.

3. If you have clicked the Page Break Preview button, you will see Fig 12.22 shown later in this section.

4. Drag the page break lines if you wish to change them. Click **OK** if satisfied to return to your worksheet.

Fig.12.21 shows a Print Preview screen where you can see the Menu bar buttons arranged along the top. The buttons have been described earlier in this section. You can also see the margin lines. You can drag these lines to change the portion of the worksheet that will be printed.

The bottom two-thirds of the figure contains a preview of the worksheet at 100% zoom, that is, at normal size.

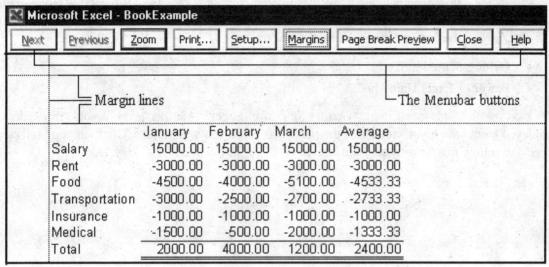

*Fig 12.21 Print Preview Screen*

In addition to the Print Preview that you have seen in Fig 12.21, you can also display the Page Break Preview. Just as you can adjust margins as you saw in Fig 12.21, you can also adjust the page breaks before printing.

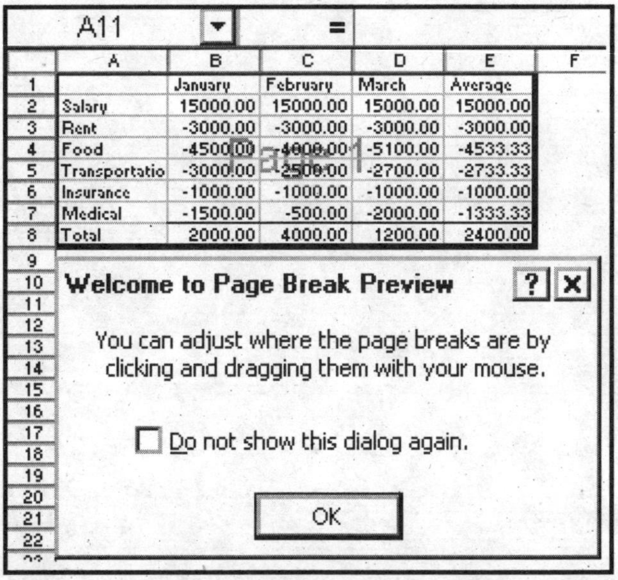

*Fig 12.22 Page Break Preview Dialogue Box*

As explained in the Page Break Preview dialogue box in Fig 12.22, click and drag the page breaks as required and then click **OK**.

After you have positioned the page breaks to your satisfaction, click **OK** to close the dialogue box.

**CD-ROM**

To learn more about Microsoft Excel 2000 in a multimedia environment, insert the accompanying CD-ROM in your computer, select the **Interactive** mode in the opening screen. The main menu will appear. To go to the section on Excel, click the button **Excel**. You will see a sub-menu containing the following topics:

- Getting Started in Excel
- Power of Excel Unleashed

Click on the first sub-menu item, "Getting Started in Excel". Another level of sub-sub-menus is displayed from which you can select the particular topic you want to see. Click on your selected topic and follow instructions on your screen.

# 13. Managing Worksheet and Data

**In this chapter:**

☞ You learn efficient ways of entering data in a worksheet. You also learn techniques to filter the data using AutoFilter and other advanced filtering methods.

☞ You are shown how to make the information in the data more meaningful by sorting the data. You learn about custom sorting and validating the data as it is entered. You are shown how you can tell Excel to respond with helpful hints if wrong data is entered.

☞ To avoid entering data from scratch, you are shown how you can import data from other sources into your Excel worksheet. You learn how to use Microsoft Query.

☞ After entering data, you are shown how to manage the data by summarising, outlining and consolidating data.

☞ You learn about one of the most powerful features of Excel, Pivot Tables and Pivot Charts. You learn how to create, display and interact with data using Pivot Tables and Pivot Charts.

☞ You are shown how to use a set of analytical tools such as Goal Seek, Solver and Scenarios.

# Managing Data

We have already discussed the basics of data entry and data editing in Chapter 12, *Introducing Excel 2000*. Now, we look at worksheet and data management in greater detail in this chapter.

## Transposing Data

After you have entered or imported data into a worksheet, you may find that it is necessary to transpose the data matrix so that the rows become columns or the columns become rows. This kind of change is often necessary for charting the data in the form of graphs, or for creating Pivot Tables.

1. Select the **cells** that you want to switch.
2. Click **Copy**.
3. Select the **upper-left cell** of the paste area. The paste area must be outside the copy area.
4. Click the **arrow** to the right of Paste and then click **Transpose**.

| City | Month | Sales Nos. | | City | Calcutta | Bombay | Madras |
|------|-------|-----------|---|------|----------|--------|--------|
| Calcutta | Feb | 200 | | Month | Feb | Feb | Feb |
| Bombay | Feb | 245 | | Sales Nos. | 200 | 245 | 300 |
| Madras | Feb | 300 | | | | | |

Column headings on the left are converted to row heading on the right

*Fig 13.01 Transposing Worksheet Data*

In Fig 13.01, the two worksheet tables show the effect of transposition. The table on the left, with cities down the first column, has been transposed in the table on the right, with cities along the top row.

## Using a Data Entry Form

If you wish to use Excel regularly as a database for processing small volumes of data that have to be entered regularly, for example, payroll data of a small company with 10 employees, you can streamline data entry by using a data entry form in Excel. A data form is a dialogue box that gives you a convenient way to enter or display one complete row of information, or record, in a list at one time. In this example, you can see a database or list and the corresponding data entry form.

Before you can use a data form to add a record to a new list, you must prepare a spreadsheet page with labels at the top of each column. Excel will use these labels to create fields on the data entry form.

To add a new record, to delete an existing record, or to change an existing record, proceed as follows:

1. Click a **cell** in the list you want to add the record to.
2. On the Data menu, click **Form**.

### *To Add a Record*

1. Click **New**.

2. Type the **information** for the new record.

3. When you finish typing data, press **ENTER** ↵ to add the record.

4. When you finish adding records, click **Close** to add the new record and close the data form.

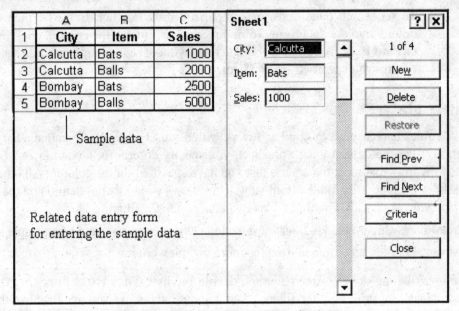

*Fig 13.02 Sample Data and Data Entry*

## To Change a Record

1. Find the **record** you want to change.

2. Change the **information** in the record.

**NOTE**

Fields that contain formulas display the results of the formula as a label. The label cannot be changed in the data form.

If you change a record that contains a formula, the formula is not calculated until you press ENTER or click Close to update the record.

1. To move to the next field, press **TAB**. To move to the previous field, press **SHIFT + TAB**.

2. When you finish changing data, press **ENTER** ↵ to update the record and move to the next record.

3. When you finish changing records, click **Close** to update the displayed record and close the data form.

## To Delete a Record

1. Find the **record** you wish to delete.

2. Press the **Delete** key.

3. To locate records, you can use the tips given below:

**TIP**

- To move through records one at a time, click the **scroll bar arrows** in the dialogue box. To move through 10 records at a time, click the **scroll bar between the arrows**.

- To move to the next record in the list, click **Find Next**. To move to the previous record in the list, click **Find Prev**.

- To set search conditions, or comparison criteria, click **Criteria**, then enter the criteria into the data form. To find records that match the criteria, click **Find Next** or **Find Prev**. To return to the data form without searching for records based on the criteria you specified, click **Form**.

# Filtering Data

Filtering is a quick and easy way to find and work with a subset of data (also called a list) on your worksheet. To filter the data in your worksheet, you specify criteria for a column and Excel will display only the rows that meet the criteria that you have specified for the column. All other data in your worksheet is temporarily hidden from view. This allows you to focus attention on the data you wish to display or work with. Excel provides two commands for filtering lists:

- AutoFilter, which includes filter by selection. This command is used for simple criteria.
- Advanced Filter, a command used for more complex criteria.

Unlike sorting, filtering does not rearrange the data in the list. When Excel filters rows, you can edit, format, chart, and print only the filtered data without having to rearrange or move the rest of the data in your entire spreadsheet.

## *AutoFilter*

You can apply the AutoFilter command to the data in a worksheet (called a list) as follows:

1. Select any cell in the **worksheet** that contains data and, therefore, is part of the list of data you wish to filter. Make sure that you have only one list in a worksheet if you intend to filter its data.

2. Click **Data** on the Standard Tool Bar.

3. Click **Filter** and then click **AutoFilter** in the drop-down menu that appears.

Drop-down arrows appear next to the column heading. *See Fig 13.03*. Click on the drop-down arrow next to the column you wish to filter. You will see some filtering options (All, Top 10 and Custom). Below the options, the items in the list will appear, sorted in the default order.

You can remove the filtering by repeating steps 1, 2 and 3. By clicking AutoFilter once again, you will remove filtering from the list.

The unfiltered list is shown at the left. Thereafter, the list is filtered with criteria set in column titled "Sales" to show only sales figures less than 1000. The list is shortened to only four rows, representing sales less than 1000. You could also set other criteria such as displaying only rows that contain sales data for the month of "Mar" or March.

Note that the data of the original list is intact. Therefore, the total is still the same as for the complete list. If you click on the drop-down arrow next to "Sales" and select the criteria "All", the full list will be displayed again.

| City | Month | Sales |
|------|-------|-------|
| Calcutta | Jan | 1,000 |
| Mumbai | Feb | 1,100 |
| Delhi | Mar | 900 |
| Chennai | Mar | 875 |
| Hyderabad | Feb | 1,200 |
| Bangalore | Jan | 1,050 |
| Chandigarh | Feb | 750 |
| Cuttack | Mar | 600 |
| Total | | 7,475 |

| City ▾ | Month ▾ | Sales ▾ |
|--------|---------|---------|
| Delhi | Mar | 900 |
| Chennai | Mar | 875 |
| Chandigarh | Feb | 750 |
| Cuttack | Mar | 600 |

Drop-down arrows

*Fig 13.03 Drop-down AutoFilter Arrows*

## Advanced Filter

Before invoking the advanced filter command, it is a good idea to determine the filtering criteria and the location of the output, which is the filtered list. You can sort the earlier list, selecting three cities like Calcutta, Hyderabad and Cuttack, specifying a convenient location on the worksheet for the filtered list to appear. We see the Criteria and the Filtered list side by side in Fig 13.04. The original, unfiltered list is the same as the one in the previous example.

| Criteria | | Filtered list | | |
|----------|--|---------------|--|--|
| City | | City | Month | Sales |
| Calcutta | | Calcutta | Jan | 1,000 |
| Hyderabad | | Hyderabad | Feb | 1,200 |
| Cuttack | | Cuttack | Mar | 600 |

Criteria for filtering

Resulting filtered list

*Fig 13.04 Criteria and Filtered List*

# Sorting

We have already seen methods of listing data that meet certain criteria in the previous section on filtering. Sorting is another method of displaying data in your worksheet with the rows sorted according to criteria that you may assign to the contents of a selected column. Thus, a list of cities containing sales data, for example, may be sorted by arranging the city names in alphabetical order. Or, the rows can be sorted in ascending or descending order of sales. We may also sort columns, assigning criteria to the rows. We look at the most commonly used sorting methods in this section.

## Sort Rows (A or D)

1. Click a **cell** in the column you wish to sort by, say the column containing the city names.
2. On the Standard Tool bar, click **Data** and then **Sort**.
3. On the Sort dialogue box that appears, choose the **Ascending** or the **Descending** radio button.
4. To complete the sorting, click **OK**. *See Fig 13.05.*

### *Set Custom Sort Order*

While the most common sort orders will be ascending (A to Z and 0 to 9) or descending (Z to A and 9 to 0), you can also use custom sort orders that you can define. You have to first set up a criteria list on the worksheet and then use this list for custom sorting. Proceed as follows:

1. In a range of cells, enter the **values** you want to sort by, in the order you want them, from top to bottom. For example:
   - Data
   - High
   - Medium
   - Low

2. Select the **range**.

3. On the Tools menu, click **Options**, and then click the **Custom Lists** tab.

| Unsorted "City" Column ---- | | | | | Sorted "City" Column ---- | | |
|---|---|---|---|---|---|---|---|
| **City** | **Month** | **Sales** | | | **City** | **Month** | **Sales** |
| Calcutta | Jan | 1,000 | — Unsorted | | Bangalore | Jan | 1,050 |
| Mumbai | Feb | 1,100 | data | | Calcutta | Jan | 1,000 |
| Delhi | Mar | 900 | | | Chandigarh | Feb | 750 |
| Chennai | Mar | 875 | | | Chennai | Mar | 875 |
| Hyderabad | Feb | 1,200 | The same | | Cuttack | Mar | 600 |
| Bangalore | Jan | 1,050 | data after | | Delhi | Mar | 900 |
| Chandigarh | Feb | 750 | sorting | | Hyderabad | Feb | 1,200 |
| Cuttack | Mar | 600 | | | Mumbai | Feb | 1,100 |
| Total | | 7,475 | | | Total | | 7,475 |

*Fig 13.05 Unsorted and Sorted Data*

4. Click **Import**, and then click **OK**.

5. Select a **cell** in the list you want to sort.

6. On the Data menu, click **Sort**.

7. In the Sort by box, click the **column** you want to sort.

8. Click **Options**.

9. Under First key sort order, click the custom list you created. For example, click **High**, **Medium**, **Low**.

10. Click **OK**.

11. Select any other sort **options** you want, and then click **OK**.

# Validating Data Entry

One of the major problems in working in Excel is that fairly large amounts of data must be entered in the spreadsheet. It is easy to make a mistake when a series of similar data must be entered one after another. Therefore, we need a method to ensure that the data we have entered is correct. In short, we need to validate the data we have entered.

There are several ways that you can set up criteria that Excel can use to validate data that you enter. The most commonly used criteria are:

- Allow only data that match a value in a pre-selected list. Thus if the reselected list contains the names of the seven days of the week, then if you misspell a day name while entering, it will be rejected and you will see a warning message.

- Allow numbers that lie between pre-selected high and low values. Thus, if you pre-select 10 and 100, any number smaller than 10 or greater than 100 will be rejected.

- Allow dates between pre-selected first and last dates. Dates earlier or later than the range selected will be rejected.

- Allow values depending on the value of another cell. For example, you could specify that if the data entered in the "Source" column in a list equals "Local", then no entry in the "Import Duty" column will be accepted other than zero.

In addition to validation criteria, you can also specify the error message that will be displayed to guide the user if he enters incorrect data.

## *Designate Valid Cell Entries*

1. Select the **cell** to validate.
2. On the Data menu, click **Validation**, and then click the **Settings** tab. *See Fig 13.06*.
3. Specify the type of **validation** you want. This includes:

   - Data from a list. See "Custom List to Validate Data" later in this section.
   - Data between preset limits.
   - Value depending on another cell.
   - Value allowed by a formula.

4. Specify if the **cell** can be left blank. See Block Blank Entries later in this section.

5. To display an optional input message when the cell is clicked, click the **Input Message** tab and make sure the **Show input message when cell is selected** check box is selected, and fill in the **title** and **text** for the message.

6. Specify how you want Microsoft Excel to **respond** when invalid data is entered. See "Specify Excel's Response" later in this section.

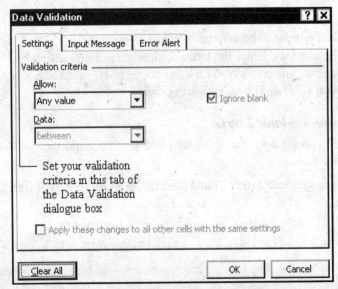

*Fig 13.06 Data Validation Dialogue Box*

## *Custom List to Validate Data*

To restrict data that the user can enter in a cell, you can create a drop-down list that appears when the user clicks the drop-down arrow. The user can then choose an entry from the list that appears. Here are the steps for creating a drop-down list and applying it to a selected cell in your worksheet:

1. Type the **entries** for the drop-down list in a single column or row. Do not include blank cells in the list. If you type the list on a worksheet that is different from the one on which you have your data entry cell, define a **name** for the list.

2. Select the **cell**, **range of cells**, or **nonadjacent selections** that you want to name.

3. Click the **Name box** at the left end of the formula bar.

4. Type the **name** for the cells.

5. Press **ENTER** ↵.

6. Select the **cell** where you want the drop-down list.

7. On the Data menu, click **Validation**, and then click the **Settings** tab.

8. In the Allow box, click **List**.

   - If the list is in the same worksheet, enter a **reference** to your list in the Source box.

   - If the list is elsewhere, enter the **name** you defined for your list in the Source box.

   - Make sure the reference or name is preceded with an equal sign (=).

   - Make sure the In-cell **drop-down check box** is selected.

   - Specify whether the cell can be left blank: Select or clear the **Ignore blank** check box.

   - To display optional input instructions when the cell is clicked, click the **Input Message** tab, make sure the **Show input message when cell is selected** check box is selected, and then fill in the **title** and **text** for the message.

   - Specify how you want Microsoft Excel to **respond** when invalid data is entered.

If the items to be entered in the drop-down list are not many, you can type the entries directly in the Source box. Enter the items with separator characters such as commas between the items. For example, you could type Low, Average, or High in the Source box instead of entering the three words in a separate list on your worksheet.

## *Block Blank Entries*

If you do not wish the user to skip very important cell entries, you can block blank entries as follows:

1. Select the **cell** and then in the **Standard Tool bar**, click **Data** and then **Validation** to open the Data Validation dialogue box.

2. In the dialogue box, click the **Settings** tab:
   - If you want to allow blank (null) values, select the **Ignore blank** check box.

   - If you want to prevent entry of blank (null) values, clear the **Ignore blank** check box.

## *Specify Excel's Response*

After displaying the data validation dialogue box, you can specify how Excel will respond after data is entered in a cell selected for data validation. Proceed as follows:

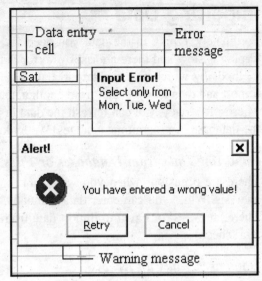

1. Click the **Error Alert** tab, and make sure the Show error alert after invalid data is entered check box is selected.

2. Select one of the following options for the Style box:

   • To display an information message that does not prevent entry of invalid data, click **Information**.

   • To display a warning message that does not prevent entry of invalid data, click **Warning**.

   *Fig 13.07 Response to Wrong Data*

   • To prevent entry of invalid data, click **Stop**.

3. Fill in the title and text for the message (up to 225 characters). If you do not enter a title or text, the title defaults to *Microsoft Excel* and the message to: *The value you entered is not valid. A user has restricted values that can be entered into this cell.* See Fig 13.07.

# Removing Data Validation

If changes occur to your worksheet, you may no longer want the constraints of data validation to continue on some cell or cells. You can remove the data validation you had imposed by first finding cells that have data validation conditions attached to them.

## *Find All Cells that have Data Validation*

1. On the Edit menu, click **Go To**.
2. Click **Special**.
3. Click **Data Validation**.
4. Click **All**.

## *Remove Data Validation*

Having found the cells, you can remove data validation as follows:

1. Select the **cells** where you no longer want to validate data.
2. On the Data menu, click **Validation**, and then do one of the following:

   • If prompted to erase current settings and continue, click **OK**, and then click **Cancel**.

   • If the Data Validation dialogue box appears, click the **Settings** tab, and then click **Clear All**.

# Importing Data

Fortunately, typing in the data you need for your spreadsheet is not the only way to enter data. Typing is slow and there are risks of error during data entry. Excel provides you with a number of methods by which you can import data into Excel from other programmes. If you use Excel to import and then analyse data from another source such as a database or a financial programme like Microsoft Money, you can refresh the data in your Excel spreadsheet whenever the original data in the database or programme changes. We look at methods for importing data this section.

### *Importing Data from Databases or Files*

There are occasions when you will want to import data from some other source into Excel for analysis. While you can enter data manually, the work takes time and chances of errors are high. There are ways for Excel to import data from certain sources that it can read and reformat into its worksheet.

### *Databases You Can Access*

Microsoft Office provides drivers that you can use to retrieve data from the following data sources:

- Microsoft SQL Server OLAP Services (OLAP provider)
- Microsoft Access 2000
- dBASE (III or IV)
- Microsoft FoxPro
- Microsoft Excel, other versions
- Oracle
- Paradox
- Text file databases

You can retrieve data from a Microsoft Exchange or Lotus 1-2-3 data source as well. However, to do this, you have to use Microsoft Visual Basic.

## Ways to Retrieve Data

You can retrieve external data from databases in the following ways:

- Using Microsoft Query.
- Using Microsoft Visual Basic.
- Using Web queries.

### *Using Microsoft Query*

You can use Microsoft Query to set up data sources and retrieve data. In Query, you can use the Query Wizard to create a simple query, or you can use more advanced criteria features in Query to create a more complex query. You can access Query directly from Excel.

## Relational Databases, Lists, and Text Files

You can use Query to retrieve data that is stored in a relational database such as Microsoft Access or Microsoft SQL Server. In addition to external databases, you can also retrieve data stored in a Microsoft Excel list or a text file.

When you retrieve data from a relational database, Excel list, or text file, you can bring together data that is organised in multiple tables. You can also specify criteria that data must meet to be included in the external data range. This allows you to exclude data that isn't relevant to your specific need. For example, you might be interested in sales figures, but only for a certain month.

If you want to retrieve all the data in a text file, you can import the text file as an external data range without creating a query.

## Install Query and Drivers

To use Query to retrieve data, you need to install Query and any additional ODBC drivers or data source drivers that your external database requires. Learn about what you need to retrieve external data.

## Importing a Text File into Excel

Use this procedure if you want to refresh the data in Excel whenever the original text file changes. If you want to copy the data into Excel without maintaining a connection to the original file, you can simply open the text file in Excel.

1. Click the **cell** where you want to put the data from the text file.

   To ensure that the external data does not replace existing data, make sure that the worksheet has no data below or to the right of the cell you click.

2. On the Data menu, point to **Get External Data**, and then click **Import Text File**.

3. In the Look in list, locate and double click the **text file** you want to import as an external data range. The Text import wizard will be launched.

   To specify how you want to divide the text into columns, follow the instructions in the Text Import Wizard.

4. Click **Finish**, and then click **Properties** in the Import Data dialogue box to set formatting and layout options for how the external data range is brought into Microsoft Excel.

5. In the Import Data dialogue box, do one of the following:

   • To return the data to the location you selected in step 1, click **Existing worksheet**, and then click **OK**.

   • To return the data to a new worksheet, click **New worksheet**, and then click **OK**.

Microsoft Excel adds a new worksheet to your workbook and automatically puts the external data range in the upper-left corner of the new worksheet.

In Fig 13.08, you can see data from a Notepad text file imported into an Excel worksheet with the help of the Data Import Wizard. The Wizard is shown in the left pane.

**NOTE**

When the original text file changes, to refresh the external data range, click **Refresh Data on the External Data tool bar**. In the Import Text File dialogue box, select your **text file**, and then click **Import**.

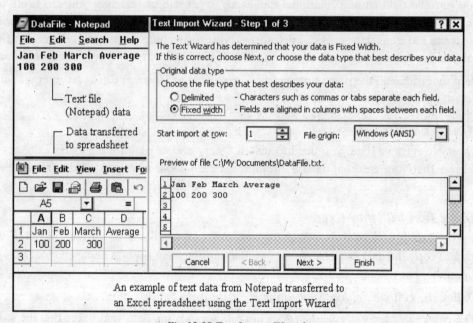

An example of text data from Notepad transferred to an Excel spreadsheet using the Text Import Wizard

*Fig 13.08 Text Import Wizard*

To change the settings you have made in the Text Import Wizard, click **Edit Text Import on the External Data tool bar**. Select your **text file**, click **Import**, and then make the changes you want in the wizard.

If you want to import only part of the data in a text file as a refreshable data range, you can create a query to retrieve the data.

# Analysing and Managing Data

With the early versions of spreadsheets, you could only enter data, calculate using the data and display results. Only some rudimentary formatting was possible. In contrast, modern spreadsheets such as Lotus 123 Millennium Edition or Excel 2000 go far beyond such "bare-bones" functions. In addition to basic calculations, they provide sophisticated ways of summarising, analysing and presenting data. In the remainder of this chapter, we will examine summarising data, what-if analysis and the use of pivot tables as well as techniques for creating and using data entry forms.

## Summarising

Worksheet data is usually in the form of lists or tables. The most common task for the spreadsheet is to summarise the data contained in a table or list. Excel has many features to assist you in this task.

## *Automatic Subtotals*

As you enter data in a list or table, Excel can be configured to create subtotals and grand totals automatically. When you insert automatic subtotals, Excel outlines the list so that you can display or hide the rows containing the details. By hiding the detail rows, you can create a summary report that highlights just the subtotals or grand totals, without the details cluttering your screen.

To insert subtotals, you have to first sort your list so that the rows you want to subtotal are grouped together.

You can then calculate subtotals for any column that contains numbers.

## *Subtotal Calculation*

Use built-in Excel functions such as Sum or Average to calculate subtotals. Grand totals are calculated by summing all the raw data, not just the subtotals. This ensures that if you calculate averages for each sub-group, the grand average is a true average of all the original data and not just the average of the sub-group averages. Whenever you change any of the detail data, Excel automatically recalculates the affected subtotals and grand totals.

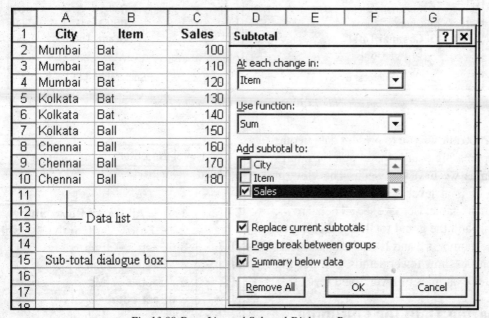

*Fig 13.09 Data List and Subtotal Dialogue Box*

## *Nesting Subtotals*

You can insert subtotals for smaller groups within existing subtotal groups. In Fig 13.09, subtotals for each sports item are in a list that already has subtotals for each region. Before inserting nested subtotals, be sure to sort the list by all the columns for which you want subtotal values, so that the rows you want to be subtotalled are grouped together.

The data list you saw in Fig 13.09 has been subtotalled, first by "City" and then by "Item" in Fig 13.10. Notice how the subtotals are nested appropriately.

Then, in Fig 13.11, you can see an example of outlining taken down to three levels. All the three figures are based on the same set of data.

## Outlining

A worksheet may contain large amounts of data. While you do have to look at and work with all the data, for the viewer of the worksheet, too many details can be a distraction.

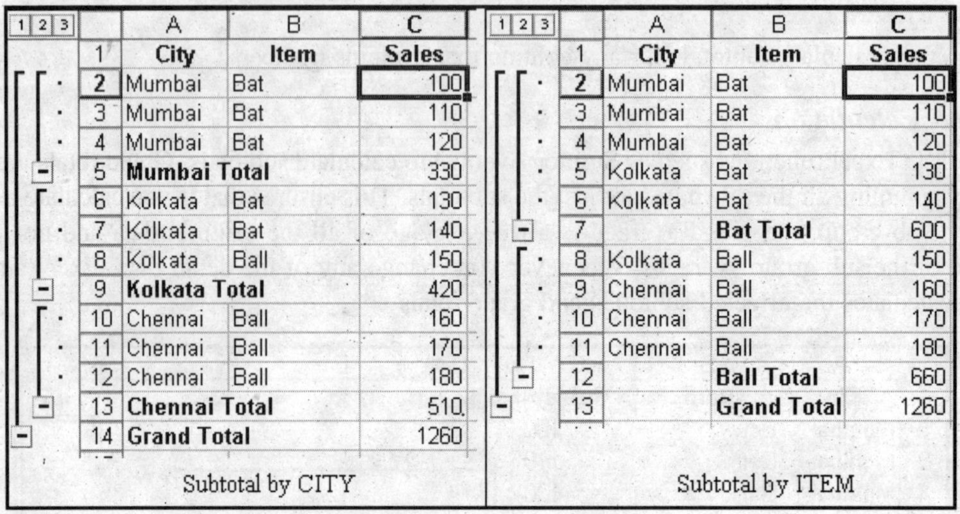

| 1 2 3 | | A | B | C |
|---|---|---|---|---|
| | 1 | City | Item | Sales |
| | 2 | Mumbai | Bat | 100 |
| | 3 | Mumbai | Bat | 110 |
| | 4 | Mumbai | Bat | 120 |
| | 5 | **Mumbai Total** | | 330 |
| | 6 | Kolkata | Bat | 130 |
| | 7 | Kolkata | Bat | 140 |
| | 8 | Kolkata | Ball | 150 |
| | 9 | **Kolkata Total** | | 420 |
| | 10 | Chennai | Ball | 160 |
| | 11 | Chennai | Ball | 170 |
| | 12 | Chennai | Ball | 180 |
| | 13 | **Chennai Total** | | 510 |
| | 14 | **Grand Total** | | 1260 |

Subtotal by CITY

| 1 2 3 | | A | B | C |
|---|---|---|---|---|
| | 1 | City | Item | Sales |
| | 2 | Mumbai | Bat | 100 |
| | 3 | Mumbai | Bat | 110 |
| | 4 | Mumbai | Bat | 120 |
| | 5 | Kolkata | Bat | 130 |
| | 6 | Kolkata | Bat | 140 |
| | 7 | | **Bat Total** | 600 |
| | 8 | Kolkata | Ball | 150 |
| | 9 | Chennai | Ball | 160 |
| | 10 | Chennai | Ball | 170 |
| | 11 | Chennai | Ball | 180 |
| | 12 | | **Ball Total** | 660 |
| | 13 | | **Grand Total** | 1260 |

Subtotal by ITEM

*Fig 13.10 Subtotal by City and by Item*

Excel 2000 allows you to present data in outline suppressing details to aid quick comprehension as we have just seen. The view in Fig 13.11 is at level 3, the highest level of detail in this table. Here we see all detail rows, subtotals and the grand total. By clicking on the level numbers 2 and 1, on the top left corner, you can show fewer details. See also Fig 13.12 for examples of level 2 and level 1.

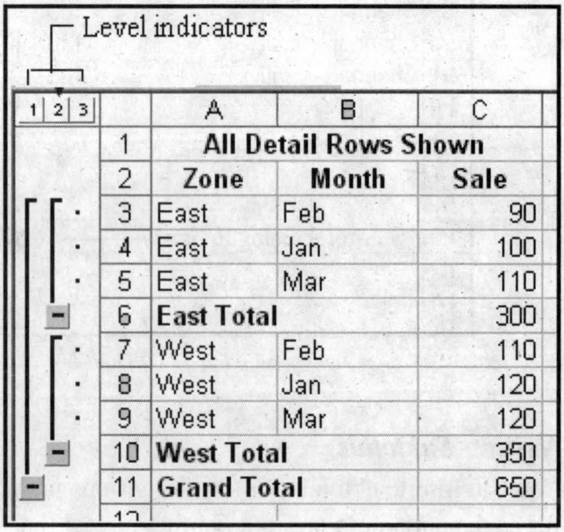

## Preparing Data for Outlining

Data to be outlined should be in list format, where each column has a label in the first row and contains similar facts, and there are no blank rows or columns within the list.

Before outlining, you may need to sort the data so that rows to be grouped are together.

Level indicators

| 1 2 3 | | A | B | C |
|---|---|---|---|---|
| | 1 | **All Detail Rows Shown** | | |
| | 2 | **Zone** | **Month** | **Sale** |
| | 3 | East | Feb | 90 |
| | 4 | East | Jan | 100 |
| | 5 | East | Mar | 110 |
| | 6 | **East Total** | | 300 |
| | 7 | West | Feb | 110 |
| | 8 | West | Jan | 120 |
| | 9 | West | Mar | 120 |
| | 10 | **West Total** | | 350 |
| | 11 | **Grand Total** | | 650 |

*Fig 13.11 Outline in Three Levels*

In Fig 13.12, the list was sorted by region and then by month, so that the detail rows for March and April within the East region are together, and the rows for each month within the West region are together. The level 2 table shows subtotals and the grand total. Level 1 shows only the grand total.

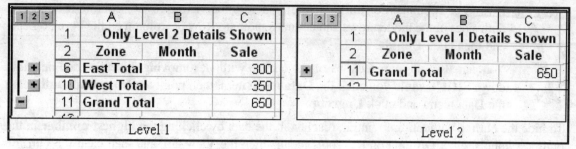

Fig 13.12 Separate Level 1 and Level 2 Views

## Displaying and Hiding Levels

Although the sample shown here has only three levels of detail, an outline can have up to eight levels, with each inner level providing details for the preceding outer level. To display only the rows for a particular level, you can click the number for the level you want to see.

# Methods of Outlining

You can outline a table either manually or automatically. It is better to use the manual method unless you are very sure that the data on your worksheet has been prepared properly for automatic outlining. For instance, the data must be sorted and subtotalled before automatic outlining can be applied.

## Outlining Automatically

If you have summarised the data with formulas that contain functions such as SUM, Excel can automatically outline the data. The summary data must be adjacent to the detail data. If you insert automatic subtotals in a list organised in rows, Excel automatically outlines the worksheet at the same time, so that you can show or hide as much detail as you need.

## Outlining Manually

If the data is not organised so that Excel can outline it automatically, you can create an outline manually. For example, you will need to manually outline data if the rows or columns of summary data contain values or descriptive text instead of formulas.

## Removing Outline

While an outline is good for presentation, if actual calculations are needed to modify data, it is best to revert to the normal worksheet format. To do so, you must remove the outline without losing any data. Proceed as follows:

1. Click the **worksheet**.

2. On the Data menu, point to **Group and Outline**, and then click **Clear Outline**. *See Fig 13.13*.

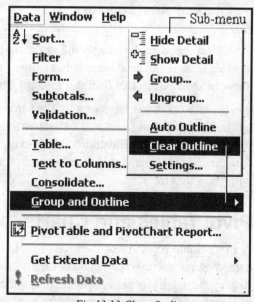

Fig 13.13 Clear Outline

**NOTE** If rows or columns are still hidden, drag across the visible row or column headings on both sides of the hidden rows and columns, point to Row or Column on the Format menu, and then click **Unhide**.

You can also ungroup sections of the outline without removing the entire outline. Hold down **SHIFT** while you click the **Data** menu item, then point to **Group and Outline** on the Data menu and click **Ungroup**.

To hide the outline without removing it, display all the data by clicking the **highest number** in the outline symbols, click **Options** on the Tools menu, click the **View** tab, and then clear the **Outline symbols** check box.

## Consolidation

To consolidate data, you combine the values from several ranges of data. For example, if you have separate worksheets containing salary figures for Manufacturing (Mfg), Sales (Sales) and Head Office (HO), you can use a consolidation to combine these figures into a corporate salary worksheet.

Excel provides several ways to consolidate data. The most flexible method is to create formulas that refer to cells in each range of data that you want to combine. Formulas that refer to cells on multiple worksheets are called 3-D formulas. In the example in Fig 13.14, there are separate tabs that contain salary details for each cost centre, with the tabs marked (for example) as Mfg, Sales, HO and a consolidation tab marked Consol. The 3-D formulas that you will need are shown in the worksheet instead of actual figures.

| 17 | A | B | C | D | E |
|---|---|---|---|---|---|
| 18 | | | Salaries | | |
| 19 | | Mfg | = Mfg!B4 | | |
| 20 | | Sales | =SalesC10 | | |
| 21 | | HO | =HOD9 | | |
| 22 | | | | | |
| 23 | | Total | =SUM(C18:20) | | |
| 24 | | | | | |
| 25 | | | | | |

◄ ◄ ► ►◄ \ Mfg / Sales / HO \ **Consol** /

*Fig 13.14 Consolidated Worksheet*

The structure of the separate worksheets need not be exactly the same, that is, the salary data may appear in different cells in each worksheet as is the case here. It is assumed that salary figures for Manufacturing are in cell B4 of the worksheet Mfg!, that of Sales in cell C10 of the worksheet Sales! And so on.

If all your worksheets have exactly the same structure, it is possible to use cell ranges, for example, on the consolidation sheet you can enter the formula "Total = SUM (Mfg:HO!C3)" instead of the formula shown in the illustration. However, it is necessary that all the worksheets have the salary data on cell C3. Note that if the structure of any one of the worksheet changes, this type of formula will generate errors.

## Pivot Tables and Charts

A Pivot Table report is an interactive table that quickly combines and compares large amounts of data. You can rotate its rows and columns to see different summaries of the source data, and you can display the details for areas of interest. Pivot Tables are surely amongst the most powerful capabilities of Excel 2000. Although they require a bit of study and understanding, they will become powerful tools that you can use to analyse and compare large amounts of data that would otherwise be very difficult to comprehend.

Use a Pivot Table report when you want to analyse related totals, especially when you have a long list of figures to sum and you want to compare several facts about each figure. Because a Pivot Table report is interactive, you can change the view of the data so that you can see more details or only summaries such as counts or averages.

Let us look at a hypothetical example involving different cities, salesmen and products to be sold (balls and bats) in the table shown in Fig 13.15. We can prepare a Pivot Table report of our choice from this data.

In a Pivot Table report, each column or field in your source data becomes a Pivot Table field that summarises multiple rows of information. In the example here, the

| City | Salesman | Item | Sales |
|------|----------|------|-------|
| Bombay | Dravid | Balls | 2500 |
| Bombay | Tendulkar | Balls | 1700 |
| Chennai | Ganguly | Balls | 1100 |
| Delhi | Tendulkar | Balls | 1750 |
| Bombay | Dravid | Bats | 1300 |
| Bombay | Kumble | Bats | 2000 |
| Calcutta | Dravid | Bats | 2100 |
| Calcutta | Kumble | Bats | 1000 |
| Calcutta | Tendulkar | Bats | 1500 |
| Chennai | Ganguly | Bats | 1500 |
| Delhi | Dravid | Bats | 1350 |

Fig 13.15 Pivot Table Data

City column becomes the City field, and sales of balls and bats are consolidated to show total sales by each salesman. A data field, such as Sales, provides the values to be summarised under Grand Total. In the example shown in Fig 13.16, data has been arranged by the Pivot Table to display information arranged to show total sales by city and by salesman. You can see the sales achieved by each salesman in each city as well as total sales in all cities for each salesman.

| 18 | Sum of Sales | Salesman ▼ | | | | |
|----|--------------|------------|---------|--------|-----------|-------------|
| 19 | City ▼ | Dravid | Ganguly | Kumble | Tendulkar | Grand Total |
| 20 | Bombay | 3800 | | 2000 | 1700 | 7500 |
| 21 | Calcutta | 2100 | | 1000 | 1500 | 4600 |
| 22 | Chennai | | 2600 | | | 2600 |
| 23 | Delhi | 1350 | | | 1750 | 3100 |
| 24 | Grand Total | 7250 | 2600 | 3000 | 4950 | 17800 |

Fig 13.16 Pivot Table Using Data

# Creating a Pivot Table

To create a Pivot Table, you run the Pivot Table and Pivot Chart Wizard. In the wizard, you select the source data you want from your worksheet list or external database. The wizard then lets you select a worksheet area for the report and a list of the available fields. As you drag the fields from the list window to the outlined areas, Microsoft Excel summarises and calculates the report for you automatically.

After you create a Pivot Table, you can customise it to focus on the information you want: change the layout, change the format, or drill down to display more detailed data.

To launch the Pivot Table and the Pivot Chart Wizard, click Data on the menu bar and then click Pivot Table and Pivot Chart Report in the drop-down menu that appears. The three-step wizard is launched. See Fig 13.17 that shows the first step of the Wizard. Follow instructions on the screen to complete the three-step process to create the Pivot Table.

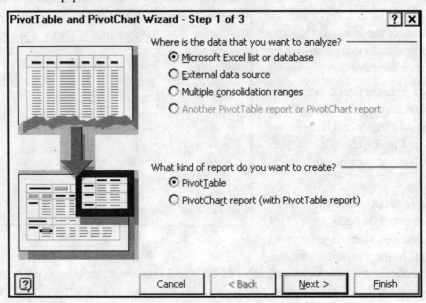

*Fig 13.17 Pivot Table Wizard (Step 1)*

# Pivot Charts

The data in a Pivot Table can be converted into a Pivot Chart by the same Wizard. Often, a graphic display enhances the impact of the data and makes it easier for the audience to grasp the essence of the meaning behind the figures that you want to convey to them.

The data from the Pivot Table showing sales by city and sales by salesmen (*see Fig 13.16*) is shown here in chart form in Fig 13.18, using the Pivot Table Wizard first and then the Pivot Chart Wizard.

In the Pivot Chart, as in the case of the Pivot Table, the variable "Sum of Sales" can be made to pivot around either the Cities (down the first column) or the Salesmen (along the top row). This gives you great flexibility in displaying your data.

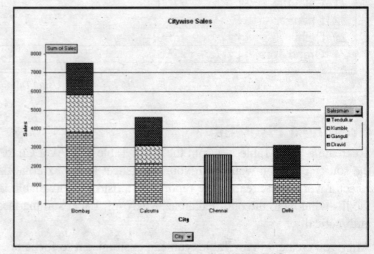

*Fig 13.18 Sales Graph from Pivot Table*

# What-if Analysis

So far, we have been dealing with different ways of presenting data in order to highlight certain information we want to extract from the data. We will now look at tools that help us analyse the data itself, with the computer carrying out repeated calculations so that you can get an answer to your query. The tools that you will use are referred to as Add-Ins to Excel 2000 and are available in the drop-down menu that appears when you click on the Tools option on the menu bar. In case the add-on you want is not already installed, Excel 2000 will prompt you to insert your Office 2000 CD-ROM so that you can install the Add-in you have selected. We look at the three most popular "Add-Ins" for Excel 2000. They will greatly enhance your problem solving and analysing skills.

In order to conserve hard disk space, you may wish to install only the Add-Ins that you need. You may even uninstall them after use. To do so, uncheck the check box of the unwanted Add-In in the Add-Ins dialogue box. For a view of Excel Add-Ins and of the Add-In manager, see Fig 13.19. The three Add-Ins discussed here, Goal Seek, Scenarios and Solver are shown framed for easy identification.

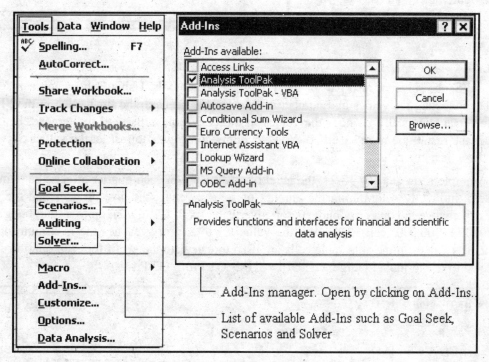

*Fig 13.19 Excel Add-Ins*

# Goal Seek

Goal seeking is a method in which Excel 2000 will vary the value of a designated cell on a worksheet until the value of another cell matches a value that you set in advance. Goal seeking is useful when you wish to find the value of a variable that will give you a known result in an equation that involves that variable. For example, if you wish to find out the interest rate that will allow you to keep your instalment repayments to a value of your choice, you can use Goal Seek. Excel 2000 will calculate automatically using several interest rates until the conditions you set are satisfied. You can launch Goal Seek by clicking Goal Seek on the Tools menu.

In the example shown in Fig 13.20, we use Goal Seek to determine the interest rate that will allow us to repay Rs. 100,000 in 180 months, paying at the rate of Rs. 900 per month. Excel 2000 automatically calculates several times with different interest rates till the desired conditions are met and then displays the required interest rate of 7.02%. By changing the target value to some figure other than Rs. 900, (say, Rs. 1,000) you can get Goal Seek to calculate the new interest rate.

**Goal Seek Exercise**

| | |
|---|---|
| Loan Amount (Rs.) | 100,000.00 |
| Period of Loan (Months) | 180.00 |
| Interest Rate (%) | 7.02 |
| Monthly Payment (Rs) | -900.00 |

**Goal Seek Status** [?] [X]

Goal Seeking with Cell E8 found a solution.

Target value: -900
Current value: -900.00

[OK] [Cancel] [Step] [Pause]

*Fig 13.20 Goal Seek Exercise*

# Solver

Like Goal Seek, Solver is also part of the What-if analysis tools. Using Solver, you can set up a formula connecting the values in a number of "Adjustable" cells to the final value in the "Target" cell. Solver automatically changes the values in the adjustable cells until the target cell formula produces the result you have specified. You can apply constraints to restrict the values Solver can use in the adjustable cells.

In the example shown in Fig 13.21, the level of advertising in each quarter affects the number of units sold, indirectly determining the amount of sales revenue, the cost of sales and the profit. Solver can change the quarterly budgets for advertising (cells C12:D12), up to a total budget constraint of Rs. 200,000 (cell E12), until the value for total profit reaches the maximum possible amount. The values in the adjustable cells are used to calculate the profit for each quarter, so they are related to the formula in target cell E14 =SUM (Q1 Profit:Q2 Profit).

| 1. Before running Solver | | | | |
|---|---|---|---|---|
| Item | Qtr I | Qtr II | Total | |
| Advertisement Budget (Rs.) | 100,000 | 100,000 | 200,000 | Constraint. Max 200,000 |
| | | | | Cells to be varied |
| Total Profit (Rs.) | | | 20,000 | Target Cell |
| **2. After running Solver** | | | | |
| Item | Qtr I | Qtr II | Total | Solver modifies Qtr I and II |
| Advertisement Budget (Rs.) | 85,000 | 115,000 | 200,000 | Adv budgets within the constraint of cell E12 to |
| Total Profit (Rs.) | | | 32,000 | maximise profit in E14 |

*Fig 13.21 Solver Example*

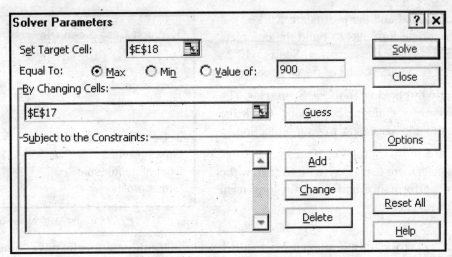

*Fig 13.22 Solver Parameters Dialogue Box*

Start Solver in an Excel 2000 spreadsheet by clicking **Tools** ➔ **Solver**. The Solver Parameters dialogue box appears.

In this dialogue box, enter the parameters for Solver to work on. Then follow the instructions on your monitor to let Solver complete the exercise. See Fig 13.22 for a view of the Solver Parameters dialogue box. The target cell value may be constrained to a maximum value, a minimum value or an exact value. You can set additional constraints for the adjustable values also.

# Scenarios

When you calculate the outcome of a worksheet such as the year-end profits, it is often necessary to look at more than one outcome because of the uncertainties in business. To look at alternatives in a convenient manner, you can create Scenarios, each showing a different outcome. Generally, the most common set of scenarios are:

- Optimistic.
- Most likely.
- Pessimistic.

You can calculate each scenario separately and save them as a set. You can then easily switch from one scenario to another to see how profits, costs or sales change as you move from optimistic to most likely or pessimistic.

## Creating Scenarios

If you want to create a budget but are uncertain of your revenue, you can define different values for revenue and then switch between the scenarios to perform What-if analyses.

In this example, since the gross revenue from sales cannot be exactly predicted, you can build two scenarios, one worst-case, where sales revenue is Rs. 100,000 and the other best-case, where the sales revenue is Rs. 150,000.

Cost of goods sold and the profits are worked out by the appropriate formulas to build the complete worst-case and best-case scenarios. See Fig 13.23 for a view of summary results of the two scenarios.

Start Scenario by clicking **Tools** ➜ **Scenarios**. The Scenario Manager dialogue box opens. Click the **Add** button to add a scenario to your collection.

Scenarios are most useful for strategy meetings where a management team may wish to review the forecast of performance and draw up long-term plans.

| 1. Worst Case Scenario | |
|---|---|
| | Rs '000 |
| Gross revenue | 100,000 |
| Cost of goods sold | 70,000 |
| Gross profits | 30,000 |
| | |
| 2. Best Case Scenario | |
| Gross revenue | 150,000 |
| Cost of goods sold | 105,000 |
| Gross profits | 45,000 |

*Fig 13.23 Example of Scenarios*

## CD-ROM

 To learn more about Microsoft Excel 2000 in a multimedia environment, insert the accompanying CD-ROM in your computer, select the **Interactive** mode in the opening screen. The main menu will appear. To go to the section on Excel, click the button **Excel**. You will see a sub-menu containing the following topics:

- Getting Started in Excel
- Power of Excel Unleashed

Click on each sub-menu item to display another level of sub-sub-menus. From these, you can select the particular topic you want to see. Click on your selected topic and follow instructions on your screen.

# 14. Excel Formulas and Functions

**In this chapter:**

☞ Having entered data in your worksheet, you learn about formulas and functions that you can use to work with the data.

☞ You are introduced to parts of a formula and methods of creating a formula to calculate the result you seek.

☞ You are shown methods of referencing data from other sources or other worksheets.

☞ You learn how to correct errors in your formulas and to use the Watch Window to spot and correct errors such as circular references.

☞ You are introduced to the many built-in functions in Excel. You learn about the Insert function dialogue box that lets you insert one of the built-in functions in a worksheet cell at the click of a mouse.

# Formulas and Functions

After having entered or imported data into your worksheet, you are now ready to use the data. To do so, you use formulas and functions just as you would when doing mathematics with pencil and paper. In addition to trigonometric functions, Excel has a large built-in library of statistical functions, financial functions and much more. We begin with an understanding of how you can use formulas to calculate in your worksheet.

# Formulas

Formulas are equations that perform calculations on values in your worksheet. A formula starts with an equal sign (=). For example, the following formula multiplies 2 by 3 and then adds 5 to the result.

   $= 2 * 3 + 5$

A formula can also contain any or all of the following: functions, references, operators and constants. Since you will almost always want to manipulate data in your worksheets by using figures for calculations, a good understanding of formulas is important for you as a user of Excel 2000.

## Parts of a Formula

Let us look closely at a sample formula:

   $= PI * A2 \wedge 2$

Here, PI is a function that returns the value of 3.142..., which is the constant value connecting radius of a circle to its diameter. A2 is a cell reference and 2 is, of course, a constant. The $\wedge$ or caret sign indicates that the contents of cell A2 are to be raised to the power 2 before multiplying it with the value of PI.

## Functions in Formulas

Functions are predefined formulas that perform calculations by using specific values, called arguments, in a particular order, or structure. Functions can be used to perform simple or complex calculations. For example, the ROUND function rounds off a number (supplied to the function as an "argument") to the specified number of digits. The structure of the function is:

   = ROUND (Cell reference, Number of digits)

Thus, to round off the contents of cell A10 and to display the result as a two-digit number, the function may be written as:

   = ROUND (A10, 2)

Notice the two arguments passed to the function. The first is a cell reference; it could also be a number. The second is the number of digits to which the first argument is to be rounded off.

## Structure of a Function

The structure of a function begins with an equal sign (=), followed by the function name, an opening parenthesis, the arguments for the function separated by commas, and a closing parenthesis.

Arguments can be numbers, text, logical values such as TRUE or FALSE, arrays, error values such as #N/A, or cell references. The argument you designate must produce a valid value for that argument. Arguments can also be constants, formulas, or other functions.

We shall study functions in more detail later in this chapter.

# Create a Formula

## A Simple Formula

You can enter a simple formula in a cell by typing an "Equal to (=)" sign followed by the formula such as = 129 + 345. The cell will contain the result of adding 129 to 345 and show 474.

The following formulas contain operators such as "+" (plus) and "^" (caret) and constants such as 129, 345, 5 and 2 as you can see in Fig 14.01. The examples show the use of numbers but no cell references.

To insert a formula in a cell, do the following:

1. Click the **cell** in which you want to enter the formula.
2. Type = (an equal sign).
3. Enter the **formula**.
4. Press **ENTER** ↵.

## Formula with a Cell Reference

The following formulas contain relative references to and names of other cells. The cell that contains the formula is known as a dependent cell when its value depends on the values in other cells. For example, cell B2 is a dependent cell if it contains the formula = C2 since the value of B2 depends on the value contained in the cell C2. In Fig 14.01, you can see examples of formulas that use cell references rather than just numbers.

| Example formula | What it does |
|---|---|
| = 128 + 345 | Adds 128 and 345 |
| = 5^2 | Squares 5 |

Formulas using numbers as in calculators

Formulas using the content of cells

| Example formula | What it does |
|---|---|
| = C2 | Uses the value in the cell C2 |
| = Sheet2!B2 | Uses the value in cell B2 on Sheet2 |
| = Asset-Liability | Subtracts a cell named Liability from a cell named Asset |

*Fig 14.01 Examples of Formulas and Cell References*

In addition to entering a formula directly in a cell, you can also do the following:

1. Click the **cell** in which you want to enter the formula.

2. In the Formula bar, type an Equal to (=) sign.

Note that the formula bar is located at the top right of your worksheet, just below the Standard tool bar.

3. To create a reference, select a **cell**, a range of cells, a location in another worksheet, or a location in another workbook. You can drag the border of the cell selection to move the selection, or drag the corner of the border to expand the selection.

4. Press **ENTER** ↵.

You can see the formula bar in Fig 14.02.

## Formula with a Nested Function

We have already seen a sample of a formula that contained the function PI, earlier in this chapter. We will now look at a more complex example containing a "Nested" function.

Nested functions use a function as one of the arguments of another function. The following formula sums a set of numbers (G2:G5) only if the average of another set of numbers (F2:F5) is greater than 50. Otherwise it returns 0.

= IF(AVERAGE(G2:G5)>50, SUM(G2:G5),0)

There are three functions used, IF, AVERAGE and SUM. AVERAGE and SUM are nested within the IF function.

To enter a nested function, proceed as follows:

1. Click the **cell** in which you want to enter the formula.

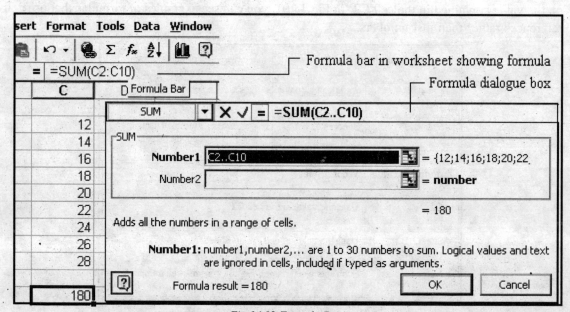

*Fig 14.02 Formula Bar*

2. To start the formula with the function, click **Insert Function** on the formula bar. See the Insert Function dialogue box in Fig 14.03.

3. Select the **function** you want to use. You can enter a question that describes what you want to do in the Search for a function box (for example, "add numbers" returns the SUM function), or browse from the categories in the **Select a Category** box.

4. Enter the **arguments**.

   • To enter cell references as an argument, click **Collapse Dialogue** next to the argument you want to temporarily hide the dialogue box. Select the cells on the worksheet; then press Expand Dialogue.

   • To enter another function as an argument, enter the **function** in the argument box you want. For example, you can add SUM (G2:G5) in the Value if true edit box.

   • To switch the parts of the formula displayed in the Function Arguments dialogue box, click a **function name** in the formula bar. For example, if you click IF, the arguments for the IF function appear.

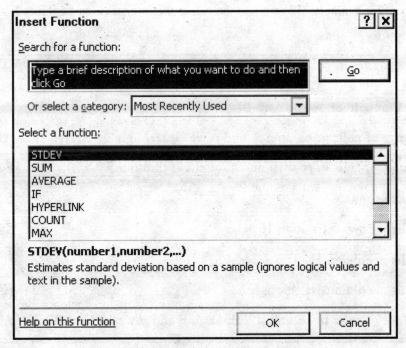

*Fig 14.03 Insert Function Dialogue Box*

You can enter the same formula into a range of cells by selecting the range first, typing the formula, and then pressing **CTRL + ENTER**.

If you are familiar with the arguments of a function, you can use the Function Tool Tip that appears after you type the function name and an opening parenthesis. Click the function name to view the Help topic on the function, or click an argument name to select the corresponding argument in your formula. In case you find the Function Tool Tip distracting, you can hide it easily. On the Tools menu, click **Options**, and then clear the Function Tool Tips **check box** on the General tab.

# Using References

We have already seen that formulas in one cell may refer to the contents of another cell. For example, a formula in cell B2 could read = A2 * 2. This means that whatever is entered in cell A2 will be doubled and entered in cell B2 by the worksheet. We say that the formula in cell B2 is "referencing" the cell A2.

A reference identifies a cell or a range of cells on a worksheet and tells Microsoft Excel where to look for the values or data you want to use in a formula. With references, you can use data contained in different parts of a worksheet in one formula or use the value from one cell in several formulas. You can also refer to cells on other sheets in the same workbook, and to other workbooks. References to cells in other workbooks are called links.

### The A1 Reference Style

By default, Excel uses the A1 reference style, which refers to columns with letters (A through IV, for a total of 256 columns) and refers to rows with numbers (1 through 65,536). These letters and numbers are called row and column headings. To refer to a cell, enter the column letter followed by the row number. For example, B2 refers to the cell at the intersection of column B and row 2. *See Fig 14.04.*

| To refer to | Use |
| --- | --- |
| The cell in column A and row 10 | A10 |
| The range of cells in column A and rows 10 through 20 | A10:A20 |
| The range of cells in row 15 and columns B through E | B15:E15 |
| All cells in row 5 | 5:5 |
| All cells in rows 5 through 10 | 5:10 |
| All cells in column H | H:H |
| All cells in columns H through J | H:J |
| The range of cells in columns A through E and rows 10 through 20 | A10:E20 |

*Fig 14.04 A1 Style of Cell Reference*

## Reference to another Worksheet

In the following example, the AVERAGE worksheet function calculates the average value for the range B1:B10 on the worksheet named Marketing in the same workbook. An exclamation mark "!" is used to separate the worksheet name from the cell range B1:B10.

= AVERAGE (Marketing! B1:B10)

## *Relative References*

A relative cell reference, such as A1 in a formula, is based on the relative position of the cell that contains the formula and the cell the reference refers to. If you change the position of the cell that contains the formula changes, the reference is changed. If you copy the formula across rows or down columns, the reference automatically adjusts to the change in position of the cell containing the formula. By default, new formulas use relative references. For example, if you copy a relative reference in cell B2 to cell B3, it automatically adjusts from = A1 to = A2.

## *Absolute References*

An absolute cell reference in a formula, such as $A$1, always refers to a cell in a specific location. Even if you change the position of the cell that contains the formula changes, the absolute reference remains the same. If you copy the formula across rows or down columns, the absolute reference does not adjust. By default, new formulas use relative references, and you need to switch them to absolute references. For example, if you copy an absolute reference in cell B2 to cell B3, it stays the same in both cells = $A$1.

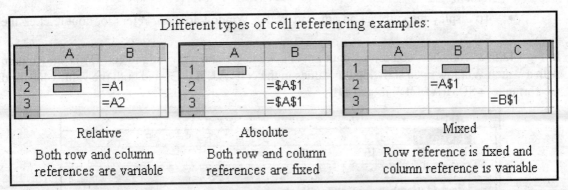

*Fig 14.05 Different Types of Cell Referencing*

## *Mixed References*

A mixed reference has either an absolute column and relative row, or absolute row and relative column. An absolute column reference takes the form $A1, $B1, and so on. An absolute row reference takes the form A$1, B$1, and so on. If the position of the cell that contains the formula changes, the relative reference is changed, and the absolute reference does not change. If you copy the formula across rows or down columns, the relative reference automatically adjusts, and the absolute reference does not adjust. For example, if you copy a mixed reference from cell A2 to B3, it adjusts from =A$1 to =B$1.

# Correcting Formulas

Formulas can be quite complex, involving cell references that span more than one worksheet, nested functions and several arguments. It is quite easy, therefore, to make a mistake. A simple error like not balancing the opening "("and closing ")" parentheses is enough to prevent a formula from working correctly. Fortunately, Excel 2000 provides you with a number of tools to correct errors in formulas. We look at the most useful tools in this section.

## *Watch Window*

By opening a Watch Window, you can watch cells and their formulas even when the cells are out of view. This is convenient in a large worksheet where you would not normally be able to see all the cells connected to your formula that you are trying to debug.

1. Select the **cells** you want to watch. To select all cells on a worksheet with formulas, click Go To on the Edit menu, click Special, and then click Formulas.
2. On the Tools menu, point to Formula Auditing menu, and then click **Show Watch Window**.
3. Click **Add Watch**.
4. Click **Add**.

You may have to do one or more of the following to adjust the Watch Window to your needs:

* Move the Watch Window tool bar to the top, bottom, left, or right side of the window.
* To change the width of a column, drag the boundary on the right side of the column heading.
* To display the cell that an entry in Watch Window tool bar refers to, double click the entry.

In Fig 14.06, a worksheet containing data in cells A1 to C1 and a formula in cell D1 is shown here with a Watch Window open showing the values in the cells A1, B1, C1 and both the value (440) and the formula "=SUM(A1:C1)" in cell D1.

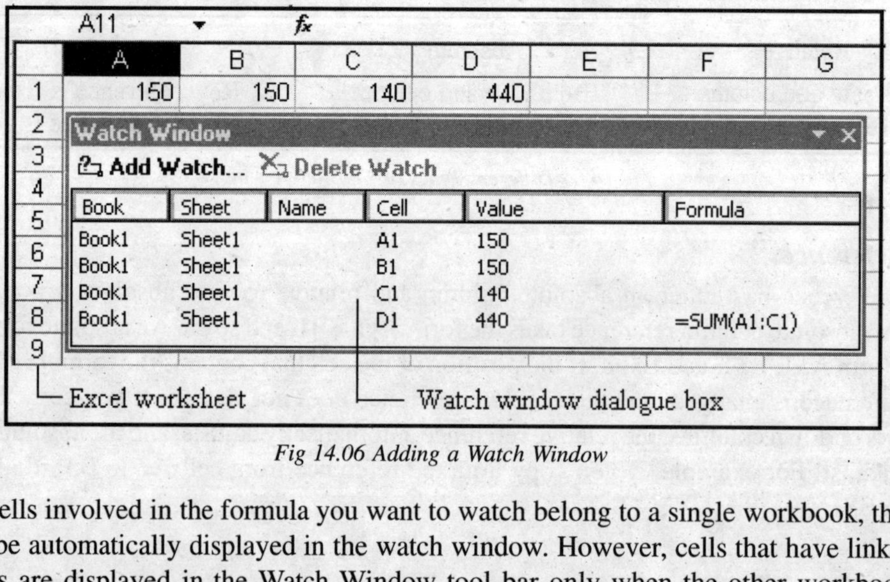

| A11 | fx | | | | | |
|---|---|---|---|---|---|---|
| | A | B | C | D | E | F | G |

Watch Window

Add Watch... Delete Watch

| Book | Sheet | Name | Cell | Value | Formula |
|---|---|---|---|---|---|
| Book1 | Sheet1 | | A1 | 150 | |
| Book1 | Sheet1 | | B1 | 150 | |
| Book1 | Sheet1 | | C1 | 140 | |
| Book1 | Sheet1 | | D1 | 440 | =SUM(A1:C1) |

Excel worksheet — Watch window dialogue box

*Fig 14.06 Adding a Watch Window*

If all the cells involved in the formula you want to watch belong to a single workbook, then all the cells will be automatically displayed in the watch window. However, cells that have links to other workbooks are displayed in the Watch Window tool bar only when the other workbook is also open. Therefore, open all related workbooks before setting up a Watch Window.

## Error Checker

In Word 2000, you can turn on the spelling checker and the grammar checker to automatically detect and report errors. Similarly, you can turn on the automatic error checking feature in Excel 2000 to detect errors in formulas.

To start the Error Checker, do the following:

1. Click **Tools** ➔ **Options** and then click on the **Error Checking** tab. You will find that there are seven check boxes to detect different types of errors automatically. Click to select the errors you want Excel 2000 to detect and report automatically as you build the spreadsheet. See Fig 14.07 for a view of the Error Checker window.

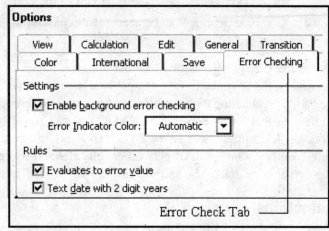

*Fig 14.07 Error Checker Window*

2. At any time, you can click **Tools ➔ Error Checking** on an open worksheet to recheck the entire spreadsheet. If you want to check only some cells and not the entire worksheet, select only the cells you want to check before opening the Error Checker.

## Circular References

While setting up a complex spreadsheet, you can accidentally insert a formula in a cell that refers back to itself, either directly or indirectly. This is called circular reference and it generates an error when the spreadsheet is calculated. This is because the formula will keep calculating in an endless loop and, hence, cannot be evaluated. If the back reference is deliberate as an intermediate step in setting up of the spreadsheet, which you intend to correct later, you may ask Excel to accept the circular reference. If the error is inadvertent, you would want Excel to find the error by pointing to the cells that have got looped together so that you may correct the situation.

### *Locate and Remove Circular Reference*

1. If the Circular Reference tool bar is not displayed, click **Customise** on the **Tools** menu, click the **Tool bars** tab, and then select the **Circular Reference** check box. The circular reference dialogue box is displayed. *See Fig 14.08.*

2. On the ·Circular Reference tool bar, click the **first cell** in the Navigate Circular Reference box.

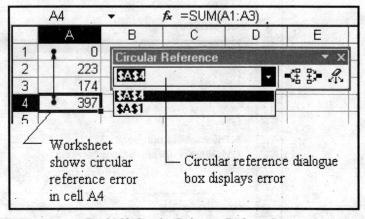

*Fig 14.08 Circular Reference Dialogue Box*

3. Review the formula in the cell. If you cannot determine whether the cell is the cause of the circular reference, click the **next cell** in the Navigate Circular Reference box.

4. Continue to review and correct the circular reference until the status bar no longer displays the word "Circular Reference".

When the Circular Reference tool bar appears, tracer arrows appear that point out the cells that depend on the formula. In the example here, tracer arrows connect "0" (in cell $A$1) and "397" (in cell $A$4) indicating the cells affected by circular reference. The head of the arrow points to $A$1 indicating that $A$4 depends on $A$1. You can move between cells in a circular reference by double clicking the tracer arrows. You can also click on the drop-down arrow next to the circular reference box which will display other cells affected by circular reference. In the example shown, the cursor is on cell $A$4 and the drop-down box indicates cell $A$1 as the other cell.

## Functions

We have already met functions as part of formulas. Functions begin with an "=" sign, followed by the function name along with arguments that are passed to functions. For example:

= ROUND (number, num_digits)

is a function for rounding off numbers to a predetermined number of digits. The function is made flexible by passing parameters (here, "number" and "num_digits") to it when the function is called in a formula. Thus, the same "Round" function can be used again and again in different formulas by passing the number to be rounded and the number of digits to be displayed as needed.

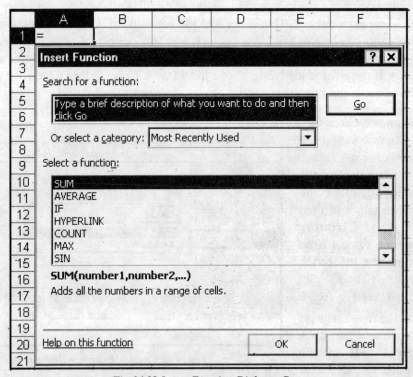

*Fig 14.09 Insert Function Dialogue Box*

You can see a list of functions available by selecting the cell where you wish to insert the function and then pressing SHIFT + F3. The Insert Function dialogue box opens. *See Fig 14.09.* In this dialogue box, you can search for a suitable function by typing its description or selecting its category (see the text that follows for function categories). You can also select from a drop-down list and seek help on the selected function by clicking on the "Help on this function" button.

## Function Categories

Excel 2000 contains a very large number of functions. They can be grouped in the following categories:

- Database
- Date and Time
- External
- Engineering
- Financial
- Logical
- Lookup and Reference
- Math and Trigonometry
- Statistical
- Text and Data

It is unlikely that you will have occasion to use all the functions that Excel 2000 contains. However, if you work regularly in a specialised area, such as engineering, financial or statistical calculations, you may wish to spend some time using Excel 2000's excellent help system to study the functions

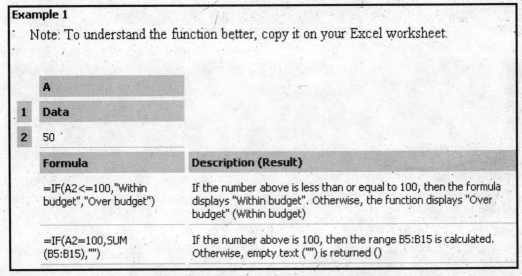

**Example 1**

Note: To understand the function better, copy it on your Excel worksheet.

| A | |
|---|---|
| **1** | **Data** |
| **2** | 50 |

| Formula | Description (Result) |
|---|---|
| =IF(A2<=100,"Within budget","Over budget") | If the number above is less than or equal to 100, then the formula displays "Within budget". Otherwise, the function displays "Over budget" (Within budget) |
| =IF(A2=100,SUM (B5:B15),"") | If the number above is 100, then the range B5:B15 is calculated. Otherwise, empty text ("") is returned () |

*Fig 14.10 Example of the Logical Function IF*

of interest to you. The syntax and meaning of each function is described in detail with one or more examples to explain how the function works.

See Fig 14.10 for an example of the Logical Function "IF".

To understand what the IF formula does in each case, read the text under Description (Result) on the right hand side of the figure.

**CD-ROM**  To learn more about Microsoft Excel 2000 in a multimedia environment, insert the accompanying CD-ROM in your computer, select the **Interactive** mode in the opening screen. The main menu will appear. To go to the section on Excel, click the button marked **Excel**. You will see a sub-menu containing the following topics:

- Getting Started in Excel
- Power of Excel Unleashed

Click on each sub-menu item to display another level of sub-sub-menus. From these, you can select the particular topic you want to see. Click on your selected topic and follow instructions on your screen.

# 15. Excel Diagrams and Charts

## In this chapter:

☞ You learn about adding diagrams to worksheets in the same way as you have learned to do in Microsoft Word.

☞ Charts are worth a thousand figures! You learn how to produce attractive charts from the figures in your worksheet.

☞ After creating a basic chart, you learn how to format the display of the chart to your liking.

☞ You are shown how to add labels such as titles, data labels and legends.

☞ You become familiar with the Chart Options dialogue box that you use to edit and modify Data Labels Legend Boxes and Text Boxes.

☞ You learn how to add data to an existing chart and to change values already in a chart.

# Diagrams and Charts

Graphics are an integral part of all types of documents including the ones that you can produce using Excel. Therefore, Excel too has a full set of tools for producing professional quality charts, diagrams and drawings. We look at these capabilities of Excel in this chapter.

# Diagrams

Excel 2000 has the same capability as Word 2000 to create, insert and edit drawings, pictures and diagrams. The drawing tool bar at the bottom of your Excel 2000 screen has the same set of icons as the drawing tool bar in Word 2000 and the same graphic capabilities.

# Charts

## Creating Charts

Since spreadsheets deal in figures, it is often necessary to represent figures in a graphic format. Creating, formatting and manipulating charts, therefore, form a major part of the skills you wish to acquire in Excel 2000. Charts are visually appealing and make it easy for users to see comparisons, patterns, and trends in data. For instance, rather than having to analyse several columns of worksheet numbers, you can see at a glance whether sales are falling or rising over quarterly periods, or how the actual sales compare to the projected sales.

In this example, you can see the tabulated data showing quarterly projected and actual sales and the corresponding bar chart using these figures. One glance at the bar chart will tell you that the second quarter actual sales are much closer to the projected sales.

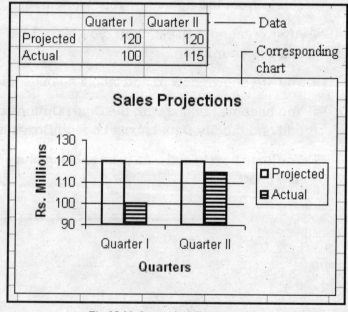

*Fig 15.01 Quarterly Sales Projections*

## Combination Charts

A combination chart uses two or more chart types to emphasise that the chart contains different kinds of information. The chart in the example shows one data series (Projected) as a column chart type and the other (Actual) as a line.

To create this kind of overlay effect, select a custom chart type in Step 1 of the Chart Wizard when you create a chart. This example uses the Line – Column Chart type. You can change an existing chart to a combination chart by selecting the data series you want to change and then changing the chart type for that series.

By using a line to display the actual sales, it is possible to emphasise the improvement in actual sales as may be seen clearly by the rising slope of the line.

Be ready to experiment with alternatives to find the combination that expresses what you have to say in the most effective manner. Incidentally, the chart wizard is a small icon on your standard tool bar, shaped like a miniature bar chart. Now let us get our hands dirty and actually create a chart!

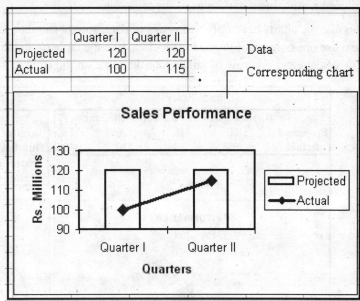

*Fig 15.02 Sales Performance Chart*

# Creating a Chart

To create a chart, the first step is to arrange your data appropriately. The arrangements will differ depending on the type of chart you wish to create. After the data has been correctly arranged, you may either:

- Customise your chart step by step, as you create it.

  Or

- Create a basic chart that you can customise later.

We shall first examine how data should be arranged to suit the chart type you have in mind.

### *Arranging Data*

Excel 2000 has a powerful, built-in chart wizard that can convert the data in your spreadsheet to a variety of professional looking charts with very little effort on your part. After the default charts have been created by the wizard, you can modify the chart and enhance its visual appeal and clarity. However, the wizard will work correctly only if the data has first been arranged correctly.

### *Column, Bar, Line, Area, Surface or Radar Chart*

For this family of charts, the data should be arranged in the form of a table. Select the entire table, including the row and column headers and then click the graph icon on the Excel tool bar to begin charting. Clicking on the icon launches the chart wizard that guides you through the charting process. We discuss the chart wizard later in this chapter.

In Fig 15.03, you will see the same data arranged in two tables. The table on the left has the data arranged in rows, while the table on the right has the same data arranged in columns. As you can see, the data has been used to create a pie chart and a doughnut chart. Both the row as well as the column arrangement can be used for charting.

Regular pie charts have only one series of data, so you should use only one column of data. You can also use one column of labels for the data, like the table on the left. Alternatively, you can have one row of data and one row of labels like the table on the right.

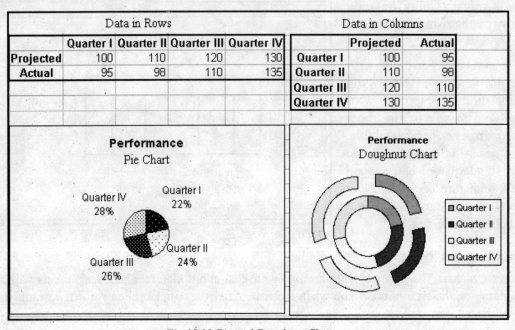

*Fig 15.03 Pie and Doughnut Charts*

## Stacked Pie or Doughnut Charts

Stacked pie charts and doughnut charts can have more than one series of data, so you can use more than one column of data, like the table on the left. Or, it may have more than one row of data like the table on the right.

| A | B | C |
|---|---|---|
| 1 | 2 | 3 |
| 4 | 5 | 6 |

| A | 1 | 2 |
|---|---|---|
| B | 3 | 4 |
| C | 5 | 6 |

## X-Y Scatter or Bubble Charts

To create Scatter and Bubble charts, arrange your data in columns. The X values should be in the first column with corresponding Y values (for scatter charts) in the second column.

For Bubble charts, the X values should be in the first column and the bubble sizes (in the column headed "Bubble") should be in the second column as shown in Fig 15.04. Scatter charts or X-Y charts are useful for showing correlation between two variables while a bubble chart is used for comparing sizes such as market share of two competitors.

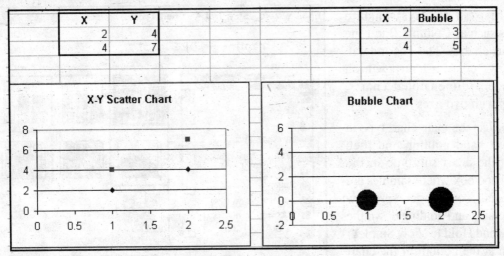

*Fig 15.04 Scatter and Bubble Charts*

### Stock Quotations

Stock quotations generally display the High, Low and Closing values of Stocks and Shares. You can display the share value of several companies on the same day by plotting the values against the company names. Or, you can show the price movement of shares of the same company spread over a period of time.

Arrange your data in columns, with the company name or date in the first column, followed by High, Low and Closing values. You can see the data for price movement of the shares of the same company spread over three days in Fig 15.05.

| Dates | High | Low | Closing |
|-------|------|-----|---------|
| 10-Apr-03 | 110 | 98 | 100 |
| 11-Apr-03 | 115 | 100 | 112 |
| 12-Apr-03 | 110 | 100 | 105 |

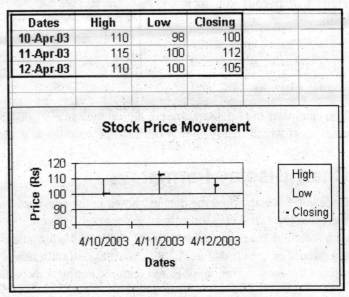

*Fig 15.05 Stock Chart*

### TRAP

Excel 2000 evaluates dates correctly only if you use the Month/Date/Year format and not the more common Date/Month/Year format we use in India. Therefore, before sorting a date column make sure that it is in the Month/Date/Year format. Otherwise, you will get wrong results.

## The Chart Wizard

We have already referred to the Chart Wizard. We take a look at the chart wizard dialogue box here in Fig 15.06. When you click on the chart wizard icon on the standard tool bar of Excel 2000, you will see step 1 as seen in Fig 15.06.

The first tab displays standard charts such as Column, Bar, Line or Pie charts. The second tab displays custom charts which include 3-dimensional charts, charts with two axes etc.

First select the main chart type in the left hand column and then select the chart sub-type in the right hand box where samples are displayed. You can get a preview by pressing and holding down the "Press and Hold to View Smples" button at the bottom of the chart sub-type box. The subsequent steps will permit you to work with:

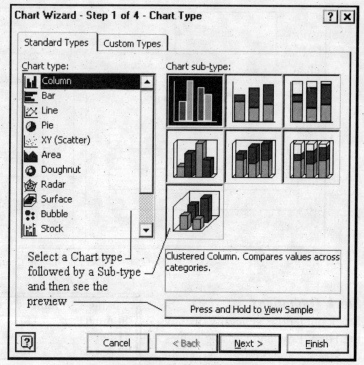

Fig 15.06 Chart Wizard

- Chart source data.
- Chart options.
- Chart location.

You can insert the finalised chart either on the same worksheet that contains data, or on a separate chart sheet which will form part of the same workbook as the worksheet.

## Chart Display Format

Once you have arranged the data as shown in the previous section, the chart wizard will produce a workable chart with very little effort on your part. However, you may wish to enhance the appearance of a standard chart to make some of the information stand out, or just to improve the general appearance of the chart. Excel 2000 provides you with many formatting tools for this purpose. We discuss the most common tools and features that will meet almost all but your very special needs.

### Fills and Lines

Use this procedure to change colours, apply a texture or pattern, or change the line width or border style for data markers, the chart area, the plot area, gridlines, axes, and tick marks in 2-D and 3-D charts, trend lines and error bars in 2-D charts, and the walls and floor in 3-D charts.

1. Double click the chart **item** you want to change.
2. If necessary, click the **Patterns** tab, and then select the options you want.

**NOTE** To specify a fill effect, click Fill Effects, and then select the options you want on the Gradient, Texture, or Pattern tabs.

Formatting applied to an axis is also applied to the tick marks on that axis. Gridlines are formatted independently of axes.

A table containing data and its corresponding column chart is shown in Fig 15.07. Some of the common elements in a chart are identified as labels such as Border for the chart area, the Chart area itself, the Plot area, which is within the chart area, the Gridlines in the plot area as well as the X-axis with its tick marks.

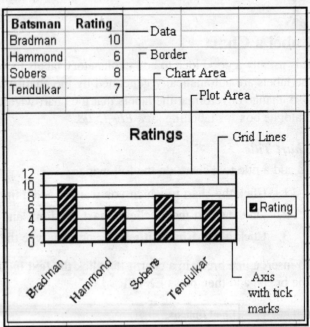

The fills and lines of the original chart produced by the chart wizard had different colours for each column and the plot area was also coloured. For black and white reproduction in this book the plot area colour has been removed and the column colours have been replaced by a hatch pattern. This is a good example of the use of different fills and lines.

*Fig 15.07 Fills and Lines in a Chart*

## Number format

You can change the number format of a chart as follows:

1. Do one of the following:
   - To format labels along an axis, double click the appropriate **axis**.
   - To format data labels or a trend line label, double click the **item**.
2. The Format Axis dialogue box appears.
3. On the Number tab, select the **options** you want.

## Change Colours

The colours used for the separate data series in your chart can have the same colour or different colours. For example, Fig 15.07 shows several batsmen's ratings. Here, you can set the same colour of the columns for the four batsmen, or you can use different colours for each batsman. To toggle the colour settings, proceed as follows:

1. Click the **data series** you want to change the colours for.
2. On the Format menu, click **Selected Data Series** or **Selected Data Point**, and then click the **Options** tab.
3. Select the **Vary colours by point** check box or the **Vary colours by slice** check box in case of a pie chart.

**NOTE**

Excel uses many colours and graded hues for its graphics. However, since the reproductions in this book are in black and white, you will only see patterns like horizontal or vertical lines and solid colours such as black, white and grey in these examples.

## Label a Chart

It is usually a good idea to add explanatory labels to your chart for better understanding. Some of the labels are automatically generated by the chart wizard; others can be added by you. You can also change or reformat the labels that the chart wizard has generated. You use the Chart Options dialogue box for labelling. *See Fig 15.08.*

### Chart Title

To add a title to a chart, do the following:

1. Click the chart to which you want to add a title.
2. On the Chart menu, click **Chart Options**, and then click the **Titles** tab.
3. Click in the **Chart title box**, and then type the **text** you want.

To insert a line break in a chart title, click the **text** on the chart, click where you want to insert the line break, and then press ENTER ⏎.

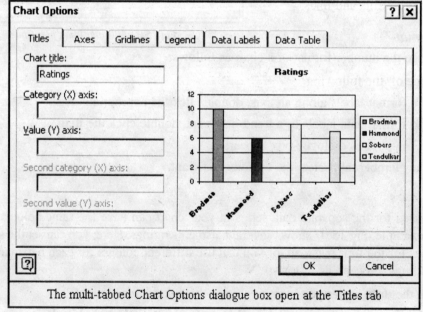

The multi-tabbed Chart Options dialogue box open at the Titles tab

*Fig 15.08 Chart Options*

### Legend

To add legends to a chart, proceed as follows:

1. Click the **chart** to which you want to add a legend.

2. On the Chart menu, click **Chart Options**, and then click the **Legend** tab.

3. Select the **Show legend** check box.

4. Under Placement, click the **option** you want.

 **NOTE** When you click one of the Placement options, the legend moves, and the plot area automatically adjusts to accommodate it. However, if you move and size the legend by using the mouse, the plot area does not automatically adjust itself.

When you use the Placement options, the legend loses any custom sizing you may have already applied.

## Chart Options Dialogue Box

The Chart Options dialogue box shown in Fig 15.08 is used for many formatting tasks. For instance, the Chart title edit box can be used to enter a new title or to change an existing one. Similarly, the Legends tab is to be selected to add legends to the chart. We shall refer to this dialogue box throughout the rest of this chapter.

Other tabs give access to formatting options of Axes, Gridlines, Legends, Data Labels and the Data table from which the chart has been created. The best way to learn the different formatting techniques is to experiment with the chart. Since you can easily delete an unsatisfactory chart and redraw it from the data table, your imagination can really be let loose.

## Data Labels

Excel plots a data as points on a chart. The point is represented as a small dot or square, called a data marker and no value is shown against it. If you want to provide additional information such as the exact value at a data point, you can use a data label as in Fig 15.09.

In order to display a data label, right click on a data point and then click Format data series on the drop-down menu. The Format data series dialogue box will appear. Click on the Data label tab. Now, by clicking on the appropriate check box, you can have the chart display the series name, the category name or the value next to the plotted data point on the chart.

If we create a column chart, using the data in the Fig 15.09 shown, by selecting the data label tab, we can add more data labels to the chart points that will display:

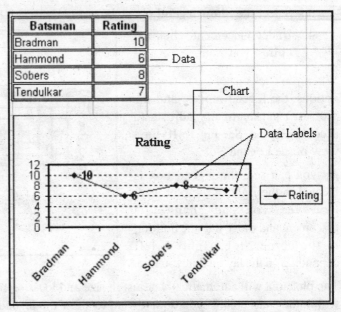

*Fig 15.09 Data Labels in a Chart*

- Series Name, which is "Rating". It is the same for each data point.
- Category Name, which will be the names of the four batsmen.
- Value, which will be the rating value for each batsman.

In this example in Fig 15.09, the rating value of each batsman has been displayed as data labels. If you wish to modify the data labels, proceed as follows:

1. Click once on the **data label** you want to change to select the data labels for the entire series, and then click again to select the **individual data label**.

2. Type the **new text or value**, and then press **ENTER** ↵.

**TRAP**

Note that if you change the data label text on the chart, it is no longer linked to the worksheet cell from which it was originally derived. This means that if you now change the text in the connected worksheet cell, the data label will not be automatically updated. You will have to make the changes yourself.

# Legend

A chart may consist of columns, bars, lines or pie slices representing data values. If many data values are plotted, it is not easy to identify a data series with the category name it represents. To clarify this relationship, you can include a legend box, which contains the category names and the identifying colour or pattern used in the corresponding columns, bars or lines in your chart.

To add legend to your chart, proceed as follows:

1. Click the **chart** to which you want to add a legend.

2. On the Chart menu, click **Chart Options**, and then click the **Legend** tab.

3. Select the **Show legend** check box.

4. Under Placement, click the **option** you want.

When you click one of the Placement options, the legend moves, and the plot area automatically adjusts to accommodate it. See Fig 15.10 for a view of the Legend Box.

As you can see, the legend box is located to the right of the plot area. However, you can change its placement and move it to the bottom, to the corner, top, right or left depending on the layout that you like.

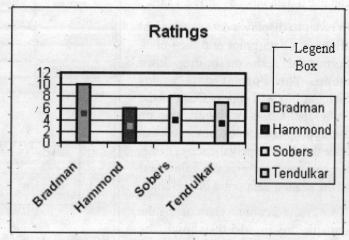

*Fig 15.10 Legend Box*

The plot area will automatically adjust in size and location to accommodate the plot and the legend within the chart area. If you do not want to show the legend box, uncheck the Show legend check box in the legend tab.

# Text Box

While a chart has a title, legends, axes titles and data labels, it is sometimes necessary to add even more explanatory information on the chart in the form of text. You add text on a chart by using the Text box.

Insert a text box in your chart as follows:

1. Click the **chart** to which you want to add a text box.

2. On the Drawing tool bar, click **Text Box**.

3. Click where you want one corner of the text box, and then drag until the box is the size you want.

4. Type the **text** you want in the box. The text will wrap inside the box. To start a new line inside the box, press **ENTER** ↵.

5. When you finish typing, press **ESC** or click **outside** of the text box.

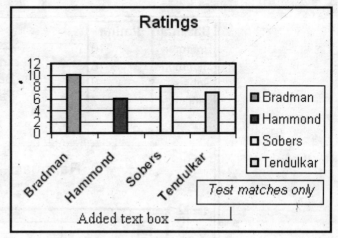

*Fig 15.11 Text Box Added On*

In Fig 15.11, a text box has been added to the chart containing the words "Test Matches only" in italics.

# Edit a Chart

When a chart is created from a range of data in a worksheet, the value of the cells on the worksheet and the plotted points on the chart are dynamically linked. This means that if you change the values in the cells, the plotted points on the chart will also change automatically to reflect the change in the data contained in the cells.

**TIP** Occasionally, you may wish to change the plotted points only, without changing the data in the cells. Such situations may arise if you wish to print out charts showing less data than what is entered in the spreadsheet without altering the spreadsheet itself. We look at procedures for adding, deleting and changing data after the data has already been used to create a chart.

## Add Data

It is sometimes necessary to add more data to an existing worksheet and to the linked chart as well.

This may become necessary if additional information is received after the worksheet and the chart had been prepared. For example, you may have prepared an initial batsman's rating table with four batsmen (Bradman, Hammond, Sobers and Tendulkar), and you may have already created a chart. (*See Fig 15.12*). Now you may want to add the statistics of S. Waugh to the same table. We discuss how you may want to do this in the following section.

**NOTE** The most common format that you will use is where the data table and the chart are both on the same worksheet, an arrangement where the chart is called an embedded chart. To add data to an embedded chart created from adjacent worksheet cells, use the colour-coded ranges that surround the data on the worksheet. Note that the illustrations in this book are in black and white, hence no colour ranges appear in the illustrations.

Fig 15.12 shows the data table and the chart before adding the details of S. Waugh. To add details about his rating to this chart, proceed as follows:

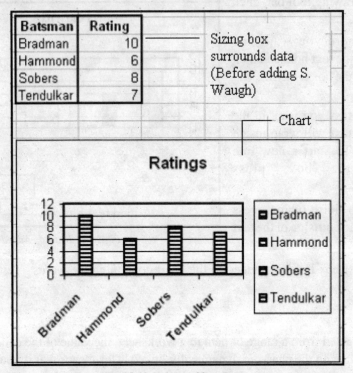

*Fig 15.12 Before Adding Data*

1.  Select the chart area by clicking the **blank area** between the border of the chart and the plot area. We have already seen these names (chart area and plot area) earlier in this section.

2.  Do one of the following:

    *   To add new categories and data series to the chart on the worksheet, drag the **blue sizing handle** to include the new data and labels in the rectangle.

    *   To add new data series only on the worksheet, drag the **green sizing handle** to include the new data and labels in the rectangle.

    *   To add new categories and data points on the worksheet, drag the **purple sizing handle** to include the new data and labels in the rectangle.

**NOTE** Note that the coloured (blue, green and purple) rectangles and handles will only appear when you click between the chart and the plot area to select the chart.

Figures 15.12 and 15.13 demonstrate the procedure we have discussed, allowing the addition of a fifth cricketer to the ratings data table and the rating chart.

If you want to delete the data you have just added, move the appropriately coloured rectangle to exclude the data you wish to remove from the chart. Thereafter, you can delete the removed data and labels in the usual manner.

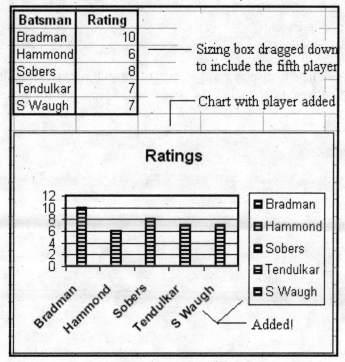

| Batsman | Rating |
|---------|--------|
| Bradman | 10 |
| Hammond | 6 |
| Sobers | 8 |
| Tendulkar | 7 |
| S Waugh | 7 |

— Sizing box dragged down to include the fifth player

— Chart with player added

*Fig 15.13 After Adding Data*

## Change Values

The values in a chart are linked to the worksheet from which the chart is created. When you change one, the other is also changed. You can change values directly in the relevant worksheet cell and the chart will automatically reflect the change. To change values directly, proceed as follows:

1.  Open the **worksheet** that contains the data plotted in the chart.
2.  In the cell that contains the value you want to change, type a **new value**.
3.  Press **ENTER** ⏎.

You will note that the chart automatically changes to reflect the change in the data table.

You have already seen an overview of charts in Excel 2000. In this chapter, we have taken you further down the road towards mastering diagrams and charts. However, you can learn many more things about making and editing and changing diagrams and charts by using Excel worksheets and charting the data yourself.

**CD-ROM**   To learn more about Microsoft Excel 2000 in a multimedia environment, insert the accompanying CD-ROM in your computer, select the **Interactive** mode in the opening screen. The main menu will appear. To go to the section on Excel, click the button **Excel**. You will see a sub-menu containing the following topics:

- Getting Started in Excel
- Power of Excel Unleashed

Click on each sub-menu item to display another level of sub-sub-menus. From these, you can select the particular topic you want to see. Click on your selected topic and follow instructions on your screen.

# 16. Getting to Know Access 2000

☞ You are introduced to the fundamentals of Access, the Database programme in the Microsoft Office 2000 suit.

☞ You learn how to open an existing database, or design a new database using special helper programmes called Wizards. You also learn to design databases from scratch, using the Design View.

☞ You learn the elements of designing a database by selecting the database tables you will use and then setting up links or relationships between them.

☞ You explore database tables, learning how to create them and enter data in them.

☞ You are shown how to create Forms and to customise them to suit your exact needs. You are also shown how to create and use Sub-forms.

☞ You learn about Queries and Reports, about their design, creation and use.

☞ You get to understand when to use Wizards and when to select Design View for creation and modification of database objects.

☞ You are introduced to other database objects that form part of a Microsoft Access database application.

# What is a Database?

A database is simply a systematic organisation of data. Let us take an example. If you are the secretary of a club and have to remind your members to pay their dues, you will need to keep their names, addresses and phone numbers on a card file so that you can find them easily. Then, you will need a standard or form letter to be used as a reminder, in which you can insert the names and addresses of the members who have not paid their dues. You may also keep a simple worksheet table in Microsoft Excel on your computer in which you will enter whether dues have been paid and the date on which payment was made. For a small club, with perhaps 20 or 30 members, this is all that you may need. However, clubs grow, memberships increase and the information becomes large and unwieldy. You may find that you are spending far too much time keeping track and often not being able to find the information you need. The time has come to organise all your information on a database.

| | | Category ID | Category Name | Descriptio |
|---|---|---|---|---|
| ▶ | ⊞ | 1 | Beverages | Soft drinks, coffees, teas, beers, an |
| | ⊞ | 2 | Condiments | Sweet and savory sauces, relishes, |
| | ⊞ | 3 | Confections | Desserts, candies, and sweet bread |
| | ⊞ | 4 | Dairy Products | Cheeses |
| | ⊞ | 5 | Grains/Cereals | Breads, crackers, pasta, and cerea |
| | ⊞ | 6 | Meat/Poultry | Prepared meats |
| | ⊞ | 7 | Produce | Dried fruit and bean curd |
| | ⊞ | 8 | Seafood | Seaweed and fish |
| * | | (AutoNumber) | | |

**Categories : Table**

Record: 1 of 8

*Fig 16.01 Sample Database*

## Using a Database for the First Time

Working with databases and database objects can be a daunting task when you first get started. The following information should help you become more familiar with the components that make up a Microsoft Access database.

## Databases: What They Are and How They Work

A database is a collection of information that is related to a particular subject or purpose, such as tracking customer orders or maintaining a music collection. If your database is not stored on a computer, or only parts of it are, you may be tracking information from a variety of sources that you have in order to coordinate and organise yourself.

For example, suppose the phone numbers of your suppliers are stored in various locations: in a card file containing supplier phone numbers, in product information files in a file cabinet, and in a worksheet containing order information...

**TIP**  If a supplier's phone number changes, you will have to update that information in all three places. In a database, however, you only have to update that information in one place — the supplier's phone number is automatically updated wherever you use it in the database. This is one of the great advantages of using a database like Access.

# Database Fundamentals

## Opening an Existing Database

If you have worked with databases before and have previously created databases on your computer then go directly to the section titled *Designing a Database*. If you are new to databases then first read what follows.

To open an existing database, do the following:

1. Make sure that Access is loaded and its opening screen is displayed on your monitor. On the file menu, click **File ➔ Open**. The Open dialogue box appears.

2. Click a **shortcut** in the left side of the Open dialogue box, or in the Look in box. Then click the **drive** or **folder** that contains the Microsoft Access database that you want.

3. In the folder list, double click **folders** until you open the folder that contains the database.

4. Do one of the following after double clicking the **database**:

   • To open the database for shared access in a multi-user environment so that you and other users can read and write to the database, click **Open**.

   • To open the database for read-only access so that you can view it but cannot edit it, click the arrow next to the Open button, and then click **Open Read-Only**.

   • To open the database with exclusive access, click the arrow next to the Open button, and then click **Open Exclusive**.

   • To open the database for read-only access and also prevent other users from opening it, click the arrow next to the Open button, and then click **Open Exclusive Read-Only**.

**NOTE**  If you cannot find the database that you want to open, click **Tools** on the tool bar in the Open dialogue box, and then click **Search**. In the Search dialogue box, enter additional search criteria. For help on an option, click the question mark and then click the **option**.

You can directly open a data file in an external file format such as dBASE, Paradox, Microsoft Exchange, or Microsoft Excel. You can also directly open any ODBC data source, such as Microsoft SQL Server or Microsoft FoxPro. Access automatically creates a new Access database in the same folder as the data file and adds links to each table in the external database.

Here are a set of useful tips:

   • To open one of the last several databases you had opened, click the file name at the bottom of the File menu. Microsoft Access opens the database with the same option settings it had the last time you opened it. If the list of recently used files is not displayed, click Options on the Tools menu, click the General tab, and then select the **Recently used file list** check box.

- To view a list of shortcuts to databases that you have opened previously, click **History** on the left side of the Open dialogue box.

- To quickly locate a file or folder in the Favourites folder, click **Favourites** on the left side of the Open dialogue box. To open a favourite file or folder, click the shortcut and then click Open. *See Fig 16.02.*

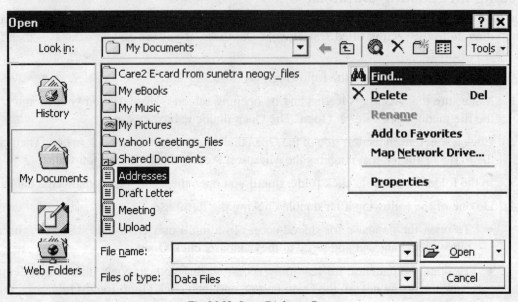

*Fig 16.02 Open Dialogue Box*

## Designing a Database

Good database design will make sure that your database is easy to maintain. You store data in tables and each table contains data about only one subject, such as customers. Therefore, you update a particular piece of data, such as an address, in just one place and that change automatically appears throughout the database.

A well-designed database usually contains different types of queries that show the information you need. A query might show a subset of data, such as all customers in Delhi, or combinations of data from different tables, such as order information combined with customer information.

Query and Table are just two database objects that you use in Access. There are other objects such as Forms, Reports and Modules. We will consider them later in this book.

**TIP** Before you use Microsoft Access to actually build tables, queries, forms and other objects, it is a good idea to first sketch out and refine your design on paper. You can also examine well-designed databases similar to the one you are designing, or you can open the Northwind sample database and then open the Relationships window to examine its design. *See Fig 16.05.*

If the Northwind sample database does not open, it has probably not been installed. To do so now, insert Microsoft Office 2000 CD-ROM in your computer when prompted, and follow instructions on your screen to install this sample database.

| Category ID | Category Name | Product Name | Product Sal |
|---|---|---|---|
| 3 | Meat/Poultry | Alice Mutton | 17,604.6 |
| 2 | Condiments | Aniseed Syrup | 1,724.0 |
| 8 | Seafood | Boston Crab Meat | 9,814.7 |
| 4 | Dairy Products | Camembert Pierrot | 20,505.4 |
| 8 | Seafood | Carnarvon Tigers | 15,950.0 |
| 1 | Beverages | Chai | 4,887.0 |
| 1 | Beverages | Chang | 7,038.5 |
| 1 | Beverages | Chartreuse verte | 4,475.7 |
| 2 | Condiments | Chef Anton's Cajun Seasoning | 5,214.8 |
| 2 | Condiments | Chef Anton's Gumbo Mix | 373.6 |
| 3 | Confections | Chocolade | 1,282.0 |
| 1 | Beverages | Côte de Blaye | 49,198.0 |
| 8 | Seafood | Escargots de Bourgogne | 2,076.2 |

Record: 1 of 77

*Fig 16.03 Sales by Category Query*

Follow these basic steps when designing your database:

## Determine the Purpose

The first step in designing a database is to determine its purpose and how it is to be used. Talk to people who will use the database. Brainstorm about the questions you and they would like the database to answer.

Sketch out the reports you'd like the database to produce.

Gather the forms you currently use to record your data.

As you determine the purpose of your database, a list of information you want from the database will begin to emerge. From that, you can determine what facts you need to store in the database and what subject each fact belongs to. These facts correspond to the fields (columns) in your database, and the subjects that those facts belong to correspond to the tables.

## Determine the Fields

Each field is a fact about a particular subject. For example, you might need to store the following facts about your customers:

- Company name
- Address
- City
- State
- Phone number

You will have to create a separate field for each of these facts. When determining which fields you need, keep the following principles of good design in mind:

- Make sure to include all the information you will need.

- Store information in their smallest logical parts. For example, employee names are often split into two fields, FirstName and LastName, so that it's easy to sort data by LastName.

- Do not create fields for data that consists of lists of multiple items. For example, in a Suppliers table, if you create a Products field that contains a comma-separated list of each product you receive from the supplier, it will be more difficult to find only the suppliers that provide a particular product.

- Do not include derived or calculated data.

- Do not include data that is the result of an expression. For example, if you have a UnitPrice field and a Quantity field, don't create an additional field that multiplies the values in these two fields.

- Do not create fields that are similar to each other.

For example, in a Suppliers table, if you create the fields Product1, Product2, and Product3, it will be more difficult to find all suppliers who provide a particular product. Also, you will have to change the design of your database if a supplier provides more than three products. You need only one field for products provided that you put that field in the Products table instead of in the Suppliers table.

## Determine the Tables

Each table should contain information about one subject. Your list of fields will provide clues to the tables you need. For example, if you have a HireDate field, its subject is an employee, so it belongs in the Employees table. You might have a table for Customers, a table for Products, and a table for Orders.

## Determine Which Table Each Field Belongs To

When you decide which table each field belongs to, keep these design principles in mind:

- Add the field to only one table.

- Do not add the field to a table if it will result in the same information appearing in multiple records in that table. If you determine that a field in a table will contain a lot of duplicate information, that field is probably in the wrong table.

For example, if you put the field containing the address of a customer in the Orders table, that information will probably be repeated in more than one record, because the customer is likely to place more than one order. However, if you put the address field in the Customers table, it will appear only once. In this respect, a table in a Microsoft Access database differs from a table in a flat file database such as a worksheet.

**NOTE**

When each piece of information is stored only once, you update it in one place. This is more efficient, and it also eliminates the possibility of duplicate entries that contain different information. Therefore, always avoid storing the same information in more than one table.

## Identify the Field or Fields with Unique Values in Each Record

To make sure that Microsoft Access is able to connect information stored in separate tables — for example, to connect a customer with all the customer's orders — each table in your database must include a field or set of fields that uniquely identifies each individual record in the table. Such a field or set of fields is called a primary key.

### Form: Customers

| ID | First Name | Surname | Phone |
|---|---|---|---|
|  |  |  |  |
|  |  |  |  |
|  |  |  |  |

### Form: Products

| ID | Name | Unit Price | Stock |
|---|---|---|---|
|  |  |  |  |
|  |  |  |  |
|  |  |  |  |

*Fig 16.04 Two Tables with Primary Keys*

## Determine the Relationships Between Tables

Now that you've divided your information into tables and identified primary key fields, you need a way to tell Microsoft Access how to bring related information back together again in meaningful ways. To do this, you define relationships between tables. *See Fig 16.04.*

You may find it useful to view the relationships in an existing well-designed database such as the Northwind sample database. Fig 16.05 gives you a view of the relationships between tables used to design the Northwind database.

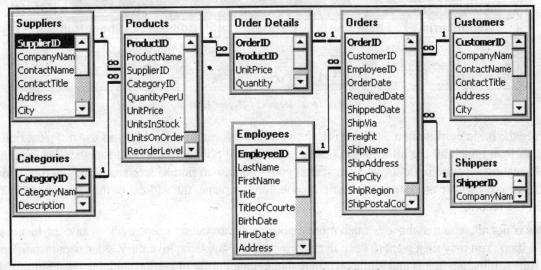

*Fig 16.05 View Relationships in Northwind Database*

### Refine Your Design

After you have designed the tables, fields, and relationships you need, it's time to study the design and detect any flaws that might remain. It is easier to change your database design now than it will be after you have filled the tables with data.

Use Microsoft Access to create your tables, specify relationships between the tables, and enter enough sample data in your tables, so that you can test your design.

**TIP**

To test the relationships in your database, see if you can create queries to get the answers you want. Create rough drafts of your forms and reports and see if they show the data you expect. Look for unnecessary duplications of data and eliminate them.

### Enter Data and Create Other Database Objects

When you are satisfied that the table structures meet the design principles described here, then it is time to go ahead and add all your existing data to the tables. You can then create other database objects such as queries, forms, reports, data access pages, macros, and modules.

We shall look at the important database objects such as tables, queries, forms etc in more detail later in this chapter. First, however, we would like to examine Access as a database from the point of view of the principles of a good database that we have just discussed.

# What is Special About Access?

Like all databases, the heart of an Access database is a table containing records and fields. Let us look at our old friend, a card file of names, phone numbers and addresses of the members of your club. A record will be all these three information about one member while the name, the address and the phone number will each be a field in the record.

| MasterList : Table | | | | |
|---|---|---|---|---|
| **MemberId** | **FirstName** | **LastName** | **Address** | **PhoneNumber** |
| 1 | Jayant | Neogy | South Avenue | 0124 2360999 |
| (AutoNumber) | | | | n |

Record: |◀ ◀     1   ▶ ▶| ▶* of 1

*Fig 16.06 Members Master List*

Since the basic purpose of a database is to let you find information quickly, you use different fields rather than bunch all the information (name, address and phone number) all together. By keeping information separate in fields, you can search your database to find a record using any of the fields. That is, you can use any one from the first name, the last name, the address or the phone number to find the record.

This is not all. You may have a much more elaborate database that keeps track of say, the business of a shop. You may then want to keep lists of customers, suppliers, inventory, sales persons, orders, invoices, bills, payments and all those things that keep an army of clerks and an accountant or two busy. You then set up a Relational database. In a relational database, information is stored in tables.

You use matching values from two tables to relate data in one table to data in the other table. In a relational database, you typically store a specific type of data just once. Access also provides many options for working with other database programmes such as Microsoft SQL Server. See Fig 16.04 earlier in this section in which the tables *Customers* and *Products* are similarly linked.

# Relationships in a Database

After you have set up different tables for each subject in your Microsoft Access database, you need a way of telling Microsoft Access how to bring that information back together again. The first step in this process is to define relationships between your tables. After you've done that, you can create queries, forms, and reports to display information from several tables at once. For example, after you have set up relationships between the following five tables:

1. Contacts
2. Calls
3. Tickler
4. Company
5. Ship To

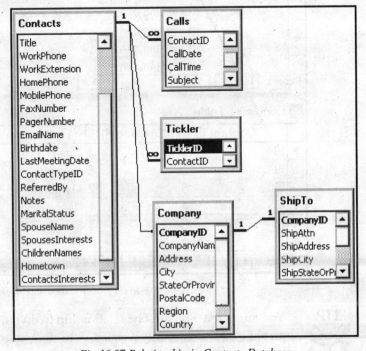

*Fig 16.07 Relationship in Contacts Database*

After the tables have data in them, you can set up queries that pull out information from each table.

## *How Relationships Work*

In the previous example, the fields in five tables must be coordinated so that they show information about the same contact. This coordination is accomplished with relationships between tables. A relationship works by matching data in key fields — usually a field with the same name in both tables. In most cases, these matching fields are the primary key from one table, which provides a unique identifier for each record, and a foreign key in the other table. For example, contacts can be associated with calls made by creating a relationship between the ContactID fields.

In Fig 16.08 you can see the linkage between the two tables.

You will notice that:

- ContactID appears in both tables.
- It is a primary key in the Contacts table and a foreign key in the Calls table.
- A one-to-one relationship.

In a one-to-one relationship, each record in Table A can have only one matching record in Table B and each record in Table B can have only one matching record in Table A. This type of relationship is not common, because most information related in this way would be in the same table.

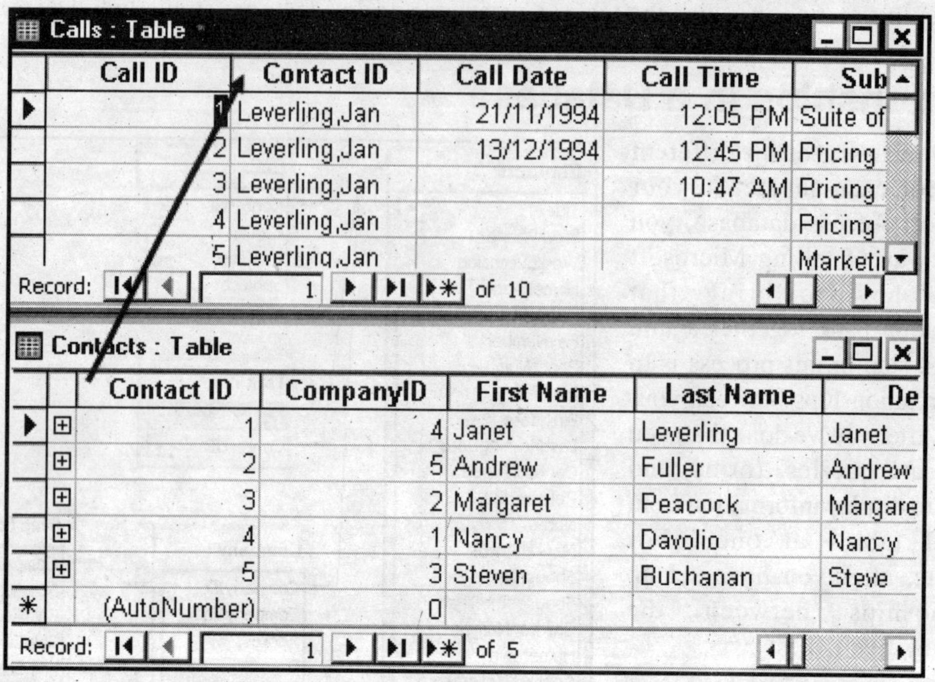

| Calls : Table | | | | |
|---|---|---|---|---|
| **Call ID** | **Contact ID** | **Call Date** | **Call Time** | **Sub** |
| 1 | Leverling,Jan | 21/11/1994 | 12:05 PM | Suite of |
| 2 | Leverling,Jan | 13/12/1994 | 12:45 PM | Pricing |
| 3 | Leverling,Jan | | 10:47 AM | Pricing |
| 4 | Leverling,Jan | | | Pricing |
| 5 | Leverling,Jan | | | Marketi |

Record: 1 of 10

| Contacts : Table | | | | | |
|---|---|---|---|---|---|
| | **Contact ID** | **CompanyID** | **First Name** | **Last Name** | **De** |
| ⊞ | 1 | 4 | Janet | Leverling | Janet |
| ⊞ | 2 | 5 | Andrew | Fuller | Andrew |
| ⊞ | 3 | 2 | Margaret | Peacock | Margare |
| ⊞ | 4 | 1 | Nancy | Davolio | Nancy |
| ⊞ | 5 | 3 | Steven | Buchanan | Steve |
| ✻ | (AutoNumber) | 0 | | | |

Record: 1 of 5

*Fig 16.08 How Relationship Works*

**TIP** 
You might use a one-to-one relationship to divide a table with many fields, to isolate part of a table for security reasons, or to store information that applies only to a subset of the main table. For example, you might want to create a table to track employees participating in a fundraising soccer game. Each soccer player in the Soccer Players table has one matching record in the Employees table.

You will find it easier to understand table design by studying one-to-one relationships although they are not very common in real life. See Fig 16.09 for a sample of a one-to-one relationship.

## A One-to-Many Relationship

A one-to-many relationship is the most common type of relationship. In a one-to-many relationship, a record in Table A can have many matching records in Table B, but a record in Table B has only one matching record in Table A.

For instance, in Fig 16.08, the Calls table shows many calls by one caller. However, a particular call is made by only one caller.

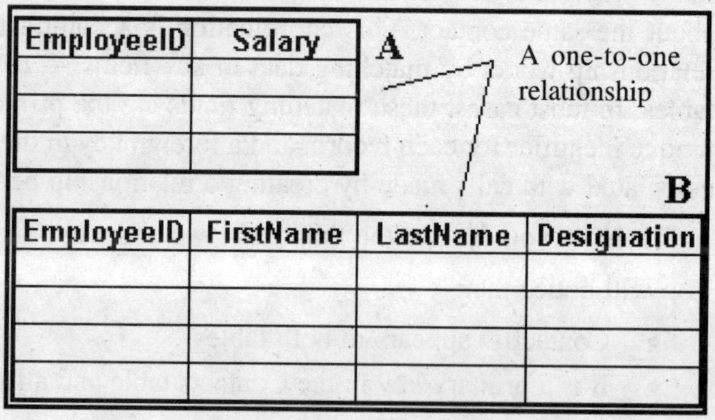

| EmployeeID | Salary | A |
|---|---|---|
| | | |
| | | |
| | | |

A one-to-one relationship

| EmployeeID | FirstName | LastName | Designation |
|---|---|---|---|
| | | | |
| | | | |
| | | | |

B

*Fig 16.09 One-to-One Relationship*

### A Many-to-Many Relationship

In a many-to-many relationship, a record in Table A can have many matching records in Table B, and a record in Table B can have many matching records in Table A. This type of relationship is only possible by defining a third table (called a junction table) whose primary key consists of two fields — the foreign keys from both Tables A and B. A many-to-many relationship is really two one-to-many relationships with a third table. For example, the Orders table and the Products table have a many-to-many relationship that is defined by creating two one-to-many relationships to the Order Details table. One order can have many products, and each product can appear on many orders.

In most cases, we come across the one-to-many relationship in the business application databases that we have to deal with.

### Pivot Tables and Pivot Charts

A special feature of Access is that like Microsoft Excel (that we discussed earlier in this book), Access can generate Pivot Tables and Pivot Chart views to tables, queries, views, stored procedures, functions, and forms. With Access 2000, you can perform data analysis and build rich Pivot Table and Pivot Chart view solutions more quickly than ever before. Pivot Table and Pivot Chart views can be saved as data access pages that can be viewed by anyone who has Microsoft Internet Explorer 5.0 or later.

## Exploring Tables

A table is a collection of data about a specific topic, such as products or suppliers. Using a separate table for each topic means that you store that data only once. This results in a more efficient database and fewer data-entry errors.

## How Data is Organised in Tables

Tables organise data into columns (called fields) and rows (called records).

For example, each field in a Products table contains the same type of information for every product, such as the product's name. Each record in that table contains all the information about one product, such as the product's name, supplier ID number, units in stock, and so on. *See Fig 16.10.*

| Product Name | Supplier | Category |
|---|---|---|
| Chai | Exotic Liquids | Beverages |
| Chang | Exotic Liquids | Beverages |
| Aniseed Syrup | Exotic Liquids | Condiments |
| Chef Anton's Cajun Seasoning | New Orleans Cajun Delights | Condiments |
| Chef Anton's Gumbo Mix | New Orleans Cajun Delights | Condiments |
| Grandma's Boysenberry Spread | Grandma Kelly's Homestead | Condiments |
| Uncle Bob's Organic Dried Pears | Grandma Kelly's Homestead | Produce |
| Northwoods Cranberry Sauce | Grandma Kelly's Homestead | Condiments |

*Fig 16.10 Products Table, Northwind Database*

## Table Design View

In Table Design View, you can create an entire table from scratch, or add, delete, or customise the fields in an existing table.

If you want to track additional data in a table, add more fields. If an existing field name is not descriptive enough, you can rename the field.

Setting a field's data type defines what kind of values you can enter in a field. For example, if you want a field to store numerical values that you can use in calculations, set its data type to Number or Currency.

You use a unique tag, called a primary key, to identify each record in your table. A table's primary key is used to refer to related records in other tables.

Field properties are a set of characteristics that provide additional control over how the data in a field is stored, entered, or displayed. Which properties are available depends on a field's data type. See Fig 16.11 to see the Products Table in Design View.

| Field Name | Data Type | Description |
|---|---|---|
| ProductID | AutoNumber | Number automatically assigned to new product. |
| ProductName | Text | |
| SupplierID | Number | Same entry as in Suppliers table. |
| CategoryID | Number | Same entry as in Categories table. |
| QuantityPerUnit | Text | (e.g., 24-count case, 1-liter bottle). |
| UnitPrice | Currency | |
| UnitsInStock | Number | |

Field Properties

General | Lookup

| Field Size | Long Integer |
| New Values | Increment |
| Format | |
| Caption | Product ID |
| Indexed | Yes (No Duplicates) |

A field name can be up to 64 characters long, including spaces. Press F1 for help on field names.

*Fig 16.11 Products Table in Design View*

## How to Relate Two Tables

A common field relates two tables so that Microsoft Access can bring together the data from the two tables for viewing, editing, or printing. In one table, the field is a primary key that you set in Table Design View. That same field also exists in the related Table as a foreign key.

1. In the Suppliers Table, you enter a supplier ID, company name, and so on for each supplier. SupplierID is the primary key that you set in Table Design View.

2. In the Products Table, you include the SupplierID field, so that when you enter a new product, you can identify its supplier by entering that supplier's unique ID number. SupplierID is the foreign key in the Products Table.

# Table Datasheet View

In a table or query, Datasheet View provides the tools you need to work with data. The tools are described below. *See Fig 16.12.*

## Table Datasheet and Query Datasheet Tool Bars

The Table Datasheet and Query Datasheet tool bars provide many of the tools you need to find, edit, and print records. You can use these tool bars to:

- Print or preview data.
- Check spelling.
- Cut, copy, or paste selected text, fields, whole records, or the entire datasheet.
- Sort records.
- Filter records, and find or replace values.
- Add or delete records.

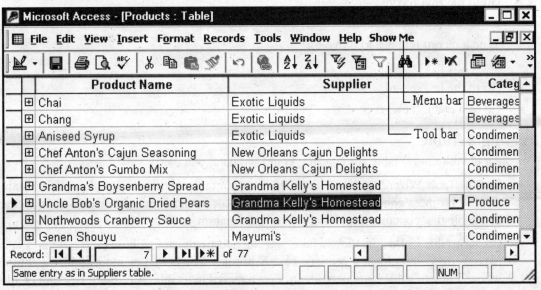

*Fig 16.12 Tools in Datasheet View*

## Columns, Rows, and Sub-datasheets

You can find tools for working with columns, rows, and sub-datasheets in the datasheet itself, or by right clicking a column selector. A sub-datasheet is a datasheet that is nested within another datasheet and that contains data related or joined to the first datasheet. A column selector is the horizontal bar at the top of a column. You can click a column selector to select an entire column in the query design grid or the filter design grid. You can also do the following:

- Use the column selector to move, hide, or rename a column.
- Resize columns or rows.
- Use sub-datasheets to view related data.
- Freeze the left-most column so that it is displayed as you scroll to the right.

### Moving Through Records

You can use the navigation tool bar to move through the records in a datasheet. *See Fig 16.13.*

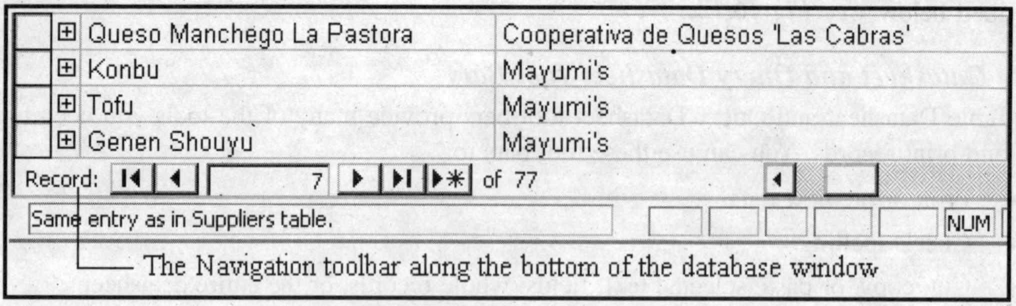

| | ⊞ Queso Manchego La Pastora | Cooperativa de Quesos 'Las Cabras' |
| | ⊞ Konbu | Mayumi's |
| | ⊞ Tofu | Mayumi's |
| | ⊞ Genen Shouyu | Mayumi's |

Record: ◄◄ ◄ 　7　 ► ►◄ ►* of 77 ◄

Same entry as in Suppliers table. 　　　　　　 NUM

The Navigation toolbar along the bottom of the database window

*Fig 16.13 Navigation Tool Bar*

You can use the navigation tool bar to:

- Go to the first record.
- Go to the previous record.
- Type a record number to move to.
- Go to the next record.
- Go to the last record.
- Go to a blank (new) record.

## Creating a Table

To create a blank (empty) table for entering your own data, you can:

- Use the Table Wizard to choose the fields for your table from a variety of predefined tables such as business contacts, household inventory, or medical records. A field is an element of a table that contains a specific item of information, such as a last name.

- Create a table in Design View where you can add fields, define how each field appears or handles data, and create a primary key. A primary key is one or more fields or columns whose value or values uniquely identify each record in a table. A primary key cannot allow nill values and must always have a unique index. A primary key is used to relate a table to foreign keys in other tables. A Design View is a window that shows the design of any of these database objects: tables, queries, forms, reports, macros, and data access pages. In Design View, you can create new database objects and modify the design of existing ones. See Fig 16.11 earlier in this chapter for view of a table in Design View.

- Enter data directly into a blank datasheet. When you save the new datasheet, Microsoft Access will analyse your data and automatically assign the appropriate data type and format for each field. A data type is the characteristic of a field that determines what type of data it can hold. Data types include Boolean, Integer, Long, Currency, Single, Double, Date, String, and Variant (default). The format specifies how data is displayed and printed. An Access database provides standard formats for specific data types, as does an Access project for the equivalent SQL data types. You can also create custom formats.

To create a table from existing data, you can:

- Import or link data from another Access database or data in a variety of file formats from other programmes. Linking tables is an action that establishes a connection to data from another application so that you can view and edit the data in both the original application and in Access.

- Perform a make-table query to create a table based on data in a current table. For example, you can use make-table queries to archive old records, to make backup copies of your tables, to select a group of records to export to another database, or to use as a basis for reports that display data from a specific time.

### Procedure for Creating a Table

To create a table by using the Table Wizard, do the following:

1. Press **F11** to switch to the Database window.
2. Click **Tables** under Objects, and then click **New** on the Database window tool bar.
3. Double click **Table Wizard**. The Table Wizard appears. *See Fig 16.14.*
4. Follow the directions in the Table Wizard dialogue boxes.

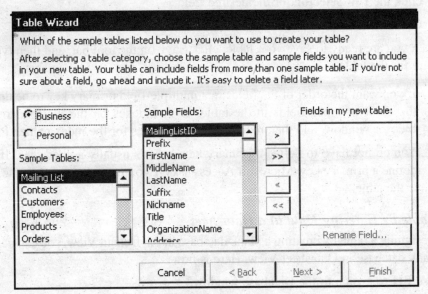

*Fig 16.14 Table Wizard*

**TIP**

If you want to modify or extend the resulting table, you can do so in Design View when you have finished using the Table Wizard.

### Create a Table in Design View

Follow these steps to create a table in Design View:

1. Press **F11** to switch to the Database window.
2. Click **Tables** under Objects, and then click **New** on the Database window tool bar.

3. Double click **Design View**.

4. Define each of the fields in your table.

5. Open the table in Design View.

   - To insert the field within the table, click in the **row** below where you want to add the field, and then click **Insert Rows** on the tool bar.

   - To add the field to the end of the table, click in the **first blank row**. See Fig 16.11 for a table in Design View earlier in this chapter.

6. Click in the **Field Name** column and type a **unique name** for the field.

7. In the Data Type column, keep the default (Text); or click in the **Data Type column**, click the **arrow**, and select the **data type** you want.

8. In the Description column, type a description of the information this field will contain. This description is displayed on the status bar when adding data to the field and is included in the Object Definition of the table. The description is optional.

9. Define a primary key field before saving your table. To do so, open a table in Design View.

   a. Select the **field** or **fields** you want to define as the primary key. To select one field, click the **row selector** for the desired field.

   b. Click **Primary Key** on the tool bar.

10. When you are ready to save your table, click **Save** on the tool bar, and then type a **unique name** for the table.

**TIP**     If you want the order of the fields in a multiple-field primary key to be different from the order of those fields in the table, click Indexes on the tool bar to display the Indexes window, and then reorder the field names for the index named Primary Key.

You do not have to define a primary key, but it's usually a good idea. If you do not define a primary key, Microsoft Access asks if you want Access to create one for you when you save the table.

## *Create a Table by Entering Data in a Datasheet*

Instead of designing a table by creating a blank database in the Design View, you can begin entering data in a blank database in Datasheet View. Here is how:

1. Press **F11** to switch to the Database window.

2. Click **Tables** under Objects, and then click **New** on the Database window tool bar.

3. Double click **Datasheet View**. A blank datasheet is displayed. The default column names are Field1, Field2, and so on.

4. Rename each column you will use: double click the column name, type a name for the column, and then press **ENTER** ↵.

5. Enter your data in the datasheet. Enter each kind of data in its own column (each column is called a field in Microsoft Access). For example, if you are entering names, enter the first name in its own column and the last name in a separate column. If you are entering dates,

times, or numbers, enter them in a consistent format so that Microsoft Access can create an appropriate data type and a display format for the column. Any columns you leave empty will be deleted when you save the datasheet.

6.  When you've added data to all the columns you want to use, click Save on the tool bar to save your datasheet. See Fig 16.12 for a table in Datasheet View earlier in this chapter.

7.  Microsoft Access asks you if you want to create a primary key. If you have not entered data that can be used to uniquely identify each row in your table, such as part numbers or ID numbers, it is recommended that you click Yes. If you have entered data that can uniquely identify each row, click No, and then specify the field that contains that data as your primary key in Design View as you have done earlier in this chapter.

**NOTE**

You can insert additional columns at any time: click in the column to the right of where you want to insert a new column, and then on the Insert menu, click Column. Rename the column as described in step 4.

## Establishing Relationships

In a relational database like Access, the power of the programme lies in the relationships between tables that you use. For instance, you may have separate tables to list customers, products, and salespersons. To extract information like which customer buys which of your products, or which salesperson makes the most sales of one of your products, you must be able to query your database with such questions. Your database can supply the answers only if the separate tables of customers, products and salespersons are properly linked. You link the tables by establishing relationships between them. See Fig 16.07 for an example of relationships earlier in this chapter.

# Exploring Forms

Forms are special objects you use in a database. You can design a form to help the user enter data in the database. You can also use forms for many other purposes. We discuss forms in this section.

## What are Forms?

A form is a type of database object that is primarily used to enter or display data in a database. You can also use a form as a switchboard that opens other forms and reports in the database, or as a custom dialogue box that accepts user input and carries out an action based on the input.

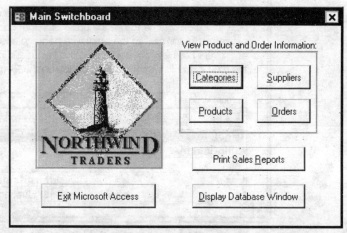

*Fig 16.15 Switchboard Form*

Forms may be of many types such as a data entry form or a switchboard form. Switchboard forms are used in database application like the main menu. As the name implies, data entry forms are used to simplify entering data in a database.

Most forms are bound (or connected) to one or more tables and queries in the database. A form's record source refers to the fields in the underlying tables and queries. You can select the fields from the underlying database that you wish to show on the form. It need not contain all the fields from each of the tables or queries that it is based on.

A bound form stores or retrieves data from its underlying record source. Other information on the form, such as the title, date, and page number, is stored in the form's design.

You create a link between a form and its record source by using graphical objects called controls. The most common type of control used to display and enter data is a text box.

*Fig 16.16 Data Entry Form*

In this form you can see the use of text boxes for entering data such as Product name, Supplier, Categories etc. The information you enter in the text boxes will be stored in the underlying database. The graphics and the layout is, however, stored in the design view of the form itself.

See Fig 16.17 for a Pivot Table view of a database.

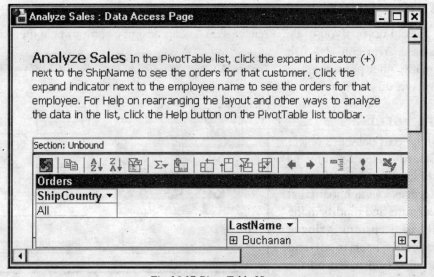

*Fig 16.17 Pivot Table View*

**TIP** You can also open a form in Pivot Table view or Pivot Chart view to analyse data. In these views, you can dynamically change the layout of a form to present data in different ways. You can rearrange row headings, column headings, and filter fields until you achieve the desired layout. Each time you change the layout, the form immediately recalculates the data based on the new arrangement.

In Pivot Table view, you can view detailed or summarised data by arranging fields in the filter, row, column, and detail areas. You can also display data visually by selecting a chart type and viewing data by arranging fields in the filter, series, category, and data areas.

## Creating a Form

You can create a form quickly by using the AutoForm command or a wizard. AutoForm creates a form that displays all fields and records in the underlying table or query. A wizard asks you questions and creates a form based on your answers. You can then customise the form the way you want it in Design View. The Design View window shows the design of tables, queries, forms, reports, macros etc. In Design View, you can create new database objects and modify the design of existing ones.

## Customising a Form

You can modify your form to suit the user's exact needs. The modification or customisation can either be done in Design View or in Pivot Table or Pivot Chart View. Both methods are described below.

### In Design View

You can customise a form in Design View in the following ways:

**Record Source:** Change the tables and queries that a form is based on.

**Controlling and Assisting the User:** You can set form properties to allow or prevent users from adding, deleting, or editing records displayed in a form. You can also add Custom Help to a form to assist your users with using the form.

**Form Window:** You can add or remove maximise and minimise buttons, shortcut menus, and other Form window elements.

**Sections:** You can add, remove, hide, or resize the header, footer, and details sections of a form. You can also set section properties to control the appearance and printing of a form.

**Controls:** You can move, resize, or set the font properties of a control. You can also add controls to display calculated values, totals, current date and time, and other useful information on a form.

### In Pivot Table or Pivot Chart View

You can customise a form in Pivot Table or Pivot Chart View in the following ways:

**Add, Move, or Remove Fields:** You can add fields to the filter, row, column, and detail areas in Pivot Table View, and to the filter, category, series, and data areas in Pivot Chart View. You can also move fields from one area to another and remove fields from the view.

**Filter Records:** You can filter data displayed in the view by adding or moving a field to the filter area. You can also filter a field in the row and column area.

**Sort Records:** You can sort items in row or column fields in ascending or descending order. You can also sort items in custom order in Pivot Table View.

**Group Records:** You can group items in row or column fields on intervals, or create custom groups.

**Format Elements and Change Captions:** In Pivot Table View, you can change the font settings, alignment, background colour, and number format of a field. You can also change the captions of fields and custom groups. In Pivot Chart View, you can change the chart type, format data markers, and more.

# Creating a Form

You can create a form in three different ways. You can use the AutoForm feature of Access, use a Form Wizard or you can create a form based on your own design view. We examine each method here.

### From a Single Table or Query Using AutoForm

AutoForm creates a form that displays all fields and records in the underlying table or query. If the record source you select has related tables or queries, the form will also include all the fields and records from those record sources.

Here is how:

1. In the Database window, click **Forms** under Objects.
2. Click the **New** button on the Database window tool bar.
3. In the New Form dialogue box, click one of the following **Wizards**:
   - **AutoForm: Columnar**. Each field appears on a separate line with a label to its left.
   - **AutoForm: Tabular**. The fields in each record appear on one line, with labels displayed once at the top of the form.
   - **AutoForm: Datasheet**. The fields in each record appear in row-and-column format, with one record in each row and one field in each column. The field names appear at the top of each column.
   - **AutoForm: Pivot Table**. The form opens in Pivot Table View. You can add fields by dragging them from the field list to the different areas in the view.
   - **AutoForm: Pivot Chart**. The form opens in Pivot Chart View. You can add fields by dragging them from the field list to the different areas in the view.
4. Click the **table** or **query** that includes the data you want to base your form on.
5. Click **OK**. The form is created.

**NOTE** Microsoft Access will apply the last AutoFormat you had used, for the next form you create. If you have not created a form with a wizard before or have not used the AutoFormat command on the Format menu, it uses the Standard AutoFormat as default. You can view the Form Wizard in Fig 16.18.

### From One or More Table or Query with a Wizard

The wizard asks you detailed questions about the record sources, fields, layout, and format you want and creates a form based on your answers.

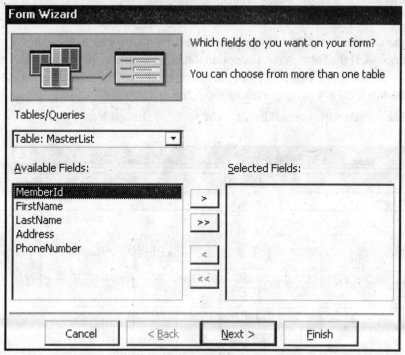

*Fig 16.18 Form Wizard*

Here is how:

1. In the Database window, click **Forms** under Objects.
2. Click the **New** button on the Database window tool bar.
3. In the New Form dialogue box, click the **Wizard** that you want to use. A description of the Wizard appears in the left side of the dialogue box.
4. Click the **name** of the table or other record source that includes the data you want to base your form on.
5. Click **OK**.
6. Follow the instructions in the Wizard.

**NOTE**

If you want to include fields from multiple tables and queries in your form, do not click **Next** or **Finish** after selecting the fields from the first table or query in the Form Wizard. Repeat the steps to select a table or query, and pick fields that you want to include in the form, until you have selected all the required fields.

## Using Design View

In this example, you will create a basic form and then customise it in Design View to suit your requirements.

Here is how you can proceed to create a form. The blank form looks like Fig 16.19.

1. In the Database window, click **Forms** under Objects.

2. Click the **New** button on the Database window tool bar.

3. In the New Form dialogue box, click **Design View**.

4. Click the name of the table or other record source that includes the data you want to base your form on. If the form is not to contain data (for example, if you want to create a form to use as a switchboard to open other forms or reports, or if you want to create a custom dialogue box), do not select anything from this list.

5. Click **OK**. Microsoft Access displays the form in Design View.

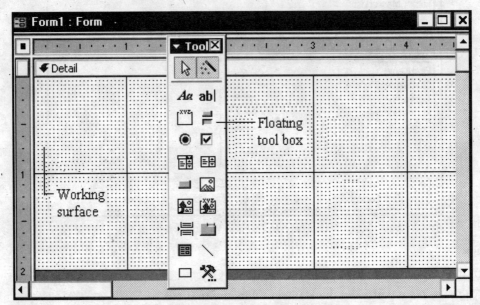

*Fig 16.19 Blank Form in Design View*

# Using Sub-forms

A sub-form is a form that is inserted in another form. The primary form is called the main form, and the form within the form is called the sub-form. A form/sub-form combination is often referred to as a hierarchical form, a master/detail form, or a parent/child form.

Sub-forms are especially useful when you want to show data from tables or queries with a one-to-many relationship. For example, you could create a form with a sub-form to show data from a Categories table and a Products table. The data in the Categories table is the "one" side of the relationship. The data in the Products table is the "many" side of the relationship — each category can have more than one product.

The main form and sub-form in this type of form are linked so that the sub-form displays only records that are related to the current record in the main form. For example, when the main form displays the Beverages category, the sub-form displays only the products in the Beverages category.

# Creating a Sub-form

Although sub-forms can be created and attached to the main form later, it is easiest if the two are designed and created at the same time. You can follow these steps to create a form and a sub-form together:

1. In the Database window, click **Forms** under Objects.

2. Click the **New** button on the Database window tool bar.

3. In the New Form dialogue box, double click **Form Wizard**.

4. In the first Wizard dialogue box, select a **table** or **query** from the list. For example, to create a Categories form that displays products for each category in a sub-form, select the Categories table (the "one" side of the one-to-many relationship).

5. Double click the **fields** you want to include from this table or query.

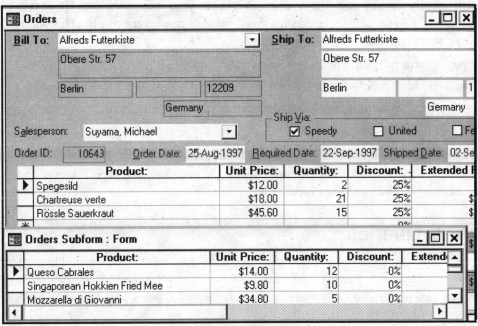

*Fig 16.20 Form with Sub-form*

6. In the same Wizard dialogue box, select another **table** or **query** from the list. Using the same example, select the Products table (the "many" side of the one-to-many relationship).

7. Double click the **fields** you want to include from this table or query.

8. When you click **Next** and then set up the relationships correctly before starting the Wizard, the Wizard asks which table or query you want to view by. Using the same example, to create the Categories form, click **By Categories**.

9. In the same Wizard dialogue box, select the **Form With sub-form(s)** option.

10. Follow the directions in the remaining Wizard dialogue boxes. When you click **Finish**, Microsoft Access creates two forms, one for the main form and sub-form control, and one for the sub-form. *See Fig 16.20.*

## Create a Sub-form and Add to Another Form

If you wish to add a sub-form later, here is the procedure:

1. Open the form that you want to add the sub-form to in Design View.
2. Make sure the **Control Wizards tool** in the toolbox is pressed in.
3. Click the **Sub-form/Sub-report tool** in the toolbox.
4. On the form, click **where** you want to place the sub-form.
5. Follow the directions in the Wizard dialogue boxes.
6. When you click **Finish,** Microsoft Access adds a sub-form control to your form. It also creates a separate form for the sub-form.

## Show a Calculated Value

A form will usually display only the selected data from your main database. However, you may design your form to do some calculations for you as well as display the results. This is how you can display a calculated value in a form or report:

1. Open a **form** or **report** in Design View.
2. Click the **Text Box tool** in the toolbox.
3. In the detail section, click **where** you want to place the text box.
4. Do one of the following:
   - Place the insertion point in the text box and type an **expression** that calculates a total.
   - Select the text box, click **Properties** on the tool bar, and type the **expression** in the ControlSource property box.

# Exploring Queries

We have seen in the previous section how data in database tables may be queried to give you only the relevant information that you want. You use queries to view, change, and analyse data in different ways. You can also use them as a source of records for forms, reports, and data access pages. There are several types of queries in Microsoft Access.

## Select Queries

A select query is the most common type of query. It retrieves data from one or more tables and displays the results in a datasheet where you can update the records (with some restrictions). You can also use a select query to group records and calculate sums, counts, averages, and other types of totals.

## Parameter Queries

A parameter query is a query that displays its own dialogue box when run, prompting you for information, such as criteria for retrieving records or a value you want to insert in a field. You can design the query to prompt you for more than one piece of information; for example, you can design it to prompt you for two dates. Access can then retrieve all records that fall between those two dates.

Parameter queries are also handy when used as the basis for forms, reports, and data access pages. For example, you can create a monthly earnings report based on a parameter query. When you print the report, Access displays a dialogue box asking for the month that you want the report to cover. You enter a month and Access prints the appropriate report.

## Crosstab Queries

You use crosstab queries to calculate and restructure data for easier analysis of your data. Crosstab queries calculate a sum, average, count, or other type of total for data that is grouped by two types of information — one down the left side of the datasheet and another across the top.

## Action Queries

An action query is a query that makes changes to or moves many records in just one operation. There are four types of action queries:

**Delete Queries:** A delete query deletes a group of records from one or more tables. For example, you could use a delete query to remove products that are discontinued or for which there are no orders. With delete queries, you always delete entire records, not just selected fields within records.

**Update Queries:** An update query makes global changes to a group of records in one or more tables. For example, you can raise prices by 10 per cent for all dairy products, or you can raise salaries by 5 per cent for the people within a certain job category. With an update query, you can change data in existing tables.

**Append Queries:** An append query adds a group of records from one or more tables to the end of one or more tables. For example, suppose that you acquire some new customers and a database containing a table of information on those customers. To avoid typing all this information into your own database, you'd like to append it to your customers' table.

**Make-Table Queries:** A make-table query creates a new table from all or part of the data in one or more tables. Make-table queries are helpful for creating a table to export to other Microsoft Access databases or a history table that contains old records.

## SQL Queries

An SQL query is a query you create by using an SQL statement. You can use Structured Query Language (SQL) to query, update, and manage relational databases such as Access.

When you create a query in Query Design View, Access constructs the equivalent SQL statements behind the scenes for you. In fact, most query properties in the property sheet in Query Design View have equivalent clauses and options available in SQL view. If you want, you can view or edit the SQL statement in SQL view. However, after you make changes to a query in SQL view, the query might not be displayed the way it was previously in Design View.

Some SQL queries, called SQL-specific queries, can not be created in the design grid. For pass-through, data-definition, and union queries, you must create the SQL statements directly in SQL view. For sub-queries, you enter the SQL in the Field row or the Criteria row of the query design grid.

# Creating Queries

When you open a query in Design View, or open a form, report, or datasheet and show the Advanced Filter/Sort window, you see the design grid, which you can use to make a variety of changes to get the query results you want. In Design View, you can create new database objects and modify the design of existing ones. The Design View is a view window that shows the design of such database objects as tables, queries, forms, reports, etc. The Advanced Filter/Sort window is a window in which you can create a filter from scratch. You enter criteria expressions in the filter design grid to restrict the records in the open form or datasheet to a subset of records that meet the criteria.

Fig 16.21 shows a Select Query (Products by Category) in Design View.

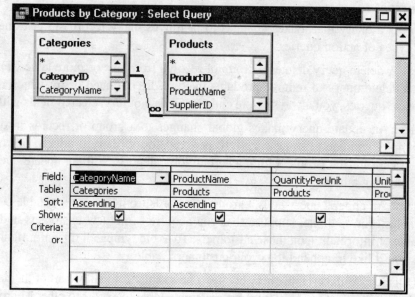

*Fig 16.21 Query in Design View*

## Add or Remove Tables, Queries, and Fields

You can add a table or query if the data you need is not in the query, or remove a table or query if you decide you do not need them. Once you add the tables or queries you need, you can then add the fields that you want to work with to the design grid, or remove them if you decide that they are not required.

## Calculate Amounts

You can add the values in a field or do other computations with the data by specifying the type of calculation to perform.

You can use an aggregate function, such as Sum or Average, to calculate one amount for all the records in each field in the design grid. Use Group By to calculate separate amounts for groups of records in a field.

## Limit Results by Using Criteria

You can limit the records that you see in the query's results or the records that are included in a calculation by specifying criteria.

Here are some of the things you can do to limit results by using criteria in query building:

- To limit the records in the query's results, enter criteria in one or more fields.
- Use the Or row for alternative criteria in the same field.
- Enter criteria for different fields. For example, for orders between 1/6/2001 and 15/6/2001.
- Calculate total order amounts, but display only those that are more than Rs.1,00,000.

# Sort Records

You can sort the query's results by specifying a sort order in the design grid. In Fig 16.22, you will observe that the design grid (bottom pane) has provision for specifying the sort order. Click the drop-down ▼ arrow next to sort and select Ascending or Descending as your sort order. If you specify a sort order for more than one field, Microsoft Access sorts the leftmost field first, so you should arrange the fields you want to sort from left to right in the design grid.

## *Use Asterisk in the Query Design Grid*

To include all fields from a table in a query, you can either select each field individually or use the asterisk (*) wildcard character. Selecting the asterisk has an advantage over selecting all the fields: When you use the asterisk, the query results automatically include any fields that are added to the underlying table or query after the query is created, and automatically exclude fields that are deleted.

When you use the asterisk, you must add fields along with the asterisk to the design grid before you can sort records or specify criteria for those fields.

When you drag more than one field at a time, Microsoft Access places each field in a separate column. If you drag the asterisk to the grid, Microsoft Access places the table or query name in one column and attaches a period and asterisk to the name (for example, Categories.*). After either operation, the datasheet looks the same.

If you type an asterisk in the Field row rather than dragging it, you must type the table name also. For example, type Customers.*.

# Calculations in a Query

There are many types of calculations you can perform in a query. For example, you can calculate the sum or average of the values in one field, multiply the values in two fields, or calculate the date three months from the current date. You perform calculations in a query using:

**Predefined calculations**, called "totals", to compute the following amounts for groups of records or for all the records combined in the query: sum, average, count, minimum, maximum, standard deviation, or variance.

**A custom calculation** to perform numeric, date, and text calculations on each record using data from one or more fields. You need to create a new calculated field directly in the design grid for these types of calculations.

When you display the results of a calculation in a field, the results aren't actually stored in the underlying table. Instead, Microsoft Access reruns the calculation each time you run the query so that the results are always based on the most current data in the database. Therefore, you can't manually update the calculated results.

## Calculations with Aggregate Functions

To display the results of a calculation in a field, you can use a predefined calculation that Access provides or custom calculations you define. Use the predefined calculations, called aggregate functions or "totals", if you want to compute the following amounts for all records or for groups of records: sum, average, count, minimum, maximum, standard deviation, or variance. You choose one total calculation for each field you want to calculate.

You can calculate some types of totals using the Simple Query Wizard. Or you can calculate all types of totals using the Total row in the query design grid, where you select the aggregate function for the calculation you want to perform on a field.

In the query design grid, you can also specify criteria to affect the calculations and produce different query results. By adding criteria, you can limit the:

- Groups, before performing calculations on those groups.
- Results, after calculations on the groups are performed.
- Records, before they are grouped and before calculations are performed.

# Custom Calculations and Calculated Fields

With a custom calculation, you can perform numeric, date, and text calculations on each record using data from one or more fields. For example, with a custom calculation, you can multiply one field's values by a set amount, find the difference between two dates stored in separate fields, combine several values in a Text field, or create sub-queries. Using the options in the Total row in the design grid, you can perform the calculation on groups of records and calculate a sum, average, count, or other type of total on the calculated field.

For custom calculations, you need to create a new calculated field directly in the design grid. You create a calculated field by entering an expression into an empty Field cell in the query design grid.

For example, you can enter in the Order Amount field the expression: Quantity x Unit Price. The expression can be made up of multiple calculations as the following example shows:

Sum([UnitsInStock]+[UnitsOnOrder]).

You can also specify criteria for a calculated field to affect the results of the calculation.

You do not have to display the results of a calculation in a field. Instead, you can use them as criteria to determine the records the query selects or to determine which records to perform an action on. For example, you can specify the following expression in the Criteria row to tell the query to return only records that have values in the Required Date field that are between today's date and three months from today's date.

**Greeting Card List**

| Birthdate | Name | Address |
|---|---|---|
| 10/10/1990 | Davolio, Daniel | 507 - 20th Ave. E. Apt. 2A |
| 07/14/1965 | Leverling, Janet | 722 Moss Bay Blvd. |
| 07/14/1965 | Peacock, Margaret | 4110 Old Redmond Rd. |

*Fig 16.22 Address Labels Report*

# Exploring Reports

A report is an effective way to present your data in a printed format. Because you have control over the size and appearance of everything on a report, you can display the information the way you want to see it and fit it conveniently in the space you have.

Fig 16.22 shows a report containing address labels for greeting cards generated from an address book database.

Most reports are connected (or bound) to one or more table and query in the database. A report's record source refers to the fields in the underlying tables and queries.

A report need not contain all the fields from each of the tables or queries that it is based on. A bound report gets its data from its underlying record source. Other information on the form, such as the title, date, and page number, is stored in the report's design.

A typical report is shown in Fig 16.23. The notes on the right explain where the information shown on the report comes from.

You create the link between a report and its record source by using graphical objects called controls. Controls can be text boxes that display names and numbers, labels that display titles, or decorative lines that graphically organise the data and make the report more attractive.

Here are some of the visual enhancements that you can add to your report:

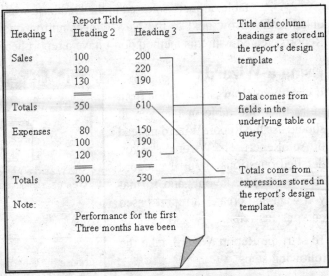

Fig 16.23 Parts of a Report

- Decorative lines.
- Labels with descriptive text.
- Text boxes to display data including calculated totals.

## Creating a Report

You can create different types of reports quickly by using wizards. Use the Label Wizard to create mailing labels, the Chart Wizard to create charts, or the Report Wizard to create a standard report. The Wizard asks you questions and creates a report based on your answers. You can then customise the report the way you want it in Design View.

There are three ways to create a report. You can use the AutoReport feature of Access, you can use a Report Wizard or you can create the report on your own Design View. We look at each method below.

### Using AutoReport

If your report is based on a single table or query, use AutoReport. It will create a report that displays all fields and records in the underlying table or query. To do so, here are the steps:

1. In the Database window, click **Reports** under Objects.

2. Click the **New** button on the Database window tool bar.

3. In the New Report dialogue box, click one of the following Wizards:

   • **AutoReport: Columnar**. Each field appears on a separate line with a label to its left. See Fig 16.24 for a view of this wizard.

   • **AutoReport: Tabular**. The fields in each record appear on one line, and the labels print once at the top of each page.

4. Click the **table** or **query** that contains the data you want to base your report on.

5. Click **OK**.

**TIP**   Microsoft Access applies the last AutoFormat you used to the report. If you have not created a report with a Wizard before or have not used the AutoFormat command on the Format menu, it uses the default, Standard AutoFormat.

You can also create a single-column report based on the open table or query or on the table or query selected in the Database window. Click AutoReport on the Insert menu, or click the arrow next to the New Object button on the tool bar, and then click AutoReport. Reports created with this method don't have a report header and footer or a page header and footer.

## Using a Wizard

If your report draws information from more than one table or query, you should use the Report Wizard instead of AutoReport. The Wizard asks you detailed questions about the record sources, fields, layout, and format you want and creates a report based on your answers.

To start the Report Wizard, take the following steps:

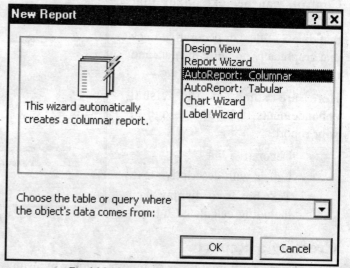

*Fig 16.24 Wizard for AutoReport Columnar*

1. In the Database window, click **Reports** under Objects.

2. Click the **New** button on the database window tool bar.

3. In the New Report dialogue box, click the **Wizard** that you want to use. A description of the wizard appears in the left side of the dialogue box.

4. Click the **table** or **query** that contains the data you want to base your report on. You do not need to do this step if you have clicked Report Wizard in step 3. Instead, you can specify the record source for the report in the wizard.

5. Click **OK**. Follow the instructions in the Wizard. See Fig 16.25 for a view of the Report Wizard.

The Wizard produces a standard format from its design template and from the data available in the underlying table or query. In case you want to modify the format, you can do so by opening the table in Design View.

## Using Design View

If you wish to quickly create a basic report and customise it later, then you may want to do so in Design View rather than use the Wizard. To do so, switch to design view for report creation. This is the better approach if you expect to modify your data source tables later.

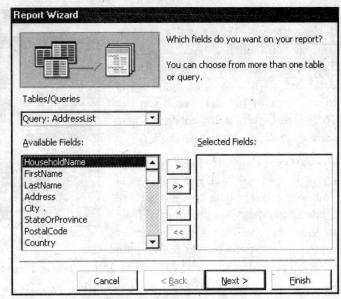

*Fig 16.25 Report Wizard*

Here are the steps:

1. In the Database window, click **Reports** under Objects.
2. Click the **New** button on the database window tool bar.
3. In the New Report dialogue box, click **Design View**.
4. Click the **table** or **query** that contains the data you want to base your report on. (If you want an unbound report, that is, a report that is not connected to any table or query, then do not select anything from this list.)
5. Click **OK**.
6. Microsoft Access displays the report in Design View. *See Fig 16.26.*

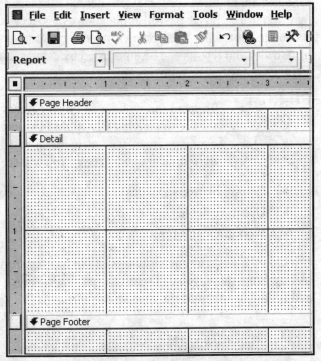

*Fig 16.26 Report in Design View*

## Other Database Objects

We have already looked at some of the objects or items that go into a database programme. In addition to Tables, Forms, Queries and Reports, there are some additional database objects that may be used to put together an Access database project or application. We take a brief look at some of these objects such as Switchboards, Data Access pages, Macros and Modules in the following section.

**Switchboards**: These are specially designed forms. They usually open as soon as you launch an Access project. The Switchboard is like a menu for the database. It will let you navigate easily to any part of the database. See Fig 16.27 for a view of a Switchboard object for the "Address Book" database.

**Data Access Page**: This is a Web page created in Access that you can post at your Website. The data access page will allow an Internet visitor to your Website to view data you have posted, enter replies to questions or edit the data on

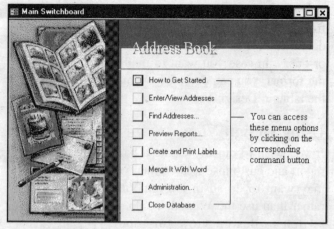

*Fig 16.27 Switchboard of Address Book Database*

the Web page. In short, you can create an interactive form so useful for e-business on the Internet.

**Macros**: These are useful for automating tasks in Access. A very useful application of a macro is to attach it to a button on an Access form. When a user clicks on the button, the associated macro will perform a predetermined task for the user such as display another form, or print out the form on the screen. Macros can make Access forms more user-friendly.

**Modules**: They are programming modules written in a special programming language called Visual Basic for Applications (VBA). VBA modules can perform much more complex tasks than macros. Modules are required for large commercial business applications using Access. For instance, you may design a complete payroll application using Access. The application will work like any complex accounting software. The complex operations required for payroll preparation and the generation of statistics and reports can be automated by using a combination of macros for the simple task and VBA modules for the more complex tasks.

## CD-ROM

To learn more about Microsoft Access 2000 in a multimedia environment, insert the accompanying CD-ROM in your computer, select the **Interactive** mode in the opening screen. The main menu will appear. To go to the section on Access, click the button marked **Access**. You will see a sub-menu containing the following topics:

- Getting Started in Access
- Updating Tables
- Working with Forms

Click on the first sub-menu item, *Getting Started in Access*, to display another level of sub-sub-menus. From these, you can select the particular topic you want to see. Click on your selected topic and follow instructions on your screen.

# 17. Using Your Access Database

**In this chapter:**

☞ You get familiarised with Access databases, learning how to start and exit Access and open and close databases.

☞ You learn to create and build new databases.

☞ You examine objects like Tables, Forms and Reports that work together to form a database application.

☞ You learn techniques of using your database. You learn to navigate a Form and find specific records. You also learn to switch different Views of the database objects.

☞ You learn about Filters including Filter by Selection and Filter by Form.

☞ You are shown how to print your Access Report.

# Familiarisation with Access

In Chapter 16, *Getting to Know Access 2000*, you have been given a basic understanding of the Access database programme. We get hands-on experience with Access in this chapter as we create database tables, set up relationships and enter data in the database programme. At the end of this chapter, you will be ready to build database applications on your own.

## Starting and Exiting Access

Depending on how Microsoft Office has been set up on your computer, you may start Access in a number of different ways. If you have the Access icon on your desktop, you can launch Access by double clicking on the icon. If you have installed the MS Office shortcut bar, then you can click on the Access icon on the shortcut bar instead. If you do not find the icons anywhere, you can launch Access from the desktop of your computer by clicking on the **Start** button at the bottom left of your opening screen and then clicking **Programs** ➔ **Microsoft Access**.

If you have Access databases already on your computer (identified by the filename extension of ".mdb"), then you can use Windows Explorer to locate the file and double click the file's name in the Explorer.

If you launch access by clicking on a ".mdb" file, Access will launch and the database will be loaded in Access automatically. You will then see the opening screen of the application on your monitor's screen. For instance, you can see the opening screen or the Main Switchboard of an

Access application entitled Address Book in Fig 16.27 in the previous chapter (Chapter 16, *Getting to Know Access 2000*).

In all other cases, only the Access application software will be launched without any database opening automatically. You will then see an opening screen like in Fig 17.01. Click on the File menu item and a drop-down list will appear. Click on File to open another dialogue box that lets you select an existing ".mdb" file. For a blank database, click on New. Like all other MS Office applications, the bottom of the drop-down menu will show a list of recently used files. If the file you want is in this list, simply click on it to open.

You can exit the Access programme in a number of ways as well. If the application programme you have been

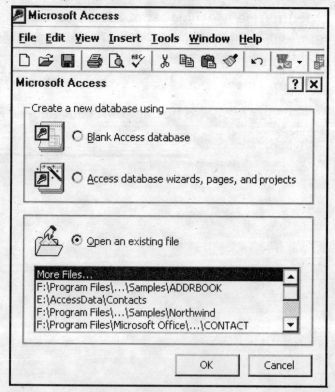

*Fig 17.01 Microsoft Access Opening Screen*

using has a Switchboard, it will have an option or a button marked Exit. Otherwise, you can click on the File menu and select Exit. A third possibility is to click on the close button ⊠ at the top right of your Access screen.

## Opening and Closing Database Files

Unlike other Microsoft Office applications, you can only have one Access file open at a time. If you open a second Access database with one already open, then the first one will close automatically.

As we have discussed already, you can launch a database file directly from Windows Explorer by clicking on the file. If you have Access already open, you can open a dialogue box by clicking **File** ➔ **Open** in the File drop-down menu. The dialogue box will show you the drive and directory where Access saves databases. Click on the filename of the database you wish to open. Fig 16.02 in the previous chapter shows an Open dialogue box.

At the bottom of the File drop-down menu, you will see a list of recently used database files. You can click on the filename you want.

The simplest way to exit a database is to open another database or to exit Access.

If the database you have opened has a Switchboard, you can use the Exit option on the Switchboard.

See Fig 16.27 in the previous chapter for a view of the Main Switchboard of an Address Book database.

## Opening and Closing Database Objects

After you have opened a database, you will see a dialogue box displayed that contains a list of all the database objects in the open database. Select the object you want in the list; for example, you can select Tables or Forms. On the right pane of the dialogue box, you will see a list of all the tables or forms that are part of the database. Click on the specific table or form you want to open. See Fig 17.02 for a view of the dialogue box for the Northwind Database. The left pane lists database objects such as Tables, Queries, Forms etc. As you select one of the objects, the full list appears on the right pane. Click on the one you need.

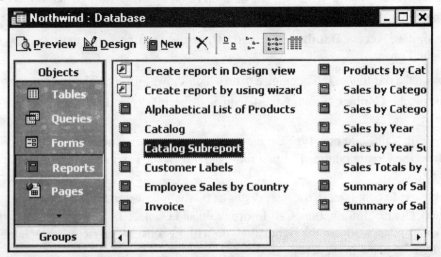

*Fig 17.02 Northwind Database Objects*

Each object opens as a separate window. You can move, resize, drag and close these object windows like any other window on your monitor's screen. You can also open more than one object on your screen at the same time, which is often very convenient if you wish to cross-check data contained in say, two tables.

Close any database object you do not need by clicking on the close ⊠ button on the top right. You can also shrink the object to your task bar at the bottom of your screen by clicking on the minimise button _ of the object window.

# Creating a New Database

In the previous chapter, we had a preliminary understanding of what a database is all about. We will now use this knowledge to create our own database. You can design a database entirely from scratch. To do so, you design each database object such as tables, forms, queries, reports, switchboards and so on using the Design View. However, the procedure is quite time-consuming. You will probably want to leave that to a professional software programmer.

Instead, you can harness the built-in power of Access by using the database wizard. In this chapter, we will use the wizard to create a Contacts Management database. This programme will allow you to make a list of your business or personal contacts and store contact information such as addresses and phone numbers. You can also use this database to keep a record of all the calls you make to them. You can ask the programme to print out a report of the list of contacts or a list of calls you have made. As you can see, this programme may be very useful for someone who contacts many people daily.

In this section, we will list the steps necessary to create the My Contacts database using Access 2000. The steps you learn here are applicable to any other database project.

## Build Database

Use the following procedure to create your My Contacts database using Access 2000:

Open Access by clicking on the **icon** on your desktop or on the Microsoft Office shortcut bar. The Access dialogue box appears.

Click on the option, **Access Database Wizard**. The pages and projects and the New Database dialogue box will open.

1. Click on the **databases tab** opening a pane which shows all the available database templates.
2. Click on the **Contact Management icon** and the File New Database dialogue box will appear.
3. In the File Name edit box, type the name of your database, which is My Contacts, and then click on the **Create** button. The first dialogue box of the Database Wizard will appear. *See Fig 17.03.*
4. Click **Next** to continue. In the next dialogue box you will see the names of the three tables created, Contact Information, Call Information and Contact Type. These names will appear in the left pane, while on the right pane you will see a list of the fields in each table as you highlight its name in the left pane.

5.  Add any of the **optional fields** that you need. The names of the optional fields will appear in italics at the bottom of each field list. After you have finalised the selection of fields for all the three databases, click **Next** to continue.

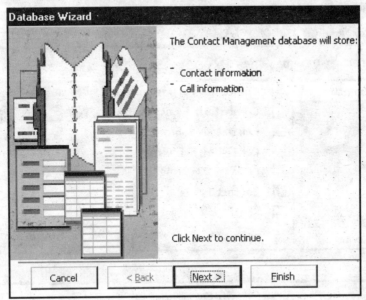

*Fig 17.03 Database Wizard First Page*

6.  In the next two dialogue boxes, you can choose the style of the **screen display** and the style for the **printed report**. In each case, the options appear in the right pane and the preview of the option in the left pane. After each selection, click **Next** to continue.

7.  Enter a **title** for your database, for example, "My Database" and click **Next** to continue.

8.  Click **Finish** on the last screen and after a short while, your newly created database application will be ready for use.

In the following sections, we shall open, enter data and study the database that we have just created. See Fig 17.04 for the second page of the database wizard. Fields already included are on your right and the left pane has optional fields that you can add.

Fig 17.05 shows the database objects included in the My Contacts database you have just created.

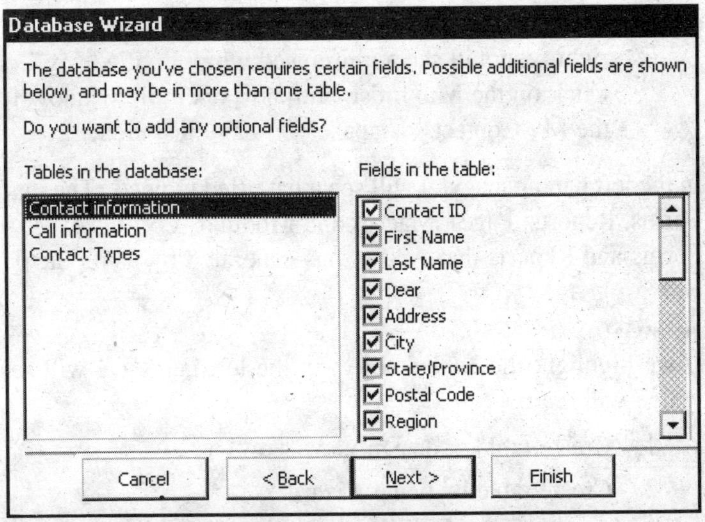

*Fig 17.04 Database Wizard Second Page*

In this illustration, you can see the forms created by the database wizard for My Contacts.

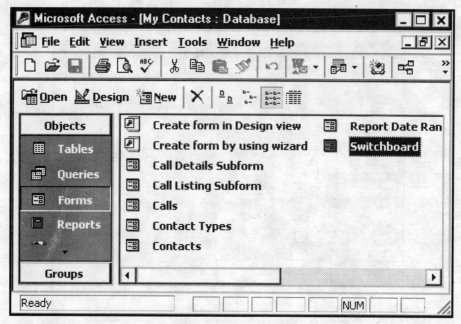

*Fig 17.05 My Contacts Database Created*

# Examining Database Objects

The database you have just created and titled My Contacts, contains a number of database objects. We will examine each object to understand how they function.

1. Open Access and click on the **New File** icon under the Open a File option in the New File Task pane.

2. The Open dialogue box appears. Click on **My Contacts** in the list of database files and the main switchboard of My Contacts will open. At the bottom of the Access screen, at the right, you will see a minimised window titled My Con. (Shortened form of My Contacts). Click on the **Maximise** button to open the window fully. This is the database window for the My Contacts database you have just created.

In the left hand pane, you will see a list titled Objects. The items listed under it are: Tables, Queries, Forms, Reports, Pages, Macros and Modules. For this exercise, we will concentrate on the Tables, Forms and Reports that Access has generated by using the database wizard.

## Tables

If we highlight the Tables object in the left pane, we will see a listing of tables in the right pane which will read:

1. Create table in design view
2. Create table by using wizard
3. Create table by entering data

4. Calls

5. Contact Types

6. Contacts

7. Switchboard Items

The first three items are creation options for tables while the last four are the actual table objects created by Access. Of the creation options listed, you will recall that we have used the Create table by using the Wizard option.

The main table is Contacts. If you open this by double clicking on its button, you will see a table much like a spreadsheet that contains the six records you have entered. Instead of using the Contacts form for entering or editing data, you can also append a record directly in this table.

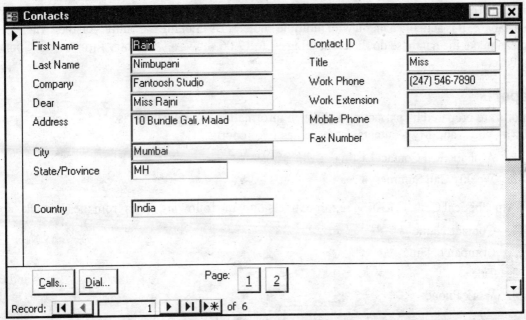

*Fig 17.06 Contacts Data Entry Form*

The two table creating options, using design view or by entering data, are alternative ways of setting up an Access database. Experienced programmers sometimes prefer to use one of these methods rather than use a Wizard. However, for our purpose, we will prefer the Wizard method.

# Forms

If we highlight the Forms object on the left pane, we will see a listing of the forms in the right pane, under two alternative methods for designing forms without the help of a wizard. The listing reads like this:

1. Create form in Design View

2. Create form by using Wizard

3. Call Details Sub-form

4. Call Listing Sub-form
5. Calls
6. Contact Types
7. Contacts
8. Report Date Range
9. Switchboard

The first six forms are associated with tables and are used for entering records. Forms allow you to enter a record in the same manner as you would enter information in a written record. Furthermore, fields in the form can be provided with data validation rules so that the user is stopped from entering wrong data. For example, a date field will not accept alpha characters.

The last form in the list above is a special form called Switchboard. This is the main switchboard for the database. It is actually a menu with multiple choices. By clicking the buttons on the switchboard, you can make the database do different things. Fig 17.06 shows a Data entry form for the Contacts database.

## Reports

Reports are prepared by extracting only such information from the database and arranging them in the way you want. My Contacts database has two reports:

1. Alphabetical Contact Listing
2. Weekly Call Summary

The Alphabetical Contact Listing report extracts only the following fields from the Contacts table:

1. Contact Name
2. Company Name
3. Title
4. Work Phone

The report then arranges the records alphabetically. The data in a report (like the data in a query) is a subset of the entire volume of data in the main database.

Similarly, the Weekly Call Summary report asks you to specify the week beginning and ending dates and then displays only the following information for the calls made within the period specified:

1. Date
2. Time
3. Contact Name
4. Subject

If you like, the reports can be printed.

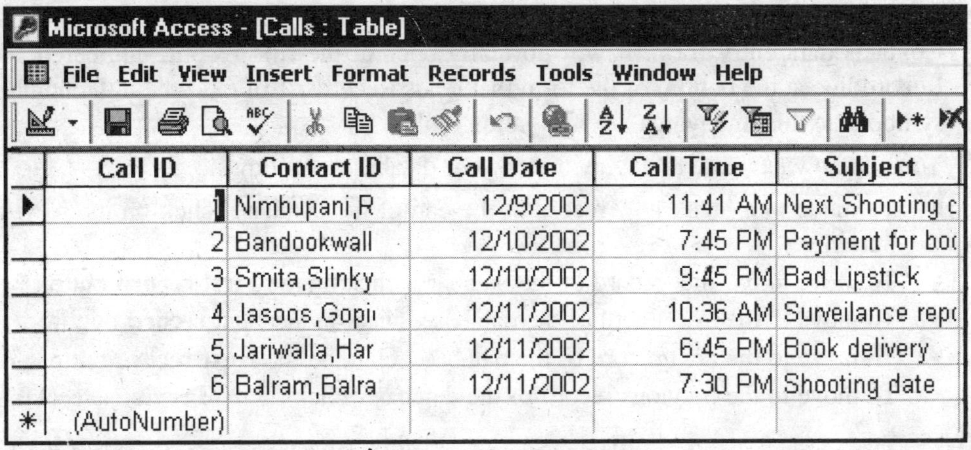

*Fig 17.07 Calls Database*

**NOTE** The My Contacts database does not automatically create any other objects such as queries, macros etc. However, it is possible to create them subsequently if you so wish. So far, we have confined ourselves to a wizard for creating our database. In addition to tables, forms and reports have been created automatically. This is no doubt convenient, and perhaps the best way to be introduced to the capabilities of Access. However, we may often need to create database objects that are precisely tailored to our needs. We will examine these issues in Chapter 18, *Customise Your Database*.

# Using Your Database

We have already practised entering data in our My Contacts database. However, there are a number of actions that we have to master to use a database effectively. We discuss some of these actions and manipulations in this section.

## Navigating in a Form

We begin by examining forms. Forms are used for a variety of purposes. For instance, the main menu of your My Contacts database is a form called Switchboard. Also, entering data on the contacts, such as their names, addresses and telephone numbers, is done using a data entry form titled Contacts that you have seen already. In this section, we look at the techniques of navigating a form.

1. Open Access if it is not already open and launch **My Contacts** as described earlier.

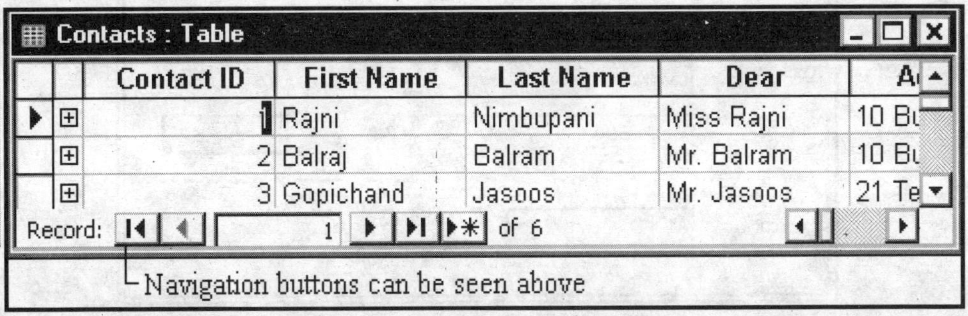

*Fig 17.08 Navigation Buttons in a Table*

2. Click on the button marked **Enter/View Contacts** on the main switchboard to display the Contacts data entry form. It will normally open at the first record, numbered 1 on the Record line at the bottom of the form that reads Records: 1 of 6. Look at the numbers and symbols on this line which are navigation tools.

3. You can now navigate to any record in your database as follows:

   • To move to a blank new record at the end of the database, click on the **New record** button.

   • To move to the first record of the database, click on the **First record** button.

   • To move to the last record of the database, click on the **Last record** button.

   • To move to the next record of the database, click on the **Next record** button.

   • To move to the previous record of the database, click on the **Previous record** button.

**TIP**  To navigate fast to a selected record, sort the database. To do so, select the field on which you wish to sort the database, say LastName, and then select either Sort Ascending or Sort Descending by clicking on the appropriate button on the tool bar. You will notice that the record numbers will no longer be in sequence. Instead, the records will be arranged according to ascending or descending last names.

4. After having located the desired record, you can edit or change the data in the form by selecting the field you want to change and adding to or modifying what is already there. When you finish and close the form, the modifications will get transferred to the main database table automatically.

## Finding a Specific Record

Your My Contacts database contains only six records and it is easy to find the record you want simply by navigating up or down as we saw in the earlier section. However, if you had a very long contacts list, say with several hundred records on it, this method of sequential navigation will be very inefficient. You need a better way to quickly reach the particular record you want.

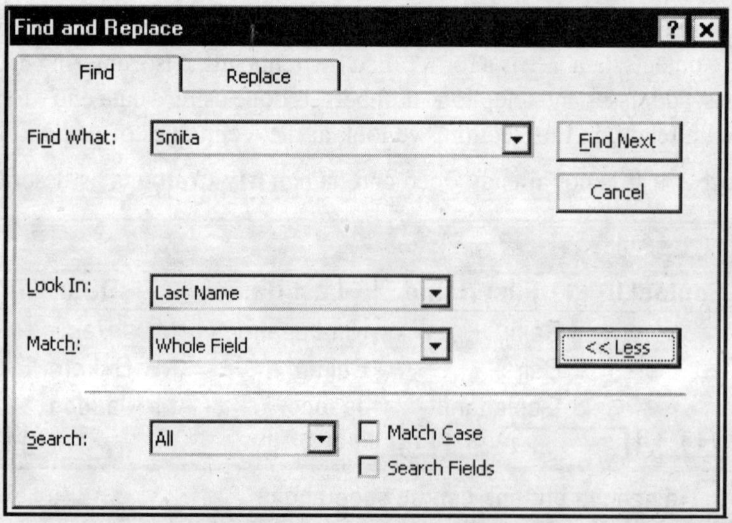

*Fig 17.09 Find and Replace Dialogue Box*

To find a specific record using the My Contacts (or any other) data entry form, do the following:

1. Open **Access**, then the database **My Contacts** and finally the data entry form **Contacts** from the main switchboard as described earlier.

2. Click in the **field** you wish to use for searching the database, for example, LastName.

3. Click **Edit** on the Access menu bar and in the drop-down menu, click on the Find option. The Find and Replace dialogue box will appear with the LastName of the current record displayed in the **Find What** edit box.

4. Type the **last name** you are looking for and then click the **Find Next** button. The record containing the selected last name will be displayed in the Contacts form.

5. Close the Find and Replace dialogue box by clicking on the **Cancel** button.

**TIP** If you index the database first using the field you intend to search on as described in the previous tip, your search will go much faster. If you wish to look at all records fulfilling a particular condition, such as belonging to the same city, first index the database on the City field. You can then search for the first record belonging to the city you choose. You will find that all other records belonging to the same city are now neatly grouped together one after the other.

## Switching Views

You have seen the Contacts form view on your screen. In this view, you will see one record at a time, organised like information is usually arranged on a printed paper form. It is very convenient for someone not very familiar with Access, but used to the old style paper forms.

Sometimes, you may wish to see more records at one time, especially when you are designing databases. To do so, you can switch to the datasheet view as follows:

1. Open **Access** ➜ **My Contacts** ➜ **Contacts form** as described already.

2. With the form open click on the **View** option on the Access menu bar and click on the **Datasheet View** in the drop-down menu. A spreadsheet-like table will appear showing all the fields and all the records. You may have to navigate the Access window using the slider bars on the right and bottom of the screen to see all the data.

3. To go back to the Form view, click on the **View** option on the Access menu bar and click on the **Form View** option.

# Using Filters

Let us say that you wish to see only a subset of all your records, for example, all your contacts living in Mumbai. You can do so through one of two filtering methods that you can use either in the Form View or Datasheet View.

### *Filter by Selection*

You use this method if you are looking at one record in your database, say in Datasheet View and want to see only those records that match some criteria of the record you are looking at. For example, you may be looking at record No. 3, of Mr Balram who lives in Mumbai and you want to see only the other contacts that also live in Mumbai. This is how to do it:

1. Make sure that you are in the **database view** of your My Contacts database. If not, get there following the instructions in the previous section.

2. Click on the **City** field and then click on the **Filter by Selection** icon on the Access tool bar. The records in the datasheet view will shrink to just two, these being the two contacts you have living in Mumbai.

3. Click on the **Remove Filter** icon on the same tool bar to restore all the datasheet records as before. *See Fig 17.10.*

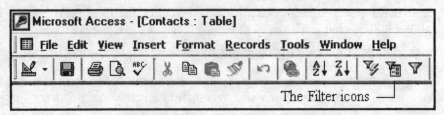

*Fig 17.10 Filter Icons on Access Tool Bar*

You can use the very same technique for selecting a subset of records in the Forms view. However, since you see only one record at a time, all that you will notice is that the bottom line on your form will change from Record: 1 of 6 to Record: 1 of 2 (Filtered). Restore all the records in your database by clicking on the Remove filter icon on the Access tool bar.

## Filter by Form

If you wish to find a subset of your database by designing a more complex set of criteria such as meeting two criteria at the same time, you have to utilise a more complex method where you use a special form for filtering your database.

Let us assume that you wish to find the contacts in your database who are both female and live in Kolkata. In that case, only by selecting "Miss" as the title, you will not get more than the desired record as both record numbers 2 and 4 will qualify. You need to set up a filter that will accept complex criteria such as "Title and City". This is how you proceed:

1. Open the **Contacts Form** if it is not already open.

2. Click on the **Filter by Form** icon on the Access tool bar. A new form titled "Contacts: Filter by Form" will open on your screen. All the fields should be blank. If there are any remnants from an earlier filtering operation, delete the entries. *See Fig 17.11.*

3. At the bottom of the form you will see a tab marked "Look for". Click on this **tab**.

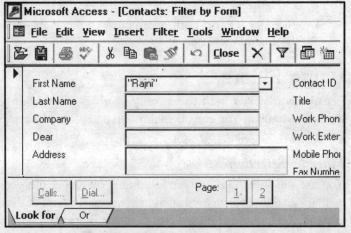

*Fig 17.11 Filter by Form Dialogue Box*

4. Now click on the **Title** field. A drop-down list will appear showing two options, "Miss" and "Mr". Select Miss. It will appear in the field captioned Title.

5. Click on the field captioned **City**. Another drop-down list will appear listing all the cities in your database. Select Kolkata.

6. Apply the filter by clicking on the **Apply Filter** icon on the Access tool bar. A fresh Contacts form will appear with just one record on it, that of Slinky Smitha, that fulfils both the criteria of being a Miss and also living in Kolkata.

7. Click on the **Remove Filter** icon to restore all the records on your database.

This example shows the use of the "AND" operator for creating a complex filtering criteria. You can also use the "OR" operator, for example, to locate all your records that meet both the criteria that the person is a Miss or lives in Mumbai. If you do so, you will see three records since these fulfil new criteria. Here is how you set up the filtering criteria:

1. Follow the **first four steps** of the previous example so that you have "Miss" selected in the Title field.

2. Click on the "**OR**" **tab** at the bottom of the form.

3. Click on the **City field** and select "**Mumbai**" from the drop-down list.

4. Apply the filter by clicking on the **Apply Filter** icon. You will be left with three records, numbers 2, 3 and 4, since they fulfil the criteria of either living in Mumbai or being titled Miss.

5. Click in the **Remove Filter** icon to restore the database to its original state.

# Printing Reports

In the Contacts database, the database wizard automatically creates two predefined reports. You can view and print these reports if you need a hard copy for distribution or filing. The two default reports created by the wizard are:

1. Alphabetical Contact Listing

2. Weekly Call Summary

To preview and print these reports, proceed as follows:

1. Call up the **main switchboard** of My Contacts as described earlier.

2. Click on the **Preview Reports** button. The Reports switchboard will open having the following options:
   - Preview the Alphabetical Contact Listing Report
   - Preview the Weekly Call Summary Report
   - Return to main Switchboard

3. Open the **report** you want. Let us open the Alphabetical contact listing report in this case. To do so, click on the **appropriate button**. After a short while, the preview of the report appears in a window titled Alphabetical Contact Listing.

4. After you have previewed the report, you can print it by clicking on the **printer icon** on the Access tool bar. The Print dialogue box opens, allowing you to select options for printing your report. *See Fig 17.12.*

The printing procedure is the same for printing any file in Windows.

5. Close all **forms** and **windows** and then exit **Access** using the Exit this database option from the main switchboard.

**TIP**

You will notice that the report is in small print and hard to read. However, the cursor has changed to a magnifying glass. By clicking the cursor when it is located on the report, you can magnify the report to normal size. Navigation bars will now appear at the bottom and right margin of the report window so that you can move the report within the window ("pan" the report) to see all of it.

As you can see in Fig 17.12, you can select the printer, the printer properties, the print range and the number of copies to be printed. Select the options you need and print your report as for any other Windows application.

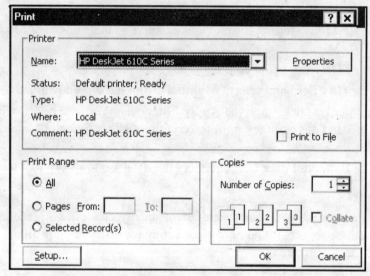

*Fig 17.12 Print Dialogue Box*

**CD-ROM**

To learn more about Microsoft Access 2000 in a multimedia environment, insert the accompanying CD-ROM in your computer, select the **Interactive** mode in the opening screen. The main menu will appear. To go to the section on Access, click the button marked **Access**. You will see a sub-menu containing the following topics:

- Getting Started in Access
- Updating Tables
- Working with Forms

Click on any of the sub-menu items to display another level of sub-sub-menus. From these, you can select the particular topic you want to see. Click on your selected topic and follow instructions on your screen.

# 18. Customise Your Database

*In this chapter:*

☞ You learn about creating and editing Tables manually and by using the Table Wizard.

☞ You are shown how to modify the structure of a Table created by the Table Wizard so that it suits your exact requirements.

☞ You learn how to query your database, so that you can extract precisely the information you want. You learn to do so by creating and modifying Queries.

☞ You are shown how to create and modify Custom Forms using the Form and the Design View. Forms are used for data entry, as a Switchboard and for a variety of special uses.

☞ You learn how to use drawing objects, List Boxes and Combo Boxes in Forms. These features enhance the appearance and utility of Forms.

☞ You are shown how to format and validate data as it is entered in a Form. You learn how to warn and guide the user of your Data Entry Form should he or she make a mistake.

☞ You learn how to create Reports and how to print the Reports you have created.

# Customising Your Database

So far, we have been discussing databases created by wizards. These are generated by standard templates in Access. For simple applications, they are usually sufficient, perhaps with slight modifications. However, for specialised database applications, you may have to customise the database so that it suits your requirement exactly.

In this chapter, we will learn how to customise the key components in a database, that is Tables, Forms, Queries and Reports.

# Creating and Editing Tables

In this chapter, you will learn how to alter the database objects you have created using the Wizard so that it has exactly the properties that you need. We begin with the basic component of the database, the Table.

## Relationships Between Tables

To modify a database to suit your exact needs you may either have to add more tables to your database or modify an existing table. For instance, in the My Contacts database you have already created, if no categories exist for your contacts, you may wish to add a new field in the Contacts table called "Categories". You may also want to create a drop-down list for the Categories field from which the user can select the appropriate category without having to type it in every time. To do this, you will have to add a drop-down list in the data form and add a small table which contains all the category values you want to use.

After you have created the Categories table, you will have to specify how this table relates to the Contacts table. That is, you will have to set up a relationship between the two tables.

The Wizard sets up a relationship between the Calls table and the Contacts table. This relationship is needed because you will make a number of calls, some to the same person in the Contacts table, and others to another person. The database must be able to go through all the calls you make, collect only the calls to a specified individual and display them together. This ability of your database comes through the use of a one-to-many relationship that the Wizard has set up for you already.

To see the relationships that already exist in the My Contacts database, proceed as follows:

1. Start **Access** and then open the **My Contacts** database as described earlier. You will see the main switchboard of My Contacts on your screen.

2. Press the **F11** function key on your keyboard. The My Contacts database window opens.

3. Click the **maximise** button if the window is not maximised already. You will now see the database window tool bar with its Relationship button. Click on this **button** to open the relationships window displaying the relationships between Contact types (or Categories), Contacts and Calls.

4. Close all **open windows** and exit the **database** by clicking on the Exit this database button on the main switchboard.

See Fig 18.01 and also Fig 16.07 (earlier in this book) for a view of the relationships in the Contacts database.

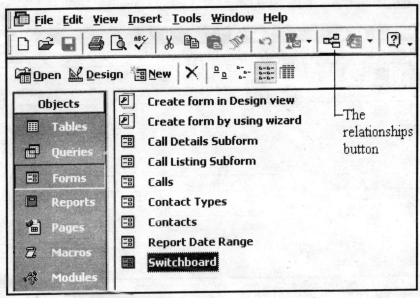

*Fig 18.01 Relationships Button on Tool Bar*

## Creating Tables Manually

We will assume that the Wizard created the My Contacts database without the categories field. We will now go through the necessary steps required to create a small table manually that will add the categories field to your database. Proceed as follows:

1. Open the **My Contacts** Database in Access. The main switchboard will be displayed.

2. Press **F11** on your keyboard. The My Contacts Database dialogue box will be displayed.

3. On the left of the dialogue box you will see a list of database objects. Move the highlight to **Tables**. The right pane will now display three options for creating tables followed by a list of tables already created by the Wizard.

4. Select the **third option** (Create a table by typing in data) by double clicking on this option. A blank, spreadsheet-like table (titled Table1 : Table) will now be displayed with 8 columns and 22 rows.

5. Click on the **View menu item** on the Access menu bar and select the **Design View** option. The table view will change to Design view. *See Fig 18.02.*

6. Type the word "**Category**" in the first row of the Field Name column. Click the **Data Type** column, which is set at its default format of Text. Do not change the format since categories will be text entries.

7. The General tab at the bottom left of the form will display a number of default settings. These settings are appropriate for our Categories database. So, **change nothing**. In the last column captioned "Description", you can optionally add a description for the entry such as "Contains categories for the Contacts".

8. To prevent duplicate entries in the table, click the **Primary Key icon** on the Table1 : Table tool bar so that Categories are assigned the primary key. The primary key is used to index the database and, therefore, no duplicate entries are allowed.

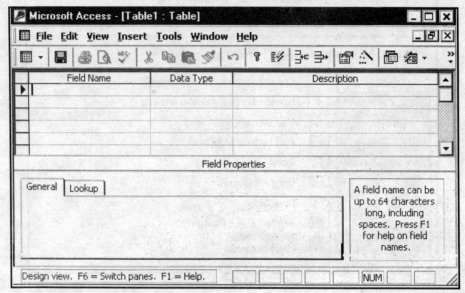

*Fig 18.02 Design View [Table1 : Table]*

9. Click the **Save icon** and assign the name "**Categories**" in the Save As dialogue box that appears. Click **OK**.

10. Click on the **File ➜ Close** option on the File drop-down menu to return to the My Contacts database window.

## Using the Table Wizard

To create complex tables, it is generally more convenient to start with the Table Wizard.

1. To start the **Wizard**, at step 4 in the previous exercise, select the **second option** ("Create table by using Wizard"). The Table Wizard window will appear.

2. In the Table Wizard dialogue box, select the "**Business**" **radio button**. Then scroll down the **Sample Tables list** till you highlight "**Tasks**". The Sample Fields window will show five items:

   • TaskID

   • TaskDescription

   • StartDate

   • EndDate

   • Notes

3. Transfer all the **field names** to the Fields in My New Table window by clicking on the **Select All button [>>]**.

4. Scroll to the **TaskDescription** field name and click the **Rename Field** button. A small dialogue box titled Rename field appears. Type the name **VisitDescription** and click **OK**. The name of the field changes to VisitDescription.

5. To link the visits to the names of the Contacts visited, you need to insert the ContactID field in this new database. To add this field, scroll to **Contacts** in the Sample Tables, highlight **Contact ID** in the Sample Fields and click on the **Add Fields [>] button** to add the ContactID field to the new database. The list of fields in the Fields in My New Table window will now contain six items. See Fig 18.03 for a view of the Table Wizard at this stage.

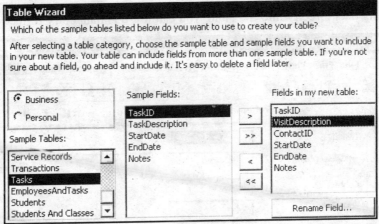

*Fig 18.03 Table Wizard in Use*

6. Click **Next** to return to the Table Wizard. Enter the name "**Visits**" and select the **radio button** marked Yes, set a primary key for me. Click **Next** to continue.

7. The next Table Wizard (*See Fig 18.04*) will show relationships. Notice that since you have used the same ContactID key in the Visits table and the Contacts table, a relationship with Contacts has already been created. Click **Next** to accept the default and to continue.

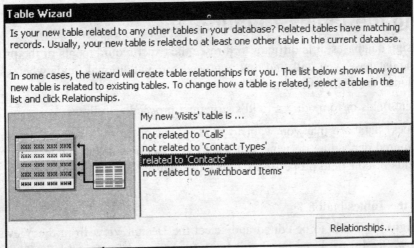

*Fig 18.04 Relationship Shown by Table Wizard*

8. In the last Wizard table that appears, select the **method** you would like to use to enter data in the table such as:

   • Modify the table

   • Enter data directly in the table

   • Have the Wizard create a form for you

9. After selecting the **option** by clicking its **radio button**, click **Finish**. The table is created. If you choose the option for the Wizard to create a data entry form, the form will also be automatically created. *See Fig 18.05.*

Instead of entering data directly into the table, you can use this data entry form.

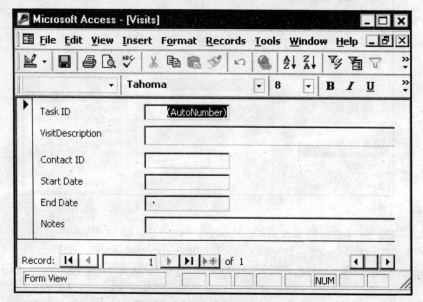

*Fig 18.05 Visits Data Entry Form*

# Modifying the Table Structure

When you design databases, it is difficult to foresee the exact requirements of the project. As you begin using the database, you will find that you need some additional fields whereas some fields originally included are really superfluous.

To add or delete fields or to modify a field's structure, proceed as follows:

**Open** the Access database that you want to modify and go to the database window. Different actions are required depending on what you want to do, such as delete fields, insert fields, move fields, edit fields or edit field properties. **Choose** the appropriate action after step 2 as explained below.

1. Click the **Tables** button.

2. Highlight the **Table** to be edited and select the Design View from the Views drop-down window. See Fig 16.11 earlier in this book for an example of a table in Design View.

- To delete a field, highlight the **field row** by clicking on the **box** at the left of the table. The entire row will be highlighted. Press the **Delete** key on your keyboard and confirm the delete in the **dialogue box** if it appears. You can also right click on the **highlighted row** with your mouse and click on the **Delete Row** option on the drop-down menu that will appear.

- To insert a new field, highlight the **row** below the one to be inserted as before. Now press the **Insert key** on your keyboard. A new blank field will be inserted above the existing, highlighted field. You can also right click on the **highlighted row** and select the **Insert Row** option on the drop-down menu that appears. You must enter the field name, data type and properties for the new field before closing the table.

- To move a **field row**, highlight it as before. Move your mouse pointer to the **left-most box** on the highlighted row. A white arrow [>] appears in the box. Click on this **arrow** with your mouse and drag the **entire row** up or down as required. Release the left mouse button to anchor the **row** in its new location. This change will also alter the position of the field in the associated data entry form if there is one.

- To edit a field, click in the **field's cell** (Field Name, Data Type etc). A blinking cursor will appear in the cell you have selected. Type the required **changes**.

- To edit a field's properties, click in the **field** as before. The field's properties are displayed at the bottom right of the table. Edit the **field's properties** as needed. See Fig 18.06 where you can see the field properties of the Contacts table.

| | Title | Text |
|---|---|---|
| | WorkPhone | Text |
| | WorkExtension | Text |
| | MobilePhone | Text |
| | FaxNumber | Text |
| | EmailName | Text |

Field Properties

General | Lookup

| Field Size | Long Integer |
| New Values | Increment |
| Format | |
| Caption | Contact ID |
| Indexed | Yes (No Duplicates) |

*Fig 18.06 Contacts Table Field Properties*

# Common Data Types

Here are the most common data types you will meet in Access databases. In this list, we have put down for you what they are and how to use them:

**TEXT**: Use for text such as names or for numbers not used for calculations such as phone numbers.

**MEMO**: Use for long notes or comments. Memo fields cannot be sorted.

**NUMBER**: Use for all numbers except currency. You can do calculations using numbers.

**DATE/TIME**: Use for dates and times. Be sure to use the correct format such as mm/dd/yy (month/date/year) by setting the input mask to the desired format in the table design view.

**CURRENCY**: Use it for monetary values.

**AUTONUMBER**: This is the identifier (ID) field. It must be unique for each record. Access increments the value of this field automatically as records are entered into the table.

**YES/NO**: Also called a Boolean field, it is used for storing True/False, Yes/No values.

# Common Field Properties

In Design View, if you scroll down the fields for any record, you will see the applicable field properties displayed at the bottom left of your monitor's screen. The field properties vary with the data type. That is, the field properties for a Text data type will be different from those of a Time/Date data type. We give here the most common field properties with explanations about their use.

**FIELD SIZE**: Decide on the field size for text (number of characters) based on the largest text you want to enter. For example, in a name field, provide enough size to take the longest name you are going to use. Usually, the default length of 50 characters is quite sufficient.

For numeric fields, Integer is sufficient in most cases. Select Long Integer to store numbers larger than 32,000. For decimal numbers, use Single.

**FORMAT**: In the field properties text box, if you enter [<] in the format row of the field properties column, then all that you enter in that field will be automatically converted to lower case. If you enter [>], then the entries are forced into upper case.

In case of Date, Currency and number fields, click on the field property text box to cause a drop-down list to appear. Select the appropriate format from this list.

**DEFAULT VALUE**: If you want a value to be automatically entered in each new record, enter it in the Default Value text box. The user can overwrite the default value if required.

**VALIDATION RULE**: Use this text box to set rules that the data must meet in order to be accepted. For example, in a number field, if you enter >50, only numbers greater than 50 can be entered. You can also force the entry to be limited to a series of choices. For example, in a State Code field, you can restrict entries to Maharashtra, West Bengal or Delhi by entering a string that reads = "MH" or "WB" or "DL". In all cases where you set up a validation rule, the user will get a warning if the rule is violated. You can use the default message that Access creates for you, or create your own message as explained in the next paragraph.

**VALIDATION TEXT**: This is the text that the user will see if a validation rule is violated. If you set the ValidationRule property but not the ValidationText property, Microsoft Access displays a standard error message when the validation rule is violated. If you set the ValidationText property, the text you enter is displayed as the error message. Usually, the text should give the user a hint as to how the mistake should be corrected.

**TIP**

You can also use the input mask Wizard to help with formatting tasks. To start the Wizard, click on the drop-down arrow ▼ next to the input mask item in the Field properties pane of the design view of a table you are modifying. You can then follow the sequence of instructions on your screen to provide an input mask for a field such as a Phone Number or a Pin Code. See Fig 18.07 for a view of the Input Mask Wizard.

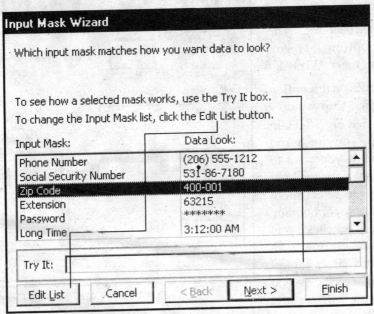

*Fig 18.07 Input Mask Wizard*

**TIP**

For more information on a field property, while in the design view, **click** on a text box of a field property. The blinking cursor appears in that text box. Now you can press the F1 key on your keyboard in order to display a help window containing information on the field property you have selected.

# Querying Your Database

In Chapter 17, *Using Your Access Database*, under the topic "Using Filters" we have seen how to create a sub-set of the records in your entire database. The sub-set only contains those records that meet a certain criteria. For example, in the My Contacts database, you can create a sub-set of only those records in which the contact lives in Mumbai. If you have a very large database with hundreds of records, the advantage of being able to create smaller and more manageable sub-sets can be seen easily.

A general procedure for creating sub-sets that meet criteria you establish is called querying your database. We will study querying in detail in this section. The most common type of query is a "Select Query". You query your main database and ask Access to select only those records that meet your criteria. In response, Access creates a sub-set of records called a "recordset". You can create a recordset from more than one table in your database. You can save a recordset and call it again in the future. If the data in the different tables that contribute to the recordset are changed, the recordset is updated automatically.

## Create a Query

Here is how you can create a simple select query:

1.  Open the **Access database** and navigate to the database window. For example, you can open the My Contacts database and move the highlight in the **left pane** to Queries in the objects list. You will see two Create Query options on the right hand pane. The second option lets you launch a **Query Wizard**.

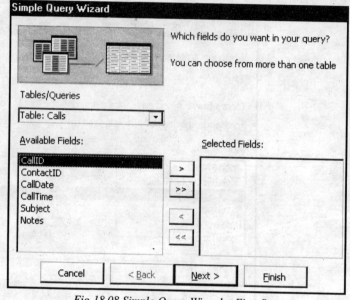

*Fig 18.08 Simple Query Wizard – First Step*

2.  Double click on this **option** and its first step window appears. *See Fig 18.08.* In this step, you are asked which fields you want to include in your query. Note that you can select more than one table for building your query by clicking in the drop-down arrow ▼ in the text box under Tables/Queries. For each table you select, you will see the available fields in the left pane under Available Fields. Transfer the **fields** you want to the right pane under Selected Fields by highlighting the field and clicking on the [>] button. If you want to transfer all the fields, click on the [>>] button instead. In our example, we select Call Date, Call Time and Subject from the Calls table and First Name and Last Name from the Contacts table to build our query.

3.  Click **Next** and in the next Wizard window, name the **query**. You can accept the **default name** given to the query by Access, which is Calls Query in this case.

| Microsoft Access - [Calls Query : Select Query] | | | | |
| --- | --- | --- | --- | --- |
| Call ID | Contact ID | Call Date | Call Time | Subject |
| 1 | 1 | 12/9/2002 | 11:41 AM | Next Shooting c |
| 2 | 5 | 12/10/2002 | 7:45 PM | Payment for boc |
| 3 | 4 | 12/10/2002 | 9:45 PM | Bad Lipstick |
| 4 | 3 | 12/11/2002 | 10:36 AM | Surveilance repc |
| 5 | 6 | 12/11/2002 | 6:45 PM | Book delivery |
| 6 | 2 | 12/11/2002 | 7:30 PM | Shooting date |

*Fig 18.09 [Calls Query : Select Query]*

4. Select the **radio button** "Open the query to view information" and click **Finish**. The query will be displayed in Table View.

## Modify the Query

If you want to apply selection criteria to the query, you will have to modify the query by opening it in design view. This is how you modify the query:

1. In the table view, click on the **View** option in the menu bar and select **Design View** in the drop-down list. The query appears in Design View. *See Fig 18.10.* The top half of the window shows the two tables used, Calls and Contacts, and the bottom half of the window has a table for entering selection criteria.

2. In the criteria text box below the appropriate field, enter the **criteria** you wish to specify. For instance, in the text box in the FirstName column, if you enter Rajni, the query will select calls made only by the Contact(s) with the first name Rajni. If you want to enter a criterion in a number column, enter an operator such as =, >, < followed by the value. Thus entering = 50 will restrict the query to records containing 50 in the specified numbers column.

3. After you have finished all the criteria you want, click the **Save** icon on the Access tool bar to save the query.

   Once a query has been saved, it will appear in the database window as a database object.

4. To display all the queries you have saved, scroll down to the **Queries** object on the left of the window. The right pane will list all saved queries. To open the query, you have simply

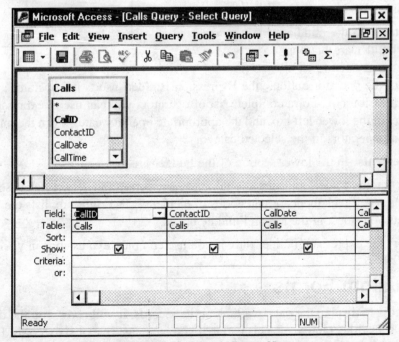

*Fig 18.10 Calls Query in Design View*

to double click on its **name**. The query window is displayed, which is "Calls Query: Select Query" in this case. The display is like a worksheet window with the fields along the columns and the calls along the rows. See Fig 18.09 earlier in this section.

5. Return to the **main switchboard** and shut down the database by clicking on the **Exit** this database button. Shut down **Access** thereafter.

## The Expression Builder

In the design view of your query, you can design complex criteria by using the Expression Builder Wizard. Click in the Criteria text box of the desired field. When the blinking cursor appears, right click your mouse to launch the Expression Builder. *See Fig 18.11.*

The Expression Builder has three sections, running from top to bottom. They are:

**Expression box:** In the upper section of the builder is an expression box where you build the expression. Use the lower section of the builder to create elements of the expression, and then paste these elements into the expression box to form an expression. You can also type parts of the expression directly into the expression box.

**Operator buttons:** In the middle section of the builder are buttons for commonly used operators. If

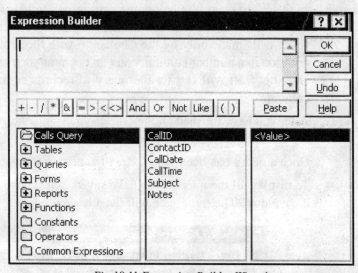

*Fig 18.11 Expression Builder Wizard*

you click one of the operator buttons, the Expression Builder inserts the operator at the insertion point in the expression box. For a complete list of operators you can use in expressions, click the Operators folder in the lower-left box and the appropriate operator category in the middle box. The right box lists all operators in the selected category.

**Expression elements:** In the lower section of the builder are three boxes:

The left box contains folders that list the table, query, form, and report database objects. The middle box lists specific elements or categories of elements The right box lists the values, if any, for the elements you select in the left and middle boxes.

You will require the expression builder only if you use complex expressions in your query.

## Using Custom Forms

If you ask Access to display the data available in its records, it will show you the default format, which is like a spreadsheet in Excel. This is fine if you have just five or six records. However if the database is large, you will probably require a better organised format for easier reading. Similarly, for entering data, most of us find it easier to use a form similar to a printed form that we are already familiar with.

Fortunately, Access can easily create custom forms just the way you want it so that you can enter or view data very conveniently. You have already seen how Access will automatically create a set of tables and forms when you use a predefined database template as we did in Chapter 17, *Using Your Access Database*, when we created the My Contacts database. However, you can edit or modify any form created automatically to make it better suited to your exact needs. For instance, you can:

- Add default values that will be automatically displayed whenever a new record is created for data entry.

- Add control objects such as check boxes and drop-down list boxes which allow you to select from a predefined list.

- Add validation rules so that the user cannot enter wrong information. For instance, you can stop the user from entering a value below a minimum you specify and warn the user of his mistake by displaying an error message.

To do all these, you have to learn how to create forms, edit them and add control objects. We practise all this using the My Contacts database you have already created in Chapter 17. What you will learn is not confined to this database alone. You will be able to apply these skills to any future Access database project that you may undertake.

## Creating a Form

As you have already seen, the best way to get started is to use a Forms wizard to create a form for you. You can then switch the form to its design view and modify the form the way you want. It is possible to design a form entirely from scratch. However, you may wish to do so after gaining some more experience in the use of Access. Let us now begin an exercise on creating forms using the Form Wizard.

We select the My Contacts database we have created earlier and proceed with the creation of a custom form.

Do the following:

1. Open the **My Contacts** database in Access and navigate to the database window. If the database opens at the Main Switchboard, click on the **maximise** icon on the minimised database window you will see at the bottom left of your screen.

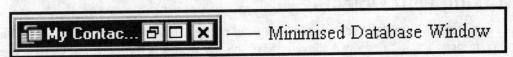

2. Click the **Forms** button in the Objects pane on your left and then click the second **Create form** button in the right pane. The Form Wizard will be launched and you will see the first step on your screen. See Fig 16.18 earlier in this book for a view of the Form Wizard.

3. In this step, you tell the Wizard the table on which the form will be based. Scroll through the **tables** list under Tables/Queries and select **Contacts**. The available fields in the Contacts database will appear in the Available Fields list.

4.  Select **ContactID** through to **PostalCode** by highlighting them one by one and clicking on the [>] to transfer each selected field to the Selected Fields window. Click **Next**. The next step window appears.

5.  In this window, choose **columnar** field layout for your form by clicking on the appropriate **radio button** and click **Next**. The next step window appears.

6.  In this window choose the **style** for your form. Select **International** in this step and click **Next**.

7.  In this window, you can name your form or accept the default name. Name the form **My Contacts**. If you want to use the form immediately, **click** the **radio button** labelled Open the form to view and enter information. Click **Finish** completing the exercise. The completed form is displayed.

8.  Close the **form**, navigate back to the **main switchboard** and exit the **database**. If you reopen the database window and click on Forms under the list of objects, you will see My Contacts listed along with other forms.

## Editing a Form

While the form created by the Wizard can be both functional and attractive, you can modify the form so that it looks and behaves just the way you want.

### Form and Design View

To modify a form, you must have the form opened in Design View. To do so, proceed as follows:

1.  Open the **My Contacts** database and navigate to the database window. Select the **Form** object under objects in the list in the left pane and double click on the **My Contacts** form in the right pane to open it. The My Contacts form appears on the screen.

2.  Click on the **View** option on the Access menu bar and select the **Design View**. If the tool box is not displayed, click the **View** option again and click on the **Tool box** option. The tool box with its set of tools appears as a floating tool bar on your desktop. See Fig 16.21 earlier in this book for a view of the Tool box in Design View.

3.  Click the **View** menu item again and select **Form View** to return to Form View. You must be in Form View to enter data in the form.

## Working with Objects

As a first step, let us practise selecting, moving and sizing objects on a form in its Design View and complete steps 1 and 2 described above to have the My Contacts form open in Design View with the tool box visible. *See Fig 18.12.*

### Selecting

Select an object or objects as follows:

*   Click on the **object**. Small black squares called Handles will appear round the object you have selected.

- To select more than one object, click the **first**, then hold down the shift key and click the **next** and so on till all the objects you need are selected. Handles will appear around each of the objects you have selected.

- If the objects you want are contiguous with no unwanted objects in between, you can select them all at the same time by clicking the mouse pointer near to (but not on) the **group of objects** and drag a black bordered rectangle that will form to include all the objects you want. Release the mouse pointer and the objects within the black bordered rectangle will be selected.

- To deselect an object, click on any **blank part** of the form.

- To delete an object, select it as described above and then press the **delete** key on your keyboard.

- To move an object or a group of objects, first select the **object** or **objects**. Then move the mouse pointer to the edge of the object (but not on a handle). The mouse pointer will turn into an open hand. Now drag the **selection** to its new location. Release the mouse button to anchor the objects to their new location.

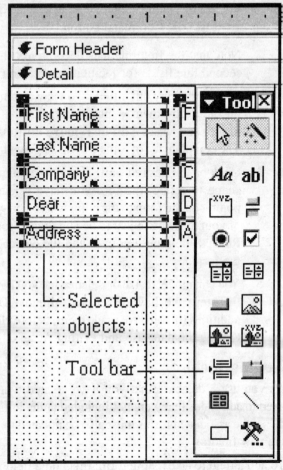

*Fig 18.12 Selected Items and Tool Box*

- To change the size of an object, select it and then position the mouse pointer on an appropriate handle. Drag the **handle** to change the size of the object. Release the mouse button when done.

## Adding Drawing Objects

You can add two basic types of drawing objects to a form. The first type is associated with a field in a table. These drawing objects include: Text boxes, Option boxes, Combo boxes, List boxes and Option buttons. They are used to simplify data entry. The other type is not associated with any field. These drawing objects include: Text labels, Lines and Graphic shapes. These objects are mainly to decorate the form and make it look more attractive.

To add a drawing object, proceed as follows:

1. Open the **My Contacts** form in Design View after launching Access and My Contacts database as discussed earlier. Make sure that the Tool box is open. If not, click on the **View** menu item and click on the **Tool box** drop-down item.

These are the most common tools you will use:

- Label, Text box, Image, Line, Rectangle.
- Toggle button, Option button, Check box, Combo box, List box, Command button.

Note that the first line lists decorative controls while the second line list is for facilitating data entry.

There are many other tools. To view a complete list, click on the drop-down ▾ button next to the Tool box title header and select **Add or remove buttons ➜ Tool box**. The complete list of tools will be displayed. *See Fig 18.13.*

2. Click on the desired **tool**. The mouse pointer will change shape to reflect the tool you have selected. Move the pointer on the form to the point where you want one corner of your drawing object to be and drag to form a rectangle. Release the mouse pointer and the object will appear on the form.

3. You can move, resize or delete what you have added using the steps we have discussed already. Delete the two additions (if you have made them) before closing the form, closing the database and exiting Access.

# Adding Fields

As you use a database that you have created, you may find the need to add fields that were not included at the initial stage. If you do so, the associated forms must also be updated to accommodate the new field(s).

To add a field to an existing form, first add a field in the table on which the form is based. Then, add it to the form. To carry out this task, proceed as follows:

1. Open the Table **Contacts** in the database My Contacts within Access. Switch to **Design View** as described earlier.

2. In Design View, **add** a new field below Notes and name it "NickName". Accept the default Data type of **Text** for the field. If you now switch back to the Datasheet View, you will see that a new field titled NickName has been added as the last column in the table. *See Fig 18.14.*

3. Open the **Contacts** form in Design View as described earlier. Make sure that the Tool box is visible. If not, click on the **View** Menu item on the Access menu bar and click on **Tool box**.

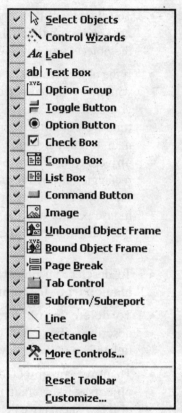

*Fig 18.13 Complete Set of Tool Box Tools*

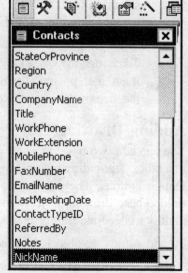

*Fig 18.14 Field List Button and Fields*

4.  Click on the **Field List** button. The list of available fields in the Contacts table will become visible. Scroll down until you see the newly added last entry, **NickName**.

5.  Before you can add this field on the form, you will need to create space for it, just below the LastName field. To create space, click on **empty space** close to the field labelled Dear. Create a selection window by dragging the mouse cursor to enclose all the fields from Dear to Country. Handles will appear around all the fields selected.

6.  Move the cursor in the selected area so that the cursor changes to an open palm. Now drag all the fields down by approximately 1/2" to create space for one field below the field captioned Dear.

7.  Drag down the field **NickName** from the Field List window to the empty space you have just created. Move the new field if required to get the correct alignment and spacing in relation to all the existing fields. *See Fig 18.15.*

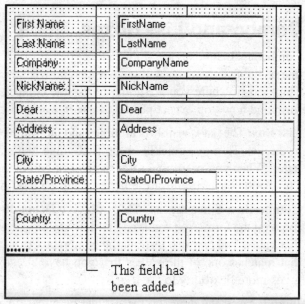

*Fig 18.15 Contacts Form with NickName Field Added*

8.  When entering data, you will want the cursor to move from field to field in the sequence they appear on the form as you press the Tab key after entering data in each field. Although NickName has been added at the bottom of the table in the table design view in the form, you would like the cursor to move in the sequence seen. That is, you want the cursor to move from LastName to NickName before moving to Dear.

9.  To do this, you reset the Tab order by clicking on **View** on the Access menu bar and clicking on **Tab Order** on the drop-down menu that appears. The Tab Order window appears. *See Fig 18.16.*

10. Notice that in the window, NickName appears at the bottom of the list. Click on the **Auto Order** button at the bottom of the window and the position of NickName will

*Fig 18.16 Tab Order Dialogue Box*

change to match the position on the form. Now, you will be able to tab through the form in the same sequence as it appears on your screen.

11. Now your My Contacts table and the My Contacts data entry form will both contain the new field NickName. Close all **windows** and exit **Access**.

# Combo and List Boxes

Combo and List boxes are features that you can add to a form to simplify data entry. Before you add one of the features, you will have to decide whether you should create a list box or a combo box. Think about where you are going to use the control, how you want the control to appear on your form and how you expect people to use it. Each control offers its own advantages:

**List Box:** The list is visible at all times and the value of the control is limited to the set of alternatives in the list. To move quickly to the first value that starts with a particular letter, you can type that letter. When you're using a form to enter or edit data, you cannot add a value that is not in the list. This is obviously useful if the list box will be used by users not familiar with Access.

**Combo Box:** Since the list of a combo box is not displayed until you open it, the control uses less room on the form. You can type the first few characters of a value in the combo box to quickly find that value. You can also instruct the combo box to accept any value that can be entered, or only text that matches one of the values that you have already entered in the combo box list. This feature gives more flexibility to the user.

In both cases, the items on the list can be either typed, or can be based on a separate table which contains the items. It is generally better to base the list box or combo box items on a separate table since you can add, delete or alter the items that appear by changing the items in the table without having to modify the form itself.

In the design view of a form, the Tool box shows the Combo box and the List box as two controls that you can install on the form. See Fig 16.19 in Chapter 16, *Getting to Know Access 2000*, earlier in this book for a view of the tool box.

In our MyContacts database, let us assume that your contacts only live in the four Metro cities and Pune. If so, instead of having to fill in the City field manually, you may decide to replace the field by a combo box which already contains the five city names. If you are certain that you will never have to use any other than these five names, you can also use a list box. However, a combo box is recommended since it lets you add any additional city if required at a later date.

## *Adding Combo or List Boxes*

Follow the procedure given below to add a combo box or a list box in the form My Contacts instead of the City field:

1. Create a new table called **City** by entering the My Contacts database, selecting **Table** on the left pane and create the table by specifying field name, data types etc in the right pane.

2. In the Design View, name the field **CityName** and accept the default data type as **text**. Save the table, entering the table name as **City** and allowing Access to create the **primary key** for you.

3. Enter the four **Metro city names**, Chennai, Kolkata, Mumbai and New Delhi. Add **Pune** to the list. Save the **table**.

4. Open the **Contacts** form in Design View and make sure that the tool box is visible.

5. Click on the **City** field so that the handles appear. Press the **delete** key on your keyboard to delete this field.

6. Click the **Combo box** tool or the list box tool on the tool box. Move the curser to where you want the top left corner of the combo or list box to be and then drag the cursor to create the box of appropriate size. Try to match the original size of the City field so as to retain the original layout. The first step of the combo box Wizard appears. *See Fig 18.17.*

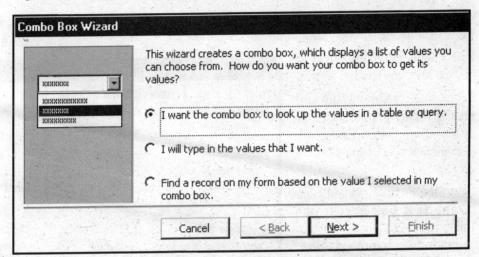

*Fig 18.17 Combo Wizard Dialogue Box*

7. In this select the **first** radio button which lets your combo box read values from a table and click **Next**. The next step of the Wizard appears.

8. Select the table **City** in this step and click **Next** to continue. The third step of the Wizard appears. In this, select the **CityName** field from the Available fields pane and transfer it to the selected fields pane on the right by clicking on [>]. Click **Next** to continue.

9. In the next step of the Wizard, you will see the table with the city names included. Accept the **default** which recommends that the key column is excluded. Adjust the **width** if required and then click **Next** to continue.

10. Type <City> when prompted for a label for the combo box and click **Finish** to complete the exercise.

11. Switch back to **Form View**. You will see that the City field has been replaced by the Combo box field. Click on the down arrow ▾ to cause a drop-down box to appear which contains the five city names you have already entered. *See Fig 18.18.*

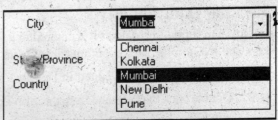

*Fig 18.18 Combo Box with City Names*

**NOTE**

Instead of replacing an existing field, if you add a new field through a Combo box, you will have to reorder the tab order by going through the same steps as you did in case of the example of adding a field (NickName) as you have already learned in the previous section on adding a field.

## Formatting Data

You can control the format of the data being entered into your database by changing the properties of the fields in which data is being entered. You do so by opening the form in the design mode.

Proceed as follows:

1.  Open the **Contact** form by opening the My Contacts database in Access. Select the **Design View** by clicking on the Design button.

2.  Select the **E-mailName** field so that the selection handles appear.

3.  Right click on the **field** and select **Properties** from the drop-down list. The Text box E-mailNames appears. *See Fig 18.19.*

4.  Select the **Format** tab and click on the **text box** next to the Format label. Now you can insert format commands here. Type [>] in the text box. It will force the entry to be only in lower case as required for e-mail names. Other formatting commands include:

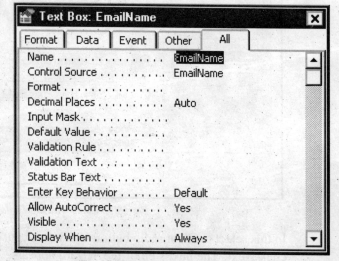

Fig 18.19 E-mailNames Dialogue Box

-   To force text to upper case, use [< ].

-   If the field is a number or date, use the down arrow ▼ in the text box to display the options available for formatting. Choose the appropriate one.

5.  Close the **Properties** window when finished and save the **form**. Close all **windows** and close **Access**.

## Checking Data Validity

In addition to formatting data as it is entered in a form, you can instruct Access to check the data for errors and to warn the user about mistakes by an error message. To do so, proceed as follows:

1.  Open the **form** to be edited in Design View.

2.  Double click the **field** and from the drop-down list, select **Properties** to display the Properties window.

3.  Click to open the **Data** tab and in the Validation rule text box, enter the **data validation rule** you want. For example:

    *   To ensure that the entry will be one of a list of permissible choices, enter the choices enclosed in quotes separated by the operator "or". For example, in the State field, you may enter "MH" or "WB" or "ND" to represent the states of Maharashtra, West Bengal and New Delhi, in that order. See Fig 18.20 for the Validation Rules text box.

    *   To specify limits of a numeric value, you can use validation rules such as <50, >0 to specify less than 50 or greater than zero respectively.

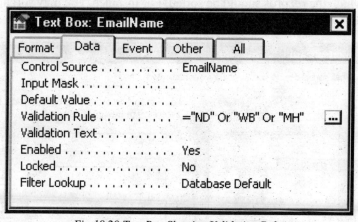

*Fig 18.20 Text Box Showing Validation Rule*

4.  If you wish to enter a special warning message for the user, click in the **validation text** box and enter your **message**. If you leave this box blank but set up a validation rule, Access will display a default warning message in case the validation rule is violated.

5.  Close the **Properties** window when done.

6.  Close all **windows** and exit **Access** in the usual way.

# Creating Reports

While queries and forms can display data from your database in the manner you want, it is necessary to use another database object to create printed information from your database. This object is the Access Report. Once again, we can get help from a Wizard, the Access Report Wizard, to easily create a report tailored to our needs. In a report, you can summarise data, displaying sub-totals and grand totals of numeric data. You can also sort the data using any of the fields in your database.

To create a report using the Access Report Wizard, follow these steps:

1.  Open the **Access** database you wish to use, navigating to the **database** window. Select the **Reports** object on the left of the window, under Objects.

2.  On the right pane, select the **option** for creating a report using a Wizard.

3.  The First step of the Report Wizard is displayed in which you are asked to select the **table** that will form the basis of your report. This step is followed by selecting the **fields** that will

be displayed in your report in the same way as you select tables and fields for a Query or a Form. See Fig 16.25 in Chapter 16, *Getting to Know Access 2000*, earlier in this book.

4. In the next step, you can decide on any grouping of data that you may want. For instance, if the report contains sales information along with customer's names, you can group according to **customers** to get the sub-total of sales by customers in addition to the grand total sales. Click **Next** to continue.

5. In the third step of the Report Wizard, you have the option of sorting the records for display in the report. *See Fig 18.21.* You can specify up to four fields to sort and also select the order in which the records should be sorted. For instance, you may sort an address database first by Pin Code, then by last name and finally by first name. Click **Next** to continue.

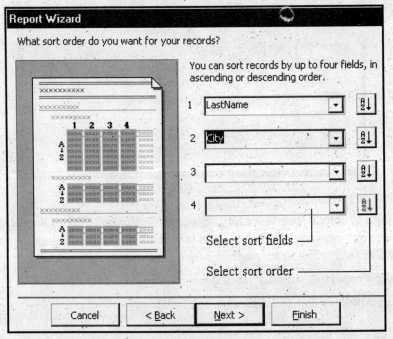

*Fig 18.21 Select Sort Fields and Order*

6. In the next step, you select the **layout** and the orientation of the report. As you select a layout by clicking on its radio button, a sample appears in the pane on the left to give you a preview. Select between **portrait** and **landscape** orientation by clicking on the appropriate **radio button**. Click **Next** to continue.

7. In the next step, you select a **style** for the report, watching the preview pane on the left to help you decide. Click **Next** to continue.

8. In the last step, you **select** a title for your report and decide if you wish to preview the report or modify the report's design. Click **Finish** to complete the exercise.

9. The completed report is displayed on your screen if you select the **preview** option. *See Fig 18.22.* Close the **window** to return to the database window.

# Printing

After you have created and previewed your report, you can print the report if you have a printer attached to your computer. Follow these steps to preview and then print any report that has been already created and saved as an object in your database:

1.  In the database window, click the **Reports** button to display all the reports saved in your database. The list will appear in the right pane.

2.  Select the **report** you wish to preview by double clicking on it. The report is displayed on your monitor's screen. See Fig 18.22 for a sample report.

| *Contacts* | | | | | |
|---|---|---|---|---|---|
| *Last Name* | *City* | *First Name* | *Address* | *State/Pro* | *Email Name* |
| Balram | Mumbai | Balraj | 10 Bundle Gali, Malad | MH | bbalram@vsnl.com |
| Bandookwalla | New Delhi | Bundledass | 77 Aziz Road | ND | bbandook@hotmail. |
| Jariwalla | Kolkata | Haribhai | 67 Paper Lane | WB | hjariwalla@hotmail. |
| Jasoos | Pune | Gopichand | 21 Teli Gali | MH | gjasoos@vsnl.com |
| Nimbupani | Mumbai | Rajni | 10 Bundle Gali, Malad | MH | rnimbupani@vsnl.c |
| Smita | Kolkata | Slinky | 11 Taltolla Road | WB | ssmitta@yahoo.com |

*Fig 18.22 Sample Report from Contact*

3.  Click the **Print** button (icon) on the Access tool bar to begin printing out the selected report. *See Fig 18.23*. The report is printed.

4.  Close the **database** and exit **Access**.

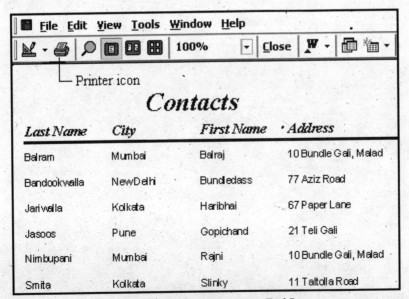

*Fig 18.23 Printer Icon on Access Tool Bar*

**CD-ROM**  To learn more about Microsoft Access 2000 in a multimedia environment, insert the accompanying CD-ROM in your computer and select the **Interactive** mode in the opening screen. The main menu will appear. To go to the section on Access, click the button marked **Access**. You will see a sub-menu containing the following topics:

- Getting Started in Access
- Updating Tables
- Working with Forms

Click on any of the sub-menu items to display another level of sub-sub-menus. From these, you can select the particular topic you want to see. Click on your selected topic and follow instructions on your screen. Material discussed in this chapter will be found mainly in items 2 and 3 of the sub-menu.

# 19. PowerPoint 2000 Basics

**In this chapter:**

☞ You are introduced to the powerful new features of PowerPoint 2000. The features include personalised menus that show the frequently used commands, new and enhanced clip art gallery, a projector wizard to help you set up a multimedia projector and multiple language support.

☞ You learn how to start and exit PowerPoint. You understand the elements of the PowerPoint window and learn their functions. You also learn how to use different views of your slides.

☞ You are shown how to create a new presentation and how to open existing ones. You learn how to use built-in design templates to give your slides a professionally uniform look. You also learn how to import outlines for your presentation from other documents such as Word 2000.

☞ You learn how to edit presentations and to move between slides, adding and deleting slides as required.

☞ You are shown how to add text to a slide, both in the outline pane and in the slide view.

☞ You learn how to insert data in your presentation in the form of tables and charts on your slides.

# What is New

In this chapter, we will cover all the basic aspects of Microsoft's presentation software, PowerPoint 2000. The more advanced features are covered in the next chapter, Chapter 20, *Customising Your Presentation*, where we tell you how to make a really professional slide show.

Before going into details, we take a quick look at the improvements in PowerPoint 2000 over its earlier versions.

Along with the other members of Microsoft Office 2000 suit of programmes, PowerPoint 2000 also has many improvements over its earlier (PowerPoint 95 and 97) versions. For those of you upgrading from an earlier version of PowerPoint, the significant improvements are summarised here.

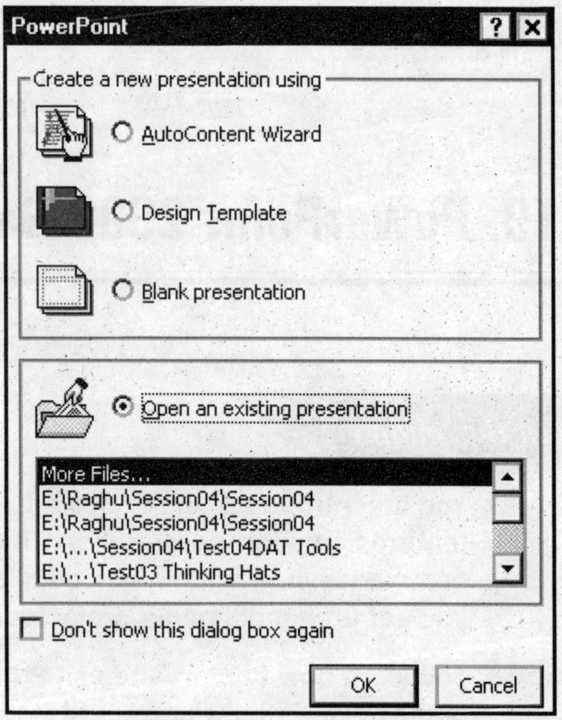

*Fig 19.01 PowerPoint Opening Screen*

## Faster Document Access

With the improved Open and Save dialogue boxes in the File menu, you can see more files at one time and access them faster in every Microsoft Office programme. Use the Places Bar to get to the folders and locations you use the most. Click History to see the last 20 to 50 documents and folders that you've worked with. Then click the Back button to easily return to folders that you've used recently.

## Display Frequently Used Commands

Only the items that you use most often are prominently featured on the new personalised menus and tool bars in Office 2000. You can easily expand the menus to reveal all commands. After you click a command, it appears on your personalised menu. Tool bars share space in a single row on the screen, so you have more room for your work. When you click a button on a tool bar, that button is added to the personalised tool bars on your screen. You can easily customise your tool bars by dragging command controls onto them. See Fig 19.01 showing the opening screen.

See what documents you have open and then use the Windows task bar to switch between open Office documents. Each document is represented by an icon on the task bar.

## New Clip Art Gallery

With the new Clip Gallery you can organise pictures into selected categories.

You can assign key words to pictures, drag images into your presentation, and leave the Clip Gallery open in a smaller window while you're working on your presentations. The new Clip Gallery can also store sounds and movies. If you use a picture, sound, or movie often, you can add it to the Clip Gallery so that you can find it easily.

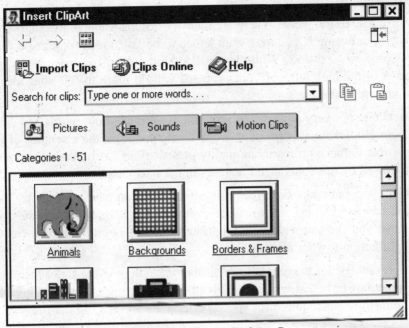

*Fig 19.02 Insert Clip Art Dialogue Box*

## Graphics and Objects

You can add graphics on Web pages easily with PowerPoint 2000. These graphics are automatically stored in GIF, JPEG, PNG, or Vector Mark-up Language (VML) format. Even after you save your presentation as a Web page, you can still edit the graphics and objects when you open your Web page in PowerPoint.

## Projector Wizard

The Projector Wizard automatically sets and restores the correct screen resolution for the projection system that you are using. Most of the popular projection systems are supported.

## Multiple Languages

You can enter, display, and edit text in all supported languages in any language version of Microsoft PowerPoint 2000. As of now, supported languages include European languages, Japanese, Chinese, Korean, Hebrew, and Arabic. Future versions are likely to support some of the major Indian languages as well.

If you have the Microsoft Office 2000 MultiLanguage Pack, you can change the language of the user interface and the contents of the Help screens. For example, your multinational corporation might have standardised an English user interface to simplify internal training and troubleshooting. But if you prefer to read Help in your native language and the language is supported by the Multilanguage pack, then you can display the help screens in your chosen language.

# Getting Started

## PowerPoint Presentations

A picture is worth a thousand words. There are many occasions when you want to inform others in a persuasive way. For example, you may want a loan to be sanctioned for a project, or get support from your boss for a new product. While you will submit a detailed report, a well-prepared half-hour presentation of the highlights of your proposal will do more to sell your idea than the 100 pages or so of your report!

Microsoft PowerPoint is a very powerful programme for presentation. In this and the next chapter, Chapter 20, *Customising Your Presentation*, we will help you learn the essentials of PowerPoint so that you will be able to make professional quality presentations easily. We will cover the basics in this chapter, followed by more advanced features in the next chapter.

With PowerPoint, you can make on-screen presentations if you have a computer available at the site. If not, you can use PowerPoint to make overhead projector transparencies or 35mm film transparencies that you can use with an appropriate projector. In addition, you can prepare paper handouts for distribution to your audience.

You use a PowerPoint file for making your presentation. In the file are slides that are projected on the screen. A slide may have text, graphics, clip art or video clips containing movie and sound. In addition, all the instructions required for special effects are included in the file.

Slides can be prepared from scratch or by using professionally prepared Design Templates (available as "New Presentations") that are included with your copy of PowerPoint. These templates are colour coordinated and complete with background graphics. You can add text or your own graphics to quickly put an attractive presentation together.

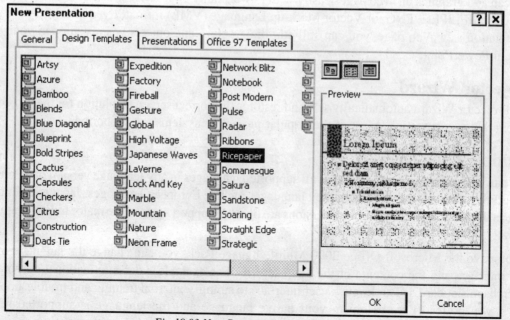

*Fig 19.03 New Presentation Dialogue Box*

In Fig 19.03, you can see PowerPoint's collection of design templates. The one you choose is previewed in the right pane.

After selecting a design template and a colour scheme for your presentation, you can put together a set of slides such as Title slides, Bulleted slides and slides containing clip art, graphs and charts or any combination of these. By using a template, you can make sure that your slides have a consistent style and colour scheme across the entire set of slides.

## Starting PowerPoint

To get familiar with the way PowerPoint works, begin by starting PowerPoint and create a blank presentation. Do the following:

1.  Start PowerPoint by clicking on its icon on your desktop or on the Microsoft Office Shortcut bar. Alternatively, you can launch the application by clicking **Start → Programmes → Microsoft PowerPoint**. The opening dialogue box appears. See Fig 19.01 earlier in this chapter.

2.  Select the Blank presentation radio button and click **OK**. The New Slide dialogue box appears. *See Fig 19.04.*

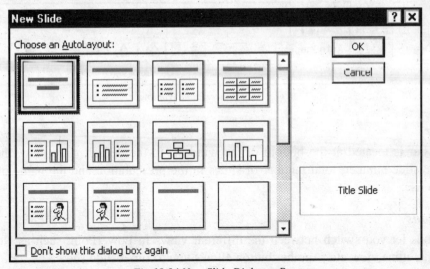

*Fig 19.04 New Slide Dialogue Box*

3.  In the gallery of slides, the title slide at the upper left is highlighted by default. Click **OK** to create a blank title slide. You can type the title and sub-title in the slide.

4.  Close PowerPoint by selecting **File** in the Menu bar and clicking on **Exit** in the drop-down menu that appears.

## The PowerPoint Window

Let us study the PowerPoint window that appears when you create a new slide or open an existing one. You will notice that many of the tool bar and menu items are similar to the Office 2000 family of menus and tool bars. However, some are unique to PowerPoint, such as the Status Bar and the

View Buttons. These two are explained below. See also Fig 19.05 for an explanation of the parts of a PowerPoint window.

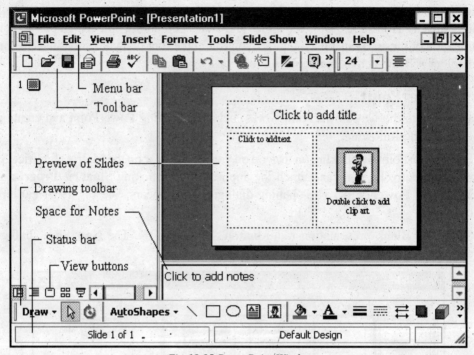

*Fig 19.05 PowerPoint Window*

### Status Bar

The status bar is located at the bottom of the window. In the default slide view, the status bar displays the slide number, total number of slides in the presentation and the name of the design template in use.

### View Buttons

These buttons let you switch between the different views in PowerPoint such as Normal view, Slide view, Outline view etc. Another button allows you to run a slide show.

The rest of the window is similar to other Microsoft Office applications. For instance, the Drawing tool bar is the same as in Microsoft Word or Excel.

## PowerPoint Views

Microsoft PowerPoint comes equipped to show you your PowerPoint presentation charts in different views to help you while you are creating a presentation. The two main views you use in PowerPoint are Normal view s Slide Sorter view. To easily switch between views, click the buttons at the lower left of the PowerPoint window. See Fig 19.06 which also shows the Outline pane and the Slide Show button.

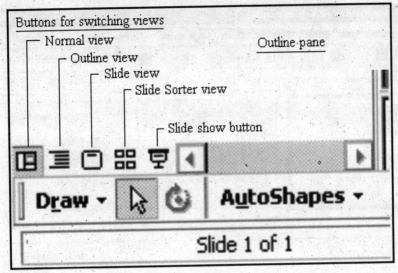

*Fig 19.06 View Buttons*

# Normal View

Normal view contains three panes: the outline pane, the slide pane, and the notes pane. These panes let you work on all aspects of your presentation in one place. You can adjust the size of the different panes by dragging the pane borders. The function of each pane is described below.

For a view of the panes in Normal View, see Fig 19.05.

**Outline Pane:** Use the outline pane to organise and develop the content of your presentation. You can type all the text of your presentation and rearrange bullet points, paragraphs, and slides.

**Slide Pane:** In the slide pane, you can see how your text and graphics will look on each slide. You can add text, graphics, movies, and sounds, create hyperlinks, and add animations to individual slides.

**Notes Pane:** The notes pane lets you add your speaker notes or information you want to share with the audience. If you want to have graphics in your notes, you must add the notes in notes page view.

These three panes are also displayed when you save your presentation as a Web page. The only difference is that the outline pane displays a table of contents so that you can navigate through your presentation.

# Slide Sorter View

In slide sorter view, you see all the slides in your presentation on screen at the same time, displayed in miniature. *See Fig 19.07.* This view makes it easy to add, delete, and move slides, add timings, and select animated transitions for moving from slide to slide. You can also preview animations on multiple slides by selecting the slides you want to preview and then clicking Animation Preview on the Slide Show menu.

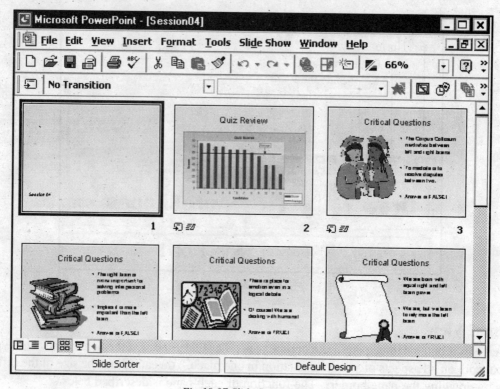

*Fig 19.07 Slide Sorter View*

You can start your slide show and preview your presentation by clicking Slide Show at any time while you are creating your presentation. Alternately, you can click on the Slide Show button shown in Fig 19.06.

## Slide View

The Slide view contains the same three panes as the normal view. However, in the default setting, the slide occupies most of the screen. You can view your slides in any order by clicking on the slide icons in your outline pane.

## Outline View

By switching to the Outline view, you can expand the pane containing the text in each of your slides. It is very convenient to use this view if your slides have substantial text and you want to edit them and ensure continuity and uniformity in what you have written as text.

As you gain experience in the use of PowerPoint, most of the time you may find yourself using the normal view for working on individual slides and the slide sorter view for arranging the sequence of your presentation.

# Creating a Presentation

We shall now get down to the nuts and bolts of creating a presentation in the following section of this chapter.

You can create a new presentation in several ways. You can start by working with the AutoContent wizard, in which the presentation you begin will contain content and design suggested by the wizard. You can also start with an existing presentation and change it to suit your needs. Another way to start a presentation is by selecting a design template that determines the presentation's design, such as the layout and the colour scheme but does not include either text or graphics.

You can also begin with an outline you import from another application such as Microsoft Word. Lastly, you can begin from scratch with a blank presentation where you choose layout, colour scheme and content. You may begin with an AutoContent wizard, where many decisions have already been taken for you. However, as you gain more experience, you may switch to a blank presentation to give maximum scope to your own creative talents.

## *Using the AutoContent Wizard*

To use the AutoContent wizard, take the following steps:

1. On the File menu, click **New**. The New Presentations dialogue box opens. Click the **General** tab.

2. Double click **AutoContent Wizard**. PowerPoint opens a sample presentation where you can add your own words and pictures.

3. Follow the **instructions** in the wizard. *See Fig 19.08.*

4. Click on the **Next** button to navigate the different options starting with Presentation type, Presentation style and Presentation options till you come to the Finish stage. To start a basic presentation quickly, you can select the **default** option in each stage.

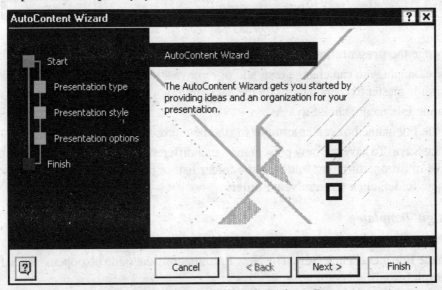

*Fig 19.08 AutoContent Wizard's Dialogue Box*

5. Change the **Sample Presentation** to suit your needs. For example, type **your text** in place of the sample text, add or delete **slides**, and add **pictures** or **other items** that you want.

6. When you finish, click **Save** on the File menu.

7. Name your presentation, and then click **Save**. To see how your slide show will look, click the **Slide Show** button at the lower left of the PowerPoint window.

### Use an Existing Presentation

To use an existing presentation, follow these steps:

1. On the Standard tool bar, click **Open**, and find and open the presentation you want in the Open dialogue box. *See Fig 19.09*.

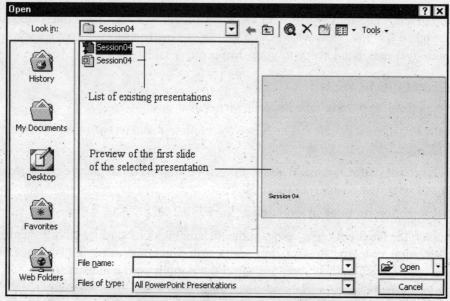

*Fig 19.09 File Open Dialogue Box*

2. Change the **presentation** to suit your needs.

3. For example, you can change text, add or remove slides, change the colour scheme, or use the slide master to change items on the background or to change the appearance of the font.

4. On the File menu, click **Save As**.

5. In the File name box, enter a **name** for the new presentation.

6. Click **Save**. To save the new presentation in a different folder, click a different **drive** in the Save in list or a different **folder** in the folder list, or both. To save the new presentation in a new folder, click **Create New Folder**.

### Use a Design Template

To use a Design Template to create a new presentation, do the following:

1. On the File menu, click **New**. The New Presentations dialogue box opens. Click the **Design Templates** tab.

2. Scroll to see all the **Design Templates**, click the one you want, and then click **OK**.

**TIP** You can see the preview of the template you select in the left pane of the New Presentation window. You can also find more templates at additional locations. See Fig 19.03 for a view of the New Presentation dialogue box which shows PowerPoint's built-in templates.

3. Scroll to see the **slide layouts**, and then select a **layout** for your title slide.

4. Type the **title** and any other **content** you want on the title slide.

5. On the Formatting tool bar, click **Common Tasks**, click **New Slide**, and then select a **layout** for the next slide.

6. Add the **content** you want.

7. Repeat steps 5 and 6 for each new slide.

8. When you finish, click **Save** on the File menu.

9. Name your presentation, and then click **Save**. To see how your slide show will look, click **Slide Show** at the lower left of the PowerPoint window.

### *Import an Outline*

To import an outline from a Word document, do the following:

1. On the File menu, click **Open**.

2. In the Files of type box, click **All outlines**.

3. In the Name box, double click the **document** you want to use.

The imported outline opens in PowerPoint. Each major heading appears as an individual slide title, and each point appears as body text.

**TIP** For best results, use a document formatted with heading styles, as in Microsoft Word. PowerPoint can use these styles to create slides more efficiently. If you have already prepared the outline of a presentation in Microsoft Word, you can easily use this outline to prepare a slide show. In Word, open the document, point to **Send To** on the File menu, and then click **Microsoft PowerPoint**. Each paragraph formatted with the Heading 1 style becomes the title of a new slide, each paragraph formatted with the Heading 2 style becomes the first level of text, and so on.

### *Create from Scratch*

As you gain experience, you will come to the stage when you may wish to control all aspects of your presentation, such as its layout and the colour scheme in addition to the text and graphics. You are now ready to start from scratch! Proceed as follows:

1. On the Standard tool bar, click **New**, opening the New presentations dialogue box. Make sure that the **General** tab is open. Now select the **Blank presentation** option and click **OK**. The New slides dialogue box opens allowing you to preview the layout styles available. See Fig 19.04 earlier in this chapter for a view of the New Slide dialogue box. You will see 24 options ranging from title slides to graphic slides that are designed to hold up to four objects. You will also see a preview of each layout in the left bottom pane. Select the **layout** you want for your title slide.

2. Type the **title** and any other **content** you want on the title slide. You can add **text** in either the slide pane or the outline pane.

3. Click the **New slide** icon on the Formatting tool bar, the New slides dialogue box opens once again to allow you to choose the layout for the next slide. Scroll to see more layouts, and then select a **layout** for the next slide.

4. Add the **content** you want.

5. Repeat steps 3 and 4 for each new slide.

6. Change the **presentation** to suit your needs.

7. When you finish, click **Save** on the File menu.

8. Name your presentation, and then click **Save**. To see how your slide show will look, click the **Slide Show** button at the lower left of the PowerPoint window.

**TIP**

No matter which method you choose for slide creation, remember to save your work-in-progress. You can switch to the slide show at any stage to observe the slides and the transition effects you have created, so that you can change them as required.

## Opening, Saving and Closing

Before you use presentations, you should get some practice in:

• Opening presentations on your hard disk for editing or modification.

• Saving your presentation after you have done with them.

• Closing PowerPoint.

## Opening

If PowerPoint has not yet been launched, do the following to start PowerPoint and open the presentation you want:

1. Click on the PowerPoint **icon** on your desktop or on the Microsoft office shortcut bar. If these icons are not available, click **Start ➔ Programmes ➔ Microsoft PowerPoint**. PowerPoint is launched and the PowerPoint opening dialogue box appears. See Fig 19.01 earlier in this chapter for a view of the Opening dialogue box.

2. Click on the **radio button** captioned "Open an existing presentation". In the display window in the bottom half of the dialogue box, you will see a list of available presentations.

3. Move the highlight to the **presentation** you want and double click to launch the **selected presentation**.

If you are already working in PowerPoint and the Open dialogue box is not on your screen, do the following:

1. Click on the **File** menu item on the PowerPoint menu bar and click on the **Open** option that appears in the drop-down menu. Another Open dialogue box appears with the available presentation files listed in the left pane and a preview of the selected presentation file in the right pane. See a view of the File Open dialogue box in Fig 19.09.

2. Click the **Open** button to launch the selected presentation.

# Saving and Closing

As you work on your presentation, your progress is retained in the computer's memory. To make sure that you do not lose the work done in case of a power failure, save your presentation from time to time. At the end of a work session, save your work before shutting down the computer.

Unless you specify the folder where you wish to save your work, it will be saved in the default folder, which is My Documents on your hard drive. To use this default folder, do the following:

1. Click **File** on the PowerPoint menu bar and click **Save As** in the drop-down menu that appears. The Save As dialogue box appears. *See Fig 19.10.*

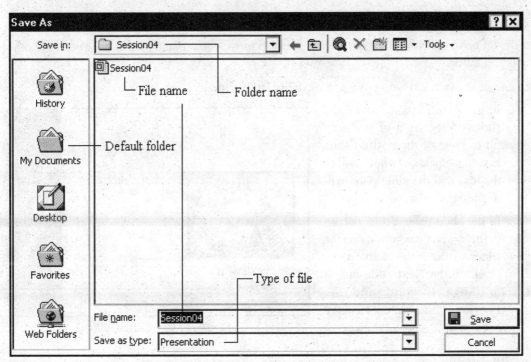

*Fig 19.10 Save As Dialogue Box*

2. Type the **name** you wish to give your presentation in the File name text box and then click on the **Save** button. The presentation is saved in the default folder with the name you have given it.

**TIP** After you have saved your work for the first time, you can save subsequent modifications simply by clicking on the Save icon on the PowerPoint tool bar. Or, you can click on the File menu item on the PowerPoint menu bar and click on the Save option that appears in the drop-down menu. In either case, the Save As dialogue box will not appear.

If you want to retain the previous version of the presentation after you have made some modifications, then follow the steps for Save As like we have seen earlier. Use a different file name to save the modification. For instance, if the existing file name for your presentation is MyPresentation, save the modified version as MyPresentation02.

After you have saved your presentation, you can close PowerPoint by selecting File from the PowerPoint menu bar and clicking on Exit in the drop-down menu that appears.

# Editing Presentations

After you have selected a layout and colour scheme for your presentation, you will work on individual slides, their text and graphics, the various transition effects you need and the sequence of the slides. Collectively, all these steps are like editing a movie. We look at the key steps in editing in this section.

## Moving Between Slides

You should be in the Normal or the Outline view to move conveniently from one slide to another in your presentation.

Take one of the two following steps to navigate from slide to slide:

- In the outline pane, move the slider on the right of the pane till the text of the desired slide appears. Click anywhere within the text and the slide pane will display the selected slide.

- In the slide pane, go to the >> or the << vertical buttons on the slider to the right of the pane. Click on the **Next** slide button to move forward and the **Previous slide** button to move back in your presentation.

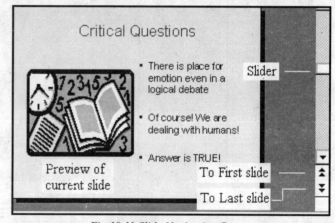

*Fig 19.11 Slide Navigation Buttons*

## Adding Slides

Whether you start with a blank presentation or begin with a design template, initially your presentation will contain only one slide. To add more slides, proceed as follows:

1. Make sure that you are either in the Normal or the Outline view. Click on one of these **view buttons** to open one if required.

2. Move the slider on the right of the outline pane till you see the slide, say slide #4 after which you wish to insert the new slide. Position the cursor at the end of the last line of the text for slide #4 and click on the **New Slide icon** on the PowerPoint tool bar. A new slide dialogue box opens to let you choose **AutoLayout** of the new slide, with the current layout already selected as the default.

3. Accept the **default** or select the layout you want and click **OK**. A new slide (slide #5 in this case) is added to your presentation with the current colour scheme and current layout.

# Deleting Slides

You may wish to modify an existing presentation for a different purpose by deleting some of the slides and adding new ones. To delete slides from your presentation, proceed as follows:

1.  Change to the **Slide sorter** view. You will see all the slides in your presentation laid out as thumbnails. You may have to use the slider bar on the right of the window to move to the slides you wish to delete. See Fig 19.07 earlier in this chapter for the Slide sorter view.

2.  Click the **slide** you want to delete. The selected slide will be highlighted with a border.

3.  Do one of the following:

    *   Press the **Delete** key on your keyboard.

    *   Click on the **Edit** item on the PowerPoint menu bar and click on the **Delete Slide** option that appears on the drop-down menu.

The selected slide is deleted from your presentation and the sequential numbering of your slides is automatically adjusted after each slide addition or deletion.

# Changing Slide Layouts

As we have seen, once you have chosen a style and layout for your presentation, they remain constant, appearing as the default for any slide you may add later. While this ensures uniformity in your presentation, you may wish to deliberately change the layout of any slide. To do so, proceed as follows:

1.  **Click** the Slide View button to change to slide view if required. On the left edge of the window, you will see icons with running slide numbers representing the slides you have. The preview of the slide will appear in the right pane.

2.  **Navigate** to the slide you want to change by **clicking** on the slide icon with the desired slide number.

3.  Click on the down arrow ▼ next to the Common Tasks button on the formatting tool bar. A drop-down menu will appear.

*Fig 19.12 Common Tasks Drop-down Menu*

4.  **Click** on the Slide Layout option to display the Slide Layout dialogue box containing the 24 layout options available to you.

5.  **Select** the layout option you want to change the existing layout of the selected slide.

While experimenting with different layouts, if you wish to undo a change, press **Ctrl + Z** on your keyboard or click on **Edit ➔ Undo**.

# Adding Text

After you have decided on the style and the layout of a slide, the next step is to add the text you want the slide to display. If the wizard or template generates some sample text, you will want to replace this with your own text.

To make sure that you prepare a striking presentation, it is a very good idea to carefully decide the text that you wish to display. Generally, the title slide will have a one-line or two-line title and sub-title. Subsequent slides will have a title, some bulleted text and there may be some graphics as well.

The bulk of your slides will be text slides with titles and bulleted text. You may add clip art, charts and graphs to the text slide itself or on separate slides to emphasise the text. A typical arrangement may be:

1. Title slide
2. Text slide
3. Text slide
4. Chart
5. Text slide
......and so on.

We will now examine different ways to work with text in your slides.

## In the Outline Pane

As we have discussed, a majority of slides in a presentation will probably be text slides containing a title and bulleted text. To alter or edit the existing text in such slides, it is convenient to use the Outline view and work in the Outline pane. So change to Outline View if you are not already in that view by clicking the Outline View button. Then click in the Outline pane. You will be amongst the existing text of the slide, making it convenient to add, edit or delete text. Do one of the following:

- To replace existing text, first select the **text** and then **type over** the selection to replace it.
- To move a slide up or down in the sequence, click on the **slide icon** and **drag** the icon up or down.
- To create a new slide, move to the end of the last line of the text in your last slide and press **Enter** ↵. A new slide will be created, based on the layout and style currently in use.
- If you wish to insert a new slide in the midst of a series of existing slides, click at the end of the text of the preceding slide and press **Enter** ↵. A bulleted blank line is created. Press **Shift + Tab** to change the line to a new slide.
- To select text, drag the mouse pointer over the **text**. To select an entire bulleted text, click on the **bullet**. To select all the text on a slide, click on the **slide icon** to the left of the title of the slide.

## In the Slide View

If you are beginning with a blank slide, you may prefer to select the Slide View for adding text to your slides.

If there is a title in the layout you have selected, the cursor will be positioned in the middle of the dotted box marking the space for the title. Here are the things you can do:

- After you finish entering the title, click the mouse button where the message "Click to add text" appears. The cursor is now positioned for entering text for the first bullet.

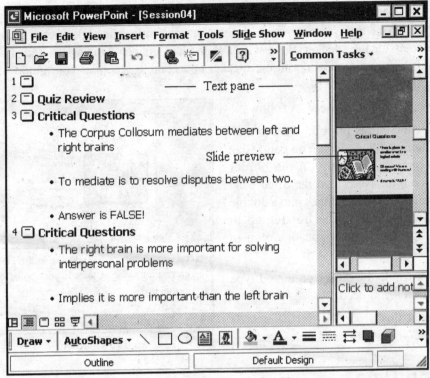

*Fig 19.13 Text Pane in Outline View*

- Hit **Enter** ↵ to start the second bullet and so on.

To edit existing text in Slide View, proceed as follows:

o Click the mouse button in the **text area**. A text box appears surrounding the text already present on the slide.

o Move the cursor to the text you want to edit by clicking on the text or by using the arrow keys on your keyboard.

o Select the text by dragging the mouse pointer over it.

o Delete selected text by pressing the delete key.

o Insert text by clicking mouse pointer at the point of insertion and then typing the text you want to add.

o Insert a new bulleted point by moving to the end of the previous bulleted text and pressing Enter.

o Insert a sub-bullet by moving to the beginning of the bulleted line you have just created and pressing Tab.

    o   Toggle the bullets on and off by clicking on the Bullets button on the PowerPoint tool bar. You will notice that the icon is the same as for Microsoft Word and other MS Office applications.

    o   Click outside the text box to deselect the slide you have been working on.

## Speaker Notes

There is a Notes pane that you can access in the Normal, Outline or Slide View. This pane allows you to type notes for the speaker along with a thumbnail image of the associated slide. After the presentation is finalised, you can print the speaker notes and use them as your guide while making the presentation. *See Fig 19.14.*

To create speaker notes, proceed as follows:

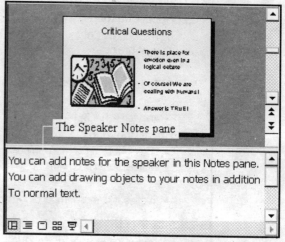

1. Click the **Notes pane** in the Normal, Outline or Slide view. You can resize the pane by clicking on the border between the Notes and the Slide pane so that the cursor changes into a double arrow. Now drag the **border** up to enlarge the Notes pane or down to reduce it.

2. Click inside the **Notes pane** and type the **notes** you need.

3. Repeat this procedure for each slide where you want to add notes.

*Fig 19.14 Speaker Notes Pane*

# Including Data

In your presentation, you will want to liven your text messages with clipart so that the pages look attractive. In addition, you may reinforce the text messages by adding charts and graphs. For instance, while speaking on sales performance, you may include a table showing the sales figures and a graph showing sales against time or by regions. In this section, we will learn how to make your presentation special by including data in different forms.

## Inserting Clip Art

The best way to include clip art on the same page as text is to select an appropriate layout when beginning work on a presentation. The New slide dialogue box gives you two options to choose from, clip art on the left (Clip Art and Text) or clip art on the right (Text and Clip Art). Double click on the clip art pane to open the clip art library for inserting clip art. See Fig 19.04 earlier in this chapter for a view of the New Slide dialogue box.

**NOTE**

Should you get a message that the clip art library is not already installed, then insert the MS Office 2000 CD-ROM and run Setup again. Select "Add or Remove Features" and change the setting to "Run from My Computer" or "Run from CD/Network". After the setup has been completed, you will be able to access the clip art gallery as described above. We will discuss clip art in much greater detail in the next chapter, Chapter 20, *Customising Your Presentation.*

## Adding Tables

You can easily insert a table of data in your slide by first selecting a Table AutoLayout template in the new slides dialogue box. Now proceed as follows:

1.  Select **File ➔ New** from the PowerPoint menu options to open the New Presentation dialogue box and choose new presentations. If you have already started a presentation and wish to add a table slide, then with a new slide open, click on the **Format** menu item on the menu bar to open the **Slide Layout** dialogue box.

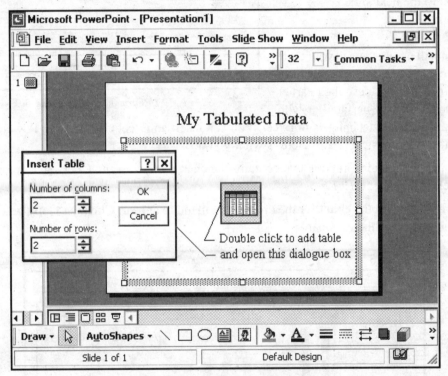

*Fig 19.15 Insert Table Dialogue Box*

2.  In the New Slide dialogue box choose the **Table** option and click **Apply**. The slide will change to display a Title text box and a table icon asking you to double click to add table. See Fig 19.15 for a view of a Table slide.

3.  Double click on the **icon** to display an **Insert Table** dialogue box in which you can choose the number of rows and columns you want. Click **OK** after making your selection. A table containing the specified rows and columns appear. The cursor changes to a pencil icon indicating that data may be entered.

4.  Format the chart by right clicking on the **chart element** you may want to format. A drop-down menu appears allowing you to select a formatting option. For instance, you can click

on the Borders and Fills option to display the Format Table dialogue box. Here, you can choose cell and table borders, fill colour for cells and text alignment within the cells. *See Fig 19.16.*

5. Click anywhere **outside** the chart to complete the work on the chart so that you can move on to the next slide.

## Adding Charts

Often, you will use the data in your table to create charts or graphs. If you have used Microsoft Excel, described earlier in this book, you will be familiar with

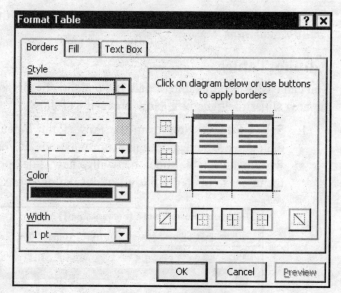

*Fig 19.16 Format Table Dialogue Box*

charting and graphing techniques in Excel. You can insert an Excel chart in your PowerPoint slide by using the Windows clipboard. Here is what you do:

1. Open the Excel workbook that contains the chart that you want. Click once on the **chart** to select it. *See Fig 19.17.*

2. Right click on the **chart** for the drop-down menu to appear. Click the **Copy** button to copy the chart into the clipboard.

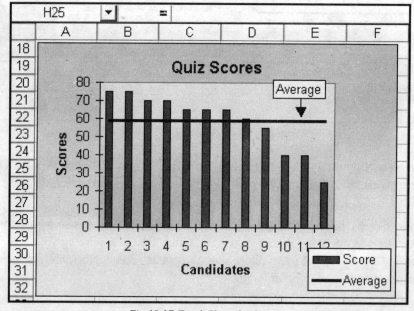

*Fig 19.17 Excel Chart for Import*

3. Switch to PowerPoint and move to the chart slide in your presentation that will receive the Excel Chart and click the **chart object** to select it. Right click in the selected **chart** to display the drop-down menu and click on the **Paste** option to paste the chart you have copied from Excel into the PowerPoint slide. You may move or resize the chart to fit your slide correctly. See Fig 19.18 for a view of the chart embedded in the PowerPoint slide.

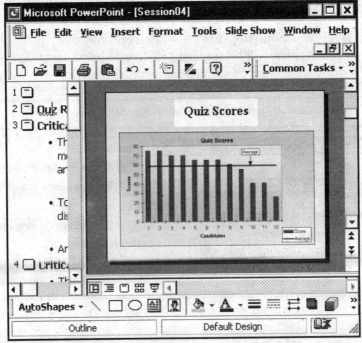

*Fig 19.18 Excel Chart Embedded in PowerPoint*

If you expect the data in your Excel chart to change, you may link the embedded chart in PowerPoint to the table and chart in Excel. If you do so, any change you make to the data in Excel at a future date, that changes the chart, will also be reflected in the chart you have pasted in PowerPoint.

## Importing Documents

If you have an agenda or a similar document consisting of points in a Microsoft Word document, you can easily import the document into PowerPoint to provide the basis for preparing a presentation.

Each item in your document will be converted into a title for a new slide. For instance, consider the following agenda items taken from a sales conference document:

- This Year's Sales Performance
- Sales by Quarters
- Sales by Regions
- Strong Product Lines
- Opportunities
- Threats
- Conclusion

You can easily see how each line will make a good title for a slide. You can then add bulleted text, clip art, charts and graphs to make your presentation really impressive.

To import a Word document to create a PowerPoint presentation, proceed as follows:

1. Open the **Word document**.

2. Format the sentences to be used for titles as **Heading 1 style** and the sentences to be converted into bulleted text as **Heading 2 style**.

3. In Word, click **File -> Send to -> Microsoft PowerPoint**. *See Fig 19.19*. A new Microsoft PowerPoint presentation will be automatically created with text titles and slides. You can now add formatting, clip art etc to improve your presentation.

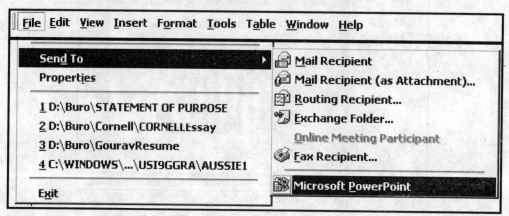

*Fig 19.19 MS Word Option for Making PowerPoint Slide*

# Printing a Presentation

PowerPoint presentations are prepared on a computer's monitor screen. For a small audience, you may use the same monitor to make your presentation as well. However, for larger audiences, other methods have to be used. For instance, you may use a multimedia projector that can be connected to a computer to display your presentation on a large screen. If you have an overhead projector, then your presentation can be printed and converted into overhead transparencies (by photocopying the prints on acetate sheets) and then displayed with the overhead projector. This is a common method used for larger audiences. At the same time, you can print handouts for the participants and speaker notes to guide the speaker during the presentation.

## Presentations

To print your presentation, proceed as follows:

1. After you are satisfied with the presentation, with PowerPoint open, click on **File ➜ Page Setup** in the drop-down menu that appears. The Page setup dialogue box opens. Select the **slide size and the orientation** of the slides and the **notes** for printing. Click **OK** when done.

2.  Click **File** ➜ **Print** and the Print dialogue box will open. *See Fig 19.20*. You will notice that the Print dialogue box is almost the same as for Microsoft Word except for "Handouts". Select the slides to be printed, whether to print in colour or grey scale, number of copies etc. Click **OK** to commence printing.

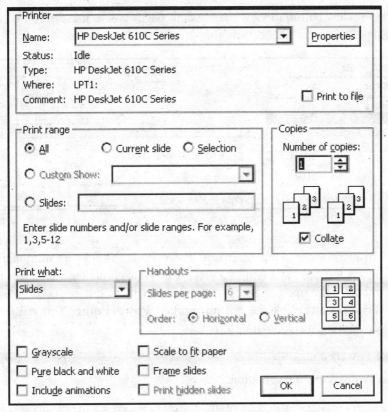

*Fig 19.20 Print Dialogue Box*

## Handouts and Notes

You may wish to distribute handouts of the slides you intend to display to your audience. To save paper, you can print more than one slide on a single sheet of paper. Since the bulleted text on your slides use large font, even 4 or 6 slides per page will be readable.

In case of speaker notes, the slides are printed as one per page, but reduced in size. The space at the bottom of the page is used to print the speaker notes that you may have included while creating each slide. In this manner, the speaker will have a full slide-by-slide briefing in hand while making the presentation.

To print handouts or notes, proceed as follows:

1.  Choose **File** ➜ **Print** and the Print dialogue box appears. *See Fig 19.21*.

2.  In the Print What drop-down list choose **Handouts** or **Notes**. Next, if you choose handouts you can choose **Slides per page** (under Handouts), which varies from 1 to 9. Next to this option is a choice for the printing order. Choose **horizontal** or **vertical**. If you choose Notes, these options will be unavailable.

3. Under the Print What window is the Colour/Grey Scale drop-down list allowing you to choose either **Colour**, **Grey Scale** or **Pure Black and White** for printing.

4. Three check boxes allow you to select whether to Scale to fit paper, Frame slides and Include comment pages. Check the **options** you need.

5. Click the Preview button to view the handout pages and to make sure that everything is in order. Click **OK** to commence printing.

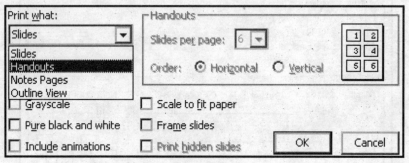

*Fig 19.21 Handout Printing Setup*

**CD-ROM** To learn more about Microsoft PowerPoint 2000 in a multimedia environment, insert the accompanying CD-ROM in your computer and select the **Interactive** mode in the opening screen. The main menu will appear. To go to the section on PowerPoint, click the button marked **PowerPoint**. You will see a sub-menu containing the following topics:

- Basics of PowerPoint

- Creating Professional Presentations

Click on the first topic, "Basics of PowerPoint" to display another level of sub-sub-menu. From the items in this sub-sub-menu, you can select the particular topic you want to see. Click on your selected topic and follow instructions on your screen.

# 20. Customising Your Presentation

## In this chapter:

☞ You learn how to customise your presentation and to emphasise selected slides in your show to maximise its effect on the audience.

☞ You are shown how to work with slide objects such as text, drawing objects and clip art.

☞ You learn to manipulate drawing objects on your slides to get the most effective arrangement you want.

☞ You are shown how to edit text and the frame of the text, called a text object.

☞ You learn how to prepare and then show your presentation for maximum impact, enhancing your slide show with animation and transition effects.

☞ You are shown how to embed music, sound and video clips in order to turn your slide show into an outstanding multimedia presentation.

☞ You learn to pack and transport your slide show to other venues and to run your slide show on other computers using the PowerPoint viewer. You also learn how to use a multimedia projector coupled with your laptop computer.

# Customising Your Presentation

In the previous chapter, *PowerPoint 2000 Basics*, you have learned how to put a basic presentation together. As you continue to use PowerPoint and become familiar with its capabilities, you will want to improve your presentations, by adding features and effects to make them more striking.

The key to persuade an audience is often the quality of the visual aids that reinforce the spoken word. To become a more effective presenter, therefore, you will like to build upon the basic skills you have already learned in the last chapter and move much beyond basics. In this chapter, we will show you how to produce professional quality electronic slide shows.

After some experience in preparing presentations, you will probably decide on your own unique style that you want to use in future presentations. To customise your presentation, you have to change your design template on which your presentation is based. A customised slide template will make sure that the slides you create will have similar looks. For example, you may select a certain colour background and display your company logo in all your slides.

## Changing the Template

Ordinarily, you will use a favourite design template for your presentations. However, to create an impact, or to suit a particular audience, you may want to make a particular presentation more flamboyant or more conservative than usual.

This is what you do to introduce a new style in a particular presentation:

1. Open the **presentation** you want to change in PowerPoint. Click **Format** ➜ **Apply Design Template** in the drop-down menu. Or, you can click on **Common Tasks** and then click on the **Apply Design Template** option. The Apply design dialogue box appears. *See Fig 20.01.*

2. Select a **design** to preview it in the right pane of the dialogue box.

3. Double click on the **design of your choice** to change the presentation design to the new format.

**TRAP**

Note that the design of all the slides in your presentation will change to this new format. You may have second thoughts after selecting a new design. It may look well in your title slide, but not appropriate for subsequent text or graphics slides. If so, click on the Undo button on the menu bar to go back to the earlier design.

## A Standard Slide

You may find that you are using a standard title slide to begin all your presentations. For instance, there may be company information, standard disclaimers and author information that remain constant while only the title of the presentation changes. If so, you can make and save a standard title slide to be used over and over again. For each new presentation, you need to insert a different title only.

To create and save such a standard (or "boilerplate") slide, proceed as follows:

1. Open a **presentation** in PowerPoint based on your favourite template design.

2. Insert a **blank slide** by scrolling to the last slide and pressing **Enter ↵**. The blank slide will inherit the colour scheme and layout of your favourite template.

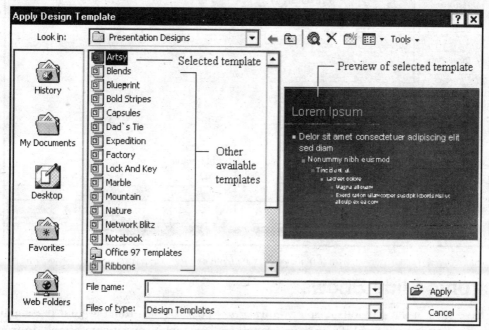

*Fig 20.01 Apply Design Template Dialogue Box*

3. Insert the **common text** that you want to use in all your title slides. In addition, you can enter a **guiding text** for the title such as "Enter the Presentation Title Here" so that you can locate where to enter different titles.

4. Delete **all other slides** from the presentation since you wish to save only the common slide.

5. On the PowerPoint menu bar, click on **File**, then click on **Save As** in the drop-down menu. The Save As dialogue box appears. *See Fig 20.02.*

6. In the Save As Type list box at the bottom of the window, scroll down and choose **Design Template**. The default folder for saving PowerPoint presentations will change to the Templates folder.

7. Enter a **name** for the template and click **Save**. Now you can begin a new presentation using this template. You will get a semi-finished title page along with your favourite layout and colour scheme.

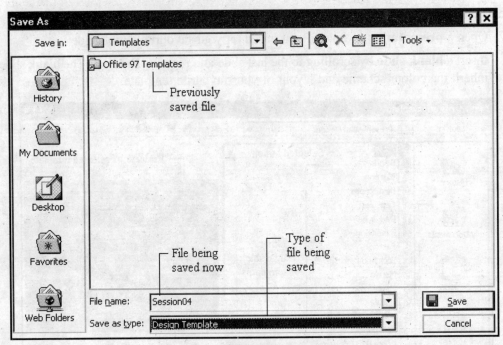

*Fig 20.02 Save As Dialogue Box*

# Electronic Slide Shows

As we have seen in the previous chapter, *PowerPoint 2000 Basics*, running your presentation on the computer is adequate only if you have a small audience who can sit comfortably in front of a single monitor's screen. For larger audiences, you will need an overhead projector or a multimedia projector. You can get transparencies made from your computer-based slides. However, overhead projectors cannot reproduce the transition effects, the animation or the embedded multimedia clips that can transform your presentation into a major experience. To get the full benefit of these effects, you have to attach a powerful computer with a multimedia projector and a speaker system. Computer and multimedia technology has now brought the required equipment within the reach of many. Today, your audience expects a multimedia, electronic slide show rather than a simple presentation with static slides. In the remaining part of this chapter, you will learn how to produce them.

## Working with Slide Objects

In addition to the text that you have worked with so far, you will want to include more slide objects such as clip art, specially formatted text, shapes and lines to enhance the impact of your slides. We look at each of these objects in turn.

### *Clip Art*

The Microsoft Office 2000 suit comes complete with a clip art gallery. PowerPoint can access this gallery just like other Microsoft Office programmes such as Word or Excel. The clip art gallery allows you to organise clip art on your hard disk in suitable groups so that you can easily find the clip you need. You can, of course, insert clip art from other sources as well, but the gallery makes it more convenient.

If clip gallery is installed in your computer, you will see an icon on the PowerPoint standard tool bar along the bottom of your screen. If not, the clip gallery feature must be installed first. Follow the usual procedure of installing Microsoft Office components from your CD-ROM. See Chapter 3, *The Windows Operating System*, for more information.

Follow these steps to insert a clip from the gallery (after its installation, if required):

1. Switch to **Slide view** if necessary and navigate to the **slide** where you want to insert clips.

2. Click **Insert ➜ Picture ➜ Clip art**. The Insert Clip art dialogue box will appear. See Fig 19.02 in the previous chapter for a view of this dialogue box.

3. Select the appropriate **category** (such as Business, Animals, Academic etc) in which you expect the clip art to be. Scroll through the images you see till you find the one you want for your presentation. Click the **Insert Clip** button on the shortcut menu and the image is inserted on your slide.

4. Move and resize the **image** on your slide as described under "Manipulating Objects" later in this chapter.

## Drawing Objects

The Drawing tool bar in PowerPoint allows you to add several basic shapes and lines to your slides. You can use the drawing tools to modify clip art that you have inserted in your slides. The drawing tool bar is the same as the one that appears in Word and Excel. In earlier chapters of this book, you can read more about the drawing tool bar.

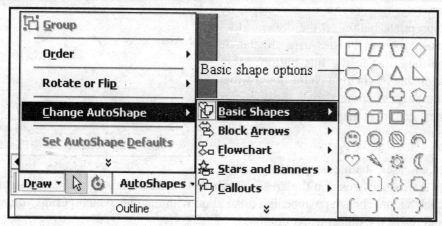

*Fig 20.03 Drawing Tool Bar with Basic Shapes Selected*

The drawing tool bar will be visible along the bottom of your PowerPoint screen. If it is not, click **View ➜ Tool bars ➜ Drawing** from the menu bar and the drop-down menus to make the drawing tool bar visible.

## Inserting Basic Shapes

The Drawing tool bar will permit you to add many shapes to your slide. We begin by inserting a line in a blank slide as follows:

1. Open a new **presentation** in PowerPoint and switch to **slide view** on a blank slide. Make sure that the **drawing tool bar** is visible. If not, follow the instructions in the previous paragraph to make it visible. *See Fig 20.03*.

2. Click on the **line** button on the drawing tool bar. The mouse pointer will change into a crosshair.

3. Move the crosshair to the **insertion point** on the slide where you wish to start the line.

4. Drag the pointer to the **terminal point** where you want the line to end and release the mouse button. The pointer changes back to its default shape and the line appears on the slide. The selection handles remain on each end of the line until you click the mouse pointer in the slide again.

While the handles are visible, you can change the line width and style by clicking on the Line style button on the design tool bar and selecting a width or style.

**TIP** If you double click on the line button, it will remain selected until you click on the button again. This will let you draw a series of lines on the slide without having to click on the line button every time.

If you keep the shift key pressed down while you drag the mouse pointer, you will create straight horizontal, vertical or inclined lines without any squiggles in them.

You can draw rectangles or other basic shapes by using the appropriate button on the drawing tool bar. For instance, you will find the Arrow, Rectangle and Oval buttons next to the line button. More shapes are available by clicking on the down arrow ▼ on the AutoShapes button, also on the drawings tool bar. Some common shapes are shown in Fig 20.04.

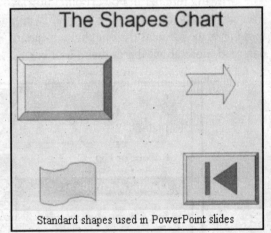

The Shapes Chart

Standard shapes used in PowerPoint slides

*Fig 20.04 Slide with Shapes*

**NOTE** In all cases, the mouse pointer changes to a crosshair. Position the crosshair where you want the selected shape to appear and click again. The shape appears on the slide with handles which permit you to position and resize the object as required.

## Editing Drawing Objects

As we have seen in case of the line, you can edit a drawing object, changing their outline or fill attributes. You can add text within a drawing object. The text will move and will get resized along with the drawing object. Before you can edit a drawing object, you must select it by clicking on it. When selected, you will see selection handles around the object.

If you have created a complex object consisting of several basic objects, you will probably group them together so that they can be moved and resized at the same time. If so, you will first have to ungroup the objects, perhaps more than once, till you get down to the basic shapes before you can edit the attributes of the objects. For instance, if you have created a circle inside a triangle and have grouped them, then you will not be able to change the outline thickness of the triangle unless you first ungroup the two so that you can select only the triangle for editing. We will discuss "Grouping Objects" later in this chapter.

## Editing Line Attributes

A drawing object has a border separating it from the background. This border is a line. The line can be invisible, or visible, of varying thickness and colour. When we edit the line attribute of a drawing object, we make changes to its thickness, colour or visibility. Here is how you can proceed:

1. Select the **object** to be edited. Selection handles appear around the object.

2. Click the **Line colour** button. A pop-up menu showing line colours will appear.

3. You can choose No Line, Automatic or a Basic Line Colour. You can also choose Patterned Lines or More Line Colours to select from a choice of patterns or from a colour palette.

4. Click on the **Line Style** button on the tool bar to select the line style (for example, a single or a double line) or line thickness. Select the desired style or thickness from the pop-up menu. Click on the **More Lines**... option at the bottom of the pop-up menu to open the Format AutoShapes dialogue box for even more options.

   • Next to the **Line Style** button is the Dashed Style button that gives you access to a variety of dashed line styles.

   • The next button is the **Arrow Style** button which lets you select different arrow heads.

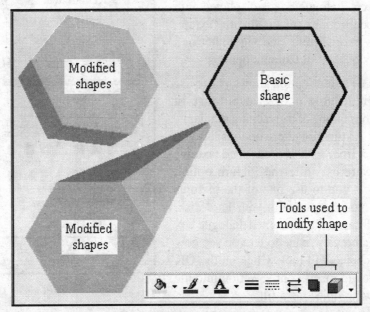

*Fig 20.05 3-D Effect Examples*

- You can add a shadow to the selected drawing object by clicking the **Shadow** button and selecting the shadow orientation you want from the pop-up menu.

- You can add a three-dimensional effect to the drawing object by clicking the **3-D** button and selecting the **effect** you want from the pop-up menu. *See Fig 20.05.*

## Editing Fill Attributes

As we have seen in the previous section, drawing objects have an outline and you can change the default outline using its line attributes. Similarly, the inside of an object may be filled with colours, patterns or nothing at all. We can edit the fill attributes of drawing objects much the same way as we edit their line attributes.

Let us work on a simple drawing object such as a square and modify its fill attributes. Proceed as follows:

1. Open a **blank slide** in a new presentation in PowerPoint.

2. Click on the **rectangle** button on the Drawing tool bar and draw a **square** on the slide.

3. Make sure that the selection handles are visible around the square. If not, click on the **square** to select it.

- To change the fill colour, click on the **Fill Colour** button on the drawing tool bar to display the pop-up menu. *See Fig 20.06.* You can now select No Fill, Automatic, choose from a set of basic colours or click on the **More Colours**... to display a colour palette for a very large number of options.

- To use a pattern as a fill, select the **Fill Effects**... option in the colour pop-up menu that is displayed in step 4. A Fill Effects dialogue box is displayed with tabbed options for Gradient, Texture, Pattern or Picture. See Fig 20.06 for a view of the Fill Colours options.

- The **Gradient** option allows you to use a single colour or two colours in various fading or brightening gradients. The Texture or Pattern options lets you select from a set of predefined textures or patterns while the Picture option allows you to use one of the pictures that you may have in your hard disk. In all cases, the concerned dialogue box has a preview pane to let you see how the choice will look. Click on the **OK** button to insert your selection into the drawing object as a fill.

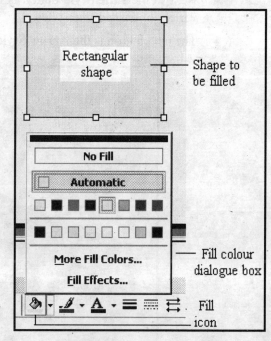

*Fig 20.06 Fill Colours Dialogue Box*

- The **Variants** option at the bottom right pane provides you with some more options of showing the direction of the gradient selected under the Gradient tab. *See Fig 20.07.*

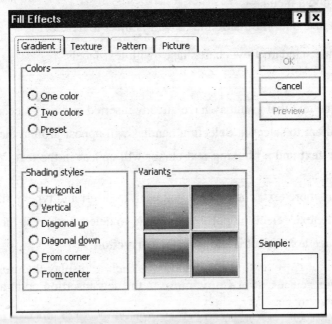

*Fig 20.07 Fill Effects Dialogue Box*

# Adding Text

Instead of adding a fill, you can insert text inside a drawing object. You can use this feature very effectively in preparing a flow chart which contains a number of shapes, each with a label describing its function.

Here is how you may add text inside a drawing object:

1. Follow **steps 1 and 2** in the previous example to create a square on a blank slide in a new presentation. Make sure that the square is selected and the selection handles are visible.

2. Right click on any of the **sides** of the square and a pop-up menu will appear with options that include **Add Text**. Click on this option and the cursor will be centred inside the square.

3. Type the **text** you want to add. The matter will get centred in relation to the square's boundaries. Take care to make sure you do not exceed the boundaries of the square while typing.

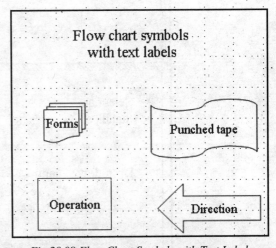

*Fig 20.08 Flow Chart Symbols with Text Labels*

4. To change the default text alignment which is centred, select the **text** and click the **Format** menu option and select from Centred, Left Aligned, Right Aligned or Justified that appears in the drop-down menu.

5. Click the mouse button **outside** the drawing object to deselect it.

Fig 20.08 shows some standard flow chart shapes with text labels.

## Editing Text

If you wish to edit the text that you may have already inserted earlier, proceed as follows:

1. Click the **object** to select it. Selection handles will appear around the object.

2. Click on the **text** and a blinking text cursor will appear in the text. You can now edit the text as follows:

   • To **insert** more text, click where you want to insert and type in the **new text**.

   • To **delete** text, select the portion you want to delete and press the **delete** key.

   • To **replace** text, select it and type the **correction**.

   • To **move** or **copy** text, select it and right click to display the drop-down menu. From this menu, select **Cut** or **Copy**, move to the new insertion point and click paste in the drop-down menu.

3. Click the mouse button **outside** the drawing object to deselect it after you finish.

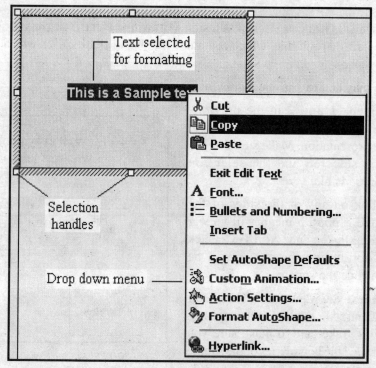

*Fig 20.09 Drawing Object with Text Selected and the Drop-down Menu*

# Changing Font Attributes

After selecting text in a slide, you can change its font attributes such as its size, style, colour and add some additional effects. This is useful in a slide containing bulleted text, where you wish to have a specific line or some words stand out.

To change the font attributes of selected text, proceed as follows:

1.  Click the Format option on the PowerPoint menu bar and click on the **Font** option. The Font dialogue box opens. *See Fig 20.10.* In this box, you can select:

    *   The **Font** such as Times New Roman.
    *   The **Font Style** such as Bold underlined or Italic.
    *   The **Font Size** in points, such as 11, 14, 24, 36 etc.
    *   **Effects** such as underline, shadow, emboss etc.
    *   **Colour** such as basic colours or from a standard or custom colour palette.

2.  Select the appropriate **options** and then click on the **OK** button to apply the new font attributes. If you want the new attributes to apply to all subsequent text, check the **"Default for new objects"** check box.

3.  Deselect the slide by clicking **outside** it after you finish.

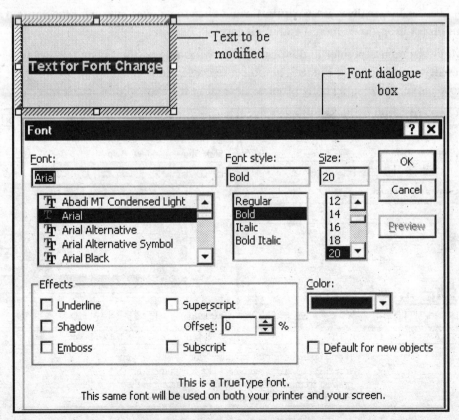

*Fig 20.10 Text with Font Dialogue Box*

## Moving and Copying Objects

In addition to inserting clip art, we can insert graphics from one slide to another or from one presentation to another. We can also copy and paste objects from other programmes, such as drawings from Microsoft Paint or charts from Microsoft Excel. To cut and paste like this, we use the Windows Clipboard. Here is how to use the Clipboard:

1.  Select the **object** to be moved or copied in a slide while in Slide View. Selection handles appear around the object. Fig 20.09 shows selection handles.

2.  You can either click **Edit ➜ Cut** or **Edit ➜ Copy** starting with the PowerPoint menu bar, or right click on the **selected object** to cause a drop-down menu to appear and click **Cut** or **Copy** in this menu. In both cases, the selected object will be copied in the Clipboard.

3.  Click **Edit ➜ Paste** after moving the cursor to a new location on the active slide, or open a new slide and click **Edit ➜ Paste**. A copy will be created in the new location or new slide.

If you have two windows open at the same time on your desktop, let us say one of PowerPoint and one of Word, you can select and copy an item from the PowerPoint slide to a Word document or vice versa.

Now do the following:

1.  Select the item in the **source window**, right click the mouse button for the **context sensitive menu** (or drop-down menu) and click **copy**.

2.  Move the mouse pointer to the **destination window** and right click to display the **context sensitive menu**. Click **Paste**. The object is copied into the destination window. You may now move, resize and change font as desired in the PowerPoint window.

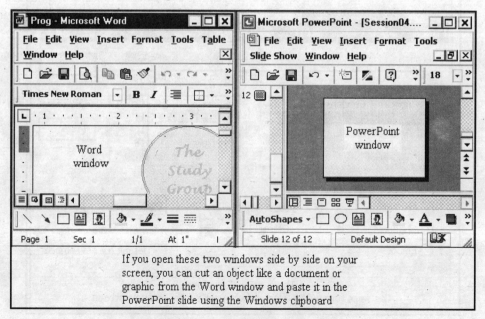

If you open these two windows side by side on your screen, you can cut an object like a document or graphic from the Word window and paste it in the PowerPoint slide using the Windows clipboard

*Fig 20.11 Word and PowerPoint Windows*

**NOTE**

If you select Cut instead of Copy in the source window, the object will be removed from there. This is useful if you do not wish to save a copy in the source programme after the item has been moved to a PowerPoint slide.

# Manipulating Objects

After you have inserted objects in your PowerPoint slide, you may want to move or resize the objects you have inserted. Before any of these actions can take place, you must select the object or objects. If there is more than one object and you want them to retain their relative positions while you move them, you may have to group the objects so that they behave as a single object. We look at these actions one by one.

## Selecting Multiple Objects

We have already seen that in the Slide view, you can select an object by clicking on it. Selection handles will appear around an object when it is selected. To select more than one object at the same time, either:

- Click them **in sequence** while holding down the **Shift** key.
- Alternatively, click the mouse pointer just **outside** one of the objects and drag the pointer to create a **dotted rectangle**. Extend the rectangle to **include** the objects you wish to select. When you release the mouse button, selection handles will appear around all the objects enclosed by the dotted rectangle.

## Grouping Objects

When you move a group of objects together, you can make sure that they do not lose their positions relative to one another. To do so, you must first group the objects. To group a set of objects on a PowerPoint Slide, proceed as follows:

1. Select **all the objects** in the group as described in the previous section.

2. Right click on any of the **selected objects**. A context sensitive menu will appear, which includes an option to **Group** the objects. Click on this **option** to create a group. *See Fig 20.12.*

Now to move all the objects in the group together, do the following:

1. Click on **any of the objects** in the group. Selection handles will appear around the entire group of objects.

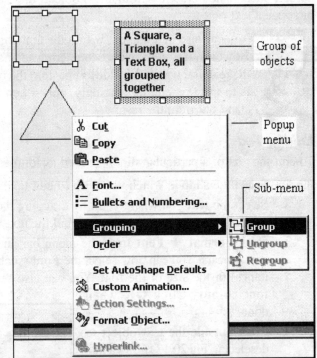

*Fig 20.12 Square, Triangle and Text Box Grouped*

2. Click on **any of the objects** and the cursor will change into a **four-headed arrow**.

3. Drag the **entire group** to a new location and release the mouse button.

### Resizing Objects

**NOTE** To resize an object, you have to select it in the usual manner so that the selection handles are visible around the selected object.

If the object to be resized is part of a group, you must first ungroup the object before you can resize it. However, you can resize the entire group at the same time without ungrouping the individual objects.

To resize a selected object, proceed as follows:

1. Select the **Object** or the **group** you wish to resize. The selection handles will appear.

2. Place the mouse pointer on **one of the handles** and resize as follows:
   - Drag a **side handle** to resize in one direction only, either horizontally or vertically.
   - Drag a **corner handle** to resize both horizontally and vertically at the same time.

3. Press and hold the **Shift key** while dragging a corner handle to resize while maintaining the proportions (aspect ratio) of the object.

## Editing Text and Text Objects

When text is added in a PowerPoint slide, it is contained within an invisible boundary since, by default, there is no border or fill in a text object. Like drawing objects, you can delete, copy, move or resize a text object.

**TRAP** You can also edit the text within the text object and change its font size, colour or style. However, if you have chosen a template and a layout for your presentation, by altering the text you will make it different from the other slides in your presentation. Our advice is to use text editing sparingly, only when some words or sentences really deserve to stand out from the rest.

### Editing Text

To edit the text of a particular slide, proceed as follows:

1. Select the **slide** in which you wish to edit text. You should be in Slide or Normal view.

2. Select the **text** you wish to edit by dragging the cursor across the text. You can select just one letter, a word, an entire line or all the text in the slide.

3. Click **Format** ➜ **Font** from the menu bar and the drop-down menu. The Font dialogue box appears. You can now select the **Font** (such as Times New Roman), the **Style** (such as italics) or the **size** of the font. You can also select special effects such as **Underline** and font **colour**. Click **OK** when done.

4. Click **outside** the text object to deselect it. Fig 20.13 shows a line with just one word edited.

A Line with one **word** edited

*Fig 20.13 Line with One Word Edited*

## Editing Text Objects

As we have mentioned, the text in a PowerPoint slide is enclosed by a normally invisible text object frame or boundary. The frame decides the length of the text before the text warps. When you align the text, the alignment (such as right aligned or centred) occurs in relation to the Text Object boundary. The boundary becomes visible as a thick, hatched line when you click on the text.

You may need to edit the Text Object boundary in two situations:

1. When you enlarge the font of the text, you may need to **enlarge** the Text Object to ensure that the text will fit within it.

2. When you shift the location of the text. To do so, you have to **drag** the Text Object rather than only the text.

To resize or move a Text Object, proceed as follows:

1. Click on the **text**. The Text Object boundary frame appears along with selection handles around it.

   - To **resize** the frame, click on the **handles** and drag the frame to the **new size** in the same way as you did to resize drawing objects earlier in this chapter.

   - To **move** the frame, click on the **frame**, but not on any of the handles and drag the object, along with the text, to the new location.

2. Click **outside** the text object to deselect it when you are done.

**NOTE**

You cannot change the size of the text by dragging the handles of the Text Object even though the size of the frame changes. The text will merely change its alignment to try to fit within the new shape.

## Showing the Presentation

After your presentation is ready, you can show it to your audience. The equipment you will need depends on the size and location of your audience. See the table below for different situations:

| Audience | | Equipment Needed |
|---|---|---|
| **Size** | **Location** | |
| Small | In your Office | Your Computer and Monitor |
| Medium | In your Office | Your Computer attached to a Multimedia Projector |
| Large | Not in your Office | A Laptop Computer attached to a Multimedia Projector |

Before beginning your slide show, you may want to specify the presentation settings and the viewing options. After the settings have been done, begin the show by clicking **View ➜ Slide Show** from the menu bar and from the drop-down menu that appears.

## Presentation Settings

To specify the presentation settings, click **Slide Show** on the menu bar followed by **Set Up Show** on the drop-down menu. The Set Up Show dialogue box appears. *See Fig 20.14.*

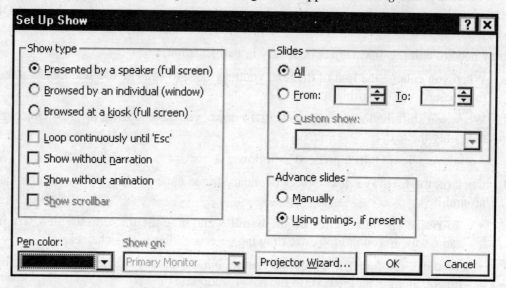

*Fig 20.14 Set Up Show Dialogue Box*

You can specify a number of options in this dialogue box such as:

- **Show Type:** You can select **full screen** (presented by a Speaker or browsed at a kiosk) or in a window (browsed by an individual). You can also decide if the show will loop continuously and run with or without animation.

- **Number of Slides:** You can specify **all slides** or **selected slides** only.

- **Mode of Slide Advance:** Select either **Manually** or **Automatic Advance** after preset time intervals.

## Viewing Options

You can preselect a number of viewing options before you begin your slide show. Here are the important options that you can use:

- After you have loaded the presentation in PowerPoint, you can begin the show by clicking **Slide Show** on the menu bar followed by **View Show** on the drop-down menu. You can also press the **F5** function key while in Normal View or Slide View. The opening slide expands to fill the whole screen. Pressing the **PgDn** key on your keyboard thereafter will advance the slides one step at a time. Pressing the **PgUp** key will move you backwards one step at a time. You can also click on the left mouse key to advance the slides one step at a time.

- To jump to a specific slide, while the show is on, right click anywhere on the screen to bring up a context menu. On this, click **Go → Slide Navigator**. The Slide Navigator dialogue box opens, with a list of all available slides in the presentation. Highlight the slide you wish to see and click the **Go To** button at the top right. The selected slide will open on the screen. *See Fig 20.15.*

- You can also use this right clicked context sensitive menu to navigate slides by clicking on **Next** or **Previous** options. However, unless you have no keyboard, this method is not as convenient as using the PgDn and PgUp keys on your keyboard.

- Click **Esc** at any time during the presentation to terminate the show.

- You can **right click** during the show to display the context sensitive menu. Select **Pointer Option → Pen → Pen colour** for selecting an online pen which will draw freehand on the slide in the selected colour. This is a very convenient way to highlight some text or object on a slide. The markings you apply with the pen are not permanent and will disappear as you move to the next slide.

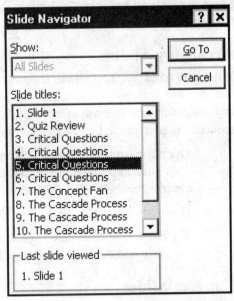

*Fig 20.15 Slide Navigator Dialogue Box*

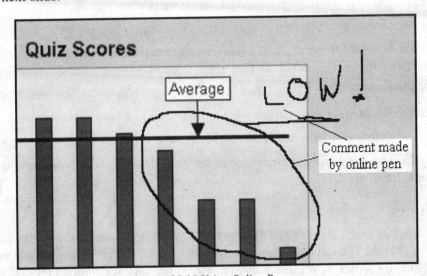

*Fig 20.16 Using Online Pen*

**TIP** To blank out a slide on the screen, right click and select **Screen → Black Screen** from the context sensitive menu. The screen goes black. You can then use the mouse pointer like a chalk on a blackboard to write any message for the viewer. Right click and select **Screen → Erase Pen** to remove your message from the black screen. Select **Screen → Unblack Screen** to restore the slide back on the screen.

# Electronic Slide Show

Some preparation before an electronic slide show will ensure that your presentation is attractive, flawless and full of impact. We look at some of the key preparatory steps here.

## Arranging Slides

When you have prepared all the slides you need for your presentation, you will want to make sure that they are arranged in the sequence you want them to appear. Although it is possible to jump to any slide during the show using the Slide Navigator, your presentation will be smoother if the sequence is prearranged. Here is what you do to prearrange the slides:

1. Open the **presentation** in PowerPoint and switch to the **Slide Sorter view**. You will see each slide as a miniature or thumbnail, arranged in sequence. See fig 19.07 in the previous chapter for the Slide Sorter view.

2. If any slide needs to be shifted, **click and drag** the slide to its correct position.

3. If you have an unwanted slide in the set, you can delete that slide in this view by selecting the **slide** and clicking the **Delete** key on your keyboard.

## Copying Slides

If you use a standard slide in all your presentations such as a Company logo, you can copy this slide from another presentation you have prepared earlier. Here is what you do:

1. Open the **source presentation** in slide sorter view and locate the **slide** you want to copy.

2. Click on the **slide** to select it. If you want to select more than one slide, click them in sequence while holding down the Ctrl key.

3. Click **Edit** on the menu bar and then click **Copy** on the drop-down menu.

4. Switch to the **target presentation** where you want to add the copied slide(s).

5. Click the **slide sorter icon** and in this view, click the slide **before** the slide(s) to be inserted.

6. Click **Edit** on the menu bar and **Paste** in the drop-down menu. The slide(s) is inserted in the new location.

## Hidden Slides

In a presentation, you may have data that you may or may not need, depending on the questions that the audience might ask. You can put the information that you may need in such a situation on a slide or slides and hide the slides. If you leave them hidden, you can click through these slides without displaying them. However, if you do decide to show them, you can unhide them as required. Here is how you hide and display a slide:

1. Move to the slide you want to **hide** in the Slide view and click **Slide Show** in the menu bar and then click **Hide Slide** in the drop-down menu.

2. Go through the presentation as usual. If you take no special action, the slide remains hidden.

3. At any time during the presentation, if you wish to display a hidden slide, right click anywhere on the screen and click **Go** ➔ **Slide Navigator**. The hidden slide will be found in the Slide

Navigator list. See Fig 20.15 earlier in this chapter for a view of the Slide Navigator dialogue box.

4.  Click on the **slide** you want to display.

# Enhancing Your Slide Show

After you have prepared your basic slide show, you can enhance the impact of your show by adding a variety of effects to your presentation. You can use a variety of special visual, sound, and animation effects. However, do use moderation. While you want your audience to be impressed, you do not want them to pay more attention to your techniques than to the contents of your presentation!

Here are some of the techniques for show enhancement that you can use:

## Animations and Transitions

Transitions are special effects that introduce a slide in a slide show. You can choose from a variety of transitions and vary their speed. You can change the transition effect to indicate a new section of a presentation or to emphasise a certain slide. Animations are special sound or visual effects that you can add to text or other objects, such as a chart.

**TIP**

If your audience uses a language (like English) that reads from left to right, you might design your animated slides so that your points appear from the left. Then, to emphasise a particular point, bring it in from the right. The change will grab the audience's attention and reinforce your point.

## Music, Sounds, and Videos

An occasional burst of music or sound during a transition or animation can bring back the attention of the audience to your slide show. You can also play videos that might include part of a company's commercial or training film. But remember not to overdo it. Frequent use of special effects can draw attention away from the content of your presentation. Learn more about adding music, sound and video later in this section.

## Animation

You can animate text, graphics, sounds, movies, charts, and other objects on your slides so that you can focus on important points, control the flow of information, and add interest to your presentation. You can set up how text or an object will appear on your slide. For example, the text can fly in from the left and it can appear by the letter, word, or paragraph. You can also choose whether the text or objects should dim or change colour when you add a new element to the slide.

You can change the order and timing of your animations, and you can set them to occur automatically without having to click the mouse. You can preview and fine tune your presentation to make sure that everything in it will work together.

Here is how you animate text and objects:

1. In normal view, display the **slide** that has the **text** or **objects** you want to animate.
2. On the Slide Show menu, click **Custom Animation**. The Custom Animation dialogue box appears.
    - Click the **Effects** tab. *See Fig 20.17.*
    - Or, if you are animating a chart created in Microsoft Graph, click the **Chart Effects** tab.

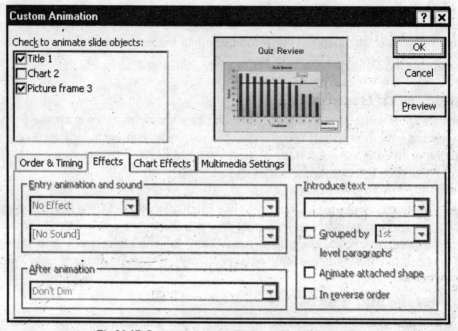

*Fig 20.17 Custom Animation Dialogue Box: Effects Tab*

3. Under Check to animate slide objects, select the **check boxes** next to the text or object you want to animate.
4. Under Entry animation and sound select the **options** you want from the drop-down list. If you are animating text, then under Introduce text, select the **options** you want.
5. Similarly, select the **sound effect** you want and then under After Animation, select desired **action** after animation (such as Dim the text).
6. Under Start Animation, select **how** you want animation to start, **automatically** or on mouse click.
7. Repeat **steps 3 and 4** for **every object** you want to animate.
8. Click the **Order and Timing** tab.
9. The Animation Order pane will open showing the items in your slide arranged in their default order of appearance. *See Fig 20.18.* Do one of the following:
    - To change the order of animation, select the **object** you want to change under Animation order, and then click one of the **arrows** to move the object up or down in the list.

- To set the timing, select the **object** and then do one of the following:
  - To start the animation by clicking the text or object, click **On mouse click**.
  - To start the animation automatically, click **Automatically**, and then enter the **number of seconds** you want to have elapse between the previous animation and the current one.

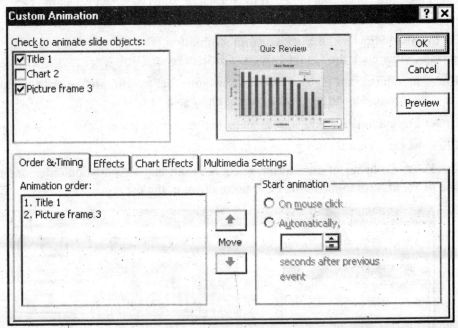

*Fig 20.18 Custom Animation Dialogue Box: Order and Timing Tab*

10. To preview animations, click **Preview**. The chart animation will run in the preview pane of the Custom Animation dialogue box.

**TIP**

A quick way to create basic animation is to select the object you want to animate in normal view, click the **Slide Show** menu, point to **Preset Animation**, and then click the **option** you want for animation.

## Editing Text or Object Animation

1. Display the **slide** in which you want to change an animation.

2. On the Slide Show menu, click **Custom Animation**.

3. Under Check to animate slide objects, select the **object** you want to change. To remove the animation from the object, clear the **check box** next to the object name.

4. On the Effects and Order and Timing tabs, make the **changes** you want.

5. Repeat **steps 3 and 4** for each object you want to change.

6. To preview the changes you made, click **Preview**.

# Animating the Elements of a Chart

You can animate the elements of a chart created with Microsoft Graph or Microsoft Excel. We have already discussed how to insert objects from Microsoft Excel or Word in your PowerPoint presentation earlier in this chapter. To animate the elements of a chart that you have copied from an Excel worksheet and pasted in your presentation, proceed as follows:

1.  Open the **slide** containing the chart in Normal or Slide view and select the **chart** you want to animate.

2.  On the Slide Show menu, click **Custom Animation**. The Custom Animation dialogue box appears. Now click the **Chart Effects** tab. *See Fig 20.19.*

3.  Under Introduce chart elements, select how you want to **animate** the chart. Options in the list will change depending on the type of chart selected.

4.  Under Entry animation and sound, select the **options** you want.

5.  Click the **Order and Timing** tab.

6.  To change the **order of animation**, select the chart under Animation order, and then click one of the **arrows** to move the chart up or down in the list.

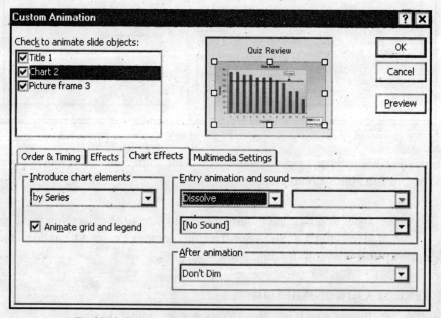

*Fig 20.19 Custom Animation Dialogue Box: Chart Effects Tab*

7.  To set the **timing**, select the chart and then do one of the following:

    •   To start the animation by clicking the text or object, click **On mouse click**.

    •   To start the animation automatically, click **Automatically**, and then enter the **number of seconds** you want to have elapse between the previous animation and the current one. The timing you set is also the time that will elapse between each animated element of the chart.

### *Viewing the Effects in a Slide*

1.  Display the **slide** you want to view in Slide View. Click on **Show Slide** in the drop-down menu. A full-sized window appears and the slide show plays, complete with transition and animation.

2.  You can also press **F5** on your keyboard while the selected slide is positioned in the Slide View mode.

# Music, Sounds and Video

Sounds, music, videos, and animated GIF pictures are available in the Clip Gallery. To use the Clip Gallery, point to Movies and Sounds on the Insert menu, and then click either Movie from Gallery — to insert movies and animated GIF pictures — or Sound from Gallery to insert music and sounds. There are additional locations on your computer or on the Internet from where you can get music, sounds, and videos.

You insert a music, sound, or video clip on a slide where you want it to play during a slide show. You can choose either to have the sound or video start automatically when you move to the slide, or to have the sound or video start only when you click its icon during a slide show. To change how the clip starts or to add a hyperlink to the clip, click Action Settings on the Slide Show menu.

You can also add animation effects and change play settings by clicking Custom Animation on the Slide Show menu. For example, you can set a sound or video to play automatically in an animation sequence.

 **NOTE** Sounds, music, and videos are inserted in your slides as Microsoft PowerPoint objects. If PowerPoint does not support a particular media type or feature, you may have to use Media Player (already installed as part of Windows) to play the file. To play a sound or video as a Media Player object, click Object on the Insert menu, and then click Media Clip. By doing so, you will use the Media Player to run the sound or video.

You will need speakers and a sound card on your computer to play music and sounds. To find out what is installed and what settings are in use, check both the Multimedia and Sounds categories by opening the Control Panel.

### *Insert Music or Sound on a Slide*

To add music or other audio clips to a slide, do the following:

1.  Display the **slide** you want to add music or sound to.

2.  On the Insert menu, point to **Movies and Sounds**.

3.  Do one of the following:

    *   To insert a sound from the Clip Gallery, click **Sound from Gallery**, and then locate and insert the sound you want.

    *   To insert a sound from another location, click **Sound from File**, locate the folder that contains the sound, and then double click the sound you want.

4. A sound icon appears on the slide. A message is displayed. If you want the sound to play automatically when you go to the slide, click **Yes**; if you want the sound to play only when you click the sound icon during a slide show, click **No**.

5. To preview the sound in normal view, double click the **sound icon**. *See Fig 20.20.*

### *Insert a video on a slide*

You can add a video clip to a slide. To do so, proceed as follows:

1. Display the **slide** you want to add the video to.

2. On the Insert menu, point to **Movies and Sounds**.

3. Do one of the following:

   • To insert a video from the Clip Gallery, click **Movie from Gallery**, and then locate and insert the video you want.

   • To insert a video from another location, click **Movie from File**, locate the folder that contains the video, and then double click the video you want.

4. A message is displayed. If you want the movie to play automatically when you move to the slide, click **Yes**; if you want the movie to play only when you click the movie during a slide show, click **No**.

5. To preview the movie in normal view, double click the **movie**. *See Fig 20.20.*

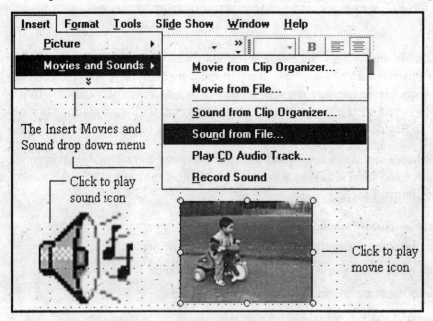

*Fig 20.20 Inserting Sound and Video on a Slide*

### *Insert an Animated GIF Picture on a Slide*

You can insert animated GIF (Graphic Interchange Format) pictures or motion clips on your slide. The picture will move when the slide is displayed. Proceed as follows:

1. Display the **slide** you want to add the animated GIF picture to.

2. Do one of the following:

   - To insert an animated GIF picture from the Clip Gallery, click **Insert Clip Art** on the Drawing tool bar and then click the **Motion Clips** tab.

   - To insert an animated GIF picture from a file, on the Insert menu, point to **Picture**, and then click **From File**.

3. Do one of the following:

   - If you clicked Insert Clip Art in step 2, click the **animated GIF picture** you want to add to your slide, and then click **Insert Clip** on the menu that appears.

   - If you clicked From File (Insert menu, Picture sub-menu) in step 2, locate the folder that contains the animated GIF picture you want to insert, and double click the **picture**.

4. To preview how the animated GIF picture will appear in the slide show, click **Slide Show** at the lower left of the Microsoft PowerPoint window.

# Transporting Your Slide Show

You may have to give your slide show on another computer, which may be connected to a multimedia projector. You have to then carry your slide show on floppy disks or some other removable media. At the place of the show, you may also have to set up the multimedia projector if you are required to use one. In the last section of this chapter, we discuss how you can do both.

## Pack and Go Wizard

When you want to run a slide show on another computer, you can use the Pack and Go Wizard to pack your presentation. The Wizard packs all the files and fonts used in the presentation together on a disk. When you intend to run your show on a computer that does not have Microsoft PowerPoint installed, you have the option of including the PowerPoint Viewer in your package. You can include all connected files as part of your package, and if you use True Type fonts you can include them as well. If you make changes to your presentation after you use the Pack and Go Wizard, just run the Wizard again to update the package.

After you pack the presentation, you can unpack the presentation to run on another computer.

Here is how you can pack your presentation for transport:

1. Insert a blank, formatted 1.44 Mb **floppy disk** in your floppy disk drive. If your presentation contains a large number of slides, keep a few extra blank and formatted floppy disks handy.

2. Open the **presentation** you want to pack.

3. On the File menu, click **Pack and Go**. See Fig 20.21 for a view of the Pack and Go Wizard.

4. Follow the **instructions** in the Pack and Go Wizard. If prompted, insert another blank, formatted **floppy disk**.

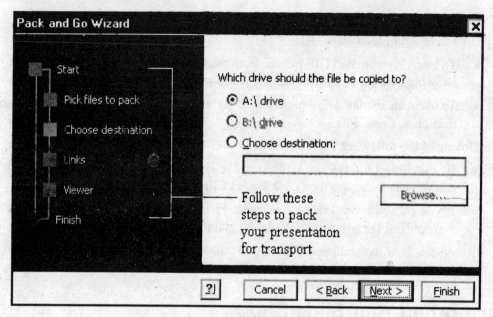

*Fig 20.21 Pack and Go Wizard*

At the destination computer, unpack your presentation as follows:

1. Insert the **disk** you packed your presentation on.

2. In Windows Explorer, go to the location of the packed presentation, and then double click the file named **Pngsetup**.

3. Enter the **destination** you want to copy the presentation to.

4. To run the slide show later, locate the presentation in the folder you unpacked it to, right click the presentation and then click Show on the shortcut menu.

**TRAP**

If the Show command is not available, neither Microsoft PowerPoint nor the PowerPoint Viewer is installed on this computer. If so, then you must repack your presentation again and this time, include the PowerPoint viewer. There is more information on the viewer in the following section.

## The PowerPoint Viewer

The PowerPoint Viewer is a programme used to run slide shows on computers that do not have Microsoft PowerPoint installed. You can add the Viewer to the same disk (or additional disks) that contains a presentation by using the Pack and Go Wizard. Then you can unpack the Viewer and presentation together and run the slide show on another computer. You can also create a play list to use with the Viewer so that you can run multiple presentations, one after another.

The Viewer, PPView32.exe, or PPView97.exe, comes with PowerPoint and is located in the PFiles\MSOffice\Office\Xlators folder on your MS Office CD-ROM. If you have installed the Viewer when you installed PowerPoint, the Viewer is located in the programme Files\Microsoft Office\Office\Xlators folder on your hard disk.

### Run the PowerPoint Viewer

Before you can give a slide show with the Viewer, you must install the Viewer on the computer that will run the slide show. To do so, proceed as follows:

1. In Windows Explorer, **locate** and double click the **PowerPoint viewer**.

2. **Locate** and select the **presentation** you want to show, and then select any other **options** you want.

3. Click **Show**.

You can show one or more presentations sequentially by creating a play list. In the Viewer, enter the file name of the document that contains the play list, and click **Show**.

## Set Up a Laptop and a Projector

Use this procedure when you want to make a presentation to a large audience as the screen of your laptop will be inadequate for viewing by many persons.

1. Connect the **external display port** on the laptop computer to the **projector**. For information about connecting external devices, see the **documentation** for your laptop computer.

2. In Microsoft PowerPoint, open the **presentation** you want to run.

3. On the Slide Show menu, click **Set Up Show**. The Set Up Show dialogue box opens. The Projector Wizard button is at the bottom of the dialogue box.

4. Click **Projector Wizard** and follow the instructions in the Wizard to set up the presentation for the type of projector that you are using. The Wizard will guide you through the steps required to detect and install the projector, to test sound and adjust the computer parameters to work properly with the projector. *See Fig 20.22.*

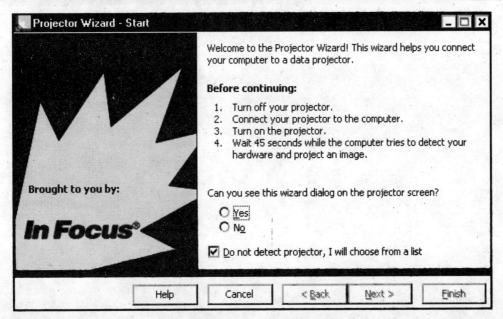

*Fig 20.22 Projector Wizard*

**CD-ROM**

To learn more about Microsoft PowerPoint 2000 in a multimedia environment, insert the accompanying CD-ROM in your computer and select the **Interactive** mode in the opening screen. The main menu will appear. To go to the section on PowerPoint, click the button marked **PowerPoint**. You will see a sub-menu containing the following topics:

- Basics of PowerPoint
- Creating Professional Presentations

Click on the second topic, "Creating Professional Presentations" to display another level of sub-sub-menu. From the items in this sub-sub-menu, you can select the particular topic you want to see. Click on your selected topic and follow instructions on your screen.

# 21. Introducing Outlook 2000

*In this chapter:*

☞ You are introduced to Outlook, its features, the system of files and folders and the elements of the Outlook Screen.

☞ You are shown how to move around in Outlook using the keyboard and the mouse. Different Outlook views require different strategies to navigate and these are explained to you.

☞ You are shown the meaning of the icons or symbols that you meet in different views of Outlook.

☞ You are shown how to configure Outlook to start automatically. You can also have Outlook go to specific views as soon as you open Outlook so that you can start immediately with what is important to you. For example, Outlook can open in the communications mode, displaying the fax or e-mail messages you have received. Or, Outlook can open to show you the calendar and the list of your tasks for the day.

☞ You learn to set up your communication centre Outlook so that you can send and receive faxes and e-mails.

# Introducing Outlook

Specialised programmes such as Word (Word processing), Excel (Spreadsheet) or Outlook Express (E-mail) each do one job well. With Outlook, however, Microsoft has created a multi-faceted programme that does a number of jobs. In Outlook you have a package that contains all that you need to communicate with others via E-mail and Fax, organise your time with schedules and tasks and regroup your own computer's files and folders for easy location. All these are features designed to increase your own productivity.

Outlook is a powerful Personal Information Manager (PIM) combined with an equally comprehensive communication system. In the Microsoft Office suit, compared to Word or Excel, Outlook is often neglected, but if you wish to organise yourself and enhance your productivity, Outlook will prove an invaluable ally.

## Outlook's Features

Outlook has the following basic features:

- **Address Book:** Where you can store-mail, e-mail and fax addresses of your contacts.

- **Task Pad:** Where you can list tasks and follow them up, providing reminders as needed.

- **Calendar:** In which you can plan the whole year, or a month at a time.

- **Notepad:** In which you can store notes for future use.

See Fig 21.01 for a view of the default opening screen of Outlook where you can see the calendar and the Task pad displayed.

In addition to the above, you can do the following with Outlook:

- Exchange e-mail through the Internet and interact with other e-mail systems such as Microsoft mail, Yahoo or Hotmail.

- If you have a fax-enabled modem, you can send and receive faxes as easily as e-mail.

- Use Word as your e-mail editor to produce advanced formatting in your communication.

- Retrieve addresses automatically from Outlook's address book by typing just a few initial letters.

- Recall e-mail messages already sent and arrange e-mail received and their replies in separate folders for easy identification.

*Fig 21.01 Default Opening Screen*

- Maintain a journal that tracks all the activity you want on your computer such as mail sent, files used etc.

Outlook excels as a desktop information manager. Here are some of the features in Outlook 2000 that make it so special:

- **Universal Address Book:** A single address book can be accessed by MS Word to create a mail-merged list, by e-mail or fax. Or, you can simply find telephone numbers of your contacts to call them up.

- **The Journal:** This is a new concept in Outlook 2000. You can configure journal to keep track of many things such as files opened by other MS Office applications or people you contact via e-mail or fax and thus keep track of your activity which you can play back later. See Fig 21.02 for a view of the Journal's timeline.

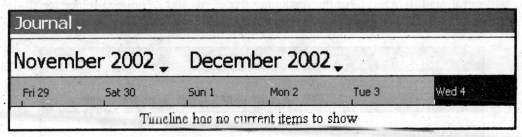

*Fig 21.02 Outlook Journal's Timeline*

- **File Manager:** You can use Outlook to view your files and folders just as you can in the Windows Explorer without leaving Outlook. You can search for, filter and group together files using criteria such as Author, Subject Key words etc, giving you greater power than Explorer. See Fig 21.03 for File View in Outlook.

- **Integration:** All components of Outlook are integrated. For instance, if you drag a contact's name to a date on your calendar, a scheduling will be automatically created. Similarly, by

| My Documents ▾ | | | | |
|---|---|---|---|---|
| Name △ | Author | Type | Size | Modified |
| Care2 E-card fro... | | Folder | | Tue 7/30/2002 5:38 PM |
| My eBooks | | Folder | | Mon 9/9/2002 8:48 AM |
| My Music | | Folder | | Sat 6/15/2002 9:43 PM |
| My Pictures | | Folder | | Sat 6/15/2002 9:40 PM |
| Shared Documents | | Briefcase | | Tue 11/26/2002 10:30 AM |
| Yahoo! Greetings... | | Folder | | Fri 11/1/2002 9:14 AM |
| Addresses | | Text Document | 257 B | Wed 11/13/2002 9:36 AM |
| Care2 E-card fro... | | HTML Document | 11 KB | Tue 7/30/2002 5:38 PM |
| Draft Letter | | Text Document | 1 KB | Thu 11/7/2002 4:47 PM |
| Meeting | | Text Document | 2 KB | Tue 11/19/2002 7:31 PM |
| Upload | | Text Document | 4 B | Wed 12/4/2002 5:35 PM |
| Yahoo! Greetings | | HTML Document | 7 KB | Fri 11/1/2002 9:14 AM |

*Fig 21.03 Outlook in File View*

dragging an e-mail to a task icon, you will automatically create a task based on the contents of the e-mail. Such capabilities allow you to avoid duplication and minimise the risk of forgetting some important task or appointment.

## Items and Folders

In Outlook, things are organised as items. Items may be further organised in Folders. To use Outlook efficiently, we need to understand what items and folders mean in Outlook's context. The main items in Outlook are: mail messages, appointments, contacts, tasks, journal entries and notes. Each item can be used to create activities and events. We will study each item in detail later in this book.

Each item is stored in a folder. For some items, there may be more than one folder. For example, for the e-mail item, there are four mail folders created as default when Outlook is first set up in your computer. The four folders are: Inbox, Outbox, Drafts and Sent Items. So, Outlook will generate four folders for mail, five more for the remaining five items and a common folder for all deleted items, ten folders in all. For a view of the folder structure displayed by Outlook, *see Fig 21.04.*

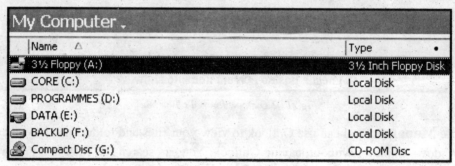

*Fig 21.04 Folder Structure in Outlook*

## The Outlook Screen

When you start Outlook, you may see the Outlook Today or the Inbox, depending on how you have configured Outlook. You will choose Outlook Today if you want to see a summary of the Calendar, Tasks and Messages. This is the screen to choose if your focus is on tasks and appointments rather than mail messages. Alternatively, you can begin with the Inbox if your focus is on communications such as e-mails. *See Fig 21.05.*

To understand the different components of the Outlook screen, we look at the Inbox. The important parts of the screen are discussed below:

**Outlook Bar:** On the left of your screen, the Outlook bar contains icons that are shortcuts to the commonly used folders. The easiest way to switch between folders is to click on its icon in the Outlook bar. The icons you see will depend on the bar you select. There are three, My Shortcuts, Outlook Shortcuts and Other Shortcuts. In Fig 21.05, you can see the My Shortcuts icons. The two hidden bars, Outlook Shortcuts and Other Shortcuts, can be opened by clicking on their buttons at the bottom of the currently open bar.

**Group Icons:** The two hidden group icons contain their own set of icons. Thus, My Shortcuts include Inbox, Draft, Journal and Outlook Updates, while Other Shortcuts contain My Computer, My Documents and Favourites. With the help of group icons, the display space for icons can be kept narrow, allowing more space for the information viewing area.

**Information Viewer:** What you will see in this viewing area will depend on the folder you have opened by clicking on its icon on the Outlook bar. For instance, in Fig 21.05, the Inbox is shown open. As you can see, the top half of the viewing area displays the headers of the-mails in your inbox while the bottom half contains the details of the topmost mail, which is opened by default.

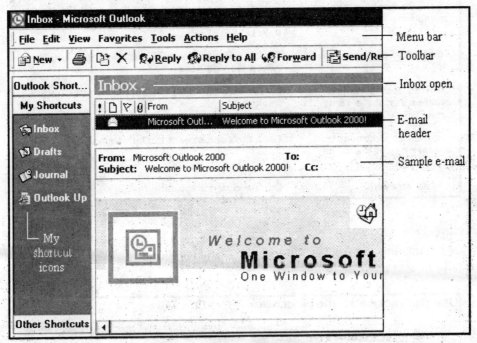

*Fig 21.05 Outlook Screen*

# Moving Around In Outlook

You can move around in Microsoft Outlook by using your mouse or keyboard shortcuts. Some views in Outlook have specific key combinations or mouse functions. These will only work in a particular view. However, most of the key combinations or mouse functions work in all views.

## Using the Mouse

You can move around in Outlook by using either your mouse or the new Microsoft IntelliMouse pointing device.

The IntelliMouse gives you more mouse features. It has a wheel or wheel button that you can rotate or hold down to make navigation easier. However, since most users have the standard two or three button mouse, what we will describe here will apply to such a mouse.

### The Day/Week/Month View

If you click the calendar icon on the Outlook bar, you will see the day/week/month view. The table in Fig 21.06 describes how to navigate in this view using your mouse:

| Use the mouse to move around in day/week/month view | |
|---|---|
| **To** | **Do this** |
| Open the appointment. | Double-click the appointment move handle. |
| Change an appointment start or end time. | Select the appointment, and then drag the top or bottom borders of the appointment (when viewing days). |
| Reschedule an appointment. | Click the left border of the appointment and drag (when viewing days). |
| Copy an appointment to another day at the same time. | Press CTRL and drag the appointment to Date Navigator. |
| Move an appointment to another day at the same time. | Drag the appointment to Date Navigator. |
| Create an event. | Double-click the top of a day. |

*Fig 21.06 Navigation with Mouse in Calendar View*

## The Timeline View

You will see the timeline view if you click on the journal icon in the Outlook bar. The table in Fig 21.07 explains how to navigate in this view.

| Use the mouse to move around on a timeline | |
|---|---|
| **To scroll** | **Do this** |
| Forward by the units of time visible on the time scale | Click the right scroll arrow on the horizontal scroll bar. |
| Back by the units of time visible on the time scale | Click the left scroll arrow on the horizontal scroll bar. |
| Forward in time by approximately one screen | Click to the right of the scroll box on the horizontal scroll bar. |
| Back in time by approximately one screen | Click to the left of the scroll box on the horizontal scroll bar. |
| Quickly to view items on a timeline | Drag the scroll box left or right on the horizontal scroll bar. |
| To any day on a timeline | Click the down arrow next to the month and year on the upper time scale, and then click the day you want in the small calendar. |

*Fig 21.07 Navigating with Mouse in Timeline View*

# Using the Keyboard

You will need the keyboard to enter data in Outlook, such as type an e-mail, or enter a task. If you prefer to continue using the keyboard for navigation instead of switching back and forth between keyboard and mouse, you can use keyboard shortcuts. However, the mouse is so much more convenient.

If you do wish to use the keyboard to navigate, the details of how to move around in tool bars using keyboard shortcuts are given in Fig 21.08.

While you should use the mouse or the keyboard (or a combination) as it suits you best, we recommend the mouse for fast navigation.

| On a toolbar, to | Press |
| --- | --- |
| Make the menu bar active. | F10. |
| Select the next or previous toolbar. | CTRL+TAB or CTRL+SHIFT+TAB. |
| Select the next or previous button or menu on the toolbar. | TAB or SHIFT+TAB (when a toolbar is active). |
| Open the menu. | ENTER (when a menu on a toolbar is selected). |
| Perform the action assigned to a button. | ENTER (when a button is selected). |
| Enter text in a text box. | ENTER (when the text box is selected). |
| Enter a name in the **QuickFind** box. | F11 |
| Select an option from a drop-down list box or from a drop-down menu on a button. | Arrow keys to move through options in the list or menu; ENTER to select the option you want (when a drop-down list box is selected). |

*Fig 21.08 Keyboard Shortcuts for Tool Bars*

## Symbols in Outlook

Some common symbols are used to add meaning to messages, events and tasks and so on. Like icons, many events and tasks are also identified by symbols. Some commonly used symbols for Calendar are given here. It will be easier to use Outlook if you become familiar with them. See the table in Fig 21.09 for symbols and an explanation of their meaning:

| Symbols in Calendar | |
| --- | --- |
| Symbol | Description |
| | Appointment |
| | Click to see calendar items that do not fit in the current view |
| | Meeting |
| | Meeting request |
| | Recurring appointment |
| | Recurring meeting or appointment |
| | Reminder for the appointment or meeting |
| | Private meeting or appointment |
|  | Start and end times of the appointment or meeting |
| | Calendar item has an attachment |

*Fig 21.09 Common Symbols Used in Calendar*

# Configuring Outlook

Each one of us has different needs when we work with our computers. Our computers too will differ somewhat. Therefore, for optimum efficiency with Outlook, you should configure Outlook to suit your needs. You may require a different set up, if:

- You have more than one user on your computer; you will need to set up individual user profiles in the multi-user mode.
- You have a phone connection and want to use the fax and e-mail capability; then you will want to configure Outlook accordingly.

**NOTE**

For this discussion, we will assume that you are a single user and wish to utilise fax and e-mail with Outlook using your existing telephone line and Internet connection. We do not discuss networking here because your system administrator will probably handle the networking configurations.

## Start Options

Depending on your preferences, you can configure how Outlook will start on your machine. For instance, you can have:

- Outlook to start automatically when you start your computer (Auto Start).
- A selected folder to open automatically when you start Outlook. (Start-up Options).

Let us examine these configuration steps.

### *Auto Start*

To make sure that Outlook starts automatically when you switch on your computer, do the following:

1. Click the **Start** button, point to **Settings**, and then click **Task bar & Start menu**. The Task bar and Start Menu Properties dialogue box opens. *See Fig 21.10.*

2. Click the **Advanced** tab, and then click the **Add** button. The Create Shortcut dialogue box opens.

3. Click **Browse**. The Browse dialogue box opens.

4. In the Look in box, click the **drive** that Microsoft Outlook is installed on.

5. In the folder list, double click the folder that contains **Outlook**. The folder opens, displaying the programmes in the folder.

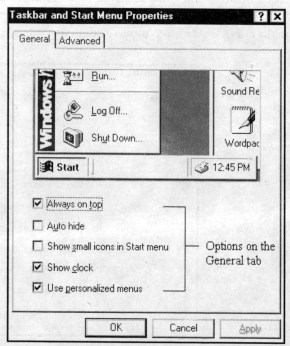

*Fig 21.10 Task Bar and Start Menu Properties*

6. Double click **Outlook**, and then click **Next**. The Select Programme Folder dialogue box opens.

7. In the folder list, click **Start Up**, and then click **Next**.

8. In the Select a name for the shortcut box, type a **name** for the shortcut (for example, Microsoft Outlook) and then click **Finish**.

Outlook is added to your start-up folder. The next time you switch on your computer, Outlook will load and run automatically.

### Start-up Options

You can configure Outlook to start with certain specific options of your choice. For instance, you can have Output create an e-mail message immediately after starting up, or start with a folder of your choice visible on the screen.

When Outlook is installed on your computer, usually as part of the installation of Microsoft Office 2000, a desktop icon is automatically created which is a shortcut you can click to start Outlook from your desktop.

You can call up the properties dialogue box of this shortcut to configure Outlook's start-up options. Here is how:

1. Right click on this desktop **shortcut** and then click **Properties**. The shortcut's Properties dialogue box opens.

2. Click the **Shortcut** tab.

3. In the Target box, type a space after the path, and then type one or more of the command-line options that you need from the table in Fig 21.11 and then click **OK**.

Use this shortcut to start Outlook and the start-up options you have selected will be activated automatically.

| To start Outlook and do this | Type this command-line option |
|---|---|
| Hide the Outlook Bar | /folder |
| Have the specified folder visible | /select *"path/folder name"* |
| Create an e-mail message | /c ipm.note |
| Create a post | /c ipm.post |
| Create an appointment | /c ipm.appointment |
| Create a task | /c ipm.task |
| Create a contact | /c ipm.contact |
| Create a journal entry | /c ipm.activity |
| Create a note | /c ipm.stickynote |
| Prompt for default manager of e-mail, news, and contacts | /checkclient |
| Create an item with the specified file as an attachment | /a *"path/file name"* |

*Fig 21.11 Command Line Options*

**TRAP**  Paths that include spaces between words, such as C:\Programme Files, must be enclosed in quotation marks (" ") and are case sensitive. To specify a path in Outlook, precede the path with "Outlook:\\". For example, to open the My Documents folder when you start Outlook, the complete entry should read "C:\Programme Files\Microsoft Office\Outlook.exe" /select "C:\My Documents".

## Communications (Fax and E-mail)

If you are part of a network, the network server will be configured for fax and e-mail. Alternatively, you may have a dial-up telephone connection and you may be using Outlook Express as your e-mail client. But if you want both fax and e-mail capability from a single programme, you can use Outlook instead of Outlook Express as your default communications software.

## Configuring Fax

Before configuring for fax, make sure that your dial-up modem is capable of sending and receiving fax. Such modems are classified usually as Data, Fax and Voice modems. Check the documentation that came with your modem.

Your fax service is configured the first time you use it. To call up fax service, do the following:

1.  Click **File ➜ New ➜ Fax Message** starting from the File menu item on Outlook's menu bar. A dialogue box opens asking you if you want to install Symantec's Fax Starter Edition. This software is part of Microsoft Office 2000.

2.  Click **Yes**. The set-up Wizard appears. Follow directions on your screen to install the required options in Outlook. See Fig 21.12 for a view of the set-up Wizard.

To send a fax, click the **File** menu, point to **New**, and then click **New Fax Message**. Outlook installs the fax feature the first time you use it. Once the fax service has been installed, sending a fax with Microsoft Outlook is as easy as sending an e-mail message.

You can also send almost any document from any of the Office 2000 programmes as a fax, and you can easily include both a cover page and any additional files you want.

### Send a Fax

You can send and receive faxes by using Microsoft Outlook. You can send an e-mail message as a fax, send faxes with cover pages, and include files with a fax.

To send a fax without a cover page, do the following:

1.  In Outlook, on the **File** menu, point to **New**, and then click **Fax Message**. The Send dialogue box appears.

2.  In the To box, enter the **name** of the contact, the recipient of the fax.

3.  If the recipient's fax number is not in your contact list, type the **fax number** in the To box.

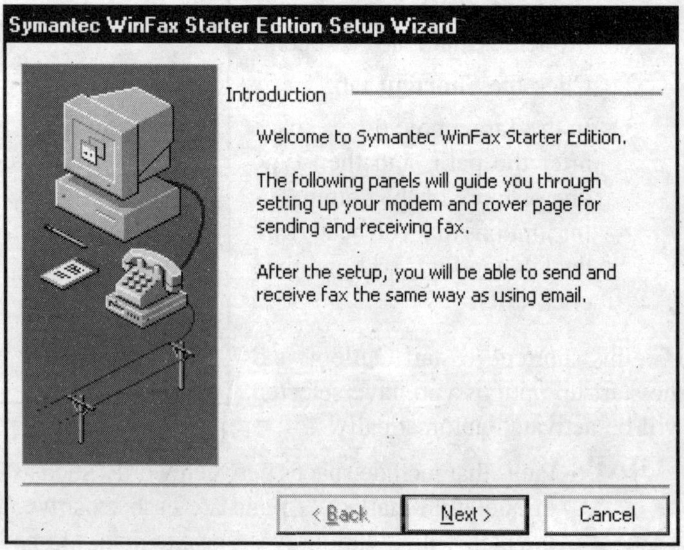

*Fig 21.12 Symantec Fax Starter Edition Set-up Wizard*

4.  In the Subject box, type a **brief description** of the fax.

5.  In the message window, type your **message**. If you have included a cover page, your message appears on it; otherwise, it appears on the first page of the fax.

6.  Click **Send**.

To include a cover page with your fax, do the following:

1. On the Tools menu, click **Options**, and then click the **Fax** tab.

2. Click **Template**.

3. Select the **Send Cover Page** check box.

4. In the Template list, click the **cover page** you want to use for all faxes. A preview of the cover page appears directly below the list. See Fig 21.13 for a view of the Cover Page Properties dialogue box.

5. If you wish to change the information on the **Fax** tab, under **Cover Page Information**, click **Edit**.

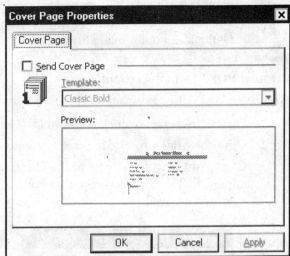

*Fig 21.13 Cover Page Properties Dialogue Box*

### Receive a Fax

To receive faxes in Microsoft Outlook, you must run Outlook with fax reception enabled. You cannot receive faxes when Outlook is not running or when fax reception is not enabled.

To enable fax reception, proceed as follows:

1. On the **Tools** menu, click **Options**.

2. Click the **Fax** tab. Fig 21.14 shows the Fax tab of the Options dialogue box.

3. Select the **Automatic receive fax** check box.

4. In the **Answer after** list, select a **number of rings** before the programme takes over.

### *Configuring E-mail*

If you have already set up an e-mail account for use with Outlook Express as described in Chapter 5, *E-Mail and Chat*, then you will have to decide if you wish to continue using Outlook Express as your default e-mail client or wish to switch to Outlook.

For this discussion, we assume that you have not set up an e-mail account using Outlook Express, or wish to use Outlook instead with a fresh e-mail account.

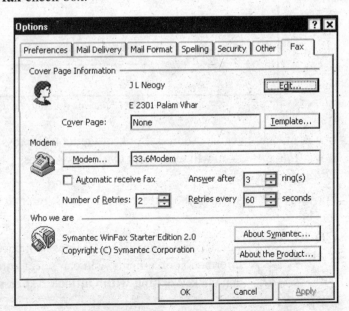

*Fig 21.14 Fax Tab: Options Dialogue Box*

**NOTE** Before you begin the configuration, you will need the Internet Protocol (IP) address of your Internet Service Provider's (ISP) POP3 and SMTP server, the dial-up telephone number you must use to connect to your ISP's server as well as the user name and password allotted to you by your ISP. After collecting this information, you can proceed to set up Outlook as your e-mail client.

**Create a POP3 E-mail Account**

To create a Post Office Protocol (POP3) e-mail account, proceed as follows:

1. On the **Tools** menu, click **Accounts**.
2. Click the **Mail** tab. The Internet Accounts dialogue box will open. *See Fig 21.15.*
3. Click **Add**, and then click **Mail**. The first step of the Internet Connection Wizard will appear. Follow the instructions on your screen, clicking the **Next>** button to move to the next step as required.

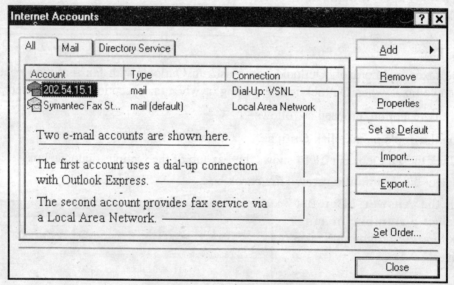

*Fig 21.15 Internet Accounts Dialogue Box*

If you already have an Address Book in Outlook Express, Outlook can update its own Address Book from there. You will read about Outlook's Address Book in the next chapter, *Communicating Through Outlook*.

For more information on the Internet and e-mails, refer to Chapter 5, *E-Mail and Chat*, earlier in this book.

**CD-ROM**  The accompanying CD-ROM does not cover Microsoft Outlook 2000. For general information on e-mails, you can select **Internet** from the CD-ROM's main menu and click **Working with Outlook Express** in the sub-menu that appears.

# 22. Communicating Through Outlook

## In this chapter:

☞ You learn the basics of communicating with Outlook 2000.

☞ You are shown how to create and set up your Address Book. You can either enter the data manually or you can import the data from other address books, such as the one you may have already created for Outlook Express, which is part of Windows.

☞ You keep your Address Book current by finding and editing entries as well as adding and deleting entries in your Address Book.

☞ You learn how to sort and filter the names and addresses in your Address Book and to organise your information into separate categories such as business, personal etc.

☞ If you have a phone line, you are shown how to use your Address Book to dial the phone number of persons in your Address Book.

☞ You learn to use Outlook's Inbox window where all fax and e-mail messages you receive are displayed.

☞ You learn how to send and receive fax and e-mail messages using Outlook.

# Communicating Through Outlook

You can use Outlook as your communication centre. You can keep track of your contacts and their correspondence, sending follow-up e-mails and faxes directly from Outlook. To keep track of the addresses, phone and fax numbers and e-mail addresses, you can use Outlook's Address Book.

The Address Book is an electronic database where useful information about your business associates, friends and relatives can be easily stored, edited and retrieved for a variety of purposes such as sending e-mails, dialling a phone number or sending a fax.

The Address Book can be used without an Internet connection for inserting names and addresses in letters drafted in Microsoft Word. With a telephone connection, you can dial numbers or send faxes. With an Internet connection, you can also send e-mails. In short, the Address Book along with Outlook's Inbox will provide you with all the connectivity you need for business or personal work.

## The Address Book

You can type in data or import it into Outlook's Address Book from another programme such as the Address Book of Outlook Express. You can also view the Address Book data in a variety of ways. For example, you can ask the Address Book to list all names and telephone numbers if you are planning to dial a contact.

### The Address Book Window

In your Outlook Shortcuts tool bar, there is an icon labelled Contacts. By clicking on this label, you can display the contents of your Address Book in the viewing window. The default view will display the information as Address Cards, much like business cards that people exchange. However, you can change the view to any one of the following:

**Address Cards:** This view shows just name and e-mail address. *See Fig 22.01.*

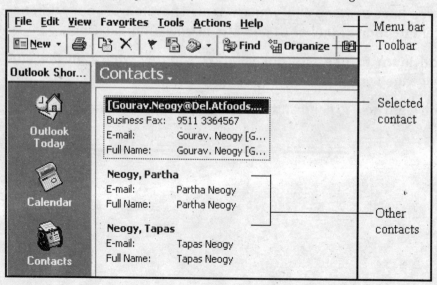

*Fig 22.01 Address Card View of Contacts*

**Detailed Address Cards:** More information is shown in this view. In both address card views, you can right click the name and click **Open** in the drop-down menu for the Contact dialogue box to open. Here you can edit, add or alter any data that may be in the database under the selected name.

**Phone List:** In this view, only the names and the phone and fax numbers are listed. By right clicking a **name** and clicking on **Call Contact** in the drop-down menu, you can open a Call Contact dialogue box to initiate a phone call.

**By Category:** After you have classified your contact information by categories such as Business, Personal, International, Key Customer etc, you can change the Address Book view so that it displays information only about contacts of a category that you select. For example, you can ask it to show only your personal contacts. You can create additional categories if you want.

## Creating Your Address Book

The structure of your Address Book is automatically created as soon as you install Outlook in your computer. To start using the Address Book, you must first enter data in it either manually, or by importing information from some other programme such as Outlook Express. We look first at entering the data manually. Do the following:

1. In any view, click **File →**
   **Now → Contacts** using the
   menu bar and the drop-
   down menus. The
   "Untitled: Contacts"
   dialogue box opens. See
   Fig 22.02 for a view of this
   dialogue box.

2. Enter information in each
   box, using the **Tab** and the
   **Shift + Tab** keys to
   navigate the form.

3. Click **Save** and **Close** in the
   dialogue box after data
   entry is completed.

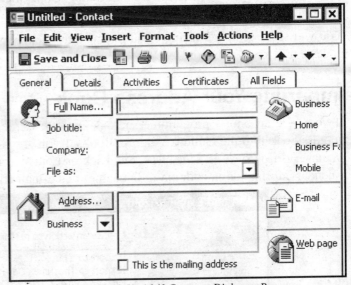

*Fig 22.02 Untitled Contacts Dialogue Box*

You will note that most of the boxes have drop-down ▼ arrows next to them. Click these to display additional options such as Home or Business address, e-mail addresses etc. In case of name and address, the drop-down arrows will reveal detailed data entry dialogue boxes such as the Check Full Name and the Check Address dialogue boxes. The boxes will automatically appear if you make an error in entering details.

## Categories

By clicking the Categories button at the bottom of the Contacts dialogue box, you can open the Categories dialogue box. *See Fig 22.03.*

To assign a category to a contact, check the **box** next to the category and click **OK**. You can check more that one check box. If you do so, the contact will appear in both the categories lists.

If you want to add new categories in addition to the default ones, click the **Master Category List** button at the bottom of the Categories dialogue box. In the Master Category List dialogue box that opens, type the new category in the Edit box and click **OK**.

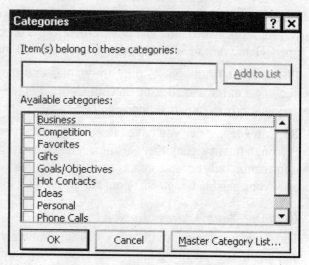

*Fig 22.03 Categories Dialogue Box*

### *Activities*

You can display all activities concerning any selected contact by right clicking on the contact name in the address card (or any other) view and clicking on Open. In the Contact dialogue box, make sure that the Show dialogue box and the Activity tab is selected.

You will see a complete listing of all interactions such as calls, e-mails and letters etc, displayed under a timeline.

# Importing Your Address Book

If you have an e-mail programme such as Outlook Express, you can import the data from its address book into the Outlook Address Book. If you are using some other Personal Information Manager (PIM) such as Schedule+, SideKick or Lotus Organiser, you can also import tasks and calendar information in addition to the names and e-mail addresses.

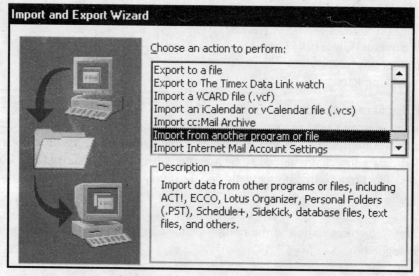

*Fig 22.04 Import and Export Wizard*

Follow these steps:

1.  On the menu bar, click **File** then **Import and Export** in the drop-down menu. The Import and Export Wizard dialogue box appears. *See Fig 22.04.*

2.  Select the **file type** for import, depending on the source programme. If you select Import from another programme or file, you will see the next step, Import a file. *See Fig 22.05.*

3.  Select the **type of data** to be imported. Click **Next**. The next step in importing files will appear.

4.  Specify the **file(s)** to be imported. You can browse the folders and files to choose your target files if required. Click the desired **radio button** under Options to decide whether to overwrite duplicates, allow duplicates or not import duplicate entries. Click **Next** when you finish.

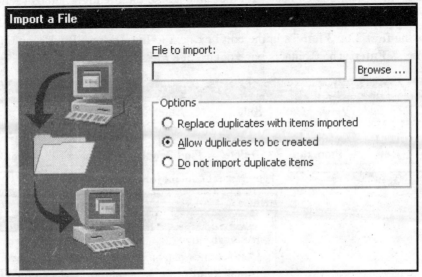

*Fig 22.05 Import a File Dialogue Box*

5.  The next step will depend on the type of the source of data. For instance, if you are importing data from a PIM, then calendar data, address list, task list and notepad data will be imported into their corresponding slots in Outlook. Click **Next** to continue.

6.  If the category of the source data is not recognised by Outlook, you will be required to map the custom fields of the source data into standard Outlook fields. If so, click on the **Map Custom Fields** button on the Import a File dialogue box. The Map Custom Fields dialogue box will open.

7.  In this dialogue box, the source fields will appear in the window to the left under the heading From... while the Outlook fields will be listed in the window on the right under the heading To Microsoft Outlook... You will notice that fields sharing the same name are already mapped for you. You will be required to map the additional fields not already matched by Outlook. Click **OK** when done to continue.

8.  You will be back in the Import a File dialogue box. Click **Finish** to begin the actual data import.

# Maintaining Your Address Book

There are a few operations that you should perform regularly to keep your Address Book current. For instance, you will need to find, edit and delete entries. To organise the information in your Address Book, you will also need to group, sort and filter the entries. We look at these activities one by one.

### Finding Entries

Do one of the following:

- Click on the **Address Book** icon on the Outlook tool bar. The Address Book window opens. In the edit box captioned "Type name or select from list", begin typing the **name** you want. As soon as you type the first few letters, the highlight will jump to the name. If there is more than one contact with the same name, the highlight jumps to the first of the names on your list.

- Type the **first 2 or 3 letters** in the edit box next to the Address Book icon on the tool bar and press **Enter**. The Contacts page opens. *See Fig 22.06.*

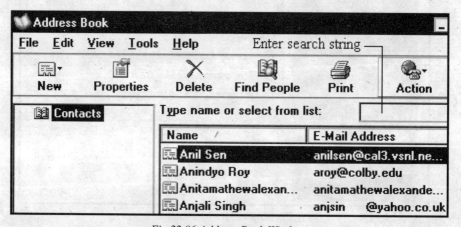

*Fig 22.06 Address Book Window*

- Open Contacts view by clicking on the **Contacts** icon on the Outlook tool bar. In this view, click on the **Find** icon. The Find pane opens. Enter the name in the edit box captioned "Look for:" and check the box captioned "Search all text in the contact". Then click the **Find Now** button. The desired data appears in the pane below. *See Fig 22.07.*

### Editing and Deleting

Having found the entry you want, right click the entry and click Open on the drop-down menu to display the Contacts dialogue box. All data related to the selected contact is displayed. You can now edit or delete individual data or even delete the entire contact.

### Sorting Contacts

You can sort your Address Book by any of the fields. For instance, you can have the entries sorted in ascending order of the last name so that you can look alphabetically. To sort your contact list, proceed as follows:

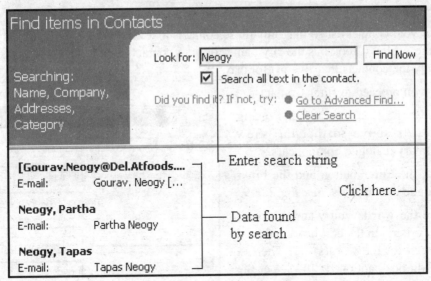

*Fig 22.07 Find Pane and Entries Found*

1. Click the **Contacts** icon on the Outlook tool bar, the contacts list will appear. Click **View** on the Outlook menu bar and click **Current View** ➔ **Customise Current View** in the drop-down menus. The View Summary dialogue box will appear. *See Fig 22.08.*

2. Click **Sort** and the Sort dialogue box will appear.

3. Choose the **field** you want to sort with from the "Sort items by" drop-down list. Select **Ascending** or **Descending** as the sort order by clicking the appropriate radio button and then click **OK**. Click **OK** again to complete the sort and display the contact list after sorting.

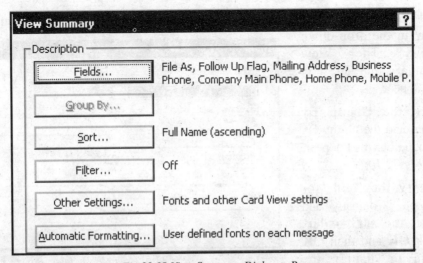

*Fig 22.08 View Summary Dialogue Box*

## Filtering Contacts

You can filter your contact list so that only those contacts that meet your criteria are displayed. For instance, if the Address Book has the city names of your contacts as a field, you can set your filter to display only the contacts that live in Bombay.

Here is how you proceed to filter Contacts:

1. Repeat the first step under Sorting Contacts above so that the View Summary dialogue box appears.

2. Click the **Filter** button and the Filter dialogue box appears. *See Fig 22.09.*

3. Type the **words** you want to use as filter criteria in the edit box captioned "Search for the word(s)…". Then in the edit box captioned "In" **select** the field from the drop-down list.

4. Click **OK** and then **OK** again to display the filtered list of contacts.

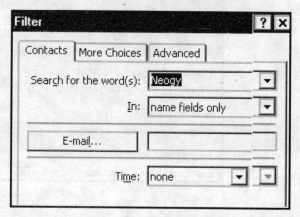

*Fig 22.09 Filter Dialogue Box*

## Grouping Contacts

Grouping contacts is useful for using table views such as the Phone List. For instance, by grouping your contacts by the company name, you can view all the names and phone numbers of the contacts you have in a particular enterprise.

Here is how you can group your contacts:

1. Display the Contacts list and select **View ➔ Current View ➔ Phone List** by clicking the Outlook menu bar followed by the required items in the drop-down menus.

2. Click **View** on the Outlook menu bar and click **Current View ➔ Customise Current View** in the drop-down menus. The View Summary dialogue box will appear.

3. Click the **Group By** button and the Group By dialogue box will appear. *See Fig 22.10.*

4. Specify the **field**, for example, "Company" and select the **sort order**. Click **OK** and then **OK** again to display the grouped contacts.

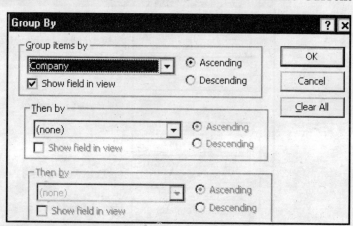

*Fig 22.10 Group by Dialogue Box*

# Using Your Address Book

You can use your Address Book in many ways to get your work better organised. For example, you can:

- Use it with Microsoft Word for mass mailing of letters to your contacts in the Address Book.

- Schedule a meeting with some of your contacts or assign tasks to them.

- Dial a phone number of a contact.

- Create an e-mail message or a fax.

- Print a telephone or address list of your contacts.

Mass mailing or mail merging is discussed in Chapter 11, *Using Word Efficiently*. The other tasks are either discussed later in this chapter, or in Chapter 23, *Using Outlook's Features*, that follows.

## *Dial a Contact*

If your modem has a regular telephone attached on the same telephone line, you can automatically dial one of the contact numbers and then have a phone conversation.

Here is how:

1. Switch to Contacts and to the **Address Cards** view. Select the contact you wish to telephone. Right click the selected **address card** and the drop-down menu appears.

2. Click the **Call Contact** option and the **New Call** dialogue box appears. *See Fig 22.11.*

3. Use the drop-down arrow ▾ to the right of the edit box for the number and select the **number** (such as business, home etc) you wish to dial.

4. Click the **Start Call** button to initiate the call. If you want Outlook to keep an automatic record of the call, **check** the box next to the caption "Create new journal entry when starting new call".

5. Click the **End Call** button when you finish.

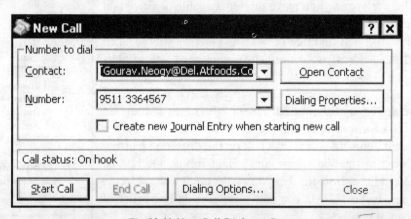

*Fig 22.11 New Call Dialogue Box*

### *Print Telephone or Address List*

If you wish to send a copy of the telephone numbers or addresses of your contacts, you can print the list by following these steps:

1. Make sure that your printer is connected and powered on. Insert printing paper in the printer.

2. Click **File** on the menu bar and click **Print Setup** on the drop-down menu. Setup options for the matter to be printed will appear. For example, for a phone list, you may choose between Table or memo styles.

3. Click **Print** on the same drop-down menu to begin printing. *See Fig 22.12.*

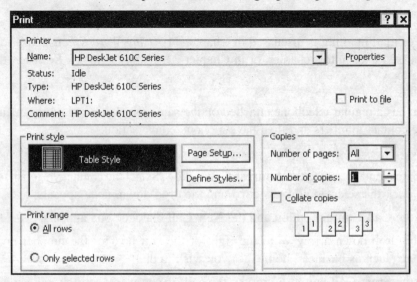

*Fig 22.12 Print Dialogue Box*

## Using Inbox

You can communicate via e-mail or fax from the Inbox of Outlook. You will require a telephone line and a modem capable of voice and fax communication to take full advantage of Outlook's communication capabilities. You will find that messaging is really simple since the Inbox and the Address Books are fully integrated within Outlook.

*Fig 22.13 Large Icon and Drop-down Menu*

 **NOTE** The Inbox also contains a Sent Messages folder, an Outbox for messages waiting to be sent and a folder for deleted items. In any view, click on the drop-down arrow ▾ next to the View icon and select Inbox, Outbox or Deleted Items from the drop-down list to view the selected folder. In Fig 22.13, you can see the drop-down list of personal contacts.

You will use the Inbox for actions such as:

- Send e-mail or fax.
- Read and reply to e-mails.
- Manage your e-mail.

Before you begin using the Inbox, it is necessary to understand the Inbox window. We do so in the next section.

## The Inbox Window

As we have already seen, the Inbox contains more than one folder. Within Inbox, you also have the Outbox folder for messages waiting to be sent, the Drafts folder for incomplete messages, the Sent Items folder for messages already sent and the Deleted Items folder for where deleted messages are temporarily stored so that you may retrieve one of them if required.

See the note in the previous section that explains how to display the folders we have discussed. In addition to displaying different folders, you can also display the contents of any open folder in different ways. To change the default view of an open folder, click on View on the menu bar and then click **Current View ➜ Customise Current View** in the drop-down menus that will appear. You can group, sort or filter the messages to suit your needs.

From Current View in the pop-up menu, you can also select a number of options such as Messages, which will display only the message headers, Messages with AutoPreview, which will also display the first three lines of the messages or Last Seven Days, which displays messages received in the last seven days and so on. *See Fig 22.14.*

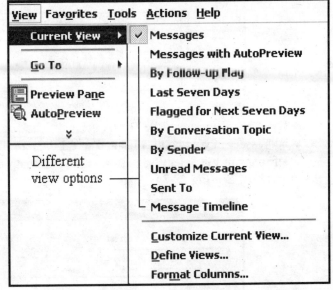

*Fig 22.14 Different View Options on Drop-down Menu*

## Messaging

We will now examine sending, responding, receiving and organising messages in Outlook. We can create both e-mail and fax messages in Outlook and the procedures are very similar. Therefore, we will deal with both forms of messaging at the same time. We assume, of course, that you have a telephone line, an Internet connection and a fax, voice and data modem installed and operational.

# Sending Messages

If you have a stand-alone computer, you can send e-mails and fax using Outlook. If you are part of a network, you can send internal Microsoft Mail messages in addition to e-mails and fax. To send a message, proceed as follows:

1. Click the **main icon** in whatever view you may be and click **Inbox** in the drop-down menu. The Inbox folder opens.

2. Click the **New Mail Message** button. The Message dialogue box appears. *See Fig 22.15.* All the boxes such as To, Cc, Subject and the body of the message will be blank. On the other hand, if you have highlighted a message in your Inbox and then clicked the Reply button, the Message dialogue box will already have the To box filled with the e-mail address and the body will contain the e-mail message you have selected in the Inbox.

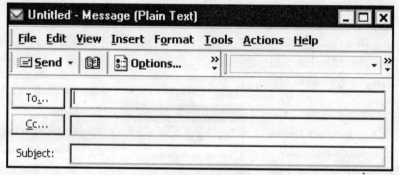

*Fig 22.15 Message Dialogue Box*

3. If it is a new message (the To box is blank) click on the **To** button to open your list of e-mail addressees in your contact list and select the **name** you want from the drop-down list in the left pane of the Select Names dialogue box that opens. You can also type the name in the edit box. *See Fig 22.16.*

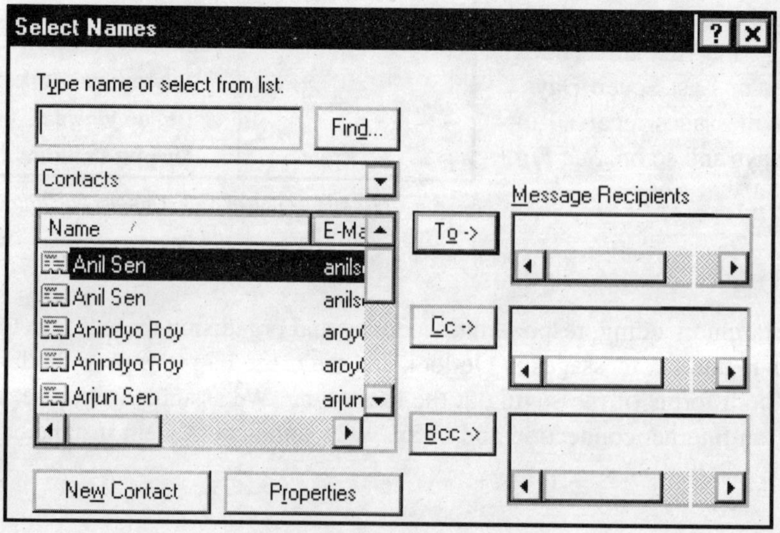

*Fig 22.16 Select Names Dialogue Box*

4.  Click on the **To>** button on this form to transfer the selected name to the right pane under "Message recipients". Click **OK** to continue. You are returned to the Message dialogue box.

5.  Enter a **subject** in its box and type the text of the message in the large edit box in the bottom part of the dialogue box.

6.  Click the **Options** button to open the Message Options dialogue box shown in Fig 22.17. Here you can set the Message, Security, Delivery and Tracking options of your message. You decide the delivery mode of the message in this dialogue box by clicking on the drop-down arrow ▼ in the box captioned "Send message using…". You can either choose the fax or the e-mail option at this stage.

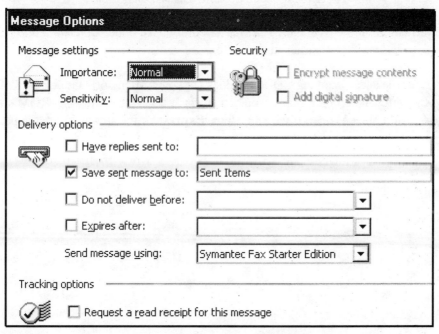

*Fig 22.17 Message Options Dialogue Box*

7.  Click the **Close** button after you have set desired options to return back to the Message dialogue box.

8.  Click the **Send** button to start message delivery. If you have chosen fax, the Symantec Fax Starter Edition dialogue box will open requesting you to confirm the fax number shown as default. *See Fig 22.18.* **Modify** or **Accept** the default number and click the **Send** button to start despatch of your message.

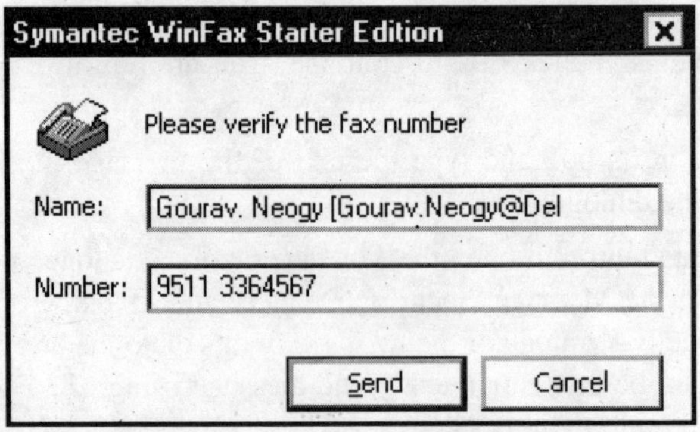

**Symantec WinFax Starter Edition**   ☒

Please verify the fax number

Name: | Gourav. Neogy [Gourav.Neogy@Del

Number: | 9511 3364567

Send | Cancel

*Fig 22.18 Symantec Fax Starter Edition Dialogue Box*

For more information on the Symantec Fax Starter edition, see under *Communications* in Chapter 21, *Introducing Outlook 2000*, earlier in this book.

**CD-ROM**  The accompanying CD-ROM does not cover Microsoft Outlook 2000. For general information on e-mails, you can select **Internet** from the CD-ROM's main menu and click **Working with Outlook Express** in the sub-menu that appears.

# 23. Using Outlook's Features

## In this chapter:

☞ You are introduced to the set of programmes that make Outlook such a powerful Personal Information Manager, helping to schedule and organise your daily tasks.

☞ You learn how to use the Calendar, which is central to Outlook's powerful scheduling and reminding features. You are shown how to use the Calendar window and schedule appointments, meetings and events.

☞ You are shown how to use the Task window, create tasks and edit tasks, setting start and end dates and setting reminders.

☞ You learn how to use the Journal to keep track of your daily activities. You are shown how to open, create and edit journal entries.

☞ You are introduced to Notes, the electronic equivalent of sticky notes that you can use to jot down information and post reminders to yourself.

# Using Outlook's Features

As we have already seen, Outlook is a combination of programmes and utilities designed to help you organise your tasks, schedules, communications and to keep track of all your activities in a journal of events.

In this chapter, we familiarise ourselves with the features that make Outlook such a powerful Personal Information Manager (PIM). We begin with the Calendar in Outlook.

## Using Calendar

In the last chapter, we have looked at the communication capabilities of Outlook using e-mail and fax. We have also seen how Outlook can be used to manage your business and personal contacts. In this chapter, we will study additional capabilities of Outlook that make the programme such a powerful PIM.

Outlook can be made a pivot point around which you can organise your daily business and personal activities. If you work by yourself, you can maintain your appointment book and track your tasks using Outlook. If you are a member of a team, Outlook will help you schedule meetings with others in your team, assign tasks and track the progress of these tasks. With the journal, you can maintain a timeline that records the files you handle, the calls you make and the messages you send and receive.

To track your tasks and to plan your appointments, you use Outlook's Calendar. See Fig 23.01 for a view of the Calendar window showing an hourly appointment list.

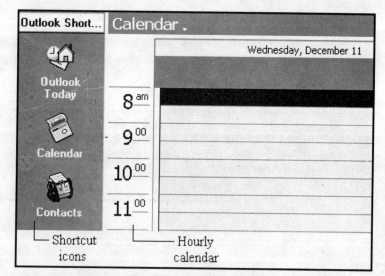

### Scheduling with Calendar

The Calendar is the basic scheduling tool you use as an individual or as a member of a workgroup. In Calendar, you carry out three basic types of activities: Appointments, Meetings and Events.

*Fig 23.01 View of Calendar*

### Appointments

Appointments are activities where you do not invite other people or reserve resources like a meeting room. You can set reminders for your appointments. You can also specify whether you will be shown as busy, free, tentative, or out of office on your calendar when others view your appointments. You can schedule recurring appointments. Clicking an appointment selects it, and double clicking the left move handle opens it. You can view your appointments by day, week, or month.

When you select start and end times for an appointment, the Autodate function of Calendar will insert the correct date even if you enter text such as "next Tuesday" or "noon" instead of typing an exact date or time.

If you are part of a network along with other colleagues, other users can give you permission to schedule or make changes to appointments in their Calendars. You can also make appointments private so that others cannot view the details.

## Meetings

A meeting is an appointment for which you invite people or reserve resources. You can create and send meeting requests and reserve resources for face-to-face meetings or for online meetings. To create an online meeting, such as a NetMeeting, select the This is an online meeting check box on the Appointment tab of your meeting request. When you create a meeting, you identify the people to invite and the resources to reserve, and you pick a meeting time. Responses to your meeting request from your networked colleagues will appear in your Inbox. You can also add people to an existing meeting or reschedule a meeting.

## Events

An event is an activity that lasts 24 hours or longer. Examples of an event include a trade fair, the Olympics, a vacation, or a seminar. An annual event, such as a birthday or anniversary, occurs yearly on a specific date, while a standard event occurs once and can last for one day or several days. Events and annual events appear in banners in your calendar. While an all-day appointment will show your time as busy, an event or annual event will show your time as free.

## *Calendar Window*

We need to understand the elements of a Calendar window to schedule appointments, meetings and events. Make the Calendar window appear by clicking on the Calendar icon on the Outlook shortcut bar. By default, the Calendar window will show the Day view. However, you can modify the display so that the Calendar window opens in the Calendar view or Table view. The Table view is good for displaying tasks or schedules since the items appear arranged neatly in a table.

## *Calendar Views*

Though the default is the Day View, you can show the Work Week View with five days, the Week View with seven days and the Month View which is the same as a month on a wall calendar. The Day or Week View gives you space to display hourly appointments. The Month View is best for an overview of the entire month rather than details. The Day or Week View has space to display the Task Pad as well. *See Fig 23.02.*

You can navigate from day to day in the Month View by clicking on the desired day's rectangle. Then, by clicking the Day View, the full details of that day are revealed.

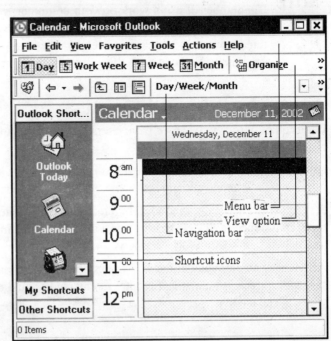

*Fig 23.02 Calendar Day View*

## *Table Views*

Active appointments are best displayed in Table View. Table Views are also used to display Events, Annual Events, Recurring Appointments and Appointments by Category. To switch to the Active Appointments View, proceed as follows:

1. Click **View** on the menu bar. The drop-down menu appears.
2. Click **Current View** ➔ **Activate Appointments** to display its Table View. *See Fig 23.03.*

| Calendar ▾ | | | | | | |
|---|---|---|---|---|---|---|
| 🗋 | 📎 | Subject | Location | Start △ | End | Recurrence Pattern |
| ⊟ Recurrence : (none) (1 item) | | | | | | |
| | 🕐 | Annual Sales Mee... | Main Co... | Thu 12/12/20... | Thu 12/12/20... | |
| | | └── Sample appointment | | | | |
| | | | | | | |
| | | | | | | |
| | | | | | | |
| | | | | | | |

*Fig 23.03 Appointments in Table View*

You can scroll through the list of your appointments using the vertical scroll bar on the right of the window. Using the View Summary dialogue box, you can sort, filter or group the appointments as you prefer.

**NOTE** If a number of users work on your computer, you can create separate Calendars for each user showing the user's own appointments. If you are the only user, you can create separate business and personal Calendars that show your business and personal appointments separately. You can save the calendars in separate folders.

# Appointments and Events

Let us quickly review what we have learned about schedules, appointments and events at the beginning of this chapter.

An appointment is an activity that you schedule in your Calendar that does not involve other people or resources. A recurring appointment occurs on a regular basis.

A meeting is also an appointment. In a meeting, you invite people over or reserve resources such as time, conference rooms etc that you will need for a meeting. If your group happens to be connected to a network or has Internet access, you can send meeting requests via e-mails from Outlook.

An event is an activity that lasts 24 hours or more. An annual event, such as a birthday or anniversary, occurs yearly on a specific date. Events and annual events do not appear as blocks of time in your Calendar view.

# Schedule a Meeting

To schedule a meeting using Outlook, proceed as follows:

1. Click the **Calendar** icon on your Outlook tool bar. The Calendar View appears, usually in the Day View format. If the meeting is for a later day, click the appropriate **Month** button to display the month you need.

2. On the menu bar, click **Actions**, then click **Plan a Meeting** in the drop-down menu. The Plan a Meeting dialogue box appears. *See Fig 23.04.*

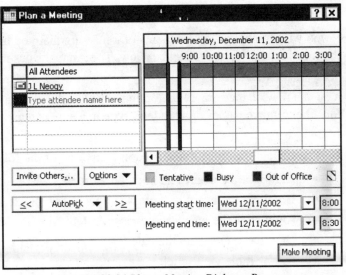

*Fig 23.04 Plan a Meeting Dialogue Box*

3. Invite attendees by typing in **names** in the right hand box, or click the **AutoPick** button and choose an option from the drop-down list.

4. Select the **Start** and **End** times in the boxes below the left pane. The left pane time chart will reflect your timings.

5. Click **Make Meeting**. The untitled Meeting dialogue box opens. *See Fig 23.05.*

6. In the Subject box, type a **description** of the meeting such as "Annual Sales Conference".

7. Schedule a meeting room by entering its **location** in the Location box, such as "Main Conference Room".

8. Select other **options** you want such as typing a brief note to yourself in the blank edit box near the bottom of

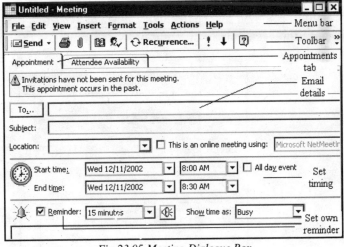

*Fig 23.05 Meeting Dialogue Box*

the dialogue box. If you wish to add to the list of participants, click the **To...** button and select the **names** from the drop-down list. You can also set a **reminder** to yourself including an audible alarm.

9. Select the way the meeting will appear to others by choosing **options** from the drop-down box captioned "Show time as".

10. Click **Send** to initiate dispatch of the e-mails to the participants of the meeting.

**NOTE** If you return to the Month view on your Calendar, you will see that the meeting is now displayed in the appropriate Date box.

You can attach an agenda for the meeting or attach minutes of a previous meeting to your e-mails by attaching an appropriate file to your meeting request before e-mailing the meeting request.

## Edit Events

If you wish to change any elements of a meeting that you have already scheduled, double click on the meeting entry in the Calendar view. The Annual sales meeting dialogue box (that you had just filled up) will open.

You can now change any of the options displayed. For example, you can click on the To... button to add or remove names of attendees, type in a new venue or change the timing of the meeting. *See Fig 23.05.*

You can delete the entire event by doing any one of the following:

- Highlight the **event** and click on **Edit → Delete**.
- Highlight the **event** and press the keyboard **Delete key**.
- Right click the **event** and choose **Delete** from the **shortcut menu** that appears.
- Drag the **event** from the calendar to the **Deleted Items icon** on the Outlook shortcut bar.
- In any Table view, click the **event's row** and then press the Keyboard's **Delete key**.

## Change Timings

The most common change that will happen to a meeting or any event is a change in timing. You can change timings easily in different ways depending on the view. For example:

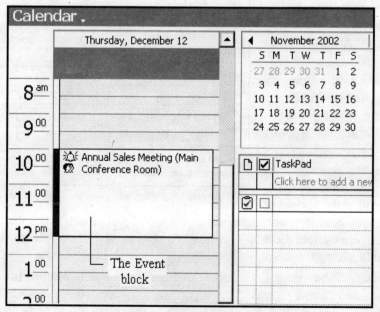

*Fig 23.06 Event Block in Day View*

- In the Day view, click the left blue border of the block surrounding the event and drag the event up or done to change its start date. To change the start time, click on the top blue border and drag it up or down. Do the same with the bottom blue border to alter the finishing time of the event.

- In the Week or Month view, drag the event to the new day. Double click the event to open its dialogue box for more detailed modifications.

## Recurring Appointments

If you have meetings or appointments that occur regularly, for example, a monthly staff meeting or a meeting with the parents and teachers at a school, you can easily schedule such recurring meetings in Outlook. Here is how to proceed:

1. Click the **Calendar** icon on the Outlook tool bar. The Calendar view opens.
2. On the Actions menu, click **Plan a meeting**. Alternatively, you can open an existing meeting schedule for editing.
3. Invite **attendees** and book **resources**. See the following section for the invitation procedure.
4. Click **AutoPick**, and then click an **option** from the drop-down list.
5. Click the **Make Meeting** button. The Meeting dialogue box appears.
6. In the Subject box, type a **description** for the meeting.
7. If you did not schedule a room, enter the **location** in the Location box.
8. Select other **options** you want.
9. On the Actions menu of the Meeting dialogue box, click **Recurrence** in the drop-down list. The Appointment recurrence dialogue box appears. *See Fig 23.07.*
10. Select the recurrence pattern and range of recurrence **options** you want.
11. Click **OK**, and the Recurring Meeting dialogue box appears. In this dialogue box, click **Send**.

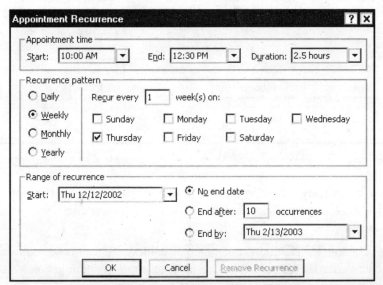

*Fig 23.07 Appointment Recurrence Dialogue Box*

# Invite Attendees and Resources

For a meeting, you need to select the attendees and any resource person that may be necessary. To invite attendees and resource persons to a meeting, proceed as follows:

1. Click the **Calendar** icon on the Outlook tool bar. The Calendar view opens.

2. On the Actions menu, click **Plan a Meeting**. The Plan a Meeting dialogue box opens.

3. Click the **Invite Others** button. The Select Attendees and Resources dialogue box opens. *See Fig 23.08.*

4. In the Type name or select from list box, enter the **name** of the person or resource you want at the meeting.

5. For each name entered, click the **Required**, **Optional** or **Resources** buttons to classify the persons. In the Plan a Meeting dialogue box, the Required and Optional attendees appear in the To box on the Appointment tab and the Resources appear in the Location box.

6. Click **OK**, and then use the scroll bars to view the free/busy time for invitees.

7. Click a **time** when all invitees are available. You can use **AutoPick** to find the next available free time for all invitees.

8. Click **Make Meeting**.

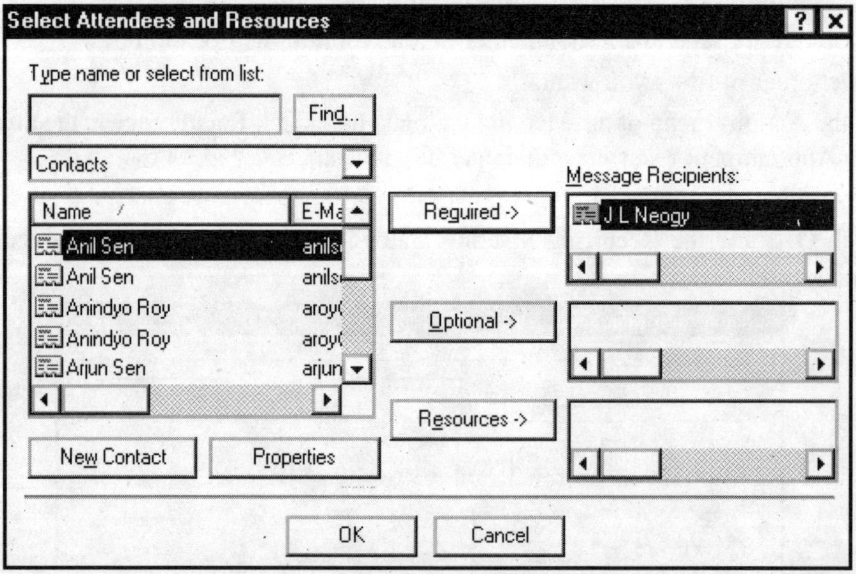

*Fig 23.08 Attendees and Resources Dialogue Box*

**TIP** You can quickly schedule a meeting with someone in your Contacts list. In Contacts, click the Contact, click the Actions menu, and then click New Meeting Request to Contact.

To schedule physical resources such as conference rooms or audio-visual equipment, create a user ID for each resource on your e-mail system just as you would for a real person. You can then schedule them for your meeting just like a person.

# Requesting a Meeting

We have seen in the previous section how to make an appointment or schedule a meeting using Outlook. Requesting a meeting is very similar. The important difference is that all the attendees and resource persons you need must be free at the same time. This is easy if all the attendees and resource persons are networked together and using Outlook for scheduling their own meetings and appointments.

**NOTE** If other attendees are not networked with you, or are not using Outlook, you will not be able to see their appointment calendars while online. In such a case, you will have to e-mail or fax requests and await their replies before the meeting can be finally scheduled.

If you do have access to the Outlook calendars of the others, proceed as follows:

1. Proceed as before to Plan a Meeting and then click **Make a meeting**. The Meeting dialogue box will open.

2. Click the **Attendee Availability** tab. The engagements of the invitees will be displayed as bar charts in Calendar view. *See Fig 23.09.*

3. Click the **AutoPick** button for Outlook to find a free time for all attendees.

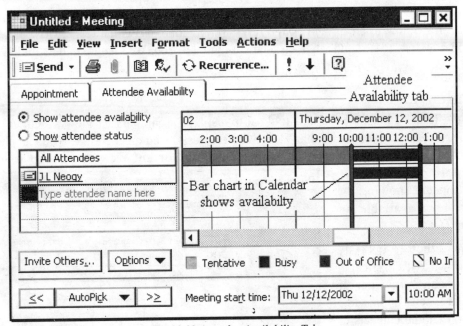

*Fig 23.09 Attendee Availability Tab*

# Tracking Responses

The nature of responses to your invitation to a meeting will depend on whether the invitee or resource person is also an Outlook user or not. We examine both situations.

## *Outlook Users*

If, as an invitee, you are an Outlook user connected to a network, you will receive both an e-mail and an item in your calendar indicating the tentative date of the meeting or appointment.

To accept or decline the appointment, open the e-mail message and click on the **Accept** or **Decline** button. You can add an **optional message** for the meeting organiser and then click on the **Send** button. The message will go to the meeting organiser's Inbox and your status (Accept or decline) will be automatically recorded in the organiser's calendar.

## *Non-Outlook Users*

If you send meeting invitations to non-Outlook users via e-mail, fax or by telephone, you will probably receive a reply in the same way. In this case, however, your calendar will not be automatically updated. After receiving the message, you will have to update your calendar manually.

# Using Tasks

Your business and personal life involves carrying out many tasks. Outlook is well equipped to list tasks, to prioritise them, allot them to other members of your team and to keep track of the progress of tasks.

In order to use Outlook's tasking capabilities, you have to understand the Task window first. You should also learn how to create and assign tasks. If someone else is the leader of your team, you must also know how to respond when tasks are assigned to you. We take up understanding tasks in this section.

## The Task Window

Click on the **Tasks** icon on the Outlook tool bar to display the Simple List View which will open by default. *See Fig 23.10*. This is a Table View, with one task listed on each line. You can change the view by clicking **View** on the menu bar and then clicking **Current View** on the drop-down list. In turn, another drop-down window appears showing the different views available for displaying tasks.

You can select a task by scrolling down to it and clicking on it. You can sort, filter or group tasks exactly in the same way as you handle contacts or appointments. To separate tasks belonging to a particular project, or to separate business and personal tasks, you can put each category of tasks in separate task folders.

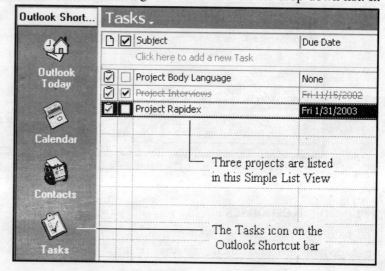

*Fig 23.10 Simple List View of Tasks*

# Create a Task

To create a new task in your Outlook Tasks list, proceed as follows:

1.  Open the Task window by any one of the following methods:

    *   In any Task table view, click **Actions** on the menu bar and then select **New Task** from the drop-down menu.

    *   Double click next to the **caption** "Click here to add a new task" on the top line of the Simple List View.

    *   Double click any **blank row** in the Simple List View.

    The Task dialogue box opens. *See Fig 23.11.*

2.  Fill in the **Subject**, **Due date**, **Start date**, **Priority** and **% Complete** fields as appropriate.

3.  Check the **Reminder** check box if you want to be reminded about the task. Add a **date** and **time** for the reminder.

4.  Enter **explanatory notes** for the task if desired by typing in the notes in the edit box. You can **categorise** the task or assign the task to a member of your team by clicking the appropriate button and filling in the dialogue box that appears.

5.  Click the **Save** and **Close** button when done. The task will now appear in your Task list.

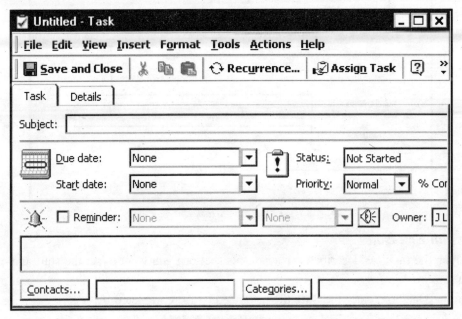

*Fig 23.11 Task Dialogue Box*

## *The Details Tab*

The Details Tab in the Task dialogue box lets you enter details such as Date completed, Billing information etc, after the task has been completed. In the Task dialogue box, click on the Details Tab to display this dialogue box. *See Fig 23.12.*

## Edit Tasks

Once you have tasks on your Task list, you can edit and modify these tasks following the steps given below.

### Open a Task

1. Click the **Tasks** or the **Calendar** icon on the Outlook tool bar.
2. Find the task in the Task list, and then double click the **Task** icon.

### Set Reminders

1. On the Tools menu, click **Options**, click the **Other** tab, and then click **Advanced Options**.
2. Click **Advanced Tasks**.
3. To have a reminder automatically turned on for new tasks, select the **Set reminders on tasks with due dates** check box.

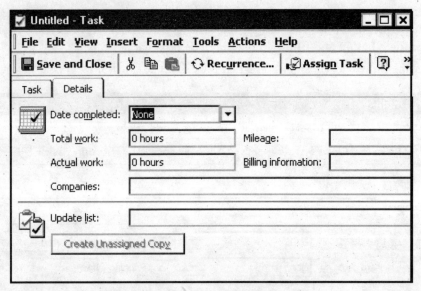

*Fig 23.12 Details Tab on Task Dialogue Box*

### Set Start and End Dates

1. Open the **task** (as described earlier in this section) you want to set the start and end dates for.
2. In the Due box, enter the **date** the task needs to be completed by.
3. In the Start box, enter a **date** to start work on the task.

**NOTE** To reset the start date without changing the due date, enter **None** in the Start date box, press **Enter** ↵ and then type the new **start** date.

Instead of typing a date, you can type a brief **description** such as "next Monday" or "one month from today".

## *Delete a Task*

1. In the Task list, select the **tasks** you want to delete.
2. Right click on your **selection** to display the drop-down menu.
3. Click **Delete**.

**NOTE**

Deleting a task that you have assigned to someone else removes it only from your Task list. The task remains in the list of the person who accepted it. You will no longer receive status reports for an assigned task; the assignee will have to keep you informed of its progress. See more on assigning tasks in the section below.

## *Assigning Tasks*

After you have created a set of tasks, you may wish to assign some or all of them to other members of your group. To assign a task, proceed as follows:

1. To create a new task, on the File menu point to **New**, and click **Task Request**. To assign an existing task, in the Task list, open the **task** you want to assign, and click **Assign Task**.
2. In the To box, enter the **name** of the person you want to assign the task to. To select the name from a list, click the **To** button. *See Fig 23.13.*
3. For a new task, in the Subject box, type a **task name**. (In an existing task, the Subject box is already filled in.)
4. Select the **due date** and **status options** you want.
5. Select or clear the **"Keep an updated copy of this task on my task list"** check box and the **"Send me a status report when this task is complete"** check box.
6. If you want the task to repeat, click the **Actions** menu, click **Recurrence**, select the **options** you want, and then click **OK**. For Help on an option, click the question mark (?) and then click the **option**.

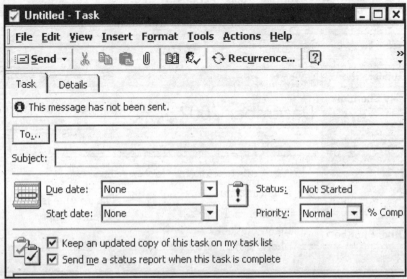

*Fig 23.13 Assign Task Dialogue Box*

7. In the body of the task, type **instructions** or **information** about the task.

8. Click **Send**.

If the assignee is an Outlook user and is connected to your network, his or her Outlook task list will display the assigned task.

If the assignee is a non-Outlook user, he or she will receive an e-mail or fax (as decided by you) informing him or her of the task assignment.

If you are the assignee, you can send a status report on the task(s) assigned to you by opening the task and clicking **Task** ➔ **Send Status Report** or by clicking the Status report button.

# Using Journal

You can use the Journal in Outlook if you wish to keep track of your daily activities against a time scale or timeline. In addition to logging your activities in Outlook, you can set up Journal to track all the files you open in the other Microsoft Office components such as Word, Excel, Access, PowerPoint etc. Even if you do not open Outlook, the Journal will keep track of the duration for which other Office application files were open. The entries are grouped by application as well as your e-mail sessions. Since you can find or filter the journal entries in the same way as tasks and appointments, Journal gives you a very powerful tool to keep track of all that you do. Records like these are very useful if you are a consultant and want to bill customers based on the time you spend working on each project.

As with other Outlook components, you can switch between the Timeline View and other Table views in Journal such as Entry List, Last Seven Days, Phone Calls etc. You can also group, filter and sort journal entries as required. See Fig 23.14 for a Timeline View of Journal.

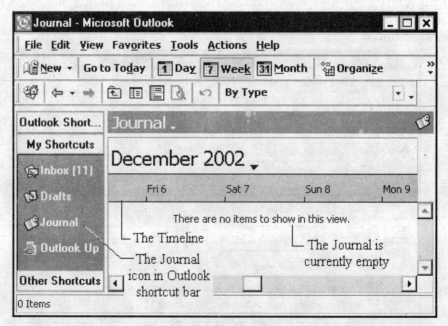

*Fig 23.14 Timeline View of Journal*

**TRAP** Before you can use Journal, you have to activate it. Since Journal keeps a log of not just your Outlook activities but of all that you do with other Microsoft Office programmes, you should be certain that you want to leave such detailed records in your computer.

## Activating Journal

To automatically record items for your contacts in Journal, do the following:

1. On the Tools menu, click **Options**.
2. On the Preferences tab, click **Journal Options**. The Journal Options dialogue box opens. *See Fig 23.15.*
3. In the "Automatically record these items" box, select the **check boxes** for the items you want automatically recorded in Journal.
4. In the "For these contacts" box, select the **check boxes** for the contacts you want the items automatically recorded for.

To turn off automatic recording of journal entries for a contact, open the Journal Options dialogue box as before and in the "For these contacts box", clear the check box next to the contact you want to stop automatic recording for.

# How to Use Journal

### *Open a Journal Entry*

To open a Journal entry, proceed as follows:

1. Click the **Journal** icon on the Outlook shortcut bar.
2. Right click the journal **entry** and then click **Open Journal Entry** or **Open Item Referred To** on the shortcut menu.

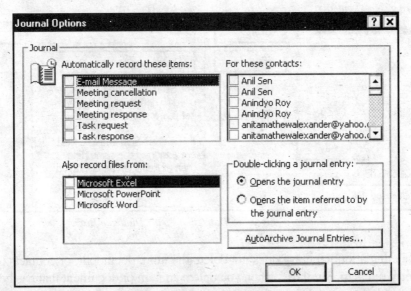

*Fig 23.15 Journal Options Dialogue Box*

To specify whether the journal entry or the item is opened when you double click journal entries, click the **Tools** menu, click **Options**, and then click the **Preferences** tab. Click **Journal Options**, and then click **Opens the journal entry** or **Opens the item referred to by the journal entry** to set your preference.

### Change the Fields Used to Display Items

When you view items and documents on a timeline, each item and document is shown at the specific time it was created, saved, sent, received, opened, or modified, according to which of these fields are used to display each item. You can change the fields used to display items on a timeline. As a result, both the location and the duration of the items may change on the timeline. To do so, proceed as follows:

1. On the View menu, point to **Current View**, and then click **Customise Current View**. The View Summary dialogue box opens.
2. Click **Fields**. The Date/Time Fields dialogue box opens. *See Fig 23.16.*
3. In the "Select available fields from" box, click the **field set** you want.
4. In the "Available date/time fields" box, click the **field** that contains the time you want to use for the item start date, and then click **Start**.
5. In the "Available date/time fields" box, click the **field** that contains the time you want to use for the **item end date**, and then click **End**.

### Delete a Journal Entry

To delete a journal entry you no longer need, proceed as follows:

1. In Journal, select the **journal entry** as described in "Open a Journal Entry" above.
2. In the Edit menu, click **Delete**.

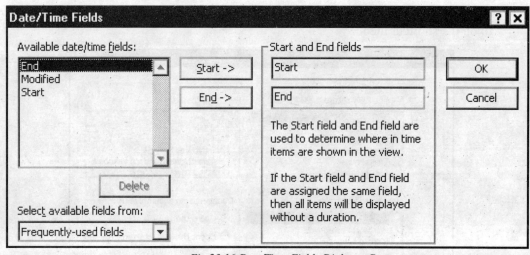

*Fig 23.16 Date/Time Fields Dialogue Box*

**NOTE**

Deleting a journal entry does not delete the item, document, or contacts that the journal entry refers to. Similarly, when you delete an item or document that has been recorded in Journal, the journal entry for that item or document is not deleted.

# Using Notes

Notes are the electronic equivalent of sticky notes that you may stick to a document or on your monitor's frame to remind you of something important. You can use notes to jot down questions, ideas, reminders, and anything you would write on note paper. Notes are also useful for storing bits of information you may need later, such as directions or text you want to reuse in other items or documents.

You can leave notes open on the screen while you work. When you change a note, the changes are saved automatically.

## Create a Note

To create a new note, proceed as follows:

1. On the File menu, point to **New**, and then click **Note**. A new note (usually in its default yellow colour) appears on the screen.

2. Type the **text** of the note.

3. To close the note, click the **note icon** in the upper-left corner of the Note window, and then click **Close**.

## Open a Note

To open an existing note, proceed as follows:

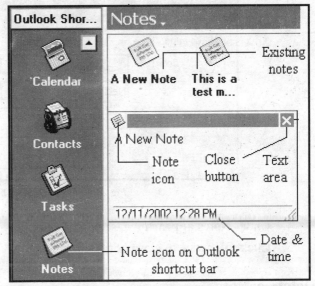

*Fig 23.17 A New Note*

1. Click the **Notes icon** on the Outlook shortcut bar. Small icons of your existing notes will appear in the right-hand pane. *See Fig 23.17.*

2. Select the note you want to open by clicking on its **icon**.

3. On the File menu, point to **Open**, and then click **Selected Items** in the pop-up menu.

## Change the Colour of a Note

All notes are coloured yellow by default. However, you may wish to distinguish some urgent notes by changing their colour. To do so, proceed as follows:

1. Open a **note** as described in the previous section.

2. At the top of the note, click the **note icon**. A pop-up menu appears.

3. Point to **Colour**, and the colour pop-up menu appears.

4. Click the **colour** you want.

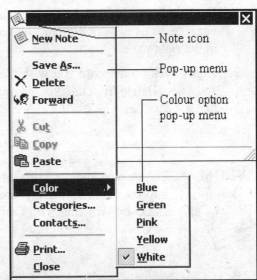

*Fig 23.18 Colour Option*

# Change Format Options for New Notes

You may wish to distinguish your new notes from old ones that were created some time ago. One way to do so is to change the format options for the new notes. Follow these steps:

1. On the Tools menu, click **Options**. The Options dialogue box appears.
2. Click the **Preferences tab** if this tab is not already open.
3. Click **Note Options**. The Notes Options dialogue box opens. *See Fig 23.19.*

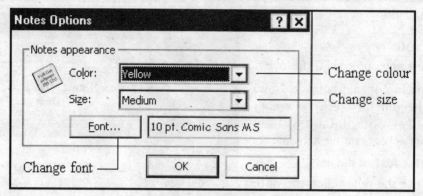

*Fig 23.19 Notes Option Dialogue Box*

4. Under **Notes appearance**, select the **options** you want, such as **colour**, **size** and **font**.
5. Click **OK** twice to close both dialogue boxes.

# Delete a Note

To delete a note you no longer need, proceed as follows:

1. Click the **Notes icon** on the Outlook shortcut bar. The icons of your current notes appear in the right pane.
2. **Right click** on the **note** you wish to delete and select **Delete** from the drop-down menu that appears. *See Fig 23.20.*

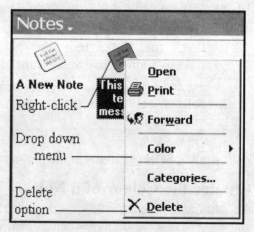

*Fig 23.20 Note Delete Option*

**CD-ROM** The accompanying CD-ROM does not cover Microsoft Outlook 2000. For general information on e-mails, you can select **Internet** from the CD-ROM's main menu and click **Working with Outlook Express** in the sub-menu that appears.

# 24. Utilising Windows Accessories

## In this chapter:

☞ You are introduced to the four most popular Windows accessories that are already Installed on your computer along with your Windows operating system.

☞ In your study of Windows accessories, you are shown how to use Notepad and WordPad for editing and how to use the two versions of the Calculator (standard and scientific) in your computer.

☞ You also learn how to use Paint for a variety of drawing and editing tasks.

# Windows Accessories

Microsoft Windows comes with a bundled set of utility programmes that are of great help to a computer user. Of these, the first two, Notepad and WordPad, are simple word processing programmes. The third programme, the Calculator, comes with two built-in versions, Standard and Scientific. With their help, you can carry out all the calculations you will need without having to pull out your pocket calculator. The last utility, Paint, is a quite sophisticated drawing and editing programme that you can use to create new drawings, paintings or edit drawings or photographs that you have scanned and loaded in your computer.

All four utilities can be found in the Accessories sub-directory of your Windows programme. For instance, to launch Notepad, you can do the following:

1. Click **Start** ➔ **Programmes** ➔ **Accessories** to display the pop-up menu that shows the Windows Accessories loaded in your computer. *See Fig 24.01.*

2. Click **Notepad**, the Notepad window opens on your desktop.

By substituting WordPad, Calculator or Paint in step 2 above, you can launch the other three utility programmes.

We take a closer look at each of these utilities in the following sections, beginning with Notepad.

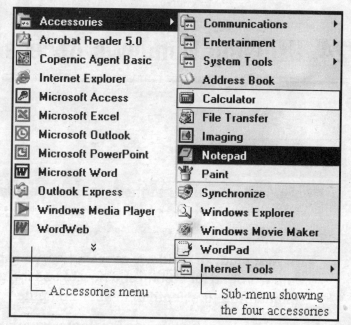

Fig 24.01 Accessories Menu and Sub-menu

# Notepad

You can use Notepad to create or edit text files that do not require formatting and are smaller than 64K (kilobytes). Notepad opens and saves text in ASCII (text-only) format. To create or edit files that require formatting or are larger than 64K, it is better to use the other text processing utility, WordPad, also supplied with Windows.

You can start Notepad as follows:

Click **Start** ➔ **Programmes** ➔ **Accessories** ➔ **Notepad**

The Notepad window appears. See Fig 24.02 for a view of the Notepad window. You will notice that the window has a title (usually the file name), menu bar, work space for typing and edition text as well as horizontal and vertical scroll bars and the standard Windows command buttons at the top right-hand corner that include minimise, maximise and close.

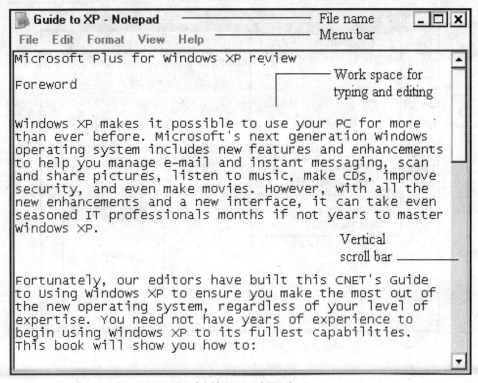

*Fig 24.02 Notepad Window*

## Editing with Notepad

Although simple, Notepad does have some useful editing capabilities. You will be able to master them quite easily. Here are some of the capabilities that you will wish to learn.

You would have noticed in Fig 24.02 that Notepad's menu bar has the following menu items: File, Edit, Search and Help. By clicking on any one of them, you can make the associated drop-down menu appear, which has additional options. For instance, in Fig 24.03, you can see the drop-down menu associated with the Edit menu item.

**TIP**

To edit text, you should first select the text in the Notepad window and then, with the pointer inside the selection, right click your mouse to display a context sensitive pop-up menu. The pop-up menu has many editing options such as Undo, Cut, Copy, Paste, Delete and Select All. You can select the appropriate item to edit your text. See the context menu at the bottom right of Fig 24.03. In addition, specific editing tasks are discussed.

### *Cut, Copy, Paste, or Delete Text*
- To cut text, select the text, click the **Edit** menu, and then click **Cut** in the drop-down menu.
- To copy text, select the **text**, click the **Edit** menu, and then click **Copy**.
- To paste text you have cut or copied, click **where** you want to paste the text, click the **Edit** menu, and then click **Paste**.
- To delete text, **select** the text, click the **Edit** menu, and then click **Delete**.

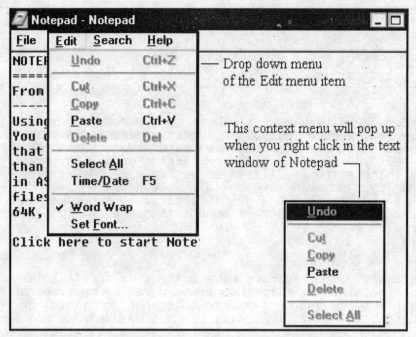

*Fig 24.03 Notepad Edit Drop-down Menu*

### Go to a Specific Line

1. Click **Edit**. The Edit drop-down menu appears.
2. Click **Go To**.
3. In the Go to line, type the **line number** you want the cursor to jump to. You do not need to have line numbers in your document for this command to work. Lines are counted down the left margin beginning at the top of the document.

### Wrap Text to the Window Size

On the Edit menu, click **Word Wrap**.

You should note that wrapping text makes all text visible on the screen, but it does not affect the way text appears when it is printed.

### Insert the Time and Date

1. Click **where** you want to add the time and date.
2. Click the **Edit** menu.
3. Click **Time/Date**. The current time and date (according to your computer's internal clock) is inserted.

# WordPad

If your formatting needs are more than the simple capabilities of Notepad, but you do not want to use a very complex word processor such as Microsoft Word, then WordPad is just the application for you.

WordPad is a text editor for short documents. With WordPad, you can format documents using various font and paragraph styles.

Start WordPad as follows:

Click **Start** ➔ **Programmes** ➔ **Accessories** ➔ **WordPad**

The WordPad window opens as shown in Fig 24.04.

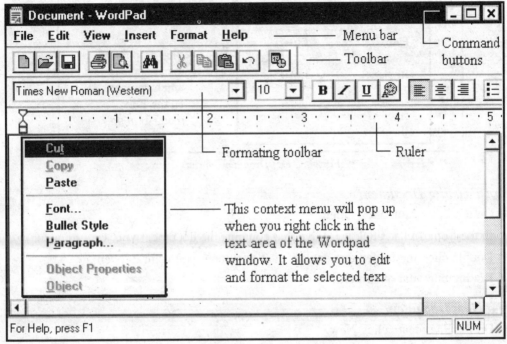

*Fig 24.04 WordPad Window*

## Working with a Document

Let us see how you can start working with a document using WordPad. Here are some of the basic steps such as creating a new document, saving changes and opening an existing document. Before you begin, take a look at the Menu bar, the Standard tool bar, the Formatting tool bar and the Ruler, all important elements of the WordPad window.

As it is the case with all the Windows Accessories and even Windows itself, you can display a drop-down menu by clicking on a menu item such as Edit. This drop-down menu is shown in Fig 24.05.

**TIP**

A document created in WordPad can be opened later in Microsoft Word. Thus, you may find it very convenient to create a draft document in WordPad and after the text is to your satisfaction, save and close WordPad, opening the same document in Word thereafter for the final stages of formatting, inserting graphics and so on.

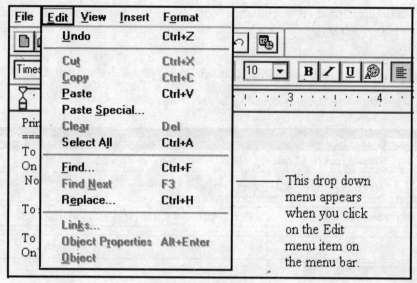

This drop down menu appears when you click on the Edit menu item on the menu bar.

*Fig 24.05 Edit Drop-down menu*

## *Open an Existing Document*

1. On the File menu, click **Open**.

2. In the Look In list, click the **drive** that contains the document you want to open.

3. Double click the **folder** that contains the document you want to open.

4. Double click the **document**.

## *Create a New Document*

1. On the File menu, click **New**.

2. Click the **type of file** you want to create, click **OK**, and then begin typing.

3. To save the file, click the **File** menu, click **Save**, and then type a **name** for the file in the File name box.

## *Save Changes to a Document*

• On the File menu, click **Save**.

• You can also save an existing document with a new name by clicking **Save As** and then typing a new **name** in the File name box. You can also choose the format of the file in the Save As format box.

• When you start WordPad, you can just begin typing in the window. Then when you save the file, you can choose the format of the file in the Save As format box. You can open a document you opened recently by clicking its name on the File menu.

# Setting up the WordPad Window

See Fig 24.04 for a view of the WordPad window showing its key elements. In order to use WordPad effectively, you may wish to set up the WordPad window exactly the way it suits you. To change the main elements such as the tool bar, the format bar or the ruler, proceed as follows:

### *Show or Hide the Tool Bar*

1. On the View menu, click **Tool Bar**.
2. A check mark appears when the tool bar is visible.

### *Show or Hide the Format Bar*

1. On the View menu, click **Format Bar**.
2. A check mark appears when the format bar is visible.

The buttons on the format bar are shortcuts for formatting text, such as making text bold or underlined, or changing the paragraph style. To format text, select it, and then click the appropriate button on the format bar.

You can drag the format bar and the tool bar to any location in the window.

### *Show or Hide the Ruler*

1. On the View menu, click **Ruler**.
2. A check mark appears when the ruler is visible.

You can use the ruler to set tab stops by clicking anywhere on the ruler where you want a tab stop. You can delete tab stops by dragging them off the ruler.

You can set margins by dragging the margin markers on the ruler.

To change the ruler settings from inches to centimetres, points, or picas, click the **View** menu, and then click **Options**.

# Working with Text

Having set up the WordPad window entirely to your satisfaction, you can move on to the actual editing and formatting of text.

### *Editing Text*

We look at editing basics such as searching and replacing text, deleting text, undoing the last action you have taken and inserting current date and time in your document.

### Select and Deselect Text

Click the left button of your mouse and drag the mouse to select text. Click anywhere in the blank document to deselect text.

By right clicking the mouse button on selected text, you can make a pop-up menu appear that lets you edit the text such as cut, copy or paste. You can also format the text by selecting font, bullet style or paragraph formatting.

### Undo Your Last Action

On the Edit menu, click **Undo**.

**Delete Text**

Select the **text** you want to delete. Then do one of the following:

1.  To remove text so that you can place it in another part of the document, click the **Edit** menu, and then click **Cut**.

2.  Or, to remove text entirely from the document, press **Delete**.

**Search for Text**

1.  Click **where** you want to start searching.

2.  On the Edit menu, click **Find**.

3.  In the Find what box, type the **text** you want to search for, and then click **Find Next**.

4.  To find additional instances of the same text, continue to click **Find Next**.

**Search for and Replace Text**

1.  On the Edit menu, click **Replace**.

2.  In the Find what box, type the **text** you want to replace.

3.  In the Replace with box, type the **text** you want to replace it with.

**Insert the Current Date and Time**

1.  Click **where** you want the date and time to appear.

2.  On the Insert menu, click **Date and Time**. *See Fig 24.06.*

3.  Double click the **format** you want.

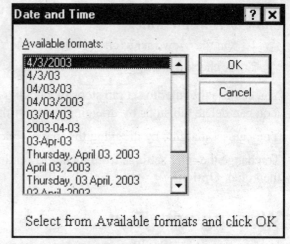

*Fig 24.06 Insert Date and Time*

**NOTE**

If you want to delete all text in a document, click the Edit menu, and then click Select All. You can also search for and replace text by clicking the Edit menu and then clicking Replace. To replace all instances of the text, click Replace All. To replace each instance of the text individually, click Find Next, and then click Replace.

## *Formatting Text*

After you have typed text in your document and edited it to your satisfaction, you may wish to improve the appearance of your document by formatting the text. For instance, you may wish to set the way the lines wrap, add bullets, change the style, size and font of the characters or even format an entire paragraph.

**Change Word Wrap**

1.  On the View menu, click **Options**. The Set View Options dialogue box appears. *See Fig 24.07.*

2.  Under Word Wrap, click the **option** you want.

The wrapping options affect only how text appears on your screen. When printed, the document uses the margin settings specified using the Page Setup command.

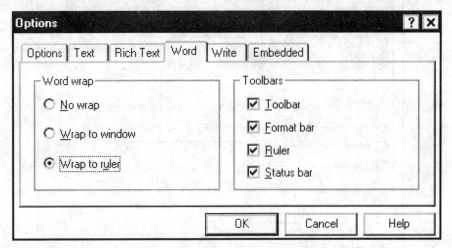

*Fig 24.07 Set View Options Dialogue Box*

### Create a Bulleted List

1.  Click a **blank line** where you want the bulleted list to start.
2.  On the Format menu, click **Bullet Style**, and then type your text. When you press **ENTER** ↵, another bullet appears on the next line.
3.  To end the bulleted list, press **ENTER** ↵ after the last line, and then click the **Format** menu and **Bullet Style** once more.

You can also click in a paragraph and then apply the bullet style.

### Change a Font Type, Style, or Size

1.  Select the **text** whose format you want to change.
2.  On the Format menu, click **Font**. The Format Font dialogue box appears. *See Fig 24.08.*
3.  Click the **options** you want.

### Format a Paragraph

1.  Click anywhere in the **paragraph** you want to format.
2.  On the Format menu, click **Paragraph**.
3.  Enter the **indentation** and **alignment** options you want.

### Set or Remove Tab Stops in Paragraphs

1.  Select the **paragraphs** in which you want to set tab stops.
2.  On the Format menu, click **Tabs**.
3.  Do the following, as needed:
    *   To set a tab stop, type the **measurement** for a new tab stop (for example, .5, 1, or 2.4 inches) in the Tab stop position box, and then click Set.

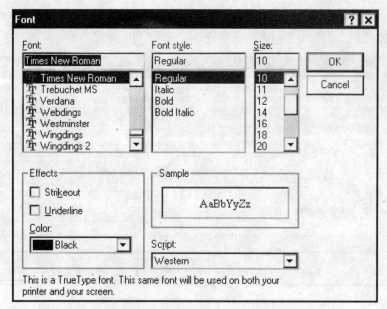

*Fig 24.08 Format Font Dialogue Box*

- To delete a tab stop in the selected paragraph, click it in the **list**, and then click **Clear**.
- To delete all tab stops in the selected paragraph, click **Clear All**.
- You can delete tab stops by just **dragging them off** the ruler.

**NOTE** You can set different word wrap options for each of the text formats in which you can save documents by clicking the appropriate tab in the dialogue box. You can specify font settings for new text by clicking the options before you begin to type. You can change the font settings for an entire document by clicking the Edit menu and then clicking Select All before carrying out step 2 above.

By default, tab stops are set for every half inch. To change the ruler settings from inches to centimetres, points, or picas, click the **View** menu, and then click **Options**.

# Printing

After you have edited and formatted your document, you are ready to print it for distribution to others. You can preview your document, set page margins or select printing options before you begin printing. The dialogue boxes for printing are very similar to what you see with other Window appliances.

## *Preview Your Document*
1. On the File menu, click **Print Preview**.
2. To return to the previous view, click **Close**.

## *Set Page Margins*
1. On the File menu, click **Page Setup**.
2. Type **new values** under Margins.

### *Change Printers and Printing Options*

1.  On the File menu, click **Page Setup**.
2.  Make the **changes** you want:

    *   If you have more than one printer installed, you may wish to select the **printer** you want for the document you want to print. To change printers, click **Printer**, and then click a **printer** in the Name box.

    *   To change paper specifications, type the **settings** you want under **Paper**, **Orientation**, and **Margins**.

# Calculator

All of us are familiar with the common hand-held calculator. It may be a simple calculator or a scientific calculator that has many additional statistical and geometric functions. Windows includes a calculator as an accessory. You can display the calculator on your monitor's screen by clicking **Start ➔ Programmes ➔ Accessories ➔ Calculator**.

Actually, you have a two-in-one calculator in Windows, the simple one and the scientific one. You can easily switch between the two by choosing **View ➔ Standard** or **View ➔ Scientific**. *See Fig 24.09.*

You can use Calculator in standard view to perform simple calculations, or in scientific view to perform advanced scientific and statistical calculations.

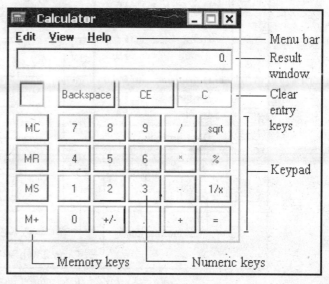

Fig 24.09 Standard Calculator

## Performing Calculations

Let us perform some simple calculations using the calculator, first with the Standard version and then with the Scientific version.

### *Simple Calculations*

We use the standard calculator for this exercise.

1.  Enter the first **number** in the calculation.
2.  Click **+** to add, **-** to subtract, **×** to multiply, or **/** to divide.
3.  Enter the next **number** in the calculation.
4.  Enter any remaining **operators** and **numbers**.
5.  Click **=**. The result is displayed in the result window.

To use your numeric keypad to enter numbers and operators, press NUM LOCK, and then type the number or operator.

## Statistical Calculations

We use the scientific calculator for this exercise.

1. On the View menu, click **Scientific**. The scientific calculator is displayed. *See Fig 24.10.*

2. Enter your first piece of **data**.

3. Click **Sta**, and then click **Dat**.

4. Enter the rest of the data, clicking **Dat** after each entry.

5. Click **Sta**.

6. Click the button for the statistics function you want to use. The result is displayed in the result window.

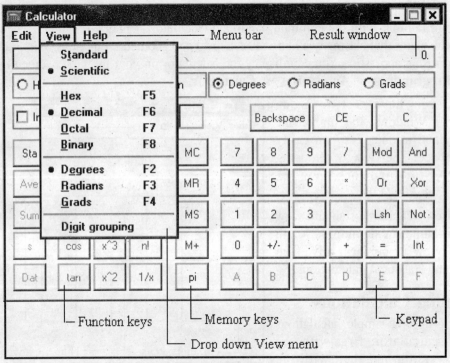

*Fig 24.10 Scientific Calculator*

## Scientific Calculations

1. On the View menu, click **Scientific** if the scientific calculator is not displayed.

2. Click a **number system**.

3. Enter the first **number**.

4. Click an **operator**.

5. Enter the next **number** in the calculation.

6. Enter any remaining **operators** and **numbers**.

7. Click =. The result is displayed in the result window.

*Convert a Value to Another Number System*

You will need this facility if you are a programmer and require hexadecimal or binary equivalent of decimal numbers. To convert numbers, do the following:

1. On the View menu, click **Scientific**.
2. Enter the **number** you want to convert.
3. Click the **number system** you want to convert to, such as Hex for hexadecimal, Bin for binary etc.

# Tips and Tricks

Here are some tips to help you with the use of your calculator.

### *To Work with Numbers Stored in Memory*

1. Click **MS** to store the displayed number in memory.
2. Click **MR** to recall a stored number.
3. Click **MC** to clear the memory.
4. Click **M +** to add the displayed number to the number already in memory.

### *To Transfer Numbers Between Standard and Scientific View*

1. To store the displayed number, click **MS**.
2. On the View menu, click the **view** you want.
3. To recall the stored number in the new view, click **MR**.

**NOTE** When you store a number, an M appears in the box above the memory options. If you store another number, it replaces the one currently in memory.

Calculator clears the display when you switch between standard and scientific view.

A number entered in hexadecimal, octal, or binary format will be converted to decimal format when transferred from scientific to standard view.

# Paint

Windows contains a fairly useful graphics programme called Paint. While there are many more powerful software programmes to draw or paint with your computer, Paint is powerful enough for your daily needs. For instance, all the graphics used in this book that contain explanations or notes on the picture have been created or edited using Paint.

In addition to creating and editing line drawings, you can also view and edit pictures or scanned photographs. Editing photographs, especially in colour, requires a good understanding of colour palettes. Furthermore, you will require a fairly high screen resolution to handle photo retouching successfully.

You can open the Paint window by clicking **Start ➔ Programmes ➔ Accessories ➔ Paint**. Or, if you have the Paint icon on your desktop, you can click that as well. The opening screen of Paint appears. *See Fig 24.11.*

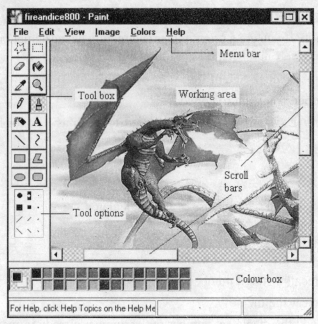

*Fig 24.11 Paint Window*

## Drawing Lines and Shapes

Paint is quite versatile if you want to create drawings consisting of lines and shapes that you may use to illustrate a technical article such as operation instructions. Given below are the basic drawing methods in Paint.

### Draw a Straight Line

In Fig 24.12, you can see an enlarged view of the Paint tool box with name tags explaining each tool. To draw a straight line, proceed as follows:

1. In the tool box, click the **Line** tool.
2. At the bottom of the tool box, click a **line width**.
3. To draw the line, drag the pointer from the **start** to the **end** of the line. You can draw a perfectly horizontal, vertical, or 45-degree diagonal line by pressing and holding down the SHIFT keyboard key while dragging with the mouse.

Fig 24.12 identifies the set of tools you have available in the Paint tool box. In this case, the Brush tool is shown selected. The rectangle below the main tool box contains the different sizes and shapes of brushes you can choose. The contents of this rectangle change to suit the tool you select. For instance, if you select the line tool, you will see lines of five different thicknesses that you can choose from.

### Draw a Free-form Line

1. In the tool box, click the **Pencil** (or **line**) tool.
2. To draw a free-form line, drag the pointer from the **start** to the **finish** of the line.

The Pencil or line tool has a fixed width. *See Fig 24.12.*

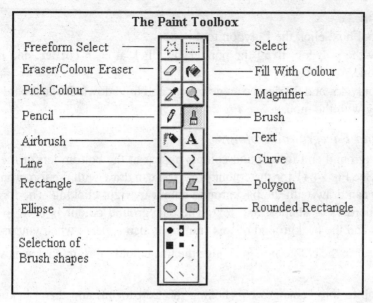

*Fig 24.12 Paint Tool Box*

## To Draw a Curve

1. In the tool box, click the **Curve** tool.
2. At the bottom of the tool box, click a **line width**.
3. Draw a **straight line** by dragging the pointer.
4. Click where you want **one arc** of the curve to be, and then drag the pointer to **adjust** the curve. Repeat this step for a **second arc**. Each curve must have at least one arc, but no more than two. *See Fig 24.12.*

## Draw an Ellipse or Circle

1. In the tool box, click the **Ellipse** tool.
2. Drag the pointer **diagonally**.
3. You can draw a perfect circle by pressing and holding down the keyboard SHIFT key while you drag with the mouse. *See Fig 24.12.*

## Draw a Rectangle or Square

1. In the tool box, click the **Rectangle** tool to create a square-cornered shape, or click the **rounded rectangle** tool to create a round-cornered shape.
2. To draw a rectangle, drag the pointer **diagonally** in the direction you want.
3. To draw a square, press and hold down the keyboard SHIFT key while dragging the mouse pointer. *See Fig 24.12.*

**NOTE**

The border width of the box is the same as the thickness selected for the line tools. To change the border thickness, click the line or curve tool in the tool box, and then click the thickness you want in the box below the tool box.

### *Draw a Polygon*

1. In the tool box, click the **Polygon** tool.
2. To draw the polygon, **drag** the pointer and click at each **corner**, and then **double click** when done.
3. To use only 45- and 90-degree angles, press and hold down the keyboard SHIFT key while dragging with the mouse. *See Fig 24.12.*

### *Background and Foreground Colours*

The default background and foreground colours appear at the bottom left of the Paint window in the colour box. See Fig 24.11 for the colour box. You can draw with the foreground colour by left-clicking, or you can draw with the background colour by right clicking. The foreground colour is used for lines, borders of shapes, and text. The background colour is used to fill the inside of enclosed shapes and the background of text frames. It also appears when you use the eraser.

Click a new colour in the colour box to change the line colour, or right click a new colour to change the fill colour.

You can undo up to three changes by clicking the Edit menu, and then clicking Undo for each change.

## Using Paint to Work with Pictures

You can work with pictures, such as .jpg, .gif, or .bmp files using Paint. You can paste a Paint picture into another document you have created, or use it as your desktop background. You can even use Paint to view and edit scanned photographs and add captions to them.

To work with a picture in Paint, proceed as follows:

1. Open the picture you wish to work with by **launching** Paint as you would any other Windows accessory and then clicking **File ➔ Open**.
2. The Open dialogue box appears, usually showing the default My Documents folder.
3. Click on the **picture** you wish to load. If the picture you want is located elsewhere, you can navigate there using normal Windows Explorer commands.

### *Putting Text in a Picture*

Whether you have created a drawing using Paint, or you have opened an existing picture as described above, you can add text to your drawing or picture in the same way as described below.

#### Type and Format Text

1. In the tool box, click the **Text** tool.
2. To create a text frame, drag the pointer **diagonally** to the size you want.
3. On the text tool bar, click the **font**, **size**, and **style** you want for the text.
4. Click inside the text frame, type or paste the **text**, and then do any of the following:
   - **Move** or **enlarge** the text frame.
   - Click a **colour** to change the colour of the text.

- Click in the **tool box** to insert the text on a coloured background. Then **right click** in the colour box to change the background colour.

**NOTE** You can view the text tool bar by clicking the View menu, and then clicking Text Tool bar. If it obscures part of the Paint window, you can drag the tool bar to any location in the window.

You can enter text into a picture only in Normal view. You can insert text into the picture by clicking outside the text frame. When the text tool is selected, you can paste text only. You cannot paste graphics.

You can undo up to three changes by clicking the Edit menu, and then clicking Undo for each change.

## Working with Colours

Paint comes with a colour palette of 48 basic colours that includes white and several shades of grey. In addition, you can call up a colour mixing palette by clicking on the Define Custom Colours button in the Edit Colours dialogue box. *See Fig 24.13.*

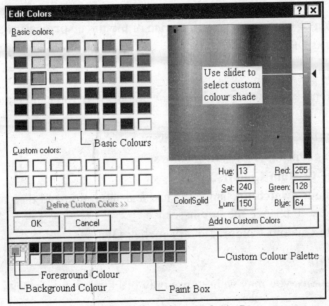

*Fig 24.13 Edit Colours Dialogue Box*

The right half becomes visible after you click the Define Custom Colours button.

In this section, we look at ways of setting colours, colour filling and the use of several colouring tools such as the brush and the airbrush.

### Set Default Foreground and Background Colours

1. To set the **foreground** colour, **click a colour** in the colour box.

2. To set the **background** colour, **right click a colour** in the colour box.

## Fill an Area or Object with Colour

1. In the tool box, click the **Fill with colour** tool.
2. Click the **area** or object you want to fill.

**NOTE**

If the shape being filled has any breaks in its border, the filling colour leaks through to the rest of the drawing area. You can find and close any openings by clicking the **View** menu, pointing to **Zoom**, and then clicking **Large Size** or **Custom**.

## Paint with a Brush

1. In the tool box, click the **Brush** tool.
2. At the bottom of the tool box, click to choose the **brush shape** you want to use. The pointer changes to a crosshair.
3. To paint, **drag** the pointer.

## Create an Airbrush Effect

1. In the tool box, click the **Airbrush** tool. The pointer changes to an airbrush symbol.
2. At the bottom of the tool box, click on one of the three **spray sizes** available.
3. To spray, **drag** the pointer.

## Create Custom Colours

In addition to the 48 basic colours provided in the colour box, you can create a variety of custom colours as follows:

1. In the colour box, click the **colour** you want to change.
2. On the Colours menu, click **Edit Colours**.
3. Click **Define Custom Colours**.
4. Click the **colour swatch** to change the hue and saturation and then move the **slider** in the colour gradient to change the luminescence.
5. Click **Add to Custom Colours**, and then click **OK**.

## Use Black and White

For technical illustrations, you may want to use only black and white instead of colours. To do so, follow these steps.

1. On the Image menu, click Attributes. The Attributes dialogue box appears. *See Fig 24.14.*
2. Click Black and White. If you change back to colour, only new work will be in colour.

## Invert all the Colours in a Picture

You can invert colours in a picture, that is, change each colour (foreground and background) to its complementary colour by clicking in the **Image** menu and clicking on **Invert colours** on the drop-down menu. *See Fig 24.15.*

Each colour is replaced by its colour complement. For example, red becomes cyan, and blue becomes yellow. This method will affect all the colours in the picture.

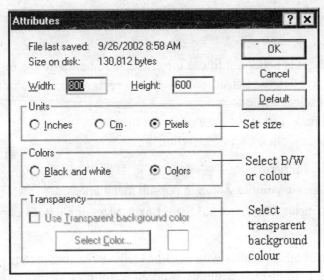

*Fig 24.14 Attributes Dialogue Box*

# Erasing

Inevitably, you will want to erase some of the work you have done. Paint provides you with an Eraser tool with four different eraser sizes to help you do the job well. You can use the eraser tool for working with small areas of your drawing.

## Using the Eraser Tool

1. In the tool box, click the **Eraser** tool.
2. At the bottom of the tool box, click an **eraser shape**. The pointer will change to a square representing the size of the eraser shape you have just selected.

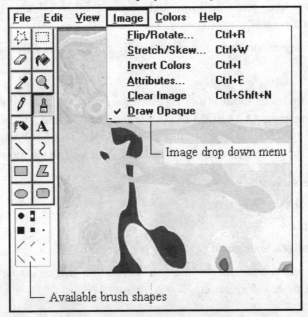

*Fig 24.15 Image Drop-down Menu*

3. Drag the pointer over the **area** you want to erase.

### Erase a Large Area

For erasing large areas, it is better not to use the eraser tool, but to do the following:

1. In the tool box, click the Select tool to select a **rectangular area** or click the **Free Form Select** tool to select a free-form area.
2. Drag the pointer to **select** the area you want to erase.
3. On the Edit menu, click **Clear Selection**.

### Zoom In or Out of a Picture

1. On the View menu, point to **Zoom**, a pop-up menu appears.
2. In the pop-up menu, click **Normal Size**, **Large Size**, or **Custom** as required.

### Display Gridlines

To align text or copies of other pictures with existing elements in your picture, you can use gridlines as guides for alignment. To display gridlines, proceed as follows:

1. On the View menu, point to **Zoom**, and then click **Custom**.
2. Under Zoom to, click **400%**, **600%**, or **800%**, and then click **OK**.
3. On the View menu, point to **Zoom**, and then click **Show Grid**.

You can remove the gridlines by repeating step 3 and clearing the **Show Grid check mark**, or by clicking **View**, pointing to **Zoom** and then clicking **Normal Size**.

## Print a Picture

* To print a picture, on the File menu, click **Print**.

* You can see how the picture will look before you print by clicking the **File** menu, and then clicking **Print Preview**.

* You can set margins or change orientation by clicking the **File** menu, and then clicking **Page Setup**.

**CD-ROM**   To learn more about Windows Accessories in a multimedia environment, insert the accompanying CD-ROM in your computer and select the **Interactive** mode in the opening screen. The main menu will appear. To go to the section on Accessories, click on the button marked **Windows**. You will see a sub-menu that reads:

* Windows Overview
* Getting Control over Windows
* Windows Utilities
* Power of Windows Unleashed

Click on the third and fourth items. In the sub-sub-menus that will be displayed, pick the accessory about which you want more information.

# 25. Protecting Your Computer From Virus

**In this chapter:**

☞ You get a detailed view of virus protection. We begin with an understanding of what computer viruses are and describe the harm they can do and how to protect your computer from virus damage.

☞ We explain in detail the popular anti-virus programme PC-cillin.

☞ We include instructions for configuring the software to meet your needs. We also speak of other anti-virus programmes.

# Virus Protection

## What is a Computer Virus?

Simply put, a computer virus is a programme that replicates (or makes duplicates of) itself in the hard disk of the infected computer. To copy itself again and again, the virus attaches itself to other programme files (for example, .exe, .com or .dll) called host programmes. Whenever this host programme is run, the virus programme will also run. In addition to replication, many viruses will also cause damage to the infected computer. The damage is caused by a small programme called the damage routine or the payload. Damage includes overwriting of programmes and data, consuming memory or processor time and other activities that slow down the performance of your computer. The partition tables of your hard disk may be damaged, or you may see taunting messages and pictures on your screen.

Computer viruses are small software programmes often written by disgruntled software programmers who may either be former employees carrying a grudge against the employer or just an antisocial programmer with malice.

Even without a "damage routine", if viruses are allowed to remain on your computer you will suffer from unexplained system crashes or sudden and unpredictable behaviour.

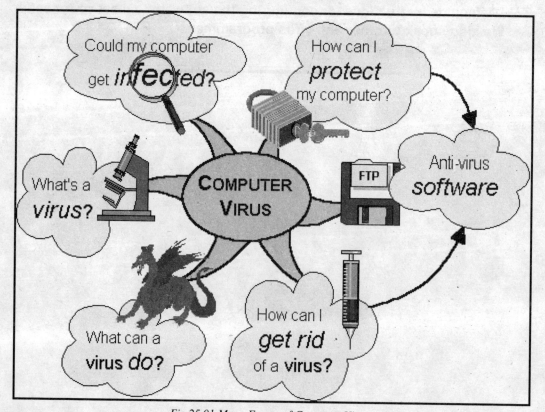

*Fig 25.01 Many Facets of Computer Virus*

Some viruses do not make their presence known for months. Instead of causing damage right away, these viruses do nothing but replicate until its preset trigger day or event. Then they unleash their damage routines.

For reliable performance of your computer, therefore, it is so very essential to prevent virus infection. In case you still get infected, it is equally important to eradicate the virus. In this chapter, we will discuss this key aspect of computer operations.

## How Viruses Spread

There are many ways for a virus to enter your computer system. Some of the common ones are listed below:

- As e-mail attachments.
- While surfing the World Wide Web (WWW) sites.
- While downloading files from File Transfer Protocol (FTP) sites.
- From an infected file in the network to which your computer is connected.
- Demonstration software that you may have installed in your computer.
- Pirated software that may contain corrupted files or intentionally infected files.
- Electronic Bulletin Boards (BBS) that you surf to post or download messages.
- From infected floppy disks that you may use to swap data or programmes.

Of these, the most likely virus entry points are e-mail, Internet and network connections, floppy disk drives, and modems or other serial or parallel port connections. In today's increasingly interconnected workplace (Internet, intranet, shared drives, removable drives, and e-mail), virus outbreaks can now spread faster and wider than ever before.

## Anti-virus Software

Just as viruses are malicious code, there are anti-virus programmes that can detect and eradicate viruses. Basically, anti-virus programmes consist of three parts:

- The virus detection engine.
- An encyclopaedia of virus signature files that helps the engine detect a virus.
- A set of utility programmes used to remove virus from an infected file, or to quarantine or delete the infected file if the virus cannot be eradicated.

Since new viruses are being written every day, the anti-virus programme requires addition to its signature files in order to remain up to date. Good anti-virus programmes have the capability of downloading and installing the new signature files from time to time.

In addition, the anti-virus programme is configurable so that you can select the nature and extent of virus protection that you wish to provide your computer system. Later in this section, we shall examine PC-cillin 2000 anti-virus software in detail in order to understand these aspects of anti-virus protection.

# Risky Files

All computer programmes and data are organised as files. The following types of files are most likely to carry a virus:

.exe, .com, .xls, .doc, .mdb

These files are especially dangerous because the virus hiding in these files do not require any special conversion or triggering process to make them active. Any of these files, if infected, will immediately release the damaging payload as soon as it is run.

Makers of anti-virus software estimate that almost 99% of computer virus infection is due to one of these types of files.

Here is a complete list of files in which a virus may lurk.

EXE - (Executable file), SYS - (Executable file), COM - (Executable file), DOC - (Microsoft Word), DOT - (Microsoft Word), XLS - (Microsoft Excel), XLA - (Microsoft Excel), XLT - (Microsoft Excel), MDB - (Microsoft Access), ZIP - (Compressed file), ARJ - (Compressed file), DRV - (Device driver), OVL - (Windows overlay file), BIN - (Common boot sector image file), SCR - (Microsoft screen saver).

**TRAP**

Therefore, be very careful before you load a file with any of these extensions (especially the five types listed at the beginning of this section) from the Internet, your network or a floppy disk. Later in this chapter, we will discuss methods of scanning a file source before file transfer to protect your computer from virus infection.

# Introducing PC-cillin

After our acquaintance with viruses and their methods of spreading, let us look at a good anti-virus software to understand how the threat from virus infection can be minimised if not eliminated. We will also learn what to do if, in spite of your best precautions, your computer is unfortunately infected. We look at PC-cillin, to see what it can do for us.

Here is what PC-cillin will do "straight out of the box" as soon as you install it in your computer:

- Check for viruses every time you Open, Copy, Move, or Save a file.
- Protect against downloading infected files from the Internet or FTP sites.
- Guard against malicious Java applets and ActiveX controls while web surfing.
- Monitor your Word and Excel sessions for macro viruses.
- Scan and clean all files on your hard drive once a week (default is Friday).
- Scan all programme files for viruses once every month.
- Check all your saved documents for macro viruses.

In addition, here is what you can do with just the click of a button:

- Scan every file on your system and clean any infected files.
- Scan any file from Windows Explorer or My Computer by right clicking the file icon.

- Scan floppy diskettes and clean any infected files.
- Check all of your Word and Excel document(s) for macro viruses.
- If you use Outlook Express 4.0 or above or Eudora Pro 4.0 or above as e-mail clients, PC-cillin will scan your e-mail message attachments as they are being downloaded from the POP3 e-mail server.
- Manually scan message attachments in your local Outlook 97/98/2000 folders.

If you take the time to customise your software, you can configure PC-cillin to perform many other tasks. You can "set and forget" as many tasks as you see fit. For each task, you can select the file types you want to scan for viruses, the action PC-cillin will take upon finding a virus (such as, Clean the infected file, Delete it, Quarantine it, Pass it, or Rename/Deny Access to it), as well as the timing and frequency of virus scans.

Viruses are detected using PC-cillin's 32-bit, multi-threaded scanning engine and a process called pattern matching. In addition to catching known viruses, PC-cillin detects and intercepts previously unknown polymorphic, or mutation viruses.

Additional layers of protection come from MacroTrap, PC-cillin's macro virus scanning engine, which detects and removes both known and unknown macro viruses.

## Keeping Your Computer Virus Free

The default settings pre-adjusted in PC-cillin is already set up to keep your system virus-free. Therefore, after installing the software, you do not have to take any more steps to ensure that your system remains virus-free.

*Fig 25.02 Virus Infection is Serious Business*

PC-cillin gives you this protection by providing three layers of protection. The layers are described below:

- The default scheduled Scan will check all those files on your computer that are most likely to be infected by viruses such as Internet and executable files.

- The real-time scanning option is switched on by default. This scanner watches over your computer file system continuously. Real-time scanning takes place automatically each time you Open, Copy, Save, or Move a file. The real-time scan will detect a virus as soon as it arrives at your computer. As soon as a virus is detected, you will get a visual and audible alarm.

*Fig 25.03 A Sick Computer*

- If the automatic pattern file update is left on, PC-cillin will automatically dial-up and connect to the Trend PC-cillin website to download the latest virus signature files and any other update that may have become available. However, if you are not continuously connected to the Internet, you should update the software periodically.

## Scanning E-mails

For many Internet users, e-mails are often the most common source of virus infection. E-mail scanning, therefore, is an important part of your virus protection plan.

PC-cillin protects your computer system in two different ways depending on the e-mail setup that you have, Outlook (part of Microsoft Office) or Outlook Express (part of Windows). The two methods are described below.

## Outlook 2000 Users

Microsoft Outlook creates a set of mail folders on your hard disk drive. They include the default Inbox and individual mail boxes that you may have created. Every time you download e-mail from the Internet, these mail boxes are updated by Outlook. PC-cillin can be configured to scan these folders after e-mails are downloaded and sent to them.

### Scanning Outlook Folders

The procedure below applies only to Outlook. It will not protect Outlook Express users. For Outlook Express virus protection, see the next section.

**NOTE** In this configuration, PC-cillin will only scan the Outlook mail folders in your computer's local hard disk. If your computer is connected to a network and the downloaded e-mails are stored in the hard disk of the network server, this procedure will not clean virus from the server's hard disk. If you are on a network, keep the real-time scanning option enabled

so that if any virus infected e-mail or attachment is opened in the computer, PC-cillin will detect the virus, quarantine it safely and warn you of the virus.

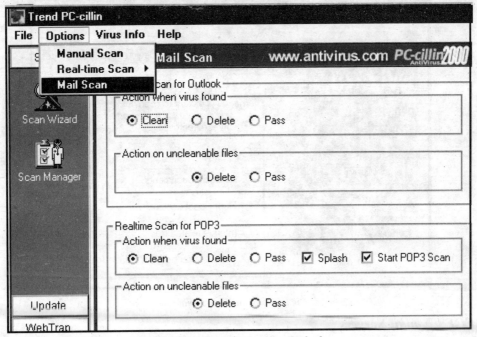

*Fig 25.04 Scan Options for Outlook*

## Configure Scan of Outlook Folders

Follow these steps to configure PC-cillin to scan Outlook's local folders:

1.  On the main screen of PC-cillin, click **Options** on the menu bar. The drop-down menu appears.

2.  Click **Mail Scan**. The Mail Scan dialogue box opens. *See Fig 25.04*.

3.  In the "Action when virus found" section, select the appropriate **radio button**. Your options are: **Clean** (recommended), **Delete** (if Clean fails) or **Pass** (if you know that the file is clean and it is a false alarm).

4.  In the "Action on uncleanable files" select between **Delete** (recommended) and **Pass** (if you know that the virus alarm is false).

5.  Ignore the remaining options since they only apply to Outlook Express files. Click the Apply button to save your changes.

## Scan Folders in Outlook

1.  Select **File ➔ Scan ➔ Scan Wizard** from the main menu on the PC-cillin main screen. The first Scan Wizard dialogue box opens. *See Fig 25.05*.

2.  Under "What do you want to scan?" click the **"Outlook attached files in local folder"** radio button. Click **Next>** to continue.

The Scan progress window will load and give information about the outcome of the virus scan.

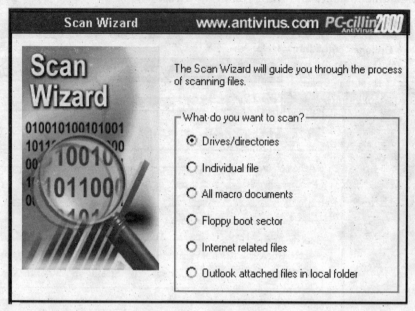

*Fig 25.05 Scan Wizard Window*

### Scan POP3 E-mail Servers

This section only applies if you are using Microsoft Outlook Express 4.0 or later versions as well as Eudora Pro 4.0 or a later version as your e-mail client.

Post Office Protocol3 or POP3 is a standard protocol for receiving e-mail. In this protocol, your Internet Service Provider or ISP (such as VSNL) receives e-mail on your behalf and stores it for you until you connect to the Internet and download your e-mail.

If your computer is part of a medium or large office, then it will be connected to a Local Area Network (LAN). In that case you may have POP3 or some other protocol on your LAN. Check with your network administrator about how to protect your computer from virus attack.

### TRAP

Make sure that the POP3 Scan feature is enabled before downloading e-mail from your ISP. The virus scan must take place while messages are being downloaded by your se-mail client (such as Outlook Express). If you download any e-mail before enabling the POP3 scan feature, subsequent scanning will not detect a virus.

### Enabling POP3 E-mail Scan

1. Select **Options** ➜ **Mail Scan** from the main menu. The Mail Scan dialogue box appears. See Fig 25.04 earlier in this section.
2. Under "Real-time Scan for POP3" group, select the **Action** you want PC-cillin to take when a virus is found.
3. Enable or disable the **Splash screen** option.
4. If you want to start the POP3 Scan every time you start PC-cillin, enable the **Start POP3 Scan** option button.

5. If you choose Clean as your preferred action when a virus is found, select an **Alternative Action** such as **Delete** or **Pass** for uncleanable files.

6. Click **Apply** to save your changes. Downloaded messages will be scanned for viruses the next time you connect to your e-mail server.

## Recommended Settings

PC-cillin is very flexible and you can easily configure it to suit your exact needs. However, the following recommended scan settings will give you effective protection in most cases. These settings are:

- Scan all file types; also activate the Include boot sector option.
- Choose "Clean files" and "Backup before cleaning".
- Quarantine files that cannot be cleaned.
- Leave Real-time Scan, Web Security and Start-up Scan on.
- Schedule Weekly or Monthly automatic virus pattern updates.

## Using Scan Manager

A very convenient feature of PC-cillin is that it comes pre-configured. In other words, it will run all the critical scans to protect your computer as soon as it is installed, without your having to take any action. However, you can also decide which scans to run and when. All you have to do is highlight the Description of the task you want to run in PC-cillin's Scan Manager and click Run. You can also create your own scanning tasks.

Here is how to use the Scan Manager:

1. On PC-cillin's opening screen, click the **Scan icon** on the PC-cillin shortcut bar. The Scan Manager window opens. *See Fig 25.06*. You will see a row of icons along the top of the window while a pane at the bottom captioned "List:" shows the recent scans run on your computer.

2. Click the **New Task** icon, the "Select what to scan" window opens.

3. In the edit box, type a **name** for the scanning task you wish to create, for example, "Core Scan". Under the caption "Select what to scan", select the **drive** you want to scan, for example, drive C:\ and click **Next** to continue. The "Choose scan options" dialogue box appears.

4. Select **scanning options** as you have done under "POP3 E-mail Scan" earlier in this chapter and click **Next** to continue. The "Schedule the Task" window appears.

5. Specify how often you want the scan task to run and fill in the **time/date option** as appropriate.

6. Click **Finish** to return to the Scan Manager window. The task you have just created will now appear at the bottom of the list in the "List:" pane. If you check the "Do you want to run this task now?" check box, the task will run automatically as soon as you click **Finish**.

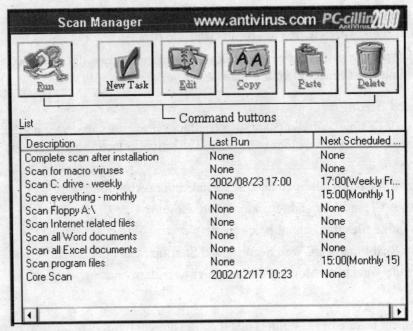

*Fig 25.06 Scan Manager Window*

## The Real-time Scan

As we have discussed, the Real-time scan option scans for virus and protects your computer automatically as long as this option is "turned on". You may, however, wish to modify the default options of Real-time scan.

To toggle between enabled and disabled mode for Real-time scan, do the following:

On the main menu of PC-cillin, click **Options** ➔ **Real-time Scan** ➔ **Scan Options**. The Real-time Scan window appears. *See Fig 25.07.*

**Check** or **uncheck** the check box captioned **"Enable real-time scanning"** to enable or disable this feature.

Set scanning properties such as Files to scan, Action when virus found and Action on uncleanable files as you have done before.

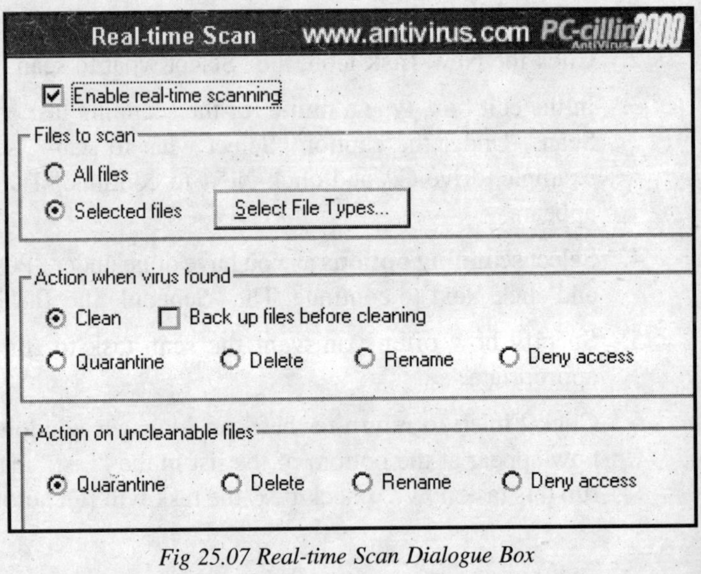

## Handling Infected Files

In spite of all your precautions, you may periodically pick up a virus that will infect one or more files in your computer. We discuss how to treat these infected files in this section.

*Fig 25.07 Real-time Scan Dialogue Box*

If PC-cillin detects a virus, it is best to clean the infected file by "killing" (deleting) the virus. If your virus signature files are current, PC-cillin should be able to detect any virus. Here is how you can tackle infected files:

- If you run one of PC-cillin's pre-set tasks, infected files will be cleaned automatically. You have to do nothing else except check the virus log at the end of the run.

- If you run an immediate scan using the Scan Wizard, you can configure PC-cillin to take one of the following actions on any virus that turns up:

  o Clean infected files. You can make a back-up copy of infected files before it is cleaned as a precaution.

  o Quarantine the infected file.

  o Delete the virus, file and all.

  o Pass over the file; you can then Quarantine, Delete, etc on a case-by-case basis.

  o Deny Access to the infected file so it cannot be used.

  o Rename the file so it has a .VIR extension, for future action.

It is recommended that the infected files are cleaned by deleting the virus. Sometimes, a file cannot be cleaned because it is corrupted or because of the nature of that particular virus. In such a case, the safest thing to do is to quarantine the file.

## Quarantined Files

If you select the option to quarantine infected files after PC-cillin fails to remove the virus in any of the scan procedure that we have discussed earlier, then the infected file(s) will be segregated in a special folder called Quarantine. By doing so, PC-cillin prevents the virus from spreading to other parts of your computer. You can open the quarantine folder to view the infected files and decide what you want to do with them.

You can display the Quarantine folder as follows:

1. On the PC-cillin opening screen, click on the **Quarantine shortcut bar**. Two icons are displayed, Quarantine and Back-up Items. *See Fig 25.08.*

*Fig 25.08 Quarantine Dialogue Box*

2. Click on the **Quarantine** icon and the quarantine screen is displayed showing the files in quarantine, if any. Along the top of the screen, note the Clean, Restore and Delete icons.

3. If the file is infected, click on the **Clean** icon. If this action fails to remove the virus, delete the infected file by clicking the **Delete** icon. If the file gets cleaned, you can restore it to its original drive/directory on your computer by clicking the **Restore** icon.

# Protection While Surfing

While surfing the Internet, make sure that your real-time scan is enabled as discussed earlier in this chapter. In addition, you can use the Web Security feature of PC-cillin.

## Using Web Security

Web Security protects you against malicious Java and ActiveX applets (or small applications) on the Internet. Like viruses, these applets can download themselves in your computer without your knowledge, while you are surfing the Internet. Although most websites are completely harmless, it is possible that someone will create a small programme and set it to run invisibly in the background whenever their web page is accessed. These applets may destroy data or steal your passwords and financial data. PC-cillin's Web Security protects you against these threats.

Here is how you can use Web Security:

1. On the opening page of PC-cillin, click the **Web Trap shortcut bar**. The two icons, Web Security and Web Filter are displayed.

2. Click the **Web Security** icon. The Web Security dialogue box is displayed. *See Fig 25.09.*

3. Check the box captioned **"Enable web security"**.

4. You can select between **"Block Programme"** and **"Prompt for action"** by clicking on the appropriate radio button. The choice depends on whether you want PC-cillin to act on its own or to prompt you for action.

5. Click **File** ➔ **Exit** to exit the programme.

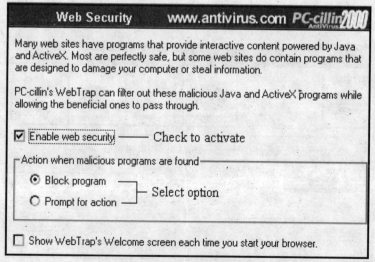

*Fig 25.09 Web Security Dialogue Box*

With Web Security enabled, PC-cillin will monitor all Java and ActiveX applets that may be silently downloaded to your computer whenever you are browsing the Web.

## Updating Pattern Files

Computer viruses are being written every day. The virus pattern or signature files that the anti-virus programme uses to detect virus become outdated very soon. Therefore, it is important that you download the latest addition to the virus pattern (or signature) files on a regular basis so that your anti-virus software does not go out of date.

To download and install the latest pattern files and other upgrades, proceed as follows:

1. Connect to the **Internet** by clicking on the **Internet connection icon** on your desktop.
2. After connection has been established, launch **PC-cillin** and click the **Update** shortcut bar on the main menu. The Update Now and Update Later icons are displayed.
3. Click on the **Update Now** icon and the Update Wizard dialogue box will be displayed. *See Fig 25.10.*
4. Click the **Next>** button and follow the instructions on your screen to download and install the latest updates.

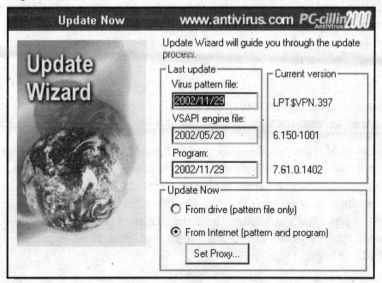

*Fig 25.10 Update Wizard*

# Other Anti-virus Software

PC-cillin is only one of a host of anti-virus software that you can install on your computer. Here is a listing of some of the top quality software that you may wish to consider for your computer.

**Norton Anti-virus 2003 Professional**
Website: http://www.symantec.com

Features: Live update, malicious script blocking, scanning of e-mail attachments and automatic scanning of outgoing and incoming mail.

Size: 38.3 MB

This software is featured in the accompanying CD-ROM. For details of how to access the multimedia presentation on the CD-ROM, see the end of this chapter.

**Mc-Affee VirusScan 7.0**
Website: http://www.mcaffee.com

Features: Malicious script blocking, integrated firewall, programme is well integrated with Microsoft products such as Windows and Office software suit.

Size: 41.1 MB

**Panda Anti-virus Titanium**
Website: Http://www.pandasoftware.com

Features: Automatic updates, good capability to repair files damaged by virus infection.

Size: 15.4 MB

## General Guidelines

Since you can get trial versions of most of these anti-virus software, you may wish to try out some of the popular ones. If you are using an operating system such as Windows XP, you will find that it comes with a built-in firewall, which protects your computer from virus attack and from malicious code to a great extent. If so, you may select a product that does not have an integrated firewall. Space available on your hard disk and the cost of the product will be other important considerations.

You may want to give weightages to the following factors:

- Ease of use.
- Convenience of updating the virus signature files from the website of the company.
- Space required on your hard disk.

**TRAP** A final word of warning! You may read opinions by Internet experts that no single anti-virus software can definitely detect each and every virus. Therefore, some experts suggest that you should use two or more anti-virus software simultaneously. However, different products may not always be compatible with each other. They may actually interfere with each other's working. Therefore, the best course appears to be to install one product, the best you can afford and add firewall protection, especially if you rate your virus exposure risk to be high.

**CD-ROM** To learn more about Anti-virus programmes in a multimedia environment, insert the accompanying CD-ROM in your computer and select the **Interactive** mode in the opening screen. The main menu will appear. To go to the section on Anti-virus software, click on the button marked **Computer Viruses**. You will see a sub-menu that reads "How They Work". Click on this to display the sub-sub-menu that reads:

- How Viruses Work
- Familiarity with Norton Anti-virus
- Scanning HDD
- Live Update

Click on your selected topic and follow instructions on your screen.

# ANNEXURE: The Self-learning CD-ROM

## In this annexure:

☞ We introduce you to the multimedia CD-ROM that accompanies this book, supplementing what you read with a rich audio-visual interactive learning experience that will make the pages of this book come alive.

☞ We describe the contents of the CD-ROM and show you how to navigate the main menu and the sub-menus so that you can quickly go to the lesson or topic that interests you.

☞ We specify the minimum and recommended requirements of the computer you will need to make sure that all the audio-visual capabilities of the CD-ROM can be fully experienced.

☞ We explain the cross references that allow you to quickly jump to a topic on the CD-ROM that you may be reading in the book.

☞ We explain how you can also use the CD-ROM as a stand-alone learning tool if you so desire.

# The Accompanying CD-ROM

The accompanying CD-ROM is a unique feature of this book. The book is laid out like a standard text and reference book. In addition, the CD-ROM contains an exciting multimedia experience; rich in visuals and sound that helps you learn computer-related topics in an interesting and easy way.

You can run the CD-ROM on your computer, independent of the book, to learn at a speed of your choosing and in the sequence that best suits your needs.

You can watch the screen graphics and listen to the audio instructions to add to what you read in the book. But that is not all—you can also interact with the programme just as you would with a teacher in a real classroom. Taken along with the book, the combination of written text, on-screen graphics, voice-over instructions and interaction creates a learning environment that is indeed second to none.

Instead of merely repeating the text of the book in the same sequence, the CD-ROM has been designed for interactive learning in a rich multimedia environment. As a result, you can either read the text, or run the CD-ROM independently of each other and derive benefit from two different forms of learning. However, it is strongly recommended that you read the book first and then go through the CD-ROM for better and faster understanding of the topics covered.

However, if you wish to jump from a topic in the book to its corresponding lessons in the CD-ROM, you can easily do that as well. Just look for the CD-ROM icon to the left of the page as you see below. A note that reads as follows, appears with appropriate navigating instructions:

**CD-ROM**

To learn more in a multimedia environment, insert the accompanying CD-ROM in your computer, select the **Interactive** mode in the opening screen. The main menu will appear. To go to the section on *How Viruses Work*, for example, click **Computer Viruses → How Viruses Work**. In the sub-menu that opens, click on the topic of your choice and follow the navigation instructions on your screen.

## Contents

The CD-ROM has been prepared using the latest multimedia technology to provide you with a rich learning experience. The following topics have been covered in the CD-ROM:

1. Computer Fundamentals
2. Windows
3. DOS
4. Word
5. Excel
6. PowerPoint
7. Access
8. Internet
9. Computer Viruses

*Fig Anx.01 Main Menu*

Each topic is further divided into sub-topics. For example, this is what is included under the main topic of Computer Fundamentals:

1. How Computers Work
2. Essential Components of Computers
3. Optional Components of Computers
4. Inside the Computer
5. Use of Computer Components

You can click on the topic of your choice to open it. Then follow the navigation instructions on your screen. See Fig Anx.01 for a view of the main menu.

# Minimum Requirements

Since the CD-ROM has sound, voice over, animation and all the features required to enrich your multimedia learning experience, you have to make sure that you use it in a computer with appropriate specifications. See below the minimum and recommended specifications that your computer should have:

- The computer should at least have a Pentium I central processing unit (CPU) running at 166 MHz. It should have a good pair of stereophonic speakers and sound capability built into the motherboard, or on a separate sound card. We recommend, however, a Pentium II CPU running at 433 MHz or faster. Otherwise, the lessons may run slowly.

- The computer should have a CD-ROM drive with 40x read speed or better.

- Your monitor and video card should support a minimum screen resolution of 800 x 600 pixels.

# Installation and Navigation Tips

## *Installation*

Installation is quite simple. Just open the CD-ROM tray and insert the CD-ROM and close the tray. The programme will load itself and in a short while, the opening screen will appear followed by the menu containing the topics on the CD-ROM.

In case the CD-ROM does not run automatically, do the following:

1. Click the **Windows Explorer** icon on your desktop.
2. Navigate to your **CD-ROM drive** and click on the Plus **+** sign to its right.
3. In the list of files that will now be revealed, double click on the file marked **Start.exe**.
4. The programme on the CD-ROM will now load and run.

## Navigation

The menu screens have menu items shaped like buttons that you click with the mouse pointer to select the topic or lesson you wish to see. Once you select a lesson, you will see navigation instructions on your screen. These instructions will tell you how to go forward or back in your lesson and how to quit the lesson or go back to the main menu. For some topics, the menu will have a sub-menu as well.

## Viewing Modes

You can select the linear viewing mode or the interactive viewing mode when you start the programme. *See Fig Anx.02 below.*

Fig Anx.02 Select Your Viewing Mode

In the demo mode, you select the lesson of your choice and it runs in sequence without requiring any inputs from you. This mode is recommended for a quick preliminary overview of a topic of your choice.

In the interactive mode, you select the lesson as usual and then you can control the sequence and speed of the lesson, navigating back and forth as you want. In addition, some of the lessons contain interactive sessions when you are prompted to carry out tasks, usually by appropriate mouse clicks. The interactive view is recommended for a more intensive study of a topic along with an interactive practice session where available.

## Cross Reference with the Book

While the CD-ROM provides you with a self-contained multimedia learning experience that you can experience independently of the *Rapidex Computer Course* book, you may wish to combine the

# Introduction

## to

In keeping with the successive upgradation of Windows Operating System versions and the feedback received from our readers, we have added a new chapter to this book. This chapter deals exclusively with *WindowsXP* – the latest version of the Windows Operating System. *Windows 98* and *ME* have already been dealt with at length in Chapter 3. Therefore, in the new 'bonus' chapter, we have highlighted the additional features of *WindowsXP*. After reading this chapter, those already working on the *WindowsXP* version, will find a number of useful tips and suggestions. These tips will help them get the best out of their new operating system. However, this chapter is sure to prove a boon for those, who are yet to shift to *WindowsXP*. The chapter weighs judiciously the pros and cons of upgrading to this version of Windows – especially, in terms of the cost involved and the likely benefits from it. Some key information provided in the chapter will also work as a true guide for taking the right decision, once and for all.

# About XP

There are four versions of Windows XP: Professional, Home, Tablet PC and Media Centre. The first two are more popular by far. In comparison to the Home version, the Professional version contains additional features useful to business user. The Tablet PC version is meant for mobile computers and the Media Centre version requires many additional hardware items for all its features to work. Therefore, we will mainly concentrate on the Professional and Home versions here.

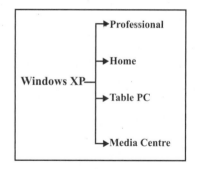

# Why XP Only

After the initial teething problems have been overcome, you will find the "Experience" of using Windows XP rewarding indeed. So, if your budget permits it, we strongly recommend that you upgrade to Windows XP.

Here are some of the plus and minus points of Windows XP in comparison to earlier versions of Windows.

| Why You Need XP | Why You Can Avoid XP |
|---|---|
| 1. Windows XP is faster, more stable and reliable than all other Windows operating systems excepting Windows 2000. | 1. XP is resource hungry. It requires a faster Central Processing Unit (CPU), more Random Access Memory (RAM) and a bigger hard disk. |
| 2. XP gives you true multi-tasking power. You can run a spreadsheet calculation while also surfing the Internet, simultaneously. | 2. If you upgrade to Windows XP on your old computer, some of your old hardware may be found not compatible with Windows XP. Also, some old software, such as DOS-based computer games, may not run on Windows XP. |
| 3. XP has better anti-virus protection including built-in "Firewall" software that filters the Internet traffic and stops viruses from entering your computer. | 3. Windows XP is expensive. It may cost three times as much as Windows 98. |
| | 4. You will need greater expertise to install and troubleshoot Windows XP. Some XP-related problems may be troublesome even for a software professionl. |

# Check if Your Computer is Suitable

Windows XP requires more computing power in terms of Central Processing Unit (CPU) speed, Random Access Memory (RAM) and hard disk space. It is also important that your computer's hardware is compatible with the NT technology, which forms the core of Windows XP. Therefore, before the upgrade, you must make sure that your computer is suitable for Windows XP.

Here is Microsoft's (and our) hardware recommendation for the users of Windows XP Professional:

- PC with 300 megahert (MHz) or higher processor clock speed is recommended. 233 MHz processor is the minimum requirement (single or dual processor system). You can select either a CPU from the Intel Pentium or Celeron family, or AMD K6/Athlon/Duron family, or any other compatible processor. We recommend at least a Pentium III 600 MHz machine.

- 128 megabytes (MB) of RAM or higher. We recommend 256 MB.

- 1.5 gigabytes (GB) of available hard disk space. We recommend at least 5 GB.

- Super VGA (800×600) or higher-resolution video adapter and monitor.

- CD-ROM or DVD drive. We recommend a CD-RW drive.

Microsoft has an excellent tool that will allow you to test your system's hardware and software compatibility even before you purchase the new operating system. Called the Upgrade Advisor, it runs on Windows 98, Windows ME, Windows NT 4.0 and Windows 2000. You can download the Upgrade Advisor (31.7 MB) from the Microsoft website.

If you are connected to the Internet, the Upgrade Advisor will go to the Microsoft website and download the latest information about compatible hardware and software. If you have a slow Internet connection, you can skip this step without too much risk. It will then run a compatibility check and then present you with a report showing any hardware or software that may have problems in compatibility with Windows XP. Reported mismatches may require you to buy a newer version or download either "patches" or "Drivers" from the manufacturer's website to overcome the problems.

There are other non-Microsoft readinesses testers also, such as the PC Pitstop's Readiness Test that you can use to check your computer's suitability. However, you cannot download this test. To use it, you must stay connected to the Pitstop website.

# Installing Windows XP

Once you are sure that your computer can run Windows XP, you are ready to install it.

## Installation ■■■■■■

To start the installation, proceed as follows:

1. Turn your computer on.
2. Scan for viruses using any anti-virus software that you may have installed.
3. Insert the Windows XP CD into your computer's CD-ROM drive.
4. After your computer automatically launches the programme, click **Install Windows XP.**
5. When you're asked to choose the type of installation you want, select **Upgrade** and then click **Next.**
6. Review the licence agreement and if you agree, accept it.
7. Enter the Product Key code from the Windows XP documentation.
8. Review the text for performing Dynamic Update. If you wish to perform Dynamic Update, select Yes, and then click Next. Windows installation starts. You must have an active Internet connection to perform Dynamic Update.
9. When the "Welcome to Windows" screen appears, follow the instructions to complete your upgrade (see Fig. XP 01).

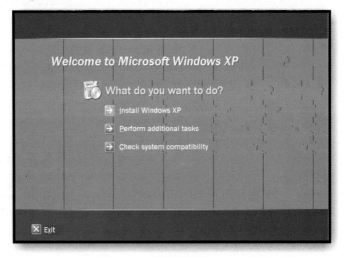

*Fig. XP 01*

NOTE

You may choose not to perform Dynamic Update during installation, since to do so, you have to stay connected to the Internet for a long time. Instead, you may update later, choosing those updates and software "patches" you need. See later in this section for more information on registration and updates.

# What is new in XP

Windows XP is now available in four versions. They are: Home, Professional, Tablet PC and Media Centre. While the Tablet PC version is meant for portable computers, the recently (2004) released Media Centre version is useful only if you have a fully equipped media centre computer (PC) with several additional hardware items required for multimedia facility. For our present discussion, we will concentrate on the two most popular versions, the Home and the Professional editions of Windows XP.

When you start, Windows XP will present you with an opening screen or Desktop that looks very different from what you may be used to on Windows 98 (see Fig. XP 02).

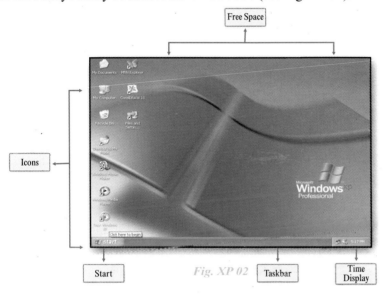

Fig. XP 02

Clicking on the Start button will display a Start Menu, which will also look different from what you are accustomed to. If you prefer the old Windows 98 (Classic) look Start menu, you can easily change to it as follows:

1. Click **Start.**
   The Start menu appears.

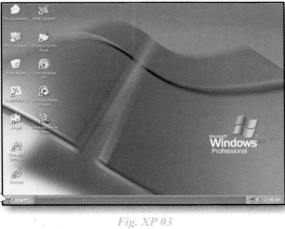

Fig. XP 03

2. Right click on any vacant portion and click on **Properties.** The Taskbar and Start menu Properties dialogue box appears.

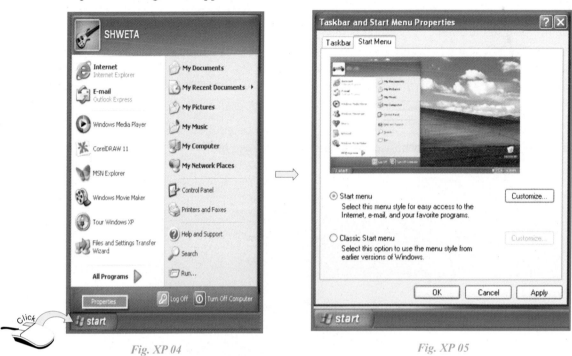

Fig. XP 04                                           Fig. XP 05

3. Click on the **Start** menu tab and then select the radio button captioned "Classic Start Menu".

Fig. XP 06

4.  Click **Apply** and then click **OK** to close the dialogue box. The familiar Windows 98 style Start Menu will now appear.

*Fig. XP 07*

## ▶ Differences Between Home and Professional Editions

Targeted for the home user, the Home version has fewer features and is cheaper. While the NT core and many features are common, the Professional version has many additional powerful capabilities. Thus, if you wish to use any of the following on your computer, you will have to install the Professional version:

- Remote Desktop that allows you to control a remote computer connected to yours in a Local Area Network (LAN).

- Dual Processor Control that allows you to run a computer (usually a LAN Server) that has two Central Processing Units (CPU).

- Built-in Fax Capability that lets you send and receive faxes through a modem over a telephone line without any additional fax software.

- Multilingual Capability that will help you run the same installation of Windows in two or more languages.

In addition, the Professional edition is more robust and secure. Buy this edition rather than the Home edition unless you have budget constraints. You can also upgrade from the Home to the Professional edition at a later date. However, this option is more expensive overall, than buying the Professional edition right in the beginning.

# New Features of Windows XP

Let us review the main enhancements in Windows XP (applicable to both Home and Professional versions) over earlier versions, in particular, Windows 98.

 ## New Look

We have already described changes to the Desktop and the Start menu. The Control Panel too has a new look. Instead of a general display, the applet icons in the Control Panel are arranged by categories. However, you can easily change back to the familiar Windows 98 look by clicking on the "Switch to Classic View" option under the Control Panel task list on the left of the Control Panel window (see Fig. XP 08).

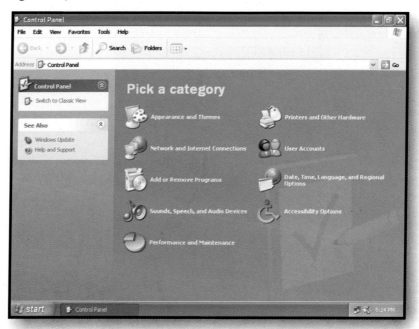

*Fig. XP 08*

 ## Greater Reliability

Older versions of Windows were built by adding a Graphic User Interface (GUI) on top of a DOS kernel. However, Windows XP uses the tested New Technology (NT) at the core of its operating system. NT technology has already proved very successful in Windows NT and Windows 2000. Therefore, Windows XP is very reliable and you can count on it to keep your computer up and running. If there is a problem, Windows XP helps you to recover easily using its System Restore feature (see Fig. XP 09).

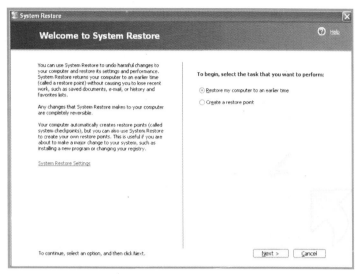

Fig. XP 09

# Improved Performance

Compared to Windows 98, you will find that after installing Windows XP, your computer will:

- Start and log you on faster
- The software applications on your computer will also run faster.
- When you run more than one task at the same time, such as drafting one document and printing another, the computer will run faster and will not crash as often as before.

# Greater Security

Windows XP's file system is more secure and robust, because it supports the New Technology File System (NTFS), which is faster and more reliable than the older FAT 16 or FAT 32 (File Allocation Table, 16 and 32 bit, respectively) file systems used by Windows 98, Windows ME or other earlier versions. However, you can continue to use the older FAT 32 system with Windows XP if you choose.

# Increased Safety

Windows XP has a built-in "Firewall". This is a special software programme that monitors all incoming and outgoing data. It protects your computer from the most common viruses, whether from the Internet or from a Local Area Network (LAN), to which your computer may be connected. The Firewall is normally off, but you can turn it on easily. The exact procedure for turning on the firewall is described later in this chapter.

# Improved Media Support

You can use audio, video or picture files more efficiently and easily in Windows XP. You can use these features of Windows XP in your business applications, such as a multimedia business presentation, consisting of slides, audio and video clips. You can also use these features for your personal entertainment by playing audio CDs, video CDs or DVD films using proper hardware, along with your computer.

The main device for playing multimedia is the Windows Media Player. It brings your digital media activities together in a central place, so that you can watch Windows Media and DVD video, play and record CDs, listen to Internet radio, transfer your media to devices, and much more (see Fig. XP 10 for a view of the Media Player).

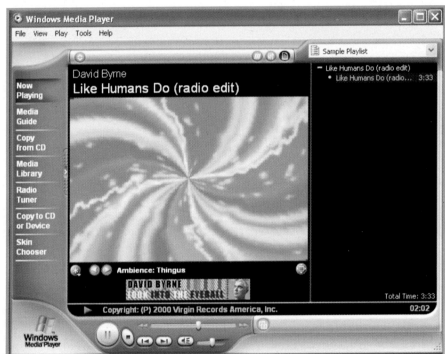

*Fig. XP 10*

# CD Burning

With Windows XP, saving critical information to a Compact Disk (CD) is as easy as saving it to a floppy disk or the hard disk. You use the CD Writing Wizard as described below.

By selecting a folder of documents, music, photos, or even software in the My Computer window and starting the CD Writing Wizard, you can quickly and easily create your own CDs.

Follow these steps to copy files and folders to a CD:

1. Insert a blank, writable CD into the CD recorder.
2. Open **My Computer.**
3. Click the files or folders you want to copy to the CD. Under File and Folder Tasks, click **Copy this file, Copy this folder** or **Copy the selected items.**
4. If the files are located in My Pictures, under Picture Tasks, click **Copy to CD** or **Copy all items to CD.**
5. In the Copy Items dialog box, click the **CD recording drive,** and then click **Copy.**
6. In My Computer, double-click the CD recording drive. Windows displays a temporary area where the files are held before they are copied to the CD. Verify that the files and folders that you intend to copy to the CD appear under **Files Ready to be Written** to the CD.
7. Under CD Writing Tasks, click **Write these files to CD.** Windows displays the CD Writing Wizard. Follow the instructions on your screen.

 # Simple Networking

Networking lets you share devices, such as printers, scanners and digital cameras if you have more than one computer. You can also share a single Internet between two or more computers connected through a network.

Launch the Network Setup Wizard by clicking **Start,** then right clicking "My Network Places", clicking **Properties** and then clicking "Setup a home or small office network". The Windows XP Network Setup Wizard is launched. Follow the instructions on your screen to set up a simple network.

 # New Features in Internet Explorer 6.0

The **Internet Explorer version 6.0 (IE 6.0)** is installed automatically along with Windows XP. With many new features, this version of the Internet browser is faster and more secure than earlier versions. However, the browser is vulnerable to Internet virus attacks. Therefore, it is essential to keep it updated by installing the latest security patches. We look at some of the important new features of IE 6.0.

The **Image or Picture toolbar** allows you to quickly and easily save, e-mail and print pictures that you find on Web pages as well as view all your saved pictures in the My Pictures folder. When you point to pictures on Web pages, the toolbar appears (see Fig. XP 11).

The **Media Pane** on the left of the IE 6.0 window provides a convenient way for locating and playing different kinds of media files within the browser window. You can also play music, video or mixed-media files without having to open a separate window. Besides, you can control the audio volume, choose which media files or tracks to play and access different media files on your computer, or on the Microsoft Internet network.

The **Image Resizing** feature will resize the pictures on a website you are browsing to fit automatically in the browser window even if the pictures are too large for the browser.

The **Security** tab of the Internet Properties dialogue box can be used to raise or lower the safety protection of your computer as you surf. For instance, you can categorise the websites you visit as "Trusted" or "Restricted", depending on how well you know and trust the site. Windows XP automatically provides high protection when you go to a "Restricted" site. Similarly, by enabling the Content Advisor in the Contents tab of the Internet Properties dialogue box, you can set levels of language, nudity, sex or violence that will be displayed as you browse the Internet.

*Fig. XP 11*

# Optimising Windows XP

After upgrading to Windows XP from an earlier version, the first thing you will notice is a more attractive and colourful user interface. In addition, Windows XP will start and shut down more quickly and other programmes will run faster than before.

However, there is room to improve performance even further. Windows XP comes to you with "default" settings meant for the average user. If you feel confident about "tweaking" or making fine adjustments to your copy of Windows XP, you can extract more speed and/or performance from your computer. In this section, we show you how.

Tweaking is not for everyone. If you are a first-time user and you like things as they are, you may not wish to experiment. Some of the tweaks we discuss may be hard to change back. So, do exercise caution. If you wish to go ahead, create a "Restore Point" before trying each change. If things go wrong, it will let you restore your computer to the pre-tweak state.

# Creating a Restore Point

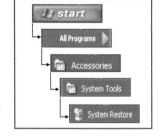

To create a Restore Point, do the following:

1. Click **Start**, then click on **All Programs**, go to **Accessories**, then **System Tools** and click on **System Restore**.
2. Select **Create a Restore Point** in the dialogue box that opens. Then click **Next** (see earlier in this chapter).
3. On the next screen, enter a name for the restore point in the **Edit** box and click the **Create** button.
4. Click **Close** to come out of **System Restore**.

After setting up System Restore, you are ready to start.

Study the tweaks given below and select the ones you want to try. To help you decide, we begin each tweak's description with a statement of the benefit you may get from it.

# Visual Appeal Versus Speed

If you select the default setup options, Windows XP will be installed with a number of visual effects, such as drop shadows, window animation, smooth fonts and more. The effects are pleasing to the eye, but very power-intensive. They can slow down Windows, especially programmes, such as AutoCAD and similar programmes that draw figures on your monitor's screen.

There are two things you can do to speed up your computer:

| Lower Color Quality | Reduce Desktop Animation and Visual Effects |
|---|---|
| Lower the color quality of your display to Medium (16-bit) rather than Highest (32-bit) as follows: | To speed up Windows, reduce Windows XP's Desktop animations and visual effects as follows: |
| 1. Right click anywhere on an empty portion of your Desktop. Then select **Properties** from the popup menu that appears. | 1. Right click on **My Computer** and select **Properties.** In the **System Properties** dialogue box, click the **Advanced** tab and click **Settings** under **Performance**. The **Performance Options** dialogue box will be displayed. |
| 2. The **Display Properties** dialogue box appears. Click on the **Settings** tab. The Settings page appears. | 2. Click the radio button marked "Adjust for best performance" and click **Apply** and then **OK** and then click **OK** again to close all dialogue boxes. |
| 3. In the Color Quality drop down box, select **Medium** (16-bit) and click **Apply** and then click **OK** to close the dialogue box | |
| The 16-bit setting is enough for all common computer tasks. You need the highest setting (32-bit) only for photo or video editing. | |

Fig. XP 12

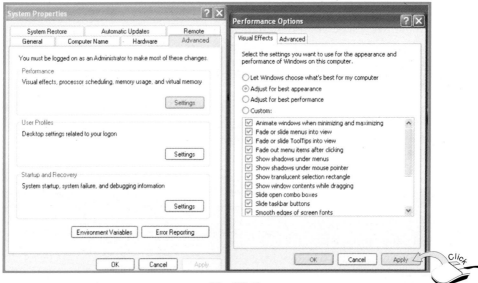

Fig. XP 13

**TIP**

You can choose to activate or deactivate individual items in the list below the radio buttons by clicking on the check boxes instead of using the radio buttons. By doing so, you will be able to get just the right balance between appearance and performance that suits you.

# Faster Boot Up

If you are the only user of your computer, you can shorten the time your computer takes to boot up every time you start it. It involves two steps: (1) Using Windows Welcome screen instead of the Classic Log-on screen, and (2) Turning the Fast User Switching feature off.

To do these, proceed as follows:

1. Click **Start**, then go to **Run.**
2. In the **Run** dialogue box, type "control user passwords" (without the quotation marks) and click **OK.** The **User Accounts** dialogue box appears.
3. Click "Change the way users log on or off". The second page of the User Accounts dialogue box appears.
4. Select the check box captioned "Use the Welcome Screen" and uncheck the box captioned "Use fast user switching".

Click **Apply Options** and then close the User Accounts dialogue box. Your boot up speed will improve now.

 # Turn Off Auto-update

Microsoft regularly publishes patches (corrections for software errors) and updates for Windows. To keep your operating system updated and safe from viruses, it is recommended that you download and install them as they become available. To make it convenient for the user, Windows XP has an auto-update feature that will try to connect to the Microsoft website and automatically download the latest patches and updates whenever you are on-line.

NOTE

Since many downloads are very big, unless you have a really fast broadband connection, it is not practical to download every update. You may want to pick and choose depending on the patch or update's criticality and size. Therefore, you may prefer to update Windows manually.

To turn off the auto-update feature, do the following:

1. Right click the **My Computer** icon and select **Properties** from the context menu that appears (see Fig. XP14).
2. The **System Properties** dialogue box appears. Click on the **Automatic Update** tab (see Fig. XP15).
3. Under **Notification Settings**, select the radio button with the caption "Turn off automatic updating. I want to update my computer manually".
4. Click the **Apply** button and then click **OK** to close the dialogue box.

Fig. XP 14                                          Fig. XP 15

 ## Shut Down Using the Power Button

If you accidentally switch off your computer's power supply before going through the familiar **Start→Turn Off Computer** process, you will see messages telling you that the computer was improperly shut down the last time and will be asked to wait while the computer's hard disks are checked for error. To avoid this, all of us should use the mouse and/or keyboard to shut down.

 There is a way to cut this process short. After changing the settings as shown below, all you will have to do is just push the computer's power button off and the entire system will shut down in an orderly manner and you will face no messages or delays when you start the next time!

Here are the required setting changes :

1. Click **Start** and go to the **Control Panel**. The **Control Panel** appears.
2. Click the **Power Options** applet. The **Power Options Properties** dialogue box opens.
3. Click on the **Advanced** tab. Under the **Power Buttons** section, move down to the drop down list box captioned "When I press the power button of my computer".
4. Click the arrow at the right of the box and from the options that appear, select **Shut Down.**
5. Click **OK** to accept the changes and close the **Control Panel**.

Now, all you have to do to shut down your computer is to press the power button on the front of your computer's cabinet to switch off power and the computer will shut down normally.

Do remember to shut all open programs and save all your work before you do this.

# READER'S FEEDBACK
# RAPIDEX COMPUTER COURSE

Name: _____

Address: _____

City: _____ Pin code: _____

Phone: _____ Fax: _____ E-mail: _____

Profession: ☐ Student   ☐ Working   ☐ Businessman   ☐ Professional

How did you get to know about the book?

☐ Brand Rapidex   ☐ Friend   ☐ Hoarding

☐ TV commercial   ☐ Advertisement in newspaper   ☐ Bookshop

Name of the shop you purchased the book from.

_____

What is your first impression about the book?

_____

Did you find the course up to your expectations?   ☐ Yes   ☐ No

Was the course worth the price you paid for it?   ☐ Yes   ☐ No

Details of shortcomings in the book.

_____

_____

Suggestions for further improvement in the book.

_____

_____

_____

Suggestions for further improvement in the CD.

_____

_____

1. Fill this form online at our website: **www.pustakmahal.com**

2. Send the filled form in an envelope to PUSTAK MAHAL, J-3/16 (Opp. Happy School), Daryaganj, New Delhi-110002.

Fax: 011-23260518      E-mail: Info@pustakmahal.com

cut it from here

**48/-**
Demy size, pp: 120

**96/-**
Demy size, pp: 192

**80/-**
Demy size, pp: 128

**60/-**
Demy size, pp: 144

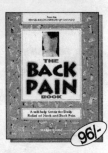
**175/-**
Big size, pp: 428

**96/-**
Big size, pp: 228

**80/-**
Demy size, pp: 152

Vol-I: pp: 140 • Rs. 96/-
Vol-II: pp: 224 • Rs. 135/-

**68/-**
Demy size, pp: 128

**88/-**
Demy size, pp: 224

**120/-**
Big size, pp: 232

**110/-**
Big size, pp: 152

**48/-**
Demy size, pp: 96

**88/-**
Demy size, pp: 240

**68/-**
Demy size, pp: 136

**60/-**
Demy size, pp: 116

**95/-**
Big size, pp: 224

**135/-**
Big size, pp: 224

**96/-**
Demy size, pp: 224

**80/-**
Demy size, pp: 224

**80/-**
Demy size, pp: 120

**68/-**
Demy size, pp: 136

**135/-**
Big size, pp: 208

**96/-**
Big size, pp: 184

## POSTAGE: RS. 15 TO 25/- EACH

# HEALTH, BEAUTY CARE, HERBS & POPULAR SCIENCE

**80/-**
*Demy size, pp: 248*

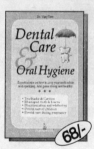
**68/-**
*Demy size, pp: 136*

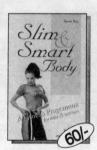
**60/-**
*Demy size, pp: 128*

**68/-**
*Demy size, pp: 128*

**68/-**
*Demy size, pp: 152*

**90/-**
*Big size, pp: 232*

**80/-**
*Demy size, pp: 184*

**68/-**
*Demy size, pp: 128*

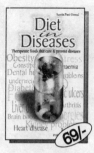
**69/-**
*Demy size, pp: 104*

**60/-**
*Demy size, pp: 120*

**96/-**
*Demy size, pp: 132*

**96/-**
*Big size, pp: 176*

**120/-**
*Big size, pp: 224*

**80/-**
*Big size, pp: 168*

**120/-**
*Big size, pp: 304*

**96/-**
*Big size, pp: 124*

**80/-**
*Demy size, pp: 96*

### Fact Books in Herbs
*Discover the Amazing power of:*
- Brahmi
- Ashwagandha
- Spirulina
- Vilayati Imli
- Salai guggal
- Amla

*Demy size*
Price: Rs. **30/-** each
Postage: 10/- each

## Popular Science & Science Tricks

**120/-**
*Big size • pp: 120*
*Also available in Hindi (With CD)*

**96/-**
*Big size • pp: 196*

**48/-**
*Big size • pp: 120*

**48/-**
*Big size • pp: 120*

**36/-**
*Big size • pp: 104*

**36/-**
*Big size • pp: 104*

## POSTAGE: RS. 15 TO 25/- EACH

10

**Everything You Wanted to Know About ASTHMA**
Dr Ashok Birbal-Jain, MD
Dr Aruna A Birbal-Jain, MD
80/-
Demy size, pp: 168

**Soul HEALING**
Dr. Bruce Goldberg
88/-
Demy size, pp: 280

**CHAKRA WORKOUT** For Body, Mind & Spirit
88/-
Demy size, pp: 240

**Healing the Past For a Vibrant Future**
68/-
Demy size, pp: 180

Dr. Bruce Goldberg
**Self-Defence against psychic attacks & evil spirits**
96/-
Demy size, pp: 242

**CHAKRA & KUNDALINI WORKBOOK**
96/-
Demy size, pp: 264

**A Beginner's Guide to ACUPRESSURE (SHIATSU Technique)**
36/-
Demy size, pp: 64

**Auras** See Them in only 60 Seconds!
80/-
Demy size, pp: 144

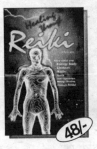

**Healing Through Reiki**
48/-
Demy size, pp: 104

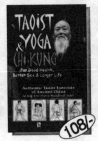

**TAOIST YOGA & CHI-KUNG** For Good Health, Better Sex & Longer Life
108/-
Demy size, pp: 304

**The Magic of Aromatherapy**
108/-
Demy size, pp: 264

**THE ACUPRESSURE HANDBOOK**
135/-
Big size, pp: 264

**The Miracle of COLOUR THERAPY**
48/-
Demy size, pp: 84

**the healing touch of Reiki**
68/-
Demy size, pp: 112

**MASTER APPROACHES TO NEW AGE ALTERNATIVE THERAPIES**
80/-
Demy size, pp: 200

**WATER A Miracle Therapy**
68/-
Demy size, pp: 112

**Magneto Therapy The miraculous healing power**
68/-
Demy size, pp: 128

**THE PRACTICAL BOOK OF REIKI** HEALING THROUGH UNIVERSAL LIFEFORCE ENERGY
96/-
Big size, pp: 168

**The miracle of Music Therapy**
80/-
Demy size, pp: 144

**21 Power Tools of Reiki** A guide to maximise the power of Reiki
60/-
Demy size, pp: 136

**Magic Therapy of COLOURS** Holistic healing through colour
60/-
Demy size, pp: 128

**Healing Heart Disease Naturally**
96/-
Demy size, pp: 200

**Relaxation Techniques**
195/-
Demy size, pp: 272

**The Healing Power of Mudras** The Yoga of the hands
68/-
Demy size, pp: 112

# DICTIONARIES & ENCYCLOPEDIAS

Big size, pp: 48
(In colour)

Demy size, pp: 136

Big size, pp: 231

Big size, pp: 58
(In colour)

Big size, pp: 98
(Double colour)

Big size, pp: 520

Big size, pp: 384

Demy size, pp: 344

Demy size, pp: 128

Big size• pp: 52 (In 4 colour)
Deluxe Binding
Also available in Hindi

Demy size, pp: 352

Demy size, pp: 184

Demy size, pp: 456

Demy size, pp: 128

Demy size, pp: 152

Demy size, pp: 196

Demy size, pp: 128

Demy size, pp: 232

POSTAGE: RS. 15 TO 20/- EACH

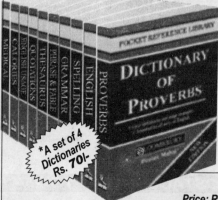

# Bloomsbury Dictionaries

- Dictionary of Phrase & Fable
- English Thesaurus
- Spelling Dictionary
- Dictionary of English Usage
- Medical Dictionary
- Dictionary of Calories
- English Dictionary*
- Dictionary of Grammar*
- Dictionary of Proverbs*
- Dictionary of Quotations*

*A set of 4 Dictionaries Rs. 70/-

Pocket size • Pages: 256
Price: Rs. 30/- each • Postage: Rs. 10/- each

12

# COMPUTER BOOKS

**196/-**

Big size, pp: 520
(FREE CD-ROM, SMS Joke
Book & Mouse Pad),

Also available
in Hindi

**150/-**

Big size, pp: 224
Also available in Hindi

**175/-**

Big size. pp: 448

**195/-**

Big size, pp: 520

**95/-**

Big size, pp: 144

**99/-**

Big size, pp: 136

**68/-**

Big size, pp: 264

**195/-**

Big size, pp: 360/-

**68/-**

Big size, pp: 192

**195/-**

Big size, pp: 416

**225/-**

Big size, pp: 444

**225/-**

Big size, pp: 392

**90/-**

Big size, pp: 184

**125/-**

Big size, pp: 252

**140/-**

Demy size, pp: 296

**120/-**

Demy size, pp: 164

## *RAPIDEX* Straight to the point series

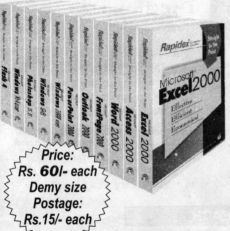

Microsoft Excel 2000

Access 2000

Word 2000

FrontPage 2000

Outlook 2000

PowerPoint 2000

Windows 2000 User

Windows 98

PhotoShop 5.5

WindowsNT4 User

Flash 4

**Price:
Rs. 60/- each
Demy size
Postage:
Rs.15/- each**

## *RAPIDEX* Condensed Users Guides

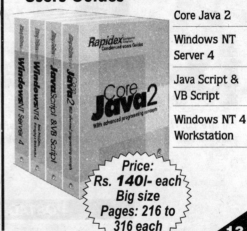

Core Java 2

Windows NT
Server 4

Java Script &
VB Script

Windows NT 4
Workstation

**Price:
Rs. 140/- each
Big size
Pages: 216 to
316 each**

13

# FUN, FACTS, HUMOUR, MAGIC & HOBBIES

Demy size, pp: 184

Demy size, pp: 115
also available in Hindi

Demy size, pp: 152
also available in Hindi

Demy size, pp: 112
also available in Hindi

Demy size, pp: 104
also available in Hindi,
Bangla, Kannada &
Assamese

Demy size, pp: 115
also available in Hindi

Demy size, pp: 104

Demy size, pp: 176

Demy size, pp: 128

Demy size, pp: 152

Demy size, pp: 128

Demy size, pp: 120

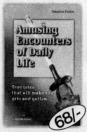

Demy size, pp: 124

Demy size, pp: 115

Pages: 144

Pages: 120

Pages: 200

Demy size, pp: 248
(Hardbound)

Big size, pp: 112
(Full colour book)

Demy size, pp: 112
also available in Hindi,
Kannada and
Marathi

Demy size, pp: 124
also available in Hindi

Demy size, pp: 124
also available in Hindi,

Demy size, pp: 124
also available in Hindi

Big size, pp: 120
also available in Hindi

## POSTAGE: RS. 15 TO 25/- EACH

14

# COOKERY, HOUSEHOLD & PARENTING

Nutritious Mushroom Recipes
96/-
pp: 96

COOKING MADE EASY
60/-
Demy size, pp: 104

OVER 100 FAT-FREE RECIPES
80/-
Demy size, pp: 120

101 All time Savoury Snacks
60/-
Demy size, pp: 102

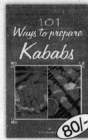
101 Ways to prepare Kababs
80/-
Demy size, pp: 136

MODERN COOKERY BOOK
68/-
Big size, pp: 144
Also available in Hindi

101 ways to prepare Curries
60/-
Demy size, pp: 140

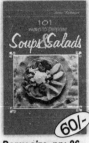
101 ways to prepare Soups & Salads
60/-
Demy size, pp: 86

101 Mix & Match recipes with Vegetables
60/-
Demy size, pp: 144

101 Chinese Recipes
60/-
Demy size, pp: 112

Cooking for Diabetics
80/-
Demy size, pp: 115

Wide range of delicious vegetarian and non-vegetarian Dishes and Desserts from four corners of India
80/-
Big size, pp: 86

1000 Household Hints
96/-
Big size, pp: 192

HOME HINTS
How to save time and money
40/-
Big size, pp: 32

FIRST AID FOR EVERY HOME
40/-
Big size, pp: 32

SPOT CHECK
How to cope with household stains
40/-
Big size, pp: 32

HOUSE PLANTS
How to care for your indoor plants
40/-
Big size, pp: 32

Rapidex HOME MANAGEMENT GUIDE
150/-
Big size, pp: 296

## Books on PARENTING

How to shape your Kids Better
It is in parent's hands to mould their children into perfection
68/-
Demy size, pp: 124

The Art of Successful Parenting
68/-
Demy size, pp: 140

PRACTICAL PARENTING TIPS
Over 1,500 Helpful Hints for the First Five Years
68/-
Demy size, pp: 208

The Joy of Parenting
80/-
Demy size, pp: 144

DISCIPLINE YOUR CHILD Without SHOUTING Or SPANKING
Practical Solutions to the Most Common Pre-school Behaviour Problems
Jerry Wyckoff, Ph.D. and Barbara C. Unell
80/-
Demy size, pp: 152

Bringing up a Dream Child
Gentle ways to discipline your child
75/-
Demy size, pp: 118

Raising a Daughter in 21st Century India
60/-
Demy size, pp: 136

In Press
Juhi Aggarwal
Feed Me I'am Yours

## COOKERY (a set of 4 books)

you save 20%
Pay Rs. 200/- instead of Rs. 240/- for complete set of 4 books priced Rs. 60/- each

- 101 Mix & Match Recipes with Vegetables
- 101 Chinese Recipes
- 101 Ways to Prepare Curries
- 101 Ways to Prepare Soups & Salads

Demy size books.

15

# MISCELLANEOUS BOOKS

## Religious & Spiritual Books

**Pearls of Spiritual Wisdom**

80/-

Demy size, pp: 158

**Dehypnotic Meditation**

96/-

Demy size, pp: 132

**VEDA**

80/-

Demy size, pp: 144

**Know the Vedas At a Glance**

80/-

Demy size, pp: 136

**The Yoga of GITA**

80/-

Demy size, pp: 152

**KNOW THE UPANISHADS**

80/-

Demy size, pp: 120

**Glory of Spiritual India**

80/-

Demy size, pp: 224

**50 Flowers from BHAGAVAT GITA**

75/-

Demy size, pp: 208

**Vedantic Truth Revealed**

48/-

Demy size, pp: 104

## Furniture Catalogue, Gates, Grills, Windows, Railings....

Hardbound

**New STEEL FURNITURE CATALOGUE**

195/-

**NEW FURNITURE CATALOGUE**

120/-

**GATES GRILLS RAILING SETS**

60/-

**Window Grills & Rolling shutters**

60/-

**MORE AND MORE DESIGNS OF GATES, GRILLS, RAILINGS & STAIRCASES**

90/-

**How best to Plan & Build YOUR HOME**

120/-

**DESIGNS OF WINDOWS**

60/-

**DESIGNS OF GATES**

60/-

**DESIGNS OF RAILINGS**

60/-

All in big size

16

## World Famous Series

**WORLD-FAMOUS DISCOVERIES**

Discoveries

**WORLD-FAMOUS 101 GREAT LIVES**

Great Lives (3 vols.)

**Strange Mysteries**

Strange Mysteries

**WORLD-FAMOUS GHOSTS**

Ghosts

**GREAT TREASURES**

Great Treasurers

**WORLD-FAMOUS Scientists**

Scientists

**World-Famous Unsolved Mysteries**

Unsolves Mysteries

**World-Famous Anecdotes**

Anecdotes

**WORLD-FAMOUS ADVENTURES**

Adventures

**Mythologies**

Mythologies

**PROPHESIES & Predictions**

Prophecies & Predictions

**Supernatural Mysteries**

Supernatural Mysteries

**FAMOUS INDIANS OF THE 20TH CENTURY**

80/-

Famous Indians of 20th Century
Pages: 224

**The world's greatest SEERS & PHILOSOPHERS**

80/-

The World's Greatest Seers & Philosophers
Pages: 142

Demy size
Pages: 120-160
in each
Price:
Rs. 48/- each
Postage: 15/- each
Postage FREE on
6 or more books
All books in
Hindi also
Four books in
Bangla & Kannada